★ THE HISTORY OF ★

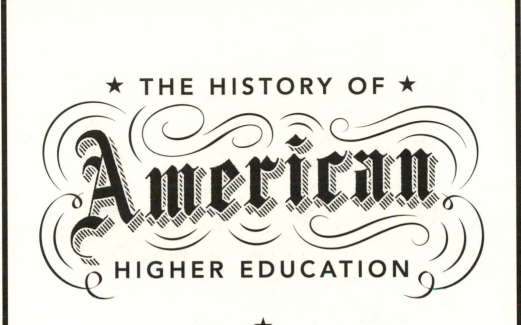

American

HIGHER EDUCATION

★

LEARNING AND CULTURE
FROM THE FOUNDING
TO WORLD WAR II

★

★ Roger L. Geiger ★

PRINCETON UNIVERSITY PRESS
Princeton & Oxford

press.princeton.edu

Jacket design by Chris Ferrante

Library of Congress Cataloging-in-Publication Data

Geiger, Roger L., 1943–
The history of American higher education : learning and culture
from the founding to world war ii / Roger L. Geiger.
pages cm.
Includes index.
ISBN 978-0-691-14939-4 (hardcover : alk. paper)
1. Education, Higher—United States—History. I. Title.
LA226.G395 2015
373.73—dc23
2014007439

British Library Cataloging-in-Publication Data is available

This book has been composed in Garamond Premier Pro,
Avenir LT Std, and Blackletter 686

Printed on acid-free paper. ∞

Printed in the United States of America

1 3 5 7 9 10 8 6 4 2

✦ Contents ✦

3

REPUBLICAN UNIVERSITIES

4

THE LOW STATE OF THE COLLEGES, 1800–1820

5

RENAISSANCE OF THE COLLEGES, 1820–1840

6

REGIONAL DIVERGENCE AND SCIENTIFIC ADVANCEMENT, 1840–1860

7

LAND GRANT COLLEGES AND THE PRACTICAL ARTS

8

THE CREATION OF AMERICAN UNIVERSITIES

9

THE COLLEGIATE REVOLUTION

10

MASS HIGHER EDUCATION, 1915–1940

11

THE STANDARD AMERICAN UNIVERSITY

12

CULTURE, CAREERS, AND KNOWLEDGE

INDEX

PREFACE

RESIDENT BARACK OBAMA ANNOUNCED A GOAL OF having every American child obtain at least 1 year of higher education and having the nation produce 8 million additional college graduates by 2020. These objectives reflect the reality that going to college has both an economic and an iconic status in American society. Economically, the knowledge acquired in postsecondary education is described as "a prerequisite for the growing jobs of the new economy" and "the clearest pathway into the middle class."[1] As an icon, college has always symbolized the acquisition of advanced knowledge, access to careers more or less connected with such knowledge, and the assimilation of middle- or upper-middle-class culture. *Knowledge, careers,* and *culture* are and always have been not only the quintessential objectives of American higher education, but also the external factors that have shaped its development. For this study, they offer keys to delve more deeply into how American colleges and universities have been affected by currents in American society—and how they, in turn, have affected American life. This book is about how, why, and where Americans went to college over the course of three centuries and, particularly, about the institutions they attended to realize their aspirations.

The history of American higher education has been often told, but the richness and variety of this subject cannot be exhausted. This study is intended to enlarge and extend appreciation of that history from the beginnings of colonial colleges to the eve of World War II. Specifically, it seeks to explain how institutions of higher education changed over time in response to their contemporary contexts. The institutions that began in an isolated, provincial colonial society evolved into a system that served an incipient economic powerhouse by 1940. For the first two centuries, colleges existed in a preindustrial economy and a largely rural society. After the Civil War, they gradually adapted to an industrializing economy, an urbanizing society, and a global knowledge regime.

The colleges in colonial North America developed a single, powerful tradition in terms of mission, curriculum, governance, and student culture. Anchored in Reformed Protestantism, the colleges differed in distinctive and significant ways but were essentially variations on a single theme. This model was buffeted first by Independence and then by the post-1800 awakening of evangelical religion, but it endured nonetheless. The first significant aberration occurred with the formation of separate, largely autonomous professional schools, first for medicine

---

1   http://www.whitehouse.gov/issues/education/higher-education. Accessed 8/19/2013.

and later for theology and law. The central collegiate tradition was redefined and reinforced by the Yale *Reports* of 1828, which supplied a unifying formula just as colleges began to proliferate. However, in the middle decades of the century, additional differences appeared as regional traditions of collegiate education diverged significantly in the Northeast, the South, and the trans-Appalachian West. Still, dramatically different paths would emerge following the Civil War.

In the last three decades of the nineteenth century, American higher education was broadened by three coeval and seemingly contradictory revolutions. The land grant movement sought to introduce the teaching of applied subjects and broaden social access. The academic revolution joined American scholars with international learning and organized them into disciplinary communities to better pursue the advancement of knowledge. Given the freedom to organize their own activities, students brought about a collegiate revolution that transformed campus life and at times overshadowed classroom studies.

Each of these areas evolved differently after 1900. A movement for liberal culture endeavored to enhance the positive features of campus social life and collegiate learning while repudiating the excesses of vocational curricula, academic specialization, and collegiate hedonism. The emergence of mass higher education considerably extended the possibilities for teaching applied subjects, but now in the cities more than the countryside and in new kinds of institutions. And American scholars and scientists, substantially aided by philanthropic foundations, emerged as intellectual leaders in basic scientific fields. The exuberance of the Roaring Twenties pulled American higher education in several directions, but the pall of the Great Depression had the opposite effect—encouraging contraction, consolidation, and greater systemwide organization. By 1940 the systemic features of American higher education had crystalized in webs of associations for different types of institutions, academic fields, and types of personnel. Additional external organizations complemented core functions, particularly research. Although contemporaries could scarcely have realized it, an inchoate foundation for the postwar explosion of American higher education was largely in place.

By 1940 American higher education had achieved four results unmatched elsewhere in the world. It had preserved and entrenched a tradition of liberal education as a fundamental attribute of a college education for all students, not just an elite. It had augmented that tradition by incorporating applied and practical studies on the same collegiate and postgraduate levels. It thus produced the first system of mass higher education, largely through individual public and private institutions responding independently to student demand. It also developed the capacity to teach and advance academic subjects on the highest level, achieving world-leading status for American science.

The story of the development of American higher education is presented chronologically in the following eleven chapters, with a twelfth chapter summarizing the arguments. Most chapters consist of four or five sections, each addressing a particular facet of a period—developments affecting students, different kinds of institutions, or the state of knowledge. The first two chapters on the colonial era treat, respectively, the first three colleges of the Puritan century and the more eventful years after 1740. The next four chapters each encompass roughly 20 years, extending to the Civil War. In a previous article, I had divided the evolution of American higher education into 30-year "generations."[2] In this case, 20-year periods provide a more nuanced picture. In both cases, the goal is to emphasize change over time, the essence of historical analysis. After the Civil War, the American system became "wider" as different kinds of colleges and universities emerged with different purposes and cultures. Chapters 7–9 portray three largely simultaneous "revolutions," generated by the land grant movement, the emergence of research universities, and the hypertrophy of collegiate culture. Chapters 10 and 11 focus on disparate developments largely after 1915, especially the formation of mass higher education, the maturation of research universities, and the state of higher education as of 1940. There are fifty sections in all; each has a particular story to relate and may be read independently to appreciate each of these subjects. Grouped in chapters, they reveal the multiple dimensions of American higher education at each point in time.

A work of this scope has no simple provenance. I began writing about the history of American higher education some 30 years ago while part of the Yale University Program on Nonprofit Organizations. In 1987 I joined the Higher Education Program at Pennsylvania State University, where I have taught the history of American higher education almost every year since, as well as more focused historical seminars.[3] This book and those courses are two manifestations of the same knowledge stock. I am grateful for the stimulation and motivation provided by the successive cohorts of history scholars. I also benefited in 1993 from the opportunity to assume the editorship of the *History of Higher Education Annual*, which since 2005 has been entitled *Perspectives on the History of Higher Education*. Originally organized by the community of scholars in this field to provide a venue for new approaches to the history of American higher education, the journal has continued that tradition by giving particular

2   Roger L. Geiger, "The Ten Generations of American Higher Education," in Philip G. Altbach, Patricia J, Gumport, and Robert O. Berdahl, eds., *American Higher Education in the Twenty-First Century: Social, Political, and Economic Challenges,* 3rd ed. (Baltimore: Johns Hopkins University Press, 2011), 37–68.

3   Roger L. Geiger, "Becoming a Historian of Higher Education," in Wayne J. Urban, ed., *Leaders in the Historical Study of American Education* (Rotterdam: Sense Publishers, 2011), 95–106.

encouragement to new historians. It has given me an invaluable window onto the evolving historical literature and brought awareness of heretofore unsuspected topics.

From this background and my own previous writings, I began planning this volume with a definite conception of patterns and events that formed the development of American higher education. Although I was more than familiar with the general outline, I still had a great deal to learn about how and why events developed as they did. I sought such knowledge wherever I could, in institutional histories, biographies, and other historical studies, but in the words of contemporaries whenever possible. These sources are indicated in the book's footnotes, although I have tried to keep these to a minimum. However, every historian is aware that studies rest upon more detailed monographs and documents. Thus, a general history such as this endeavors to distill precious ores from mountains of previous scholarship. I am thus indebted and truly grateful to those hundreds of scholars whose contributions have made this study possible.

I owe more specific, personal thanks to the many individuals who have assisted in some aspect of producing this study. My history doctoral students not only have contributed to my understanding of particular topics, as acknowledged in the footnotes, but they have also engaged with me in ongoing dialogue about the history of American higher education. In chronological order, they are Roger Williams, Dorothy Finnegan, Susan Richardson, Christian Anderson, Julianna Chaszar, Jordan Humphrey, and Nathan Sorber. Many historical colleagues have provided strategic support, council, and advice, especially Bruce Leslie, Harold Wechsler, David Potts, Katherine Chaddock, Doris Malkmus, and Les Goodchild. James Axtell provided helpful comments on an earlier draft. I owe particular thanks to David R. Jones for critical reading and severe editorial guidance on several iterations of this study.

PROLOGUE:
UNIVERSITIES, CULTURE, CAREERS, AND KNOWLEDGE

IGHER EDUCATION HAS ALWAYS DENOTED A particular level and kind of learning in modern Western societies. It has been defined by officially designated institutions—universities—which alone have been given the power to confer the degrees that certify acquisition of such knowledge. Higher education has aspired to provide access to the most advanced learning of an age. Such learning implies a distinctive culture that marks educated persons and prepares them for respected positions in society. Higher education thus constitutes a gateway to valued careers—some, like the learned professions, that require mastering sophisticated systems of applied knowledge and others that rely on acquiring general knowledge and intellectual powers. Culture, careers, and knowledge represent the most basic social purposes of higher education. Each has a dynamic of its own with respect to higher education and to the larger society. Each is also contingent on time and place, so that higher education's relation to culture, careers, and knowledge changes with historical context. Hence they present three largely independent dynamics that shape higher education. This study employs these perspectives to probe and examine the evolution of higher education in the lands that became the United States. They largely shaped this history from the inception of the first degree-granting entity in the seventeenth century to the emergence by 1940 of the institutions of the world's first system of mass higher education.

★   ★   ★

Culture, careers, and knowledge were parts of the English heritage that shaped the earliest colleges of the American colonies. The institutions and curriculum were set by medieval precedents and further elaborated during the Renaissance. The "educational revolution" of the sixteenth and seventeenth centuries expanded the incidence of higher education in England to an extraordinary degree. The religious turmoil of the Protestant Reformation made theological doctrines the critical sphere of intellectual controversy. And the close identification of state, church, and college generated tensions and conflict that plagued the governance of the early colleges.

Universities were an enduring legacy of medieval European civilization. The University of Paris took form in the twelfth century and inspired the formation of similar organizations at Oxford and Cambridge. These institutions began as groups of clerical scholars, or masters, who taught and also certified their pupils to teach. They became the first Northern European universities when they were given separate legal incorporation by Popes or monarchs and accorded the right to confer degrees. In addition to professional degrees, which had been issued by forerunners at Bologna and Salerno, the Northern universities offered a general arts course that foreshadowed modern undergraduate and graduate studies.

The medieval arts course for a bachelor's (undergraduate) degree consisted largely of the trivium of the ancient liberal arts—grammar, rhetoric, and logic—and the three philosophies of Aristotle—mental, moral, and natural philosophy. Grammar meant mastering Latin, the universal language of learning and the sole medium of academic communication. Students were ready for matriculation only when they had been prepared in Latin, and much of their first year was devoted to polishing those skills. Logic was the next subject to master, with the specific goal of preparing students for a ritualized form of debate called disputations. When an initial threshold of competence was achieved, a second-year student became a "sophister," eligible to engage in disputations. Third- and fourth-year students were known as junior and senior sophisters. They broadened their learning by studying Aristotle's three philosophies while further developing their skills at disputations. Displaying these skills was an important part of the graduation ceremony for the bachelor's of arts (AB) degree. Yet, this degree was equivalent to an apprentice certificate; students who wished to acquire a license to teach or to proceed to a professional faculty studied for an additional 3 years, largely on their own, to be admitted master of arts. Thus, the complete arts course spanned 7 years. When completed, "this course put the student in touch with some of the greatest minds of antiquity . . . the cream of the world's knowledge . . . and gave him the intellectual tools for using knowledge for good profit."[1]

The medieval arts course was significantly altered during the Renaissance. Objecting to the narrow scholasticism of the Church, Renaissance writers advocated additional content in order to appeal to a broader audience. Under the rubric of humanism, they sought to encourage the study of Greek and Latin literatures but especially emphasized reading Greek authors in their original language. Mastery of Greek thus became an additional requirement for the arts course. This "polite learning" was deemed to contribute to the formation of character

---

[1] Samuel Eliot Morison, *The Founding of Harvard College* (Cambridge: Harvard University Press, 1935), quote p. 33.

and judgment as well as worldly knowledge—and was thus lauded as the proper education of gentlemen. Appreciation of this new cultural aim penetrated the English universities by the latter fifteenth century, and they gradually incorporated the study of Greek, wider reading of classical literature, and greater emphasis on rhetoric and oratory. This "new" education was particularly attractive to the growing ranks of wealthy families, who sought to mold their sons to be not only gentlemen, but men of affairs as well. This development was furthered by the transformation of the organization of English universities.

From the late Middle Ages, the English universities had benefited from large gifts to establish endowed colleges. Originally meant to support "fellows"—resident scholars—they soon took in fee-paying students and provided both residence and instruction. By the end of the 1400s, the colleges had assumed the entire responsibility for education. College tutors directed small groups of students through the whole course of study. This decentralization of teaching actually spawned considerable diversity across the universities. Each college was founded on different terms by its particular benefactor. The college master dominated their operations, including the choice of fellows. The actual teachers—the tutors—had considerable discretion in choosing which materials their students would study, so long as they were properly prepared for disputations. The English AB course thus had a definite structure but much internal latitude. Hence, colleges developed distinctive personalities—and later distinctive stances toward religious controversies of the day. Emmanuel College, Cambridge, founded in 1584 to train preaching ministers, was foremost in nurturing English Puritanism and in supplying leaders for the Massachusetts Bay Colony—including John Harvard.

The rise of the colleges also changed the nature of university life. No longer the calling of ascetic churchmen, college living entailed a degree of luxury befitting future gentlemen. Besides providing comfortable rooms, board, and good fellowship, colleges owned extensive grounds, often with bowling greens, ponds for fishing and bathing, and tennis courts. Students even played a crude, and physical, version of football. By the sixteenth century, college populations spanned a broad social range: high-ranking "fellow-commoners," who paid double fees and dined at the high table with the fellows but seldom took the trouble to graduate; commoners, or regular fee-paying students; and sizars, the equivalent of work-study students who paid reduced fees. This social diversity was product of the remarkable expansion of university attendance in the sixteenth and seventeenth centuries.

Enrollments at Oxford and Cambridge shot upward during the Elizabethan era and remained at high levels for nearly a century. A peak of sorts occurred during the 1630s, the decade of the Puritan migration to the Massachusetts Bay

Colony. Historian Lawrence Stone has calculated that entrants to higher education, including students of law at the Inns of Court, represented 2.5 percent of 17-year-old males in 1640; and that England in these years may well have been "the most literate society the world had ever known."[2] Perhaps half of these students came from noble or gentry families, who had assimilated the cultural value of polite learning and an arts education. But the other half of the students were sons of bourgeois, professional, or plebian families, who sought the status of gentleman and secure careers in church or state. Their path to higher education was smoothed by growing wealth and economic opportunity, widely available schooling supported by grassroots philanthropy, and an intensifying preoccupation with religion. Most dissenters from the Church of England, including the Puritans, were especially supportive of education. When the Puritans held power during the Civil War and Interregnum (1640–1660), they offered proposals to expand educational opportunities, including the establishment of a third university. However, the reaction to Puritan rule after the Restoration seems to have translated into suspicion of popular education and narrowing of the educational franchise. Instead, the legacy of aspirations for wide common education and liberal access to higher education passed to New England with the Puritan emigrants.

The Protestant Reformation in England was a political event, instigated by King Henry VIII to secure a divorce from his first wife but also, not incidentally, to enhance royal authority. Its immediate result was a centralized state church with a hierarchy of archbishop and bishops as well as liturgy and rituals little changed from Catholicism. True Protestantism soon arrived with apostles of John Calvin and Martin Luther, who advocated the simplicity of early Christian worship, reliance on Biblical authority for all religious practice, and faith as the chief means of salvation. The religious doctrines of church and state oscillated violently from Henry's Protestant son Edward VI (1547–1553) to his Catholic daughter Queen Mary (1553–1558) before Henry's remaining child, Queen Elizabeth (1558–1603), managed a compromise that preserved a Protestant national church with loosely interpreted liturgy. But under Elizabeth's successor, religious feelings gradually became further polarized. James I was a Protestant—the patron of the King James Bible—but he also regarded the state church as an essential arm of royal authority. One religious faction, which included his son Charles I (1627–1649), wished to move the Church of England closer to Catholicism in terms of episcopal authority, theology, and ritual. Sentiment among England's

2   Lawrence Stone, "The Educational Revolution in England, 1560–1640," *Past and Present*, 28 (July 1964): 41–80; 57, quote p. 68. "In quantitative terms, English higher education did not get back to the level of the 1630s until after the first World War; did not surpass it until after the second" (p. 69).

Calvinist Protestants developed in the opposite direction, rejecting bishops, vestments, and all forms of ritual. At the extreme, "separatists" wished to opt out of the Church altogether and worship in individual congregations of the faithful guided by a minister of their own choosing. Among the most radical separatists, the Pilgrims emigrated to Holland in 1608 and to the Plymouth Colony in 1620.

The Calvinist faith of the Puritans was based upon the grim convictions that the world and its inhabitants were inherently corrupt as a result of Adam's fall, and salvation was reserved for only a few. Theologically, the signature doctrine of Puritan Calvinism was predestination—the belief that an all-powerful God had predetermined whether an individual would be saved or damned. Only those having faith might experience an inward conversion (regeneration) that marked a person as among the elect, but even then continual striving to overcome sin and lead a godly life was expected without any possibility of certainty. This severe doctrine invited endless explication and interpretation. In this respect, Puritanism continually sought to maintain an unstable equilibrium between doctrines emphasizing the conversion experience of the elect (antinomianism), on one side, and arguments admitting some limited role for good works (Arminianism) on the other. In practice, Puritans depended heavily upon their ministers. Hence, the social unit of Puritanism was the congregation and minister, joined in a solemn covenant, as they imagined the early Christian churches. New England Puritanism combined a rigid moral code that eschewed frivolity and demanded strict observance of the Sabbath; intense introspection to sort out the nuances of faith, sin, and inward conversion; and intellectual challenge to read and interpret the Scriptures in light of Calvinist doctrine. Above all, the Puritans considered learning indispensable to lead them through these daunting tasks.

English Puritans under Charles I recoiled from what they perceived to be the corruption and "popery" of the Anglican Church and rampant immorality in English society. Yet they were reluctant to separate from the Church. Many chose instead to create a godly community in New England that "shall be as a city upon a hill, the eyes of all people . . . upon us." These words of John Winthrop, leader of the Massachusetts Bay Colony, imply that the colonists sought not to reject England but to recreate it in more perfect form. The colony was barely settled when the persecution of nonconformists in England intensified. In reaction, Puritans fled to Massachusetts by the boatload—20 ships per year from 1634 through 1638, a total of 12,000 settlers by 1640. This population was self-selected on the basis of religious zeal but otherwise represented the broad middle ranks of English society, from yeoman to gentry but below the nobility and above the rural poor. They were relatively well educated, with an estimated one in forty households led by college graduates, or about the same proportion as college students in England in 1640. Moreover, it was a community that valued education and was accustomed to supporting it through charity. Common schools taught literacy so that all could read the Bible; Latin grammar schools prepared students for higher studies; and only a college was needed "to advance Learning and to perpetuate it to Posterity." Moreover, a model was readily at hand in the university college and the arts course. Thus, a college was not an ornament but a necessary element in "a city upon a hill."[3]

The Puritans carried not only Reformation theology to the New World, but also patterns of governance characteristic of the Reformation era. In England and across northern Europe, the Reformation brought the domination of the state over national churches. In the process universities became "territorial institutions."[4] Whereas medieval universities had been organized as guilds to protect their autonomy against local towns and bishops, the polity of the seventeenth century regarded state, church, and university as forming a single compound entity. In reality, relations among these organizations were often contested, with consequences that produced two kinds of dynamics for early colonial colleges. Contention between secular and church authority was one source of tension with inescapable ramifications for colleges. A second source was the struggle to define or maintain orthodoxy in the face of doctrinal drift or challenge. For the first three colonial colleges—the colleges of the Reformation era—conflicts surrounding such issues shaped their first century.

---

3   This phrase is from a sermon by John Winthrop aboard the *Arabella* en route to Massachusetts (1630).

4   Jurgen Herbst, *From Crisis to Crisis: American College Government, 1636–1819* (Cambridge: Harvard University Press, 1982), 1–4.

★ THE HISTORY OF ★

American

HIGHER EDUCATION

★ 1 ★

THE FIRST CENTURY OF THE AMERICAN COLLEGE, 1636–1740

HARVARD COLLEGE

IGHER EDUCATION IN BRITISH NORTH AMERICA was conceived on October 28, 1636, when the Great and General Court of Massachusetts Bay "agreed to give 400£ towards a schoale or colledge." Despite the ambiguity of this wording, there is no doubt that the Puritan leaders intended to provide education comparable to that of Oxford and Cambridge, with which they were familiar. Provision had already been made for a preparatory grammar or Latin school in Boston; the new founding was intended for "instructing youth of riper years and literature after they came from grammar schools." This relatively generous appropriation triggered a train of events that led to the erection of Harvard College and its first commencement 6 years later, in 1642.[1] However, the path was far from easy.

Further steps were taken late in 1637 when the Court directed that the college be located at Newtown and added "that Newetowne shall henceforward be called Cambrige."[2] It confided the responsibility for the college to a "committee" of six magistrates and six ministers—who soon became the Board of Overseers. Newtown had grown rapidly in the early 1630s and even functioned briefly as the capital. But its first settlers found the area too cramped and left in 1636 for Connecticut.

The college was intended to uphold orthodox Puritanism, as interpreted by the General Court, the governors of the colony, and this consideration seems to have played a role in placing it in Newtown. Religious controversy was present from the start. The Colony had been shaken that same year by what was deemed heretical teachings by Anne Hutchinson. In increasingly popular

---

1   The following draws upon Samuel Eliot Morison, *The Founding of Harvard College* (Cambridge: Harvard University Press, 1935) and *Harvard College in the Seventeenth Century* (Cambridge: Harvard University Press, 1936). Quotes, *Founding of Harvard*, 168, 449. These works are summarized in *Three Centuries of Harvard* (Cambridge: Harvard University Press, 1936).
2   Morison, *Founding of Harvard*, 188.

discussion groups she had advocated a more severe, antinomian version of Calvinism, which meant stricter criteria for determining who belonged to the elect and hence qualified for full church membership. This approach threatened the governance of both churches and the General Court. Reverend Thomas Shepard of Newtown played a prominent role in opposing Hutchinson's views when she was tried and ultimately banished. The fact that Shepard was named to the overseeing committee and that the college was placed next to his dwelling would seem to be linked with his role in this controversy. Producing ministers with the proper interpretation of Puritanism was understood to be the mission of the new college.

Finding qualified leaders for the college was a challenge throughout the seventeenth century. The ministers of existing congregations were committed by covenant to remain with their congregations, making newcomers the most likely candidates at first. In the summer of 1637 Nathaniel Eaton arrived with some attractive credentials. He was just 27 years old, and his older brother had helped to organize the Massachusetts Bay Company. Although he had dropped out of Trinity College, Cambridge, he subsequently studied at the Dutch University of Franeker with William Ames, the Puritan's most revered theologian. Considered a "rare scholar" for having written a tract on observation of the Sabbath, Eaton was named master and charged with launching the college. He seems to have begun instructing about ten first-year students in the summer of 1638. The little that is known of this initial effort is all bad. Eaton routinely whipped his charges, and his wife failed to provide them with adequate beef and beer. The overseers were apparently blind to these practices, but when he savagely beat an assistant, the whole fiasco came to light. Eaton was tried and dismissed but still managed to abscond with some college funds. The college closed after just 1 year of operation, and students returned to their homes.

Before this tumult, John Harvard had taken an interest in the inchoate college. A graduate of Emmanuel College, Harvard probably crossed over on the same ship as Eaton and undoubtedly visited the new college. When he succumbed to consumption shortly after the college opened, he bequeathed it half of his estate and his entire library. Six months later, a grateful General Court ordered "that the colledge agreed upon formerly to bee built at Cambridg shalbee called Harvard Colledge."[3] But the college still awaited a teacher.

Its needs were met when Henry Dunster arrived in August 1640. A Bachelor and Master (1634) of Magdalene College, Cambridge, who had preached and taught in England, Dunster consented to become the first president of Harvard College just 3 weeks after disembarking—"a meer stranger in the Country," in

3 Ibid., 221.

his words.[4] Reassembling the students almost immediately, he was responsible not only for shepherding them through to the commencement of 1642 but for organizing enduring forms of teaching, living, and governance.

Dunster originally established a 3-year course of study for the AB degree, loosely modeled on those of the Oxford and Cambridge colleges. The major components were philosophy (logic, ethics, and politics), the classical languages and literature, and other subjects suitable for a gentleman's education in the arts. Latin and Greek had quite different roles. Latin was the language of instruction and communication, so that students had to be able to read, write, and speak it as a condition for admission. Beginning students needed only a basic grounding in Greek grammar since this proficiency was developed in all 3 years. Students began by emphasizing logic in order to develop a facility for the disputations that were central to the arts course. Each class devoted one day per week to rhetoric, which prepared students for the flourishes of oratory known as declamations. Saturdays were devoted to divinity. The original Dunster course included Oriental languages (Hebrew and a smattering of Chaldean and Syriac), his specialty, as well as single terms that addressed history, botany, physics, astronomy, and geometry. After a decade, Dunster felt compelled to extend the course to 4 years, like the AB course in England. The fact that the additional year was appended to the beginning of the course and was used for honing skills in Latin and Greek, suggests weak student preparation.

Several aspects of the original Harvard course are notable. First, it was meant to convey a liberal education in the arts for the first degree. Despite the intense piety of the Puritans, the arts were considered essential to the culture of an educated gentleman. Future clergymen were expected to earn a second degree, the master of arts, by reading divinity for 3 years, whether in the college or elsewhere. But the paucity of resources in seventeenth-century Massachusetts made it difficult for most students to complete their education. Second, the course provided a largely literary education. Scientific subjects were only touched upon, in a manner that did not yet reflect the intellectual advances of the seventeenth century. Mathematics was confined to arithmetic and geometry in the last year. The corpus of knowledge transmitted at Harvard College was considered fixed, and inquiry after new knowledge was beyond imagining. Third, in spite of the static conception of knowledge, the pedagogy demanded what today would be called active learning. Students studied their texts, kept notebooks to organize this knowledge, and copied key concepts or phrases for future use in declamations or disputations. These latter two exercises occupied significant parts of the week for all classes, and performance in these exercises largely determined a

4   Ibid., 448.

3

student's standing. Finally, the graduation protocols provided both accountability and a capstone experience as the commencers publicly "demonstrated their proficiency in the tongues and the arts" with declamations and disputations that addressed previously publicized "*theses* and *quaestiones*."[5]

Harvard's first commencement in 1642 consecrated the initial success of Dunster's efforts. In an impressive ceremony, the governor, magistrates, ministers and other educated citizens endured a full day of Greek and (mostly) Latin presentations. Nine students who had begun their studies under Nathaniel Eaton were awarded the first degree of bachelor of arts. It is often noted that the college had no authority to award degrees, since it lacked a royal charter. However, Harvard degrees had the backing of the colony, which created the college as one component of its self-sufficient existence. Given the universal nature of the arts course and President Dunster's qualifications as a master, Harvard degrees were soon recognized elsewhere as well.[6]

The commencement also marked the public debut of the college building. This structure allowed the students, who had been "dispersed in the town and miserably distracted," to be united in the "collegiate way of living."[7] The graduates of Cambridge and Oxford who organized the college viewed this arrangement as essential for a college of arts: teachers and scholars living together under a common discipline and sharing in meals, chambers, prayers, and recreation—a kind of total immersion in a setting devoted to learning. The building itself soon came to be known as the Old College. A four-story wooden open quadrangle, shaped like an *E*, it was so poorly designed and constructed that it required constant repairs and lasted fewer than 40 years.[8] The first floor contained a large hall where the entire college assembled for prayers, meals, and college exercises, as well as rooms for storing, preparing, and serving food. The library was on the second floor. Student chambers were scattered throughout, mostly on the upper stories. Students lived three or four to a chamber, which also contained individual cubicles as studies.

In 1650 Dunster was able to solidify the governance of the college by obtaining a charter of incorporation from the General Court. The eminent Overseers could seldom be gathered for college business, so the Charter of 1650 established

---

5 "Theses are propositions on the several liberal Arts and other subjects studied in the undergraduate course, which any member of the graduating class, if challenged, was supposed to be able to defend, in Latin, by the recognized rules of syllogistic disputation . . . . The quaestiones were defended or opposed by candidates for the Master's degree, at Masters' Commencement on the afternoon of Commencement Day": *Harvard College*, 580.

6 Morison, *Founding of Harvard*, 257–62.

7 Ibid., 448.

8 Bainbridge Bunting, *Harvard: An Architectural History* (Cambridge: Harvard University Press, 1985), 5–12.

a corporation, consisting of the president, treasurer, and five fellows, to be responsible for the affairs of the college and particularly its finances. The Overseers remained as a second, dominant external board, with responsibility to approve the actions of the Corporation. Dunster no doubt envisioned active teaching fellows filling out the Corporation. However, because the college could support only two such positions in the seventeenth century, outside ministers were enlisted. Whether the fellows should be instructors or external representatives would be a future bone of contention. The Charter of 1650 has endured as the basis for governing Harvard, the oldest continuous corporation in the Western Hemisphere.

Dunster resigned the presidency in 1654 under circumstances that exposed the realities of college governance perhaps better than the charter. He was first disturbed by the General Court's assertion of authority over the college. When Dunster had complained of insufficient funds, the court ordered a review of all income and expenditures. The resulting report found no wrongdoing on Dunster's part, but the court nevertheless affirmed the Overseers' authority over the corporation in financial matters. Dunster doubtless had assumed that his charter accorded greater powers to the president and corporation, and he complained of this slight in his letter of resignation. However, it was a theological matter that made his position untenable. Dunster had become convinced that there was no scriptural justification for infant baptism. The notion that baptism should signify adult religious commitment was a heresy associated with Anabaptists, who were outlawed in the Colony and banished to Rhode Island. Dunster could have retained the presidency had he kept his beliefs to himself, but he would not suppress what he held (with Biblical justification) to be truth. The court finally reacted by announcing that no one should teach in school or college who "manifested themselves unsound in the faith."[9] Given the Reformation melding of state, church, and college, Dunster had to go. But the problem of the state determining what was sound or unsound in the faith was not so easily dismissed—as subsequent developments would show.

When Dunster withdrew in 1654 he left a flourishing, if impecunious, college of about fifty students. Harvard degrees were recognized in England, and its students hailed from New England and beyond. In just 15 years Dunster had created the fully functioning arts college that the Puritan founders had envisioned. Yet it had already assumed distinctive American features. The collegiate way of living was sparer in Cambridge, Massachusetts, but in some ways more intense. Students thrown together with their classmates for 4 years developed lasting bonds,

9 *Harvard College*, 302–14; Jurgen Herbst, *From Crisis to Crisis: American College Government, 1636–1819* (Cambridge: Harvard University Press, 1982), 10–18.

so that the class became a stronger source of identity in America than in England. Tutors turned over rapidly given their meager stipends, so that the president dominated teaching in the American college. And, while Oxbridge colleges enjoyed endowments and a significant degree of autonomy, Harvard emanated from a self-defined community that expected to both support and control the institution.

Dunster was replaced by the learned but elderly Charles Chauncy (1654–1672), who provided solid if uninspired leadership until his death at age 80. The difficulties facing Chauncy and Harvard were not of his making. The outbreak of the English Civil War in 1640 had brought the dissenters to power. With an end to persecution, Puritans were no longer driven to emigrate to the Bay Colony. The absence of newcomers and new money brought the economy near to collapse. The dearth of new settlements also shrunk the need for new ministers. Instead, Puritan rule in England during the 1650s under the Protectorate of Oliver Cromwell generated a huge demand for Puritan ministers there. A reverse migration took place that chiefly attracted the young and the educated. Reverend Richard Mather of Dorchester, for example, saw three of his four Harvard-educated sons take parishes in England and only the youngest, Increase, return to Massachusetts after the Restoration.[10] As the constituency of Harvard evolved from first-generation immigrants to indigenous families, educational aspirations waned. College enrollments fell by half during Chauncy's tenure; graduates fell to five or six per year (and none in 1672), and fewer bachelors completed the master's degree. These relative doldrums persisted until the 1680s. By then a pattern for seventeenth-century Harvard was set.

Roughly 300 students attended Harvard under Dunster and Chauncy (1640–1672), and almost 200 of them graduated. In the next 35 years the college enrolled about 360 students, most of them after 1690, when class size grew to around 15.[11] Dunster's students were distinctive in being the sons of English exiles, if not exiles themselves. Sons of ministers or magistrates were a majority, and the rest came from gentry families. These classes contained a number of older students, as well as students from England and other colonies. Under Chauncy, however, Harvard quickly became a New England institution. The ministerial connection, unsurprisingly, was central to both recruitment and careers. Almost one-quarter of Harvard students were sons of Harvard-trained ministers. But, overall only about two-thirds of students came from gentry or college-educated fathers. Included in this group were a few fellow-commoners, as at Oxbridge, who paid double tui-

10 Michael G. Hall, *The Last Puritan: The Life of Increase Mather* (Middletown, CT: Wesleyan University Press, 1981), 41–48.
11 Morison, *Harvard College*, 70–80, 448–52.

tion and dined with the fellows and resident bachelors, a practice that continued into the early eighteenth century. Still, it seems remarkable that one-third of students came from the common people of New England. One reason for this may have been the availability of schooling. Samuel Eliot Morison found the largest numbers of students hailing from, respectively, Boston, Cambridge, Ipswich, and Roxbury—towns that maintained grammar schools in the same order of size. Other students would typically have been prepared individually by local ministers and even then would face the costs of tuition and living expenses at Harvard. Total costs for 4 years at Harvard in the seventeenth century approximated 2 years' income for a common laborer—not too different from the price of a residential public university education in 2010.[12]

A professed mission of Harvard College was to educate a learned Puritan ministry, but the college was never a seminary and always committed to an arts education. Becoming a minister was the only distinctive "career" existing in seventeenth-century New England. More than half of Harvard students entered the ministry until about 1720, but ministerial preparation occurred after the bachelor's degree. A few students remained at Harvard to read for the master's degree, while most apprenticed with local ministers. Entrance into the profession required both acceptance by a congregation and ordination. The large number of graduates that pursued this demanding route reflects the prominence of ministers in Puritan society. Conversely, the variety of callings followed by the remaining graduates suggests mixed rather than fixed occupations. College graduates by definition assumed the status of gentlemen. As such they were expected to fill public offices in their community (although Harvard graduates were exempt from military service). Similarly, most probably raised a good portion of their own food and traded goods. Many young graduates spent some time as teachers, but only a handful became career educators. Fewer than 10 percent became physicians, as few settlements were large enough to support a medical doctor. Finally, the law did not become a distinct profession in America until the middle of the next century.[13]

In the hierarchical society that the Puritans brought from England, education and property were markers of status. A college education signified high social status, but also the expectation to play a prominent role in community or church affairs. The Harvard College curriculum inculcated the culture associated with this status. On one hand, the omnipresence of God and His handiwork

---

12 Marjory Somers Foster, *"Out of smalle Beginnings . . .": An Economic History of Harvard College in the Puritan Period* (Cambridge: Harvard University Press, 1962), 83–84; James Axtell, *The School upon a Hill: Education and Society in Colonial New England* (New Haven: Yale University Press, 1974), 207–18.

13 Morison, *Harvard College*, 556–65; Bailey B. Burritt, "Professional Distribution of College and University Graduates," U.S. Bureau of Education, Bulletin No. 19, 1912.

permeated their intellectual world, and what the Puritans called godliness was an expected outcome for a college graduate. But learning itself—the basic arts curriculum—was universally recognized as the foundation of the culture of a gentleman. The polite learning acquired from ancient literature was certainly a part of this culture. But the College also inculcated a sense of *eupraxia* (well-acting), the Aristotelian notion embedded in Puritan theology that the end of knowledge is praxis, or knowing how to act.[14] This gentleman's culture was the implicit content of a Harvard education for ministers as well as laypeople. It permeated status relationships and everyday life in Puritan society. It was explicitly celebrated on special occasions like Harvard's annual commencements, where educated men from throughout the colony gathered to ritually induct graduates into the culture of gentlemen.

YALE COLLEGE

The Puritan settlers of Connecticut were an offshoot of their counterparts at Massachusetts Bay, and they too felt the need for a college to uphold and perpetuate religion and learning. Hopes of founding a college centered on New Haven, but the only serious attempt to launch such a school foundered around 1660 for lack of students or support. The small and dispersed settlements in the colony frustrated any concerted effort. Instead, aspiring ministers endured the difficult and expensive trip to Cambridge, where they comprised 12 percent of Harvard graduates. However, by century's end conditions finally seemed propitious for the colony to have a college of its own.

The governor of Massachusetts described Connecticut, circa 1700, as "thirty-thousand souls, about thirty-three towns, all dissenters, supplied with ministers and schools of their own persuasion." It was a homogeneous Puritan society in which church and state functioned as parts of a coordinated whole. Under its corporate charter the colony enjoyed self-government with an elected governor and general assembly. The social and political units were actually the forty-six independent church congregations. All residents paid taxes to support the Congregational churches. Ministers took the initiative to launch a college. Led by James Pierpont of New Haven, ministers from several coastal towns met and agreed upon the desirability of such an effort. At this juncture the status of the American colonies was under scrutiny in England. Fearful of taking any step that

14 Morison, *Harvard College*, 163–64; Perry Miller, *The New England Mind: The Seventeenth Century* (Cambridge: Harvard University Press, 1963), 190; Norman Fiering, *Moral Philosophy at Seventeenth-Century Harvard: A Discipline in Transition* (Chapel Hill: University of North Carolina Press, 1981), 44–47.

might disturb Connecticut's relative autonomy, they sought legal advice about the possible status and scope of a college. The responses offered cautious encouragement, but recommended a low profile—giving the "Accademie as low a name" as possible and the master a title "which shows Least of Grandeur." With this timid backing, ten ministers brought the plan to the General Assembly, which on October 9, 1701, passed "An Act for Liberty to erect a Collegiate School."[15]

This entire process was encouraged through an ongoing exchange of letters and advice from conservative Harvardians in Massachusetts. In 1701 the staunchly Puritan minister and statesman Increase Mather was being forced from the Harvard presidency (see below), and he and his supporters were eager to see an alternative school established that would uphold Puritan orthodoxy. Early in that year an anonymous letter, attributed to his son Cotton, suggested that Connecticut establish a university to be called "The School of the Churches," with the pastors of twelve churches serving as external government. In September Increase Mather, no longer president, wrote to provide his encouragement. Interestingly, both Mathers advocated an institution quite different from Harvard. They envisioned a college entirely controlled by Congregational ministers, who could be trusted to preserve the "purity of religion." They rejected the collegiate way of living in favor of having students room in the town as they did in continental universities. And they condemned the boisterous public commencements that had become the custom at Harvard and "of late years proved very expensive & are occasion of much sin." More direct assistance was provided by Massachusetts Judge Samuel Sewall (H. 1671). Upon request of the Connecticut ministers, he provided a draft charter for the college. With only slight editing, this was the document enacted by the General Assembly.[16]

The charter of the Collegiate School gave its sponsors the authority and powers needed to found an institution but left other particulars open for the trustees to determine. The purpose was clear: "the founding, suitably endowing & ordering of a Collegiate School within his Majesties Colony of Connecticut wherein Youth may be instructed in the Arts & Sciences who thorough the blessing of Almighty God may be fitted for Publick employment in both Church and Civil State." Complete authority over the institution was accorded to ten named trustees, all senior ministers of the larger colony towns, with the right to name their successors in perpetuity. The General Assembly granted the new school an annual grant of £120 country pay (i.e., in kind), and the right to acquire and

15 Richard Warch, *School of the Prophets: Yale College, 1701–1740* (New Haven: Yale University Press, 1973), quotes pp. 41, 25, 24, 30; Brooks Mather Kelley, *Yale: A History* (New Haven: Yale University Press, 1974), 3–10.

16 These documents are presented in George Wilson Pierson, *The Founding of Yale College: The Legend of the Forty Folios* (New Haven: Yale University Press, 1988), 3–12.

own other assets. As for the school itself, the trustees were to hire a rector and tutors, as well as "grant degrees or Licenses" as they deemed proper. Subsequent controversy over whether Yale was a public or private institution would invoke different interpretations of these events. However, for Connecticut Puritans the churches and civil state were each playing their accustomed roles in adding a college to the polity.

The trustees wasted no time, gathering in Saybrook, at the mouth of the Connecticut River, only 1 month later to lay the foundation for the school. It was here, according to venerable Yale legend, that the trustees allegedly pledged their own books—some forty folios—to give the college its first tangible property.[17] They designated Saybrook as the provisional locus of the college and named one of their number, Abraham Pierson of nearby Killingsworth, as rector. Curriculum was not an issue, since all but one of the trustees were Harvard graduates and well understood that their purpose was to teach the "liberal arts and languages" and to confer bachelor's and master's degrees. Having all attended during the Chauncy era, they replicated Harvard of the 1650s. This November meeting in Saybrook marks the true founding of what became Yale College.

The early years of the Collegiate School were disorderly, but the resolve of the trustees and the general support of the colony preserved a viable and growing enterprise. At the outset, Rector Pierson was unable to secure a release from his Killingsworth congregation to move to Saybrook, so the students instead came to him. He began instructing the first student in his home in 1702, and that same year the school awarded its first degrees, both BA and MA, to an exceptionally well-prepared student. It thereby asserted its status as a true college despite its unassuming title. Pierson provided sound leadership and instruction, although finding satisfactory tutors proved difficult. In the first 5 years of operation, the school enrollment rose to seventeen undergraduates and produced fourteen graduates. However, when rector Pierson died in 1707, new arrangements had to be made. The college finally moved to Saybrook, but there teaching was conducted by tutors since, again, no rector could be persuaded to relocate. The college persisted in Saybrook for 8 years, although in far from satisfactory conditions. In 1716 the unhappy students dispersed to study with ministers independently, most going to Wethersfield (near Hartford) or New Haven. The trustees from the Hartford churches then asked the General Assembly to locate the college there permanently. For a year, students were instructed in three different places—Wethersfield, New Haven, and a few still in Saybrook. At this point New Haven made a concerted effort to claim the college and began erecting a true college building for its new home. The General Assembly finally intervened,

17   For the circumstances and significance, see Pierson, *Founding of Yale College*.

eventually deciding in favor of New Haven, but both Saybrook and Hartford contested the decision for another 2 years.

While still in this precarious state, the college had the good fortune to receive a major gift from Elihu Yale, an English Anglican originally from New England who had grown quite wealthy in the India trade. Cotton Mather had written to Yale promising him a naming opportunity: "what is forming at New Haven might wear the name of YALE COLLEGE." Jeremiah Dummer, a Harvard graduate who was the London agent for Connecticut and Massachusetts, secured Yale's donation. Dummer convinced the Anglican Yale to support a dissenter college since, Yale reasoned, "the business of good men is to spread religion and learning among mankind without being too fondly attached to particular Tenets, about which the World never was, nor ever will be agreed"—a sentiment shared by no one connected with the Collegiate School.[18] In August, 1718, his donation arrived in Boston: a large box of books, a portrait of King George I, and goods from the East Indies that sold for more than £500. The new college building was quickly named for Yale, and soon the institution itself was called Yale College. By 1720 the Collegiate School had a new name, a permanent home, and a building for the collegiate way of living. It also obtained a resident rector for the first time. The Reverend Timothy Cutler was considered one of the colony's most effective preachers and just the sort of leader who could discipline the students and overcome the previous fissiparous tendencies.

Yale College thrived in its new home and quickly grew. It averaged twelve annual graduates in the first half of the 1720s and sixteen in the second half. It also became somewhat more worldly. Whereas almost three-quarters of earlier graduates entered the ministry, that proportion fell to around one-half from the 1720s onward. Yale was fulfilling its mission of fitting youth for employment in both church and civil state. However, its parallel mission of upholding the purity of Puritanism would prove more challenging.

THE COLLEGE OF WILLIAM & MARY

Virginia was chartered in 1606 as a Crown colony with Anglicanism as the established church. Hence, affairs of church and state were legally set in London, including provisions for education. Only 10 years after Jamestown was settled in 1607, King James asked his subjects to contribute toward "the erecting of some Churches and Schooles for the education of children of those Barbarians."[19] This

18   Warch, *School of the Prophets,* quotes p. 85.
19   For Colonial William & Mary, Thad W. Tate, "The Colonial College, 1693–1782," in *The College of William & Mary: A History, vol. I (1693–1888)* (Williamsburg: King and Queen Press, 1993), 3–162;

initiative blossomed into a plan for a full-fledged university inland from Jamestown at Henrico. Land was secured, settlers were brought in, and in 1622 a rector was named. Before he could set sail, however, the unappreciative Barbarians massacred the settlers, and the venture was abandoned. Not until William and Mary assumed the throne in the Glorious Revolution of 1688 would conditions in London again be propitious for planting a college in Virginia. That these conditions were exploited to create the College of William & Mary was the single-handed accomplishment of an individual who today might be labeled a policy entrepreneur, James Blair.

Son of a Scottish minister, Blair was educated in the arts and theology at the University of Edinburgh before assuming his own parish. A liberal Anglican, he was purged from that position for not supporting the Stuart monarchy. Moving to London, he established good relations with Anglican opponents of the Stuarts. In 1685 Blair was persuaded to accept a parish in Virginia, which was always in need of clergy. He apparently distinguished himself among rather undistinguished peers and also married into a powerful Virginia family. He was a rising political force within the colony when the Glorious Revolution brought his patrons to power in London. Blair was appointed commissary, or head of the Anglican clergy in Virginia, and at his first convocation in 1690 he secured a resolution to establish a college. He soon enlisted the support of the colony and in 1691 traveled to England to secure a royal charter. Nearly 2 years of bureaucratic wrangling ensued, but in 1693 Blair succeeded in having the monarchs issue a charter for a college bearing their names.

Certainly the College of William & Mary was less premature than the Henrico venture 70 years earlier, but it was nevertheless created for a land that had little use for advanced education. Virginia by the 1690s had a dispersed population of large plantations that were growing wealthy through tobacco and slaves. In many ways still a frontier society, it lacked both towns and schools, and it had large numbers of unattached and unruly young men. No doubt Blair and officials in London felt the need for a college so that—in the words of the charter—"the Church of Virginia may be furnished with a Seminary of Ministers of the Gospel, and that the Youth may be piously educated in good Letters and Manners." But these were wishful thoughts. Whereas the early colleges of New England were founded and supported by their communities, the chartering of William & Mary was an act of a distant government. Still, obtaining a

---

J. David Hoeveler, *Creating the American Mind* (New York: Rowman & Littlefield, 2002), 79–100; Arthur P. Middleton, "Anglican Contributions to Higher Education in Colonial America," *Pennsylvania History*, XXV, 3 (July, 1958): 49–66, quote p. 52. Most records of colonial William & Mary were destroyed in successive fires, so there is much uncertainty about many aspects of the college.

royal charter was something of a feat—unmatched by any other college in the American colonies.

The college charter specified four levels of instruction—a grammar school to teach basic Latin, a school of philosophy in which collegiate subjects would be taught, and a school of divinity to prepare Anglican ministers. A separate endowment provided for an Indian school as well. The charter also specified a faculty of six—single teachers for the grammar and Indian schools, professors of moral and natural philosophy, and two professors of divinity. The institution was to be liberally supported with land grants and shares of various royal revenues. Just as Oxford and Cambridge each elected a member of the House of Commons, the college could elect a burgess to the Virginia legislature. Initially, a board of trustees was responsible for the college assets until the terms of the charter were fulfilled; those powers would then revert to the president and faculty of the college. However, more than 30 years passed before this occurred. In the meantime, James Blair was in full control. He was named president of the college for life, which turned out to be 50 years. He also served on the board of trustees and the Board of Visitors that succeeded it. Unlike northern college presidents, he never taught in the college. This was but one of many anomalies in the unique model of the College of William & Mary.

The early years of the college saw three notable accomplishments. First, Blair succeeded in hiring an able schoolmaster for the grammar school, and instruction commenced in 1694. Second, with the funds promised for the founding of the college, an impressive collegiate building was erected over the next 5 years. Third, as complications grew at the Jamestown settlement, Blair helped arrange the relocation of the colony capital to Williamsburg, close by the college. Twenty-nine registered students were reported in 1702, all in the grammar school, but the situation soon deteriorated. Blair's growing involvement and power in the colony came with neglect of the college. He quarreled (victoriously) with succeeding royal governors and alienated the grammar schoolmaster. Enrollments shrank (Blair withdrew his own nephew), and the trustees withheld Blair's substantial presidential salary due to lack of progress in fulfilling the charter. Then, in 1705, the college building burned to the ground, followed shortly by the resignation of the only teacher.

Barely a decade after its founding, the College of William & Mary was close to collapse. But it slowly recovered over the next decade. The Indian school was organized for the first time, fulfilling the obligation of its endowment. It appeared to serve its purpose for a number of years before the unrealistic expectations of the English toward Native Americans became evident. A new master was retained for the grammar school, although one less reliable than his predecessor. And a new college edifice was slowly raised—the building that now stands in restored form at the College. For a short time (1717–1721) the college even managed to retain a professor of mathematics and natural philosophy. But Blair's political intrigues caused the college to dissolve into factionalism once more. For at least two decades, James Blair's ongoing political battles had made the founder more of a liability than an asset. However, at this juncture he endeavored to revive the college and fulfill the terms of its charter.

In order to have the charter transferred to the college, thus giving sovereign authority to the president and faculty, Blair had to obtain the six professors or masters originally specified. Only in 1729 was he able to make a pretense of doing so. His most solid appointee was a recent Oxford graduate, William Dawson, who was made professor of moral philosophy. Dawson filled that post for 14 years and succeeded Blair as president (1643–1652). The masters of the grammar and Indian schools also counted. To fill out the faculty he appointed two parish clergy to the chairs in divinity, although they had no apparent duties. The chair in natural philosophy was awarded to an Edinburgh graduate who was otherwise occupied on a surveying expedition. On his demise in 1731 a competent replacement was named, who actually did teach in the college. Historians of the colonial college doubt that the six charter masters were ever in the same room together, but on paper they were sufficient to fulfill the terms of the charter.[20]

In 1729 the royal charter, amended with additional statutes (1727), was transferred from London to Williamsburg.[21] The college now had both a grammar school and a school of philosophy with two qualified teachers. Moreover, since the college's founding, Virginia had evolved into a society with growing numbers of wealthy planter families, now more appreciative of cultural gentility and some kinds of practical learning. According to the statutes of the college, the grammar school offered a 4-year course, capped by an examination at or about age 15. Two more years of study in the school of philosophy could lead to a bachelor's degree (extended to 4 years in 1758). But, in fact, the sons of Virginia had little desire for so long a course or for formal degrees. Most probably acquired some Latin from local tutors or ministers and then attended for two or three years in the grammar school and possibly in philosophy, but apparently none graduated. Nor did the faculty offer any encouragement for them to do so.[22] As for preparing ministers

20 Tate, "Colonial College," 62–72.

21 August 15, the date of the transfer, was henceforth celebrated as Transfer Day, an event similar to commencements at northern colleges.

22 The absence of graduates presents a puzzling contrast with other colonial colleges. Most William & Mary masters were the product of Oxford colleges, which provided instruction but not degrees. The university conducted examinations and awarded degrees. Without the sanction of examinations and degrees, instruction was most likely offered and received in a casual manner. Only in 1770 were efforts made to upgrade the course of study, and the first BA degrees were awarded in 1772: Tate, "Colonial College," 113.

of the gospel, ordination into the Anglican clergy could be performed only by a bishop, which meant travel to England. Among early William & Mary students, only a handful seem to have followed that path, and they all finished their education in England. Total enrollments rose to around 60 in the 1730s and fluctuated near that level for the rest of the colonial era.

Throughout the history of the colonial college, the grammar school enrolled the largest number of students. Presumably most of these students would have been age 11 to 15, and they no doubt set an unfortunate tone for residential life in the college. The college building also included quarters for philosophy students, but they were not required to live there. It is difficult to compare the college course with that in New England or, for that matter, Oxbridge, the putative model for William & Mary. The grammar school was intended to prepare students in Latin and Greek for collegiate studies, but apparently not many proceeded to the school of philosophy. There, all the other subjects of the collegiate course were taught by the two professors in unknown sequences, if any. In striking contrast with the northern colleges, tight class cohorts were entirely absent, as were the recitations that structured students' daily life. Only at the end of the colonial period was a regular plan of lectures in place. Before then, the rapid turnover of masters must have precluded a consistent or complete curriculum.[23] In one sense, the College of William and Mary offered the amount and kind of advanced education that eighteenth-century Virginia could assimilate. However, the principal constituencies could not agree on a formula that met their divergent interests, with consequences that will be seen below.

CONFLICT AND NEW LEARNING
IN THE EARLY COLLEGES

The first three colleges of British North America followed the pattern of Reformation Europe, in which universities were territorial organizations under the combined authority of an established church and the civil state. Each college was configured somewhat differently but retained the same common elements. Teaching was under the supervision of members of the clergy, and all learning was placed in a religious context. Representatives of the established church provided some or all of the external governance of the institution. And representatives of the civil government were involved as overseers at all but Yale. The colonies provided financial support and had ultimate oversight over the colleges.

---

23   Robert Polk Thomson, "The Reform of the College of William and Mary, 1763–1780," *Proceedings of the American Philosophical Society*, 115, 3 (June 1971): 187–213.

This model of joint church-state effort worked well enough for the establishment of these "schools of the Reformation," as historian Jurgen Herbst has termed them.[24] However, problems soon developed. As new ideas emerged questioning the reigning dogmas of the churches, the ramifications were quickly transmitted to the colleges. Further, the ambiguous sharing of clerical and secular authority proved inherently unstable. Thus, the early histories of these institutions were characterized not by the unity of church, state, and college, but by conflict and controversy.

The seventeenth century experienced greater intellectual advancement than any previous era in human history, marked above all by the scientific revolution, embodied in the Royal Society of London (f. 1662), and the beginnings of the Enlightenment, the dominant intellectual movement of the next century.[25] Neither of these developments affected the curriculum of colonial colleges for some time. The arts course was largely frozen in the trivium and what was still largely Aristotelian philosophy. Moreover, the deeper purpose of the college course and the overriding preoccupation of the institutions were to demonstrate the truth of Christianity. The new learning affected attitudes toward religion first, church polity second, and colleges third.

The new ideas of the late seventeenth and early eighteenth centuries are best described as the Early Enlightenment, to distinguish them from later, more vigorous phases. The two intellectual giants who symbolized the movement in England were John Locke (1632–1704) and Sir Isaac Newton (1642–1727). Their achievements were monumental. Newton's *Principia Mathematica* (1689) described the physical laws governing matter and motion and superseded all previous formulations. Locke's *Essay Concerning Human Understanding* (1690) ignited an ongoing reappraisal of how and what the human mind knows; his *Two Treatises on Government* (1690) anchored the Whig tradition of limited monarchy in England and was later an inspiration for the American Declaration of Independence. For contemporaries, however, the contributions of both men had a multitude of possible meanings. According to historian Norman Fiering, "Locke's philosophy and Newton's discoveries were important in early America only in highly qualified ways, and neither the *Essay* . . . nor the *Principia* . . . may be considered crucial documents for comprehending the development of thought in America before about 1735." This was largely because the intellectual leaders of New England sought initially "new forms of integration of reason and religion." In this quest, Fiering proposes, they were

24   Herbst, *From Crisis to Crisis*, 3–16.
25   Peter Dear, *Revolutionizing the Sciences: European Knowledge and Its Ambitions, 1500–1700*, 2nd ed. (Princeton: Princeton University Press, 2009).

more immediately inspired by a contemporary of the two giants, John Tillot-son (1630–1694).[26]

Elevated to Archbishop of Canterbury in 1691, Tillotson was known above all for his widely admired sermons. Published in various forms and editions beginning in 1664, he was considered "not only the best preacher of his age, but seemed to have brought preaching to perfection."[27] These sermons were probably the most widely read religious literature in the American colonies from 1690 to 1750, not only for their literary qualities but because they also had a generic appeal that transcended religious dogma. They conveyed two principal ideas. First, "nature itself, including human nature, is a revelation of God that may be trusted as an independent source of divine truth." This idea was consistent with Protestant theology, which had always regarded the universe as a manifestation of God's work. Now Newton (or more accurately the popularizers of Newton) had shown the cosmos to be an even more glorious creation than previously realized. But with Tillotson the idea of natural religion distanced itself from other Protestant doctrines. Second, the free exercise of reason could be a guide to religion in itself, without reference to theological commentary. None other than John Locke furthered these arguments with *The Reasonableness of Christianity* (1695), where reason guided by the New Testament yields the simple moral truths of Christianity.[28] Tillotson, whom Locke greatly admired, had also joined reason and revelation by arguing that "the law of God requires nothing of us, but what is recommended to us by our own reason." These sentiments, embellished by Tillotson's literary flair and broad appeal, established a foundation for what Fiering calls "philosophical Anglicanism"—a broad reorientation of the Church of England toward an inclusive, tolerant posture, otherwise known as latitudinarianism. In America, James Turner calls this tradition more simply "reasonable religion."[29]

Numerous other writers contributed to this movement, but the result was official endorsement for a benevolent and intelligent deity, whose guidance for humankind could be known through nature and reason. This was a far cry from

26   Norman Fiering, "The First American Enlightenment: Tillotson, Leverett, and Philosophical Anglicanism," *New England Quarterly* 54, 3 (Sept. 1981): 307–44, quotes pp. 332, 334. See also, Henry F. May, *The Enlightenment in America* (New York: Oxford University Press, 1976), esp. 10–13: May identifies these developments as the beginning of the "Moderate Enlightenment," which reconciled reason and Protestant religion and spanned most of the eighteenth century. He identifies the rational Christianity of Samuel Clarke as foundational, whose influential lectures given a decade after Tillotson's death and developed these themes further: 13–14.

27   Quoted in Fiering, "First American Enlightenment," 310n; Tillotson's sermons were sold to a publisher after his death for £2,500, the largest sum paid to date for rights to an English book. The fourteen volumes were reprinted as late as 1735.

28   Roger Woolhouse, *Locke: A Biography* (Cambridge: Cambridge University Press, 2007), 336–44.

29   James Turner, *Without God, without Creed: The Origins of Unbelief in America* (Baltimore: Johns Hopkins University Press, 1985), 28–34.

the vengeful God of Calvinism. For New England Puritans this view was a challenge quite different from the persecution of the Stuart church; it was rather the challenge of seduction. However, the implications were not apparent until the end of the century. Before then, even Increase Mather admired "the great and good Archbishop Tillotson." And so did Mather's future nemesis, John Leverett, who brought these same ideas into Harvard College.[30]

★　★　★

HARVARD COLLEGE, 1685–1724. Following the death of President Chauncy in 1672, Harvard's weak enrollments were compounded by a series of short-term, ineffective leaders and increasing intellectual isolation from England. Its fortunes began to change, however, when Increase Mather, minister of Boston's Second Church, accepted the presidency (1685–1701). Mather was one of the most learned and prominent figures in the colony—so prominent, in fact, that he had little time for the college. He declined to relinquish his pastoral post or to reside in Cambridge. Moreover, the years of his presidency coincided with a long-running constitutional crisis. In an attempt to reorganize the New England colonies, London abolished the original charter of the Massachusetts Bay Company (1684) and with it the Harvard charter of 1650. The college continued to operate, as did the colony, but Mather was continually involved in negotiations to resolve this situation, including 4 years spent in London. In the meantime, the governance of the college by Corporation and Overseers was uncertain at best. The college nevertheless gained renewed vigor under the direction of two dedicated tutors, John Leverett and William Brattle.

Leverett and Brattle both belonged to prominent Boston families. They were educated together at the Boston Latin School and Harvard (1680). Appointed tutors in 1685 and 1686, respectively, they resided in the college and taught all subjects until both resigned in 1697, Brattle to become pastor of the Cambridge church and Leverett to rise in public office to Speaker of the House of Representatives. During these years the size of the college roughly doubled,[31] but more importantly the two tutors opened the college to the new ideas of the age, especially those of liberal Anglicans. Given Boston's frequent intercourse with the mother country and its growing merchant class, it could scarcely remain isolated from English thought, but Leverett and Brattle were key agents in implanting those ideas. They prompted some modernization of the curriculum, with Brattle

---

30　Quoted in Fiering, "First American Enlightenment," 340, 314.
31　In the decade before 1685, Harvard averaged ca. twenty-five students and six annual graduates; in the 1690s, ca. fifty undergraduates and twelve bachelor's.

contributing an introductory text for Cartesian logic that was used almost until the Revolution.[32] They probably had a greater impact by setting the intellectual tone for the college community. At nightly meals masters and divinity students and other recent graduates joined Leverett and Brattle for stimulating conversation. They thus had a profound influence on numerous Harvard graduates and future ministers, introducing them especially to "episcopal" literature and philosophical Anglicanism.[33] This influence led to the emergence of a distinctly liberal faction, with consequences for the colony and the college.

The liberal Puritans emerged as a distinct party with the organization of Boston's fourth church in 1699. This effort was bankrolled by Thomas Brattle, William's brother, who was also treasurer of Harvard. It gathered liberal Harvard graduates, including its new minister Benjamin Colman, who had studied in England. The new church remained faithful to much of Puritan theology but broke decisively with prevailing church practices by relaxing requirements for membership and foregoing religious tests. Inclusiveness, greater doctrinal flexibility, and the "catholick spirit" better suited the predilections of the city's growing merchant class, who were also gaining influence in the government. The liberals next succeeded in ejecting Increase Mather from the Harvard presidency. The pretext was the long-simmering issue of mandatory residence in the college. Presented with an ultimatum, Mather finally moved to Cambridge, but he could endure it for only 6 months. When he returned to Boston in 1701, the presidency was considered vacated. His successor, Samuel Willard (1701–1707), was also unwilling to forego his Boston congregation. Instead, he was appointed vice president with no residential requirement, merely a promise of regular visits. During these years the college operated much as it had previously; Leverett's former students were tutors, and both Leverett and Brattle were close at hand, residing literally next door. Upon Willard's death in 1707, the corporation defied tradition by electing Leverett, a layman, to a post that had always been filled by Puritan ministers. This act alienated the orthodox Puritans, led by the Mather clan, from the liberals; but the deal was sealed by the colony governor, who offered to reinstate the Charter of 1650 if Leverett were made president. In a stroke, Harvard acquired an on-site leader of enormous stature in the community and resolved the

---

32 "In nearly every discipline—logic, metaphysics, ethics and natural philosophy—the Aristotelian Scholastic inheritance was largely abandoned": Fiering, "First American Enlightenment," 322; however, Morison considers the elements of the curriculum to have been quite stable: *Harvard College*, 147; on Brattle, 192–93; Thomas Jay Siegel, *Governance and Curriculum at Harvard College in the Eighteenth Century*, PhD Diss., Harvard University, 1990, 372–88. Siegel provides a detailed sequel to Morison for issues of governance and curriculum.

33 Morison, *Harvard College*, 504–9; Specifically, they introduced doctrines of rational Christianity of Cambridge Platonist Henry More: Fiering, "First American Enlightenment," 322–23; Hoeveler, *Creating the American Mind*, 44–47.

uncertainties of its governance. These steps established a solid foundation for its efflorescence in the remainder of the colonial era and beyond.[34]

To Samuel Eliot Morison he was the "Great Leverett," who "was steadfast in preserving the College from the devastating control of provincial orthodoxy . . . kept it a house of learning under the spirit of religion . . . [and] founded the liberal tradition of Harvard University."[35] Indeed, his control over the college was challenged by Puritan conservatives until the end of his presidency. The greatness of President Leverett (1708–1724) did not stem from pedagogical or organizational innovation. Rather, his personal charisma and complete devotion to the institution served as aegis under which the college prospered, grew, and changed with the times.

Harvard College roughly doubled in enrollments during the Leverett years. In 1721 it counted 124 students, including resident graduates. Only Yale and Harvard attained larger enrollments in the colonial era, and the size of the average American colleges would not exceed this figure until the 1890s. The General Court voted funds for Massachusetts Hall (1720) to accommodate these students in the college. A good part of this growth apparently came from the rising merchant class of the region, whose sons often wished above all to become gentlemen. Their presence enlivened extracurricular life at the college with clubs, the first student periodical, and abundant illicit activities. This behavior was sufficiently notorious that a 16-year old Benjamin Franklin satirized these would-be gentlemen who left Harvard "as great Blockheads as ever, only more proud and self-conceited." Those destined for the ministry declined from nearly two-thirds at the end of Leverett's tutorship to under one-half at the end of his presidency—still by far the college's largest constituency.[36]

Leverett seems to have had less impact on the curriculum as president than he did as a tutor. That he hired a permanent instructor in Hebrew suggests how traditional the arts course remained. But within that structure unmistakable progress occurred. During these years tutors served increasingly lengthy tenures, led by Henry ("Father") Flynt, who held that post for 55 years, abused by students and beloved by graduates. Thomas Robie, who tutored from 1713 to 1722, made important contributions to advancing science in the college. His scientific observations brought election to the Royal Society, and he resigned to practice medicine, which he taught himself. These older and more professional teachers were more competent than the typical tutors—recent graduates, usually

34   Hall, *Last Puritan*, 292–301; Morison, *Harvard College*; Morison, *Three Centuries*, 45–53.

35   Morison, *Three Centuries*, 53–75, quote pp. 74–75.

36   Morison, *Three Centuries*, quote p. 61; Burritt, "Professional Distribution"; John D. Burton, "Collegiate Living and Cambridge Justice: Regulating the Colonial Harvard Student Community in the Eighteenth Century," *Perspectives on the History of Higher Education*, 23 (2003–2004): 83–106.

preparing for ministerial careers.[37] Of greater significance was the creation of permanent professorships. This academic milestone was made possible by the gifts of a London Baptist, Thomas Hollis. At the urging of Benjamin Colman, now a fellow of the Corporation, Hollis endowed a professorship of divinity in 1722. Although he stipulated only that the chairholder be accepting of adult baptism, Harvard's governors insisted on strict religious tests before appointing Edward Wigglesworth—further evidence of the limits of "liberal" Puritanism. But Hollis fortunately ignored this slight, and Wigglesworth, during his 41-year incumbency, subtly chipped away at bedrock Calvinist doctrines. In 1727 Hollis donated a second chair in mathematics and natural philosophy, this time encouraged by a recent Harvard graduate studying in England, who was then named to fill it. Isaac Greenwood strengthened the teaching of science and mathematics during his short tenure (1727–1738) before succumbing to intemperance; and his successor, John Winthrop (1738–1779), achieved far more.[38] The Hollis professorships gave an American college an intellectual foundation for the first time. These individuals had a secure position in which to develop expertise in their subjects and to convey that expertise not only to students but to the community at large. The eighteenth-century holders of these chairs thus played a crucial role in overcoming the outmoded worldview of Puritanism and bringing the Enlightenment to America.

★　★　★

YALE, 1718–1740. New Haven proved more resistant to intellectual advancement. Boston was a thriving seaport in constant intercourse with England. Many Harvard graduates, like Colman and Greenwood, traveled to the mother country for further study and there imbibed the prevailing spirit of toleration, reason, and scientific inquiry. Connecticut remained quite insular, even as its Puritan homogeneity slowly eroded. In addition, while the transformation of Harvard had been led by secular leadership on its governing boards, Yale was effectively under the thumb of its clerical trustees. The congregational church, moreover, had solidified its internal discipline by adopting the Saybrook Platform in 1709. Drawn up by church leaders who were also trustees of the Collegiate School,

37 John D. Burton, "The Harvard Tutors: The Beginning of an Academic Profession, 1690–1825," *History of Higher Education Annual*, 16 (1996): 5–20; Clifford K. Shipton, *New England Life in the Eighteenth Century* (Cambridge: Harvard University Press, 1963), 6–12; Frederick G. Kilgour, "Thomas Robie (1689–1729), Colonial Scientist and Physician," *Isis*, 30, 3 (Aug. 1939): 473–90.

38 Morison, *Three Centuries*, 66–68; Theodore Hornberger, *Scientific Thought in the American Colleges, 1638–1800* (Austin: University of Texas Press, 1945), 44–51; Hoeveler, *Creating the American Mind*, 215–36.

the platform specified traditional Calvinist articles of faith and established consociations to oversee the individual congregations. Concerned above all with disorder within their churches, Connecticut Puritans were only dimly aware of the new ideas of the Moderate Enlightenment, which were closer at hand than they realized.[39]

Just 4 years before he secured Elihu Yale's gift, Jeremiah Dummer had assisted the Collegiate School by gathering a large donation of books (1714). Well connected himself, he managed to acquire gifts from London's leading men of letters, including a second edition of the *Principia* from Sir Isaac Newton. In all, he dispatched nine crates of books containing more than 800 volumes. The school suddenly possessed perhaps the largest and most up-to-date library in the colonies, but given its disorganized state there were few beneficiaries. Early colonial college libraries were off limits to undergraduates and used chiefly by master's or divinity students. However, one recent graduate took a keen interest and began to peruse the collection.

Samuel Johnson graduated from the Collegiate School in Saybrook in 1714. He began teaching in nearby Guilford and borrowing books from the new collection. Johnson had a penchant for constructing comprehensive philosophical systems from his student days to his later writings. However, confronting the new learning was like leaping across centuries from the outdated curriculum he had just studied. He abandoned the geocentric Ptolemaic cosmology for the Newtonian universe only in 1717, for example. He initially sought to assimilate the empirical epistemology of Locke's *Essay Concerning Human Understanding* with the teleological systems he learned in college. He next attacked astronomy by reading the popularizers of Newton, but he quickly discovered he lacked the mathematical knowledge to read the master. As he read, Johnson formed discussion groups with nearby teachers and ministers and continued this practice when he became a tutor at New Haven. Johnson was a learned but unpopular tutor from 1717 through 1719, quite likely because he attempted to teach new learning that he did not fully understand himself. He was forced to leave to ensure internal peace for the new rector, Timothy Cutler, and took a post as minister in nearby West Haven. As he continued his reading, the focus shifted to philosophical Anglicans like Tillotson. Johnson's reading circle now included Rector Cutler, who as a 1701 graduate of Harvard would have been more familiar with the new learning and had already begun flirting with Anglicanism.[40]

---

39 Warch, *School of the Prophets*, 52–57; Hoeveler, *Creating the American Mind*, 55–62.

40 Joseph J. Ellis, *The New England Mind in Transition: Samuel Johnson of Connecticut, 1696–1772* (New Haven: Yale University Press, 1973), 34–75.

At the 1722 graduation, Cutler concluded prayers with a passage from the Anglican liturgy. In doing so he signaled his apostasy from the Congregational Church and acceptance of the great enemy of Puritanism, the English Church. He was joined by Samuel Johnson and five others, only one of whom followed through with his apostasy. Subsequently examined by the trustees and then by the governor, Cutler, Johnson, and a Yale tutor stood their ground. They resigned their positions and soon set sail for England to become Anglican clergy. The specific issue that had prompted the break was their doubts of the legitimacy of Puritan ordination rather than ordination by a bishop in the apostolic succession. However, behind this recondite theological issue lay the weight of the new learning, rational Christianity, and natural religion.[41]

The apostasy at Yale reverberated throughout New England, giving false hopes to Anglicans and unwarranted despair to Puritans. As for Yale, the trustees reacted predictably by imposing church discipline: They declared that all college officers would henceforth be required to swear acceptance of the Confession of Faith of the Saybrook Platform.[42] As far as its governors were concerned, Yale was a sectarian college. And, for a time it prospered as such. Elisha Williams (1726–1739) was installed as the new rector, and for his tenure Yale at last had stability to grow and prosper. Williams was recognized as an admirable college leader. The number of graduates rose by half to average 18 per year, and the colony provided ample support. A church-state consensus upheld Puritan orthodoxy, which now emphasized a heightened guard against "Arminianism." This doctrine implied that salvation could be achieved in some measure though good works and had always been rejected vehemently by Calvinists in favor of predestination. But Arminianism was now the de facto creed of the Anglican Church, if not liberal Puritans. When Williams resigned to follow other pursuits, the trustees chose as successor Thomas Clap (H. 1722), a young Connecticut minister who had distinguished himself through fierce opposition to Arminianism. Clap (1740–1766) was the first Yale rector to have a normal succession and the first as well to assume the direction of a tranquil and settled college. It would not remain so for long. Clap would spend his tenure in a futile struggle to uphold Puritan orthodoxy—to preserve a school of the Reformation in an age of Enlightenment.

41   Existing historiography emphasizes Samuel Johnson, his reading of the Dummer collection, and his subsequent reading circles for the apostasy. However, it seems more likely that Cutler led the actual break, possibly after receiving assurances from Anglicans of appointment as minister to the new Anglican Church being erected in Boston. In that position, Cutler subsequently became a strident conservative, alienating both Harvardians and liberal Anglicans: Shipton, *New England Life*, 79–101.

42   Ironically, the same year that Harvard imposed a rather superficial religious test on one individual, Edward Wigglesworth, Yale imposed a more stringent test on all future teachers.

WILLIAM & MARY. The Virginia college felt no such tension between Calvinism and philosophical Anglicanism. James Blair was aligned with church liberals who triumphed in the Glorious Revolution and even corresponded with John Locke. Later, William & Mary would embrace enlightenment thinking as a matter of course. However, new learning and old learning were scarcely issues when the institution was only a grammar school; nor did sympathy toward the new learning spare it from conflict afterward. Rather, an ambiguous governance structure and the political fault lines of the colony produced repeated, debilitating confrontations.

James Blair seems to have set a pattern with his clashes with the colony's governors, which were symptomatic of a latent antagonism between the interests of the Anglican clergy and those of native Virginia planters. After a period of relative calm during the aged Blair's final years and the tenure of his successor, William Dawson, this conflict intensified. The charter accorded the president and faculty control over the college. Once a full faculty was resident, they became more assertive. Most were products of Oxford colleges, where they had absorbed a strong sense of entitlement. Being members of the Anglican clergy, answerable to the Bishop of London, gave them additional independence. They provoked the ire of governors by taking stridently partisan positions on local political issues. In the college, they defied prohibitions against marriage and ministering to local parishes for extra income. They also resisted residing in the college and refused to take responsibility for disciplining the (mostly grammar school) students. The Board of Visitors, representing the Virginia political elite, held powers of appointment but was otherwise frustrated by its inability to intervene in the operations of the college. The 1750s and 1760s witnessed a continual battle between these two sides. Typical of this stalemate, a confrontation in 1757 culminated with the Board of Visitors firing the entire faculty, only to have their action reversed on appeal to London 6 years later. Both sides invoked the interests of the college: the faculty claimed the right to control teaching and students, while the Visitors sought to rectify what they considered low standards and lax discipline. Ineffectual and self-serving actors on both sides exacerbated these conflicts, but basically their differences were fundamental.

The William & Mary charter envisioned a school of the Reformation in which the interests of state and church were joined, but this unity of purpose was never achieved in colonial Virginia. Instead, the Anglican clergy and the planters who dominated the Virginia polity each pursued their own vested interests. Worse, neither side's interests supported the integrity of an institution of advanced learning. The faculty defined its role as "training up Youth, who are intended to be qualified for any of the three learned Professions, or to become Gentlemen, and accomplished Citizens."[43] Yet the college prepared few "Ministers of the Gospel," as specified in the charter, and those few finished their training elsewhere; also, it taught neither medicine nor law. Students had no incentive to complete a college course even if one had been defined. For the colony's elite families, the college assumed a purely cultural role, serving as a finishing school where their sons acquired the patina of gentlemen. They too had no need for college degrees. Only at the end of the colonial era did the Virginians take an interest in raising curricular standards and granting degrees.

This tardy development can be seen in the contrasting experiences of two of the college's most accomplished citizens. Thomas Jefferson, after a rigorous preparation in an academy, came to the college at age 16 for a leisurely 2 years (1760–1762), which happened to be a hiatus in the faculty wars. He studied classics, philosophy, and law but otherwise had a student experience like no one else. Jefferson was essentially tutored by the lone professor of philosophy, William Small, a rare noncleric who was aloof from the church's battles. Jefferson often joined his professor at the governor's table for "rational and philosophical conversations." Jefferson treasured this experience but also seems to have left the college convinced of the need for its complete restructuring.[44] Just 10 years later, James Madison, second cousin to the future U.S. president and subsequently president of the college, received the first bachelor's degree awarded by William & Mary. He had studied at the college for 4 years and was a mature 23 years old in 1772. By that date considerable agreement existed on the desirability of separating the grammar school and expanding the collegiate offerings.[45] Reform would await the Revolution, but Virginia would persist with its own distinctive interpretation of American higher education.

THE EMBRYONIC AMERICAN COLLEGE

The college founders of the first century had sought to re-create the English patterns of higher education with which they were familiar, but the small scale of operation, limited resources, scarcity of qualified teachers, and closeness of external governors all skewed the development of the colleges. These factors made the three original colleges differ from each other, but they nevertheless shared similarities of mission, aspiration, and operations. By 1740 these, in turn, produced

---

43 Faculty statement of 1770 attributed to John Camm: Tate, "Colonial College," 116.

44 Mark R. Wenger, "Thomas Jefferson, the College of William and Mary, and the University of Virginia," *Virginia Magazine of History and Biography*, 103, 3 (July 1995): 339–74, quote p. 359.

45 Tate, "Colonial College," 112–20. See below, chapter 2.

in embryonic form the distinctively American patterns of collegiate education and governance.

The American model of a strong president under the authority of an external governing board with a relatively weak faculty was the product of evolution rather than design. The starting point for this process lay with the efforts of Henry Dunster and James Blair to design quite similar structures of governance. The Oxbridge colleges were largely controlled by their masters and permanent fellows, subject to the oversight, if any, of a Visitor. Accordingly, Dunster devised a Harvard Corporation consisting of the president, treasurer, and five fellows, who he assumed would in the future be the teachers in the college. The William & Mary charter similarly placed control of the college in the hands of the president and masters. Both charters gave broad, loosely defined powers to the external boards: the Overseers had the right to review and approve all actions of the Harvard Corporation, and the Visitors had authority to enact laws and rules for William & Mary. Behind both boards stood the governments of the respective colonies, which became involved on infrequent but important occasions.

The original presidents dominated their fledgling institutions for lack of alternatives, but other possibilities soon emerged. William & Mary was atypical in acquiring more or less permanent masters by the 1730s. But these individuals soon contended for control of the college, challenging at different times the authority of the president, the Visitors, and even the governor. Harvard before Leverett and Yale before Elisha Williams endured extended periods of weak or absent heads. In those cases tutors basically conducted day-to-day affairs but never acquired governing powers. Unlike the fellows in the Oxbridge colleges, the tutors/fellows did not have permanent posts. They were essentially candidates for future positions, usually as ministers. For this reason, local dignitaries were recruited to also be fellows of the corporation. By controlling appointments, presidents could assure themselves of a cooperative board. Leverett took this approach after the charter was reinstated, but then unusual circumstances found the college with three "career" tutors who preferred the college to a pulpit—Flynt, Robie, and an ex-minister, Nicholas Sever. When the latter was not appointed to the corporation, he launched a prolonged campaign to have tutors automatically named as fellows. Had he succeeded, Harvard might have evolved toward faculty governance—a discouraging prospect considering the self-serving rule of fellows at Oxbridge colleges and the subsequent example of William & Mary.

Instead, the American pattern of strong college presidents began to crystallize with Leverett's presidency. After the long drift under absentee heads, he solidified the operations of the college and foreshadowed the dominant role of presidents: "Leverett did not articulate the separate functions of the college government, preferring instead to place himself at the center of the governing system and to exercise all functions himself."[46] For most of his tenure, he worked with a friendly corporation and minimized the opportunities for Overseers' inputs. Only in the last years, during the Sever affair, did this change. The Overseers became far more intrusive, even conducting a formal visitation in 1723. The Sever controversy also embroiled the college in colony politics—one of the potential liabilities of external governance. Although Leverett's death stilled this controversy, the president and Overseers contended for authority throughout the colonial period, but the relative authority of president and corporation largely endured. This pattern of strong presidents was confirmed at Yale in a different manner.

Connecticut largely followed Cotton Mather's advice in establishing a "school of the churches" with a single, clerical governing board, as they sought to avoid the ascendancy of secular interests that was occurring at Harvard. Even so, the colony repeatedly intervened in college crises. Preponderant trustee power over the institution produced dismal results. The college head was only designated "rector," not president. Having the college run by tutors brought discontent and ultimately disintegration. Stability was achieved only when an effective head, Elisha Williams, was in place; but the rector's office was apparently not attractive enough to retain him. Finally with Thomas Clap, Yale obtained a powerful campus leader. Clap, in fact, wrote a new charter incorporating the "President and Fellows of Yale College in New Haven" (1745), thus giving the president a seat on the board. Although the new title changed little in daily operations, it empowered President Clap for the forceful role he would fulfill for the next 2 decades.

The American college president evolved as a complement to powerful external governors and weak, temporary teachers. The external governing boards represented the social support that sustained the colleges. Originally, at least for Massachusetts and Connecticut, the colleges drew support from unified Puritan communities, but over time that support increasingly reflected powerful groups within those communities. In either case, a strong executive figure was the necessary intermediary to keep the college faithful to the interests of its patrons—a role the independent faculty of William & Mary disdained. Events also seemed to prove that a strong resident president was needed for internal management. In the hierarchical societies of the English colonies, a president of high social standing and dignified personal bearing seemed a necessity. A person of equivocal stature could be mercilessly harassed by socially superior students, as sometimes happened to tutors. The president's prestige was, in fact, a critical factor in upholding respect for the entire "immediate government" of the college. Finding

---

46   Siegel, "Governance and Curriculum," 20.

an appropriate figure to fill this position was a grave problem for the early colleges and a persistent difficulty throughout the colonial era.

For students the distinctive experience of the American college, at least the northern ones, was what Cotton Mather called the collegiate way of living and the strong loyalties of class cohorts. Residential colleges seemed necessary to anchor the schools as permanent institutions. Colleges without them tended to fare poorly in the first century (Yale) and later. These structures were meant to copy the Oxbridge colleges, but they quickly acquired a distinct character. The tutors who also dwelled there were young recent graduates, unlike the scholarly fellows in England. Each tutor assumed instruction for a single class of students rather than a self-selected group. These individuals went through their entire academic exercises as a unit and thus acquired a strong sense of solidarity that often endured through their lifetimes. By the same token, hazing and class rivalry tended to discourage bonds across classes. In addition, class cohesion allowed the curriculum to assume a standardized form for each separate class.

Both the objectives and the methods of seventeenth-century colleges had been refined for centuries but are quite remote from modern education. The colleges took as their fundamental purpose that "the main end of [a student's] life and studies is, *to know God and Jesus Christ which is eternal life,* Joh. 17.3."[47] For Puritan educators, everything in the world was an idea in the mind of God—a single unified body of knowledge, which man in his fallen state could grasp only imperfectly. They assumed, consistent with Aristotle, that everything had a purpose and that knowledge of purpose could be deduced through logic.[48] This approach had been most fully developed by Peter Ramus, a sixteenth-century French humanist, in his *Technologia*. This all-encompassing system of logic reduced all knowledge to 1,267 propositions. As taught in the colleges, the *Technologia* was the system of logical deduction that progressively revealed the mind of God. Students had to master this approach in order to earn a bachelor's degree and become scholars in their own right. Hence, students had a great deal to learn before they could "know God and Jesus Christ," and the curriculum was designed to impart this knowledge.

---

47 *New England's First Fruits* (London: 1643), quoted in Morison, *Founding of Harvard*, 434; the Yale college laws stated: "Every student shall consider the main end of his study to wit to know God in Jesus Christ and answerably to lead a Godly sober life": Warch, *School of the Prophets*, 191. The following account of curriculum draws on Morison, *Harvard College*; Siegel, "Governance and Curriculum"; Morgen, *Gentle Puritan*, Warch, *School of the Prophets*; and Carl A. Hangartner, *Movements to Change American College Teaching, 1700–1830*, PhD Diss., Yale University, 1955.

48 Morgan quotes as example: "The end of the Sunne, Moone, and stares is, to serve the Earth; and the end of the Earth is, to bring forth Plants, and the end of Plants is, to feed the beasts": *Gentle Puritan*, 54.

In most basic terms, the college course can be seen as imparting three kinds of learning—linguistic skills, logical argument, and general knowledge. Latin, of course, was the language of learning and instruction. Proper preparation was the prerequisite for college studies, and polishing these skills occupied much of the first year. Greek was largely employed to read the New Testament, and Hebrew was limited to reading and translating the Psalms. The study of these languages thus complemented the religious mission of the colleges. When students made sufficient progress in the "tongues," they began the study of logic, which was the focus of the second year. The aim was to develop the skill to engage in syllogistic [using logical deduction] disputations. These were stylized debates, conducted in Latin, in which students rehearsed arguments for and against propositions, largely drawn from the *Technologia*. Disputations continued during the third and fourth years, incorporating material drawn from the philosophical subjects covered in those years.[49] These exercises were central to the curriculum and featured in graduation ceremonies. For commencement, students would publish a list of *theses* that they were prepared to defend, thus demonstrating their fitness as scholars. It is largely from these lists that historians have deduced what was taught in the early colleges. Finally, general knowledge was drawn from Aristotle's three philosophies—mental, moral, and natural—and subsequent elaborations. This was the content knowledge that informed the propositions of the *Technologia*. Various subjects might be incorporated. However, content knowledge in this scheme played a limited role, and for that reason advances in knowledge did little to drive change in the curriculum until the last years of the colleges' first century.

The organization of the curriculum reveals how the basic aims were accomplished. Dunster, who had to teach all three classes himself, treated a separate subject each day. Monday and Tuesday were devoted to disputations and philosophy; Greek and Hebrew filled the next two days; Friday was devoted to rhetoric and declamations, Saturday, to divinity, and the Sabbath was observed on Sunday. This basic pattern endured and was reproduced at Yale as well. At the end of Leverett's presidency, disputations were still held on Mondays and Tuesdays, and rhetoric and divinity occupied Fridays and Saturdays, respectively. Friday's declamations were an important exercise. Each student in turn had to compose (and later memorize) a brief Latin oration and "declaim" before the whole college once every 6 or 8 weeks. These speeches were written and turned in as well, thus developing both oratory and composition. Content knowledge was conveyed to students in lectures, usually by the president, and recitations were conducted by the tutors. Originally, when books were scarce and expensive,

49 For example, the Harvard plan of study for 1723: Morison, *Harvard College*, 146–47.

recitations were intended to repeat and clarify materials from lectures or texts that students had copied. As books became more widely available, tutors used recitations for oral questioning, in which students had to demonstrate that they had mastered the day's lessons. Hence, schedules usually allotted 2 hours of preparation time before each recitation. The material for which the tutors were responsible—linguistic skills, learning logic, and fairly basic subjects—did not require advanced or specialized knowledge and thus should have been within the competence of inexperienced recent graduates to teach, if not very well. Tutors apparently might or might not bother to explain the material in recitations. In fact, tutors who attempted to push students beyond these basics, such as Samuel Johnson, proved more unpopular than those who offered no guidance. In recitations all students were expected to master, or memorize, the lesson (no scholar left behind); students had opportunities to display their "genius" in declamations and especially disputations.

The fundamental historical question is how and when the college course began to incorporate the new learning and a more secular outlook. To appreciate why this process was so slow, one must recognize the effectiveness of this course for its primary purpose as well as its deep immersion in Puritan Protestantism. First, the content and the exercises of the course gave graduates the cultural grounding and the oratorical skills for future careers. Second, even before formal training for the ministry, all graduates were saturated with Christian doctrines.

Consider the fixtures of the college course. Each day included morning and evening chapel, which consisted of prayers and scripture. Saturday and Sunday were devoted entirely to religion. On Saturdays students heard lectures on scripture or divinity and recited on classic works of Puritan theology. On Sundays they heard two sermons, which they later had to explicate. Work in Greek and Hebrew focused almost entirely on the Bible as students learned to translate passages of the New Testament back and forth from English, Latin, and Greek. And the ubiquitous disputations reflected the theocentric propositions of the *Technologia*. This grounding in Puritan doctrines prepared graduates to serve the "church and civil state" but particularly the church. The majority of students who attended Harvard and Yale in the first century undoubtedly aspired to the ministry. The proportion that attained pulpits, cited before, actually undercounts these aspirants, since it fails to account for those with unknown careers and an appreciable number, like Flint and Robie, who prepared for the ministry but did not obtain a pulpit.

Given this rigid and time-honored structure, new knowledge was not easily incorporated. A consensus exists among historians that the new learning only began to make significant inroads at Harvard and Yale in the 1720s and that meaningful change in the college course occurred after 1740.[50] During those years the gradual acceptance of new ideas along with the decline of Ramean thinking can be charted in commencement theses. Acceptance of the Newtonian revolution and experimental science is most readily documented. These doctrines did not encounter philosophical barriers but rather a scarcity of individuals capable of fully comprehending and utilizing them. At Harvard the foundation seems to have been laid by tutor Robie. He became a self-taught Newtonian and was also responsible for the acquisition of philosophical apparatus. These activities seem to have occurred toward the latter years of his tutorship, when he no doubt taught Newtonian disciples Thomas Clap (H. 1722) and Isaac Greenwood (H. 1721). The latter acquired much deeper knowledge by studying in London from 1724 to 1726. As the first Hollis Professor of Natural Philosophy in 1727, he was a committed Newtonian who brought the new science to the college and the public. He advanced the woeful teaching of mathematics in particular and employed the college's growing collection of instruments for experiments. When John Winthrop succeeded Greenwood in the Hollis professorship (1739–1779), the new science was not only a permanent part of the curriculum, but experiment and observation were accepted as the means to access an open and growing body of knowledge. Yale, which began the century in far more benighted condition than Harvard, soon caught up. Newton was incorporated into the course by 1730, and in 1734 rector Williams led a concerted effort to acquire philosophical apparatus. His successor, Thomas Clap, was an enthusiastic proponent of Newtonian science and especially devoted to astronomy.

The basic ideas of John Locke were more difficult to assimilate since his emphasis on empiricism challenged not only the *Technologia*, but the more advanced rationalism of Descartes. However, Lockean perspectives, or at least the spirit of empiricism, were just as necessary as philosophical apparatus for opening inquiry to observation and experiment and for challenging adherence to a fixed body of knowledge. A turning point was the English publication in 1725 of a logic text by Isaac Watts, a dissenter and scholar well known to the American colleges. Watts' *Logick: Or, The Right Use of Reason* incorporated basic Lockean views into a more traditional framework but still highlighted key concepts like the importance of experience as a source of new truth. By the 1730s Locke had become part of the curriculum at both Yale and Harvard. In 1743, Harvard students were assigned Locke's *Essay* itself, which quickly became standard practice.

---

50   Morison, *Harvard College*, 139–284; Siegel, "Governance and Curriculum," 155–468; Warch, *School of the Prophets*, 186–249; Morgan, *Gentle Puritan*, 47–57; Hornberger, *Scientific Thought*. See also chapter 2.

These developments were important in themselves but also symptomatic of a larger transformation taking place. The new learning of the eighteenth century was beginning to penetrate the American colleges, not as triumphal doctrines but as additional materials in an increasingly cluttered course of study. As colonial historian Edmund Morgan observed: "Students were not presented with opposing views and asked to choose between them. Instead they were expected to assimilate Aristotelian rhetoric, Ramist theology, Berkeleyan metaphysics, and diluted Newtonian physics. These were all incompatible in varying degrees and on different levels. . . . [I]t would have required a real genius merely to ascertain the precise points of conflict among the various parts of the Yale curriculum."[51] Or Harvard's, for that matter. However, at the end of their first century, American colleges had transcended the closed world of Puritan theology and were about to embark on a new Age of Enlightenment.

---

51 Morgan, *Gentle Puritan*, 56.

COLONIAL COLLEGES, 1740–1780

NEW COLLEGES FOR THE MIDDLE COLONIES

I N THE MID-EIGHTEENTH CENTURY, COLLEGES IN the American colonies doubled in number and changed in character. The College of New Jersey (1746), King's College in New York (1754), and the College of Philadelphia (1755) were chartered and began instruction. The new colleges on the New York–Philadelphia axis were products of the rapid growth of the economies and populations of the Middle Colonies, although each reflected the distinctive demography and religious character of its surroundings. Unlike the settings of the first three colleges, the entire region was populated by diverse peoples with differing Protestant beliefs. However, initially only a few of these groups had any interest in colleges. The growing number of Presbyterians had close roots in Scotland and Ireland, where ministers were expected to be highly educated. In the two cities, upper-class members of the Church of England sought institutions to solidify their social position and ties with English culture. Still, these foundings were interconnected. The Presbyterian initiatives in New Jersey kindled the efforts in New York and Philadelphia. The latter sought Samuel Johnson for its head before he opted to lead King's; and William Smith's meddling in the planning for King's led to his appointment as provost in Philadelphia. Each of these campaigns took nearly 7 years to create a college, and these prolonged processes affected the outcomes. Ultimately, the colleges of the Middle Colonies represented the learning and spirit of the American Enlightenment. But strangely, the catalyst for these developments was the Great Awakening of evangelical religious fervor.

Historians have accorded the Awakening a large role in shaping colonial colleges. However, the most vigorous outbursts of revivalist preaching occurred in the early 1740s, and the lasting schisms they provoked in major churches overlapped with other social and political fault lines. The central figure was George Whitefield, a young Anglican minister who acquired notoriety for his revivalist preaching in London during 1738–1739 while raising funds for a Georgia orphanage. When he returned to America late in 1739, his reputation preceded him.[1] Whitefield relied on the publicity of his revivalist exploits in colonial news-papers and the regular publication of his own *Journal* to heighten public antici-pation of his appearances. The colonial equivalent of a rock star, his act and tours were thoroughly orchestrated. Starting around Philadelphia, he delivered nearly 350 sermons during 3 tours lasting through 1740. He estimated that on 61 occa-sions he preached to crowds of 1,000 or more, and a few reportedly as large as 20,000—more than the population of the largest American cities. He preached in every colony but achieved a huge response only in the Calvinist "revival belts," consisting of mostly Presbyterians in the Middle Colonies and Congregational-ists in Connecticut and Massachusetts—the location of his third tour.

Whitefield was clearly an orator of great talent, able to make listeners acutely aware of the perils of damnation and desperate to improve chances for salvation. He espoused a crude version of old-time Puritanism but sidestepped predestina-tion by offering listeners the possibility of salvation through the conversion ex-perience. The conversion of souls at these revivals was regarded as evidence of the "Work of God," an interpretation sanctioned by the colonies' foremost theo-logian, Jonathan Edwards.[2] The transient appearances were part of the perfor-mance. He gave only a few well-rehearsed sermons in each locale, stirring religious passions, before moving on and leaving local clergy to deal with the aftermath of anguished souls. These and later revivals had a cumulative effect, becoming more intense in preaching tactics and spiritual impact in the following years.

Whitefield himself seems to have been an amiable fellow who got on well with a spectrum of hosts, especially in his later tours.[3] He befriended Benja-min Franklin, for example, who shared none of his "enthusiasm" but admired his eloquence—and may have appreciated the boost Whitefield's publicity gave to his printing business. Whitefield ingratiated himself with contemporary Puritans by claiming to espouse traditional Calvinism and railing against the Arminianism of Tillotson and the Church of England. However, a crucial tac-tic of Whitefield's self-advertisement was to foment controversy, and here the message contained a poison pill. To dramatize his own piety compared with the laxness of existing churches, he made reckless accusations that present ministers were unconverted—lacked a conversion experience—and hence unfit to lead their parishioners to salvation. Although he was cordially welcomed at Harvard and Yale, they received the same treatment. In his published *Journal* he wrote,

1   Frank Lambert, *Inventing the "Great Awakening"* (Princeton: Princeton University Press, 1999).
2   Edmund S. Morgan, *The Gentle Puritan: A Life of Ezra Stiles, 1727–1795* (University of North Carolina Press, 1962), 20–41.
3   After an initial visit to Georgia in 1738, Whitefield had six American tours—starting in 1739, 1744, 1751, 1754, 1763, and 1769. During his later tours, although still preaching fire and brimstone, he was regarded as a religious statesman.

"As for the Universities [*sic*] . . . Their Light is now become Darkness—Darkness that may be felt—and is complained of by the most godly ministers."[4]

Whitefield was soon followed by a succession of imitators, itinerant revivalist preachers who were more extravagant in their preaching and blatant in their attacks. Thus, the Awakening quickly evolved from an apparent Work of God to a challenge to the churches and the two northern colleges. The radicalism and blatant emotionalism of the Awakening soon divided the Reformed churches into New Light adherents and Old Light defenders. Nowhere was the schism more dramatic than at Yale College.

Whitefield spent 3 days in New Haven (October 24–26, 1740), preaching in the college and the town. He was warmly greeted by Rector Thomas Clap, who approved of the spiritual agitation he inspired in Yale students. Among the itinerant preachers who followed, Gilbert Tennent preached for a week in the spring of 1741. A leader among the New Light Presbyterians in New Jersey, he had collaborated with Whitefield, who explicitly encouraged him to "blow up the divine fire" in New England. Tennent was even more emotive than Whitefield and was especially damning toward allegedly unconverted ministers. The Awakening spawned increasing numbers of itinerant preachers, like Reverend Eleazer Wheelock (Yale 1733), who exulted after one revival, "the Whole assembly Seam'd alive with Distress[,] the Groans and outcrys of the wounded were such that my Voice Co'd not be heard." Perhaps the worst was James Davenport, demented and self-anointed, who one knowledgeable commentator called "the *wildest Enthusiast* I ever saw." Thus, the Awakening assumed a radical form that divided congregations, repudiated an educated ministry, and reduced religion to raw "enthusiasm."[5]

At this point Clap had seen enough. He helped the colony promulgate a ban on itinerant preachers and eventually deport Davenport as non compos mentis. At Yale, student preaching and proselytizing had completely disrupted the college order. Clap first expelled one of the New Light leaders, David Brainerd, for allegedly saying that a tutor had "no more grace than a chair." Then, in 1742, he was compelled to close the college and send students home. When it reopened, with the most zealous New Lights pursuing salvation elsewhere, order was restored and the crisis appeared to be over. But Clap was unrelenting against New Light influence in and around his college. He sought to discredit both Gilbert Tennent and Jonathan

---

4 Quoted in Richard Hofstadter, *America at 1750: A Social Portrait* (New York: Vintage: 1971), 288.

5 Louis Leonard Tucker, *Puritan Protagonist: President Thomas Clap of Yale College* (Chapel Hill: University of North Carolina Press, 1962), quotes pp. 123, 126; Edmund S. Morgan, *The Gentle Puritan: A Life of Ezra Stiles, 1727–1795* (University of North Carolina Press, 1962), 30; Brooks Mather Kelley, *Yale: A History* (New Haven, Yale University Press, 1974), 50–55; Edwin Scott Gaustad, *The Great Awakening in New England* (New York: Harper & Brothers, 1957), quote p. 47: "Enthusiasm" had a specific meaning of personal revelations of divine impulses or visions, as well as 'religious frenzy': Gaustad, *Great Awakening*, 77–78.

Edwards. In 1744 he expelled two brothers for attending a New Light service while home with their parents. Like the Brainerd affair, this arbitrary act was widely publicized and fanned controversy throughout the colonies. When the student protested that he broke no college law, Clap replied, "The laws of God and the College are one." In truth, these were the laws of Thomas Clap, who embraced intolerance and autocracy at a time when colleges were moving in the opposite direction.[6]

Whitefield attracted enormous crowds in Boston, but the response of the college was much cooler.[7] The Harvard faculty flatly rejected his condemnation of Tillotson, and relatively few students were affected. When Whitefield's disparaging *Journal* remarks appeared, battle lines were drawn.[8] Whitefield returned to New England in 1744 but was now excluded from the pulpits of Harvard and Yale. He responded with renewed attacks. On this occasion, he was answered with a "Testimony" of the president and faculty of Harvard "against the Reverend Mr. George Whitefield, and his Conduct" (1744). This pamphlet condemned him for "*Enthusiasm*," for claiming "greater Familiarity with God than other men," and for "Arrogance . . . that such a young Man as he should . . . tell what books we shou'd allow our Pupils to read." Whitefield's ineffectual rejoinder was countered by a more thorough denunciation by Hollis Professor of Divinity Edward Wigglesworth. In addition to a blow-by-blow refutation of Whitefield's accusations, he upheld the college's Calvinist credentials and accused Whitefield, despite his evasions, of antinomian heresy.[9]

This incident is testimony to the growing maturity of Harvard College. The appointment of its president, Edward Holyoke (1737–1769), was considered a victory for the liberal faction, and his long tenure was notable for modernizing the curriculum (discussed below). The advancing spirit of the Enlightenment was evident in the Harvard argument that "Reason, or . . . Revelation of the Mind of God" are better trusted than Whitefield's "sudden Impulses and Impressions." Harvard reflected the cosmopolitanism of a great seaport, rather than the religious enthusiasm of the common people who flocked to Whitefield. Harvard also had a professor of divinity with the authority to oppose the celebrity upstart. All these qualities were lacking at Yale.[10]

---

6 Tucker, *Puritan Protagonist*, 133, 139.

7 Josiah Quincy, *The History of Harvard College* (Boston, 1860), 39–71.

8 Edwin Scott Gaustad estimated that the high tide of the Awakening in New England lasted 2 years, but a severe reaction quickly followed. Arguments against the Awakening and its prophets were well developed by the time Whitefield returned: *Great Awakening*, 61–79.

9 J. David Hoeveler, *Creating the American Mind: Intellect and Politics in the Colonial Colleges* (New York: Rowman & Littlefield, 2002), 215–22.

10 Richard Hofstadter and Wilson Smith, eds., *American Higher Education: A Documentary History* (Chicago: University of Chicago Press, 1961), quotes pp. 62–63; Samuel Eliot Morison, *Three Centuries of Harvard* (Cambridge: Harvard University Press, 1936).

Old Lights dominated colonial government in Connecticut, and they rewarded Clap in 1745 with prompt approval of a new charter that made him a member of the trustees. Although this represented a formal elevation of Clap's status, he increasingly behaved as if he had become sovereign ruler. In an effort to enforce religious conformity, he required all students to attend religious services in the college rather than the town. To justify this action, Clap wrote: "Colleges are Societies of Ministers for training up persons for the work of the *Ministry*." And Clap himself became the arbiter of the nature of that training. He stiffened the religious tests for all teachers and denied students access to liberal books in the library. Clap's obsessions may have been reactions to the Awakening, but they soon became more personal than theological. Withdrawing Yale students from New Haven's First Church alienated Old Lights, but he failed to placate New Lights, even when he reversed course and welcomed Whitefield into the college in 1754. Clap's autocratic ways earned him increasing numbers of enemies, which would be his undoing when he lost control of the college in the 1760s.[11]

★   ★   ★

The split between old-light and new-light Presbyterians in the middle colonies began before Whitefield's arrival and from the outset raised the issue of ministerial education. Most local ministers had been trained in Scotland or New England, but by the 1730s their numbers could not match the rapid growth of congregations. Some new ministers, especially among recent Scots-Irish immigrants, were trained individually by local ministers, and almost all favored a new-light style of preaching. This was especially the case with William Tennent, Sr., a master's graduate of Edinburgh who trained Gilbert and three other sons for the ministry. He then instructed additional ministerial aspirants in a log structure that adversaries dismissively called the "Log College." The classically educated Tennent instructed his charges in Latin, Hebrew, and a good deal of Bible study; they also imbibed his fervent pietism, to the increasing displeasure of the Philadelphia Synod.[12] Both factions attempted to alter requirements for ordination to either facilitate or obstruct these new-light candidates. The conflict prompted the synod in 1739 to consider establishing a school or seminary. The arrival of Whitefield inflamed these tensions and led in 1741 to the expulsion from the synod of new-light presbyteries of New Brunswick and New York. The

---

11   Kelley, *Yale*, 55–70, quote p. 62; Tucker, *Puritan Protagonist*, 173–97.

12   The Log College operated from 1735 to ca. 1744 and produced about 20 ministers: "William Tennent," *Dictionary of National Biography Online*; Hoeveler, *American Mind, 102–12*. Presbyterian infighting is explicated most thoroughly in Leonard J. Trinterud, *The Forming of an American Tradition: A Re-examination of Colonial Presbyterianism* (Philadelphia: Westminster Press, 1949).

dominant figure in the former was Gilbert Tennent, who now led the opposition of the Scots-Irish New Lights. The area around New York was home to a group of "New England Presbyterians," led by Yale graduate Jonathan Dickinson. Each side soon sought the means to educate its own ministers.

In 1743 the Philadelphia Synod officially sponsored an academy in New London, Pennsylvania, under Francis Alison, reputedly the finest classical scholar in the colonies and an opponent of the Awakening despite his Scots-Irish background.[13] The school sought to teach at both preparatory and collegiate levels, but the synod's clear intention was to prepare old-light ministers. The school was supported by the churches and charged students no tuition. An attempt was made to have Yale award its students degrees (which would have made it America's first branch campus), but Thomas Clap was not encouraging. Alison's school struggled financially and never attempted to obtain a charter. After he joined the Academy of Philadelphia in 1752, the school migrated to nearby New Ark, Delaware.[14]

In the New York region, Elizabethtown minister Jonathan Dickinson was an articulate advocate of new-light positions similar to those of Jonathan Edwards. He was appalled by President Clap's vendetta against the New Lights, but overcrowded Yale was no answer in any case to the need to educate more Presbyterian ministers. On the other hand, Dickinson sought a moderate approach that would bypass radical New Lights, whose excesses had tarnished the movement. This precluded a log-college type of seminary. In 1745 Dickinson formed a group of Presbyterians and Anglicans from both sides of the Hudson who pledged £185 and began formulating a charter for a prospective college. Anglicans soon fell out of this coalition, most likely over the issue of control, but this initiative seems to have planted a desire for their own institution in New York City.[15] Seven Presbyterian ministers and laymen persisted and by the end of the year presented a charter to the royal governor. A staunch Anglican, the governor promptly rejected it, stating that he had no authority to authorize a "dissenter's college." However, he died in May, and the interim governor was advised by friends of the college. On October 22, 1746, a charter was granted to the College of New Jersey, and classes began the following May in the parsonage of Jonathan Dickinson.

13   For Alison, see Douglas Sloan, *The Scottish Enlightenment and the American College Ideal* (New York: Teachers College Press, 1971), 73–102.

14   For the New Ark Academy, see Elizabeth Nybakken, "In the Irish Tradition: Pre-Revolutionary Academies in America," *History of Education Quarterly*, 37, 2 (1997): 163–84.

15   Bryan F. Le Beau, *Jonathan Dickinson and the Formative Years of American Presbyterianism* (Lexington: University Press of Kentucky, 1997), 173–74; Robert A. McCaughey, *Stand Columbia: A History of Columbia University in the City of New York, 1754–2004* (New York: Columbia University Press, 2004), 8–9.

The original charter named seven trustees—three New Jersey ministers and one from New York and three Presbyterian laymen residing in New York—six Yale graduates and one son of Harvard. Thus, the college from its birth was academically a lineal descendant of the New England colleges, offering a "plan of education as extensive as our circumstances will admit."[16] But its organization was distinctive. The trustees had the authority to name five additional members, and they quickly moved to invite Gilbert Tennent—who had mollified his radical views—and three other log-college ministers. By incorporating the most prominent Scots-Irish, the college presented a solid front of new-light Presbyterians stretching from New York to Pennsylvania. Nonetheless, the college proclaimed itself open to "those of every religious denomination," which was consistent not only with New Jersey freedom of religion but also the practices of Yale and Harvard. Its all-Presbyterian trustees resembled the monolithic governing board of Yale; however, the latter represented the colony's established church, which was not the case in New Jersey. The new governor, Jonathan Belcher, perceived the weakness of the charter, particularly in the face of Anglican opposition. A new light himself and avid supporter, he worked with the trustees to devise a stronger charter. The new charter of 1748 created a mixed board of twenty-three trustees representing the colony as well as the Presbyterian founders. The governor presided as an ex-officio member, but Presbyterians were assured of a majority. Its church-state governance now paralleled Harvard's Overseers but had far greater control. Thus, the College of New Jersey constituted a distinctive governance model of a provincial college.

The efforts of Mid-Atlantic Presbyterians to educate ministers for their growing needs resulted, through the efforts of Dickinson, in a liberal arts college open to all. Both these traits proved invaluable for the further development of the college. Efforts to secure Presbyterian control had resulted instead in a mixed governing board that made the college a "public" institution, at least in a colonial sense. However, despite the close identification with New Jersey, it had an intercolonial board. Nor did the province ever support the college; Governor Belcher proposed a lottery to raise funds, but the New Jersey Assembly voted it down.

Jonathan Dickinson died only 4 months after opening the college, but instruction was quickly transferred to founder Aaron Burr's parsonage in nearby Newark. At this point the college was merely an enlargement of the classical

---

16 The original trustees wrote: "Though our great intention was to erect a seminary for educating ministers of the gospel, yet we hope it will be a means of raising up men that will be useful in other learned professions—ornaments of the State as well as the Church." Jurgen Herbst, *From Crisis to Crisis: American College Government, 1636–1819* (Cambridge: Harvard University Press, 1982), quote p. 84. The following also draws on Hoeveler, *American Mind*; and Thomas Jefferson Wertenbaker, *Princeton, 1746–1896*, with a new preface by John Murrin (Princeton: Princeton University Press, 1996 [1946]).

schools that both reverends had provided at their homes (an arrangement little different from Yale's early days in Killingworth). But the college's legitimacy was soon confirmed in 1748 when the trustees gathered in Newark for the first commencement exercise. Aaron Burr was elected president, and he then proceeded to award six bachelor's degrees and a master of arts to Governor Belcher. The new college offered a curriculum nearly identical to that of Burr's alma mater, Yale.[17] Still, the founders were aware that a real college required a permanent home and, above all, a collegiate building. From the outset Governor Belcher had favored "Princetown" in the center of the colony. In the event, the town had to outbid rivals in order to secure the college in 1753. To raise the funds for a building, Gilbert Tennent and Samuel Davies, a new-light minister from Virginia, were sent to England for a year of fund-raising. Old-side Presbyterians and Anglicans attacked Tennent for his former radical views, but the pair succeeded by emphasizing the college's religious freedom for English audiences and lauding its mission of training Presbyterian ministers for donors in Scotland and Ireland.[18] The £4,000 they raised financed Nassau Hall, the grandest collegiate structure in colonial America. When it was occupied in 1756, the College of New Jersey achieved permanence and legitimacy. By then it also had rivals in New York and Philadelphia.

★ ★ ★

The founding of these two colleges was triggered by the events in New Jersey, and each followed a different path to a similar outcome. The New York Assembly authorized a lottery to raise funds for a college the day after the first New Jersey charter was signed, and the Pennsylvania effort followed quickly upon the college's 1748 consecration. Both Anglicans and old-light Presbyterians were threatened by what they called the "Jersey College," since, in their apocalyptic views, a monopoly of collegiate education by New Lights could undermine their churches. However, behind the churches in both cities stood emerging social elites, increasingly aware of the cultural advantage of colleges; if there were to be colleges, these groups felt that they should control them. They were defined by their considerable wealth, in most cases derived originally from commerce but also by positions in government and society that consolidated their status. In New York, many of the key figures were vestrymen in the Anglican Trinity

17   Francis L. Broderick, "Pulpit, Physics, and Politics: The Curriculum of the College of New Jersey, 1746–1794," *William and Mary Quarterly*, 3rd series, 6, 1 (Jan. 1949): 42–68.
18   George William Pilcher, *Samuel Davies: Apostle of Dissent in Colonial Virginia* (Knoxville: University of Tennessee Press, 1971), 135–57; Sloan, *Scottish Enlightenment*, 116.

Church—the men who managed the affairs of the Church. In Philadelphia, a party coalesced among supporters of the Proprietor, Thomas Penn, against the Quakers who dominated the local Assembly. Besides holding important official posts, they became trustees of the College of Philadelphia and belonged to other exclusive organizations.[19] Finally, elite plans for these colleges did not go uncontested; in each city they were challenged and influenced by individuals with different ideas about education. In the end, though, wealth and social status prevailed.

When the possibility of a New York college arose, Anglicans in the region took the lead.[20] Neither the established church in the province nor more than one-seventh of the congregations, they nonetheless regarded the Church of England as an extension of royal government and a natural leader of society. Foremost among them was Samuel Johnson of Connecticut. Following his notorious 1722 conversion, Johnson became a settled minister in Stratford, where he vigorously promoted the Church among hostile Congregationalists. He was responsible for preparing 5 percent of Yale graduates to become Anglican ministers (1725–1748). He also spearheaded Anglican condemnation of the "strange, wild enthusiasm" of the Awakening and regarded the Jersey College as a "fountain of Nonsense." As a leading colonial intellectual, Benjamin Franklin avidly sought to recruit Johnson to the Philadelphia Academy and published his philosophical treatise, *Elementa Philosophica* (1752). Prominent Anglicans initially debated the best location for the college. However, the lottery funds were voted by the Assembly rather than the royal governor and consigned to a commission. The location issue was resolved in 1752 when Trinity Church offered to donate a choice piece of real estate on what was then the northern fringe of the city.[21]

At this juncture a formidable adversary emerged in the person of William Livingston, scion of wealthy upstate landholders, a Yale graduate (1741), and with family ties to the College of New Jersey. He embraced Enlightenment views toward liberty and intellectual progress, and he seemed equally opposed to the presumptuous hegemony of Trinity Church and the Anglican families that dominated its vestry. In 1753 he and his associates launched a journal of opinion, the *Independent Reflector*, to oppose the planned college. A member of the Lottery Commission himself, Livingston condemned Anglicans for seeking to establish a "Party-College" or the "College of Trinity Church." As an alternative,

---

19   Stephen Brobeck, "Revolutionary Change in Colonial Philadelphia: The Brief Life of the Proprietary Gentry," *William and Mary Quarterly*, 3rd Series, 33, 3 (July 1976): 410–34; Ann D. Gordon, *The College of Philadelphia, 1749–1779: Impact of an Institution* (New York: Garland, 1989); David C. Humphrey, *From King's College to Columbia, 1746–1800* (New York: Columbia University Press, 1976), 25–30.

20   See Humphrey, *King's College*; Robert A. McCaughey, *Stand Columbia*, 4–25.

21   Humphrey, *King's College*, 25.

he advocated the creation of a public, nondenominational institution. Since the college was funded with public lottery funds, he argued, it should be controlled by the legislature. That body should elect the trustees, who would in turn choose a president. The college should not teach the doctrines of any sect, and students would be free to attend the church of their choice. Anglicans responded that the established church, as they considered themselves, deserved preference in the college. For much of the year this war of words escalated. There was zero likelihood of establishing a nondenominational college governed by the popularly elected legislature, but the anticlerical arguments of the *Reflector* found considerable sympathy among the majority of non-Anglicans. Thus, as in New Jersey, the controversy shaped the organization of the college.

Behind the scenes, the Anglican elite pressed their advantage. They silenced the *Independent Reflector* by forcing its printer out of business. They secured the support of the Dutch Reformed Church, traditionally a close ally. Finally, they issued an ultimatum that the college must have an Anglican president and liturgy or else the land would revert to Trinity Church. When this stipulation was accepted by the lottery commission (largely the same individuals), the founding of the college was assured. Samuel Johnson began teaching the first class in July 1754, and several months later lieutenant governor James De Lancey (another ally) signed the charter in the name of the King.

The "College in the Province of New York . . . in the City of New York in America . . . named King's College" conceded several points to its critics. It granted assurances that it would be open to all Christian believers and would not attempt to impose the beliefs of any sect upon its students. These were principles that President Johnson had long upheld and fought for in Connecticut. The college was governed by forty-one trustees who represented the public, though not the elected assembly that Livingston had championed. Seventeen ex-officio members included the royal governor, holders of several public offices, and the senior ministers of Trinity Church and the Dutch Reformed, Presbyterian, French, and Lutheran churches. Twenty-four governors were named in the charter to serve without term, their successors to be chosen by the board. This latter group consisted largely of Trinity vestrymen and their Dutch Reformed allies. They and their successors would hold a firm majority for the life of the college. King's was thus not the instrument of the Anglican Church that its initial proponents had sought and that its critics had denounced. Only three Anglican clerics sat among the governors—the Archbishop of Canterbury (in absentia), the rector of Trinity Church, and the Anglican president. King's College instead was owned and operated by the powerful families that patronized Trinity and the Dutch Reformed churches. Moreover, the charter gave the governors powers ordinarily exercised by colonial college presidents, such as choosing the books that would be used and presiding over meetings of the board.[22] But why did these gentlemen feel the need to control a college?

A modern answer would be for social reproduction. No less than Massachusetts Puritans a century before, the dominant figures in New York's hierarchical society hoped a college would perpetuate their community and the social order. By the 1750s, though, cultural ideals had changed. The New York elite envisioned some combination of learning, gentility, virtue, and piety with which to imbue the next generation of lawyers, judges, merchants, and statesmen. Although New York was noted for its philistine preoccupation with business, the spirit of Enlightenment had taken root. Several of King's founders had amassed enormous libraries, and a few had signed on to Benjamin Franklin's inchoate philosophical society. William Livingston, among the younger elite (and no less elitist than his foes), had organized a "Society for the Promotion of Useful Knowledge." Learning had become an expected adornment of a gentleman. The English model of gentility represented another cultural ideal for social climbers in the provinces, one tangibly exemplified in the aristocracy of the mother country. Familiarity with the classics and literature was deemed essential for forming the manners and taste of a gentleman. "Virtue" was an explicit, if less concrete, outcome expected from the college. This meant producing "truly good men" guided by devotion to duty, selflessness, and righteousness. Samuel Johnson placed foremost the goal of offering a "truly Christian education," but this was inextricably linked with the inculcation of virtue at King's and elsewhere. Indeed, the entire college curriculum was infused with moral purpose stemming from this association of piety and virtue. More practically, the college was intended to produce the professionals who would be leaders of society. The legal profession had clearly emerged as the pathway to elite positions in and out of government. Even as the college was forming, New York lawyers established the requirement of a bachelor's degree to become an apprentice. In the next decade, the King's College Medical School was organized in an effort to dominate that profession. Thus, there was a direct connection between the cultural ideals the college was expected to cultivate and entry into the upper ranks of New York society. This social reality, more than denominational doctrines or interests, lay behind the bitter controversy over the organization of the college.[23]

In one sense, the critics' polemics against the college proved to be self-fulfilling: they so tarnished the enterprise that almost no students from outside Anglican and Dutch Reformed circles chose to attend. However, Anglican hopes were disappointed too. The college failed to provide the ministers needed

22 Ibid., 68.
23 Ibid., 152; McCaughey, *Stand Columbia*, 33–44.

for Anglican congregations, producing an average of just one per year. Nor did Anglicans from other colonies send their sons to New York. Of the 226 students who matriculated from 1754 to 1776, three-quarters resided within 30 miles of the college, most within walking distance. Fully one-quarter of students were related to governors of the college, and others came from the same social circles. King's charged the highest tuition of any colonial college and, unlike the College of New Jersey, insisted on 4 years of matriculation to graduate. These factors no doubt helped to depress the graduation rate to near 50 percent.[24] Moreover, the governors were unperturbed by this situation. A narrow gateway to the upper ranks of society certainly suited their family interests, but they also regarded it as part of the natural order—as did their counterparts in Philadelphia.

The Proprietary Party in Philadelphia faced a more amiable foe. Self-made and self-educated Benjamin Franklin was exquisitely sensitive to the gradations of social hierarchy that he himself had surmounted but also somewhat skeptical toward colleges, which he had ridiculed as a young man. As an indefatigable proponent of intellectual advancement, Franklin naturally came to address the city's educational vacuum. His principal concern was to establish an English-language school that would teach modern languages, history, and science, thus preparing students "for learning any Business, Calling or Profession, except such wherein Languages are required." He broached such a project in 1743, the same year he launched the American Philosophical Society, but found no support. Assured of backing in 1749, he published an extensive *Proposal* to establish such an academy that would provide all students with a thorough grounding in the English language and, he conceded, instruction in Latin and Greek for those aspiring to "Divinity . . . Physik [or] Law." In November, twenty-four trustees gathered to draw up a "Constitution for the Public Academy in the city of Philadelphia" following Franklin's plan. These self-perpetuating trustees represented the non-Quaker elite of the city: three-quarters were Anglicans; the others were powerful old-side Presbyterians, plus Franklin as president, and one token Quaker. It soon became apparent that the trustees were far more interested in classical than English schooling. Nonetheless, the Academy opened in early 1751 with three instructors responsible for "schools" in Latin and Greek, mathematical subjects, and English. It was described by contemporaries as a "collection of schools."[25]

24   Humphrey, *King's College*, 194.
25   John Hardin Best, ed., *Benjamin Franklin on Education* (New York: Teachers College, 1962), quotes pp. 146, 171; Edward Potts Cheyney, *History of the University of Pennsylvania* (Philadelphia: University of Pennsylvania Press, 1940), 72; Mark Frazier Lloyd, "The College, Academy, and Charitable School in the Province of Pennsylvania: Simultaneously Franklin's Triumph and Defeat" in John H. Pollack, ed., *'The Good Education of Youth': Worlds of Learning in the Age of Franklin* (New Castle, DE: Oak Knoll Press, 2009), 150–67.

From the outset, the trustees envisioned a higher institution, but the path to creating a college had to be trod carefully.[26] When Thomas Penn received Franklin's *Proposal*, he initially found it too ambitious, likely to "prevent . . . application to business," where only a "good common School education" was needed. But Penn needed supporters on the ground in his struggles with the Quaker-dominated Assembly, and the trustees were his natural allies, soon to be known as the Proprietary Party. He consecrated their work in 1753 by issuing a charter for the Academy, including a Charity School. By then, Francis Alison had been hired and was already teaching collegiate subjects in the "philosophical school." At this juncture, the Philadelphia project intersected with coeval efforts in New York in the person of William Smith.

A product of Aberdeen University, Smith came to New York in 1751 as a tutor. He quickly inserted himself into the college controversy by publishing a pamphlet supporting the Trinity party, the faction most likely to advance his own situation. He then wrote a more ambitious piece, *A General Idea of the College of Mirania* (1753). The first American treatise on higher education, it described an educational system for mythical Mirania that embodied Enlightenment values still novel in America. Miranians divided the population into "two grand classes." Those designed for the learned professions, including the "chief offices of the state," received thorough training in Latin and some Greek to prepare them for college. The first 3 years of the College of Mirania provided extensive coverage of classical authors, mathematics, contemporary philosophy, and science. A final 2 years were devoted to applying this knowledge, first through polishing speaking and writing skills and finally by studying agriculture (applied science) and history (applied philosophy). All subjects were suffused with natural religion, which provided such a solid base that "revealed religion" in the form of "the general uncontroverted Principles of Christianity" was touched on only once a week on Sunday evenings. As for the rest of the Miranians, they were educated in a Mechanic's School that is "much like the English School in *Philadelphia*, first sketched out by the very ingenious and worthy *Mr. Franklin*."[27] This volume so impressed Franklin and the trustees that Smith was recruited to teach in the philosophical school. But first, Smith returned to England to be

---

26 On the College of Philadelphia, see Gordon, *College of Philadelphia*.

27 William Smith, *A General Idea of the College of Mirania, with a Sketch of the Method of Teaching Science and Religion in the Several Classes* (New York: 1753), quotes pp. 15, 59. The title page addressed the volume "to the consideration of the Trustees nominated by the Legislature to receive Proposals, etc., relating to the Establishment of a College in the Province of NEW-YORK." Albert Frank Gegenheimer, *William Smith: Educator and Churchman, 1727–1803* (Philadelphia: University of Pennsylvania Press, 1943); Roger L. Geiger and Nathan M. Sorber, "Tarnished Icon: Provost William Smith and the College of Philadelphia," *Perspectives on the History of Higher Education*, 28 (2011): 1–31.

ordained as an Anglican priest. His ordination appears to have been a reward for his efforts on behalf of King's College rather than a reflection of his piety, but he also considered this status appropriate for leading a college. More important, Smith met with Thomas Penn and struck a deal: Penn would support Smith and the establishment of a college, and Smith would work as the Proprietor's unofficial agent in Philadelphia. In May 1754, Smith was appointed provost; a year later a new charter established the "College, Academy, and Charitable School of Philadelphia, in the Province of Pennsylvania." The founding of the college was an amicable, consensual affair, but Smith's new role ensured that this would not be the case for long.

The College of Philadelphia was unique in having neither religious nor government ties. It was led by its assertive provost, who was a political rather than a theological Anglican. He was balanced by vice provost Francis Alison, a committed old-light Presbyterian who shared Smith's disdain for religious enthusiasm. The college was open to all denominations, as promised in its charter. It considered itself a public institution, despite being governed by a self-perpetuating board of individuals who represented only themselves. Moreover, the trustees exerted tight control over the institution. They created no president, and they reserved to themselves all powers over admissions, appointments, and finance. In this respect, the college was dominated by a social elite as much as King's, but only some of the outcomes were the same. The college was, by comparison, a thriving, multitiered institution. Around 1760, Smith reported 100 students altogether in the college and Latin and Greek schools, plus an additional 90 students studying English and mathematics in the academy. But like King's, the college produced few graduates—just 154 from 1757 to the Revolution. More than one-third came from Philadelphia, and many of them were related to the trustees. But the college also drew Anglicans and Presbyterians from the hinterland and surrounding states. Some 20 percent of graduates became ministers, 14 Presbyterian versus 12 Anglican. Some sons of wealthy families attended for several years but felt no need to graduate before pursuing careers.[28] Taken as a whole, including the charitable elementary schools for boys and girls, the institution provided substantial education for the region and especially the city, while also serving the purposes of its elite governors. No doubt it could have done more.

By the time the College of Philadelphia was chartered, William Smith had already plunged into provincial politics on behalf of his patron. In anonymous pamphlets, soon unmasked, he attacked the democratic nature of the assembly and advocated greater authority for the proprietor. This offensive included gratuitous slurs of Franklin, who was backing the other side. This struggle grew more

28   Gordon, *College of Philadelphia*, 213–41.

acrimonious as additional issues accentuated the polarization. Most important here, Smith's aggressive Anglican and proprietary positions gave the college a political coloration, which was confirmed when the trustees stood behind him. Franklin was eased out of the board presidency in 1756. He later complained, "Everything to be done in the Academy was privately preconcerted in a cabal.... The Trustees had reaped the full advantage of my head, hands, heart and purse . . . and when they thought they could do without me they laid me aside."[29] The bitterness of this conflict was exemplified in 1758, when the assembly had Smith jailed for alleged complicity in a libelous attack. The trustees authorized him to teach his students from his confinement, thus thumbing their noses at the assembly. Smith had to go to England to be absolved of the charges, where he was honored with doctorates from the universities of Oxford and Aberdeen. Smith apparently assumed, correctly, that he was protected in his aggressive behavior by the backing of the trustees and proprietor. But the college was not so fortunate. Both Alison and Franklin complained that Smith's strident Anglicanism was the cause of low enrollments and dwindling participation in its lotteries. As Smith made himself "universally odious," in Franklin's words, he could scarcely help but make the college appear partisan.

The irony of this situation was that, aside from its political association, the College of Philadelphia had in Alison and Smith the strongest faculty of any colonial college, save Harvard. Both provost and vice provost were products of the Scottish Enlightenment and introduced the moral philosophy of Francis Hutcheson (discussed below). Smith was the most progressive college leader of the colonial era. His *College of Mirania* was informed by the midcentury curricular reforms at the University of Aberdeen. In a *Postscript* to the second edition (1762), he explained that the Mirania plan had been implemented at the College of Philadelphia. Only the first 3 years of the Miranian scheme were taught, but this streamlining of the college course was in itself a significant innovation.[30] Smith personally focused on belles lettres and science. A poet himself, he stressed the importance of mastering composition and style in English; he also organized student plays, which were forbidden elsewhere, for public audiences. For science, he became a patron of the famous instrument maker David Rittenhouse and collaborated in gathering data from the celebrated 1769 transit of Venus. The printed course of study for the college was accompanied by a long list of "books recommended for improving the youth" during "private hours,"

29   Cheney, *University of Pennsylvania*, quote p. 109; Robert Middlekauff, *Benjamin Franklin and His Enemies* (Berkeley: University of California Press, 1996), 42–54.

30   Thomas R. Adams, ed., *Account of the College, Academy and Charitable School of Philadelphia in Pennsylvania* by William Smith, (Philadelphia: University of Pennsylvania Library, 1951).

including "Spectator, Rambler, &c. for the improvement of style and knowledge of life." Thus, the College of Philadelphia had the potential to provide intellectual leadership for the American colonies, a role that the College of New Jersey would belatedly fill. However, given the predominance of dissenters, few wished to follow a truculent, self-serving Anglican. The hollowness of Smith's strategy would become apparent when the crisis with Britain arose.[31]

The founding of the three mid-Atlantic colleges established a pattern that had not been apparent before 1740, when just three dissimilar institutions existed. This pattern, though, did not consist of simple characteristics but rather of a series of appositions that reflected the tacit spread of Enlightenment thinking. First, either formally or in public opinion, they were considered public institutions, but they operated as if owned by particular groups. Ownership was vested in the external boards, or the faculty in the case of William & Mary; but although there could be differences of opinion among these owners, their collective authority was never shaken under colonial rule. Second, the general acceptance of Enlightenment notions of toleration coexisted with a distinct denominational commitment— "toleration with preferment" in the words of historian Jurgen Herbst.[32] Thomas Clap's atavistic resistance—and its ignominious failure—was the exception that proves this rule, as will be seen. Within the colleges, students largely managed to deal with whatever tensions might arise from differing creeds (at least post-Awakening), but contradictions were never entirely resolved among external constituencies, especially where Anglicans were involved. Finally, the spread of Enlightenment doctrines forced the colleges to assimilate the new knowledge into cultural and curricular templates that had been shaped by ancient Greece and Rome. Coming to terms with the American Enlightenment was the most dynamic influence shaping colonial colleges before the Revolution.

ENLIGHTENED COLLEGES

As provincial outposts of the British Empire, the American colonies were slow to appreciate the rich outpouring of ideas from eighteenth-century Britain. When these doctrines were assimilated with dissenting religious traditions, the resulting fusion of ideas has been called the Moderate Enlightenment.[33] For new ideas to leap from the pages of books requires individuals to espouse them, a context in which they are meaningful, and institutions in which to embed them. For the colonial colleges, this process first needed the conviction that the new

31 Geiger and Sorber, "Tarnished Icon," 18–20.
32 Herbst, *From Crisis to Crisis,* 65 et passim.
33 Henry May, *The Enlightenment in America* (New York: Oxford University Press, 1976).

ideas should be taught, then the instructors, books, and materials to teach them. From the 1730s to the 1760s this process gradually accelerated, as trans-Atlantic communication, immigration, and domestic printing all increased. Spearheading this transformation and legitimating other forms of new knowledge was the Newtonian revolution in natural philosophy.

Incorporating Newtonian physics into American classrooms required three pedagogical advances. Explicating the Newtonian universe was perhaps the most basic. Next came the need to demonstrate physical principles through experiments performed with "philosophical apparatus." Most challenging was to elevate the teaching of mathematics to conic sections and trigonometry and, ultimately, to calculus. The Hollis Professorship of Mathematics and Natural Philosophy created the first such opportunity. Harvard graduate Isaac Greenwood, who was instrumental in obtaining the Hollis gift, studied Newtonian science in London from 1724 to 1726. Upon returning to Boston, he privately offered "An Experimental Course of Mechanical Philosophy" that included "Three Hundred Curious and Useful Experiments" to acquaint his audience "with the Principles of Nature, and the Wonderful Discoveries of the Incomparable Sir Isaac Newton."[34] Greenwood was appointed to the Hollis chair immediately afterward and began teaching the same material to Harvard students (almost 40 years after Newton published the *Principia*). Essentially a talented popularizer, he presented a general account of Newton's "Wonderful Discoveries" and employed the philosophical apparatus, also donated by the Hollis family, to demonstrate physical principles in experimental lectures. Telescopes that the college had acquired were employed to teach astronomy. Greenwood upgraded the teaching of mathematics and authored a basic textbook. Dismissed in 1738 for intemperance, he was replaced by John Winthrop, who held the Hollis chair until his death in 1779. Winthrop was easily Colonial America's foremost professional scientist, continually engaged in observation and inquiry. He published papers in the *Philosophical Transactions* of the Royal Society and led an expedition to Nova Scotia to observe the 1761 transit of Venus. In the classroom he employed a growing trove of instruments in experimental demonstrations. With Winthrop, Harvard set a standard for teaching natural philosophy that other colleges could only hope to emulate.

Harvard accumulated, through donations from the Hollis family and others, an extensive collection of philosophical apparatus.[35] These consisted of assorted

34 Quoted from title of Greenwood's course: in Theodore Hornberger, *Scientific Thought in the American Colleges, 1638–1800* (Austin: University of Texas Press, 1945), 45. See also Brooke Hindle, *The Pursuit of Science in Revolutionary America, 1735–1789* (Chapel Hill: University of North Carolina Press, 1956); and Siegel, *Governance and Curriculum at Harvard College*, 237–39, 248–53.

35 Josiah Quincy, *The History of Harvard College* (Boston, 1860), 482–83.

balances, pulleys, and inclined planes to demonstrate mechanical principles; air pumps and vessels for creating vacuums; optical instruments to show Newton's theories of light and colors; as well as microscopes, thermometers, and barometers. Winthrop demonstrated experiments with electricity in the 1740s, before Franklin popularized that subject. For the foremost Newtonian science, astronomy, Harvard acquired a collection of telescopes. Another Hollis gift supplied an orrery—a mechanical model of the solar system that showed the relative movements of the planets. When Harvard's large collection was destroyed in the 1764 Harvard Hall fire, it was more than replaced by timely donations from 150 different individuals. By that date, the scientific demonstration lecture had become an expected part of the college course. Such apparatus was deemed essential by all the colonial colleges, and they devoted scarce resources to acquire them. However, teaching this subject now required special skills. Creating these positions and finding competent teachers proved more difficult.

At the College of Philadelphia, William Smith was proficient in mathematics and astronomy and later taught natural philosophy to medical students. He employed another math teacher as well. The first professor Samuel Johnson appointed to teach these subjects was a Winthrop student, but he died after 3 years, and his replacement proved inadequate.[36] William Small, Jefferson's mentor at William and Mary, provided scientific instruction for the few years he was present (1758–1762). Later, the college commissioned him to purchase $2,000 of the latest philosophical apparatus. These instruments were used by the future president, Reverend James Madison, a 1772 graduate who became professor of natural philosophy and mathematics in 1773. At Yale, President Clap was an enthusiastic astronomer. After his departure a professorship for natural philosophy was established in 1770, but the incumbents, when the position could be filled, were competent teachers at best. A chair of natural philosophy was a high priority for the College of New Jersey's new president, John Witherspoon, which was filled in 1771. That same year, Witherspoon purchased the famous Rittenhouse orrery, originally intended for the College of Philadelphia, which then had to wait for a copy to be made. The significance and prestige of Newtonian science altered college teaching by introducing the experimental lecture employing apparatus, creating a demand for specialized professors and establishing the expectation that the curriculum should incorporate new knowledge.

The legacy of John Locke followed a more circuitous route into the curriculum of American colleges. Locke's *Essay Concerning Human Understanding* was being read in the colleges by the 1730s, but the problem of reconciling

---

36   Humphrey, *King's College*, 106–8; a third professor, Samuel Clossy, taught natural philosophy in the college but joined the medical school in 1767 (134–35).

his empiricist conception of knowledge with prevailing theology was largely ignored. In Scotland, however, moralists wrestled with the implications of Locke's doctrines. The most influential interpretation was offered by Francis Hutcheson (1694–1746), a Glasgow professor whose writings on moral philosophy became widely appreciated in the 1740s and 1750s. As a moderate Presbyterian, Hutcheson's views were compatible with the dissenting American colleges. His moral philosophy epitomized the Moderate Enlightenment's synthesis of reason and religion, which became the preferred approach in prerevolutionary colleges. Hutcheson posited that the human mind was not a Lockean *tabula rasa* but rather possessed an inherent moral sense, analogous to human physical senses like touch and smell. A moral sense that distinguished between right and wrong was compatible with revealed and natural religion, while also invoking reason to sharpen these distinctions, especially where the public good was concerned. For subsequent interpreters, this foundation for ethics was "common sense," and that term came to represent this Scottish approach to moral philosophy that would later predominate in American colleges. For Presbyterians on both sides of the Atlantic, it provided a cogent marriage of reason and religion.

Hutcheson's moral philosophy was first propounded in America by Francis Alison at the College of Philadelphia, who led students through a literal explication of his writings.[37] Philadelphia students began moral philosophy in the middle of the second year and continued it into the first term of the third (final) year. In addition to basic ethical issues, Alison later included Hutcheson's views on natural rights and social questions. Hutcheson drew upon the "Whig canon" in justifying natural rights, balanced government, and the right of resistance to tyranny; Alison, too, taught these doctrines in his classroom and later invoked them for the patriot cause. More influential in elevating moral philosophy to a central role in the curriculum and Republican ideology was John Witherspoon, the Scot who became president of the College of New Jersey in 1768. Witherspoon lectured the seniors on moral philosophy, thereby enshrining it as a "capstone" of the college course. He taught the basic doctrines of Hutcheson but was considerably more eclectic. He included recent enlightened thinkers, such as David Hume, if only to refute them; and he encouraged students to read current authors in the college library, often in the volumes that he had brought from Scotland. In Witherspoon's worldview, moral philosophy was as much a part of nature as Newtonian science. He looked forward to "a time . . . when men, treating moral philosophy as Newton and his successors have done natural, may

---

37   Douglas Sloan, *The Scottish Enlightenment and the American College Ideal* (New York: Teachers College Press, 1971), 73–102; Smith, *Account of the College*, 22.

arrive at greater precision."[38] A historian of the American Enlightenment judged that Witherspoon's "theology, philosophy, and politics were exactly appropriate to their time and place"; and his introduction of the Common Sense philosophy, in particular, was "the first promulgation of the principles that were to rule American college teaching for almost a century."[39]

The origins of the political philosophy that underpinned the Revolution are more diffuse. Historian Bernard Bailyn has explained the intellectual roots of the American Revolution as the fusion in "the decade after 1763, [of] long popular, though hitherto inconclusive ideas about the world and America's place in it . . . into a comprehensive view, unique in its moral and intellectual appeal." Sometimes called the Whig canon, it conflated and drew what seemed relevant from three congeries of thought: first, notions of natural rights and social compact drawn from seventeenth- and eighteenth-century political theorists; second, the concept of balanced government drawn from historical examples of monarchy, aristocracy, and democracy; and third, belief in the inherent liberties of Englishmen and the English constitution, shaped by that nation's tumultuous history. American colleges taught some of these constituent materials throughout the eighteenth century, added more enlightened authors by the 1760s, and allowed or encouraged students by the 1770s to explore this ideology on their own. Thus, while the colleges had little direct input to the Whig canon, they provided a milieu in which its multiple components could reinforce one another.[40]

Political theorists who rationalized theories of natural rights and the consent of the governed were read sparingly in the curriculum. Locke's *Two Treatises on Civil Government* was not used before the prerevolutionary years and then was only recommended. The widest arrays of these writings were recommended at the colleges of New Jersey and Philadelphia. Witherspoon and Smith explicitly advocated outside reading as an essential component of education and provided lists of titles that students should peruse for their own "improvement." In addition, Hutcheson's *Moral Philosophy* reinforced the Whig canon where it was taught. Undoubtedly, political theory became more pertinent as the crisis with Britain deepened after 1765. In the readings pursued on their own, students often favored histories, including the English saga of opposition to government tyranny from the Commonwealth to the Glorious Revolution. At Harvard, where

38   Sloan, *Scottish Enlightenment*, 103–45; Mark A. Noll, *Princeton and the Republic; 1768–1822* (Princeton: Princeton University Press, 1989), 36–52, quote p. 41; Hoeveler, *Creating the American Mind*, 122–26.

39   May, *Enlightenment in America*, quotes pp. 62, 64.

40   Bernard Bailyn, *The Intellectual Origins of the American Revolution* (Cambridge: Harvard University Press, 1967), quote p. 22; David W. Robson, *Educating Republicans, the Colleges in the Era of the American Revolution* (Westport, CT: Greenwood, 1985), 57–74.

there is some documentation, students read a broad spectrum of modern histories. Typically for the period, such works were written from inherently moral perspectives.[41] This was even truer of the Latin and Greek classics that had been the staple of the college curriculum since Henry Dunster.

A large part of this literature is concerned with political themes. The Greek states of the fifth century BCE, were preoccupied with wars and issues of governance; the most read Latin writers dated from the two centuries after 50 BCE that witnessed the fall of the Republic and the vicissitudes of early Empire. After 1750 college assignments included greater coverage of historical works that directly addressed such issues. Caesar's *Commentaries* and the histories of Sallust and Tacitus were now added to Cicero's political orations; in Greek, the historical writings of Herodotus, Thucydides, and Plutarch were now read. These writings were filled with republicanism, civic morality, and observations on government, which became more relevant as the crisis deepened.[42] College students in these years appeared to embrace classical studies enthusiastically, and this interest laid a foundation for the doctrine of republicanism that dominated the new nation from the time of the Revolution. Students in the enlightened colleges of the 1760s and 1770s found immediate relevance in the ancients even as they sought to assimilate the new learning of their own century.

The intellectual currents of the eighteenth century favored the increasing attraction of belles lettres in prerevolutionary colleges. The term encompasses work in the English language—literature as well as the perfecting of writing and speaking that was also called rhetoric. Literature included imaginative writings, particularly drama, history, and essays. Especially popular were the writings of Joseph Addison and Richard Steele in *The Spectator*, a short-lived literary journal (1711–1714) that was widely reprinted. *The Spectator* was admired for its literary style, for popularizing basic Enlightenment ideas, and for applying them to everyday life. William Smith reflected this perfectly when he recommended students read it for self-improvement. Smith was an early advocate of belles lettres, making command of the English language a goal of both the *College of Mirania* and the College of Philadelphia. Belles lettres thus connoted both the cultivation of useful skills, particularly public speaking, and assimilation of the sophisticated culture of the mother country. These objectives were so attractive to students that they pursued them independently through the organization of literary societies (discussed below). Harvard students showed increasing interest in plays, poems, and novels, and they organized a drama club in 1758. The

---

41   Robson, *Educating Republicans*, 87–89.

42   Ibid., 77–81; Carolyn Winterer, *The Culture of Classicism: Ancient Greece and Rome in American Intellectual Life, 1790–1910* (Baltimore: Johns Hopkins University Press, 2002).

restocked Harvard library after the Harvard Hall fire contained ample works of contemporary literature, and in 1771 Harvard created a chair in rhetoric and oratory.[43]

Yale students were late in manifesting an interest in politics but took a lively interest in belles lettres. These interests were encouraged by two tutors, future president Timothy Dwight (Y. 1769) and the poet John Trumbull (Y. 1767). They challenged the prevailing view that "English poetry and the belles-lettres were . . . folly, nonsense and an idle waste of time." Students responded by petitioning the Yale Corporation to allow Dwight to offer special instruction in rhetoric and belles lettres.[44] Trumbull produced a remarkable satire of the traditional Yale student, "The Progress of Dulness or the Rare Adventures of Tom Brainless." The protagonist is a country boy prepared and sent to college by his parents. Incapable of benefiting from the experience, he

> Read ancient authors o'er in vain,
> Nor taste one beauty they contain.
> Four years at college doz'd away
> In sleep, and slothfulness and play.

Tom graduates despite these failings and, unfitted for anything else, becomes a teacher:

> He tries, with ease and unconcern,
> To teach what ne'er himself could learn.

Tom's natural progression is to become a soporific country preacher, who

> On Sunday, in his best array,
> Deals forth the dullness of the day.[45]

Trumbull's mockery of what had hitherto been the modal Yale student reveals how Enlightenment culture had displaced orthodox Calvinism in the late-colonial colleges.

---

43   William Smith, *Account of the College, Academy, and Charitable School of Philadelphia* (1762), quote p. 23; Thomas Jay Siegel, *Governance and Curriculum at Harvard College in the 18th Century*, PhD Diss. Harvard University, 1990, 306, 466–67.

44   Kenneth Silverman, *A Cultural History of the American Revolution* (New York: Crowell, 1976), 221–22.

45   John Trumbull, *The Progress of Dulness, or the Rare Adventures of Tom Brainless* (Carlisle, 1797 [1772]), quotes pp. 9, 12, 19; on student political involvement, Robson, *Educating Republicans*, 83.

Trumbull and Dwight, both ardent patriots, exemplified how the power-ful lure of belles lettres fused with American pride and patriotism. Producing a native literature was seen not only as the maturation of colonial culture but more grandly as the fulfillment of America's destiny. America shall be "The first in letters, as the first in Arms . . . . This land her Steele and Addison shall view, the former glories equaled by the new," wrote Trumbull, and Dwight foresaw the emergence of "more glorious ROMES." At the College of New Jersey com-mencement of 1771, graduates Philip Freneau and Hugh Henry Brackenridge recited *A Poem on the Rising Glory of America*:

> I see
> Freedom's established reign; cities, and men,
> Numerous as sands upon the ocean shore,
> And empires rising where the sun descends!——
> The Ohio soon shall glide by many a town
> Of note; and where the Mississippi stream
> By forests shaded, now runs weeping on,
> Nations shall grow, and states not less in fame
> Than Greece and Rome of old!

Originally justified to polish the speaking skills of ministers and statesmen, belles lettres transcended that role, capturing the imagination and enthusiasm of collegians to craft their own indigenous literature.[46]

★ ★ ★

Finally, medical education provides an entirely different example of the impact of trans-Atlantic learning on American colleges. Interest in establishing medical schools arose among physicians in New York and Philadelphia in the 1760s. In both cases, impetus came from recent medical graduates of Edinburgh Univer-sity. The medical school in Edinburgh had been organized only in 1726, but it quickly became renowned for its excellent instruction and the favored locus for American students. Few university-trained MDs practiced in colonial North America, and almost all were located in the largest cities. They competed there against practitioners with various levels of training and even more varied ap-proaches to healing. University-educated MDs possessed higher status and

---

46 Kenneth Silverman, *A Cultural History of the American Revolution* (New York: Crowell, 1976), 219–235, quotes, 231; Philip Freneau, *A Poem, The Rising Glory of America*, Early Americas Digital Ar-chive (2003).

wealthier patients—as well as an inflated confidence in their own medical acumen.[47] Thus, young men with European training seized the initiative to upgrade medical instruction in American cities.

William Shippen Jr. and John Morgan were sons of elite Philadelphia families who took MDs at Edinburgh in 1762 and 1763, respectively. Shippen returned to Philadelphia and began offering private lectures in anatomy. Morgan capped his education with a grand tour of the Continent, where he discussed medicine with famous physicians and had audiences with both the Pope and Voltaire! He returned to Philadelphia with a detailed plan to establish medical education in conjunction with his alma mater, the College of Philadelphia. Morgan's social standing eased acceptance of his plan. He brought letters of support from Franklin, Thomas Penn, and several college trustees. In 1765 he was appointed Professor of the Theory and Practice of Physick. Shortly thereafter, Shippen was given a similar appointment in Anatomy and Surgery. Other appointments followed of physicians with similar backgrounds, including Edinburgh graduate Benjamin Rush, who later became the most authoritative figure in early American medicine. By 1769 a full medical faculty of five was offering courses—all Edinburgh graduates. Nor was the medical school a financial burden to the college; the professors' only compensation came from student fees.[48]

The announcement of the medical appointments in Philadelphia galvanized a group of university-trained physicians in New York to follow this "laudable Example." They included both newly minted and established MDs. In 1767 their proposal to establish six chairs in a medical school was accepted by the King's College trustees. These professorships—anatomy, surgery, theory and practice of medicine, chemistry, materia medica (or pharmacy), and obstetrics—paralleled the course at Edinburgh and (its model) the University of Leyden.[49] At both King's and Philadelphia, the new professors had an elevated conception of their mission and, as a result, made degrees difficult to obtain. The first degree was a bachelor of medicine, which required a complete course of lectures, general examination, knowledge of Latin and natural philosophy, and apprenticeship—in at least 3 years. The MD required another round of courses and examinations, plus publication and public defense of a "treatise." Ten or twelve students earned BM degrees from King's and two of them proceeded to an MD; at Philadelphia,

47   William G. Rothstein, *American Physicians in the 19th Century: From Sects to Science* (Baltimore: Johns Hopkins University Press, 1985), 26–38; Humphrey, *King's College*, 233–38. Between 1749 and 1800, 122 Americans attended medical school at Edinburgh, 49 from Virginia: William Frederick Norwood, *Medical Education in the United States before the Civil War* (Philadelphia: University of Pennsylvania Press, 1944), 27.

48   Cheyney, *University of Pennsylvania*, 96–104; Norwood, *Medical Education*, 63–78.

49   Humphrey, *King's College*, 238–63; Norwood, *Medical Education*, 109–12.

thirty-one students took the first degree and five, the second. At King's the vitality of the medical school waned after the first few classes, but attendance at Philadelphia topped thirty students before the Revolution forced a suspension of classes.[50]

Physicians in the eighteenth century "became stratified primarily by the amount and nature of education" they received; however, patients "rarely benefited . . . in proportion to the amount of training of the physician."[51] In fact, medical science made little progress during the Age of Enlightenment. Physicians, whether practitioners or professors, made diagnoses on the basis of superficial symptoms, like fever, and were hopelessly muddled regarding causation and cures. These failures, and fanciful theories of disease, made it difficult for physicians to learn from their own cases. The single area in which education and training might improve results was surgery, which was still severely constrained by ignorance of infection and anesthesia. Under these conditions, perhaps it is understandable that neophyte, European-trained doctors were overconfident about the efficacy of medical arts. This was the case with John Morgan and especially Benjamin Rush, a zealous "bleeder" who obstinately defended his convictions and was continually engaged in controversy. But the desire to introduce the "unequalled Lustre" of European medical education no doubt increased enthusiasm for medical schools. Sincerely trusting in their own knowledge, they hoped to raise the standard of medical practice and their own standing as well. Rush noted that his professorial appointment in 1769 "made my name familiar to the public ear . . . [and] was likewise an immediate source of some revenue."[52] Beyond serving their professors, the schools met with limited success. They raised the bar too high for new MDs and thus constrained access to what little knowledge the professors could offer. And the public never shared their own confidence in their art. Consequently, control over medical licensing was generally withheld from educated doctors. This tension between medical schools, the wider medical profession, and the licensing of doctors would bedevil the field for another century.

COLLEGE ENTHUSIASM, 1760–1775

When Reverend Ezra Stiles, future president of Yale, learned of the chartering of Dartmouth College, he noted that three more colleges were in the planning stage in Georgia, South Carolina, and his own city of Newport, Rhode Island:

---

50   Humphrey, *King's College*, 247–48, quotes pp. 242, 248; Norwood, *Medical* Education, 75–76, 111; Cheyney, *University of Pennsylvania*, 103.

51   Rothstein, *American Physicians*, quotes pp. 34, 36.

52   Humphrey, *King's College*, 238; George W. Corner, ed., *The Autobiography of Benjamin Rush* (Princeton: Princeton University Press, 1948), 81.

"College Enthusiasm!" he wrote in his diary.[53] Stiles was reacting to a growing public interest in colleges, particularly in places where they were lacking. This same concern had already brought existing colonial colleges under increased public scrutiny. Internal and external pressures were pushing them toward reform and modernization. The spread of Enlightenment thinking was only part of the changing environment. Expectations of religious toleration were now paramount among these church-linked institutions. More immediate, the colonial elites that composed their governing bodies were sensitive to changing conditions in colonial society. In the 15 years before the Revolution, the first six colonial colleges were prodded to adapt to rapidly changing conditions, while "college enthusiasm" produced three additional institutions. The waning of the old order was most vigorously resisted at Yale.

Thomas Clap had spent much of the 1740s opposing the New Lights of the Awakening, but in the 1750s his regime was challenged from the opposite direction—by the spreading acceptance of Enlightenment views.[54] Clap upheld contrary convictions: he rejected religious toleration within the college, censored library holdings, and argued that colleges are primarily for training ministers. This fundamental divergence lay at the heart of the Yale controversy, but it was grounded in the fractured religious polity of Connecticut and further confounded by the issue of the colonial government's authority over the college. The Old Lights, who remained a powerful force in Connecticut politics, represented the moderate wing of the Congregational churches, increasingly open to toleration and reason; and these views were further supported by a growing Anglican presence. Clap soon rejected his former allies and embraced the New Lights. But they, too, had changed and were now led by New Divinity preachers—college-educated zealots inspired by Jonathan Edwards and Samuel Hopkins. The New Divinity energized Yale's dwindling number of ministerial candidates. However, their approach proved too extreme—and esoteric—for most congregations. So here, too, Yale's sectarian emphasis was out of tune with much of Connecticut society.[55]

The campaign against Clap began in earnest in 1755 with the publication of a critical pamphlet. The not very anonymous author was Benjamin Gale (Y. 1733), a prominent physician and scientist, member of the Assembly, and staunch

---

53 Franklin Bowditch Dexter, ed., *The Literary Diary of Ezra Stiles, D.D., LL.D.*, 3 vol. (New York: Scribner's, 1901), I, 46. A college was proposed for Western Massachusetts in 1862 but squelched by the opposition of Harvard: Richard Hofstadter and Wilson Smith, eds. *American Higher Education: A Documentary History*, 2 vol. (Chicago: University of Chicago Press, 1961), I, 131–33.

54 Events at Yale are described most fully by Louis Leonard Tucker, *Puritan Protagonist: President Thomas Clap of Yale College* (Chapel Hill: University of North Carolina Press, 1962), 201–62; also, Brooks Mather Kelley, *Yale: A History* (New Haven: Yale University Press, 1974).

55 Many new-light congregations formed during the Awakening reverted to Baptism under local ministers and resented the Congregational Standing Order, of which Yale was a part.

secularist. He was closely associated with his father-in-law, Reverend Jared Eliot, the foremost critic of Clap on the Yale Corporation.[56] Gale's pamphlet first addressed Yale's finances, showing that the college had no need of the annual £100 subsidy it received from the colony. He then attacked Clap's attempts to force students to attend church services within the college and the proposed appointment of a professor of divinity—steps he called establishing an "Ecclesiastical Society." Gale found no justification in the statutes for a college church. Yale College was established by the Assembly as a secular institution for the instruction of youth, "either in *Divinity, Law, Physick*, or some other Profession." The Assembly, furthermore, was the "Overseer" responsible for the college. Gale's argument echoed Livingston's campaign for "public" governance of King's College, but in this case Clap was actually instituting the kind of denominational hegemony that Livingston had hypothetically imagined. The political question was whether or not the Assembly, as Overseers, would appoint a committee of visitation that would almost certainly undo Clap's policies.

In the event, the Assembly withdrew Yale's annual grant but went no further. Clap then proceeded to fulfill his plan. He raised funds for a professorship of divinity and brought in Naphtali Daggett (Y. 1748), who was duly installed after a trial period and intensive interrogation (1756). Despite Yale's limited faculty, Dagget's job was to preach, not teach. Yale still had no professors to assist the president in teaching substantive subjects. Clap also succeeded in creating a separate church within the college, over the opposition of Jared Eliot and several other trustees. The president had now alienated his former supporters and at this point turned to the New Light/New Divinity Party for support. He had succeeded in establishing a sectarian college but one that represented only a minority of Connecticut Christians. More ominous, opposition to Clap and his rule, led by Gale, continued to build throughout the province.

Despite the hyperbole over religious intolerance, students seemed little affected. If anything, their behavior reflected the sinking reputation of the president. College discipline degenerated in rising absenteeism, wanton vandalism, and open defiance of Clap. Despite repeated requests to intervene, the Assembly was reluctant—either to confront Clap or become embroiled in religious controversy or both. Finally, in 1763, a petition from leading citizens could not be ignored: It complained of the "arbitrariness and autocracy of the President, the multiplicity and injustice of the laws . . . and the unrest of the students"; and it requested that the Assembly review the college laws and send a visitation committee.[57] Both sides were invited to state their cases to the Assembly. Before a

---

56 A.Z. [Benjamin Gale], *The Present State of the College of Connecticut Considered* (1755).
57 Kelley, *Yale*, 67.

hall packed with spectators, Clap presented a masterful defense. Whereas his opponents assumed that the Assembly was the legal founder of the college and thus its rightful overseer, Clap provided an alternative history: the school was begun a year before the 1701 charter by a meeting of Connecticut ministers, who pledged their own books to found the college. This story was elaborated with legal citations to form an apparently convincing case. Clap further alleged that the charges of the petitioners and the (supposedly exaggerated) disorders in the college were instigated by his long-standing enemies. When the new-light-leaning Assembly declined to intervene, Clap emerged triumphant. Moreover, his dubious account of Yale's founding was long held to establish the private nature of the college.[58] But none of this lessened his problems in New Haven.

Disorder in the college continued to escalate, finally reaching open rebellion.[59] In 1766 nearly all the students signed a petition of grievances to the corporation. When the corporation declined to act, they boycotted classes and became violent. The tutors were forced not only to resign but to flee New Haven. The corporation declared an early spring vacation, but when the college reopened (with no tutors), few students returned. Faced with the ruin of the college, Clap had no choice but to resign. The rest of the school year was effectively canceled, and Clap presided over a subdued commencement as his last act. Perhaps the most consequential student rebellion before the 1960s, student resistance had succeeded where Clap's many enemies had failed. But compared with the growing vitality of other colonial colleges, Yale for long was unable to keep pace.

Unable to find a suitable replacement who would accept the position, the corporation named Daggett acting president. The scholarly Daggett had aptitude neither for administration nor for governing students, and the Corporation signaled their lack of confidence in him by closely managing college affairs, choosing the tutors, for example. Daggett, unlike his predecessor, made few enemies, and the college slowly recovered. But he had previously taught only divinity, and even as the college's sole professor did not lecture to students. Not until 1770 was an undistinguished professor of math and natural philosophy appointed to cover Clap's subjects. The college did manage to appoint effective tutors in these years (Dwight and Trumbull), who seem to have carried the instructional load. Nonetheless, the college benefited from a geographical monopoly.[60] Throughout

58   George W. Pierson, *The Founding of Yale: The Legend of the Forty Folios* (New Haven: Yale University Press, 1988).

59   James Axtell, *The School upon a Hill: Education and Society in Colonial New England* (New Haven: Yale University Press, 1974), 238–42.

60   Beverly McAnear, "The Selection of Alma Mater by Pre-Revolutionary Students," *Pennsylvania Magazine of History and Biography*, 73, 4 (Oct. 1949): 429–40. More than 75 percent of Yale students

the turmoil of the Clap years, it enrolled around 170 students. Attendance fell to almost half that number during and after the collapse but gradually rose to the previous level by the Revolution. By then, students were expecting more from their education (see below). Confronted with increasing student disorder, Daggett resigned the presidency in 1777, although not his professorship. Yale was the second largest colonial college, at times exceeding Harvard in enrollment (table 1), and was reasonably well furnished; but at best Yale offered perfunctory pedagogy and contributed nothing to learning.

Harvard prospered under the placid presidency of Edward Holyoke (1737–1769) from before the Awakening until the pre-Revolution turmoil. Ezra Stiles, who rated all the college presidents he had known, described Holyoke as having "a noble commanding presence . . . [and] great Dignity"; "Yet not of great erudition." Holyoke's own judgment on his career was more negative: "if any man wishes to be humbled and mortified, let him become President of Harvard College." [61] He never explained if this statement reflected his treatment by students or Overseers, but the progressive changes in the college during his tenure largely originated with the latter.

Harvard still retained much of the arts course of a Puritan college when Holyoke assumed the presidency, but it also had unique strengths. The two Hollis professorships ensured that college teaching would reflect up-to-date scientific knowledge and moderate interpretations of religious doctrines. A large and inventive student body found ways to pursue their intellectual interests, as will be seen in the next section. And the Board of Overseers by the 1750s contained "unusually intelligent and cultivated gentlemen" who were sensitive to educational trends. Still, a later president observed that the college adjusted "tardily" to the "impulses given to science and literature in England, during the reign of Queen Anne"; and "it was not until after the middle of the eighteenth century, that effectual improvements were introduced." [62] Beginning in 1754 the Overseers voiced concern for student attainments in oratory and classical learning. In a series of steps that were often resisted in the college, they established public exhibitions of forensic disputations—the kind of public speaking valued by gentlemen like themselves, and by students too. New prizes were awarded based on merit. It took until 1766 for these practices to become the law of the college,

---

were from Connecticut, and many more came across the sound from Long Island. Later, Yale graduates would fan out across the new nation and send sons and students back to alma mater.

61   Ezra Stiles, *Literary Diaries*, II, 336; Samuel Eliot Morison, *Three Centuries of Harvard* (Cambridge: Harvard University Press, 1936), 99.

62   Overseers included liberal Boston ministers Jonathan Mayhew and Charles Chauncy: Morison, *Three Centuries*, 89. Quincy, *History of Harvard*, II, 123: by "influences of the period" Quincy meant "impulses given to science and literature in England, during the reign of Queen Anne."

but then created an eighteenth-century version of accountability.[63] In the meantime, the Overseers began to reorganize instruction.

In a prescient move, the Overseers resolved around 1760 to create more professorships for the college by finding donors of endowments. They obtained six such pledges, all in wills. Only one was realized immediately, the Thomas Hancock Professorship of Hebrew and Oriental Languages. It was awarded in 1765 to Thomas Sewell, an accomplished linguist and instructor in Hebrew, who was rewarded for proposing a plan to upgrade the teaching of classical languages. A second appointment that year installed Edward Wigglesworth Jr. to succeed his father as Hollis professor of divinity. He was a biblical scholar but, unlike his father, not an ordained minister. He also broke precedent by being eager to teach in the college. At this same time, the Overseers decided that "tutors should function differently than they do now." A reorganization the following year assigned each tutor to teach a single subject to each class, rather than teaching all subjects to a single class. The four tutors were made responsible for Latin, Greek, philosophy (logic, ethics, metaphysics), and science (math, astronomy, natural philosophy). Each also served like a homeroom teacher, providing instruction to a single class in English language skills (elocution, rhetoric, and composition). With these reforms Harvard formalized a faculty that distinguished between introductory and advanced instruction—a structure that could accommodate both basic instruction and some advanced learning.[64]

★ ★ ★

The three Anglican colleges all had direct or indirect ties with England, although these relationships differed from New York to Philadelphia to Virginia. These colleges also wrestled with issues of curriculum and institutional control. Despite the difficulties in relations with England in the wake of the Stamp Act crisis, Anglicans aggressively upheld the interests of their colleges. Their confidence stemmed from a superficial perception of growing strength.[65] Culturally, as the upper classes of colonial cities increased in wealth and sophistication, they became more Anglicized in material goods, social conventions, intellectual culture,

---

63   Quincy, *History of Harvard*, II, 123–36: "Many other improvements, in the collegiate textbooks, exercises, and principles of discipline, may be traced to this period, and to the influence of the able men, who then guided the board of Overseers" (p. II, 136).

64   Siegel, *Governance and Curriculum at Harvard*, 253–68, quote p. 261; Quincy, *History of Harvard*, II, 130–34, 496–97.

65   This confidence was manifest most notably in the 1760s campaign for the appointment of American bishops—a movement that greatly antagonized moderate dissenters with whom Anglicans had most in common: May, *Enlightenment*, 81–87.

and church membership. Politically, the notion of a cosmopolitan British Empire was more appealing than parochial colonial assemblies. And although the Anglican Church in America was relatively weak and fragmented, its leaders usually occupied the heights of the colonial social hierarchy. They believed the *Church of England* deserved a privileged position in British Imperial society, and for them the colleges were strategic institutions.

At Philadelphia, Provost William Smith fully shared the outlook of the mostly Anglican Trustees, whose interests were aligned with those of Proprietor Thomas Penn. The college was officially nonsectarian and included old light Presbyterians among both faculty and trustees. The issue of religious balance was nonetheless delicate. When concerns were raised about Anglican domination in 1764, the trustees issued a declaration that the existing denominational representation in the college would be permanent. This step assured Anglican advantage but not for proselytizing. Smith was a virtual Deist, who dismissed theological doctrines as "Rubbish." Philadelphia was by far the most enlightened college, and that in itself may have lured students toward the lenient tenets of the Anglican Church.[66]

By the end of the 1760s William Smith was at the pinnacle of his social and intellectual eminence in America's largest and wealthiest city. He was the leading figure in the Anglican Church and the College, an author, scientist, and office-holder in numerous organizations. Typically, he staged public student dramatic presentations—the first being *Alfred, A Masque*, a glorification of Alfred the Great that concluded with the singing of *Rule Britannia*. When the American Philosophical Society was resuscitated in 1768, Smith became its permanent secretary. Although he could not match the social and financial status of the proprietary gentry, he was part of the same social circles, and so was the college. Besides attracting the sons of the non-Quaker gentry, the college drew students from large landholders in Maryland and the South. Compared with other colleges, its students paid high fees, had a low rate of graduation, and were notably youthful. Wealthy parents tended to provide thorough and early educational preparation, creating the ironic situation that one of the youngest bodies of students was taught the most advanced curriculum. Graduation was not a high priority for students whose careers would be determined by families, not credentials. The college was financed primarily through fund-raising—another art that William Smith mastered. Both the College of Philadelphia and its Provost were ideally

66   Stephen Brobeck, "Revolutionary Change in Colonial Philadelphia: The Brief Life of the Proprietary Gentry," *William and Mary Quarterly*, 3rd series, 33, 3 (July 1976): 410–34; Harold E. Taussig, "Deism in Philadelphia during the Age of Franklin," *Pennsylvania History*, 37 (1970): 217–36. Francis Alison charged that potential Presbyterian ministers were converting to Anglicanism: Trinterud, *American Tradition*, 212–17.

adapted to the Anglophile social and cultural milieu that would soon be challenged by the Revolution.[67]

The governors of King's College were less content with their learned president. Nor was Samuel Johnson happy with his position. He endured the deaths of two wives, a son, and a beloved son-in-law during his presidency (1754–1763), and he fled the city for lengthy periods during smallpox outbreaks. Between these absences and an unavoidable turnover in teachers, the college fell, in Johnson's own words, "much into disrepute." King's never had more than 30 students during Johnson's tenure, leading one trustee to ask, "what need of so many tutors for so few scholars?" By 1760, the governors became more assertive and also began looking for a successor. Tellingly, they appealed to the Archbishop of Canterbury to locate a fitting Oxonian. He recommended Myles Cooper, a 25-year-old graduate of Queen's College, Oxford, who arrived in 1762. The governors somewhat rudely hastened Johnson's departure, and Cooper became president the next year.[68]

The nature of the presidential transition signaled the governors' ascendancy over the college, and the young Cooper readily conformed to their wishes. The school's historian characterized him as "first and last that stock character of eighteenth-century English public life, a placeman." A bon vivant, he fit easily into the New York social milieu, and it was soon said, "Cooper . . . knows everybody, and everything that passes here." His distinctive contribution to the college was to make it more English, after the model of his alma mater.[69] The college course was shifted significantly toward that of Queen's College, Oxford. The reading of classical authors in Latin and Greek became the chief emphasis. In philosophy, the focus was logic, metaphysics, and Aristotle—subjects considered outdated by other colleges. In another striking departure, math and natural philosophy were deemphasized to the point of neglect. The contrast to the College of Philadelphia could not have been starker. Cooper also emphasized the collegiate way of living. Although now an American tradition, he gave it an Oxonian twist. Students were required to live in the college, wear gowns, and conform to a much stricter disciplinary regime. He walled in the college grounds and hired a porter to keep the students inside. Cooper boasted (wishfully) that discipline, which had previously been "one heavy Accusation exhibited against us," was now unsurpassed in any other college. These measures did nothing to raise the popularity of the college. Enrollments averaged just 25 students through the 1760s, and the new grammar school, which was badly needed to improve student preparation, likewise attracted few students.[70]

67   Geiger and Sorber, "Tarnished Icon: William Smith and the College of Philadelphia," 1–31.
68   Humphrey, *King's College*, 119–25, quotes pp. 119, 122.
69   McCaughey, *Stand Columbia*, 27.
70   Humphrey, *King's College*, 126–30, quote p. 130.

By 1770 prospects for King's College began to brighten. Enrollments increased moderately to around 40, but the college was now wealthy as a result of funds raised in the previous decade. And the launch of the medical department was an added boost to prestige. The governors and their president might have been apprehensive about the deteriorating relations between Britain and America; however, their reaction was just the opposite. Buoyed by the Anglican ideology, they sought a larger role by expanding King's College into a university. Once again the model was Oxford—a university structure that encompassed constituent colleges. They deluded themselves into thinking that a royal charter for such an institution would cement "the Union between Great Britain and the Colonies . . . diffuse a Spirit of Loyalty . . . [and] maintain and extend the Discipline and Doctrine" of the Church of England. Specifically, they hoped to obtain a royal gift of regius professorships, two representatives in the colonial assembly (like Oxford's seats in Parliament), and future control over any additional colleges in New York. In 1771 Cooper departed for London to sell this plan. Although the idea found some support, he brought no charter document to be approved. When he returned the next year, the governors appointed a committee to draft a charter for "the American University in the Province of New York." After 2 years, a long and complex charter proposed a King's College writ large. That is, the governing structure of the university would ensure the authority of Myles Cooper and the existing governors over the university and future colleges. They were still endeavoring to implement this plan in 1775 when Cooper, an outspoken loyalist, was run out of New York City by a patriot mob.[71]

The politics of higher education were entirely different in Virginia, where the president and faculty of William & Mary were Anglican clergy and the lay Visitors represented the province's governing elite. The faculty routinely intervened in local politics on behalf of the clergy, and the Visitors were perpetually frustrated by their inability to affect the affairs of the college. Educational issues were often submerged under these conflicts and the personal animosities they generated. In 1763 the Visitors attempted to revise the statutes to secure far-reaching control over the faculty, who naturally resisted. This battle raged for the remainder of the decade until the intervention of the Bishop of London, and perhaps exhaustion, brought some peace but little change. Then, the atmosphere in Virginia began to improve.[72]

71 Ibid., 140–151, quote p. 141.

72 Susan H. Godson et al., *The College of William & Mary: A History*, 2 vol. (Williamsburg: College of William & Mary, 1993), I, 101–26; Hoeveler, *American Mind*, 283–89; Robert Polk Johnson, "The Reform of the College of William and Mary, 1763–1780," *Proceedings of the American Philosophical Society*, 115, 3 (June 1971): 187–213.

Dissatisfaction with the college had been longstanding and widespread, but now Virginians took notice that, although the wealthiest colony, their publicly supported higher education was glaringly inferior to that in the North. Not only did the college produce no graduates and few homegrown clergy, but preparation for medicine and law in the province was scandalously haphazard. With assistance from the bishop and the governor, William & Mary began to function more like a true college. During his short-lived governorship, Lord Botetourt sought to assist rather than assault the college. He encouraged both academic achievement and the completion of bachelor's degrees by establishing two medals in 1770 to be awarded in "classical learning" and "philosophical learning." The same year the Bishop of London sent two competent faculty members, giving the college, for the first time, the full complement of masters called for in its charter. In 1772, Nathaniel Burwell and James Madison were awarded the first Botetourt medals and also became the first graduates of William & Mary.

The elevation of the level of scholarship in the college received little recognition. Rather, a crescendo of criticism and calls for reform ensued. There were three obvious targets. First, for good reason, critics wished to abolish the grammar school. It was an anomalous legacy of the original charter that mixed college students with children and caused unending problems with lodging and discipline. However, it was also the mainstay of the institution's enrollments. Second, William & Mary had an unstructured plan of studies; students were not grouped in classes or examined on their progress, so that few completed studies and took degrees. As an alternative model, critics looked to the now esteemed College of New Jersey, which offered shorter, cheaper, and better education. The faculty countered that their plan followed the superior practices of Oxford and Cambridge. But in 1775 Samuel Stanhope Smith opened Hampton-Sidney, a Presbyterian Academy, bringing the New Jersey model closer to home. Third, many critics called for more practical forms of education. The faculty responded with a self-righteous defense of classical, liberal education. But almost all laymen perceived a need for some provision for medical and legal training. These were issues that colonial William & Mary was incapable of addressing. However, the academic vitality of the early 1770s and the wider appreciation of educational developments elsewhere set the stage for significant change after the Loyalist faculty departed.[73]

★ ★ ★

The last three colonial colleges to be founded were barely launched before the Revolution. Rhode Island College commenced teaching in the president's

---

73 Thomson, "Reform of William & Mary," 201–5.

parsonage in 1766 and found a permanent home 4 years later. Queen's College purchased a tavern in which to begin instruction in 1772, with just one tutor and no president. Dartmouth College, the last to be chartered (1769), imported its initial students from Connecticut to a clearing in the wilderness in 1770. The first two of these colleges fulfilled the educational aspirations of denominational communities, while Dartmouth resulted from a unique conjuncture of individual enterprise and government sponsorship.[74]

Reverberations from the foundings of New Jersey and King's colleges affected other denominations. New Lights of the Dutch Reformed church were enraged when their old-light brethren allied with Anglicans at King's College in 1755. Their leader, Theodore Frelinghuysen, declared, "let every one provide for his own house" and called for the establishment of a college that would also prepare young men for "the sacred ministerial office in the Church of God." This faction of the Dutch church persisted doggedly until that goal was realized.[75] Baptists constituted a far larger population that included many former Congregational New Lights, but they had little internal organization. Moreover, they had little use for colleges, preferring ministers with an inner calling to those with formal education. No Baptist had graduated from a colonial college since 1734. But attitudes began to change among at least a few. The Philadelphia Baptist Association established an academy in New Jersey in 1756 and soon looked to establish a college. It found a possible leader when a product of its academy, James Manning, graduated from Nassau Hall in 1762.[76]

Rhode Island was the obvious locus for a Baptist college. The province was known for religious toleration, and Baptists were the largest denomination by far; however, the principal city of Newport was a cosmopolitan seaport where Congregationalists and Anglicans predominated. Baptist churches had grown throughout the region with the conversion of schismatic New Light congregations, but they endured discrimination from the Congregational Standing Order in Massachusetts and Connecticut. In 1763 the Philadelphia Baptists sent Manning to Newport to explore the possibilities of establishing a college. He met there with Ezra Stiles, the learned minister of the Second Congregational Church, whose own aspiration was to promote greater unity among the Calvinist-Reformed churches. The two men agreed that Stiles would write a charter for a college jointly operated by Baptists and Congregationalists. The

74 Hoeveler, *American Mind*, 181–212.

75 Herbst, *From Crisis to Crisis*, 110–13; Richard P. McCormick, *Rutgers: A Bicentennial History* (New Brunswick: Rutgers University Press, 1966), 3–24; William H. S. Demarest, *A History of Rutgers College, 1766–1924* (New Brunswick: Rutgers College, 1924).

76 Herbst, *From Crisis to Crisis*, 123–27; Walter C. Bronson, *The History of Brown University, 1764–1914* (Providence: Brown University, 1914), 1–75.

resulting document proposed two tiers of governance: *trustees* with a majority of Baptists would elect the president, and *fellows* with a majority of Congregationalists would provide academic governance. Although the draft gave Baptists majority control and veto powers, they balked at the large role reserved for Congregationalists. The Rhode Island Assembly modified the charter to ensure larger Baptist majorities and then passed what was otherwise a liberal charter (1764). Toleration was fine, but ultimately the Baptists wanted control of their own college.

James Manning assumed a pulpit in Warren, Rhode Island, and opened Rhode Island College there in 1766. Three years later the college graduated seven students. At this point a decision had to be made on a permanent home, and the issue of control surfaced again. The two contenders were Newport and Providence. In Newport Baptists would be faced with the cultural hegemony of educated and genteel Congregationalists and Anglicans, while Providence was more comfortably Baptist. Wealthy Newport made the most lucrative offer, but the Providence bid was then made competitive by the exertions of local boosters—the Browns, a family of wealthy merchants. Once again, Baptist control took precedence over all other considerations. Stiles condemned it as a "Party college," a grave insult among the enlightened, and made a futile effort to found a second college in Newport. The Browns stood by their commitment, and by 1772 a large college edifice was completed, modeled after Nassau Hall. But by 1775 the college enrolled just 41 students, a minority of them from Rhode Island.[77] The Baptists now owned a college, even though they had little use for one.

The same determination to have its own college energized the new-light wing of the Dutch Reformed Church. A smaller ethnic community, for whom Dutch was the first language, it had been irretrievably split by the Awakening. As with the Anglican Church, the governing body of the Dutch Reformed Church was across the Atlantic. While the Old Lights remained under its authority, the New Lights had formed a confederation and begun to ordain their own ministers. This "American party" sought to dispense with the Dutch language and establish a college specifically to educate ministers. In 1759 Frelinghuysen took their case to the governing body in Amsterdam, only to be denied (and lose his life in a shipwreck on the return voyage). With both the mother church and New York Old Lights opposing them, they petitioned the governor of New Jersey. At first they were rebuffed, but in 1766 Governor William Franklin (Ben's son) approved a charter. All trace of this document has been lost, and it was never

---

77 Bronson, *History of Brown*, 44–50; Under Manning (1766–1791) CRI graduated 165 students; 43 became clergy, 26 Congregational and 12 Baptist: Martha Mitchell, ed., *Encyclopedia Brunoniana* (Providence: Brown University Library, 1993), 362–63.

actually enacted. Meanwhile, the Dutch church sought to divert the project by proposing an alliance with the College of New Jersey. The evangelicals stood their ground, and in 1770 Governor Franklin issued a new charter similar to that of the College of New Jersey.

Queen's College was organized the following year. Instruction was consigned to a single tutor, Frederick Frelinghuysen, nephew of Theodore and stepson of Reverend Jacob Rutsen Hardenbergh, a trustee and later acting president who had not attended college himself. Frelinghuysen, a 1770 graduate of the College of New Jersey, was soon attracted to the law. He was replaced by his classmate, John Taylor, a Presbyterian, who remained the instructor for most of the next two decades. Prospects were dimmed when the two factions of the Dutch church managed to reconcile, but they then chose to support a professor of divinity in New York City instead of the fledgling college. On this tenuous base, the college persisted until disrupted by the Revolution. It graduated its first student in 1774 and four more the following year. It would graduate 35 more students before tutor Taylor resigned in 1790, some 15 of these graduates becoming ministers. Queen's College was a premonition of things to come in American higher education. Erected by a denominational faction to meet its own needs, it long lacked the population and resource base to offer more than a rudimentary college course and was unable to do even that for years at a time.

Dartmouth College founder, Reverend Eleazar Wheelock, was a man of pious, single-minded zeal. A 1733 graduate of Yale, the Awakening transformed him into an ardent itinerant preacher. When he returned to his parish in Lebanon, Connecticut, he discovered a second transcendent cause—educating and Christianizing Native Americans. He had been approached by a Christian Mohegan, Samson Occom, who sought a classical education and proved to be an adept student. Wheelock subsequently organized Moor's Charity School in 1754 to educate Native American youth, with hope of training teachers and missionaries. Wheelock's intentions would today be labeled cultural imperialism, predicated on a typically deprecating view of Native American peoples and cultures; but few contemporaries possessed as genuine a concern for their welfare.[78]

The path from Moor's Charity School to a college in Hanover, New Hampshire, had numerous subplots, but three developments proved key.[79] First, Wheelock's endeavors depended on philanthropy from the first gift from Joshua

---

78   Colin G. Calloway, *The Indian History of an American Institution: Native Americans and Dartmouth* (Hanover, NH: Dartmouth College Press, 2010), 1–14; James Axtell. "Dr. Wheelock's Little Red School," in Axtell, *The European and the Indian: Essays in the Ethnohistory of Colonial North America* (New York: Oxford University Press, 1981), 87–109.

79   Most fully recounted in Leon Burr Richardson, *History of Dartmouth College*, 2 vol. (Hanover: Dartmouth College, 1932).

Moor. In 1765 Samson Occom, now an inspiring pulpit orator, embarked on a fund-raising trip to England that proved hugely successful. Some £12,000 were raised for Indian education and confided to a trust presided over by the Earl of Dartmouth. Second, Wheelock had become discouraged by the inherent frustrations of educating Native Americans.[80] He resolved to relocate nearer the frontier and educate white missionaries as well, which meant founding a college. The prize of an established school with a huge endowment elicited numerous offers, but here the third development was decisive—the intervention of New Hampshire Royal Governor John Wentworth. In protracted negotiation, both men tacitly favored establishment of a college—Wheelock to educate minister-missionaries and Wentworth to secure a college for the province. In 1769 they agreed upon a large grant of land on the upper Connecticut River, a territory opened for settlement only 5 years before by the defeat of the French—and a charter for Dartmouth College. The charter provoked an outcry from the bene-factors of the Indian school, including the English trustees and Samson Occom. The former were indispensable, and Wheelock assuaged their concerns by as-suring that Moor's Charity School would use the trust funds to educate Indian youth and future missionaries separate from the new college. With legal details settled in the late summer of 1770, Wheelock embarked on the Herculean task of building a college and a community in the primeval forests at Hanover.

Wheelock brought a few students with him from Connecticut in 1770. The next year, he staged a commencement ceremony in the primitive structures that had been built, entertaining Governor Wentworth and an entourage of gentle-men. The four graduates, including Wheelock's son John, all had transferred from Yale. Despite its remoteness, Dartmouth attracted increasing numbers of students. Many came from Connecticut, either from sympathy with Wheelock's evangelicalism or disapproval of Yale. Students also came for a free education. Charity students pledged a bond for the value of their education to guarantee that they would become missionaries. In 1772 twenty-four students were enrolled in the college, with seventeen below college level, including six Indians. The Indians and twenty of the English students were on charity. Pre-Revolutionary Dartmouth had by far the highest proportion of ministerial graduates (74 per-cent), but few of the commitments to become missionaries were honored. Most charity graduates preferred pulpits in the multiplying settlements of the Con-necticut Valley, and Wheelock recovered almost nothing from their bonds.

80 Wheelock wrote in 1761: "None know, nor can any, without Experience, Well conceive of the Difficulty of Educating an Indian." By 1771 he had succeeded with "40 Indians who were good read-ers, writers and were instructed in the principles of the Christian religion. . . . [But] not more than half preserved their character unstained. The rest are sunk into as low, savage and brutish a way of living as they were before . . . and six of those who did preserve a good character are now dead." Ibid., I, 39, 78.

And what of the Indians? Wheelock was accused by contemporaries and historians of duplicity in leveraging donations for Indian education into a personal collegiate fiefdom.[81] More likely his motives were mixed. Wheelock was a zealot whose mission to the Indians remained constant through these years, yet the objective of a college for white students had become uppermost in his plans. Dartmouth College thus emerged as the dominant offshoot. Financially, although he had pledged to spend the English trust funds on Indian education, the funds seem to have been largely consumed in clearing land and erecting buildings and were exhausted by 1774. These expenditures for founding the settlement were parceled between Dartmouth, Moor's, and, for that matter, Wheelock's personal accounts. Little of this enterprise benefited Indians, to be sure, but circumstances played a large role. Wheelock was effectively excluded from the more placid Indian tribes of New York and Pennsylvania and eventually found recruits to the North among Canadian tribes. Between fifteen and twenty were in attendance before 1776, and three Indian students graduated from the college (1777–1781). Wheelock's loyal early graduates did undertake missionary work for a time. But all these activities became more difficult to support after the charitable funds were exhausted. Inevitably, he experienced the same frustrations as in Connecticut. Still, until his death in 1779, the Indian mission was kept alive. Afterward, occasional Indian students continued to be educated at Moor's School until the 1850s, supported by a Scotch charity, but few advanced to Dartmouth College.[82]

These three colleges have several traits in common. All were inspired by New Light, or Calvinist, beliefs; all the founders sought control of their colleges above all else; and all subordinated learning, particularly the new learning, to perfunctory replication of traditional curricula. These founders were no doubt correct in fearing that mixing with more learned and sophisticated groups would submerge their own particularistic goals. But Rhode Island Baptists also rejected emerging academic standards when they excluded Congregationalists. Wheelock, too, had to defend his control by deflecting attempts by Governor Wentworth to attach Anglicans to Dartmouth. In fact, academically the new colleges were distinctly inferior to their established peers. Here the opinion of Ezra Stiles is probably more accurate than accounts of later college historians. He found it "singlular" that Wheelock rose "to the figure he did, with such a small literary Furniture." He

81   Ibid., I, 122–28, 219–21 et passim; Bobby Wright, "For the Children of the Infidels? American Indian Education in the Colonial Colleges," *American Indian Culture and Research Journal*, 12, 3 (1988): 1–14.

82   Calloway, *Indian History*, 15–95. The Society in Scotland for Propagating Christian Knowledge supported Indian education in America from ca. 1730 until this mission was legally terminated in 1924: "Scottish money, raised by Samson Occom and controlled by the SSPCK, kept Dartmouth in the business of educating Indians" (p. 37).

noted that Manning was made president only 2 years out of college, "not . . . for his Literature, but because he was a Baptist"; and that he had "a superficial general Knowledge of the Languages & Sciences," besides being "very biggotted."[83] Manning's assistant followed his same educational track and was appointed "professor of natural philosophy" with no apparent qualifications 3 years after graduating (CNJ. 1766). Wheelock enlisted charity students as tutors, including his son John, as soon as they graduated, and they later became the college's first professors. Wheelock, in fact, evinced no interest in curriculum and largely reproduced the college course he had known at Yale in the 1730s.[84] Rhode Island was no better. At Queen's the entire course was confided to a single tutor, and no college graduate could be found to serve as president. Despite the advances in learning incorporated elsewhere, a minimal study of classical languages, English, philosophy, and a smattering of mathematics and science was accepted in America as a collegiate course of study for the AB degree. Of course, just such laxness had allowed Connecticut ministers to start the Collegiate School and Jonathan Dickinson to launch the College of New Jersey. But this low minimal standard set an ominous precedent for the new nation. However, on the eve of the Revolution, American colleges appeared to have bright prospects.

★   ★   ★

In the 1760s, the principal concern of "Nassau Hall," as it was familiarly known, was to preserve new-light control over the institution that embodied those convictions. President Samuel Finley's death in 1766 exhausted the supply of Awakening veterans to lead the college.[85] The schism between the new-light New York Synod and the old-light Philadelphia Synod had been papered over in 1758, but the estrangement ran deep. Now, Philadelphia Old Lights approached the trustees with an offer of badly needed financial support if their candidates were named president and professor. In near panic, the trustees elected as president, sight unseen, a Scottish minister, John Witherspoon, *before* considering (and tabling) the Philadelphia proposal. Witherspoon had an impressive reputation as a battler for the evangelical wing of Scottish Presbyterianism but no connection with

83   Stiles, *Diary* (May 24, 1779), 338–39. Student notes for 1773 report "President Manning's lectures in philosophy touched briefly on psychology, intellectual and moral philosophy, ontology, and natural philosophy, and that this instruction was completed in only a few days more than a month": Mitchell, ed., *Encyclopedia Brunoniana*, 432.

84   Bronson, *History of Brown*, 38, 102–3; Richardson, *Dartmouth*, I, 119–21, 175, 203.

85   Aaron Burr was succeeded in 1758 by Jonathan Edwards, who died within months from a smallpox inoculation. Samuel Davies (1759–1761) was followed by Samuel Finley (1761–1766), both trained in log colleges. Mark A. Noll, *Princeton and the Republic, 1768–1822* (Princeton: Princeton University Press, 1989), 16–27.

America or the College of New Jersey. He declined the honor, citing his wife's refusal to leave Scotland. For Benjamin Rush (CNJ. 1760), who was studying medicine in Edinburgh, an Old Light alternative was unthinkable. In his hyperbolic words, it would mean the triumph of "enemies of the college," "the cause of her dissolution."[86] His importuning eventually swayed both Witherspoons. The offer was renewed, and in 1768 John Witherspoon was installed with great fanfare as the college's sixth president.

In Witherspoon the college got far more than it had anticipated.[87] As a product of the Scottish Enlightenment, he brought broader knowledge, higher intellectual standards, and more sophisticated interpretations of Presbyterian doctrines. The college's shortcomings in these areas had previously worked to its advantage. Lax admission standards allowed most students to enter as sophomores or juniors, facilitating access for the many nonaffluent students. With almost half its graduates (1748–1768) joining the ministry, the perpetuation of New Light divinity was the foremost mission and the chief attraction for many students. But intellectually the drift toward New Divinity metaphysics and a subordination of the new learning to service to the faith was tarnishing its reputation. Remarkably, Witherspoon succeeded in raising the college to his standards while at the same time fortifying its mission. He modernized instruction more fully to incorporate the new learning, introduced Scottish moral philosophy, harmonized theology with the Moderate Enlightenment, and led the college in its commitment to patriotism.

Witherspoon brought more than 300 books with him, including the latest Scottish authors, to update the library and the knowledge base. One of his first acts was to personally take charge of the college grammar school in order to strengthen student preparation. An attempt to force all students to study for 4 years was abandoned, largely because most could not afford to do so; but steps were taken to tighten the granting of advanced standing. Witherspoon introduced the practice of lecturing with his own subjects—moral philosophy, divinity, history, and eloquence. He dictated his notes for students to transcribe and then elaborated on the material. History and composition were repeated for juniors and seniors. After some vigorous fund-raising, the college was able to

86   David Freeman Hawke, *Benjamin Rush: Revolutionary Gadfly* (New York: Bobbs-Merrill, 1971), 56: Rush called Rev. Francis Alison, Professor at the College of Philadelphia, "an enemy to vital religion" (ibid.). John Maclean, *History of the College of New Jersey, 1746–1854*, 2 vol. (New York: Arno Press, 1969 [1877]), I, 285–99.

87   On Witherspoon: Noll, *Princeton*, 28–58; Douglas Sloan, *The Scottish Enlightenment and the American College Ideal* (New York: Teachers College Press, 1971), 103–45; Thomas Jefferson Wertenbaker, *Princeton, 1746–1896* (Princeton: Princeton University Press, 1996 [1946]), 48–108; Broderick, "Pulpit, Physics, and Politics."

appoint a professor of mathematics and natural philosophy in 1771. Philosophical apparatus was purchased, making experimental lectures possible. Besides teaching composition and criticism, Witherspoon gave increased attention to English skills through orations and forensic disputations. For most New Jersey students, the junior-senior years were the bulk of their college education, and they largely consisted of science, public speaking, and Witherspoon.

To teach and defend true philosophy, Witherspoon felt it necessary to confront and refute false doctrines. The Common Sense philosophy that he brought from Scotland provided refutations of the philosophical idealism of the New Divinity, the skepticism of David Hume, or the incipient threat of Deism. It accommodated the learning of the Enlightenment by positing the reality of the physical world and, hence, the entire scope of natural philosophy. It accorded the moral sense an analogous scientific foundation. And it found revelation to be perfectly compatible with reason and the natural order, while remaining above reason in other respects. Witherspoon thus expounded a "new moral philosophy" that preserved Calvinist doctrines in part but repudiated a good deal of the college's New Light heritage and the drift toward the New Divinity. He thus brought the College of New Jersey to the forefront of eighteenth-century higher education and the Moderate Enlightenment.[88]

Prior to the Stamp Act crisis, college leaders supported the English monarchy as the enemy of Papist powers (namely, France) and defender of the liberties of Englishmen. They consistently urged students to become involved in public affairs. The vestigial distrust of American Presbyterians toward England was nonetheless quickened by the deepening crisis. Arriving as the crisis unfolded, Witherspoon's wholehearted commitment to the American cause provided leadership and inspiration to his students. Once familiar with the situation, he unhesitatingly opposed British policies to tax and to punish the American colonies. In 1772 he published his first political pamphlet supporting American liberties. From 1774 he became progressively involved through the local committee of correspondence and the New Jersey Provincial Assembly. Elected to the Continental Congress, he became the only clergyman to sign the Declaration of Independence. College of New Jersey students imbibed patriotism in their classrooms and from local role models and had ample opportunity to express these sentiments in public speaking.[89]

In 1772, Witherspoon decided against a fund-raising trip to the West Indies and instead penned an *Address to the Inhabitants of Jamaica . . . in Behalf of the College of New Jersey*. Although in his post for scarcely 4 years, his description

88 Noll, *Princeton*, 47; May, *Enlightenment*, 62–64.
89 Robson, *Educating Republicans*, 44–46, 58–70.

stands as the ideal of the American colonial college at the zenith of its development. The close association with the upper classes was explicit in the notion that a college education was especially needed by "the children of persons in the higher ranks of life." The purpose of a colonial liberal education was "either to enjoy life with dignity and elegance, or imploy it to the benefit of society, in offices of power or trust." Arguing the superiority of American over English education, he emphasized rigorous instruction and examinations, and since students lodged in the college with their teachers, "their morals may be more effectually preserved." He described the 4-year course of instruction as being equivalent to the English universities, but the features he stressed were science and public speaking: the numerous orations students delivered instilled "by early habit presence of mind and proper pronunciation and gesture"; and the college's philosophical apparatus, including the Rittenhouse orrery, were "equal, if not superior, to any on the continent." Witherspoon took particular pride in the fact that "the College of New Jersey is altogether independent": it consequently was not beholden to government or patrons. Further, the college was open to "every religious denomination," and "every question about forms of church government is . . . entirely excluded" from its teaching. "*A tree is known by its fruits,*" Witherspoon wrote, and Nassau Hall could point to the many "Clergy, Episcopal and Presbyterian" that it educated, as well as "gentlemen in the Law and Medical departments." Fittingly, each September's Commencement was "always attended by a vast concourse of the politest company, from the different parts of this province and the cities of New-York and Philadelphia."[90]

The institution that Witherspoon described embodied crosscutting elements of culture, careers, and knowledge. It featured the Enlightenment veneration for science as well as the now sacrosanct respect for religious toleration. It identified the professions that graduates were expected to pursue, along with public offices and the verbal skills that would assist them in their exercise. And it made repeated reference to the cultural attributes of the "higher ranks of life" that graduates would occupy as gentlemen and members of the "politest company." The feature of the colleges that Witherspoon failed to mention, but which was so prominent in the stories of the nine colleges just reviewed, was social and denominational particularism—the concerted efforts of specific constituencies to secure and maintain control over collegiate institutions. Behind these efforts lie just those factors Witherspoon emphasized—guaranteeing access for a particular constituency to the higher ranks and politest company. In reality, the role

90   John Witherspoon, *Address to the Inhabitants of Jamaica, and Other West-India Islands in Behalf of the College of New Jersey* (Philadelphia, 1772), reprinted in Hofstadter and Smith, *American Higher Education*, I, 137–46.

of colonial colleges in linking these elements was exceedingly loose and variable. Enlightened sensibilities were an intended outcome of college in Cambridge, Philadelphia, or New York. Professional careers, especially in the ministry, were paramount in Hanover, New Haven, or New Brunswick. Cultural capital was linked with family capital most strongly in Williamsburg and New York. And efforts to tie the medical and legal professions to the colleges were most overt in New York and Philadelphia. The learning that some colleges valued highly was only weakly related to these outcomes. Size, wealth, and status depended above all on a college's constituency. To appreciate how these factors interacted, and with what results, one needs to examine how they affected students.

COLONIAL COLLEGE STUDENTS

The estimated 721 students attending American colleges in 1775 represented roughly 1 percent of an age cohort of white males. A quarter-century later, in 1800, about the same proportion attended colleges. Looking backward, the proportion was similar around 1740. While precise numbers remain uncertain, the most revealing fact is clear—American colleges served a stable and quite small portion of the population for the latter two-thirds of the eighteenth century.[91] The most trustworthy numbers for this era are bachelor's degrees.[92] The number of annual graduates reached 50 in 1721 as Yale joined Harvard in graduating students. But the totals stayed at that level until the late 1750s, when the mid-Atlantic colleges began contributing. Graduates quickly rose to an average 110 per year in the 1760s and 130 from 1771 to 1775. By the 1790s graduates doubled the average of the 1760s, but the population grew faster, by 140 percent. Taking a longer view, the number of college graduates in the whole population was about 11 per 10,000 at the beginning of the century and the same at the end. That figure was only slightly higher, at 12, prior to the Revolution. Thus, the intellectual vitality of the colleges from 1760 to 1775 was only faintly echoed in demography. As a social institution, the colonial colleges never transcended a narrow social base, and the same conditions persisted well into the nineteenth century.

Several factors affected college attendance. Each college was "owned" by and oriented toward a particular group. Even while accepting outsiders, each college

---

91   Data on enrollments are available for 1775 (table 1) and 1800 (Colin B. Burke, *American Collegiate Populations*), participation rates calculated by the author for 3-year cohorts. The 1 percent figure matches that derived by Phyllis Vine Ehrenberg, *Change and Continuity: Values in American Higher Education, 1750–1800*, PhD Diss., University of Michigan, 1974.

92   Walter Crosby Eells, *Baccalaureate Degrees Conferred by American Colleges in the 17th and 18th Centuries*, Circular No. 528, Office of Education (May 1958). All degree and population data from this source.

had a distinct constituency. Attendance was further influenced by accessibility, cost, and the availability of preparatory education. Most significant by far was the limited demand for the learning and culture that colleges offered.

Preparation for college was the first obstacle faced by potential students. This meant acquiring a basic competence in Latin and rudimentary knowledge of Greek. These skills were taught, along with other subjects, at the grammar schools and academies scattered unevenly throughout the colonies, but mostly in the Northeast. Unless such a school was locally available, the cost of room and board—the principal expense associated with education—could be prohibitive. Many students instead were "fitted" for college by local ministers. Thus, students arrived at colleges with different degrees of preparation, and preparatory instruction was needed for the weaker cases. Samuel Johnson pleaded for such a school at King's, which was not created until his departure. Witherspoon turned his attention to this problem as soon as he reached Princeton. Manning opened a Latin school before the college in Rhode Island, and Wheelock used Moor's School for this purpose.

New students were examined by the college president on their classical language skills and assigned accordingly. Since the freshman year was largely a review and reinforcement of the skills required for admission, well-prepared students were placed as sophomores or sometimes higher. Advanced placement was the norm at New Jersey but less common at Harvard or Yale. For most graduates, the average time of the course was closer to 3 than 4 years. Given the anarchic modes of preparation, college students varied widely in age. Wealthy students or those with educated fathers might acquire sufficient Latin to enter at 14 or younger. Less privileged students, particularly those feeling a call to the ministry, often worked for several years and began college in their 20s. Students in the Harvard class of 1771 ranged from 12 to 27 years. The median age of graduates was 21 at Harvard, Yale, and New Jersey, but 18 at Philadelphia and 23 at Dartmouth. Of course, not all students graduated. Perhaps five of eight matriculates received a bachelor's degree, but here too the variance was huge (and the data uncertain). Almost all New Jersey students (92 percent) graduated prior to Witherspoon, compared with none at William & Mary before 1772. King's and Philadelphia graduated just above half of their students. Whether or not a student chose to complete the college course often reflected his reasons for attending in the first place.

Which college a student chose to attend might be affected by cost, proximity, or religious affinity—but such factors interacted. Most likely, especially for younger students, choices would be determined by personal or family connections. Recommendations from teachers or ministers also played an important role. Other factors were superimposed on this typical eighteenth-century matrix. Geographical proximity was the norm, since travel costs were high and family connections were more likely to be local. New Jersey is the notable exception, drawing only one-quarter of its prerevolutionary students from its namesake state. Before Witherspoon, the college attracted New Lights from New England, but such students soon disappeared. This loss was balanced by a growing number of southern students, reflecting the spread of Presbyterianism in the region but also a growing demand for collegiate education among wealthy planters.[93] Dartmouth attracted New Lights from New England. The majority of Rhode Island students also came from other states, but probably not from very far away. Both the latter schools were the cheapest to attend. Along with New Jersey, low cost was undoubtedly an attractive feature, especially for Dartmouth. It was notorious for students who worked their way through by teaching during winters, practically emptying the college. In addition, it provided the equivalent of student loans by allowing students to "run a tab." Many students owed the college significant sums by graduation, which they then had to promise to repay.[94]

Harvard represented one extreme not only in its seniority but also in the maturity of its social relations. The creation of new colleges actually narrowed its geographic catchment. Forty-one percent of prerevolutionary classes came from Eastern Massachusetts, where the prevalence of college graduates was five times the national average and numerous preparatory schools existed. For that reason, seven of ten students entered Harvard before age 18, and most students began as freshmen and took the full 4-year course. Harvard endowment funds supported about 10 percent of classes with "work-study" scholarships, frequently awarded to the sons of country clergymen.[95]

Aside from the new-light preferences for early New Jersey and Dartmouth colleges, religion does not seem decisive when proximity and family connections are taken into account. Anglicans freely attended Yale and Harvard; Baptists and Dutch Reformed were comfortable at Nassau Hall. For all the emphasis that some colleges placed on learning, academic quality seems to have had little impact on enrollment decisions. The growing reputation of Witherspoon's New Jersey for southern planters, who could afford any school, may be an exception, as would Harvard's ability to attract occasional students from abroad. The

---

93 Beverly McAnear, "The Selection of an Alma Mater by Pre-Revolutionary Students," *Pennsylvania Magazine of History and Biography*, 73, 4 (Oct. 1949): 429–40; Richard A. Harrison, "Introduction," in Richard A. Harrison, ed., *Princetonians, 1776–1783* (Princeton: Princeton University Press, 1981), xxviii–xxx.

94 McAnear, "Selection of an Alma Mater"; Richardson, *Dartmouth*, I, 239–45: these student debtors largely repaid the college.

95 Conrad Edick Wright, *Revolutionary Generation: Harvard Men and the Consequences of Independence* (Amherst: University of Massachusetts Press, 2005), 30–58.

negative case is supplied by Yale, which sustained the largest or second-largest enrollment despite "poor teaching of an incapable faculty."[96]

Why did 1 out of 100 male youths embark on the arduous path of preparing for and attending college? There can be no simple answer, since students came from a variety of social backgrounds and pursued quite different career paths. Rather, family influence and individual agency interacted to produce several distinctive patterns. With some exceptions, the motive was not preparation for careers. Every student followed an identical course; decisions and training for subsequent careers generally followed graduation. The college course provided a liberal education for young men who hoped to become gentlemen. In the enlightened age of the late eighteenth century, becoming a gentleman had a moral as well as a social meaning. John Adams defined it not as being wellborn or wealthy, "but all those who have received a liberal education, an ordinary degree of erudition in liberal arts and sciences." However, learning was insufficient by itself; gentleman was a status accorded by society. A gentleman needed to cultivate the inner virtue and the outward manners demanded by polite society, just the qualities that Witherspoon showcased in his promotional address. A gentleman knew Latin and Greek but also how to dance gracefully. Acquiring the wealth to maintain the lifestyle of a gentleman was a separate—and essential—matter. Most important, in the sharply graded social order of provincial America, gentlemen occupied positions of respect and distinction. They filled local and provincial offices, led public meetings, and were accepted in polite society and respected in the community. Young men who went to college expected at the least to attain such status or perhaps do better. [97]

Almost no college students came from the lower ranks of society, for whom such a path would be unimaginable, let alone unaffordable. For reasonably prosperous families, however, including those with substantial farms, college might be at least a possibility.[98] For this segment of society, college going represented maintaining or gaining social status. For early College of New Jersey (pre-1768), one-half of known student fathers were farmers. Although this figure fell steadily afterward, 48 percent of prerevolutionary students came from farming or non-elite backgrounds. The fact that the college drew students from such a distance

96   McAnear, "Selection of an Alma Mater," 436.
97   Quoted in Gordon S. Wood, *The Radicalism of the American Revolution* (New York: Vintage, 1993), 195; Wright, *Revolutionary Generation*, 22–25.
98   The most widely cited figure for the affordability of colonial colleges comes from an offhand estimate by Jackson Turner Main: "perhaps one in ten—could afford to send a son to college" (*The Social Structure of Revolutionary America* [Princeton: Princeton University Press, 1965], 247). The remainder of the paragraph qualifies this statement by noting wide variability across the colonies. His later study of Connecticut notes, "a college degree was available to young men of ordinary, though not really humble means" (*Society and Economy in Colonial Connecticut* [Princeton: Princeton University Press, 1985], 330).

reflected wealthier families, who predominated after 1776. At Harvard, the availability of local educational opportunity seems to have translated into social mobility. Just 23 percent of students were sons of Harvard graduates on the eve of the Revolution, while 45 percent came from farms and nonelite households.[99] Such diverse origins produced several patterns of college going.

Young men who had a conversion experience and dedicated their lives to the ministry were a distinctive type. They provided most of the mature students, belatedly obtaining preparation for college and often entering after age 20. Undertaking a ministerial calling was a serious, adult commitment. Younger students might be identified as "hopefully pious" but were not expected to take such decisions until they finished college. New Light New Jersey was a magnet for such students, and they seem to have been the predominant clientele at Dartmouth. They were also a significant presence at Harvard and Yale, where 10 and 15 percent of prerevolutionary graduates, respectively, were age 25 or over.[100]

Perhaps most difficult to characterize are those students who aspired to become "first-generation" gentlemen. Their fathers were likely to be prosperous and respectable farmers or merchants (or both) and leaders in the local community. The students had probably distinguished themselves through motivation and achievement, recognized by their families, ministers, or teachers. As the colonial economy grew, these middling strata—country gentry and urban bourgeoisie—prospered. College became affordable for their sons and promised increased social status. And for the colleges, these groups constituted an important source of students in more ways than one. The Founding Fathers were predominately first-generation college graduates—John Adams, Thomas Jefferson, Samuel Adams, James Madison, Benjamin Rush, James Wilson, and many more.[101]

For households with college-educated heads, sending sons to college was a natural form of status maintenance. Yet, this was a limited population. College-educated ministers, the largest group, were shrinking demographically; and educated lawyers or physicians were miniscule in number. The 23 percent of graduate sons at Harvard is a surprisingly small figure for the school with the most highly educated ambient population, and the proportion at Yale and New Jersey was certainly less. Little wonder that King's and Philadelphia, oriented toward elite families, had small enrollments.

---

99 These percentages are for known fathers' occupations: James McLachlan, "Introduction," *Princetonians, 1748–1768: A Biographical Dictionary* (Princeton: Princeton University Press, 1976), xxii; Harrison, "Introduction," *Princetonians, 1769–1775*, xxiv–xxv; Wright, *Revolutionary Generation*.

100 Eells, *Baccalaureate Degrees*, 46; Ehrenberg, *Change and Continuity*, 214–19; David F. Allmendinger Jr., *Paupers and Scholars: The Transformation of Student Life in Nineteenth-Century New England* (New York: St. Martin's, 1975).

101 Wood, *Radicalism*, 197.

For truly wealthy families, college was merely one of several options for their sons, and graduation was irrelevant. James Bowdoin III left Harvard in his senior year (1771) for England, where he burnished his genteel credentials by learning horsemanship, French, dancing, and fencing, followed by two grand tours of the Continent (still, he later regretted his "negligence" at college). New York Lt. Governor James De Lancey (himself educated in England) sent his eldest son directly to a merchant apprenticeship, while two other sons attended both King's and Philadelphia without graduating, before taking up the law. This pattern of attending college for a dose of culture and learning was virtually the norm for southern planters, certainly those who patronized William & Mary. This was apparently true for the Maryland landed gentry too, who reportedly sent at least 100 students to the Philadelphia Academy as of 1753 but counted only 9 graduates in the first decade of the college. Statistics on graduate occupations show relatively few idle "gentlemen" or planters, but they may have been numerous among nongraduates.[102]

Ezra Stiles thought that most Yale graduates returned from whence they came, to "mix in with the Body of the public, and enter upon Commerce, or the *Cultivation of their Estates.*" However, enumerations of known careers shows the majority of colonial college graduates entering the major professions of clergy, law, or medicine.[103] Except for those students called to the ministry, choosing among these paths was problematic. College could accomplish the first goal of forming young gentlemen but not the larger challenge of securing a livelihood. Young Benjamin Rush was typical in being undecided on a career after graduation: tentatively choosing law by process of elimination, he was finally steered toward medicine by his former teacher. Many graduates wavered between the ministry and law and in later years increasingly opted for the latter. But the years after graduation were a time for probing and further preparation. On average, more than 5 years elapsed between college graduation and certification as minister, physician, or lawyer. A few, especially future ministers, remained at college to further their learning. Fully one-quarter of Harvard graduates taught school for at least part of this time, as John Adams did. How and where one acquired professional credentials made a great deal of difference, since one could preach, plead, or attempt to heal without going to college. Professionals who were also gentlemen set themselves apart.

Detailed statistics exist for graduate occupations, though they reveal nothing of the nuance and ambiguity of actual lives. The clearest trend is the fall off in the number and proportion of ministers after 1765. This trend is evident at

102   Wright, *Revolutionary Generation*, 45, 70; Gordon, *College of Philadelphia*, 116–31.
103   Morgan, *Stiles*, 322; Bailey B. Burritt, *Professional Distribution of College and University Graduates*, U.S. Bureau of Education, Bulletin, 1912, No. 19.

Harvard and Yale but not yet at the College of New Jersey, where Witherspoon no doubt attracted ministerial candidates. Overall, the proportion of ministers dropped from 36 percent (1761–1765) to 28 percent (1771–1775). (See table 1.) The countertrend was a rise in the number of graduate lawyers, but this development was muted before the Revolution—10 percent of graduates in the 1750s, 15 percent in the 1760s. Both these trends accelerated after the Revolution and were more characteristic of that era. Becoming a physician was a steadier choice, made by about one of eight graduates.[104]

For at least half of colonial students, college represented an opportunity for social advancement. Whether these opportunities were realized depended on connections, character, circumstances, and individual ability. Colonial colleges had mixed records on recognizing merit. "Genius" was recognized only in the awarding of parts at commencement, and this was the only competition that seemed to matter for students.[105] Otherwise college was an endurance test. Those who persisted graduated, like Tom Brainless. However, students from less privileged backgrounds were somewhat more likely to possess the talents and motivation that would help them to succeed. Success in eighteenth-century society meant attaining the status and livelihood of a gentleman. Of course, many graduates did more. Each college can cite a list of graduates who held important office and contributed to the new nation, with the College of New Jersey claiming the most distinguished record.[106] But this was also a time of abundant opportunity as the Revolution opened room at the top. It was also true that many graduates achieved less. A careful reading of class biographies reveals subtle and not-so-subtle indications that numerous college graduates fell short of success—country preachers rejected by their congregations, itinerants who wandered South or West without ever establishing themselves, and individuals with pronounced eccentricities. Such cases of gentlemen manqué may account for roughly three of ten graduates. When early fatalities are added, colleges would be fortunate if more than half of their graduates achieved the expected status.[107] However, these results were hardly random; prerevolutionary students actively sought to shape their own futures.

104 Burritt, *Professional Distribution*.

105 For the role, or absence, of merit in early colleges: Joseph F. Kett, *Merit: The History of a Founding Ideal from the American Revolution to the Twenty-First Century* (Ithaca, NY: Cornell University Press, 2013), 68–91.

106 A list of eminent graduates and office holders was published by president John Maclean: *History of the College of New Jersey, 1746–1854*, 2 vol. (New York: Arno Press, 1969 [1877]), I, 357–62: This list became the basis for Woodrow Wilson's famous address, "Princeton in the Nation's Service" (see chapter 9); Robson, *Educating Republicans*. 58–70.

107 These conclusions reflect the findings of a prosopography exercise by the author's graduate seminar in colonial higher education, Penn State, Spring 2010.

TABLE 1 ★ THE NINE COLONIAL COLLEGES

INSTITUTION	YEAR OF OPENING	ENROLLMENT, 1775	GRADUATES, 1769–1775	MINISTER GRADUATES 1769–1775
Harvard College	1638	180	308	16.6%
College of William & Mary	1694	c.80	4	25%
Yale College	1702	170	188	36.2%
College of New Jersey	1747	100	150	48%
King's College	1754	40	44	4.5%
College of Philadelphia	1754	30	50	12%
Rhode Island College	1766	41	44	31.8%
Dartmouth College	1770	c.60	31	74%
Queen's College	1771	20	6	33%
TOTAL		721	825	29%

Students who embarked on the collegiate way of living in late colonial colleges entered a cloistered, artificial world, but one that replicated the hierarchical societies from which they came. On one hand, every day's activities were regimented according to a strict schedule, ruled by the college bell; on the other hand, the college was in itself a distinct social world.[108] The discipline of the college schedule was necessary for the enforcement of liberal learning, let alone maintaining order, but the social life of the college conveyed much of the learning sought by future gentlemen. Until 1767 at Yale and 1772 at Harvard, entering classes were ranked according to the social standing of each student's father.[109] The college constituted a hierarchy, headed by the president, professors, and tutors and among students determined by the seniority of the four classes. Deference was required to social superiors and encoded in social rituals and mandated customs.

An avowed aim of the colleges was to nurture their wards into gentlemen, but the means with which they encouraged manners and gentility tended to be externally imposed, like the rules upholding college discipline. Acquiring the virtues of a gentleman was instead an internal process but one that could be affected in three principal ways. First, the primary social unit of the college was the individual class, the context for most all activities over 4 years. A student's character was thus subject to the critical judgments of his classmates. In order to earn their respect, students were expected to develop and manifest gentlemanly qualities of honor, generosity, independence, and—above all—loyalty. Such qualities were associated with male maturity and contrasted with the rigid disciplinary regime aimed at controlling youth. This disjunction was the source of the most notable confrontations between students and college authorities.[110] Second, the distinctive experience of advancing in status each year conveyed powerful social messages. Freshmen entered at the bottom of the college hierarchy. They were hazed by the sophomores who gleefully forced them to assume a subordinate status, and they were also obliged to run errands for the seniors (fagging). These college customs were elaborately detailed and enthusiastically enforced, with full backing of the college government. The reward for enduring such humiliation was the opportunity to inflict it upon others in the following years. Thus, college instructed students in a most direct way to accept subordinate status when necessary but also how to exercise authority over social inferiors. By their senior year, they ascended to the pinnacle

---

108   Leon Jackson, "The Rights of Man and the Rights of Youth" in Roger L. Geiger, ed., *The American College in the Nineteenth Century* (Nashville: Vanderbilt University Press, 2000), 46–79; for colonial colleges as "total institutions," Ehrenberg, "*Change and Continuity,*" 151–200.

109   Axtell, *School upon a Hill*, 219–23.

110   Jackson, "Rights of Man"; Axtell, *School upon a Hill*, 224–30.

of the student hierarchy and the status of incipient gentlemen.[111] Finally, students took the initiative on their own or with parental encouragement to acquire genteel trappings. Most colleges offered optional instruction in French, and dancing and fencing lessons were available in the cities. However, students also demonstrated initiative in seeking the intellectual skills appropriate to their station.

The decade before the Revolution saw the creation of student literary societies, which would come to dominate campus life for nearly a century. These organizations allowed students to hone their literary skills, particularly public speaking and debate. They also expressed a provincial yearning to partake of the thriving literary culture of England. Within these organizations students assumed responsibility for their own education. Some earlier groups had sought similar ends. At Harvard, clubs had been formed to practice oratory, first by prospective ministers and later by broader groups. In the 1750s drama clubs presented plays (i.e., reading parts) privately in student rooms. These earlier groups were based on friendships and interests and thus lacked continuity. However, in 1770 students organized a debating society "to improve the art of speaking." By inviting members of all classes to join, the Speaker's Club was able to persist, albeit with subsequent mergers and name changes. But the club culture at Harvard was unique. Each club had its own purpose, so that some students joined them all.[112] Elsewhere, the signature feature of literary societies was two, secret, competing societies enrolling most of the student body.

This pattern evolved at both Yale and the College of New Jersey, absorbing some earlier clubs. The Linonian was founded at Yale on September 12, 1753, but no further trace of its existence is known before 1766, except that freshmen were not admitted. That issue provoked the formation of Brothers in Unity (1768), and both societies subsequently included all classes. At this stage, both societies admitted fifteen to twenty Yale students and seem to have met off campus in rented space or in the homes of sympathetic alums. The Linonian appears to have been the more organized of the two; Brothers was founded "for the improvement of science and friendship," but also "to procure enjoyment." The American Whig Society was formed at New Jersey in 1769 and the Cliosophic Society the next year, both evolving from predecessors that existed since about 1765. The Whig took inspiration from the pseudonym used by William Livingston to attack the threat of creating an Anglican bishop, and Clio sought to invoke "the praise of learning or wisdom." Both colleges at first disapproved of the societies. Witherspoon soon

---

111 Cf. Morgan, *Stiles.*
112 Siegel, *Governance and Curriculum at Harvard,* 301–8; Morison, *Three Centuries,* 138–41.

endorsed them and provided space in Nassau Hall, but Yale sought to restrict dramas as frivolous.[113]

As the first independent student organizations, the literary societies provide a rare insight into student mentality. Students clearly valued practicing parliamentary process, since the societies had elaborate procedures, an abundance of elective offices, and frequent elections. Multiple activities also ensured that everyone would participate. Debate was central, but it took several forms: forensic disputations (carefully prepared), extempore debates (probably less prepared), or questioning (discussion of current issues). Members also gave declamations or orations and submitted compositions. Various forms of drama were also popular, especially comedies and "humorous dialogues." The Yale societies had a decided literary emphasis. Although plays were outlawed—at Yale and throughout New England—the Linonian presented an elaborate production in a local tavern, in which "the Officers appeared dressed in Regimentals, & the Actresses [probably local girls] in full & elegant suits of the Lady's Apparel." In 1773, the Linonian staged its "anniversary" celebration at a New Haven home, including guests. Festivities began at 11 a.m. with orations and elections. A sumptuous dinner followed with appropriate libations, followed by a drama, music, humor, and one final oration, concluding at 5 p.m. This event was repeated the next year but canceled in 1775 because of the hostilities.[114]

Besides "procuring enjoyment," the deeper purpose of the literary societies was self-improvement. Although little is known of prerevolutionary activities at Nassau Hall, it appears that they provided practice for the orations and debates that Witherspoon emphasized. The societies provided a supportive setting; one Harvard club typically included in its rules, "no Member Shall presume to Impose on another or Laugh or Scoff at his performance." Developing linguistic skills was valued in all colleges. At King's, for example, Alexander Hamilton met weekly with four other students to practice composition, debate, and oratory. Queen's College, with twenty students, still established a literary society, no doubt imitating its neighbor. Literature was also cultivated by students. As soon as the societies had regular quarters they began to accumulate libraries of contemporary works.[115] Probably only at Philadelphia were such subjects

113   Edward B. Coe, "The Literary Societies" in William L. Kingsley, *Yale College: A Sketch of Its History*, 2 vol. (New York,1879), 307–23; J. Jefferson Looney, *Nurseries of Letters and Republicanism: A Brief History of the American Whig-Cliosophic Society and its Predecessors, 1765–1941* (Princeton: Princeton University, 1996).

114   Kenneth Silverman, *A Cultural History of the American Revolution* (New York: Crowell, 1976), 220; Coe, "Literary Societies," 312.

115   Thomas S. Harding, *College Literary Societies: Their Contribution to Higher Education in the United States, 1815–1876* (New York: Pageant Press, 1971), 21; Humphrey, *King's College*, 200.

incorporated into the curriculum. The founders of Whig included future novelist Hugh Henry Brackenridge and poet Philip Freneau as well as future president James Madison. This literary impulse was mobilized by societies to attack one another periodically with scurrilous doggerel. These rivalries enhanced the psychological impact of the societies, fostering greater effort and commitment.

There is little evidence that the literary societies played a significant role in the rising tide of patriotism. The societies were, after all, for self-improvement, not resolving issues. And their proceedings were secret. Students found other outlets for political expression. Students at the more rigorous colleges were well prepared to wrestle with issues of liberty, justice, and civic morality from their readings of classical authors, moral philosophy, and natural law. As the crisis deepened, orations and declamations drew increasingly pointed morals from the classical authors. Commencement theses were prominent outlets for such themes.[116] Harvard students were immersed in the escalating patriot movement from the first confrontations in Boston until British troops marched through Cambridge, pausing to ask directions, on their way to Lexington and Concord. Harvard students were consequently the earliest and most thoroughly committed to the patriot cause. At Princeton, students devised their own protests, wearing homespun to commencement as early as 1765, hiring a public hangman to ceremoniously burn a traitorous letter in 1770, and staging a tea party bonfire in 1774. Rhode Island and Yale students soon demonstrated their patriotism as well, marking these four schools as the foremost patriot colleges. Each had organized a student militia by 1774.[117] In contrast, the three Anglican colleges resisted the rush toward revolution to different degrees: Philadelphia opposed British policies but did not favor independence; the loyalist faculty of William & Mary was increasingly isolated; and only King's College was unabashedly loyalist. These three schools would be most profoundly reshaped by the Revolution, but that momentous event altered the entire landscape of American higher education.

116 Robson, *Educating Republicans*, 57–93; Hoeveler, *American Mind*, 241–81, 307–12.
117 Wertenbaker, *Princeton*, 55–58.

REPUBLICAN UNIVERSITIES

RITISH TROOPS PASSED THROUGH CAMBRIDGE ON April 19, 1775, on their way to and from the first battle of the Revolutionary War. Eight years later, the Continental Congress was meeting in Nassau Hall when it received the Treaty of Paris that ended the War for Independence. The colleges were intimately involved with the American Revolution, partly through active commitment and often by being too close to hostilities. Only remote Dartmouth avoided closing or dispersing at some point during the war. College halls were some of the largest buildings in the colonies and the first to be commandeered for barracks or hospitals. Harvard College became the army headquarters for the siege of Boston, forcing students and faculty to decamp to Concord for a year. The Rhode Island college edifice was occupied first by American and then by French troops from 1776 to 1782. A brief British invasion of New Haven in 1779 prompted Yale to disperse its classes to different parts of Connecticut. King's College was occupied by American troops in 1776 and then by the British before being gutted by fire. Nassau Hall was at the center of the battle of Princeton in early 1777, and the college could share only what remained of the structure until the end of the war. The British also seized Queen's College in 1776, and classes did not resume there until 1782. The College of Philadelphia closed before the British occupied the city in 1777; its buildings were used in turn by American and British troops. William & Mary was spared until the final campaign of the war, when it had to close for a year in 1781, turning its buildings over to French troops and also suffering a fire.[1]

All the colleges save King's in occupied New York ultimately backed the patriot cause. Throughout the colonies, however, nearly 20 percent of the white population had loyalist sympathies, and about 3 percent emigrated. In the early stages of the war, there were all shades of opinion, including Quakers and Germans who supported neither side. At Dartmouth, Eleazer Wheelock seemed reluctant to cut ties with his English patrons, and Baptists at Rhode Island College opposed the British but distrusted patriot Congregationalists, their longtime

---

1   David W. Robson, *Educating Republicans* (Westport, CT: Greenwood, 1985), 103–34.

nemesis.[2] As the new state governments were organized, a bright line was drawn between patriots and traitors. Among college alumni, only 2 percent of New Jersey graduates had loyalist sympathies, compared with 16 percent of living Harvardians and more than half of King's graduates. Loyalists, and particularly émigrés, were disproportionately represented at the highest ranks of colonial society but less so among college graduates. The latter pursued livelihoods built on ability and learning—the social stratum that had most to gain by overthrowing monarchical society.[3]

Despite disruptions, occupations, mobilization of student militias, and removals, most colleges sustained some level of operation. The malleable nature of the college course permitted cutting corners. Classes did not recite entire works but selected only passages chosen by the tutors, and these could easily be curtailed as need be. Similarly, advanced subjects lectured by presidents or professors had the same elastic nature. The quality of education undoubtedly suffered, but the total number of graduates fell by just one-third for the years 1778 through 1782. The colleges suffered far more than a loss of students. The destruction of buildings, libraries, and apparatus was accompanied by virtual impoverishment, as inflation ravished existing financial assets while tuition and government support dwindled or disappeared. But even as their physical fortunes were at low ebb, the aspirations of colleges soared. They perceived themselves, and were perceived by the new states, as having an indispensable role to play in forming republican citizens for the new nation.

The creation of an independent republic, the United States of America, presented the founders with the challenge of defining the nature of its government and the conditions that would allow it to flourish. Steeped in classical heritage, they were familiar with the moralistic accounts by Greek and Roman writers of the beauties and fragility of the ancient republics—Sparta, Athens, Thebes, and especially Rome. All knew, in theory at least, that the survival of republics depended on the *virtue* of their citizens—the capacity of individuals to put the public good—the *res publica*—above their personal interests. [4] For patriots, education seemed the best means of instilling virtue in the citizenry, but here classical authors offered little guidance. A dialogue about the proper and necessary modes of education would ensue throughout the Early Republic, complicated by assumptions about the inevitability or obsolescence of social distinctions. Another lesson of republican government gleaned from both ancient and modern

2   J. David Hoeveler, *Creating the American Mind: Intellect and Politics in the Colonial Colleges* (New York: Rowman & Littlefield, 2002), 271–81.

3   Gordon S. Wood, *The Radicalism of the American Revolution* (New York: Vintage, 1991).

4   Wood, *Radicalism*, 95–109.

history was the necessity of balanced or mixed government. Here the consensus drew lessons from the failure of balanced government in Great Britain through the supposed aggrandizement of the crown and the corruption of the aristocracy. However, all knew the perils of democracy too, its inherent tendency toward anarchy, leading to dictatorship. They accordingly advocated moderating institutions, particularly upper houses comprising men of learning and property, to hold this threat of tyranny in check. Few thought that the common people, those without property, were likely to exhibit republican virtue. Rather, the genteel qualities of virtue and disinterestedness were required of the leaders of society, qualities instilled by a liberal arts education. Thus, the colleges offered hope of reproducing the natural aristocracy of learning and talent that the founders themselves exemplified. From the outset, then, the colleges were seen as key institutions of the new republic.[5] In most states, steps were taken during or soon after the struggle for independence to bolster higher education and incorporate it into the new republican order. These efforts had three common elements: the creation of universities, close association with the state, and the incorporation of Enlightenment learning.

The penchant for university status was a reflection of these lofty aspirations and particularly the expectation that the United States would assume a respected place in the world of learning. The late eighteenth century offered diverse models of what a university might be. Most familiar to Americans were the examples of Oxford and Cambridge, where the university was an examining and certifying body for constituent teaching colleges. These peculiar arrangements had evolved in the late middle ages and could hardly be replicated. The "American University in the Province of New York" proposed by Myles Cooper varied significantly from the Oxbridge model. The university in this case was to be a parallel but superior teaching institution having the authority to govern and supervise subordinate colleges within the province. The university would thus be the controlling entity of a stratified, centralized system. In continental Europe and Scotland, universities conventionally contained four faculties—theology, medicine, law, and philosophy or the arts. American colleges defined themselves in terms of the last of these subjects, but postgraduate ministerial candidates had long read theology in the colleges, and Philadelphia and King's had added medical departments. Incorporating professional education would become an aspiration of republican universities.

---

5 Ibid., 95f; Gordon S. Wood, *The Creation of the American Republic, 1776–1787* (Chapel Hill: University of North Carolina Press, 1969), 46–75, 197–206, 237, 426–27, 479–80, et passim; Carl J. Richard, *The Founders and the Classics: Greece, Rome, and the American Enlightenment* (Cambridge: Harvard University Press, 1994), 12–38, 123–50.

The strategic importance of higher education and the ideological commitment to the public good virtually guaranteed that the new state governments would seek authority over the colleges. The colonial colleges were regarded as inherently public institutions despite de facto control by particular groups. The governance of colleges largely evolved with prevailing conceptions of "public." Governing boards in the new republic typically included government officials, supplemented by representatives of major religious denominations. This pattern resembled colonial formulas adopted by King's and Rhode Island, except for the preponderance of public representatives. Public dominance at least implied public financial support, although this proved difficult in an economy starved for currency.

Republicanism has been called the ideology of the Enlightenment, and republican universities joined in spirit the vision of America assuming a leading role in the world's intellectual progress.[6] Specifically, they hoped to further the curricular advances of the late-colonial colleges. The inculcation of virtue was to be enhanced with more attention to history, political theory, and law. Plans for professional education would be extended beyond medicine and law to practical arts like navigation, architecture, and agriculture. Modern languages, especially French, were brought into the curriculum. And the high status of science continued to be honored. Republicanism embraced the Enlightenment ideal of "useful knowledge," with little regard for the difficulties of incorporating practical subjects into the college course.

The identification of republican universities and Enlightenment ideology generated utopian expectations.[7] Not surprisingly, these aspirations would prove difficult to achieve or sustain in the Early Republic. Nonetheless, these themes dominated both thought and actions about higher education for the remainder of the eighteenth century.

MAKING COLLEGES REPUBLICAN

For the patriot colleges, the Revolution brought varying degrees of republican reform. At the College of New Jersey, overwhelming support for the Revolution and the continuity provided by President Witherspoon precluded sentiment for reform. After 1779, responsibility for the operations of the college was largely assumed by Witherspoon's son-in-law, Samuel Stanhope Smith, who epitomized the mindset of the Moderate American Enlightenment. The three newest colleges were so destitute at the end of the war that movement toward republican

---

6 Wood, *Radicalism*, 100, 191.
7 Wood, *Creation*, 53–56.

reforms was tentative and belated at best. Republican ideology had a more immediate impact at Harvard, and it dominated the reorganization of the three formerly Anglican colleges.

In Massachusetts, the writing of a new state constitution made Harvard the first republican university. The process was inspired by John Adams, who expressed as keenly as anyone the connections between education, virtue, public good, and republican government. The Constitution contained a separate section on "The University at Cambridge and Encouragement of Literature, &c." These provisions preserved the legal structure, rights, and property of Harvard College "for ever." The only change in status replaced the magistrate Overseers with the governor, lieutenant governor, council, and senate of the Commonwealth. The same six ministers remained, but the institution was now overseen by mostly public officials. For good measure, Adams wrote and inserted a remarkable paragraph, declaring,

> wisdom and knowledge, as well as virtue, diffused generally among the body of the people, being necessary for the preservation of their rights and liberties . . . it shall be the duty of legislatures and magistrates, in all future periods of the Commonwealth, to cherish the interests of literature and the sciences and all seminaries of them; especially the University at Cambridge . . . . [8]

Harvard soon became somewhat more university-like by adding a medical school. This step was preceded and abetted by the formation in 1781 of the Massachusetts Medical Society. Adams had enjoined the Commonwealth "to encourage private societies . . . for the promotion of agriculture, arts, sciences, commerce, trades, manufactures, and the natural history of the country," and Harvard was usually linked with these proliferating efforts. John Warren (H. 1771), a Revolutionary War surgeon, was instrumental in establishing the society. Appointed professor of anatomy and surgery the following year, he was joined by Benjamin Waterhouse (MD, Leyden, 1780) as professor of the theory and practice of physic. Both men were 29 years old: the well-connected Warren was trained by apprenticeship and wartime experience; Waterhouse, with 6 years of the finest European medical training, had to overcome opposition because he was not a Harvard graduate. A third professor of chemistry and

---

8   Chapter V, Sections I & II: Josiah Quincy, *History of Harvard University*, 2 vol. (Boston, 1860), II, 507–9; the Constitution also stated: "no person holding the office of President, professor, or instructor of Harvard College shall at the same time have a seat in the Senate or House of Representatives": Chapter VI, Article II.

materia medica completed the original faculty, which began instruction in the fall of 1783.[9]

Adams himself promoted the litany of societies mentioned above by inspiring the American Academy of Arts and Sciences, but here too Harvard played a role. Adams was determined that Boston should have an equivalent to Philadelphia's American Philosophical Society. As he advocated this project, a fellow of the Harvard Corporation feared creating a rival to the college. On the contrary, Adams explained, "It would be an honor and an advantage to [Harvard]. . . . the president and principal professors would no doubt always be members." Indeed, this was the case. When the academy was incorporated in 1780, sixty-two of the original sixty-four members owned Harvard degrees, and half of its quarterly meetings took place in Harvard's "philosophy chamber"—the room containing the college's philosophical apparatus. Its first president, James Bowdoin II, stated his expectation that most future members would be sons of Harvard as well. The academy was a quintessential Enlightenment creation. It defined an intellectual community of learned gentlemen, and it was dedicated to that combination of practical arts and experimental science that was expected to produce useful knowledge. And like most Enlightenment schemes, it was grander in conception than in practice. The academy, for all its local prestige, yielded only modest accomplishments (four volumes of *Memoirs*, 1785–1821). But it constituted a prominent node in a network of institutions that connected the social and intellectual elite of Eastern Massachusetts.[10] Over time, the most active and dynamic node in that network would be the University at Cambridge.

In Connecticut, the same republican impulses failed to produce a similar result. By 1777 Yale had been forced to desert New Haven, acting president Daggett had resigned, and the college was broke. Many patriots thought its clerical trustees should be replaced by public officials. An appeal to the Connecticut Assembly was received sympathetically, but the assembly conditioned any aid on the election of Ezra Stiles as the new president. Stiles was universally respected

9 Henry K. Beecher and Mark D. Altschule, *Medicine at Harvard: The First Three Hundred Years* (Hanover, NH: University Press of New England, 1977), 29–45; Peter Dobkin Hall, "The Social Foundations of Professional Credibility: Linking the Medical Profession to Higher Education in Connecticut and Massachusetts, 1700–1830" in Thomas L. Haskell, ed., *The Authority of Experts* (Bloomington: Indiana University Press, 1984), 107–41. Waterhouse was the only non-Harvardian to teach in the medical school before 1864; he also differed from his colleagues socially, politically, and professionally, and they finally forced the corporation to fire him in 1812. His later eccentricities are described by Samuel E. Morison, *Three Centuries of Harvard* (Cambridge: Harvard University Press, 1936), 222–23.

10 Walter Muir Whitehill, "Early Learned Societies in Boston and Vicinity" in Alexandra Oleson and Sanford C. Brown, eds. *The Pursuit of Knowledge in the Earl American Republic* (Baltimore: Johns Hopkins University Press, 1976), 151–73, quote p. 152; John C. Greene, *American Science in the Age of Jefferson* (Ames: Iowa State University Press, 1984), 63–70.

throughout the colonies for his learning, and his pastorate in Newport had kept him out of Connecticut's Old Light–New Light wars. Despite some support for an internal candidate, the corporation duly elected Stiles in September, but it would be another 6 months before he accepted. In the meantime, subsequent negotiations between Yale and the state foundered. Only a decade after Thomas Clap, considerable animus still existed toward Yale and its clerical trustees; and there was even talk of establishing a second, state college. The assembly sought greater control through an equal say in appointments, but it refrained from making definite commitments to aiding the college. Under the circumstances, Yale decided against connecting with the state.

While hopes were still high, Stiles addressed a letter to the senior fellow on the Yale Corporation outlining his vision of transforming Yale into a republican university. He envisioned adding six professorships to Yale's existing positions in divinity and natural philosophy: physic, law, ecclesiastical history, civil history, Hebrew and oriental languages, and oratory and belles lettres. This was a practical list, inspired in part by consultations with the Harvard president and professors. Belles lettres was already popular at Yale, although taught by the tutors. Oriental languages would duplicate the chair recently created at Harvard. Medical education was a perceived need in Connecticut, although it seems doubtful that a single professor could address this lacuna. Stiles himself wished to occupy the chair in ecclesiastical history, where he could teach his own moderate interpretation of Calvinism. Civil history would no doubt embody principles of republicanism, but this was also the aim of the proposed chair in law. Stiles did not foresee educating professional lawyers but rather hoped to fit "civilians" for Connecticut society as he knew it. During their careers, Yale graduates were likely to hold public office as justices of the peace, representatives, or delegates. Broad, general instruction in law would thus prepare them for public service. The impact would be still greater because "this Knowledge is catching, propagates to all around and transfuses itself thro' the public." Stiles thus articulated his own interpretation of how colleges contribute to republican virtue: "establishing and endowing Professorships of Law in american Universities" was essential because "it is scarcely possible to enslave a Republic where the Body of the People are Civilians, well instructed in their Laws, Rights and Liberties."[11]

As president of Yale (1778–1795), Stiles personally embodied this spirit of republican education but lacked the resources to build a university. The Yale course remained conventional, with Stiles alone teaching advanced subjects. Only in

---

11   Edmund S. Morgan, *The Gentle Puritan: A Life of Ezra Stiles, 1727–1795* (Chapel Hill: University of North Carolina Press, 1962), 292–324, quotes from Stiles to Eliphalet Williams, Dec. 3, 1777, pp. 322–23.

1792, under the ascendant Federalist consensus, did the state seek a rapprochement with Yale College. Financial support was granted in return for minority representation of state officials on the board. Stiles attributed this about-face to Connecticut's wish to emulate the steps other states had taken to support their colleges. It also signaled the restoration of confidence in Yale's ability to provide sound education. Nonetheless, the college was able to restore the professorship of natural philosophy only during Stiles's last years. In this respect, Yale illustrated the predominance of penury over ideology in the quest for republican universities.

The College of Philadelphia was the only nonsectarian colonial college, but it was dominated by its aggressive Anglican provost, William Smith, and a largely Anglican board of trustees. Smith took the side of colonial rights with characteristic energy but still hoped to preserve ties with the mother country. He was well within the patriotic mainstream in 1775, when George Washington and the Second Continental Congress took time off from raising an army to attend the college commencement. However, the next year, when the die was cast for independence, Smith, the College, and most of the trustees became isolated and suspect. Their predicament stemmed less from the national course of events than from local politics.[12]

The revolution in Pennsylvania was the most radical of any state. The peculiar bifurcated power structure of the colony abruptly collapsed in 1776. The Proprietary Party was hopelessly compromised by their wealth, privilege, and English ties, and the assembly, dominated by Quakers and their German allies, wanted no part of the Revolution or the war. Elections brought to power a determined minority of ideologically committed revolutionaries, largely from the backcountry. They had urged voters to "choose no rich men, and [as] few learned men as possible." The constitution they produced ignored republican notions of balanced government, establishing instead an all-powerful unicameral legislature elected through wide suffrage and annual elections. Soon after the British withdrew from Philadelphia, the Constitutionalists took aim at the college. Although a few of the college party had departed with the British, most joined the patriot side with varying degrees of enthusiasm. But they remained adamantly opposed to Pennsylvania's revolutionary government. The feeling was mutual, and early in 1779 the assembly appointed a committee "to enquire into the present State of the College and Academy of Philadelphia."[13]

---

12 Roger L. Geiger and Nathan M. Sorber, "Tarnished Icon: William Smith and the College of Philadelphia," *Perspectives on the History of Higher Education*, 28 (2011): 1–31; Hoeveler, *Creating the American Mind*, 333–44.

13 Richard L. Brunhouse, *The Counter-Revolution in Pennsylvania, 1776–1790* (Harrisburg: Pennsylvania Historical Commission, 1942); Ann D. Gordon, *The College of Philadelphia, 1749–1779: Impact of an Institution* (New York: Garland, 1989), 270.

The arguments for preserving or reorganizing the College of Philadelphia invoked definitions of public and private, an ambiguous distinction that would long plague American colleges. The trustees maintained that the College was a private institution, created with charitable contributions, and hence an autonomous charitable corporation. They also defended their governance as preserving its nonsectarian character. The state's radical constitution claimed state responsibility for republican education, and the Constitutionalists exploited this claim by charging the trustees with malfeasance and lack of patriotism. They asserted that "corporations compose a species of government"; and schools in particular required "a liberal foundation in which the interests of American Liberty and Independence will be advanced and promoted and Obedience and Respect to the Constitution of the State preserved." At the bottom, however, was the accusation that the college "appears to have allied itself so closely to the government of Britain." In actual charges, the trustees were accused of violating the "broad and catholic Foundation" on which the college was established, of preserving an oath of allegiance to the crown while ignoring the test oaths imposed by the state, and of tolerating traitors. These were dubious charges that ought to have been adjudicated, but amidst war and revolution the Assembly simply imposed its will.[14] The law of November 29, 1779, amended the charter and terminated the College of Philadelphia.

The new incarnation, the University of the State of Pennsylvania, would persist for 12 years. The trustees were replaced by a new board containing six ministers of the principal denominations, six state officials serving ex officio, and twelve selected laymen, including Benjamin Franklin, who refused to participate. Initially, the state promised ample funding from confiscated Tory properties, but adequate support never materialized. John Ewing, a scholarly Presbyterian minister, was named provost and David Rittenhouse, for a short time, professor of astronomy and vice provost. Interestingly, a committee was also subsequently formed to "inquire into the state of the late Medical school," but it requested "the several Medical Professors in the mean time to proceed in their lectures as heretofore." Most professors resigned in opposition to the Constitutionalists, but, after some turmoil, were persuaded to continue in 1783. In this case the government seemed to have put the continued operation of the medical school ahead of political purity.[15]

---

14 Jurgen Herbst, *From Crisis to Crisis: American College Government, 1636–1819* (Cambridge: Harvard University Press, 1982), 176–83; Gordon, *College of Philadelphia*, quotes pp. 272, 269, 271.

15 David Freeman Hawke, *Benjamin Rush: Revolutionary Gadfly* (New York: Bobbs-Merrill, 1971), 250–51; The *Medical Department of the University of Pennsylvania*, pp. 89–90; Franklin supported the claims of the college trustees: 92.

Inventing a republican university was a work in progress for the new institution. It took until 1782 to develop a curriculum calling for seven professors, the most novel being a professor of German. Chairs were also established in history and oratory and English language, but they were apparently filled for only 2 years (1782–1784). Still, a faculty of five professors (including the provost) was substantial for the 1780s. It was also more than the university could afford. The college course was extended to 4 years, but students wanting only partial courses were welcomed, too. Attendance seems to have been similar to the prerevolution decade with an average of nine graduates and a similar number of nongraduates per class; but the university was poorly run, and the quality of education clearly deteriorated. Throughout the 1780s, William Smith and the old trustees pressed their case that the college had been illegally confiscated. In 1789, with a more conservative government in place, they were vindicated. The College of Philadelphia reclaimed its property and began teaching once again. But the university persisted as well. Having two colleges in the city, neither financially viable, made no sense. With ideological passions much cooler, the faculties and trustees of the two institutions merged in 1791 to form the University of Pennsylvania. Personal animosities persisted nonetheless, to the detriment of the unified university: William Smith was dropped, and Provost Ewing was still despised by many trustees for having sided with the Constitutionalists.[16]

The College of William & Mary is known for Thomas Jefferson's efforts to create a republican university, but internally instruction was largely sustained by Reverend James Madison. He had been appointed professor of natural philosophy in 1773, a year after his graduation. Already an ardent patriot, he traveled to England in 1775 to receive ordination as an Anglican priest (where his outspoken views raised suspicion that he was a spy). In 1777, when the last loyalist was driven from the college, Madison assumed the presidency, a position he would hold for life (1777–1812). He and the professor of moral philosophy kept the college operating despite shrinking enrollment and the loss of its former revenues. During these years Thomas Jefferson, as a member of the committee that was rewriting the laws for the Commonwealth of Virginia, formulated a "Bill for Amending the Constitution of the College of William and Mary, and Substituting More Certain Revenues for its Support." In keeping with his efforts to disestablish the Anglican Church, Jefferson argued that the college should be a state institution with regular state support. He proposed eight professorships, adding ancient languages, law, medicine, history, mathematics, and modern languages. Characteristically, he further specified in some detail a multitude of topics to be covered by each professor.

---

16   Edward Potts Cheney, *History of the University of Pennsylvania* (Philadelphia: University of Pennsylvania Press, 1940), 129–50.

Thus, Jefferson envisioned a state university devoted to professional and advanced subjects. Under wartime conditions, there was no hope of implementing such a scheme, nor his more famous conception of a comprehensive system of public education in the "Bill for the More General Diffusion of Knowledge." By 1779, when Jefferson joined the Board of Visitors, the college was in dire condition. Unable to change the college charter, the Visitors now changed the professorships within the charter. In addition to natural and moral philosophy, they created three chairs for law and police, anatomy and medicine, and modern languages. Appointments were quickly made, and the college was able to open in January 1780 with professors supported solely by student fees, payable in tobacco. [17]

The reforms forged a unique version of collegiate education. William & Mary offered no instruction in Latin or Greek. Students were expected to acquire grounding in the classics before enrolling but were admitted regardless. Courses of study for degrees were set, but students could attend whichever lectures they chose, in any order. Thus, the measures taken in the early 1770s to impose some order on the college course largely lapsed. In theory, the college allowed the freedom for intellectual exploration that Jefferson admired, and under the circumstances this looseness may have been the only feasible approach. Still, some aspects of the reform clearly failed. No lectures in medicine were ever given. The professor of modern languages, a Jefferson favorite, was scarcely competent and was soon an embarrassment. But a republican education of sorts might still be had.

Reverend James Madison, who became bishop of the American Episcopal Church in 1790, had a transcendent faith in the destiny of America as a "republic of virtue."[18] He advocated a heightened fusion of Christianity and Enlightenment in which America was destined to become "the theater whereon the Providence of God is now manifested," specifically as the home of liberty and equality. After the Revolution he assumed the teaching of moral philosophy, which he infused with modern political theory, including Rousseau and Adam Smith. The polymath Samuel Miller later observed that in no other college was "political science . . . studied with so much ardour [or] considered so preeminently a favorite subject."[19] Madison was also an active scientist, by contemporary standards, and faithfully taught natural philosophy in the college. If Madison was the pedagogical mainstay

17   Robert Polk Thomson, "The Reform of the College of William and Mary, 1763–1780," *Proceedings of the American Philosophical Society*, 115, 3 (June 17, 1971): 187–213; Susan H. Godson et al., *The College of William & Mary: A History* (Williamsburg, Virginia: College of William & Mary, 1993), 121–95. Jefferson's Bill for the General Diffusion of Knowledge proposed universal primary education, grammar schools in each county, and scholarships for a few poor students to advance, ultimately to the college.

18   Charles Crowe, "Bishop James Madison and the Republic of Virtue," *Journal of Southern History*, 30, 1 (Feb. 1964): 58–70.

19   Samuel Miller, *A Brief Retrospect of the Eighteenth Century*, 2 vol. (New York, 1803), II, 504: this work is discussed later in this chapter.

of the college, its star was law professor George Wythe, who had been Jefferson's mentor and a signer of the Declaration of Independence. Wythe was venerated in Virginia for his knowledge of law and government and by his students for being a conscientious and beloved teacher. Unlike in legal courses elsewhere, Wythe trained students to be practicing lawyers through lectures and moot courts.

However, the old guard gradually reasserted its influence. They succeeded in reestablishing the grammar school to the detriment of the college. Wythe resigned in 1789 out of exasperation with these developments, and Jefferson spoke of the "demolition" and "ruin" of the college. Wythe was replaced by St. George Tucker, an able legal scholar and teacher who taught from his law office. But he, too, resigned when ordered, like a tutor, to visit student rooms to enforce parietal rules. Thus, William & Mary for a time was the first American college to offer professional legal education but was unwilling to separate it from the college. This failure exemplified the contradictions of its makeshift model. More problematic was a secular college led by an Episcopal bishop. Despite Madison's ardent republicanism, fully shared by students, the college could not dispel its ties to the old Anglican establishment. And the growing Presbyterian community distrusted both its secular politics and Episcopal influence. Abandoned by Jefferson too, the college persisted weakly after its tenuous postwar recovery.[20]

Efforts to resuscitate higher education in New York began as soon as the British departed and had strong backing from the patriot remnant of King's College supporters. They were spearheaded by James Duane, an influential lawyer, senator, mayor of the city, and ex-governor of King's. In the latter role, Duane had supported the gambit to form the American University, and the new legislation in 1784 created the same type of overarching university. The University of the State of New York was given responsibility for all schools and colleges founded in the state. It was governed by a board of regents consisting of state officials, ex officio, the mayors of New York and Albany, and two representatives from each county. At its inception, the sole institution it governed was King's successor, Columbia College. The difficulty with this arrangement was soon apparent, as the geographically dispersed board could seldom gather a quorum. To rectify this, thirty-three more representatives were named to the board, twenty from New York City, and the quorum size was reduced to nine. This board laid ambitious plans: Columbia would resemble a European university with four faculties, including seven salaried professors in the college, eight medical ones, two in law, and nine "extra professorships" (i.e., unpaid). The state provided a generous appropriation to rebuild the college and launch instruction, and Columbia College held its first commencement in 1786.

20   Godson et al., *College of William & Mary*, 165–98.

Now, however, a handful of New York City regents held the power to govern all the schools and colleges in the state (had there been any others). This situation was rectified in 1787 by the adroit Duane with legislation creating a new, separate charter for "the Trustees of Columbia College in the City of New York." Although broadly representative of the college's constituency, the Columbia trustees included no public officials and were self-perpetuating. Columbia became privately governed, focused on the city rather than the state. Nonetheless, the trustees, who dominated the institution, were no less committed to creating a republican university. It remained under the theoretical purview of the regents and still sought public support.

In its new incarnation, Columbia College was initially a great success. William Samuel Johnson, son of the founding president, became Columbia's first president in 1787. A lawyer rather than a clergyman, his appointment signaled a healing denominational neutrality. A belated patriot during the Revolution, he had become a prominent federalist statesman in Connecticut, adept at invoking the rhetoric of republican virtue. In 1792 a 5-year grant from the legislature allowed the college to create four professorships—in French, Hebrew, law, and chemistry. However, all these subjects were optional rather than part of the regular course. James Kent, a distinguished jurist, was named professor of law and sought to have future lawyers and statesmen "imbibe the principles of Republican government." An initial audience of forty students and "private gentlemen" evaporated to zero by the third year, after which Kent resigned. The professors of French and Hebrew also drew few students and were dropped when the subsidy ran out. Only chemistry was retained and incorporated into the regular course. Still, with eight college professors and a fully staffed medical school, Columbia in the 1790s came as close as any eighteenth-century institution to fulfilling the image of a republican university. Out of necessity, Columbia abandoned the collegiate way of living. Its postwar students were older, lived in the city, and had considerable freedom over much of their time. Making amends for past practice, the college announced that its tuition would be "as cheap as any other college," which meant matching that of Nassau Hall—about $15 per year. All these factors no doubt helped to boost Columbia's enrollment to 140 students in the midnineties. It graduated more students from 1791 to 1796 than King's did in three decades. But this was a high point. In 1799, the state terminated its subsidies, and the college was forced to scale back to just the president and two professors. It soon reverted to the parochialism of its forerunner.[21]

21   Humphrey, *King's College*, 1976), 267–306, quote p. 294; Robert A. McCaughey, *Stand Columbia* (New York: Columbia University Press, 2003), 49–78, quote p. 54; Elizabeth P. McCaughey, *From Loyalist to Founding Father: The Political Odyssey of William Samuel Johnson* (New York: Columbia University Press, 1980), 239–64.

EDUCATIONAL ASPIRATIONS
IN THE EARLY REPUBLIC

After the Revolution, the dialogue on education subtly shifted. Instead of notions of republican virtue, concern focused on how education might serve to unify the nation; instead of reforming existing institutions, ideas arose about creating new ones; and instead of attention to colleges and their graduates, discussion moved to educational possibilities for the rest of the population. All these themes were aired in the 1780s by Dr. Benjamin Rush, who "wrote more often and more fully than perhaps any American of the day on education."[22] Rush had already contributed to American higher education by convincing John Witherspoon to come to Princeton and by becoming a charter member of the nation's first medical school. His educational speculations were prompted for the most part by deep personal commitments superimposed on the political turmoil of the decade. Rush was an ardent and idealist patriot who sat in the Second Continental Congress and signed the Declaration of Independence. But he was acutely concerned that achieving independence did not assure a successful republic. For him, the Pennsylvania Constitution was tantamount to "mobocracy," and the Articles of Confederation were inadequate to govern the nation. "We have changed our forms of government," he lamented, "but it remains yet to effect a revolution in our principles, opinions, and manners so as to accommodate them to the forms of government we have adopted." To this end, he famously advocated employing education "to convert men into republican machines," able "to perform their parts properly in the great machine of the government of the state." Although described as a gadfly, given to quotable hyperbole, Rush was an original, if opinionated, thinker with a gift for articulating timely issues. He played an active role in promoting the federal constitution, for example, but subsequently criticized Washington and the federalists for an overconcentration of executive power. An exemplar of science and Enlightenment, he remained a devout Presbyterian and defended the role of the churches.[23]

In the 1780s Rush championed the founding of two denominational colleges in Pennsylvania, proposed a plan for a system of public education, floated the idea of a national university, and challenged the dominance of Latin and Greek

22 Robson, *Educating Republicans*, 227–53; David Freeman Hawke, *Benjamin Rush: Revolutionary Gadfly* (New York: Bobbs-Merrill, 1971), quote p. 285.

23 David Tyack, "Forming the National Character: Paradox in the Educational Thought of the Revolutionary Generation," *Harvard Education Review*, 36, 1 (1966): 29–41, quote p. 29; Benjamin Rush, "Thoughts upon the Mode of Education Proper to a Republic" [1786] in Frederick Rudolph, ed., *Essays on Education in the Early Republic* (Cambridge: Harvard University Press, 1965), 9–23, quote p. 17.

in the college course. All these endeavors seem to have been triggered by the serendipitous campaign to launch Dickinson College in Carlisle, Pennsylvania.

Local citizens had hoped to raise an existing grammar school to a chartered academy, but in 1782 Rush seized upon this initiative and inflated it to the founding of a Presbyterian college. The idea of such an institution to serve the growing numbers of Presbyterians in the backcountry had been in the air for some time, but Rush's motives were mixed with his personal vendetta against the new University of the State of Pennsylvania. At the time, Rush had resigned his chair (temporarily) in the medical school, and he was philosophically opposed to the mostly Presbyterian Constitutionalists who now ran the university and the state government. Rush held the no longer fashionable belief that "without religion . . . learning does real mischief to the morals and principles of mankind." The university suffered from "extreme Catholicism"—"as no religion prevails, so no religious principles are inculcated in it." As an alternative, Rush offered a political justification for denominational colleges in a pluralistic society. Perhaps with his alma mater in mind, he urged state Presbyterians "to entrench themselves in schools of learning. These are the true Nurseries of power and influence." Where religion was concerned, Rush seemingly rejected the model of a nondenominational republican university and offered instead the rationale that religious communities needed to establish their own institutions for their own defense and perpetuation: or, "colleges are the best schools for divinity."[24]

In arguing for the college at Carlisle, Rush also offered practical arguments. For citizens of the backcountry, Princeton was too distant and too expensive to attend; Philadelphia was also expensive and might endanger the morals of country students. Carlisle was central to the Presbyterian settlements as well as being a healthful and prosperous locale. The college was naturally opposed by the state university and by Presbyterians loyal to the College of New Jersey, and there were even misgivings in Carlisle. But Rush was relentless in pressing his case, and he recruited powerful allies in the state's premier lawyer, James Wilson, and Governor John Dickinson. Originally he had proposed an entirely Presbyterian board of trustees, but the final charter precluded church control, adding representatives from other denominations, especially the German churches. In the chaotic politics of the new state, the college charter was approved in September 1783.[25]

---

24   Benjamin Rush, "Hints for Establishing a College at Carlisle" (1782); quoted in Hawke, *Benjamin Rush*, 285–87.

25   Charles Coleman Sellers, *Dickinson College: A History* (Middletown, CT: Wesleyan University Press, 1973), Hawke, *Benjamin Rush*, 285–90. The subsequent trials of Dickinson College are described below.

Only 2 years later Rush was recruited to help found a second Pennsylvania college. Members of the Lutheran and German Reformed churches wished to establish an institution specifically for Pennsylvania's German community. Their assimilation had been a longstanding concern, addressed quite inadequately by the German professorship at the university and Rush's attempt to include them at Dickinson. Rush was eager to assist, and the effort led to the chartering of Franklin College in Lancaster in 1787. Widespread support for this solution to the "German problem" took no account of the general indifference among the Germans themselves. Franklin College functioned largely as a grammar school for 2 years and then lapsed into suspended animation, a legal entity without operations.[26]

Justifying the campaign for Dickinson College stimulated Rush to speculate more widely about the role of education in republican society. In preparation for the first trustee meeting (1784), he spent considerable time and effort composing "Thoughts upon the Mode of Education Proper to a Republic"—the source of his remark about "republican machines." However, he then felt compelled to devise an actual plan to realize those goals. In 1786 he published "Plan for the Establishment of Public Schools," which envisioned "the whole state . . . tied together by one system of education." He proposed that tax-supported free schools be established for elementary education in each township or district. Each county would establish an academy to teach the learned languages and prepare students for college. In its bare outline, Rush's plan resembled Thomas Jefferson's "Bill for the General Diffusion of Knowledge," but whereas Jefferson aimed to cull a few natural aristocrats from the masses, Rush intended to educate, or perhaps indoctrinate, all citizens. He explicitly justified the imposition of school taxes by describing the benefits of education for the entire community. His contemporaries found this aspect of "Plan" to be impractical, especially for rural and backcountry settlements. Rush countered with a more specific plan that would be feasible for Philadelphia and its vicinity. He argued that only free schools could bring education to the poor and laboring classes and, perhaps mindful of the Pennsylvania Constitution, "where the common people are ignorant and vicious . . . a republican nation can never long be free and happy." Rush would educate both girls and boys, instructing them in reading, writing, and the principles of Christianity.[27]

With this extension of his plan, Rush became a prominent advocate of female education. He was, in fact, an original trustee of the Young Ladies' Academy of

26   Sally F. Griffith, *Liberalizing the Mind: Two Centuries of Liberal Education at Franklin & Marshall College* (University Park: Pennsylvania State University Press, 2010), 6–16; Hawke, *Benjamin Rush*, 316–19.

27   Hawke, *Benjamin Rush*, 296–97, 331–32.

Philadelphia (f. 1786). In an address there, he sought to relate female education to the "situation, employments, and duties of women in America," who, unlike their British counterparts, had few servants. The duties of managing a household and instructing children created the need for a practical education. This meant mastering English-language skills, learning figures and bookkeeping, and general knowledge of the world through geography, science, and history. The Young Ladies' Academy actually taught a curriculum similar to the Philadelphia Academy for boys.[28] Above all, Rush's prescriptions for education are testimony to his faith in the ability of education to shape citizens and ultimately the republic.

Rush's plan for Pennsylvania anticipated his better-known national plan. He was clearly uneasy with the seeming repudiation of republican universities implied by his campaign for Dickinson College. In "Plan," he consequently rehabilitated the university as an institution for advanced professional training superior to the denominational colleges. For Pennsylvania, he advocated one university in the capital where "law, physic, divinity, the law of nature and nations, economy, etc." would be taught by public lectures "after the manner of European universities." Its professors should receive state salaries but would also charge fees for their lectures ("at a moderate price") as in the medical school. Beneath the university would be four regional colleges—in Philadelphia, Carlisle, Lancaster, and (some day) Pittsburgh. Like other American colleges, they would provide a liberal education and graduate bachelors' who would, "if they can afford it, complete their studies by spending a season or two attending lectures in the university." An optimist might well have mused in 1786 that Pennsylvania was evolving toward this model. But Rush immediately projected it onto the national stage.[29]

Prior to the calling of the Constitutional Convention, Rush depicted the failings of the Articles of Confederation in "An Address to the People of the United States" (1787). The essay concluded by returning to his obsession of building the social base for a republic, only now the vehicle was to be a national university. The objectives were both unity and knowledge: college graduates from all the states would be melded "together into one mass of citizens" by studying all subjects related to government "and everything else connected with the advance of republican knowledge and principles." Unlike the professional university he proposed for Pennsylvania, the national university was to be a postgraduate institution dedicated to acquiring and teaching the most advanced knowledge. Finally, in a suggestion that probably raised more opposition than support, Rush

---

28   Benjamin Rush, "Thoughts upon Female Education, Accommodated to the Present State of Society, Manners, and Government in the United States of America," in Rudolph, *Essays on Education*, 27–40, quote p. 27; Margaret A. Nash, "Rethinking Republican Motherhood: Benjamin Rush and the Young Ladies' Academy of Philadelphia," *Journal of the Early Republic*, 17, 2 (Summer 1997): 171–91.

29   Benjamin Rush, "Plan for a Federal University," *Pennsylvania Gazette*, October 29, 1788, 4.

suggested that after some years all functionaries of the federal government would have to be graduates of the national university.[30]

The idea of a federal university acquired a life of its own over the next decade. The notion that the federal legislature should be empowered to establish a university was introduced at two points in the Constitutional Convention but failed of adoption. The idea was vague, its appropriateness uncertain, and the convention had more vital matters to decide. Rush elaborated his proposal further in 1788. He expanded the list of subjects to be included, particularly the practical arts of agriculture, manufacturing, and commerce. He also specified that after 30 years, offices in the U.S. government would be restricted to graduates.[31] The basic idea was endorsed by a number of other writers. When the American Philosophical Society sponsored a competition in 1795 for devising "the best system of liberal education," both winning entries proposed educational systems topped by a national university.[32] This notion was favored by President George Washington in his first address to Congress (1790). The matter was not seriously considered until the end of his second term, when he proposed to donate fifty shares of the Potomac River Company to an endowment for such a university. Washington hoped that a national university would preclude Americans studying in Europe, where they might contract "not only habits of dissipation and extravagance, but principles unfriendly to Republican Governmt." At his urging, Congress debated authorization for this project at the end of 1796 but ultimately voted to drop the matter. The notion of a federal university would be revived periodically but to no avail. A chimera of Enlightenment thinking, it represented the aspirations rather than the realities of the Early Republic.[33]

Rush's Plan for a Federal University included only those subjects "calculated to prepare our youth for civil and public life." Classical languages and literature were not only omitted, but he concluded his essay with a snide comment that Americans were destined to progress further and faster than Europeans still preoccupied with these studies. Rush himself was an accomplished Latinist, and the classics had been included in his previous plans. But in 1789 he turned the full force of his rhetoric against the study of Latin and Greek. Here he was original chiefly in his vehemence. Franklin had been a critic for the last half-century; and although the generation of the Founders was probably the most devoted to

---

30   Robson, *Education Republicans*, 228–30; Hawke, *Benjamin Rush*, 340–43.

31   Rush, "Plan for a Federal University"; Robson, *Educating Republicans*, 230–31.

32   Samuel Harrison Smith, *Remarks on Education*, and Samuel Knox, *An Essay on the Best System of Liberal Education*, reprinted in Rudolph, *Essays on Education*, 167–223, 271–372.

33   Robson, *Educating Republicans*, 232–36; David Madsen, *The National University: Enduring Dream of the USA* (Detroit: Wayne State University Press, 1966); quote from George Washington, "Last Will and Testament" (1799).

ancient languages and history, independence brought new doubts and doubters.[34] Noah Webster, in particular, argued that the highest priority should be development and perfection of the English language and that learning Latin and Greek only detracted from that end. Rush found additional reasons. Classical languages were unnecessary for a liberal education and excluded promising students who could not or would not abide them. Spending 4 or 5 years of schooling to master these languages was worse than a waste of time. With his characteristic prudery he condemned exposing students to the salacious behavior of ancient gods and men. Moreover, like Webster, he felt that the classical languages corrupted rather than refined English usage, and their contents could be taught with translations. The attention Rush and Webster drew to this issue touched off a prolonged controversy in which the debating points listed above were refuted, defended, and reiterated. However, one point that he raised went beyond rhetoric: Greek and Latin were unpopular with the common people and requiring them for college in effect diminished access to advanced education and knowledge.[35]

Corroboration of this last point was supplied by Samuel Miller in his encyclopedic rendering of the intellectual developments of the eighteenth century.[36] Criticisms of the classics reflected and perhaps legitimized developments in the colleges. Miller repeatedly noted "the low state of classic literature in the greater number of American colleges.... [T]he popular prejudice against it is strong and growing; and there is too much reason to fear that this prejudice will at no great distance of time, completely triumph." The belief was widespread "that the time bestowed on the acquisition of these languages, if not entirely wasted, might at least be more usefully employed." Finally, Miller echoed Rush's last point: "public respect for classic literature" had diminished; and dispensing with it would "break down the 'wall of partition' between the literary and the other classes of citizens, and . . . render liberal information the common portion of all ranks in the community."[37] Clearly more than literary tastes were involved: the hegemony of Latin and Greek raised basic issues of culture and class in the Early Republic.

Indeed, although Rush had little impact on events, all four of the issues he raised in the 1780s would resonate in the expansion of higher education and complicate the original model of republican universities. His championing of

---

34 Meyer Reinhold, *Classica Americana: The Greek and Roman Heritage in the United States* (Detroit: Wayne State University Press, 1984), 116–37.

35 Ibid., 128–36; Richard, *Founders and the Classics*, 196–231; Hawke, *Benjamin Rush*, 367–68.

36 Gilbert Chinard, "A Landmark in American Intellectual History: Samuel Miller's *A Brief Retrospect of the Eighteenth Century*," *Princeton University Library Chronicle* 14, 2 (Winter 1953): 55–71.

37 Miller, *A Brief Retrospect of the Eighteenth Century*, II, 220, 221, 222. Miller found standards for Greek to be especially debased: "in some American Colleges . . . no more knowledge of Greek is required in those who graduate *Bachelor of Arts*, than that which may be derived from the Grammar and the Greek Testament": II, 405n. This is discussed further below.

denominational education reflected the wide persistence of ingrained religious belief. Applied to colleges, it reemphasized the residual religious foundations of the American college as well as Rush's recognition of their role in preserving the "power and influence" of denominations in a secular age. The federal university was a new formula for the tangled objectives of republican universities—Enlightenment goals for learning that were becoming more difficult to realize. Public systems for educating all children would increasingly be posed not as complements but as competing alternatives to government support for colleges. And within the colleges, the role of the classical languages would long survive further attacks. These matters affected new colleges and universities for the remainder of the century and beyond as they were drawn into the growing conflict between federalists and republicans.

★   ★   ★

By 1790 the world was changing. The Constitutional Convention of 1787 had fashioned a federal government that now sought to bind the nation together and deal with its many challenges. The presidential inauguration of unanimously elected George Washington, April 30, 1789, was followed within a week by the gathering in France of the Estates General—the beginning of the French Revolution. The federal Constitution was the supreme achievement of the intellectual republicanism that had guided the founders. Three branches of government provided the checks and balances that allowed the expression of democracy while guarding against mob rule. But the details had to be worked out. Secretary of the Treasury Alexander Hamilton and Vice President John Adams favored a strong federal government, especially in financial matters. In addition, they blatantly sought to preserve the traditional hierarchical social structure. Thomas Jefferson and James Madison, in opposing them, envisioned a more decentralized polity and greater scope for democratic processes. They championed popular sovereignty and assumed the mantle of republicanism. An overt split between federalists and republicans in the government opened in 1792. Up to that point, the French Revolution had been universally hailed in the United States as vindication and validation of the American Revolution. For the rest of the decade, disagreement over the radical course of the revolution, the European wars it ignited, and American relations with France served to intensify the polarization between federalists and republicans in the United States.[38] These developments

38   Henry F. May, *The Enlightenment in America* (New York: Oxford University Press, 1976), 153–222; Gordon S. Wood, *Empire of Liberty: A History of the Early Republic, 1789–1815* (New York: Oxford University Press, 2009), 95–208.

affected the colleges too, their intellectual, social, and religious foundations. With the emergence of federalist and republican parties, the "public good" could no longer be ritually invoked to favor higher education, since that notion itself was contested. Colleges themselves assumed political colorations, and they soon had to deal with oscillating majorities of federalists or republicans in state governments.

The dominant ideas of the 1780s reflected the fruition of the Moderate Enlightenment—the worldview that had gained increasing ascendancy since midcentury and had melded doctrines of reason and progress with Protestant religion. The two revolutions, however, hastened the spread of more extreme strains of Enlightenment thought. The struggle for independence gave rise to millennial interpretations of liberty and democracy; European *philosophes* like Voltaire and Rousseau began to be read; and deism assumed a more prominent and threatening guise. Most of the founders conformed to a polite, rational deism: they were scornful of theology and organized denominations, but when challenged they upheld beliefs in a deity and an afterlife, a stance generally acceptable to moderate Protestants. These attitudes were reflected in declarations of freedom of religion, toleration, and the nondenominational nature of the colleges. However, more extreme expressions of deism and atheism became increasingly common, grotesquely epitomized by Robespierre's attempt in 1794 to replace the Christian God with the Goddess of Reason. That same year, Thomas Paine published *The Age of Reason*—an unremitting attack on the Bible and Protestant theology that shocked and frightened Christian leaders across the country. The 1790s marked the zenith, and with Paine the hypertrophy, of Enlightenment doctrines and attitudes in the United States, but also, for that reason, it touched off a religious reaction. Republican colleges and universities continued to be founded, but their difficulties revealed the precariousness of these institutions.

NEW COLLEGES IN THE NEW REPUBLIC

By the end of the eighteenth century, the nine colonial colleges had been joined by thirteen additional, more or less permanent, colleges.[39] Although the origins and circumstances of each new college were unique, the prevailing ideology of republicanism supplied a common theme. While several institutions were established explicitly as state republican universities, almost all had some kind of state connection. "Public" higher education was an inchoate concept in these

---

39   Herbst, *From Crisis to Crisis*, 174–231: see appendix A for college foundings; Robson, *Education Republicans*, 187–260.

years, and its modern opposite—"private"—was inconceivable. Legal status was nonetheless an important factor in their existence, but so too were the physical realities of their settings and circumstances. With the exception of the College of Charleston, all these colleges were in rural or small-town locales, well removed from population centers and remote as well from the influence of well-educated citizens, who chiefly supported established colleges. They had difficulty too in accumulating the accoutrements of learning and, most serious, competent instructors and leaders. Each new college was also colored by some degree of denominational affiliation. However, in this Enlightened age all colleges were committed to religious toleration and none were permitted to be under church control. The diverse origins of these institutions can largely be ascribed to five interacting factors: the actions and politics of state legislatures, the aspirations of regions or localities, the interests of religious denominations, the actions of individual entrepreneurs, and preexisting academies.

The stated intention, in state constitutions or subsequent legislation, to establish republican universities reflected the same motives that transformed existing colleges. However, the universities chartered in Georgia (1785), North Carolina (1789), and Vermont (1791) had no foundations on which to build. Starting from scratch presented challenges in choosing a location and acquiring funds and buildings but also of securing a faculty and attracting students. Only North Carolina immediately began the lengthy process of realizing a state university, which stretched over 6 years from charter to opening in 1795. By then, additional colleges had opened, and two had closed.[40]

In states that already had a college, partisan political divisions were often behind measures to establish additional colleges. This was the case in Virginia, where dissenters had long chafed against the established Anglican Church and were eager to prevent William & Mary from monopolizing higher education in the state. Before the War for Independence was concluded, a degree-granting charter was awarded to Liberty Hall Academy—which kept its same name; and a similar charter was granted to Hampden-Sydney Academy, founded by New Jersey graduate Samuel Stanhope Smith, which then became a college. Both institutions were established Presbyterian schools that had been teaching some advanced subjects and wished to prepare ministers. The boards of trustees of both colleges were made independent, although still consisting of Presbyterians. The trustees were charged "to preserve in the minds of the students that sacred love and attachment which they should ever bear to the principles of the

---

40 Franklin College in Pennsylvania closed after 2 years (1787–1789), and Cokesbury College in Maryland was established by the Methodists in 1794 but closed the following year (see chapter 4): Bernard C. Steiner, *History of Education in Maryland* (Washington, D.C.: GPO, 1894).

glorious present revolution." The state regarded them as public institutions and gave Hampden-Sydney a small land grant in 1784, and Liberty Hall petitioned the legislature unsuccessfully for support. In 1796 the legislature assumed it had the authority to pass legislation changing the name and organization of Liberty Hall, transforming it into what would have been a republican university with four faculties and public members on its board. Although scarcely feasible, the legality of this action was never tested. In the face of resistance from the school, the legislature backed down. The school assumed the name of Washington Academy (1798), but it did not call itself a college until 1813.[41]

The new colleges in Pennsylvania, as already seen, owed much to the entre-preneurship of Benjamin Rush. Dickinson College would scarcely have been launched without his obsessive drive, but he merely abetted the efforts of the German Community and Lancastrians to found Franklin College in 1787. Both these colleges were motivated in part by opposition to the ruling Constitutional-ists and their control over the state university. Yet, both colleges were celebrated with republican rhetoric. The explicit hope behind Franklin College was to ac-celerate the assimilation of Pennsylvania Germans, but the founder's petition spoke of promoting the arts and sciences in order to "preserve our present re-publican system of government." Both colleges had religiously mixed boards of governors without representatives of the state, but both received state support—Franklin initially through a large land grant and Dickinson through periodic appropriations. However, neither college built upon even an academy, where students might prepare for college. In Carlisle, student demand seemed to be misaligned with the college's attempted offerings; and in Lancaster the number of advanced students never equaled the forty trustees.[42]

The most redoubtable collegiate entrepreneur was certainly William Smith. Exiled from Philadelphia to Maryland's Eastern Shore, he soon gained control of the local academy and sought a college charter. In 1782 he managed to gather £5000 in gifts and secure a charter for Washington College. From the outset he envisioned a republican university but had to deal with the political realities of Maryland's Eastern and Western Shores. He proposed that a parallel college be established on the Western Shore and the two colleges be joined in an overar-ching University of Maryland. In 1785 this plan was realized: St John's College was chartered in Annapolis, the university was created, and both colleges were granted annual appropriations. Erected on established academies, each retained

---

41 Herbst, *From Crisis to Crisis*, 191–92, 221–22; Robson, *Educating Republicans*, 196, 246–48; Frank W. Blackmar, *The History of Federal and State Aid to Higher Education in the United States* (Wash-ington, D.C.: GPO, 1890), quote p. 178; Ollinger Crenshaw, *General Lee's College* (New York: Random House, 1969), 3–33.

42 Griffith, *Liberalizing the Mind*, 6–16; Sellers, *Dickinson College*, 51–76; see below.

its own board of governors, while the University of Maryland had a public board headed by the governor. Washington College was more of an upstart, but it had the indefatigable William Smith. He imposed the College of Philadelphia curriculum, including an English-language course. He continued to raise funds for a projected, large college edifice. And he persuaded George Washington himself to attend the 1784 commencement. St. Johns was delayed in opening the collegiate course until 1789, but at that juncture the entire scheme began to unravel. When Smith foresaw being reinstated at the College of Philadelphia, he promptly deserted his Maryland enterprise. Without the force of his personality, the Washington College edifice remained unfinished, and the trustees of the University of Maryland held no further meetings. As long as state support was forthcoming, St. John's persisted as a fairly robust college but Washington less so. However, with growing republican sentiment objecting to state support for "aristocratic" colleges, the subsidies were reduced and then terminated entirely in 1805. The first University of Maryland was abolished as well. This was a devastating blow to both colleges, which struggled to survive in the ensuing decades.[43]

In Massachusetts, regional factors explain the founding of Williams and Bowdoin colleges. The former emerged from the bequest of Ephraim Williams to establish a free school in what became Williamstown in the northwest corner of the state. The school was not launched until 1791, 36 years after Ephraim's death. But then the trustees immediately sought to raise it to a college. They were emboldened by a pending project to establish a college in the territory of Maine. Securing an experienced Yale tutor, Ebenezer Fitch, to head the school may have also boosted their confidence. In their petition, they emphasized a regional role: to educate boys from Western Massachusetts who might otherwise go to Dartmouth or Yale and to provide opportunities for nearby students in Vermont and New York (areas that soon had their own colleges). Williams College was chartered in 1793, a thoroughly Congregational school that the Commonwealth regarded as a regional state college. The state reserved rights to intervene for the good of the college and provided intermittent financial subsidies. The following year, protracted negotiations in Maine culminated in the chartering of Bowdoin College. It stemmed from a general desire among the educated class of fast-growing Maine for a college to buttress republican values. The chief obstacle was determining a location. When Brunswick was finally recommended, the charter quickly followed. However, this too was a case of starting from scratch, and 8 years passed before the college opened. Founded by sons of Harvard, Bowdoin

---

43 Geiger and Sorber, "Tarnished Icon," 20–23; Steiner, *History of Education in Maryland*, 69–117; George H. Calcott, *A History of the University of Maryland* (Baltimore: Maryland Historical Society, 1966), 8–15.

was governed like their alma mater by a corporation and overseers, and it too received state support as a regional state college.[44]

When Union College began operations in 1795, it was the first such institution chartered by the New York State Regents. Compared to the haphazard chartering elsewhere, their procedures appear deliberate and informed. Attempts to found a college in upstate New York began during the Revolution, as the growing population had no wish to attend King's, nor did the numerous Dutch Reformed parishioners favor Queen's. An academy was successfully organized in 1785 under Dutch Reformed auspices, but repeated requests for a college charter were denied, chiefly because of inadequate resources. In 1793 the regents finally granted a charter for Schenectady Academy, and the town then made a concerted effort to raise sufficient funds for a college. This effort enlisted all the area churches, which according to legend gave rise to the name "Union College." A final obstacle then appeared in the form of a competing petition from an academy in Albany. After lengthy deliberations, the regents decided in favor of Schenectady, and Union College opened later in 1795. Although the college resulted from mobilizing local energy and resources, it soon turned to the state for support. In its first decade it received far more income from New York State than from private donors, and the relative solvency of the college soon helped to make it the most vigorous of all these early foundings.[45]

All the colleges described above were regional institutions, resulting from local initiatives. In contrast, legislators in South Carolina originally addressed the challenge of republican education through a deliberate regional strategy. After failing to establish a college in Charleston during the colonial era, the state was beset after Independence by rivalry between the coastal plantations and the fast-growing inland piedmont. In 1785 a bill was passed chartering three colleges—two at existing academies in the up-country that never developed into colleges and one for the College of Charleston. The latter was favored with a grant of property and ex officio seats on its board for the governor and lieutenant governor. Thus, Charleston resembled a state institution, but it took a private effort to bring it to life. The Reverend Robert Smith, an Episcopal priest, was president of the trustees and principal of an academy. In 1789 he merged his academy with the college, bringing sixty pupils and becoming principal of the college. Scion of a wealthy family and educated at Cambridge University, Smith employed his own funds to rehabilitate the college properties, technically as a loan. Just as the

<hr>

44 Herbst, *From Crisis to Crisis*, 214–17; Frederick Rudolph, *Mark Hopkins and the Log: Williams College, 1836–1872* (New Haven: Yale University Press, 1956), 4–10; Charles C. Calhoun, *A Small College in Maine: Two Hundred Years of Bowdoin* (Brunswick, ME: Bowdoin College, 1993), 4–18.

45 Wayne Somers, *Encyclopedia of Union College History* (Schenectady, NY: Union College Press, 2003), 296–99 et passim.

college opened in 1791, though, state politics produced a new charter that made the college a private entity with a self-perpetuating board. The college thus lost any hope of future assistance from the state. Smith persisted in instructing his classes, and in 1794 six of the most advanced students were groomed for graduation. However, this was the high point for the early College of Charleston. The next year Smith was elected bishop of South Carolina, and his duties soon forced him to resign as principal. Without Smith's leadership and deep pockets, the college limped along, essentially as a grammar school. Difficulty in obtaining respected teachers tarnished its prestige, and a further blow fell in 1801 when the state finally chartered a true republican university in Columbia.[46]

★   ★   ★

The "college enthusiasm" that Ezra Stiles noted before the Revolution appeared to blossom after Independence. However, in a pattern that would long characterize the proliferation of American colleges, local backing for founding the early colleges far exceeded any willingness to support and sustain institutions once established. As a result, few were able to offer a full college course taught by competent instructors. Those that came closest to this standard largely depended on state support, irregular and undependable as it was. Their semirural locations yielded little private support and comparatively few students. This was certainly the case with the Virginia colleges, which struggled for many years to offer collegiate courses. The same was true for the Maryland colleges once state support was withdrawn, even for St. John's in the state capital. Williams, in remote Williamstown, soon found its putative region occupied with more accessible colleges. Although kept solvent by state support, the trustees long contemplated closing or relocating. Bowdoin opened later (1802) on a more solid footing, and Union College soon emerged as the strongest of the early colleges, benefiting from state patronage and the economic vitality of its region.

The weakness of the College of Charleston (it closed in 1811) raises the larger question of why colleges did not flourish in American cities. Of course, Harvard (always the exception), removed from Boston proper, was becoming the cultural focal point for the region's professional and commercial classes. But Rhode Island College was sustained by the patronage of the Brown family, not local students. Columbia and Pennsylvania rested on the support and patronage of rather narrow elites, and both declined badly after 1800 before stabilizing.

46   J. H. Easterby, *A History of the College of Charleston, Founded 1770* (Charleston: College of Charleston, 1935), 1–41; Colyer Meriweather, *History of Higher Education in South Carolina* (Washington: GPO, 1889), 56–58.

Charleston was a wealthy city, even if less wealthy than before the Revolution, and the area's leading citizens adorned the college's initial board of trustees. Yet, Robert Smith seems to have been the only one to provide financial assistance. Additional giving was needed to permit the now-private college to develop, but the Charleston elite not only turned their backs, Smith's heirs hobbled the college further by demanding repayment of his "loans." The College of Charleston in some ways presaged the inhospitable environment for colleges in American cities. Wealthy families often preferred to send their sons away to more prestigious schools rather than local upstarts (as did Charleston principal, Robert Smith) and thus had little incentive to support city colleges. For nonelites, early cities offered numerous educational alternatives, cheaper and more practical than a classical college. Local reputation is difficult to gauge, but it was all-important for contemporaries. It also took considerably more resources to sustain a city college than to keep a rural venture on life support, but the rural syndrome presented a different set of problems.

The perils of the new, inland colleges are exemplified by the experience of Dickinson, which was graphically described by its first principal, Reverend Charles Nisbet (1785–1804). Benjamin Rush sought to duplicate his coup of recruiting Witherspoon to New Jersey by enticing another learned Scottish divine. Nisbet was a friend of the new republic, having favored American independence. After much cajoling, he accepted the challenge of bringing the intellectual riches of his homeland, "the most learned nation in Europe," to the Pennsylvania back country. Disillusionment set in soon after he reached Carlisle, but he persisted with fatalistic resignation, while addressing a litany of complaints to numerous correspondents.[47]

The Dickinson College charter of 1783 vested all powers in the large board of trustees, which did not include the college principal. The trustees, led by Rush, proceeded to formulate an overloaded republican curriculum without so much as consulting Nisbet. To even attempt to cover all these subjects, professors were expected to lecture as much as 7 hours a day, leaving students no time for preparation. Not that Dickinson students needed such time since they had, according to Nisbet, "a decided aversion to books and learning." Moreover, the faculty had little means to influence this behavior. Among Rush's many strong prejudices was opposition to the collegiate way of living. He purposely had Dickinson students live in the town, even though that put them beyond the college's control. There was actually no alternative; given its premature launching, the college

<hr>

47 Sellers, *Dickinson College*, quote p. 117; David W. Robson, "Enlightening the Wilderness: Charles Nisbet's Failure at Higher Education in Post-Revolutionary Pennsylvania," *History of Education Quarterly*, 37, 3 (Fall 1997): 271–89.

occupied only the grammar school building for its first two decades. Nisbet's greatest frustration was nonetheless with the trustees, who had no conception of the Scottish universities he wished to emulate. In practice, the college was governed by the local trustees, who were most responsive to the wishes of students and townspeople. Students were poorly prepared for college study, with most needing work in the preparatory class. From the outset, however, the faculty had difficulty organizing the students into distinct classes, and the trustees did not help matters by tolerating loose standards, both for instruction and graduation. In 1798 students took advantage of trustee leniency by staging a strike to demand graduation after a single year of study. To Nisbet's horror, the trustees acquiesced. For 3 years students were graduated after only a year of classes. This spectacle not only destroyed the reputation of the school but deprived it of tuition revenue as well. The situation was finally addressed in 1800, and the college course was slowly rebuilt, first by extending it to 2 years. Despite his continual vexation, Nisbet was a conscientious teacher, sincerely devoted to his students. But his lack of control over students or curriculum guaranteed a low state of learning, irrespective of the primitive conditions.[48]

Dickinson differed from other new colleges in the exceptional qualifications of its head and the misguided schemes of its founder, but in other respects its ills were all too common.[49] Competent college leaders were scarce in the Early Republic, which was one reason for intrusive trustee control. Dickinson had its share of problems finding competent faculty. Nisbet's longtime colleague, professor Robert Davidson, lacked the wit to feel Nisbet's anguish.[50] The dominant role of trustees was written into most college charters, but when they sought to control daily affairs, especially student discipline, the results were usually detrimental, as they were at Dickinson. By the end of the century, the chief curricular challenge was no longer introducing republican content but rather preventing the collapse of the college course. Overt student resistance at Dickinson and Transylvania, where similar conditions existed, was only one obstacle, but material weakness and poor student preparation made it difficult to maintain a 4-year course in most new colleges. Ironically, sustaining a traditional course poorly, as had been done originally at Queen's and Dartmouth, seemed to cause fewer problems than republican curricular experiments. The audacity of student

48   Sellers, *Dickinson College*, 77–135, quote p. 87; Robson, "Enlightening the Wilderness," 285.

49   Nisbet described the weaknesses of American colleges in a letter to Alexander Addison (May 11, 1792): Alexander Addison Papers, 1776–1803, DAR.1925.06, Box 1, Folder 42: Special Collections Department, University of Pittsburgh: Robson, "Enlightening the Wilderness."

50   Reverend Davidson taught geography by having the students memorize an acrostic verse, where the first letter of each line spelled his name. He served the college loyally for 24 years and was regarded as a peacemaker, perhaps for acquiescing to student demands: Sellers, *Dickinson College*, 72–74, 94–95.

graduation demands was a portent of rising student resistance across all the colleges. At Dickinson and elsewhere, it often assumed a political dimension. Nisbet, a staunch Federalist, likened the students to the "French revolutionary crowd," infected by the "licentious . . . spirit of the present age."[51] In general, Federalists were concerned to uphold high standards of learning in the colleges, while Republicans opposed curricula and practices that contributed to "aristocratic" airs. By the end of the century, the polarization of American political life had spilled over into the colleges.

★   ★   ★

With the opening of the University of North Carolina in 1795, state universities emerged as a new type in American higher education. Consciously intended to be republican universities, they initially differed little from existing patterns of governance, finance, or organization. And they were afflicted with the same ills besetting previous new colleges. However, their identification with their states provided some sustenance and continuity in the longer term, though not without recurring controversy. This model proved most robust in the South, but only after 1800. At that date, historian David Robson observed, "those who advocated closer ties between colleges and state could point to no working model of a state institution."[52]

North Carolina made the most determined effort to create such an institution.[53] North Carolina Federalists took advantage of their ascendancy during the ratification of the Constitution to pass legislation establishing the university in 1789. Wishing to insulate the university from state politics, they established a self-perpetuating board of forty trustees. These trustees were chosen from the leading figures in the state, including the governor, but none served ex officio. With Enlightened federalist William Davie (CNJ. 1776) as the driving force, these conservative visionaries believed that overcoming the relative backwardness of their state required the education of republican leaders. Direct tax support was out of the question, but legislation gave the university the proceeds from confiscated and escheated lands. On this slender base, a remote location in the center of the state was selected, and work was begun to fashion a college and a town.

51   Robson, "Enlightening the Wilderness," 285.
52   Robson, *Educating Republicans*, 247.
53   Darryl Lynn Peterkin, *'Lux, Libertas, and Learning': The First State University and the Transformation of North Carolina*, Ph.D. Diss., Princeton University, 1995; Kemp P. Battle, *History of the University of North Carolina*, 2 vol. (Raleigh, NC: 1907), et passim; William D. Snyder, *Light on the Hill: A History of the University of North Carolina at Chapel Hill* (Chapel Hill: University of North Carolina Press, 1992), 3–37.

Despite the many obstacles, the university made notable progress. The curriculum the trustees devised for North Carolinians was "a more liberal plan than any in America." It emphasized English and science and made the ancient languages optional. When half of the initial students were found to be totally unprepared, a preparatory school was quickly created. The university soon had more than 100 students overflowing Old East, the first college structure. It established two literary societies and graduated its first class in 1797. Attracting effective teachers to rural North Carolina was an ongoing challenge, especially given low salaries. Lacking a suitable president, the trustees appointed a succession of presiding professors. The faculty generally were young, fractious, and in some cases they held unwelcome political views. Volatile faculty chemistry and lack of effective leadership led to a disastrous confrontation at the fledgling university. Students rioted in the summer of 1799, horsewhipping the presiding professor, threatening others, and generally running amok for a week before calm was restored. The riot was a blow to the reputation of the university and the hopes of its founders.

By 1799 Republicans had gained control of the General Assembly. They had consistently opposed the university for promoting "aristocratic" attitudes and decried the federalist monopoly of selecting trustees. At the end of 1799 they repealed the legislation that had granted the university escheated lands—its only source of public funds. The trustees now faced a double challenge of rebuilding a ruined college and reconstituting relations with the state. For the first, they turned to Reverend Joseph Caldwell, a graduate and former tutor of the College of New Jersey, who had been recruited in 1796 and had proved to be the most trustworthy member of an ill-fated faculty. Caldwell, who was just 27 in 1800, held the confidence of students, and under his direction enrollments began to recover. His principal reform was a classical course: Latin was made compulsory in 1801 and Greek, in 1804. That same year, Caldwell was named president and given a seat on the board. Financially, the university scraped by during these years, while suing the state to restore its revenues. In 1805 the repeal was overturned, but the General Assembly was not through; it modified the board of trustees, making the governor the president, adding fifteen members, and having succeeding members appointed by the Assembly. From this date the university resembled other American colleges in its course of study, while it constituted a true state university in its financial and governance ties to North Carolina.

By 1805, two other versions of southern state universities were operating, a weaker one in Georgia and a stronger one in South Carolina. Georgia had bequeathed its university a charter and a large land grant in 1785, but interest in launching a college developed only at the end of the century. The location chosen was far inland on the Georgia frontier, an admirable physical setting but extremely remote. The university obtained a credentialed president in Josiah Meigs, the science professor at Yale whose outspoken republicanism had made him unwelcome in Federalist Connecticut.[54] Meigs did well to establish a functioning college in a near wilderness. He installed the Yale curriculum with particular emphasis on science, and he managed to graduate the first class in 1804. The university had a dual governing structure: public representatives acted as overseers on the "Senatus Academicus," while the college was largely governed by a self-perpetuating board of trustees. This latter body, or its local representatives, resented Meigs's republicanism, his secularism, and, no doubt, his prickly personality. They forced him out of first the presidency and then his professorship. This was an ill omen. The university largely languished for another decade, beset by denominational rivalries and the hostility of legislators toward higher education of any sort.[55]

South Carolina adopted a different approach. Politically, the state was divided between wealthy planters in the coastal region and the rapidly growing population of the piedmont areas. In an effort to promote unity, political leaders resolved in 1801 to establish a state college where, the governor hoped, "the friendships of young men would be . . . promoted and strengthened throughout the State, and our political union be much advanced thereby."[56] The institution they created, South Carolina College, was unique in three important ways. First, it was placed in the heart of the capital, Columbia, and thus avoided the rural syndrome. Second, the board of trustees included the highest officers of the state and legislature, and the balance were appointed by the legislature: the government of the state and the college were essentially the same. Third, the state provided a generous appropriation to construct the college and annual appropriations to support it. Also remarkable, the governors placed academic distinction above politics or religion to build a strong reputation, intending no doubt to appeal to the state's leading families. For a president, they lured Jonathan Maxcy, president of Union College, with a substantial raise in salary ($2,500 vs. $1,500). Although a Baptist minister, Maxcy conformed to the secular regime of the college. The trustees also aimed high with unsuccessful professorial offers to John

---

54   William M. Meigs, *Life of Josiah Meigs* (Philadelphia, 1887): to hold his professorship Meigs felt compelled to address a long political testament to the Yale Corporation qualifying his support for France and upholding his patriotism, 39–42.

55   Thomas G. Dyer, *The University of Georgia: A Bicentennial History, 1785–1985* (Athens: University of Georgia Press, 1985), 9–28.

56   Daniel Walker Hollis, *University of South Carolina: Vol. I, South Carolina College* (Columbia: University of South Carolina Press, 1951), I, 3–73; quote Governor John Drayton, p. 17; Michael Sugrue, "'We Desired Our Future Rulers to Be Educated Men': South Carolina College, the Defense of Slavery, and the Development of Secessionist Politics" in Roger L. Geiger, ed., *The American College in the Nineteenth Century* (Nashville: University of Vanderbilt Press, 2000), 91–114.

McLean, the chemistry professor at the College of New Jersey, and Joseph Caldwell at North Carolina. Initially, the college had to settle for young instructors, mostly from northern colleges. Within 3 years, South Carolina College had more than 100 students, three professors and two tutors.[57]

South Carolina College was in many ways the embodiment of a republican university. The founders explicitly intended it to educate the leaders of South Carolina society and government—"a nursery for virtue and science, the two brightest pillars of republican government."[58] The state assumed responsibility for its governance and support. Only in curricular matters were the founders less ambitious. The classical course was adopted without Enlightenment embellishments (but also fairly light on Latin and Greek), and perhaps for that reason, the institution was named a college rather than a university. After 1805, republican rhetoric might still be invoked, and Thomas Jefferson's singular creation of the University of Virginia (opened 1825) was a retrospective tribute to that model; but what had been the dominant trend in higher education since the Revolution was effectively exhausted, overwhelmed by far larger movements—the advancing democratic spirit of the nation, the material weakness of the colleges, and the attenuated demand for the instruction they offered.

★ ★ ★

These realities can be glimpsed through contemporary eyes in an extraordinary work by Reverend Samuel Miller, *A Brief Retrospect of the Eighteenth Century . . . Containing a Sketch of the Revolutions and Improvements in Science, Arts, and Literature during That Period* (1803). In two volumes and more than 1,000 pages, Miller displayed enormously wide knowledge and his own sharp judgments of the intellectual history of Europe and America over the previous century. He was keenly interested in higher education and included histories and descriptions of the existing American colleges.[59] Overall, Miller judged that "what is called a *liberal education* in the United States, is, in common, less accurate and complete" than in Great Britain or some European countries. He ascribed the blame for this weakness to both the institutions and American society. "The great majority of our Colleges have very inadequate funds," and this resulted in too few professors having to cover "too large a field of instruction." Thus, "they can convey but

---

57   South Carolina College experienced a turbulent student culture and extreme ideological bias, but fulfilled the founders' intention of unifying state leadership: Sugrue, "South Carolina College." See chapter 6.

58   Hollis, *South Carolina College*, 35.

59   See Roger L. Geiger, "The Reformation of the Colleges in the Early Republic," *History of Universities*, XVI, 2 (2000): 129–82, esp. 130–33.

very superficial knowledge" to their students, even "if well qualified themselves, which is far from being always the case." These faults were exacerbated by college trustees, who, "either from their own ignorance, or in compliance with popular prejudice, have . . . contracted the time requisite for completing a course of instruction." As for American society, the "comparatively equal distribution of property in America, while it produces the most benign political and moral effects, is by no means friendly to great acquisitions in literature and science." Hence, there were "few persons of leisure," and students passed through "what is called liberal education [in a] hurried manner" in order to begin "practical pursuits." America also offered little "encouragement to learning." "There are no rich *Fellowships* in our Universities . . . [and] Academic chairs are usually connected with . . . small salaries." Further, "the *love of gain* peculiarly characterizes the inhabitants of the United States," which tends "to discourage literature."[60]

Miller praised the unprecedented intellectual achievements of the eighteenth century—"monuments of enterprise, discovery, and improvement . . . so numerous, valuable, and splendid, as to stand without parallel in the history of the human mind." He was hopeful as well that the impediments to learning in America were declining and conditions in the colleges improving. But he added an additional and telling critical note, praising the growing freedom of inquiry, but noting that it had also been "perverted and abused . . . carried to the extreme of licentiousness." Particularly since 1780, "deliberate and systematic attacks were made on Revealed Religion, through the medium of pretended science." "Infidel philosophers"—"prating about the . . . 'triumph of Reason,' . . . the 'prefectibility of Man,' &c. &c."—had "poisoned the principles and completed the ruin of millions."[61] Thus, while celebrating the advance of secular knowledge, Miller caustically rejected the hypertrophy of "Reason"—the ideology of the Enlightenment. In taking this position, he articulated one of the salient features of the dawning era: the attack on real or imagined radical doctrines stemming from the Enlightenment by the defenders of Protestantism. Toleration, it seems, expired with the eighteenth century and with it the ambiguous neutral ground between natural and revealed religion on which the colleges had sought to operate.[62]

60 Miller, *A Brief Retrospect of the Eighteenth Century*, quotes pp. II, 404–7.

61 Ibid., II, 410, 412, 431–33. Miller at this juncture was a 'liberal' Presbyterian, supporting Jefferson and republicanism; in the next decade he would join the Princeton Theological Seminary and be known for his conservative views: Chinard, "Landmark in American Intellectual History," 55–71.

62 That is, what Henry F. May has characterized as the "Moderate Enlightenment": *Enlightenment in America*. May depicts the reaction against the "Revolutionary Enlightenment" (223–77); the United States would have a succession of Enlightened presidents from 1801 to 1829, but May characterizes their actions as a "pattern of Enlightenment qualified by political caution" (312). May terms the assimilation of the Enlightenment in nineteenth-century colleges as the "Didactic Enlightenment": 337–58.

The chimera of republican universities might linger into the nineteenth century, even exhibiting occasional vital signs. However, its principal tenets were increasingly eclipsed after 1800. The notion of anointing republican leaders was engulfed by an egalitarian tide. The dream of universities encompassing all branches of useful knowledge was confounded by the weaknesses of actual colleges. State governments repudiated or ignored the institutions they had chartered. And Enlightenment optimism and values were discredited. Henceforth, pressure would increase to make learning in the colleges compatible with religious faith.

THE LOW STATE OF THE
COLLEGES, 1800–1820

ISTORIAN GORDON WOOD CAPTURED THE PERPLEXING transformation of the Early Republic:

> The popular social forces unleashed by the Revolution . . . transformed society and culture in ways that no one in 1776 could have predicted. . . . In many respects this new democratic society was the very opposite of the one revolutionary leaders had envisaged.[1]

The idea of equality overwhelmed the republican ideals of the founders. The colleges fit awkwardly with this egalitarian spirit. Insofar as they sought to educate gentlemen, who expected deference from social inferiors, they in effect promoted inequality. This role was instinctively defended in most colleges, given the prevalence of Federalist views. However, outside the citadels of Federalism, colleges were buffeted by countertrends, increasingly espoused under the banner of Jeffersonian Republicanism. Hence, Dickinson students wanted genteel credentials *fast*; the classical languages were attacked as markers of gentility; and popularly elected representatives reflected their constituents' disdain for colleges. The result was a growing disjunction between the republican foundations of the colleges and the society of the Early Republic.

This misfit was apparent in the waning of "college enthusiasm." Aside from the colleges mentioned in chapter 3, the first two decades of the century saw the opening of marginal frontier colleges that produced few, if any, graduates—four colleges in Western Pennsylvania, four in Tennessee and Kentucky, and two in Ohio. The three academies that received charters—isolated Hamilton in New York and the Roman Catholic seminaries of St. Mary's and

---

1 Gordon S. Wood, *The Radicalism of the American Revolution* (New York: Random House, 1991), 230.

Georgetown—fared little better.[2] College attendance was dismal as well. Although enrollment figures are approximations, colleges enrolled roughly 1 percent of white male cohorts before the Revolution, and they failed to recover to that level until the 1820s. The second decade of the nineteenth century was particularly weak, with growth in college enrollments failing to match population growth. The causes of this weakness spanned culture, careers, and knowledge.

The ascendant egalitarianism of American society had a dual effect on the colleges. Insofar as it challenged the cultural distinction of college learning, it fanned hostility largely outside of higher education per se. Where these forces acquired a foothold within colleges, as at Dickinson, they debased the content of education. This situation was complicated by the resurgence of religious faith known as the Second Great Awakening, which produced three distinct camps: rapidly growing popular denominations, led by Baptists and Methodists, who eschewed college-educated ministers completely and embraced the egalitarian spirit; Federalists and traditional Calvinist denominations, who sought to impose religious orthodoxy in the colleges; and a shrinking number of republican liberals, who defended the Enlightenment heritage of nondenominational toleration and openness. During these decades the proliferation of professional schools altered the relationship of colleges to subsequent careers. Medical schools grew and multiplied, and colleges sponsored formal schools of law. A greater impact came from schools of theology created for the education of ministers. In the eighteenth century, graduation from college was the preferred preparation for professional training in all these professions, but after 1800 students entered the new professional schools after some college study or none at all. The failure of republican colleges cut American institutions adrift from frontiers of advancing knowledge. Early nineteenth-century colleges harbored few outposts of learning.[3] Thus, an additional challenge, largely overshadowed by the larger social trends, was to reestablish footholds in the world of learning.

The first two decades of the nineteenth century were a time of disorganization and meager accomplishments for American colleges. As they adjusted as best they could to cultural crosscurrents and material wants, their foremost challenge stemmed from the students they were charged to instruct.

---

2 The most substantial colleges founded from 1800–1820 were Middlebury (1800), Bowdoin (1802), South Carolina College (1805), and Hamilton (1812). Some of the frontier colleges thrived after 1820. For a complete list, see Jurgen Herbst, *From Crisis to Crisis: American College Government, 1636–1819* (Cambridge: Harvard University Press, 1982), 244–53.

3 Stanley M. Guralnik, *Science and the Ante-Bellum American College* (Philadelphia: American Philosophical Society, 1975).

THE PROBLEM WITH STUDENTS

The economy of the Early Republic long struggled to overcome the loss and destruction of the Revolutionary years, initially handicapped by the anarchic Articles of Confederation. As the economy improved, pockets of wealth emerged among Southern planters, merchants in the nation's seaports, professionals in the larger cities, and enterprising land speculators. Though the country remained overwhelmingly rural, a rising tide of internal commerce, driven by what critics chastised as a mad pursuit of money, raised the standard of living for a growing portion of the population.[4] But much of New England faced rural overpopulation on marginal farmlands; and settlers pushing westward were hamstrung by primitive transportation. Despite the prevailing spirit of democratic egalitarianism, for the vast majority of young men, a college education was neither attractive nor feasible.

Although alternatives to the classical course were proposed and tried, the expectation persisted that a liberal education should be grounded on Latin and Greek. The only academic requirements for admission to college remained the ability to translate a few standard works from Latin and Greek into English and English text into Latin. Some knowledge of basic arithmetic was often required but not everywhere. Many students were prepared for college individually, usually by local ministers. Southern families often employed tutors for this purpose. Before the Revolution, numerous grammar schools had existed in New England to prepare students in Latin, but this system deteriorated from waning public support. In its place, increasing numbers of private academies were founded. First established by individual teacher-entrepreneurs, academies taught a broad variety of subjects to boys and girls at all stages of education. Latin and Greek were usually offered, but only for the boys and often only enough for college admission. At the other extreme, some of the stronger academies duplicated parts of the college course and prepared students for advanced standing. Academy instruction improved over time, but the system was widely regarded as inadequate for college preparation before the 1820s.[5]

Colleges prepared some students themselves, either in a preparatory class or with private tutors. However, the obstacles to this and other forms of preparation were largely economic. Living costs were the chief expense of schooling

---

4 Wood, *Radicalism*, 325–27; Idem., *Empire of Liberty: A History of the Early Republic, 1789–1815* (New York: Oxford University Press, 2009), 322–24, 702–8.

5 Kim Tolley calls the schools of single entrepreneurs "venture Schools" and reserves "academy" for chartered institutions, a distinction more evident after 1820: Nancy Beadie and Kim Tolley, eds. *Chartered Schools: Two Hundred Years of Independent Academies in the United States, 1727–1925* (New York: Routledge Farmer, 2002), 3–38.

away from home. At the College of New Jersey in the 1790s, a representative example, board alone was $70 per year, and room rent was another $16, compared to tuition of $24. Living expenses were paramount whether a student left home to study with a minister, at an academy, or at a college. Hence, families sought to minimize the time their sons would be away for schooling. Few families could afford the $100+ annual cost of even the least expensive college, and the same was true for the costs of preparing a son for college.

The result was a dearth of students for the colleges and a low and declining level of student preparation. Colleges had little choice but to set admissions standards exceedingly low. Students were admitted on the basis of an oral examination, usually administered by the president. These subjective judgments tended to conform to the realities of the available clientele. Partly for this reason, the freshman year was essentially remedial, devoted to polishing the students' Latin and Greek. However, students with solid training in these languages, often from an educated parent, met entrance requirements with ridiculous ease. George Ticknor qualified for Dartmouth at age 9, although he waited until 14 to enter as a junior. More generally, this created the problem of colleges "filled with children," in Samuel Miller's words. Students became younger after the Revolution so that by 1800–1810, the colleges had their most immature clientele ever. The median age for entrants at Columbia was 14, at Harvard, 15½, and at New Jersey, 16. The entering students at Union College in 1805 were aged 12, 13, 14, 14, 16, and 22. Since younger students were more boisterous and less serious about their studies, the immaturity of students was at the least detrimental to order and learning. Francis Wayland, future president of Brown, typified the plight of many when he joined the sophomore class at Union College in 1811 at age 15: he later lamented, "I was soon hurried into studies which I could not understand, and which I had little interest. . . . the social influences about me were bad."[6]

The immaturity of students was most pronounced at the established colleges. Students from families that could afford to prepare sons at reputable academies and send them long distances to college met the low admission requirements at an early age. Indeed, sons of wealthy families became more numerous among students at these schools. At the College of New Jersey, sons of farmers declined from a third before the Revolution to just 8 percent of students in the 1790s. Wealthy Southerners were especially conspicuous at Harvard, Yale, and New Jersey. Harvard, in particular, had the highest tuition and living costs, although it did provide some aid for indigent students. At Yale, southern students resented

---

6 Samuel Miller, *A Brief Retrospect of the Eighteenth Century*, 2 vol. (New York, 1803), II, 274; Francis Wayland, *A Memoir of the Life and Labors of Francis Wayland* (New York, 1867), 32.

associating with "sons of small farmers and mechanics"; they formed their own literary society and intimidated students who spoke openly against slavery.[7] Overall, only a few colleges catered heavily to the upper class. Harvard's affluent clientele continued to be joined by rural recruits from middling social backgrounds, and Yale probably tipped further in this direction with its traditional constituency from the Connecticut countryside.[8] The College of New Jersey, however, drew most of its students from a distance, indicating a predominance of wealthy parents. The majority of Columbia students after 1800 were sons of Manhattan professional families. And South Carolina College served the most elite student body among southern institutions, at least until the University of Virginia vied for that distinction. But if these colleges played a large role in status maintenance, higher education as a whole offered social and economic advancement for the majority of its students.

Middle-class sons in the larger towns, like Francis Wayland, were often able to prepare for college at local academies and do so at an early age. A substantial number of college students undoubtedly came from such backgrounds—from families pursuing a variety of urban occupations or possessing modest amounts of property. An alternative pattern of college going characterized the newer rural colleges, one similar to that of colonial Dartmouth. Many of their students came from regional farms and rural communities. Compared with other collegians, they struggled to finance their education, entered at a mature age, and often intended to become ministers. America was a nation of farmers, most of whom owned the land they worked and produced goods for market. This "rural middle class" also produced a surplus of sons who pursued livelihoods by moving West to new lands, migrating to cities, or obtaining an education. These boys were normally obliged to work on the family farm until 18 or 21 years of age, and their schooling was typically intermittent.[9] But, especially in New England, they were often fitted for college by local ministers. They formed a significant clientele for Dartmouth, Williams, Middlebury, and other New England colleges.[10] Rural

7   John M. Murrin, "Introduction," *Princetonians, 1791–1794* (Princeton, 1990), xvii–lvii, esp. xxxvii; Samuel Eliot Morison, *Three Centuries of Harvard* (Cambridge: Harvard University Press, 1936), 183–84, 200–201; Julian M. Sturtevant, *An Autobiography* (New York, 1896), 99–101.

8   Julian Sturtevant observed of the Yale College Commons: "the families of merchant princes of New York, Boston, and Philadelphia; of aristocratic cotton planters; of hard-handed New England farmers; of Ohio backwoodsmen, and even the humblest sons of daily toil were there, sitting at the same tables.... Yale College in 1822 was the most democratic portion of American society": *Autobiography*, 79–80.

9   Joseph F. Kett, *Rites of Passage: Adolescence in America, 1790 to the Present* (New York: Basic Books, 1977).

10   David F. Allmendinger Jr., *Paupers and Scholars: The Transformation of Student Life in Nineteenth-Century New England* (New York: St. Martin's, 1975); David M. Stameshkin, *The Town's College: Middlebury College, 1800–1915* (Middlebury: Middlebury College Press, 1985), 95–98.

colleges in Pennsylvania and points south clearly relied on a similar clientele. Remarkably, such students were able to finance a college education by living very frugally and piecing together support from parents, relatives, loans, and their own labor. For the latter, teaching played a crucial role, either to accumulate savings before college or earnings while attending. All the newer colleges expected a substantial part of their student body to be teaching during winter terms, and even Harvard and Yale long made accommodations for this practice. Later, Christian organizations provided some financial support to poor but pious students. The presence of these relatively poor students sometimes weakened the collegiate way of living at these colleges. More generally, it testifies to the openness of collegiate education, despite small enrollments, to a wide range of American youth.

Students from all social backgrounds brought a democratic spirit to the colleges that conflicted with the hierarchical authoritarianism of their eighteenth-century customs. Hence, the most pressing concern for the colleges at the beginning of the new century was maintaining control over their students. Pranks and misbehavior were endemic to colonial colleges, but perhaps only the rebellion against president Clap had lasting repercussions. Students apparently behaved with increasing license after the Revolution.[11] However, these difficulties failed to prepare colleges for the wave of prolonged and sometimes violent student rebellions that began at the turn of the century. At least eight colleges, enrolling the majority of students, suffered episodes of more or less collective student defiance of college authority.

The 1798 student strike at Dickinson and the 1799 riot at the University of North Carolina were harbingers of thirteen major confrontations in the next decade.[12] In 1802 students embarked on a destructive rampage at ardently Republican William & Mary, and when Nassau Hall burned shortly afterward, the trustees suspected arson and similarly blamed the disaster on student misconduct. At North Carolina in 1805 the trustees sought to enforce discipline by appointing student monitors to inform on their classmates, but instead this action provoked the "Great Secession" by the majority of the student body. At Harvard a series of confrontations culminated in the 1807 "Rotten Cabbage

11   Samuel Miller noted the disappearance of "a large portion of that *constraint* and *servility*, and of those *monkish habits*, which were formerly connected with the diligent pursuit of knowledge, and considered a necessary part of a system of study": *Brief Retrospect*, II, 273. Leon Jackson describes four periods of "protracted disorder" at Harvard between 1787 and 1793: "The Rights of Man and the Rights of Youth: Fraternity and Riot at Eighteenth-Century Harvard" in Roger L. Geiger, ed. *The American College in the Nineteenth Century* (Nashville: Vanderbilt University Press, 2000), 46–79.

12   Roger L. Geiger, "The Reformation of the Colleges in the Early Republic, 1800–1820," *History of Universities*, (2001): 129–81; Steven J. Novak, *The Rights of Youth: American Colleges and the Student Revolt, 1798–1815* (Cambridge: Harvard University Press, 1977).

Rebellion," after which forty students were expelled or withdrew. The same year the most damaging disorder occurred at the College of New Jersey. Students presented a petition to protest the expulsion of three classmates but were then suspended themselves for forming an "unlawful combination." The confrontation quickly escalated: soon 126 students were suspended, provoking a riot, student seizure of Nassau Hall, and the closing of the college. When it reopened a month later, just half of the previous students returned. The reputation of the college was besmirched and its president, hopelessly compromised. The rebellion of 1807 tipped the college into a downward spiral that endured for more than two decades.[13]

These three confrontations were representative of growing defiance of authority on the part of students and increasing intransigence by the colleges. Colleges had promulgated more rigorous college laws in the face of student disorders, and they responded to the rebellions by imposing even more draconian regulations and punishments. *Submission and control* was the prevailing approach to the challenge of managing students in an increasingly anachronistic organization. The eighteenth-century residential college, for all its strict rules and authoritarianism, had in practice been fairly loosely run. A certain level of student misbehavior was tolerated as natural and inescapable. Witherspoon had instructed his tutors to distinguish between "youthful foibles and follies, and those acts which manifest a malignant spirit, or intentional insubordination." [14] Despite official proscriptions, student testimony describes ample opportunities for excursions outside the college and revelry within. For tutors, policing the campus was a thankless job, fraught with tacit resistance and potential retaliation and more often than not performed in a perfunctory manner. Punishments were carefully calibrated to the offense through escalating degrees of public disgrace. Students might be admonished privately, in front of their class or the entire student body, before suspension or expulsion was invoked. The aim was to elicit remorse and penitence so that the transgression might be forgiven and the student restored to an honorable place in the college.

When colleges consciously heightened enforcement and punishments they touched off a vicious cycle; aggrieved students felt that they had been treated unfairly; and when their protests were rejected, they sometimes felt honor-bound to resist unjust authority. Students invoked republican rhetoric, no doubt rehearsed in their literary societies, to justify their "rights" and to decry

---

13   Novak, *Rights of Youth*, 16–37; Mark A. Noll *Princeton and the Republic, 1768–1822* (Princeton: Princeton University Press, 1989), 214–43.

14   Howard Miller, *The Revolutionary College: American Presbyterian Higher Education, 1707–1837* (New York: New York University Press, 1976), 260–68, quote p. 176; Geiger, "Reformation of the Colleges," 179, 86n.

the "tyranny" of despotic authorities. The notion of "honor," particularly strong among southern students, was often the catalyst in turning individual transgressions into collective defiance. And there were certainly bad eggs among the classes, as Wayland had noted. The pious Julius Sturtevant considered a number of his Yale classmates "dissipated and licentious," and found it "almost incredible that the body of the students should have been so deeply imbued with the spirit of hostility to the college government." Yet the troublemakers dominated their classmates "with a terrorism seldom surpassed."[15] On the other hand, in major confrontations the student spokesmen were often class leaders. A Princeton rebel, who later recanted, thought "the finest young men have refused to return," and the same was true of the North Carolina Secession. Harvard rebellions implicated future luminaries, including Ralph Waldo Emerson. A Harvard professor later mused:

> In college rebellions the students were always right as to principle, though injudicious in their modes of [behavior]. There was not one of those rebellions in which the leaders were not among the foremost in their respective classes, in character no less than in scholarship. . . . [T]here was no form of collective protest they could make, which was not deemed rebellious. . . . [16]

The alienation of students, both good and bad, was a sign of institutional failure, but the cause and the cure were far from evident.

Colleges took countermeasures against factors they associated with student disorders. New Jersey was certain that student affluence led to dissipated behavior, particularly drinking and disruptions. They enacted regulations intended to limit the amount of money a student could have during a term. Harvard later imposed a similar rule, although in neither case was it effective. Student drinking was a problem everywhere during a period that one historian has labeled the "Alcoholic Republic." Attempts to proscribe it were ubiquitous as well. At Princeton, the college got the New Jersey legislature to prohibit taverns and merchants from selling liquor to students. Colleges recognized the incongruity of enrolling very young students, and one by one established a minimum age for entry, usually 14. They also notified other institutions of the identity of expelled troublemakers, thereby creating an effective blacklist.[17]

15 Noll, *Princeton and the Republic*, 230–32; Sturtevant, *Autobiography*, 94–95.

16 Novak, *Rights of Youth*, 36; Morison, *Three Centuries of Harvard*, 208–12, 230–31; Andrew Peabody, *Harvard Reminiscences* (Boston: 1888), 84–85.

17 W. J. Rorabaugh, *The Alcoholic Republic: An American Tradition* (New York: Oxford University Press, 1979), 138–40; Noll, *Princeton*, 235–36; Miller, *Revolutionary College*.

Tightening discipline and control were universal reactions but scarcely effective. The ideal was to occupy all of a student's waking hours. As the new president of Union College, Eliphalet Nott (1804–1866), boasted in 1804, "the week is completely filled up with collegiate, the Sabbath with religious, exercises." His belief that "no college has ever furnished such complete security to the manners and morals of youth" soon proved illusory and, predictably, prompted measures to make the college laws even more stringent. Twenty years later, the liberal George Ticknor urged the same approach at Harvard, arguing that students were corrupted by too much free time and free movement: "the best moral discipline of students is that which is laid in the careful and wise occupation of all their time and powers."[18] At loosely run William & Mary, steps were taken after the riot to house all students in the college and to impose greater discipline, also with little success. The most feasible path open to colleges was expanding studies in the classical languages and their attendant recitations. This same approach might also address the low state and disorganization of the curriculum at the start of the nineteenth century. Thus, the University of North Carolina began to require first Latin and then Greek, and William & Mary did the same. For Dickinson's new president, Jeremiah Atwater, the means for enforcing discipline lay with an emphasis on piety and classical languages as well as strict college laws.[19] In truth, colleges were unable to offer anything better if they were to extend the college course to a respectable 4 years and keep students fully occupied.

Student invocations of republican rhetoric added a further dimension to the rebellions. The northern, Federalist press was quick to ascribe the havoc at William & Mary to Jeffersonian doctrines of politics and religion (though Jefferson had by 1802 distanced himself from the college). At New Jersey, proudly patriotic trustees were shocked to have the political faith of the Revolution turned against them. Their only explanation blamed the "loathsome deformity" of the Radical Enlightenment: "the clumsy sophistry of Godwin; the pernicious subtleties of Hume, and the coarse vulgarity of Paine."[20] Here, the path back to virtue was obvious—the Revolutionary heritage had to be united with Christian faith. Thus, student protests over rotten food and arbitrary punishments were subsumed in the ideological wars of the era through a condemnation of Enlightenment doctrines and assertion of the need for greater religious faith.

18 Novak, *Rights of Youth*, quote p. 22; Codman Hislop, *Eliphalet Nott* (Middletown, CT: Wesleyan University Press, 1971), 127–28; George Ticknor, *Remarks on Changes Lately Proposed or Adopted in Harvard University* (Boston, 1825), 42: reprinted in David B. Potts, *Liberal Education for a Land of Colleges: Yale's Reports of 1828* (New York: Palgrave, 2010), 193–218.

19 Novak, *Rights of Youth*; Miller, *Revolutionary College*, 280–83; Geiger, "Reformation of the Colleges," 156–61.

20 Noll, *Princeton and the Republic*, 236; Miller, *Revolutionary College*, 271–79.

Though governance through submission and control was a significant cause of student rebellion, the colleges vainly hoped that more of the same would provide a remedy. At Yale, rebellions persisted until 1830 and at Harvard, until 1834. At southern universities, rebellions could be triggered any time that the "honor" of students was seemingly impugned. In the North, rebellions ended only with the passing of the philosophy of submission and control and the dawning of a new era of collegiate life (chapter 6). Until then, greater emphasis on student piety seemed the only viable approach.[21] In fact, abandoning dangerous Enlightenment notions and reasserting Christian piety appeared to be an answer to many college ills. Moreover, it was consistent with the welling spirit of the Second Great Awakening.

THE SECOND GREAT AWAKENING AND THE COLLEGES

The wave of religiosity that washed over most of the United States after 1800 was fundamentally different from its predecessor. The First Awakening was a short-lived outburst of revivalist preaching that left a legacy of both conversions and opposition. The Second Awakening also was characterized by revivals, but revivals that began inconspicuously in the1790s and spread widely across the country. Preachers at the great Cane Ridge camp meeting of 1801, and the many frontier revivals that followed, induced the same spiritual euphoria as had Whitefield and Tennant. But in New England the revivals were quiet and orderly—and no less effective in converting souls. Thus, the Second Awakening had more than one face as it affected common people in small towns and countrysides as well as more educated and sophisticated inhabitants of population centers. The Second Awakening also endured—growing in confidence, coverage, and influence through the first four decades of the century. Two key conditions help to account for this growth. First, at the end of the eighteenth century a substantial portion of the population was "unchurched." Enlightenment influence was less responsible for this than that the establishment of churches had not kept pace with population growth, and ministers were in scarce supply. These last two conditions would change dramatically in the succeeding decades. Second, the Awakening was sustained by the creation of religious organizations. The churches themselves were only part of this. Operating separately or jointly, they spawned a network of voluntary societies to spread the gospel and holy causes

---

21   At both Yale and Harvard in 1823, pious students (including Julian Sturtevant) were provoked sufficiently to inform upon their miscreant classmates, at some personal peril: Sturtevant, *Autobiography*; Morison, *Three Centuries of Harvard*, 230–31.

far and wide in what was called the "Benevolent Empire."[22] The colleges played a central role in the institutionalization of the Awakening, a role that changed over time. The first decades of Awakening saw increasing denominational focus at most established colleges and the creation of theological seminaries as more intensive centers of religious activity. The next decades spawned renowned evangelists like Lyman Beecher and Charles Grandison Finney, temperance societies, abolitionists, the proliferation of denominational colleges, and higher education for women. Before long, the pervasive religiosity ignited by the Awakening transformed the world in which the colleges operated.[23]

The Second Awakening ignited a phenomenal expansion of the "popular denominations"—initially the Baptists and Methodists. The number of Baptist congregants was 65,000 in 1790 and 173,000 in 1810; the neophyte Methodists grew from just 5,000 at the time of the Revolution to 65,000 in 1800 and 130,000 in1806.[24] Both denominations recruited from the largely unchurched and uneducated common people, although in different ways. At the grass roots, Baptist expansion was driven by farmer-preachers, who experienced a call to the ministry, obtained licenses to preach, and gathered or assumed a community church. The Baptists were thus inherently decentralized, with regional "Associations" playing a minor role. Methodists, in contrast, were an offshoot of the Anglican Church, tightly organized under the authority of bishops. Their agents for reaching the people were dedicated circuit riders—ministers assigned to cover set geographical areas through recurrent visits. Where converts were made, "classes" were formed to maintain worship and religious instruction between visits of the circuit rider, thus forming the kernel of future congregations. Both approaches were well suited to expand with the westward movement of the population. Both churches propounded an optimistic Reformed theology, in which salvation was open to all on the basis of faith, validated in the conversion experience and moral self-improvement. Keeping teachings simple for their

---

22   Roger Finke and Rodney Stark, *The Churching of America, 1776–2005: Winners and Losers in Our Religious Economy* (New Brunswick: Rutgers University Press, 2006). By one count, eleven interdenominational benevolent societies were established between 1810 and 1827, including the American Bible Society (1816); American Tract Society (1825); American Home Mission Society (1826); American Colonization Society (1819); and American Sunday School Union (1824): *Quarterly Register* (Oct. 1828), 133.

23   For background, see Sydney E. Ahlstrom, *A Religious History of the American People* (New Haven: Yale University Press, 1972); Daniel Walker Howe, *What Hath God Wrought: The Transformation of America, 1815–1848* (New York: Oxford University Press, 2007), 164–202.

24   From only 19 percent of church members in 1776, these denominations claimed 55 percent by 1850, with Methodist alone claiming more than one-third of the national total. In striking symmetry, the formerly dominant churches (Congregational, Episcopalian, and Presbyterian) declined from 55 percent to 19 percent: Finke and Stark, *Churching of America,* 59, 56. Revivals were generally opposed by Presbyterians, Lutherans, and Episcopalians.

unlettered audience, they looked only to the Bible for spiritual guidance. Given this approach, sophisticated college-trained ministers were unwelcome.

When the American Methodist Episcopal Church was organized in 1784, Cokesbury College was founded at the same time. Located North of Baltimore, it was named for Thomas Coke, John Wesley's personal emissary from England, and Francis Asbury, head of the American church. Basically an academy, it offered an 8-year course, mandated by John Wesley himself, extending from elementary instruction to classical languages. A fair number of students enrolled, but the school was continually under water financially. In hope of relief, it applied for and received a college charter in 1794. However, the next year the college building was consumed by fire, most likely deliberately set. By that date, substantial opposition existed to Methodist collegiate education. A disillusioned Asbury wrote: "the Lord called not Mr. Whitefield nor the Methodists to build colleges. I wished only for schools; Dr. Coke wanted a college." [25]

For the next two decades, Methodism spread like wildfire due to the exertions of dedicated circuit riders. These soldiers of Methodist Evangelism were hostile toward educated ministers, and that feeling could be mutual. Revivalist Lyman Beecher, a Yale grad, dismissed these ministers as "generally illiterate men, often not possessed of even a good English education. . . . By them, as a body, learning is despised . . . they are utterly unacquainted with Theology." Reacting to such criticism, the General Conference in 1816 directed that its ministers, who above all had to be "approved unto God": "should add an ardent desire for useful knowledge. He should strive by every lawful means to imbue his mind with every science which is intimately connected with the doctrine of salvation by Jesus Christ, and which will enable him to understand and illustrate the sacred scriptures."[26] This was still a far cry from college education. However, the Church became increasingly concerned that more prosperous and educated worshipers would desert these benighted congregations for other faiths. Not until the late 1820s did the Church contemplate sponsoring colleges, and then the rationale was to educate the laity under Methodist auspices, not their ministers. The Methodists soon became the most prolific founders of colleges, but they did not create a seminary to educate ministers until 1847, and the practice remained controversial even after that date.

Frontier Baptist preachers felt no differently about college-educated ministers than the circuit riders with whom they often competed, but coreligionists

25 Bernard C. Steiner, *History of Education in Maryland* (Washington, D.C.: GPO, 1894), 229–45, quote p. 243; Finke and Stark, *Churching of America*, 76–84.

26 Sylvanus Milne Duvall, *The Methodist Episcopal Church and Education up to 1869* (New York: Teachers College, 1928), quotes pp. 43, 41.

in eastern cities had more ambivalent views. The Philadelphia Association had sent James Manning to found Rhode Island College (Brown University in 1804), which nevertheless enrolled few Baptists. Educated converts played a conspicuous role in the church leadership. Among the latter was Luther Rice, a graduate of Williams and Andover Theological Seminary, who converted to Baptism after dedicating his life to missionary work. Rice became a tireless fund-raiser and organizer within the denomination. His conviction that missionaries needed a sound education brought involvement with the Baptist Education Society. The position of eastern Baptists was just the opposite of the one the Methodists would later take: they sought better-educated ministers but not colleges. They consequently proposed "literary and theological institutions" in which literary studies were merely preparatory for separate ministerial training. Rice had persuaded the Baptists to support such an institution in Washington, D.C., but Congress refused to charter a religious institution. Instead, he obtained a charter for Columbian University (later George Washington University) in 1821 with the usual language of openness to all religions.[27] Still, eastern Baptists preferred ministerial to collegiate education. New York Baptists chartered the Hamilton Literary and Theological Institution (later Colgate University) in 1823 exclusively for the education of ministers, a restriction it retained until 1846. In 1818, the Maine Literary and Theological Institution (later Colby College) opened in Waterville with little support from local Baptists. It quickly reverted to the college that local Republican boosters had always wanted as a counterweight to Federalist Bowdoin. The college closed its theological department in 1825 when Massachusetts Baptists founded the Newton Theological Seminary.[28]

By then, the calculus of college founding was changing as the disadvantages of eschewing learning for salvation became increasingly apparent. Spreading the gospel to the common people had been possible only for Baptists and Methodists by dispensing with the kind of college-educated ministers that were deemed essential by traditional Reformed churches. The latter were handicapped in proselytizing the frontier, even with the aid of benevolent societies, precisely because of their reliance on scarce college-trained clergy.[29] Nonetheless, this first phase

27   Elmer Louis Kayser, *Bricks Without Straw: The Evolution of George Washington University* (New York: Appleton Century Crofts, 1970), 15–26; Jonathan Going, "Outline of a Plan for Establishing a Baptist Literary and Theological Seminary in a Central Situation in New-England," (Worcester, Mass.: September 1819). The decentralized Baptists soon splintered into numerous churches in keeping with the proliferation of denominations spawned by the Awakening, or, as Howe suggests, "awakenings": *What Hath God Wrought*, 180–82.

28   David B. Potts, *Baptist Colleges in the Development of American Society, 1812–1861* (New York: Garland, 1988). Maine boosters of Colby College were Republicans who sought a counterweight to Federalist Bowdoin.

29   Finke and Stark, *Churching of America*, 55–99.

of evangelical proselytizing laid a foundation for the subsequent proliferation of denominational colleges.

★　★　★

In contrast, the Awakening in established colleges placed great emphasis on theology and the more rigorous education of ministers. The individual who most fully embodied this academic phase of the Awakening was Timothy Dwight, president of Yale College (1795–1817). Just as John Witherspoon had made the College of New Jersey America's leading college by exemplifying the values of the Republican Christian Enlightenment, so did Dwight personify and advocate the spirit of the academic Awakening. He attacked the influence of the Radical Enlightenment and especially French infidelity, and he promoted an interpretation of Reformed theology suited to the times. Moreover, he rebuilt the curricular and extracurricular foundations of the college. In theology, politics, and pedagogy, Dwight laid the foundations that made Yale the largest and most influential American college until after the Civil War.[30]

Dwight, above all, exuded the evangelical combativeness of the new age. The grandson of Jonathan Edwards and always a New Light Congregationalist, he appreciated the learning of the eighteenth century while roundly condemning the secularism that had accompanied it. He combined personal charisma with powerful preaching and his own system of theology. These doctrines harmonized easily with the Awakening in New England—sufficiently conservative to assuage old-school Calvinists but presented with a zeal befitting his New Divinity grandfather. Dwight's theology was encapsulated in 160 lectures delivered to Yale students each Sabbath morning, forty per year, so that a student heard the entire system over 4 years of college. These lectures launched the New Haven Theology, a milder evangelical Calvinism, which was developed by Dwight's students, Moses Stuart, later a biblical scholar at Andover Theological Seminary, and theologian Nathaniel Taylor, pastor of New Haven's First Church. Yale graduates preparing for the ministry studied privately with Dwight, and in order to continue this training, Yale created a Theological Department (1822) 5 years after Dwight's death.[31]

The piety that Dwight sought to foster was reinforced by the faculty he selected. He specifically chose tutors who shared his outlook, including Stuart and Taylor. Three other tutors—Jeremiah Day, James Kingsley, and Benjamin

---

30   For Dwight's life: Charles E. Cuningham, *Timothy Dwight, 1752–1817: A Biography* (New York: Macmillan, 1942); for impact on Yale, Geiger, "Reformation of the Colleges."
31   Ahlstrom, *Religious History*, 415–20; discussed below.

Silliman—advanced to professorships, and each contributed to bolstering the Yale curriculum. Day raised the teaching of mathematics beyond the rudimentary level and authored a badly needed algebra text in 1814. Kingsley expanded Greek instruction beyond the New Testament by having students read the *Iliad* and later a larger Greek reader. Because of his piety and character, Silliman was selected by Dwight to study chemistry, despite having no background in the subject. He was sent to the University of Pennsylvania Medical School to learn the subject and later to England. Silliman became a prominent scientist, but like his colleagues, a dedicated pedagogue, lecturing chemistry to juniors, seniors, and medical students. With this faculty, Yale significantly upgraded the content of the college curriculum when most colleges were struggling to offer a 4-year course.

Dwight's selection of faculty deliberately created a remarkable homogeneity in politics as well as religion, and this ambiance affected students as well. Yale experienced the first student revival in 1801–1802, apparently with discreet encouragement from Dwight's pulpit. In 1807 a revival in New Haven, prompted by the preaching of Moses Stuart, spread to the college. Two more revivals occurred during Dwight's tenure, in 1812 and 1815, although by this time they were becoming more commonplace across New England. The proportion of Yale graduates entering the ministry actually declined slightly under Dwight, but the college above all graduated devout Christians who entered all the professions, particularly education.[32]

Dwight's theology informed his staunch Federalist views, including his implacable opposition to the French Revolution and to Jeffersonian Republicans. He argued insistently that once sound religion had been undermined, political and social stability would be imperiled as well. Hence, deism and even liberal Protestantism were tantamount to atheism and subversive of the social order. These views became a dogma of the Awakening, and Yale students were immersed in them, particularly in their senior years when Dwight guided most of their instruction. His recitations included long expositions of current issues. After one such class, Silliman confided to his diary that the president "gave the democratic societies a severe and deserved trimming."[33]

Despite his deep conservatism, Dwight succeeded as a teacher and disciplinarian largely because he rejected the prevailing approach of submission and control. His ultimate objective was not outward conformity but saving students'

---

32 George W. Pierson, *A Yale Book of Numbers: Historical Statistics of the College and University, 1701–1976* (New Haven: Yale University Press, 1983), 476; Brooks Mather Kelley, *Yale: A History* (New Haven: Yale University Press, 1974), 115–39.

33 George Park Fisher, *Life of Benjamin Silliman*, 2 vol. (New York, 1866), I, 42.

souls. Dwight was a dedicated educator who taught almost continually from his graduation from Yale at age 17 (1769). He felt a genuine pastoral concern for students as individuals, seeking to instill in them a true love of learning, moral behavior, and piety. Intellectually, he sought to engage students directly by challenging the correctness of their beliefs as well as those of the authors they read. His formidable presence was an asset. He was held in awe by Yale students and by the faculty, too. He used this charisma to institute what he called the parental system of discipline. Dwight largely discarded the entire eighteenth-century panoply of graduated public disgrace (admonitions). Instead of publicly admonishing offenders, Dwight gave them private, fatherly counseling. If problems persisted, he would employ his rhetorical powers to warn a student that he was "in danger." The next level would be to inform a student's parents and work with them to rectify the situation. If all else failed, students were sent home, pending credible evidence of penitence. Dwight held Yale students to a high standard. He was especially vigilant toward new students and quick to expel any who could not establish their good character. He was the first to devise student report cards to further engage parental influence. As far as he could determine, his parental approach was unique, and Yale alone experienced no student rebellions during the years of his presidency.

Imposing less external control over students and instead according them greater responsibility for their own moral conduct was the way out of the impasse of submission and control. However, that path was not an easy one even for Yale. Under Dwight's successor, Jeremiah Day, the personal engagement with students seems to have been lost, and the college experienced two serious riots.[34] But the basic features of Dwight's college endured, so that Yale soon provided the template for American colleges.

The success of Yale contrasts with the downward spiral of the College of New Jersey. Samuel Stanhope Smith (1795–1812), the son-in-law and heir to Witherspoon, was an almost exact contemporary of Dwight. Smith too had an imposing physical presence, came from a ministerial family, was a leader of the Church, in his case Presbyterian, and was also an ardent Federalist. However, unlike Dwight's dedication to theology, Smith's thinking was formed by the Moderate Enlightenment, with particular admiration for science. And where Dwight made his mission the rehabilitation of what he called "a ruined college," Smith sought to perpetuate the success of the revered Witherspoon. One more important difference: Dwight's early success earned him a free hand from Yale trustees; but New Jersey's mounting troubles brought growing intervention from an increasingly reactionary board.

34 Julian Sturtevant, *Autobiography.*

Above all, Smith upheld the views of the Republican Christian Enlightenment that had formed the dominant American ideology from the Revolution to the Awakening. In his own writings he sought to show how these elements, particularly science and religion, reinforced one another. In a piece that earned his induction into the American Philosophical Society—*An Essay on the Causes of the Variety of Complexion and Figure in the Human Species* (1787)—he championed the scientific method of "minute and careful" observation of nature and then argued that such an approach showed that climate could account for variety in the human species. "Science" thus supported the biblical account of the unity of humanity and also vindicated the moral laws of human nature posited by the Scottish Common Sense philosophy. These same values shaped the college course. Smith's tenure began with the hiring of John Maclean, a well-trained scientist from Scotland, as professor of chemistry—the most exciting scientific field of the era. Smith sought to deemphasize classical languages, largely confining them to the first year, and devote the rest of the course to "the most *useful* branches of literature & science." In 1799, the board approved admitting certificate students for only scientific and English-language courses. Smith thus promoted the modernization of the curriculum during the heyday of republican universities. [35]

The election of Thomas Jefferson and the gains of the Democratic-Republicans prompted deep forebodings in Princeton, no less than New Haven. And the reaction was much the same: a growing conviction that education and learning, when unrestrained by religion, could be dangerous to the social order. Smith shared these views, but conservative trustees would ultimately act upon them. The burning of Nassau Hall in 1802 was interpreted as a confirmation of this pessimistic vision. Smith attributed it to the "progress of vice and irreligion." The Princeton community nevertheless rallied to support the rebuilding of Nassau Hall, and the college briefly prospered. But trustees, emboldened by the spreading spirit of the Awakening, were increasingly critical. They were especially concerned with the small number of graduates entering the Presbyterian ministry. The student rebellion of 1807 then confirmed their worst fears. From that point, the most conservative trustees dictated the fate of the college. In 1812, they forced Samuel Smith to resign and fired John Maclean as well. [36]

With the revolution of 1812, the Awakening triumphed over the Enlightenment in Princeton. Smith was replaced by Reverend Ashbel Green (1812–1822), a longtime trustee and Smith critic, who had consistently sought greater religiosity

35   Noll, *Princeton and the Republic,* 115–19, quote p. 130.
36   Noll, *Princeton and the Republic,* quote p. 158.

in the college. As president, his foremost objective was to improve the "deplorable state" of the college through spiritual renewal. He succeeded in fostering a long-sought revival in 1815, but it was sandwiched between student rebellions in 1814 and 1817. His unsurprising response was to make the draconian college laws even more draconian. Green explicitly sought to displace his predecessor's influence by purging Smith's writings from the curriculum. Unlike Dwight, the Presbyterian trustees at Princeton associated science itself with the enemies of religion. After Maclean was sacked, less science was taught. Instead, instruction in Latin and Greek was enlarged, extending through the senior year, and mandatory Bible study was introduced. The most enduring achievement of 1812 was the founding of the Princeton Theological Seminary. After 1807 both Green and fellow trustee, Samuel Miller, sought to establish an institution for the education of Presbyterian ministers "uncontaminated by the college." With the backing of the Church and the college trustees, they created a seminary that had full use of the college facilities but an entirely separate governing board. Archibald Alexander, a rigid old-line Calvinist, was appointed as the first professor, soon joined by Samuel Miller (now an archconservative). Ashbel Green became chairman of the seminary board of directors. The new regime at the College of New Jersey continued to honor the legacy of Witherspoon (Green would later write his biography), but two elements of the Republican Christian Enlightenment were now overshadowed: the sacred had eclipsed secular learning, and the college no longer aspired to educate leaders for the Republic but rather pious members of the Presbyterian Church.[37]

Liberal Harvard was virtually alone in defying the waxing spirit of the Awakening, but the impetus for this development did not come solely from within. Congregationalists in and around eastern Massachusetts increasingly sympathized with the latitudinarian openness of Anglicanism, which perpetuated the outlook of the Enlightenment. After the Revolution exorcized the English Church, they gradually abandoned the theology of Reformed Protestantism in favor of Unitarianism—what Emerson called the Boston religion. By 1800 all but one of the Boston churches were led by such liberal ministers, and they were patronized by the city's wealthy merchants. Indeed, the fusion of the area intellectuals, led by the ministers of the liberal Boston churches, with the region's prosperous merchants created the cultural class known as the Boston Brahmins.[38] The rapprochement with Harvard had been gestating since the college

---

37   Noll, *Princeton and the Republic*, quotes pp. 273, 268. Enrollment at the College of New Jersey had been more than 200 in 1807, but it steadily declined to near 70 in the 1820s; at that juncture there were more than 100 students in the Princeton Theological Seminary: Thomas Jefferson Wertenbaker, *Princeton, 1746–1896* (Princeton: Princeton University Press, 1996 [1946]), 144–80.

38   Peter S. Field, "The Birth of Secular High Culture: *The Monthly Anthology and Boston Review* and Its Critics," *Journal of the Early Republic*, 17 (Winter 1997): 575–609.

allied with Boston Federalists after the Revolution. When the longstanding split between liberals and more orthodox Congregationalists came to a head at Harvard, a Brahmin Corporation tipped the college toward Unitarianism.[39]

In 1803 Hollis Professor of Divinity David Tappan died, and before a successor could be named, President Willard succumbed as well. Battle lines were clearly drawn, but intrigue over the candidates persisted for almost 2 years. The orthodox party, led by Hebrew Professor Eliphalet Pearson, insisted that only a Calvinist could meet the stipulations of the Hollis chair and felt the same was true for the presidency, which Pearson coveted for himself. Regardless, a Unitarian, Henry Ware, was nominated by the Corporation and overwhelmingly confirmed by the Overseers. Shortly afterward, a similar process made liberal-Unitarian Samuel Webber president of Harvard (1806–1810). To the dismay of most New England Congregationalists, and Pearson, who resigned in disgust, the college was now solidly in Unitarian hands, estranged from its Calvinist heritage. The decisive votes by the Corporation and Overseers, however, indicate that this change was the work of the Brahmins—now the core constituency of the institution.[40]

Harvard's 1806 reorientation had far-reaching consequences for both sides. Freed from the incubus of Calvinism, the liberal-Unitarian constituency would spur the development of Harvard into the most fecund center of secular learning in nineteenth-century America. However, the spirit of the Awakening also found a champion as Congregationalists came together to found the Andover Theological Seminary, the first graduate school for ministerial education and a center of learning in its own right.

The spurned Eliphalet Pearson avenged his rejection by convincing a donor to redirect a large bequest for ministerial education from Harvard to Phillips Andover Academy, where it supported a professor of theology. Offering an institutional alternative for training ministers required enlisting the support of the different factions of Congregationalists, ranging from Old Lights to New Divinity. Unity of sorts was accomplished through the efforts of the combative and influential Jedediah Morse, the Yale-trained minister of John Harvard's old church in Charlestown and a noted geographer. The specter of Unitarianism not only motivated Congregationalists to overlook their previous differences, but ultimately allowed them, at least temporarily, to propound an evangelical faith with a single voice. To bypass the need for a separate charter, the seminary was attached to Phillips Andover and soon attracted funds

39 Peter S. Field, *The Crisis of the Standing Order: Clerical Intellectuals and Cultural Authority in Massachusetts, 1780–1833* (Amherst: University of Massachusetts Press, 1998).
40 Ibid., 111–40.

for buildings and three professorships. The speaker at the 1808 opening ceremony was Yale's Timothy Dwight, thus signaling the backing of Connecticut Congregationalists for the Andover coalition. The important role of theological seminaries will be examined in the next section. However, the emergence of Andover Theological Seminary as the "West Point of Orthodoxy" was a major asset to the academic Awakening. It possessed a learned and aggressive faculty, and it soon had more than 100 enthusiastic students. Initially allied with Yale, it became a major force in the advance of Reformed evangelical Protestantism.[41]

The evolution of Harvard as a predominantly Unitarian college accelerated after John Thornton Kirkland became president (1810–1828). One of Boston's liberal ministers, Kirkland also belonged to a group of like-minded gentlemen who formed after 1804 around the *Monthly Anthology*. They sought to cultivate the "literary profession" and looked to the "University at Cambridge" to further this end. Indeed, Kirkland's presidency was a major turning point in Harvard history, the beginning of the Augustan Age of Brahmin ascendancy.[42]

Unlike any other contemporary college, Harvard experienced extraordinary prosperity and expansion in the decade after Kirkland's appointment, thanks to the generosity of Brahmin donors and a 10-year appropriation (1814–1824) from a fleeting Federalist majority in the legislature. The Brahmins fully concurred with Kirkland's wish to create a "university on the extended plan . . . as a place of systematic education to the three principal professions."[43] Accordingly, the flow of their gifts permitted the medical school to be moved to Boston and put on a solid basis, the Divinity School to be realized by 1819, along with initial professorships in law. As for literary aspirations, Kirkland sponsored four faculty prospects to study at Göttingen and elsewhere. All would experience frustration in attempting to introduce European learning into the prevailing college pedagogy, but at least one, George Ticknor, established a tradition of scholarship in modern literature. By 1821, the college had 10 professors—none Congregationalist, all but one with some postbaccalaureate training. Most were, nevertheless, uninspiring pedagogues in a profession that did not yet offer prestigious careers. The nearest thing to a professional academic was an amateur

41   Natalie Ann Naylor, *Raising a Learned Ministry: The American Education Society, 1815–1860*, DEd Diss. Teachers College, Columbia University, 1971, 170–77; Ahlstrom, *Religious History*, quote p. 394.

42   Samuel Eliot Morison, "The Great Rebellion in Harvard College and the Resignation of President Kirkland," *Publications of the Colonial Society of Massachusetts* (April 1928): 54–112.

43   [John Kirkland], "Literary Institutions—University," *North American Review*, 7 (July 1818), 270–88, quotes pp. 276, 277: According to McCaughey ("Transformation," 247n, below note 44), Edward Everett actually wrote this piece.

naturalist who held the chair in Natural History.[44] Creating a true university would prove more difficult than the Anthologists had imagined, but as early as 1820 Harvard was the centerpiece of a network of private, Brahmin-dominated cultural institutions.

The Awakening made the long-standing split among Massachusetts Congregationalists into a permanent gulf. While verbal warfare between the two sides produced "one of the best theological discussions of human nature in American church history," the two sides had quite different aims. The goal of Andover was to define and enforce the precise doctrines of the correct Reformed theology. These beliefs were specified in the Andover Associate Creed, to which all teachers had to subscribe—initially and every 5 years. The oath-takers swore, among other things, their complete opposition, "not only to Atheists and Infidels, but to Jews, Papists, Mahomatans, Arians, Pelagians, Antinomians, Arminians, Socinians, Sabellians, Unitarians, and Universalists." In contrast, Unitarianism was a highly moralistic viewpoint that wished above all to dispense with theology. Its ministers expounded their own logical and rational interpretations of scripture with complete tolerance for the interpretations of others, if offered in the same spirit. The ascendancy of Brahmin culture under president Kirkland institutionalized toleration and intellectual values at Harvard. It also set a course away from the quasi-public nature of the institution toward private control by that same coalition.[45]

THE RISE OF PROFESSIONAL SCHOOLS

The relative decline of the colleges in the first two decades of the century coincided with the formation of an entirely new sector of professional schools. These schools could be alternatives or complements to existing colleges, depending on circumstances. Most important, they represented different paths of preparation for the professions than college graduates had traditionally pursued. They might be organized as separate institutions or connected, often nominally, with colleges. And they might train students who had graduated from college, had some college study, or had none at all. Professional education has generally been shaped by a reciprocal relationship between education, training, and entry credentials, on one side, and standards of practice upheld by gatekeeping bodies on the other. In the Early Republic, these conditions varied considerably from state to state. In

44   Robert McCaughey, "The Transformation of American Academic Life: Harvard University 1821–1892," *Perspectives in American History*, VII (1974): 239–332; David B. Tyack, *George Ticknor and the Boston Brahmins* (Cambridge: Harvard University Press, 1967).

45   Ahlstrom, *Religious History*, quote p. 397; Field, *Crisis of the Standing Order*, quote p. 168; Ronald Story, *Harvard and the Boston Upper Class: The Forging of an Aristocracy, 1800–1870* (Middletown, CT: Wesleyan University Press, 1980).

freewheeling Kentucky, Transylvania University offered medicine and law almost from its opening in 1799; but in Massachusetts entrenched professions had to be reckoned with. The schools themselves were often small and short lived, and the patterns were quite different for each of the "noble" professions. It would take more than a century before modern postgraduate education in university professional schools finally crystallized, but movement began in these decades.

The same conditions that constrained college attendance affected demand for professional training. The limited resources of many students made them seek quick and cheap access to careers. The prevailing egalitarianism, espoused by Republican legislators, encouraged relaxed access to the professions and professional schools. Ready opportunities enticed students to bypass collegiate education. This trend was furthered by the high cost of professional preparation, at least in law and medicine. The overall situation undermined the colonial pattern, whereby students attended college to become gentlemen and then chose a profession to earn a livelihood. Noah Webster in 1828 defined "gentleman" as a courtesy title applied to "men of education and good breeding, of every occupation."[46] In egalitarian America, the status of both gentlemen and professionals became increasingly fluid. Nevertheless, the professions were the destinations of the majority of college students, and the colleges largely identified with that role.

GRADUATE CAREERS. The careers of college graduates are known chiefly from the biographical records compiled by institutions or devoted alums. As valuable as these records can be, they are still limited. By naming a single career, they tend to overcount the well-defined noble professions. Most Americans, including college graduates, lived in small towns, where they were more active in commercial life and local government than these single categories would indicate. Tabulations of graduates also omit attendees who did not receive a degree. At the College of New Jersey, for example, where nongraduates have been traced, 70 percent of students graduated in the 1790s, a figure undoubtedly above the average.[47] The rise of professional schools and the weakening link between college graduation and professional careers meant that colleges had little influence on the professions. Thus, these records tell more about the careers of the people who went to college than about those who practiced the professions in American society.

---

46 Quoted in Wood, *Radicalism of the American Revolution*, 345.

47 Colin Burke has given more complete occupational designations to a more limited sample of graduates from all regions: *American Collegiate Populations* (New York: New York University Press, 1982); John M. Murrin, "Introduction," *Princetonians, 1784–1790*, Ruth L. Woodward and Wesley Frank Craven, eds. (Princeton: Princeton University Press, 1991). The percentage of nongraduates varied considerably at CNJ and across the colleges.

The largest compilation of graduate careers for the northern colleges indicates how students responded to trends in American society.[48] The proportion of graduates entering the ministry fell from one-third in the 1760s to near one-fifth in the 1790s. The number of graduate lawyers did not rise appreciably until the Revolution but jumped substantially from near 13 percent in the 1760s to almost 30 percent in the 1790s. Independence and the high tide of the American Enlightenment favored secular careers. Lawyers were especially favored by the collapse of colonial governments and the formation of state judiciaries. Graduates during the Revolutionary years entered "public service" in large numbers (almost 6 percent, 1771–1785), but not the next generation (1.35 percent, 1786–1800), who may have suffered from the unpopularity of their predominantly Federalist sympathies. Prospects for ministers, in contrast, were dismal in the last decades of the eighteenth century. Minister-graduates of the College of New Jersey had been 48 percent of the pre-Revolutionary classes but fell to 15 percent afterward (1784–1794). Worse, only about one-half of them had successful careers. Yale experienced a drop of one-third in minister graduates in these years (from 36 to 24 percent), and the later graduates tended to be New Divinity adherents whose abstruse theology found favor with few congregations.[49] Comfortable pulpits were in short supply for graduates of these colleges, and the substantial shortage of educated ministers in more rural territories was met to some extent by graduates of the newer colleges, who persisted longer in choosing clerical careers.

This preference for law over the ministry continued into the nineteenth century before the Awakening affected graduate careers. Among all northern colleges, lawyers outnumbered clergy almost 3:2 from 1800 to 1815 but then were exceeded by ministers for the next 25 years. Those years—from 1815 to 1840—represented the high tide of Awakening piety generally. These data are striking evidence of the gradual spread of Awakening influence and its dominant influence on American culture during that quarter-century. This period also saw the founding of large numbers of theological seminaries. Dartmouth experienced the most dramatic shifts: It sent the majority of its students into the ministry until almost 1790; then lawyers outnumbered ministers 3:1 from 1800 to 1815; but ministers then overtook lawyer graduates until 1840.[50] This same basic pattern is evident for large producers of ministers, like Williams and

---

48 Bailey B. Burritt, *Professional Distribution of College and University Graduates*, U.S. Bureau of Education Bulletin, 1912: No. 19. This discussion also draws upon Murrin, "Introduction"; Burke, *American Collegiate Populations*, and Gerald W. Gewalt, *The Promise and the Power: The Emergence of the Legal Profession in Massachusetts, 1760–1840* (Westport, CT: Greenwood, 1979).

49 Murrin, "Introduction," lvi; Morgan, *Gentle Puritan*, et passim.

50 The conflict between liberal and religious viewpoints at Dartmouth is discussed in the next section.

Middlebury, as well as more modest producers, like Union and Bowdoin.[51] The limited evidence available for Southern colleges suggests that they mirrored the national pattern in part, but that state universities prepared fewer clergy. Those universities produced a consistently high proportion of lawyers and even more planters—together a majority of southern antebellum graduates.

MEDICAL SCHOOLS. In 1800 the United States counted five aspiring medical departments, all linked with universities. The medical department of the College of Philadelphia operated almost continuously through the Revolutionary War, surviving the vicissitudes of its host until the University of Pennsylvania emerged in 1791. The Harvard medical department was proudly begun in 1783 but suffered from a feud between its two principal professors and the remoteness of Cambridge from Boston's flourishing medical community. Columbia revived the medical school of King's College, but it too languished like its predecessor. Transylvania University attempted to incorporate medical instruction within its original structure in 1799. And at Dartmouth, Nathan Smith began lecturing in a one-man medical department. A decade later, Columbia's school was about to fold, displaced by the independent College of Physicians and Surgeons; Transylvania's effort was still not organized; Smith was about to decamp to Yale; and Harvard finally resolved its difficulties by moving to Boston. In Philadelphia, however, the medical school of the University of Pennsylvania was not only thriving, with 400 students, it was the largest institution of higher education in the country.[52]

The primacy of the Penn medical school stemmed from its large and eminent faculty and its continuous operation. Unlike colleges, the reputation of individual professors proved a powerful draw for students of professional schools. Benjamin Rush emerged as the most influential medical educator of the era, but his colleagues were European trained and had respected reputations of their own. Philadelphia was also accessible to students who could afford it. Penn consequently attracted the bulk of the relatively wealthy and mobile students in the first two decades of the century. Enrollments touched 500 in the mid-1820s, when Penn was teaching one-fifth of the nation's medical students, and enrollments remained near that level for the remainder of the antebellum period. In

---

51 The number of graduate ministers was undoubtedly boosted by the American Education Society: see below and note 47.

52 George W. Corner, *Two Centuries of Medicine: A History of the School of Medicine, University of Pennsylvania* (Philadelphia: Lippincot, 1965); William Frederick Norwood, *Medical Education in the United States before the Civil War* (Philadelphia: University of Pennsylvania Press, 1944), 63–86; Edward Potts Cheney, *History of the University of Pennsylvania, 1740–1940* (New York: Arno Press, 1977), 207–16.

many years the majority of students were from the South. Even after medical schools were established in southeastern states, a large proportion of antebellum southern doctors held MDs from Penn.

The Penn medical school established the template for medical education in the United States. The basic subjects of medical education—and chairs in the school—were anatomy, surgery, theory of medicine, materia medica (or pharmacy), chemistry, and midwifery. These were the chairs at the University of Edinburgh as well as the College of Philadelphia, and subsequent adjustments merely complemented this core.[53] Students purchased tickets for lectures in these subjects for a term of 4½ winter months. A full medical course consisted of attending the same lectures for 2 years because, "no ordinary capacity . . . and no ordinary memory [is adequate] to the recollection of a full course of medical instruction by attendance upon a single course of lectures."[54] To graduate, students needed to pass an oral examination and write a thesis. To practice medicine, a graduate was expected to have at least 2 years of apprenticeship as well. All this was expensive. Tickets to lectures were $20 for each of the six courses. Fees for matriculation and graduation could add another $50; and living in Philadelphia was dear. But a complete medical education required more. There were separate fees for clinical instruction, and dissection could be learned only from private courses of anatomy with cadavers. The professors charged hefty fees to accept students as their own apprentices. Student expenses for one term have been estimated at $300 to $400 (compared with $100 minimum for a year at most colleges). Largely because of the expense, only a small percentage of students graduated with MDs at the beginning of the century, but over time the number of graduates rose substantially.

On the other side of the ledger, teaching in the medical school could be enormously lucrative for the professors, who pocketed almost all the fees. Here lay the source of weakness for antebellum medical education. The professors of the Penn medical department were the best of their day, not only in training and mastery of their subjects but also in dedication to the medical profession. However, their reliance on fee income made the medical department essentially a proprietary institution.

The financial arrangement hobbled the development of the curriculum. Professors earned fees for their lectures, but lectures by themselves were scarcely adequate preparation to practice medicine. Clinical medicine was necessarily

---

53 William G. Rothstein, *American Physicians in the Nineteenth Century: From Sects to Science* (Baltimore: Johns Hopkins University Press, 1985), 88–93. These subjects remained the basic fields of medical education in 1847, when the American Medical Association was formed, with the sole addition of "physiology and pathology," which had formerly been called the "institutes of medicine."

54 Corner, *Two Centuries*, p. 74.

slighted, and only a few students learned surgery at private anatomy courses. Nor could the apprenticeships available to most students provide the sophisticated knowledge that professors could potentially teach. On a personal level, changes in course requirements or chairs could have a significant impact on the earnings of professors. The Penn faculty, for example, divided over whether or not obstetrics should be required for graduation. Such issues, not to mention the large egos of medical professors, generated bitter rivalries within medical schools. At Penn, professors so distrusted each other's questioning of graduation candidates that examinees were placed in a specially constructed "green box" to conceal their identities. The worst consequence of professorial profit motives stemmed from the effects of competition: when enrollments were threatened by competitors, the response was invariably to lower requirements. Standards declined as medical schools defended market share. At Penn, this process was discernible as early as 1789–1791: competition between the state institution and the resurrected college prompted the dropping of the Latin requirement, opening the door to students who had not attended college. In 1811, when the new medical college in Baltimore threatened to siphon off southern students, the requirements in math and natural philosophy were ended. Previously, the Medical Department had asked the state to strengthen licensing requirements for medical practice; however, the refusal of Pennsylvania—and other states—to uphold licensing standards left medical schools defenseless against this race to the bottom. In 1847, for example, in support of the newly formed American Medical Association, the Penn department extended its course to 6 months. No other medical schools followed this example, and in 1853 the course was reduced back to the standard 4½ months. All the problems, so evident at the country's best medical school, were far more pernicious at the growing number of new schools.

Twenty-six new medical schools were organized from 1810 to 1840. Only a handful of these were associated with universities, like the Yale medical department that opened in 1813. More typical was the Medical College of Baltimore, which was organized and incorporated in 1807 by local doctors as an independent proprietary undertaking. This venture soon assumed the mantle of the University of Maryland and was quite successful for about two decades. It recruited respectable occupants for six chairs, acquired a building, and received state aid. However, it then descended into schism, tumult, and lawsuits of the kind that afflicted most urban proprietary medical schools.[55]

55   The University of Maryland chartered in 1813 was unique in attempting to create a four-faculty university on the proprietary medical school model. The College and Divinity School never functioned on this basis, and the law school was a short-lived, single-person effort. The "university" thus consisted of the medical school: George H. Callcott, *A History of the University of Maryland* (Baltimore: Maryland Historical Society, 1966), 16–83.

Country medical schools represented another distinct type, adumbrated by Nathan Smith's solo effort at Dartmouth. Rural schools usually consisted of only a handful of teachers and had no access to hospitals for clinical instruction. They nevertheless subsisted by attracting regional students who could scarcely afford the better urban schools. One exemplar, Castleton Medical College, received a charter from the state of Vermont in 1818. Organized by local doctors, it was proudly supported by townspeople and associated for a short time with Middlebury College. Castleton enrolled more than 100 students for most of its four-decade existence, a larger enrollment than most liberal arts colleges. In the 1830s it began offering two terms per year, an option that allowed students to earn an MD in a single year and was particularly attractive to transfers from other schools. Multiple terms also allowed traveling professors to teach at more than one institution. From 1818 to 1854, Castleton matriculated more than 4,500 students and graduated 1,350 MDs—a substantial addition to the stock of educated doctors. By that last date, however, Castleton was surrounded by five additional country medical schools. Such schools thrived in the first half of the nineteenth century and may have graduated one-third of the nation's MDs.[56]

In the expanding western lands, the demand for medical education probably exceeded that for collegiate study, but the medical schools proved even more unstable. Transylvania University emerged as the leading center for the midsection of the country and the lower South. A medical school had been intended from its chartering in 1799, but it began regular teaching only after 1816. Soon, like the University of Pennsylvania, the medical school overshadowed the rest of the university. In 1826, during its "golden age" under liberal president Horace Holley (1818–1827), 92 collegians were enrolled, compared with 282 medical students. The medical department consistently enrolled more than 200 before its decline and demise in the late 1850s. In total, the medical department enrolled almost 6,500 students and granted nearly 1,900 MDs. The medical department was well supported by the state and the Lexington community and thus was adequately equipped; its reputation was also burnished by a succession of renowned professors, some of whose egos may have exceeded their reputations. One stalwart of the department, Benjamin Dudley, fought a duel in 1822 against another professor. He seriously wounded his adversary and then saved his life by administering first aid. The department's meteoric path shone brightest in the 1820s, when it began publishing a medical journal (1828–1839). But it was ultimately doomed by the limitations of Lexington for clinical

---

56 Norwood, *Medical Education*, 204–8; Rothstein, *American Physicians*, 98–99.

and anatomical instruction, coupled with increasing regional competition and ever-present internal conflicts.[57]

Another prickly but talented professor was Daniel Drake, who taught at Transylvania on three separate occasions—as well as four other medical schools. Drake left Transylvania after a single year in 1818 to teach in Cincinnati—a hotbed, literally, for medical education. Despite local opposition, Drake succeeded in obtaining a charter for the Medical College of Ohio in 1819. The charter made the faculty the only governors of the institution and specified a two-thirds vote for professorial appointments. The college began instruction in 1820 with five professors, but dissension quickly emerged. In 1822 two professors resigned, and the other two voted to dismiss Daniel Drake! As was common in these vendettas, Drake then sought to drive his former colleagues out of business by forming a rival school. After a period of local pamphlet warfare, Drake found his instrument by organizing a medical department for the revived Cincinnati College (1834). A bitter rivalry ensued, "punctuated with fistic combats between students of the two schools." However, Drake was unable to hold his coalition of professors together, and the Medical College managed to muddle on. In the 1850s two additional medical schools were established, in addition to the irregular Cincinnati Eclectic Medical Institute. The latter engendered conflicts all its own, as when two rival factions battled with weapons for control of its building until one side prevailed by deploying a 6-pound cannon.[58]

Until late in the nineteenth century, medical schools expanded their role in the education of physicians but grew increasingly remote from colleges and universities. This was the case for both institutions and students. Even the best medical departments—at Penn, Harvard, and the New York College of Physicians and Surgeons—were run entirely by the faculty, entirely in their own interests. In this respect, they differed only by degree from the multitude of independent proprietary schools. Moreover, their dependence on student fees locked them into the same inadequate pedagogy. In the spirit of Jacksonian democracy, licensing laws were weakened or abolished in the 1830s and 1840s, encouraging competing medical sects and crippling any hope of enforcing higher standards. Under these conditions, the relationship between college study and medical education was further attenuated. A consistent trickle of college graduates (9–10 percent) became physicians, but they were a small portion of the profession—although

57 Norwood, *Medical Education*, 289–97; Walter Wilson Jennings, *Transylvania: Pioneer University of the West* (New York: Pageant Press, 1955).

58 Joseph F. Kett, *The Formation of the American Medical Profession: The Role of Institutions* (New Haven: Yale University Press, 1968), 79–94; Norwood, *Medical Education*, 304–21, quote p. 313; Martin Kaufman, "American Medical Education" in Ronald L. Numbers, ed., *The Education of American Physicians: Historical Essays* (Berkeley: University of California Press, 1980), 7–28.

no doubt significant for leadership. One study of the Vermont medical colleges estimated that 20 percent of the students in the second quarter of the century had any college training. Away from the Northeast, that figure probably shrank to near zero. Then too, many medical students never became doctors. Two college presidents—Francis Wayland and Mark Hopkins—took medical degrees after college before embarking on different careers. The graduation numbers for Castleton and Transylvania show only about 30 percent of students taking an MD, although many undoubtedly practiced nonetheless. Over time obtaining MDs became easier and more common. A decent secondary education was considered sufficient preparation for medical studies before the twentieth century. However, the proprietary nature of medical schools led them to eschew any responsibility for their students—to enroll "young men ... who are grossly deficient in almost all the elementary branches of knowledge." Not until the last quarter of the century, when medical science was slowly introduced into medical education, would a handful of universities lead the reformation of the medical profession.[59]

LEGAL EDUCATION. The organization of legal education in American colleges lagged well behind the other professions. As late as 1840 there were 7 law schools with perhaps 350 students. A historian of the subject warns, "generalizations about the legal profession and the role of law in the first half of the nineteenth century are hard to make."[60] With this caveat, legal edication can be found in three forms: (1) Law lectures established by colleges to complement a liberal education; (2) the expansion of law office apprenticeships into independent law schools that taught basic skills of legal practice; and (3) the award of bachelor of laws degrees (LLB) by colleges. Only the last signified the completion of a course of study in a separate school or department and thus represented the institutionalization of legal education in American higher education.

Little wonder that Republican Universities of the Early Republic were eager to incorporate the teaching of law. Its Enlightenment roots informed a good deal of republican ideology; the legal and judicial professions had assumed unprecedented prestige; and a large and growing number of their graduates sought careers in the field. However, one enormous obstacle stood between theory and practice: the control of entry to the profession by established lawyers and judges. They required long (and, for them, lucrative) apprenticeships before aspiring

---

59   The College of Physicians and Surgeons joined Columbia in 1860. Norwood, *Medical Education*, 431–33; Rothstein, *American Physicians*, quoting AMA founder Nathan Davis (1855), 117.

60   Data from Alfred Z. Reed, *Training for the Public Profession of the Law* (New York: Carnegie Foundation for the Advancement of Teaching, 1921); Robert Stevens, *Law School: Legal Education in America from the 1850s to the 1980s* (Chapel Hill: University of North Carolina Press, 1983), quote p. 6.

lawyers could be admitted to the bar. Hence, as has already been seen, well-intentioned college lectures on the law contributed little to professional aspirations and, with the partial exception of William & Mary, quickly lapsed.

Given the variability of apprenticeships in law offices and long-standing dissatisfaction with them, a clear need existed for professional preparation. This need was met in part after the Revolution first and most successfully by Tapping Reeve in Litchfield, Connecticut. He increased the number of apprentices in his law office until it was recognized as a school (ca. 1784) and produced about fifteen graduates annually for the remainder of the century. After James Gould joined Reeve as a partner in 1798, attendance peaked at more than fifty in 1813 and remained robust until the late 1820s. The school was closed in 1833.[61]

The Litchfield School provided the first systematic professional education for aspiring lawyers. Reeve and later Gould presented the law as a coherent system in daily lectures, including references to legal texts that students would later read on their own. An 1803 graduate compiled 1,514 pages of notes, which he later bound and indexed—a compendium of the law to use in his practice. The lengthiest treatments were given to contracts, real property, pleading, mercantile law, and domestic relations. Students were examined weekly on the principles underlying the rules they had covered, and they also conducted moot courts. A full course lasted between 1 year and 18 months; the first year cost $100. The reputation of the Litchfield School soon drew students from all over the nation. In 50 years, it produced more than 1,000 graduates, including 66 senators and congressmen, 10 governors, and numerous justices, 2 on the Supreme Court. Surprisingly, this success found few imitators. Independent schools appeared in Connecticut in the 1810s and in other states in the 1820s, although there was often little difference between named and informal "schools." Unlike independent medical schools, the law schools were usually operated by a single proprietor and seldom survived his passing. The material they taught was less controversial and far more effective than early nineteenth-century medicine, but their connection with certification for practice was even more tenuous. The proprietary nature of both types shaped their operations, virtually precluding any standards for admission. This condition affected college law schools as well.

The first collegiate law school at Harvard was the product of intent and serendipity. In 1781 loyalist Isaac Royall bequeathed an endowment for a professor of laws or "physick and anatomy." It took until 1815 for sufficient funds to accumulate. The Brahmin lawyers, who by then controlled Harvard, envisioned

---

61 *Quarterly Register and Journal of the American Education Society,* (May 1833), 302 [unsigned]; Reed, *Training,* 128–33, 444; Arthur E. Sutherland, *The Law at Harvard: A History of Ideas and Men, 1817–1967* (Cambridge: Harvard University Press, 1967), 25–31.

a law professor of the old type, charged with lecturing to Harvard seniors and interested citizens in order to "qualify them to become useful and distinguished supporters of our free systems of government." However, the first occupant of the chair, Chief Justice Isaac Parker, had other ideas. In his inaugural address he presented a scheme for creating a professional school, similar to Litchfield, that would teach legal principles rather than practice to "resident graduates in jurisprudence." The following year (1817), a professional school of law was created that offered an 18-month course of study and awarded a bachelor of laws degree. A full-time professor of law was also hired, supported by student fees, to provide a course of study and conduct day-to-day operations. The law course was intended to complement practical training in a law office. However, it ignored Parker's desire to teach only college graduates. The law school from the outset was open to all comers.

The role of the Harvard Law School was complicated by the need for aspiring lawyers to serve an apprenticeship in a law office and resistance among local lawyers to adapting their customs to the new school. The school nonetheless had a promising start, quickly equaling the enrollments at Litchfield. But students attended irregularly, and only one in four took a degree, which was hardly needed in any case. In the late 1820s attendance dwindled until the school was reduced to perhaps two students in 1828–1829. At this point, the School of Law was regarded as a failed experiment. Parker had resigned in 1827, and the last professor, in his letter of resignation, attributed this sorry state to the declining numbers of law students in Massachusetts and competition from the new law school at the University of Virginia and a private school in Northampton. But the Brahmins were not willing to give up on this enterprise.[62]

In 1829, as lawyer-politician Josiah Quincy assumed the presidency of Harvard, prominent lawyer and legal scholar Nathan Dane offered $10,000 to create another law professorship. Dane wished to elevate the "Law College at Cambridge" so that "the principles of jurisprudence should be taught systematically, as a science." His chief stipulation was that the chair be given to Supreme Court Justice Joseph Story. Already a fellow of the Harvard Corporation, Story had refused previous offers to join the law school. However, the offer from his friend Dane, Harvard's willingness to meet his demanding terms, and the opportunity to mold the now vacant school enticed him to accept. To conduct daily operations when the busy Story was absent, another professor was hired from the shuttered Northampton school, and he brought his students as well. The Harvard Law School once again had a distinguished jurist at its head, and its fortunes immediately revived. Under the new regime, Story's erudition was

---

62 Gewalt, *Promise of Power*, 129–58; Sutherland, *Law at Harvard*, 43–91.

accompanied by professional training needed for practice. The easing of apprentice requirements for admission to the bar in the 1830s also made the new 2-year course more valuable for prospective lawyers. Within a decade it became the largest law school in the country, and in 1844 enrollment reached 156 students. This was still a floating population, with students entering and leaving throughout the academic year.

As holder of the Dane Chair, Story was expected to write as well as lecture about the law. He soon began producing his famous *Commentaries* (ten volumes, 1832–1845) on different aspects of the law but especially the definition of commercial law for the new market economy. He also gave the school a national orientation by emphasizing federal law rather than laws of the states. Story was a dedicated and inspiring teacher, and the subsequent eminence of his students over 15 years compares with Litchfield's record over 50. Story's brilliant career at Harvard, in fact, represents a new phenomenon in American higher education—a teacher with national stature whose scholarship served to define his field.[63]

Story's great prestige and the growth of the school helped Harvard set the template for American legal education by 1840. It included the bachelor of laws degree entirely separate from the undergraduate AB degree; a course of study that was exclusively technical or professional; and degree requirements that were not linked with state requirements for admission to the bar. In addition, the law schools were basically businesses. Only a few colleges had endowed chairs like Harvard, but even there, the fees paid by students remained with the school. These four conditions gave early law schools curricular license, subject only to the discipline of the marketplace. Some cleaved closely to the skills of the law office, like Yale, which started its law school in 1823 by incorporating an independent school and its pupils. Others strove to embrace the science of law. But all had to prove sufficiently useful for students to attend of their own volition. Many ephemeral efforts clearly failed this test. The law department launched at Princeton in 1847, for example, "provided that the Professors be paid from the proceeds of the tuition fees." It drew so few students that it was not worth the efforts of the lawyer-teachers, who abandoned it in 1852. By the Civil War, 30 law schools had been started and 21 still operated; however, a large majority of the nation's 36,000 lawyers had never darkened the door of a college law school.[64]

SCHOOLS OF THEOLOGY. The first theological seminaries were established in reaction to alleged failings of the colleges. Andover Theological Seminary

---

63 Ibid., 92–139, quote p. 95; Reed, *Training*, 142–50.

64 John Maclean, *History of the College of New Jersey, 1746–1854*, 2 vol. (Philadelphia: 1877), ii, 299, 318–19; Reed, *Training*.

was dedicated to educating orthodox Calvinist clergy because Harvard would not; Princeton Theological Seminary was chartered to be at, but not part of, the College of New Jersey. Baptists sought to avoid colleges with hybrid literary and theological institutions. As institutions of professional education, however, schools of theology were more closely linked with colleges than their counterparts for medicine and law. They consciously sought to be *graduate* institutions; and, far from being proprietary, they established a firm practice of charging no tuition at all. Dependent upon endowments or gifts, theological seminaries still managed to proliferate during the quarter-century heyday of the Awakening (1815–1840).[65]

The first two theological seminaries were both national institutions. Andover was rigidly orthodox, with New Divinity leanings, but it was open to all qualified Protestants "possessed of personal piety." It drew students from the Congregational strongholds of Dartmouth, Middlebury, and, later, Amherst. It required matriculates to have a college education or equivalent preparation, and only a small minority of students fell into that latter category. The 3-year Andover course became the model for other seminaries. The first year was devoted to Bible study and required facility in both Greek and Hebrew; the second covered theology, or church doctrines, including church history; and the final year taught sacred rhetoric, or the art of preaching. Andover's wealth separated it from most other seminaries in terms of professorships, library holdings, facilities, and scholarships to assist indigent students. Most important, this wealth allowed the cultivation of advanced scholarship. Professor of biblical literature Moses Stuart became proficient in German to stay abreast of scholarly writings, despite his distaste for German theology. He also invited able students to continue their studies beyond the third year in the "resident licentiate" program. The best of these "graduate students" were encouraged to complete their studies in Germany, and many became faculty at Andover and elsewhere.[66]

The official name for the Princeton Seminary—the Theological Seminary of the Presbyterian Church—accurately identified it as belonging to the church rather than the college. Its role above all was to uphold the conservative, "Old School" interpretation of Presbyterian orthodoxy (heirs of the Old Lights). It was governed by the church's General Assembly, and each year trustees, faculty,

---

65 Glenn T. Miller, *Piety and Intellect: The Aims and Purposes of Ante-Bellum Theological Education* (Atlanta: Scholars Press, 1990); Natalie A. Naylor, "The Theological Seminary in the Configuration of American Higher Education: The Ante-Bellum Years," *History of Education Quarterly*, 17, 1 (Spring 1977): 17–30.

66 *Quarterly Register* (May 1833): 295; Miller, *Piety and Intellect*, 73–74; Jerry Wayne Brown, *The Rise of Biblical Criticism in America, 1800–1870: The New England Scholars* (Middletown, CT: Wesleyan University Press, 1969), 45–59.

and students had to swear an oath of belief in these doctrines. The Princeton Seminary was defined by the work of three long-serving professors: Archibald Alexander (1812–1851), Samuel Miller (1813–1848), and Charles Hodge (1822–1878). The latter famously boasted that no new idea was taught at Princeton during his tenure. But this conservatism was accompanied by a commitment to scholarship. They firmly supported a scientific understanding of the natural world consistent with the Common Sense philosophy, and Hodge spent 2 years in Europe (1827–1828), mostly at Halle and Berlin, studying German theology. Princeton rivaled Andover as the largest theological seminary, but its goal of a unified church proved chimerical. Presbyterians elsewhere erected their own seminaries—ten more by 1840, one-third of the national total. Still, the narrow theological doctrines of the Old School, no matter how eruditely argued, were self-defeating given the religious fragmentation of post-Awakening America. The Princeton theologians rejected the entire evangelical movement, found New Haven and Andover Congregationalists doctrinally unsound, and, therefore, condemned cooperation with other denominations in Protestant benevolent societies. In 1837 the Old School gained control of the General Assembly and expelled its New School rivals. The stalwarts of the Princeton Seminary defended this schism in the Church, and did what they could to impose Old School orthodoxy on Presbyterian colleges.[67]

The theological departments established at Harvard and Yale evolved from the older pattern of ministerial preparation but still differed considerably from each other. Harvard formally organized its Divinity School in 1819 with the aid of the Unitarian Society for the Promotion of Theological Education. A product of president Kirkland's expansive phase, the president immediately appointed his former Anthologist colleague, Andrews Norton, who embarked on a career of biblical scholarship. Since Unitarians had no church doctrines to profess, the department required "no assent to the peculiarities of any denomination of Christians." In fact, the department was only attractive to Unitarian teachers and students. Since career opportunities for Unitarian ministers were limited, enrollments were never substantial. The professors instead emphasized scholarship in oriental languages and biblical criticism. After Kirkland, the university never embraced the explicit identification with Unitarianism that the theology department expressed.[68] Such was not the case at Yale.

67   Miller, *Piety and Intellect*, 99–113; William K. Selden, *Princeton Theological Seminary: A Narrative History, 1812–1992* (Princeton: Princeton University Press, 1992); Miller, *Revolutionary College*.

68   William Wallace Fenn, "The Theological School" in Samuel Eliot Morison, ed., *The Development of Harvard University* (Cambridge: Harvard University Press, 1930), 463–71, quote p. 464; Brown, *Rise of Biblical Criticism*, 75–93; James Turner, *The Liberal Education of Charles Eliot Norton* (Baltimore: Johns Hopkins University Press, 1999), 22–36.

The Yale Department of Theology, although a separately organized unit, was closely bound in spirit and culture to Yale College. In 1822 fifteen Yale seniors petitioned for the establishment of a theology department in which to continue their studies. The faculty warmly backed this initiative and voluntarily taught in the school when it was launched the same year. Funds were raised for a professorship, which was awarded to New Haven minister and theologian Nathaniel Taylor. He was soon joined by Josiah Gibbs, a student of both Timothy Dwight and Moses Stuart, who pursued German learning in Hebrew and philology. Taylor's distinctive theology promoted a moderate Calvinism that ultimately offended both the New Divinity proclivities of Andover and the Old School orthodoxy of Princeton. But more consequential than theology at Yale was a pervasive commitment to Christian service. Yale infused a Christian culture in students that graduates of both the college and the theology department exemplified, not only as ministers but also as missionaries, as educators, and in other professional careers. Yale graduates were conspicuous in the formation of the many Christian benevolent societies that organized the work of the Awakening. The Yale theology department was somewhat larger than Harvard's and nearly as inbred; but unlike Harvard, its graduates spread widely across the nation and, indeed, the world.[69]

The establishment of these major theological seminaries inaugurated the first sustained engagement of American scholars with Germanic scholarship. The common ground was the study of the Bible. The Andover curriculum devoted the first year to biblical studies, and those who taught "Sacred Literature," despite widely divergent theologies, believed that unlocking the meaning of the scriptures was the key to establishing the word of God. Hodge wrote, "The Bible is to the theologian what nature is to the man of science. . . . In theology as in natural science, principles are derived from facts." Andrews Norton devoted much of his career to writing *The Evidences of the Genuineness of the Gospels*. Stuart and Gibbs were motivated by the same quest. To seek the truth of the Bible meant assimilating the learning of German scholars. They produced the most authoritative Hebrew grammar and were, similarly, far advanced in philology and exegesis. Beyond this scholarship, however, American scholars were often more repelled than attracted. The reigning German idealist philosophy was incomprehensible to American churchmen, and they rejected many of the conclusions German scholars drew from their studies. But the studies themselves were essential. Once dedicated to biblical scholarship, Americans could scarcely ignore these sources. Understanding the words of the Bible in their original languages

---

69   William L. Kingsley, *Yale College: A Sketch of Its History*, 2 vols. (New Haven, 1879), II, 15–28; Miller, *Piety and Intellect*, 150–53; Brown, *Rise of Biblical Criticism*, 171–77.

required an understanding of the contexts in which they were used, which in turn required an understanding of ancient civilizations. Gibbs, for one, followed this path from Hebrew to comparative philology. The biblical scholars of the theological seminaries provided one early path leading American letters out of its provincial isolation. Although not always appreciated in their own institutions, they spearheaded the building of scholarly libraries, the establishment of learned journals, and the regular monitoring of German scholarship.[70]

In 1815 the leaders of Andover Seminary founded the American Society for Educating Pious Youth for the Gospel Ministry—an organization that helped to define the structure of American higher education. The founders sought to address the "deplorable" lack of properly prepared clergy in the country by soliciting aid for "indigent young men of talents and hopeful piety, in acquiring a learned and competent education for the Gospel Ministry." For its first 10 years, the American Education Society (as it was soon renamed) publicized its mission by documenting the dearth of ministers and raised sufficient donations to support between 100 and 200 students. Recipients had to be at least 15 years old and produce "unequivocal testimonials of real indigence" and yearly evidence of "genius, diligence, literary progress, morals, and piety." However, the society made only grudging progress until it named Elias Cornelius as secretary (1825). Converted his senior year at Yale, Cornelius studied for the ministry with Dwight, Lyman Beecher, and as a resident licentiate at Andover. But rather than taking a pulpit, he became a brilliant fund-raiser for a succession of Christian organizations. He streamlined the society, established branch societies, and brought in funding to support increasing numbers of students. He also established the *Quarterly Register* (the *Chronicle of Higher Education* of its era), an authoritative compilation of data and commentary on collegiate and theological education. In particular, the *Register* promoted the society's foremost aim of institutionalizing a "thorough education" for ministers.[71]

Andover had always preferred that its students be college graduates and complete the entire 3-year course in theology. Under Cornelius, enforcing this pattern became an avowed aim of the society. From the outset, the society had wished to address the "radical deficiency in the system of classical education." Until 1827, it directed financial assistance to students in academies or colleges so that

---

70   Miller, *Piety and Intellect*, 437–55. Miller notes that only relatively wealthy seminaries could encourage scholarship. Besides the four discussed here, he would include the General Theological Seminary of the Protestant Episcopal Church (f. 1817) and Union Seminary (New York) established in 1836 by Presbyterians.

71   Naylor, *Raising a Learned Ministry*. The workings of the AES are described in Allmendinger, *Paupers and Scholars*, 64–76. The influence of the AES peaked in 1837, when it was weakened by the financial panic and the Presbyterian schism. After 1840 it reverted to a Congregational organization.

they might obtain such education. In 1828 the society also began to support students in theological seminaries.[72] These theology students were required to sign a pledge that they would complete the full 3-year course. In the 1820s, diverse patterns of collegiate and theological education still existed, such as the Baptist literary and theological institutions. The Bangor Theological Seminary in rural Maine, although Congregational, combined classical and theological instruction in a 4-year course—a sensible approach for its mature, hard-pressed students. Cornelius nonetheless pressured the seminary until it adopted a 3-year theological curriculum. Despite the shortage of clergy, the overriding objective was to "elevate the standard of ministerial qualifications," not only by enabling students to attend seven years of higher schooling but also by forcing institutions to offer a "thorough education." The American Education Society thus promoted the distinction between undergraduate and graduate-professional education as the emerging standard for American higher education.[73] The difficulty of achieving that standard is evident from the record of the theological seminaries themselves.

The four schools just described were all intended as postgraduate institutions, but elsewhere a bewildering variety of patterns existed. Many of the early seminaries were founded, like Andover, as independent institutions. Some remained independent, like Hartwick Seminary in New York (Lutheran, f. 1815), Newton Seminary in Massachusetts (Baptist, f. 1825), and the General Theological Seminary of the Episcopal Church (f. 1817) in New York City. Other independent seminaries spawned colleges, such as the Lutherans in Gettysburg, the German Reformed in starting Marshall College, and the Dutch Reformed in establishing Rutgers. But colleges also produced independent seminaries, as did Hampden Sidney in launching Union Theological Seminary. In a still different pattern, hybrid combinations of collegiate and theological education were created in Bangor and the Rock Spring Theological School in Illinois (f. 1827). The early western colleges were often founded with the hope of training ministers, and this mission was later transferred to separate theological departments. Two of the most prominent were associated with Oberlin and Jefferson colleges, but this pattern appeared across Ohio at Kenyon, Western Reserve, and Granville (later Denison). More Protestant theological schools and seminaries were opened in

---

72   In 1833 the AES supported 344 students at 17 colleges, including one-quarter of students at Middlebury, Williams, Amherst, and Miami. Other favored colleges were Yale (52 recipients), Dartmouth, Jefferson, Brown and Western Reserve. AES supported perhaps one-fifth of the 1,000 seminary students. By the 1850s, one-third of Congregational and New School Presbyterian ministers had received AES assistance. At least two-thirds of its beneficiaries served as ministers or missionaries: *Quarterly Register* (May 1833), 332–35; Naylor, *Raising a Learned Ministry*, 303.

73   Naylor, *Raising a Learned Ministry*, 216, 190. In 1830 the percentage of college graduates at the seminaries mentioned in note 70, ranged from 67 (Princeton) to 94 (Andover) but were generally much lower elsewhere: Ibid., 209.

the second and third decades of the century than colleges. By 1840, the *Quarterly Register* identified thirty-eight in operation.[74]

In the early decades of the nineteenth century the formal education of medical doctors and lawyers drifted further away from the liberal education offered by American colleges. However, this was not the case with institutions for the education of ministers. The establishment of divinity schools and theological seminaries interacted with collegiate education in four important ways. First, these schools were able to posit and enforce a clear distinction between undergraduate and postgraduate education. Second, by creating and legitimizing separate organizations for ministerial education, the secular nature of the undergraduate curriculum was insulated from denominational objectives. Third, by establishing positions for professors to study and explicate the Bible, the leading schools planted the seed of academic scholarship in American higher education. And fourth, the products of these first graduate schools, whether smitten by the charms of scholarship or not, filled the ranks of college teachers by midcentury.

WHO OWNS COLLEGES?

The Massachusetts Constitution of 1780 enshrined the University at Cambridge as a republican institution, with government officials and senators sitting on the Board of Overseers. Thirty years later, in 1810, A Federalist majority in the legislature reconstituted the board by dropping the senators and replacing them with fifteen Congregational ministers and fifteen laymen chosen by the board. The pretext for this move was apparently the criticism by Republican senators of Harvard's handling of student discipline following the 1805 riot. Ensuring an overwhelming Federalist presence eliminated this source of Republican caviling—but not for long. In 1812, a Republican legislature repealed the 1810 law and restored the senators to the Overseers. This was done without the approval of the college and accompanied by an ominous demand to inspect its records. However, in 1814 Federalists were once more in control, and a new law retained the senators but reinstated the fifteen laypeople from 1810. This created a board of seventy-seven Overseers, forty-six of them elected officials. As a further favor, the proceeds of a bank tax were used to promise Harvard a $10,000 appropriation for each of the next 10 years. As political footballs, colleges might gain or lose, but longer term the dangers were paramount.[75]

---

74 *Quarterly Register* (Aug. 1840), 116–18. Four Roman Catholic seminaries were identified, but the AES did not follow them.

75 Morison, *Three Centuries of Harvard*, 210–14 ; John S. Whitehead, *The Separation of College and State: Columbia, Dartmouth, Harvard and Yale, 1776–1876* (New Haven: Yale University Press, 1973), 16–20.

American colleges were universally regarded as public institutions. They were created by government bodies through legal charters that entitled them to perform the public function of awarding recognized degrees. From the colonial colleges to the Early Republic, it was assumed that those same governments exercised oversight of the colleges. Beyond these certainties, ambiguity prevailed. Some colleges included elected officials among their governors and some did not. Some states granted occasional financial support—and some did not. And legislatures sometimes passed laws affecting their makeup, as had happened in Pennsylvania, Virginia, and now Massachusetts. Only in this third situation did the issue arise of the relationship between these *public* institutions and elected authorities. Who owned the colleges, and under what conditions? This question did not become urgent until conflicts arose, as they did in the second decade of the nineteenth century. By then, the polarization of Federalists and Republicans had hardened into political blocs, and religious fervor sparked by the Awakening was mobilized in dedicated organizations. When colleges became aligned with a single party, they became vulnerable to political rivalries, as happened at Harvard. When religious factions contested for dominance within colleges, they became vulnerable to conflicts over ownership.

Events of the 1810s undermined the tacit relationships between colleges and states. Harvard was long regarded as a Massachusetts institution, but after the shuffling of Overseers, the state and the public were more often antagonistic than supportive. In Virginia, William & Mary forfeited its special status through maladministration and the designs of Thomas Jefferson for creating a new state university. In Connecticut, Yale's association with state Federalists had brought intermittent subsidies and blocked the establishment of competing colleges. However, such self-interested policies bolstered the growing ranks of opponents until the Congregational-Federalists were voted out of office. In 1818 a new state constitution disestablished the Congregational Church and with it the Standing Order and Yale's preferential status. With some difficulty, Yale embarked on a quest for private donors to finance its new Divinity School, for example, but also to ensure long-term funding as a self-supporting institution.[76] The most dramatic and consequential clash over college-state relations occurred between Dartmouth and New Hampshire.

The Dartmouth College case, decided by the Supreme Court in 1819, can best be understood by following the successive stages of this dispute.[77] The first

76   Jurgen Herbst, *From Crisis to Crisis* (Cambridge: Harvard University Press, 1982); Peter Dobkin Hall, *The Organization of American Culture, 1700–1900* (New York: New York University Press, 1984), 79–94.

77   See Whitehead, *Separation*, 52–76; Steven J. Novak, "The College in the Dartmouth College Case: A Reinterpretation," *New England Quarterly*, 47, 4 (Dec. 1974): 550–63; Leon Burr Richardson, *History of Dartmouth College* (Hanover, NH: Dartmouth College Publications, 1932), I, 287–346.

stage began with the estrangement of the trustees and President John Wheelock and led to the polarization of the college community. Several issues lay behind these developments, although often submerged in quotidian squabbles. John Wheelock was a capable but unpopular steward of the college. Named to the position at his father's deathbed, he assiduously attempted to acquire the learning befitting a college president; but his attainments as an autodidact earned little respect. He had a far better head for business, and various machinations of land grants eventually made the Wheelocks one of New Hampshire's richest families. After 1800, successor trustees of the college regarded him with disdain and distrust, but his resistance to the Awakening prompted an overt falling out. In 1804 the trustees appointed a young professor of divinity who exemplified the new wave of evangelical zeal. Wheelock blocked him from the college church, but he assumed the pulpit of the Hanover meetinghouse and led an intense revival in the winter of 1805–1806. From this point the college was divided between evangelical Calvinists, who opposed the president, and those who opposed the evangelicals. In 1809 the religious faction succeeded in imposing temperance restrictions, which provoked a destructive student riot. Wheelock dealt lightly with the miscreants, who were, after all, his enemy's enemy. But at this juncture the appointment of new trustees and faculty produced dominant majorities for the anti-Wheelock forces. Relations between the two sides deteriorated further, and in 1814 the trustees humiliated Wheelock by removing him from teaching the seniors. Wheelock had threatened to claim huge sums from the college for long-ago loans—with accumulated interest. He now wrote and distributed a polemical tract rehearsing past disputes, denigrating the trustees, and inviting the intervention of the legislature. This assault was too much for the trustees, and in exasperation they fired Wheelock in 1815.

In the second stage, Wheelock's dismissal became a cause célèbre in New Hampshire politics. Republicans, eager for an issue to embarrass their Federalist foes, portrayed Wheelock as a martyr to the rigid Calvinist trustees of the college, representatives of the resented Standing Order. As happened in Connecticut, the unpopularity of the college helped elect a Republican legislature and governor in 1816. The new governor, William Plumer, believed that the college should be connected with the state and that the legislature had the authority to alter the charter (as Massachusetts had done). Plumer was a lawyer and statesman in the Enlightenment tradition, a correspondent of Jefferson's, and probably more learned than anyone associated with Dartmouth College.[78] A law was

---

78 Plumer subsequently advanced a conception of a utilitarian state university, but such a notion was ahead of its time and had no support in the state: Eldon L. Johnson, "The Dartmouth College Case: The Neglected Educational Meaning," *Journal of the Early Republic* 3, 1 (Spring 1983): 45–67.

enacted, adding nine governor-appointed trustees to the existing dozen, adding a board of overseers, and changing the name to Dartmouth University. The trustees refused to recognize this legislation or to meet with the new trustees, thus denying them a quorum.

In the third stage, the two sides defied one another. At Plumer's request, additional legislation lowered the quorum to nine and permitted the governor to appoint replacements for any absent trustees. The trustees then filed suit to block these actions. The university trustees proceeded to meet under the new quorum, discharged the sitting president appointed by the old trustees, and reinstated Wheelock as president of Dartmouth University. For the next 2 years, Dartmouth College and Dartmouth University coexisted uncomfortably side by side, with occasional clashes of competing literary societies. Wheelock survived his reappointment less than 2 months, but his son-in-law, William Allen, was named acting president, thus keeping Dartmouth University in the family.

In the final legal stage, the case was brilliantly argued by both sides in New Hampshire Superior Court—a Republican versus a Federalist interpretation of government. The trustees' law team argued that Dartmouth was a private, charitable corporation with which the legislature had no right to tamper. They also insisted that it was a *college*—like an endowed English college, not like an English university that was subject to Parliament. The state argued that Dartmouth was a public corporation and that the state had the right to intervene where the public good was involved. The two sides presented mirror images of governance—one in which state legislators might pervert the intentions of donors, and another in which private trustees might subvert the public good. The Court ruled decisively for the state, reasoning that Dartmouth was a public corporation because it pursued a public purpose and as such was a proper object of legislation. Despite the setback, the trustees persisted by appealing to the Supreme Court in 1818.[79]

The trustees' case was argued dramatically by Daniel Webster, who famously emphasized the college theme by pleading, "it is a small college, and yet there are those who love it." The state did not send its victorious law team but had their case presented by locals who were unfamiliar with the details. These circumstances probably mattered little, because the justices saw somewhat different issues at stake. In his decision, Chief Justice John Marshall ruled that the original gifts to establish the college in effect chartered a corporation, which was a contract protected by the Constitution—a view the New Hampshire court had rejected. Justice Joseph Story further argued that even if it were a public corporation, the legislature could not "take away the private property of a corporation, or change the use of its private funds, acquired under the public

79 Whitehead, *Separation*, 72.

faith."[80] Marshall and Story were particularly concerned to extend the contract clause of the U.S. Constitution to private corporations; and Story, as a Harvard Overseer, may have been as concerned with Massachusetts as with New Hampshire.

By protecting the rights of corporations under the contract clause the Dartmouth College case became a landmark of U.S. constitutional law. Historians have been less certain of its impact on American higher education. For some time, historians assumed that the ruling stimulated the proliferation of private colleges that began shortly after 1819. Or, further, that this rebuke to public intervention discouraged the founding of state universities.[81] As will be seen in the next chapter, these developments had dynamics of their own. Conversely, the notion that the "decision received scant attention after it was issued" is equally mistaken.[82] Beyond the arcane legal arguments and the ulterior motives of Justices Marshall and Story, the decision seems a correct one. The New Hampshire Legislature was motivated by sordid politics, not public interest, in altering the Dartmouth charter. It scarcely served the public good to restore the college to control by the Wheelocks. If heir presumptive William Allen had assumed life tenure, like his father- and grandfather-in-law, the college would have remained a family fiefdom until at least 1868—99 years! The Supreme Court ruling precluded state intervention in private corporations without consent or due process, and that protection was a vital concern to contemporaries.

The *North American Review*, practically a Harvard organ, wrote,

> Perhaps no judicial proceedings in this country, ever involved more important consequences. . . . While the cause was pending, there was much anxiety felt for its final result by friends of our literary institutions; for it was early perceived, that they stood on no surer foundation than Dartmouth College.

The case was widely publicized and had a direct impact on college-state relations. One of the first to exploit the decision was Eliphalet Nott, the wily president of Union College. In 1805 he had traded the right to raise $80,000 through state lotteries for state representation and eventual control over Union's Board of Trustees.

---

80   Herbst, *Crisis to Crisis*, 232–43, quote p. 238.

81   Donald Tewksbury, *The Founding of American Colleges and Universities before the Civil War* (New York: Arno Press, 1969 [1932]), 64–66; 150–52; Richard Hofstadter, *Academic Freedom in the Age of the College* (New Brunswick: Transaction Publishers, 1996 [1955]), 220.

82   See John S. Whitehead and Jurgen Herbst, "How to Think about the Dartmouth College Case," *History of Education Quarterly*, 26, 3 (Fall 1986): 333–50, quote p. 334 (Whitehead).

In 1823 he invoked the Dartmouth College case to justify legislation that revoked the state's pending domination of the board and ensured private control, despite the college's deep involvement in New York State politics. In 1826 the Maryland legislature unilaterally assumed control over the proprietary University of Maryland. The medical faculty waited a decade before challenging this action, but then retained Daniel Webster, who assured them that the state's confiscation was "*void by the Constitution of the United States.*" For 2 decades after the Dartmouth decision, one-half of new college charters contained "reserve clauses" that in theory allowed states to intervene in the colleges in order to uphold the public interest, but in practice these provisions were rarely, if ever, invoked.[83]

The most notorious application of the Dartmouth College principle occurred at Bowdoin College and involved none other than William Allen. Appointed to the vacant presidency of Bowdoin shortly after losing his position at Dartmouth University, Allen soon exhibited the Wheelock traits of autocracy and arrogance. Opponents finally devised an ingenious way to get rid of him. In 1831 the legislature passed a law that required all college presidents in the state ($N = 2$) to resign after commencement and specified a two-thirds vote of trustees for reinstatement. This was no problem for Waterville College, but at Bowdoin Allen could not muster two-thirds support. He subsequently sued to retain his position, invoking the precedent of the Dartmouth College case that had cost him his previous post. The case was tried before Justice Joseph Story in 1833. In his decision, Story quoted extensively from "the great case of Dartmouth College" and emphatically reinforced the notion that the college's charter made it a private corporation and thus protected from interference by the state. The strength of Story's opinion in effect made it difficult for a state to invoke even a reserve clause. Allen was reinstated and occupied the Bowdoin presidency, unhappily for all concerned, for another 5 years.[84]

Justices Story and Marshall succeeded in establishing a bright-line distinction between public and private corporations, based on their founding rather

---

83   *North American Review* (Jan. 1820): 83; Wayne Somers, *Encyclopedia of Union College History* (Schenectady: Union College Press, 2003), 745; Codman Hislop, *Eliphalet Nott* (Middletown, CT: Wesleyan University Press, 1971), 153–65, 201–2; Callcott, *University of Maryland,* quote p. 74; Mary F. Beach, *An Analysis of the Dartmouth College Case and Its Impact on the Founding of American Colleges and Universities, 1819–1839,* PhD Diss., Boston College, 1990, 99–124. In addition, Miami University invoked the Dartmouth College Case to block removal from Oxford to Cincinnati: Peter Dobkin Hall, "The Spirit of the Ordinance of 1781: Organizational Values, Voluntary Associations, and Higher Education in Ohio, 1803–1830," ms. nd.

84   "Opinion of Judge Story in the Case of William Allen vs. Joseph McKeen" (Boston, 1833), quote p. 8; Charles C. Calhoun, *A Small College in Maine: Two-Hundred Years of Bowdoin* (Brunswick, ME: Bowdoin College, 1993), 84–90. Story concluded his opinion with a virtual apology to the college for restoring "a head, who may (*however undeservedly*) not enjoy its *highest* confidence" (p. 21).

than their purpose. Together with the application of contract guarantees to corporations, these rulings greatly aided the commercial development of the country, as intended. However, the ruling solved only one problem for colleges—protecting them from overt state intrusion. Even as private corporations, which most legally were, they continued to serve a public purpose. They thus persisted as semipublic, semiprivate institutions, a status more vexing for later historians than for contemporaries.[85] The chief entanglements with their respective states took place through publicly elected officials on boards of trustees and state financial support, both of which had myriad forms and implications.

★　★　★

States have provided financial succor for their colleges, public and private, from colonial times to the present. In the Early Republic, lack of liquid funds greatly inhibited any generous impulses, so that support depended on political will *and* financial means. Regular appropriations were a rarity; instead states supported colleges when they could with what they had. Colonial colleges sometimes received dedicated revenues—the Charlestown ferry for Harvard and tobacco taxes for William & Mary. After the Revolution, states used windfalls to support the colleges—escheated lands or confiscated Tory property. Land grants nonetheless remained the most feasible and popular way to sustain colleges. The Northwest Ordinance of 1787 provided one source of educational land grants. Still, it often proved difficult to realize cash revenue from these holdings. Lotteries were another popular form of aid. They had to be authorized and supervised by governments and hence were considered public funds. After 1800, states became somewhat more solvent and magnanimous. In South Carolina, federal reimbursements for wartime expenses created a treasury surplus that allowed the state college to be launched on generous terms. Banks were vulnerable to state exactions, and bank taxes were directed to higher education in Connecticut and Massachusetts in 1814. When state tax revenues accumulated, they typically were allotted to "literary funds" to support education. Thomas Jefferson was able to divert this treasure to the University of Virginia, but prevailing practice more often reserved these funds for common schools. Increasingly, requests for state funds were specifically linked with public purposes. Eliphalet Nott was a virtuoso at portraying to legislators how appropriations to Union College would be used for "the poor man's son of promise, taken from their obscurity and educated free of expense." Pennsylvania legislators were readily persuaded to make grants to most of the state's small colleges.

85　Whitehead and Herbst, "How to Think."

Although the pretext was usually to prepare teachers for public schools, such grants were basically political pork. [86]

For the most part, such intermittent support was not accompanied by any form of state control. Where a single institution monopolized higher education, states tended to assume the right of oversight, as in New Hampshire. Colleges were generally willing to barter board representation for state financial support. That was the quid pro quo at Yale in 1792 and Union College in 1805. Dartmouth, after defending its independence, discussed a similar arrangement with New Hampshire in the 1820s. Over time, the eighteenth-century expedient of placing public officials on college boards of trustees served little purpose. Connecticut officials remained on the Yale board after the Standing Order was terminated but had little influence. This situation seems to have prevailed elsewhere, where government officials seldom had the time or the interest to become involved. After 1819, few new charters included elected officials. Even the New York Board of Regents exerted little influence over established colleges and was strongly resisted by Eliphalet Nott in Union College matters. In general, colleges continued to seek financial support from their states, but the inclination of states for constructive involvement with colleges waned. [87]

If the "private" colleges of the early nineteenth century retained public characteristics, the ostensibly public colleges assumed a decidedly private character. The distinguishing characteristic of the "public" colleges was the appointment of the governing board by the state legislature or governor. However, in some cases these boards were accorded the right to elect successors, but in either case the boards and the presidents they selected operated much like private colleges. The two exceptions were South Carolina College and the University of Virginia, which were the only antebellum institutions supported by annual state funding—appropriations in South Carolina and proceeds from the Literary Fund in Virginia. Other state colleges subsisted on the proceeds of land grants and student tuition. [88] These early state colleges, all in newly settled territories, also succumbed to varying degrees of Presbyterian influence. Presbyterians generally proved to be the most aggressive and intolerant bearers of denominational faiths. They were a distinct minority in all of these states, but they were heavily

---

86   Frank W. Blackmar, *The History of Federal and State Aid to Higher Education in the United States* (Washington, D.C.: GPO, 1890); Whitehead, *Separation of Church and State*; Hislop, *Eliphalet Nott*, quote p. 202; Saul Sack, *History of Higher Education in Pennsylvania*, 2 vol. (Harrisburg: 1968), I, 307–9.

87   Whitehead, *Separation of College and State*, 77–88; Beach, *Dartmouth College Case*, 115–22; Hislop, *Eliphalet Nott*.

88   Tuition was similar at public and private colleges. Except for Harvard ($75), it was highest at the universities of Virginia ($75), North Carolina, and South Carolina (both $50). Elsewhere, tuition varied between $20 and $40 at the College of New Jersey (1840): *Quarterly Register* (1840), 189.

represented among the college educated who were chosen as trustees, and Presbyterian ministers predominated among individuals available and competent to be possible presidents.[89]

The most determined battle between Presbyterians and secularists occurred at Transylvania University. When chartered in 1799 the university united two existing schools and incorporated Presbyterian trustees, who dominated the institution for most of its first 2 decades. Under their stewardship the college course shrank to a single year, and they consistently defended the acting head, an embarrassing Presbyterian zealot. Lexington was divided politically, religiously, and by family alliances, and the university was a bone of contention. Finally in 1817, the legislature changed the charter and appointed a new set of trustees who were committed to creating a respectable university. The parallel to Dartmouth is striking, but Kentucky's actions were never challenged. The new board offered the presidency to Horace Holley, a highly respected Boston Unitarian minister. Under Holley the university experienced a "golden age": learned and respected professors were hired, the college course was raised to 4 years, the professional schools flourished, and enrollment exceeded 400 by 1822. Presbyterians remained adamantly hostile and soon began a campaign to discredit Holley for his liberal religious views. From 1825, Holley was also threatened by a populist governor who sought to boost his own standing by attacking the "aristocratic" university. Feeling that his position had become untenable, Holley stepped down in 1827, although he may well have welcomed the opportunity to move on.[90] Transylvania persisted with wavering success, but it was continually hampered by fluctuating denominational hegemony, the indifference of populist governments, and the economic decline of Lexington. By the Civil War its several departments had all succumbed.

Other attempts to establish state colleges in the West before 1820 fared worse than Transylvania. The charters and the initial state ties all date from the era of republican universities, when higher education was perceived to be a vital

89   The University of Georgia's first president, Josiah Meigs from Yale, proved too Republican and too liberal for the largely Federalist governors and was forced out after nine stormy years (1801–1810). The college was unsettled until Reverend Moses Waddel was appointed in 1819 and conducted it as a Presbyterian college. Much the same was true of the University of North Carolina after Joseph Caldwell, a Presbyterian, assumed the presidency in 1800.

90   James Paul Cousins, *Children of the Western World: The Illusion of Religious Control and the Making of Higher Education in Kentucky, 1780–1818*, PhD Diss., University of Kentucky, 2010; Walter Wilson Jennings, *Transylvania, Pioneer University of the West* (New York: Pageant Press, 1955), 58–153. Presbyterians reacted by founding Centre College in Danville, which became operational in 1822. The decline of the university seems to have been due to the decline of Lexington, competition from other institutions, and capricious state intervention: Alvin Fayette Lewis, *History of Higher Education in Kentucky* (Washington, D.C.: GPO, 1899).

public interest, but efforts to organize functioning colleges confronted the realities of the early nineteenth century. All received public support through land grants, but revenues were difficult to realize except through land sales, which were irregular and unpredictable. Tennessee took the approach of chartering regional colleges: Blount near Knoxville (1794), Greeneville (1794), and Washington colleges (1796), which only opened in 1804–1806. These pioneers were essentially one-man, one-room schoolhouse-colleges, elevated from similar academies. Congressional land grants in 1806 allowed East Tennessee College to supplant Blount, but the college did not open until 1820. Cumberland was forced to close for a decade in 1816 and then emerged as the University of Nashville; and East Tennessee finally managed to organize a regular college course at the end of the 1820s.[91]

Ohio employed the Northwest Ordinance land grants to charter Ohio University in the East (1804) and Miami in the west (1809). The former began instruction in 1809 and graduated its first student in 1815 while operating essentially in the one-room mode. By 1819, however, a college building and a regular college course were in place. Miami was not able to do the same until 1824, but it soon flourished. Indiana chartered Vincennes University in 1806, and several name changes later, Indiana College became fully operational in 1828.[92]

Early in the nineteenth century almost all these institutions were led by Presbyterians, regardless of the makeup of their boards. In the case of Miami, the board, the faculty, and the surrounding population were all staunch Presbyterians. At Indiana, Presbyterian control of the state college provoked rising protests from Methodists and other denominations, which soon established their own colleges. Presbyterian leadership has often been chastised, but in fact it produced mixed results. It worked in Miami's favor until the college became identified with the intolerant Old School after 1840; however, at Indiana the long-serving president quit the church in exasperation with Old School bigotry. Nashville hired Princeton Presbyterian Philip Lindsley as president (1825–1850), who championed the liberal educational tradition of Witherspoon and Smith and spoke eloquently against denominational narrowness.[93] All these schools, like Transylvania, experienced transient periods of prosperity beginning in the 1820s,

91   Herbst, *Crisis*, 196–97; James Riley Montgomery, Stanley J. Folmsbee, and Lee Seifert Greene, *To Foster Knowledge: A History of the University of Tennessee, 1794–1970* (Knoxville: University of Tennessee Press, 1984). Although colleges are dated from the times of charters, openings, or first graduates, the ability to organize separate classes and a 4-year course best signifies successful establishment.

92   Hall, "Spirit of the Ordinance": Thomas D. Clark, *Indiana University: Midwestern Pioneer, Volume 1, the Early Years* (Bloomington: Indiana University Press, 1970).

93   Lucius S. Merriam, *History of Higher Education in Tennessee* (Washington, D.C.: 1893); Hofstadter and Smith, *American Higher Education*, 328–34, 376–79.

most likely from a combination of land revenues, fairly robust demand, and a temporary lack of competitors. But longer term, these state colleges suffered from the disadvantages of both sectors. One observer later wrote of East Tennessee: "ostensibly, [the college] was to receive Government support; practically, it did not, but the belief that it was dependent upon the Government naturally tended to deprive it of the support of private individuals." The same could be said of all western state colleges in the first half of the century and beyond. They suffered not only from neglect by egalitarian state governments but also from the hostility of denominations supporting their own colleges. Of these six colleges, only Indiana avoided closing its doors later in the nineteenth century.[94]

★   ★   ★

The first two decades of the nineteenth century receive scant attention in higher education histories, but in these years the landscape of higher education was transformed in lasting ways. The ideals and pretensions of the American Enlightenment shriveled before the onslaught of emotional religion. Lost were public support for republican universities, toleration, secularism, and aloofness from theological doctrines. Surviving were a healthy regard for science, safely honored in the common sense philosophy, and legal limitations on denominational favoritism in the colleges. However, conditions for all but a handful of colleges reached their lowest ebb. Most could not sustain a 4-year course, and many newly chartered institutions were unable to begin or sustain operations. Instead, a growing demand for professional education stimulated new and enduring establishments. Medical schools thrived, although the inherent drawbacks of operating as proprietary institutions became increasingly apparent. Formal legal education emerged later, weaker and separated from the colleges. And mushrooming theological seminaries, within colleges or independent, provided ministers with professional education on a scholarly basis. Just as the Awakening inspired theological seminaries, it also brought demands for religious freedom that doomed the standing order in New England and the privileged position enjoyed by the leading colleges. The collapse of Federalism in the face of democratic egalitarianism denied the educated class the power to control social institutions through government. However, the Dartmouth decision preserved their ability to control eleemosynary (nonprofit) corporations, creating the foundation for the subsequent emergence of the private nonprofit sector.

94 Ohio University closed, 1845–1848; Miami, 1873–1885; Nashville closed its college in 1850, when Lindsley resigned, and was never able to successfully reopen; Transylvania was converted to a normal school before collapsing; and East Tennessee closed, 1862–1865.

LOW STATE OF THE COLLEGES, 1800–1820

The years from 1800 to 1820 represented a turning toward a new order in American higher education, not its realization. Most momentous for the immediate future, the next decade would experience the recrudescence of the colleges, spurred by two of the drivers of American history, the inspiration of the Awakening on religious denominations and the relentless western expansion of the nation.

★ 5 ★

RENAISSANCE OF THE COLLEGES, 1820–1840

N THE 1820S THE COLLEGE ONCE AGAIN BECAME THE focal point of American higher education. Interest in the colleges took three forms: the desire to improve and perfect the basic pattern of the American college; the desire to fundamentally change that model; and efforts by diverse groups in American society to found colleges that they could call their own. The emergence and proliferation of separate professional schools gave the colleges a clearer mission, but just how this mission ought to be accomplished provoked experiment and controversy. But the welling popularity of colleges could not be gainsaid. The number of functioning colleges jumped from 28 in 1815 to 80 in 1840; the number of students grew from 2,566 in 1820 to 8,324 in 1840. By the latter date, the United States was becoming what historian David Potts has called "a land of colleges."[1]

An economic transformation of the country accompanied and stimulated the growth of colleges. In 1819 the country experienced an economic panic and its first domestically generated depression. After the recovery, the United States experienced rapid economic growth until the Civil War, interrupted principally by the panic and depression of 1837–1843. The United States remained a preindustrial society in which education played little role in the economy but was, nonetheless, a beneficiary of its secondary effects. Above all, it was affected by the expansion of the country and the revolution in transportation.

In 1800, 300,000 Americans lived beyond the Appalachians; in 1820, 2 million. By then most of the settled territories were still considered frontier, but the onset of the transportation revolution in the 1820s began to change that. In 1818 the National Road linked Maryland and Ohio, and steamboats had begun to ply

---

1 College counts by author. There are no definitive numbers of colleges, given closings, reopenings, and "false" colleges: Colin Burke, *American Collegiate Populations* (New York: New York University Press, 1982); David B. Potts, *Liberal Education for a Land of Colleges: Yale's "Reports" of 1828* (New York: Palgrave Macmillan, 2010).

the Mississippi. The Erie Canal opened in 1825, connecting the Eastern seaboard with the Great Lakes and generating a flurry of canal building elsewhere. And in 1830 the first steam locomotives heralded future railroads. As these means of transport complemented the river arteries of the trans-Appalachian region, the products of these fecund lands reached markets in the East, and imported and manufactured goods from the East found consumers in the West. This trade shaped a distinctive American economy, comprising hugely profitable cotton plantations in the South, textile factories in New England, and a few growing urban entrepôts.[2]

However, the vast expanse of country harbored a market economy of small-scale producers of agriculture-based goods. In the words of historian Robert Wiebe, "very little in the American economy built upward. . . . Almost everything spread outward." This "commercial hinterland . . . tended to replicate the same mixture of small-scale activities in each largely autonomous region: processing farm products and manufacturing for local markets, wholesaling and jobbing, financing and transporting."[3] These activities were conducted by a burgeoning population of middle-class or protomiddle-class farmers, merchants, bankers, lawyers, and other workers needed to produce, distribute, and finance goods and services. Wiebe called these clusters "island communities." Their founders and entrepreneurs may have had little education themselves, but a cash economy required literacy and numeracy. Moreover, as they prospered, they sought greater educational opportunities for their sons and, before long, daughters. The relentless geographic and economic expansion of the United States thus expanded the population of potential students for colleges and educational institutions.

The growth of colleges and student numbers was scarcely inevitable. In Western Europe and, particularly, Britain, economic modernization did not affect higher education for some time. There, well-developed national systems of secondary education provided rigorous classical education but also served as stringent gatekeepers to universities. In the United States, common schools were locally organized and open only part of the year, and the secondary space was filled by a hodgepodge of private schools and academies.[4] As was seen in chapter 4, the

2 Daniel Walker Howe, *What Hath God Wrought? The Transformation of America, 1815–1848* (New York: Oxford University Press, 2007), passim.

3 Robert H. Wiebe, *The Opening of American Society: From the Adoption of the Constitution to the Eve of Disunion* (New York: Knopf, 1984), 259.

4 Fritz K. Ringer, *Education and Society in Modern Europe* (Bloomington: Indiana University Press, 1979), 206–59; R. D. Anderson, *European Universities from the Enlightenment to 1914* (Oxford: Oxford University Press, 2004), 119–37; Carl F. Kaestle, *Pillars of the Republic: Common Schools and American Society, 1780–1860* (New York: Hill & Wang, 1983).

early western colleges operated more as secondary schools before being able to offer a college course. American colleges thus had a far greater role in providing access to education than did European universities. This condition would persist throughout the nineteenth century, contributing to their popularity but also to the ambiguity surrounding their roles.

NEW MODELS FOR COLLEGES

Before America became a land of colleges, other forms of higher education emerged as alternatives and sometimes challengers to the traditional college course. The rise of professional schools represented one alternative, and the early attempts to form inclusive universities represented another. Other initiatives sought to broaden curricula to include more practical subjects and widen participation to the more practical minded. Some of these institutions were formed in the first two decades of the century, when the college curriculum was still in flux. The most distinctive of these was the U.S. Military Academy at West Point.

Launched by President Jefferson in his first year in office and chartered in 1802, West Point is often linked with his Enlightenment views and patronage of science. However, his motive in this case was political—to provide a Republican counterweight to Federalist domination of the armed services. Rudimentary mathematics was the only academic subject taught in the early years, and poorly educated Republican recruits were favored over better-prepared Federalists. Officially part of the Corps of Engineers, during the first decade cadets learned little beyond military tactics and field fortification. Moreover, the academy was beset with administrative turmoil, both in Washington and at the Point, causing it virtually to cease functioning from 1811 to 1813. Congress intervened with legislation in 1812 that raised educational standards: It established professors in science, mathematics, and engineering as well as instructors in French and drawing; admissions standards were set for age (15 years) and education; and the corps of cadets was organized.[5]

At this juncture, Captain Alden Partridge emerged as the dominant figure at the Academy. Partridge had graduated from the Academy in 1806 after attending Dartmouth for 3 years, and he remained at the Point as instructor and sometime acting head. Now he was promoted to professor of engineering, the country's first, and then superintendent. The vainglorious Partridge was popular with the

---

5 Theodore J. Crackel, *West Point: A Bicentennial History* (Lawrence: University of Kansas Press, 2002), 53–80; James William Kershner, *Sylvanus Thayer: A Biography* (New York: Arno Press, 1982), 100–38.

cadets, whom he relished leading on parades and military exercises, but detested by the faculty for his authoritarian streak. Administrative chaos prevailed until a successor was named in 1817 (without informing Partridge). Refusing to obey the new superintendent, he was court-marshaled but then allowed to resign. Partridge departed with the conviction that the kind of military education he had fostered at West Point could be replicated to train citizen soldiers and provide needed instruction in practical fields. He soon embarked on a career of educational entrepreneurship to promote this model.

Sylvanus Thayer, the new superintendent (1817–1833), is officially recognized as the "Father of the Military Academy." Although some reforms had been implemented earlier, he molded an effective and enduring "Thayer system." A graduate of Dartmouth before entering the Academy, Thayer had briefly observed the most advanced military education at France's École Polytechnique, which taught a concentrated course in mathematics and engineering as a foundation for later studies at "schools of application."[6] Inspired by that example, Thayer instituted a curriculum that made West Point the nation's first and foremost school of engineering. Achieving this required more than changing the curriculum.

Thayer's first challenge was to reestablish discipline after the laxness of the Partridge regime. Here he accomplished what colleges of the day could not: he imposed a strict regime of structured activities that occupied the entire day. His use of military punishments, especially courts-martial, and his own authoritarian style caused some backlash; his tenure was marked by occasional student riots. Responsibility for all academic matters was confided to the Academic Board—consisting of the faculty, chaired by the superintendent, and reporting to the Secretary of War. This was arguably the first example of shared academic governance, particularly after the autocratic Thayer departed. The Board approved dividing the class sections by proficiency, so that more capable students could study more advanced material—another first in American higher education. The most important curricular reform was establishing a 4-year course: a student's first 2 years were largely devoted to mathematics and French; the third year comprised physics, chemistry, and topographical drawing; and fourth-year students concentrated on engineering, with a smattering of collegiate subjects, including moral philosophy. Until 1824, the seniors studied only military engineering, but that year, with some prodding from Washington, civil engineering was introduced. West Point quickly became the

6   Kershner, *Thayer*, 73–99; on the École Polytechnique, Robert F. Hunter and Edwin L. Dooley Jr., *Claudius Crozet: French Engineer in America, 1790–1864* (Charlottesville: University Press of Virginia, 1989).

nation's principal source of civil engineers, who were badly needed to assist the transportation revolution.[7]

West Point differed from other colleges in significant ways.[8] The superintendent had far less power than a college president, governing instead with the academic board. The chain of command went through the army chief engineer, the secretary of war, to the president. In the populist politics of the Jacksonian era, the academy bore the unpopularity of both the professional military and higher education. The hostility of President Andrew Jackson himself drove Thayer from office, but the academic board managed to insulate the school from frequent political attacks. Most of the faculty that Thayer assembled persisted long after his departure. West Point combined academic conservatism with a commitment to academic quality. Two professors had followed Thayer's path to Europe to study military education, and the faculty was generally well qualified. Frequently criticized for overemphasizing math and engineering, the academic board responded in 1854 by adding a fifth year of study to incorporate humanistic subjects and additional military training. From Thayer until the1840s, the West Point curriculum substituted useful French for the classical languages, taught the most advanced mathematics and physical science, and had the most effective course in engineering.

Elsewhere, interest grew in military/engineering education for the nation's expanding infrastructure, but without West Point's faculty and captive audience, both teacher supply and student demand were tenuous. The most energetic promoter was Alden Partridge, who remained an inveterate foe of Thayer and West Point. In 1820 he recovered from his discomfiture to found the American Literary, Scientific, and Military Academy in his native Norwich, Vermont. This incongruous amalgam of military, collegiate, secondary, and practical instruction reflected Partridge's messianic mission to create a trained civilian militia, to employ military discipline for training and education, and to allow cadets (i.e., students) freedom to study any subject at their own pace. The academy was open to students as young as nine, and it granted only certificates for completing studies in its many subjects. And, it was a success of sorts.[9]

7   Kershner, *Thayer*, 81–106; for the negative side of Thayer's early years, Hunter and Dooley, *Claudius Crozet*, 16–30: Crozet was an École Polytechnique graduate and Napoleonic veteran who became professor of engineering under Partridge but felt he was mistreated by Thayer.

8   James L. Morrison, *'The Best School in the World': West Point, the Pre–Civil War Years, 1833–1866* (Kent, OH: Kent State University Press, 1986): Morrison emphasizes the similarities in the student experience, in and out of class, a graduation rate of ca. 50 percent, and a philosophy of a single course to shape the mind; however, the differences are significant: 102–13.

9   William A. Ellis, ed., *History of Norwich University, 1819–1911*, 3 vol. (Montpelier, VT, 1911), I, 1–90; Gary Thomas Lord, "Alden Partridge's Proposal for a National System of Education: A Model for the Land-Grant Act," *History of Higher Education Annual*, 18 (1998): 11–24.

In 1824 Partridge descended the Connecticut River to Middletown, where he convinced local citizens to provide land and buildings to relocate the academy. On its new campus, the academy swelled to more than 300 students and 20 ostensibly qualified professors and instructors. But Partridge himself seemed to be the only force that could hold this enterprise together, and he was often absent on proselytizing tours. After just 4 years the collapsing academy retreated back to Norwich, abandoning the Middletown facilities, which soon became home to Wesleyan University (1831). Partridge regrouped nonetheless and in 1834 obtained a state charter for Norwich University, which continued to offer both military and civil engineering courses, although on a much diminished scale.[10] Although Partridge was called a "consummate clown" by one observer, he inspired the founding of numerous private, mostly ephemeral, military academies or institutes in the North and the South. An indigenous tradition of military academies developed in the South, where state-supported military academies were also founded, beginning with Virginia Military Institute (1839) and the Citadel (1842). None of these schools, however, approached the effectiveness of West Point in teaching science and engineering.[11]

Another anomalous institution that reflected popular enthusiasm for science was the Rensselaer School, opened by Amos Eaton in 1825. A graduate of Williams College (1799), Eaton only became a passionate promoter of science after a disastrous law career. He retooled as a "graduate student" with Silliman at Yale before engaging in surveying and lecturing in the Albany area. The patronage of Stephen Van Rensselaer allowed the school to be incorporated in 1824. Eaton and one other professor offered a 1-year course focused on geology and natural history, leading to a "bachelor's of natural science." Their courses were apparently the first to allow students to participate in scientific activities, as opposed to attending lectures, and graduates tended to become enthusiastic teachers and practitioners. Although Eaton had great ambitions, the school remained a modest, 1-year course given by Eaton himself, with some assistance from former students. In 1835, a 1-year course in civil engineering was added, and the name was changed to Rensselaer Institute. The school benefited from the backing of local notables, including Union president Eliphalet Nott, who became the

---

10   Norwich University was chartered in association with the Universalist Church, which had sought a college: Ellis, *History of Norwich*, 7–10; David B. Potts, *Wesleyan University, 1831–1910: Collegiate Enterprise in New England* (New Haven: Yale University Press, 1992), 3–6, quote p. 5.

11   Jennifer R. Green, *Military Education and the Emerging Middle Class in the Old South* (New York: Cambridge University Press, 2008); Rod Andrew Jr., *Long Gray Lines: The Southern Military School Tradition, 1939–1915* (Chapel Hill: University of North Carolina Press, 2001); Dean Paul Baker, *The Partridge Connection: Alden Partridge and Southern Military Education*, PhD Diss., University of North Carolina, 1986, chapter 6.

absentee president in 1829. Nott resigned in 1845 when Union began offering its own engineering course. The school barely survived the death of Eaton in 1842 but revived to launch a successful 3-year engineering course in 1851 as Rensselaer Polytechnic Institute.[12]

During the 1830s, engineering professors were sometimes hired and lectures offered in liberal arts colleges, including Geneva (Hobart), Pennsylvania (Gettysburg), William & Mary, New Jersey (Princeton), and the universities of New York, Alabama, and Pennsylvania. The long depression of 1837 to 1843 seems to have undermined these initiatives, but other factors were no doubt in play. It proved difficult to retain competent engineers on college faculties, and the lectures they gave could not alone provide adequate training. After the depression, however, engineering education would finally take root beyond West Point.[13]

★ ★ ★

When the University of Virginia opened in 1825, it was both a new model for American higher education and a belated realization of the old dream of republican universities. The latter model had preoccupied founder Thomas Jefferson since the reforms of William & Mary during the Revolution. After becoming disillusioned with his alma mater, the idea of a separate state university for Virginia developed in his mind for 20 years. The University of Virginia embodied Enlightenment ideals of secularism, republicanism, and useful knowledge. But much had transpired since the Early Republic, and Jefferson's university was also shaped by his own political battles against Federalists, organized churches, and his enemies in the North. Jefferson carefully manipulated key faculty appointments, library acquisitions, and the curriculum in order to foster the right brand of Democratic Republicanism. He outmaneuvered the churches to exclude them from the university and from any official role in Virginia higher education. But above all, the University of Virginia emerged in his mind as a sectional institution. He deeply resented that Virginians sent their sons to be educated in the North. Harvard was the great rival and nemesis that turned Virginia students into "fanatics & tories." The Missouri crisis of 1819–1820 over extending slavery in the West reinforced these sentiments but also elicited sympathy in the state for securing the appropriations needed to finish constructing his spectacular

12   Samuel Rezneck, *Education for a Technological society: A Sesquicentennial History of Rensselaer Polytechnic Institute* (Troy, NY: RPI, 1968).

13   Terry S. Reynolds, "The Education of Engineers in America before the Morrill Act of 1862," *History of Education Quarterly*, 32, 4 (Winter 1992): 459–82. See chapter 6.

campus. Jefferson could not wait for the University of Virginia to develop into a good university: it had to be launched as the South's finest, a fitting rival of Harvard and Yale.[14]

The University of Virginia was thus created by Jefferson's drive and vision. Working through his agent in the legislature, he captured the state's Literary Fund, at the expense of public education, and secured authorization for the university in 1818. He led the commission that outlined a plan of studies in 1819. And, as head (rector) of the Board of Visitors, he controlled the design of the campus, its construction, and the hiring of its teachers. Jefferson's vision differed from the German universities that were emerging as centers of professional training and specialized scholarship.[15] Rather, his was an Enlightenment vision that valued breadth of knowledge. The university was launched with eight designated professorships (all it could afford), each responsible for a "school": ancient languages, modern languages, mathematics, natural philosophy, natural history, anatomy and medicine, moral philosophy, and law. These were subjects taught at other American universities, but Jefferson specified that the professors cover impossibly broad subject matter. The professor of ancient languages, besides instructing in Latin and Greek, was to teach Hebrew, rhetoric, belles lettres, ancient history, and ancient geography. The single professor of medicine was charged with subjects covered by six professors in full medical schools. When Jefferson's recruiter tried to hire European professors, he had to compromise on these broad competencies that no single individual could cover. Five professors were hired abroad, and Americans were found for natural history and moral philosophy. The chair in law could not be filled until 1826. The university opened with a young but highly competent faculty. Its distinctiveness was not in the subjects the faculty was charged to teach, but the manner in which they would be taught.[16]

Jefferson designed a campus of classical beauty that is admired to this day. The enormous rotunda, modeled on the Roman Pantheon, faced a broad lawn, flanked on either side by the professor's pavilions, with student residences close by to the rear. However, the imperfections of the academic system immediately became apparent. Students were free to enroll in the schools of their choosing, with study in three schools per session envisioned as the norm. Professors were enjoined to lecture as well as provide suitable out-of-class exercises. Rigorous examinations were given to those who wished to "graduate" from a school,

---

14   Philip Alexander Bruce, *History of the University of Virginia, 1819–1919: The Lengthening Shadow of One Man*, 5 vol. (New York: Macmillan, 1920); Cameron Addis, *Jefferson's Vision for Education, 1760–1845* (New York: Peter Lang, 2003), Jefferson quote (1820), p. 93.

15   Edward Everett, "University of Virginia," *North American Review*, 10 (Jan. 1820): 124–27.

16   The schools are described in Bruce, *History*, II, 81–197.

but no degrees were offered until 1831.[17] It was the most liberal approach to learning heretofore devised in American higher education, an idealization of Jefferson's own experience at William & Mary, but it was little appreciated by its clientele.

The class list for the University of Virginia read like a who's who of the state's most distinguished families. Even with an annual state appropriation of $15,000, it was the most expensive college in the country, and the sons of wealthy planters predominated (after 1845 the state provided a small number of scholarships). These students brought to the university the culture of the plantations, including drinking, gambling, guns, and an exaggerated sense of honor, often invoked against the professors. Disturbances and flagrant abuse of the faculty occurred almost immediately. The first student riot in 1825 provoked a famous meeting of the Board of Visitors, where three former presidents—Jefferson, Madison, and Monroe—expelled five perpetrators, including Jefferson's great-great-nephew. The disorders did not attenuate until the late 1840s, after a student had shot and killed a professor (1840) and prolonged rioting required the militia to restore order (1836, 1845). The southern state universities generally were prone to such disturbances, but none matched Virginia's infamy. These excesses were exacerbated by the privileged status of its students, their considerable freedom, and weak academic discipline. Two-thirds of Virginia students attended for 1 year or less. Very few completed a diploma; lacking such a goal, the majority put little effort into their studies.

The principal historian of the university expressed some sympathy for the frustrations faced by students, if not for their inexcusable behavior.[18] Jefferson's plan created what today would be called an upper-division university; that is, it taught material that other colleges offered to the junior and senior classes. Yet, standards of admission were lenient, and few Virginia students had adequate preparation for that level of studies, especially in Latin and Greek. Discouragement no doubt boosted the high rate of attrition. Given the difficulty of getting to and from Charlottesville, the university session (academic year) originally had only one break and none at all in the oppressive summer months. And, despite the liberality of the regime, students chafed at the requirements to wear uniforms and to surrender control of their money as well as a disciplinary code that was periodically tightened.

---

17 The master's degree, created in 1831, was awarded for earning diplomas in several schools. An MD was offered as well, and bachelor's degrees, in 1848. However, few degrees were awarded: up to the war, the university awarded 40 bachelor's degrees and 107 master's. Students who earned a diploma in any school were entitled to be "graduates of the University of Virginia": Bruce, *History*, III, 61–65.

18 Bruce, *History*, passim.

Despite the notoriety of student misbehavior, the university sought to maintain high academic standards. Faculty had to be knowledgeable in order to lecture their subjects 6 hours per week for 10 months of the year. They were very well paid for their efforts and tribulations. As faculty turned over, the new appointees maintained that high level of competence. They appear to have been completely occupied with teaching duties (and a gracious social life) and were genuinely devoted to upholding academic standards. The university had no president, another Jeffersonian innovation, but a rotating chairmanship of the faculty instead. The professors thus bore collective responsibility for academic matters, and they were usually backed by the Board of Visitors. The Visitors, for their part, took a close interest in the university and consciously sought to uphold Jeffersonian ideals. After Jefferson's death in 1826, James Madison chaired the board as rector until 1836. The professors gradually adjusted their schools to prevailing realities. Most extended their courses to 2 years, so that "juniors" were introduced to subjects and "seniors" were taught more advanced material. Examinations for those who wished to "graduate" held students to a high standard. For the minority of students who took their studies seriously, the university offered a rigorous course of instruction by devoted teachers. Students quickly augmented classroom learning by forming debating societies. However, in a case of southern sensibility preempting intellectual ideals, they were forbidden to speak on controversial topics. Although Jefferson had been the guiding spirit, Virginians created a university that suited the state's elite families: prestigious bordering on pretentious, it accommodated both serious academic study and the artifices of Southern gentility. As a model for American higher education, it could scarcely be replicated.

★ ★ ★

Virginia's putative northern rival, the University in Cambridge, faced its own frustrations in its endeavor to improve on the model of the American college. During the prosperous early years of his tenure, President Kirkland (1810–1828) was able to indulge the Anthologists' vision of creating a university that could support "a few men of genius in the pursuit of letters."[19] Kirkland, like Jefferson, recognized the superiority of European universities, but instead of seeking European professors, he sponsored four prospective faculty to study there between 1815 and 1820, principally at Göttingen. The brilliant Edward Everett was appointed professor of Greek at age 21 and immediately dispatched to Germany,

---

19 [John Kirkland], "Literary Institutions—University," *North American Review*, 7 (July 1818), 270–88, quote p. 277.

where he became the first American to earn a German PhD. His traveling companion and fellow student at Göttingen was George Ticknor, who was subsequently appointed to a new endowed chair in modern languages. A Harvard tutor, Joseph Cogswell, spent 5 years in European study, and he was joined in 1817 by a promising young graduate, George Bancroft. Upon returning, all became disillusioned in attempting to introduce the spirit of Germanic learning into the prevailing college pedagogy. Bancroft, who assumed continental airs, was hounded from his tutorship by relentless student harassment after one miserable year. He and Cogswell both left in 1823 to found the highly regarded Roundhill preparatory school. Edward Everett was demoralized by "too much . . . contact with some little men and many little things" and soon escaped by getting elected to Congress (1824). Only Ticknor endured; his professorship spared him from the drudgery of conducting recitations and disciplining students.[20]

Although somewhat removed from the fray, Ticknor was personally frustrated by his inability to control the students admitted to his lectures or examine them on the content. He became convinced that the college course at Harvard and other American colleges needed radical reform. He objected to the single fixed course: students did not study subjects, but books, or parts of books; the recitation method precluded real teaching; and the few lectures were no better since students neither prepared nor were examined on the material. Finally, dividing the class into sections alphabetically, instead of by proficiency, reduced pedagogy to the lowest common denominator. Ticknor may have been more knowledgeable about different practices in higher education than any contemporary American. Besides European-wide experience, he visited his old Dartmouth roommate, Sylvanus Thayer, at West Point, where he admired the academic as well as the military discipline. He met and corresponded with Jefferson about education and in 1824 received a personal tour of the nearly finished University of Virginia. His own views seemed to meld these two near opposites: lofty ambition to admit advanced learning to the college but hard-headed discipline to control student behavior and allow effective teaching. Ticknor advocated reform soon after he began teaching, but his opportunity came when the college was rocked in 1823 by perhaps the worst disturbance in its history.

Under the kindly Kirkland, Harvard students increasingly tested and transgressed college rules. But the class of 1823 carried revelry and defiance of authority to new levels. The "Great Rebellion" was caused nonetheless by an

---

20 Richard Yanikoski, *Edward Everett and the Advancement of Higher Education and Adult Learning in Ante-Bellum Massachusetts*, PhD Diss., University of Chicago, 1987, quote p. 18; David B. Tyack, *George Ticknor and the Boston Brahmins* (Cambridge: Harvard University Press, 1967); Thomas Adam and Gisela Mettele, eds., *Two Boston Brahmins in Goethe's Germany: The Travel Journals of Anna and George Ticknor* (Lanham, MD: Rowen & Littlefield, 2009), 1–94.

internecine conflict between a united majority of "high fellows" and a "Black List" of students whom they viciously abused for opposing their mayhem. The enmity of the rebels reached a fevered pitch over parts in commencement, and ensuing acts of violence and intransigence resulted in forty-three of the class of seventy being dismissed from the college.[21]

The governing boards and the public were now convinced that something was terribly wrong at Harvard. Ticknor took the lead in organizing discussions of reform and pressing his previous views. Two years of meetings and reports produced 153 new "Statutes and Laws of the University in Cambridge," which embodied several of the measures advocated by Ticknor. He elaborated and praised them in a subsequent pamphlet. "In the first place . . . Harvard College is now . . . thrown open to all who wish to obtain any of the instruction it offers, whether they seek to obtain an academic degree or not." Second, the laws sought to reduce vacations and keep students on campus and at their studies, practices Ticknor admired at West Point. "A third important change, and one which may be useful in many colleges . . . instruction . . . shall be given by *departments*; and . . . students shall, to a certain degree, have a choice of the studies they are to pursue." Finally, "a *fourth* important change . . . the divisions of the classes for recitations and teaching shall be made according to proficiency," which should provide a "broad cornerstone for beneficial changes in all our colleges."[22] With a partial course, electives, and grouping sections by merit, Ticknor believed that Harvard had broken the mold of the traditional course and illuminated the way for a reformation of American colleges. But he was soon disillusioned.

Harvard College teachers proved reluctant to institute these curricular reforms. Ticknor's Göttingen comrades had all departed, and most remaining professors were uninspiring pedagogues.[23] President Kirkland's enthusiasm for university building—and for Ticknor—was by this time greatly diminished. The faculty dragged its feet about establishing departments, and public opinion seemed to regard sorting students by merit as undemocratic. The college soon made the practice optional, effectively ending this reform before it began. Nor was anything done to encourage nondegree students to take advantage of Harvard instruction, and virtually none appeared. Ticknor alone pioneered the new model as head of the department of modern languages. There he felt the results

21   Samuel Eliot Morison, "The Great Rebellion in Harvard College, and the Resignation of President Kirkland," *Colonial Society of Massachusetts, Transactions: 1927–1930* (April, 1928): 54–112.

22   George Ticknor, *Remarks on Changes Lately Proposed or Adopted in Harvard University* (Boston, 1825), reprinted in Potts, *Liberal Education*, 35–40.

23   Robert McCaughey, "The Transformation of American Academic Life: Harvard University 1821–1892," *Perspectives in American History*, VII (1974): 239–332. Ticknor, in contrast, was an adopted Boston Brahmin.

vindicated the reform. The most capable students advanced rapidly to read eminent European authors, and modern languages became the most popular department. But Kirkland had asked Ticknor to refrain from citing "what has been done or proposed by others": the spirit of reform was extinguished in Harvard College.[24]

★　★　★

That spirit flared brightly, however, at the anti-Harvard—the new bastion of Orthodox Congregationalism in Amherst, Massachusetts. Started by a secession from Williams College in 1821, Amherst College had overcome the opposition of existing Massachusetts colleges to obtain a charter in 1825. It opened at the zenith of the Awakening in the Connecticut River valley, a Congregational stronghold that had hitherto looked north to Dartmouth or south to Yale. Its attendance mushroomed to more than 200, and Ralph Waldo Emerson called it an "infant Hercules." In some ways early Amherst typified the new colleges that complemented the expanding agricultural economy. Students were drawn almost entirely from the region; 40 percent needed aid from the college Charity Fund or the American Education Society; many were mature students; most were deeply pious.[25] Like many new colleges, Amherst felt an impulse for improvement. In 1826 the faculty proposed, and the trustees approved, a bold plan of reform.

Unlike the innovations just reviewed, the Amherst proposal owed nothing to European inspiration. It stemmed rather from a conviction of public dissatisfaction with the colleges for not being "sufficiently modern and comprehensive, to meet the exigencies of the age and the country." In the tradition of Franklin, Rush, and Webster, it asked why a college student should "be compelled to spend nearly four years . . . in the study of the dead Languages, for which he has not taste, [and] from which he expects to derive no material advantage . . . ?" The proposal did not reject the classical course but rather asked that an equivalent course be created to offer instruction in French, Spanish, and other modern subjects, including a "department of theoretical and practical mechanics." Such a course would be better adapted "to the taste and future pursuits of a large class of young men, who aspire to the advantages of a liberal education." In a provision that reflected local realities, the proposal strongly urged the creation of a new department to teach the "science of education," since "three fourths of [the

---

24　Tyack, *George Ticknor*, 112–23, quote p. 121.

25　*American Quarterly Register* (Apr. 1829): 224; David F. Allmendinger Jr., *Paupers and Scholars* (New York: St. Martin's, 1975).

students] expect to be teachers, in one form or another," at some point in their careers.[26]

The Amherst Trustees instituted the parallel course in 1827, but problems quickly arose. The freshman class of 1827 was the largest yet for the college, and eighteen of sixty-seven students chose the modern languages course. However, the new French instructor proved incompetent, and the regular faculty found the teaching of additional subjects onerous. Students soon sensed that this instruction was inferior to the regular course. In 1828 no incoming freshmen opted for modern languages, and the trustees terminated the experiment. Students of modern languages were absorbed into the classical course, and the principal faculty advocate resigned.[27]

The Amherst plan was one of many experiments with parallel, partial, or English-language courses in the 1820s. Despite the anticlassical rhetoric, it was a fairly conservative approach: It preserved unaltered the classical course; the classical languages were required for admission; and students in both courses took the same nonlanguage subjects. Unlike Harvard or Virginia, Amherst lacked the resources to offer a diversified curriculum. That "large class of young men" supposedly clamoring for a liberal education, or part of one, failed to materialize at Amherst or anywhere else, and the few who did attempt this course soon became aware of its cultural and pedagogical inferiority. The one college where a parallel course lasted was Union, where Eliphalet Nott created a "scientific" course—actually a misnomer—in 1828. His alternative was even more conservative, allowing students to opt for modern languages and history subjects only after the freshman year. With students taking many of the same subjects and receiving the same AB degree, no stigma seemed to attach to Union's scientific course.[28]

No lack of models for college education existed in the 1820s, but all were effectively marginalized, at least until the succeeding generation. Military education for engineers found an effective formula under Army discipline at West Point, but civilian imitations struggled before 1850, despite the best efforts of Alden Partridge. Thomas Jefferson's idiosyncratic vision produced the monument he sought, but not a model for others; and its subsequent evolution moved it closer to the mainstream. Harvard, with the greatest academic resources in the

26   *The Substance of Two Reports of the Faculty of Amherst College to the Board of Trustees, with the Doings of the Board Thereon* (Amherst, 1827), quotes pp. 5–9; reprinted in Potts, *Liberal Education,* 162–84. Many Amherst students taught school to fund their own education.

27   W. S. Tyler, *History of Amherst College during Its First Half-century* (Springfield, MA, 1873), 172–73. Amherst became conservative and declined precipitously during the depression: Claude M. Fuess, *Amherst: The Story of a New England College* (Boston: Little, Brown, 1935), 122–26.

28   Frederick Rudolph, *The American College and University: A History* (New York: Knopf, 1962), 110–35; Wayne Somers, ed., *Encyclopedia of Union College History* (Schenectady: Union College Press, 2003), 200–201.

country, could not reorganize itself to employ them more effectively, settling instead for a demonstration project in the department of modern languages. And, efforts to loosen the grip of classical languages and make college studies accessible to a larger population foundered at all major schools, save Union College. The traditional model of the American college, despite all strictures, possessed remarkable residual strength. Yet, unlike its adversaries, it seemed to lack forceful advocates—until 1828.

THE YALE *REPORTS* OF 1828

Alternative models to the traditional college course may have had few successes in the 1820s, but reverberations were felt at most new and established colleges in the form of tentative reforms, questioning of established practices, or, more often, serious breakdowns—most everywhere, that is, except at Yale. [29] There, since the presidency of Timothy Dwight (1795–1817), the faculty had consistently sought to strengthen and enlarge the traditional, classical course. Each of Dwight's professorial appointments had contributed. Jeremiah Day extended math instruction to trigonometry and surveying, besides algebra, authoring what became standard textbooks in those subjects. James Kingsley adopted an all-purpose Greek reader, the *Collectanea Graeca Majora* (1805). Benjamin Silliman soon emerged as the most renowned academic scientist for his work in geology and mineralogy. He delivered famed demonstration lectures in chemistry to juniors and seniors, attracted graduate students, and founded the respected *American Journal of Science and Arts*. After Day (1817–1846) succeeded Dwight as president, a professor of rhetoric and oratory was added, as well as another professor of math. Instruction in Latin and Greek was extended to the senior year (1824), and juniors were given an option of studying French, Spanish, or calculus (1825–1826).[30]

What did not change was the form of instruction. The course of study, at Yale and elsewhere, was anchored by three recitations per day, interspersed with lectures, especially for juniors and seniors. Recitations during the first 2 years of study consisted of little else but Latin, Greek, and math. Considerable effort was devoted to writing and speaking through compositions, translations, disputations, and declamations. Students were examined orally twice a year. The president and faculty were, like their inspirational former president, devoted

---

29   "Introductory Essay: A Land of Colleges," David B. Potts, *Liberal Education for a Land of Colleges* (New York: Palgrave Macmillan, 2010), 7–12: the fullest analysis of the Yale *Reports* of 1828.

30   Roger L. Geiger, "Context for a Compelling and Cogent Case" in Ibid., 227–34; historical data on Yale from George W. Pierson, *A Yale Book of Numbers: Historical Statistics of the College and University, 1701–1976* (New Haven: Yale University Press, 1983).

pedagogues, and Yale was the largest and most national American college. Graduate Julian Sturtevant, although a critic, later judged that "Yale was probably doing better work than any other college in the country." The Yale faculty consequently bristled at charges that the colleges were relics of the past needing to be "new-modelled" for modern America. They reacted specifically to the charges of Ticknor, coming from old rival Harvard, and the Amherst faculty, the new rival to the North. The threat hit home when a trustee resolution, whether serious or contrived, proposed that the Yale course be altered by leaving out "the study of the *dead languages*." A committee of the Yale Corporation then asked the faculty to respond, and the result was a two-part report written by President Jeremiah Day and professor James Kingsley, respectively.[31]

Day began stridently by denying that the college had been "stationary," alluding to the developments described above. He then cut straight to the purpose of college: "to lay the foundation of a superior education."[32] This was achieved through "the *discipline* and the *furniture* of the mind; expanding its powers and storing it with knowledge." Mental discipline was by far the more important, and it could be developed only by bringing "all the important mental faculties . . . into exercise." For Day, this meant the full college course, much as it existed at Yale, combining lectures, recitations, "written and extemporaneous *disputes*," and examinations. The college course should not be expected to finish a student's education but rather to teach him "*how* to learn." Day then contrasted this "thorough education" with other existing or proposed alternatives. He rejected the idea of emulating German universities since, besides being impossibly costly, they offered advanced and professional education for which American colleges provided only a foundation. He then dismissed existing suggestions or efforts to offer an accelerated ("superficial") course, a partial course, or the kind of vocational subjects advocated for parallel courses. The Yale course was superior to all these, and to try to incorporate any of them would diminish the quality and prestige, and hence the effectiveness, of a Yale education. In fact, "the multiplication of schools and academies in this country, requires that colleges should aim at a high standard of literary excellence." Their role was to furnish the culture of an educated upper class: to produce "men of superior education, of large and liberal views, of those solid and elegant attainments, which will raise them to a higher distinction, than the mere possession of property."

31 Potts, "Introductory Essay"; Julian Sturtevant, *An Autobiography* (Chicago, 1896), 90–91.

32 All quotations from Yale University, *Reports on the Course of Instruction in Yale College; by a Committee of the Corporation and the Academical Faculty* (New Haven, 1828), reprinted in Potts, *Liberal Education,* 85–140. Note the plural *Reports*.

To complete this argument, James Kingsley attempted to establish that "familiarity with the Greek and Roman writers is especially adapted to form the taste, and to discipline the mind." His claims that these subjects "form the best preparation for professional study," or that modern languages cannot instill mental discipline, were no doubt more plausible to contemporaries than to modern readers. However, he too emphasized cultural arguments that reflected realities of the 1820s. The classical languages were still regarded as essential to a liberal education, and far from declining, in Europe they seemed to be "pursued with increasing ardor." "Without a preparation in classical literature," someone in educated company "immediately feels a deficiency in his education." Kingsley concluded by explicitly contradicting Ticknor's charges, without mentioning him by name: Yale examinations were rigorous and thorough; its recitations provided genuine teaching; and its graduates departed with an intellectual foundation for success and distinction.

The report of the Corporation Committee, responding to the faculty reports, was written by Governor Gideon Tomlinson and was so warmly supportive that it seems unlikely that the Corporation ever seriously envisioned dropping the "dead languages." He added a point of his own, and one surely appreciated in New England, by observing that the neglect of the "learned languages" in France "immediately preceding and during the revolution" had "disastrous" consequences. Indeed, proponents associated the classical languages with upholding the social order. Tomlinson emphatically reiterated the principal arguments of Day and Kingsley and ended by capturing the essence of the Yale experience. For the past 25 years the classical languages at Yale had "received increased attention . . . and . . . classical and other attainments required as a qualification for admittance into the college, have been considerably augmented." The effect had been to "elevate the character of the institution, and the standard of scholarship." Yale students were now older and better prepared "more successfully to pursue the studies requiring maturity of intellect." Far from abandoning classical studies, Tomlinson foresaw future admissions requirements being raised further.

The Yale *Reports* of 1828 have been generally interpreted by historians as a rearguard action to defend an obsolete curriculum, "a fossil of eighteenth-century classicism."[33] The authors of the Reports believed and argued just the opposite— that knowledge of the classics was a critical element in the quality of a person's educational formation and that the contemporary trend was to strengthen, not

33 Caroline Winterer, *The Culture of Classicism: Ancient Greece and Rome in American Intellectual Life, 1780–1910* (Baltimore: Johns Hopkins University Press, 2002), 48. For additional views, see Stanley M. Guralnik, *Science and the Antebellum College* (Philadelphia: American Philosophical Society, 1975), 29–32, n. 37.

compromise, such studies. Indeed, admirers of the scholarly attainments of Ox-bridge or German universities noted the far more rigorous classical training pos-sessed by students entering those universities. And all three authors suggested that the preeminent position of Yale College vindicated the steps it had taken to bolster the classical course. With this central contention the authors of the *Reports* were more prescient than the critics. The classical course would dominate American collegiate education for another two generations, invariably defended by appeals to mental discipline. The study of Greek, in particular, received in-creasing emphasis in following decades, both in Germany and the United States. To understand these developments, one needs first to grasp the power of the case that the *Reports* argued before asking why its weaknesses were conveniently overlooked by contemporaries.

The *Reports* was less a presentation of original ideas than a synthesis of notions that had been recently aired, separately or incompletely.[34] The clear articulation that a college education was a *foundation* rather than a *finished* education must have struck contemporaries as at once obvious but also profound. It was espe-cially true for Yale. In the year of the *Reports*, Yale College enrolled 325 students, the medical school, 68, the department of theology, 54, and the law school, 20, and there were 7 resident graduates—in other words, just over two-thirds of students were what Yale had only recently begun calling undergraduates. More-over, three-quarters of Yale College graduates of that era pursued careers in the professions of law, clergy, medicine, or (the smallest group) education. Nearly all would pursue further education to prepare for these professions. Although it was noted in the last chapter that the relationship between college and pro-fessional school was breaking down, this was not the case for Yale students. The close alliance with the American Education Society reinforced the imperative of a *thorough education*—the phrase repeatedly invoked in the *Reports*. Also reiter-ated is the message that a classical education is the appropriate preparation for professional studies. Day asserted a new identity for colleges as undergraduate education focused on developing general mental faculties, and no other coeval forms of education could challenge that claim.

The means by which this was accomplished—instilling mental discipline—have long puzzled modern historians. Some have written this concept off as a relic of faculty psychology. On the other hand, modern neuroscience has doc-umented how repeated activities can induce physiological change in the brain, which sounds to a layperson much like mental discipline. In fact, contemporar-ies understood perfectly what Day meant and continued to use the term as he

---

34 Potts, "Introductory Essay," 36–37; e.g., the Amherst Report asserts that its parallel course "should require as great an amount of hard study, or mental discipline": p. 13.

had for the next half-century. Mental discipline was clearly a real phenomenon for Day and other educators, and it is given several formulations in the *Reports* to try to convey its essence.[35] After teaching and examining students daily for 25 years, Day certainly had a clear idea of how students managed to master a body of material, organize it, and express it. He equated this with expanding mental powers, learning how to learn, or mental discipline, and he elicited widespread agreement among educators that this was what colleges sought to accomplish. However, a fallacy lurked in this argument: if classical languages are what is taught and mental discipline a result, then mastery of these texts was believed to be the cause of mental discipline. Of course, Kingsley attempted the more diffi-cult task of proving that classical studies do this better than other subjects. Soon, critics of the *Reports* rejected his strained reasoning, maintaining that the thor-ough study of other subjects would also produce mental discipline. This latter belief gained adherents throughout the rest of the nineteenth century without swaying the convictions of the faithful.

Mental discipline was the key concept of the *Reports* because on it hinged the deeper claim for the quality of collegiate education. The authors were acutely aware of the competitive market for colleges. Day called for a "competition for excellence." Both he and Kingsley warned that Yale's standing would diminish if it should incorporate any of the less prestigious forms of education: "it will be deserted by that class of persons who have hitherto been drawn here by high expectations and purposes." Yale had specific concerns in this respect. It was fac-ing new competition on its home turf from Washington College (later Trinity) in Hartford (f. 1824) as well as Amherst, up the Connecticut River valley. Yale had also become the most national of American colleges: in 1800, Connecticut residents comprised 88 percent of its graduates, but in 1830, just 44 percent.[36] Moreover, Day emphasized the advantages of a classical over a vocational ed-ucation for "young men intended for active employment": "merchants, manu-facturers, and agriculturalists . . . are the very classes which . . . have the best op-portunities for reducing the principles of science to their practical applications." "[T]he object of the undergraduate course, is not to finish a preparation for business, but to impart that various and general knowledge, which will improve, and elevate, and adorn any occupation," which will impart "high intellectual cul-ture." The Yale *Reports* thus justified the value of a college education ultimately in cultural terms. And this was the message that, subliminally or explicitly, convinced contemporaries: a liberal education in the classical course, through

---

35   Also see Potts, "Introductory Essay," 33–35.

36   *Quarterly Register* (Apr. 1829), 226; Peter Dobkin Hall, *The Organization of American Culture, 1700–1900* (New York: New York University Press, 1984), 161–62.

mental discipline, instilled in individuals a superior culture that would enhance their capabilities and status in any career they might undertake.

If the Yale *Reports* had an Achilles' heel (to use a classical allusion), it would be the actual teaching of the classical languages. Here Ticknor was probably closer to the mark than Kingsley. Julian Sturtevant, a Yale student in the 1820s, supported the notion of mental discipline but thought it was achieved through drill, not teaching. The tutors "could hardly be said to teach at all," and Yale custom strictly forbade asking for guidance outside the classroom. He quotes Kingsley telling his class, "young gentlemen, you read Latin horribly and translate it worse." Recitations were, in fact, devoted not to understanding or appreciating literature but rather to grammatical exercises—parsing, scanning, and translating words. Students prepared about twenty lines of Greek for each recitation and one to two pages of Latin. The tutors at Yale led recitations in all subjects for the first 3 years (Harvard tutors had been teaching single subjects since 1766) and were scarcely capable of conveying deeper learning. Even learned professors like Kingsley focused on grammatical exactness, not content. The expanded study of Greek after 1800, which Kingsley spearheaded, exacerbated this situation, since reading literary Greek made greater demands on students.[37] The *Graeca Majora* was a large collection of extracts (explicated with Latin endnotes) that provided linguistic exercise without literary appreciation. Each class read different excerpts, so that there was little common learning. The Revolutionary generation had found inspiration in the content of classical literature, primarily Roman, and defended its study against critics on that basis.[38] The Yale *Reports*, in contrast, emphasized the process of studying the classical languages—in some ways an easier argument. That is, the classics in theory produced mental discipline even if badly taught in practice. This situation seems to have been the norm—so commonplace that most contemporaries failed to perceive any contradiction. Thus, Sturtevant found "the course of instruction in Yale from 1822 to 1826 . . . as very faulty and inadequate; yet it did exert a great and salutary influence over the student."[39]

But if language instruction was faulty at Yale, where it was strongest, what can be said for the rest of American colleges? The difficulty experienced by the

37 The Greek New Testament that was studied before 1800 was written in the simpler, *Koine* Greek, whereas the literature of classical Greece was in the more complex *Attic* Greek.

38 Winterer, *Culture of Classicism*, 29–49; Lyman Bagg, *Four Years at Yale* (New Haven, 1871), 558–68.

39 Sturtevant, *Autobiography*, 84–85, 90–91. The Yale authors boasted of adapting and improving the course of studies over time, but after 1828 innovation largely ceased: A professor of Greek was added in 1831, and tutors were finally allowed to specialize by teaching single subjects, but the only additional subject added in the next 15 years was two terms of law for seniors. Ironically, Yale's greatest strength was in physical science, where it was preeminent during this period (see chapter 6).

newer colleges in establishing a full college course has already been described. Yet, they embraced the message of the Yale *Reports* and with it the teaching of Latin and Greek largely through grammatical drilling. The 1820s marked the beginning of a vast proliferation of American colleges, all predicated on this notion and scarcely capable of offering anything else. Although many experimented with minor innovations, the mid-nineteenth-century American college would be based on the premise that completion of an AB degree signified a liberal education based on a classical course and produced, in theory, mental discipline and high culture. To a large degree, the colleges would be judged by the extent to which they measured up to Yale's standard of teaching Latin and Greek.

DENOMINATIONAL COLLEGES I

In 1820 and 1821, Baptists opened colleges in Waterville, Maine, and Washington, D.C. Soon, Episcopalians began instruction at new colleges in Connecticut, New York, and Ohio. The Dutch Reformed Church finally fashioned a permanent college in New Brunswick, as did evangelical Congregationalists in Amherst. Colleges by and for Friends outside of Philadelphia and Lutherans in Gettysburg followed. In 1830 the country's largest organized church—the Methodists—abandoned their distrust of higher education by sponsoring major colleges in Middletown, Connecticut, and Boydton, Virginia.[40] Although traditional in form for the most part, these institutions represented a distinct type of American college. While open to members of all faiths—a requirement of their charters—they were sponsored by churches primarily to serve a religious community. Although the education or preparation of ministers was sometimes a consideration, the chief motive was to preserve the community through the sheltered education of laypeople. This denominational defensiveness interacted with the enthusiasm of local boosters to promote the economic interests of their communities. Largely absent from this formula were state governments, other than issuing college charters on ever more permissive

---

40 These dates for opening may differ from the dates claimed for founding or charters. These institutions are:

Colby College	1820	Baptist
Columbian College	1821	Baptist
Amherst College	1824	Congregational
Rutgers College	1825	Dutch Reformed
Wesleyan University	1831	Methodist
Haverford College	1832	Quaker
Pennsylvania College	1832	Lutheran
Randolph Macon College	1832	Methodist

terms. The result was an accelerating proliferation of denominational colleges, the signature pattern of American higher education in the middle quarters of the nineteenth century.

From the time of Independence to 1820, a new college opened on average every 18 months. This rate increased in the 1820s to roughly one every 8 months and then doubled to three per year from 1830 to 1845. This rate doubled again in the next 10 years, and spurted to 10 new colleges per year in the half-decade before the Civil War. Of the approximately 180 colleges established between 1820 and 1860, just 10 were state controlled; almost all the rest were denominational colleges.[41] Of course, the population of the United States was soaring during these years. College going registered gains from 1820 to 1840, rising from about 0.8 percent of a 4-year cohort of white males to about 1.4 percent. The depression slowed enrollment growth in the 1840s, but the robust growth of the 1850s recouped those relative losses with more students and more colleges. The average college size in 1840 had reached seventy-eight students, and it was the same again in 1860. Moreover, this proliferation of denominational colleges persisted for another 2 decades, so that the average size in 1880 was just eighty-eight students. Like no other nation, the United States expanded higher education by multiplying small colleges.[42]

Several underlying factors help to account for American uniqueness. Political decentralization spurred this process. Just as the many German principalities each coveted their own university, the American colonies produced nine colleges, and the several states continued that pattern. However, when the states failed to exert authority over higher education, the religious fragmentation of the country compounded decentralization. No single denomination could claim 20 percent of the population of any state (1850), and the major denominations in fact harbored rival factions that increasingly sought their own colleges. A third factor, perhaps paramount, was the frontier—the inexorable settling of the vast interior of the continent. New colleges were not founded on the physical frontier between wilderness and settlement but rather on the real estate frontier of newly established (or projected) towns. These were the embryonic island communities described above. They sought and welcomed colleges not only as nodes of economic activity but also to fill educational and cultural vacuums. Most of these colleges began as academies, and nearly all

41 Count by author from various sources, ignoring short-lived colleges. Cf. Burke, *American Collegiate Populations*; Donald G. Tewksbury, *The Founding of American Colleges and Universities Before the Civil War* (New York: Arno Press, 1969 [1932]).

42 Author's calculations: Roger L. Geiger, "The Era of Multipurpose Colleges in American Higher Education, 1850–1880," in *American Colleges in the Nineteenth Century* (Nashville: Vanderbilt University Press, 2000), 127–52.

included preparatory departments.[43] The expansion of the United States encouraged the proliferation of denominational colleges, especially in the trans-Appalachian West.

Historian David Potts has characterized the founding of Baptist colleges as a "haphazard series of essentially local enterprises with only a partially religious character." Indeed, local and religious factors intertwined in the hundreds of unique founding sagas. Localities played three types of roles. In some cases, local boosters took the initiative in founding colleges; colleges were also founded by concentrated religious communities to provide local education of the right kind; and, as standard practice, churches solicited offers and placed new colleges in towns that promised the most attractive financial package. As for religion, some early colleges were inspired by missionary zeal on the part of individuals or groups, but as churches formed regional organizations, these bodies decided when and where to establish colleges. The growth of denominational colleges exhibited overlapping processes of extension and elaboration.[44] That is, the establishment of colleges by previously excluded denominations represented the elaboration of the institutional base of higher education. Extension denotes the founding of colleges in newly formed communities—acts of faith in more ways than one. Home missionaries from the principal denominations tended to lead this process, either inspired individuals or products of Eastern theological seminaries. Real estate speculators played a role as well, particularly in the Midwest.[45] However, in settled areas, the elaboration process produced denominational colleges for new or smaller religious sects as well as additional colleges for the major churches.

None of these processes was entirely new. Princeton had secured the College of New Jersey with the most lucrative offer. Allegheny College (f. 1817) was founded with hopes for real estate development. The eighteenth-century Presbyterian colleges in Virginia were reactions of an excluded religious minority against an Anglican monopoly. And, missionary-ministers founded would-be colleges in Appalachia from western Pennsylvania to Tennessee. However, the denominational colleges of the mid-nineteenth century differed from past practices in their orientation toward laymen, their broader educational scope, and their degree of separation from actual churches. These traits

---

43 Burke emphasizes the colleges' role in "educational upgrading": "almost every antebellum college in the West and South began as one of those ill-defined institutions, an academy": *Collegiate Populations*, 37.

44 See Geiger, "Multipurpose Colleges."

45 Colleges, too, sometimes engaged in real estate ventures in the hope of generating income: Daniel T. Johnson, *Puritan Power in Illinois Higher Education Prior to 1870*, PhD Diss., University of Wisconsin, 1974, 42–61, 76–94; David K. Brown, *Degrees of Control: A Sociology of Educational Expansion and Occupational Credentialism* (New York: Teachers College Press, 1995), 86–100.

reflected the spread of theological seminaries for ministerial preparation. In fact, these seminaries multiplied along with the colleges—some 66 founded between 1820 and 1860.[46] Sometimes linked with colleges, the seminaries were smaller and more ephemeral, but they were clear testimony to the division of labor between clerical and lay education, and encouraged an arm's-length relation between colleges and churches. With few exceptions, the churches provided no direct financial support for denominational colleges after founding. The colleges raised their own funds, largely through agents operating within the denominational community. Finally, although denominational colleges were a distinct type, the predominant nature of colleges founded after the depression of 1837–1843 shifted somewhat again, as will be seen in chapter 6. Such distinctions may appear subtle, but it would be far more misleading to lump denominational colleges together as a single phenomenon.[47] Inherently heterogeneous, they represent variations on a theme, both across denominations and over time.

The Methodists overcame their aversion to colleges in the 1820s. Although still a minority in the church, individuals in scattered localities from Maine to Illinois founded a variety of seminaries and precarious colleges. By 1830, the Annual Conferences (the regional governing bodies) actively promoted colleges. As overt anti-intellectualism waned, the Methodists feared that young men educated by other denominations were being lost to the church and the ministry. Education, furthermore, could be either "the most powerful auxiliary [of] infidelity and vice" or "a champion for Christianity." The Methodist rationale soon shifted from defending the flock to emphasizing this latter mission. As the largest and fastest-growing church, occupying the evangelical mainstream, the Methodist colleges could assume an ecumenical posture. They welcomed students of all faiths or no faith, promised not to proselytize students, and included non-Methodists on governing boards. Still, the conferences and their network of churches provided the base of support. Sponsored colleges could appeal to the faithful as Methodist institutions and their agents were permitted to preach sermons and pass a collection plate. With such official stamps of approval, Methodists began aggressively to found colleges.[48]

46   In 1860 there were 61 theological seminaries with 2,000 students; more than half of "frontier" seminaries were attached to colleges, but the majority were organized independently: Gerald G. Winkleman, *Polemics, Prayers, and Professionalism: The American Protestant Theological Seminaries from 1784 to 1920* , PhD Diss., State University of New York at Buffalo, 1975, 144–57.

47   Roger L. Geiger, "Introduction: New Themes in the History of Nineteenth-Century Colleges," in *American Colleges in the Nineteenth Century*, 1–36; Potts, *Baptist Colleges*, 4–9 and 9n.

48   Sylvanus Milne Duvall, *The Methodist Episcopal Church and Education up to 1869* (New York: Teachers College, 1928), 64–78, quote p. 75.

The establishment of the first prominent Methodist institution, appropriately named Wesleyan College, was negotiated with all the formality of an international treaty between Middletown, with an empty campus to fill, and the New York and New England Conferences, now committed to collegiate education. An agreement signed in 1830 transferred Alden Partridge's former campus to the Methodists, who agreed to open a college the following fall. The president of the new institution was Wilbur Fisk, a highly respected principal of a Methodist academy and possibly the only college graduate (Brown 1815) among New England Methodist ministers. The college soon found an eager clientele. Antebellum enrollments fluctuated between 100 and 150, though it still suffered from pervasive penury. Students tended to be older and poorer than at other New England colleges, and three-fifths became ministers or teachers.[49]

The Methodists occupied other defunct institutions by taking control of Dickinson and Allegheny Colleges in 1833. At Dickinson, the dysfunctional relations of faculty and local trustees had persisted long after Charles Nisbet's unhappy tenure. The resignation of the faculty in 1815 closed the college until 1821. Operations were again suspended in 1832. Negotiations with the Baltimore and Philadelphia Conferences resulted in Methodists replacing the former trustees. They resolved the former difficulties by making the new president chairman of the board. They named a professor of law, whose house conveniently adjoined the campus, and raised an endowment before opening the college in 1834. Dickinson was far healthier under Methodist direction, soon enrolling more than 100 students.

The third acquisition was a greater challenge. Allegheny College had been founded in northwestern Pennsylvania in 1817 by a group of local landowners, including newly arrived Timothy Alden, a Harvard graduate who aspired to found a town ("Aldenia") and a college. Literally a one-man operation, Alden's titles included trustee, president, professor, secretary of the board, keeper of the cabinet, and "Agent for soliciting benefactions of Alleghany College"—all for no salary. After graduating a class of four in 1821, including Alden's two sons, the college dwindled and closed. Donations had provided a substantial library, but no operating funds. Efforts at resuscitation proved futile, and in 1831 Alden resigned all his posts. At this point the Pittsburgh Conference stepped in and negotiated control of the board and the college. Under Methodist auspices, the college became viable—barely. It reported 100 students in 1840, surely an exaggeration, with most in the preparatory school.[50] In this and other respects, Allegheny typified precarious western colleges.

---

49 Potts, *Wesleyan*, 7–49, 238–39.

50 Charles Coleman Sellars, *Dickinson College: A History* (Middletown, CT: Wesleyan University Press, 1973), 195–208; Saul Sack, *History of Higher Education in Pennsylvania*, 2 vol. (Harrisburg, 1963),

Indiana Asbury College (later DePauw University) was a conspicuous success among the early colleges in the West. The Indiana Conference criticized Presbyterian dominance of the state college to rally support, and they obtained a charter in 1837 for a college in Greencastle—a poor and primitive settlement on territory purchased from the Indians just 18 years before. Early Methodist colleges had difficulty finding qualified instructors given the church's dearth of college graduates. In 1838 they secured Cyrus Nutt, who had just graduated from Allegheny College, to teach the preparatory classes. Unable to hire professors, Nutt taught college courses as well, later recording that he "had to hear some thirteen classes each day, besides corresponding and acting as president." In 1839 Matthew Simpson accepted the presidency (1839–1847). He had studied medicine before turning to preaching and was largely self-taught. When he sought to enroll at Allegheny, he was instead awarded an AM degree and hired to teach. In 1839–1840, Nutt and Simpson were able to offer a 4-year course to 22 college students, as well as instructing 43 "irregulars" and 58 preparatory students. Asbury benefited from strong support from the Indiana Conference, which mobilized Methodist ministers throughout the state to promote and take collections for the college. The college was chronically short of funds; nonetheless, these contacts helped to attract students. Within 15 years of opening, enrollment exceeded 400, though just 92 were in the college classes. The college soon acquired a reputation for accommodating indigent students. In one later class, one-third was entirely self-supporting, and another third earned most of their expenses.[51]

The undivided backing of the Indiana Conference made Asbury the peak of an informal Methodist educational system. As the Methodists embraced education, they founded schools of all types and levels. By one count, Methodists by 1860 had established 229 educational institutions, two-thirds still open, including 34 colleges. Methodism espoused fundamental middle-class virtues—a pious life, moral behavior, abstention from stimulants and frivolous activities— which together shaped solid citizens who were likely to prosper. Education was lauded for contributing on all counts. It raised the religious and intellectual level of the whole community, and it allowed individuals to live fuller lives. Methodist literature tirelessly reiterated these themes, and innumerable individuals

I, 65–67, 74–79. Jonathan E. Helmreich, *Eternal Hope: The Life of Timothy Alden Jr.* (New York: Cornwall Books, 2001): Alden hoped to develop the town of Aldenia on land he owned; one scheme to rescue the college, proposed by an emissary from Alden Partridge, would have created a military academy, but terms could not be agreed upon.

51 George B. Manhart, *DePauw through the Years: Volume I, Indiana Asbury University, 1837–1884; DePauw University, 1884–1919* (Greencastle, IN: DePauw University, 1962), passim, quote p. 19; James Findlay, "Agency, Denominations, and the Western Colleges, 1830–1860" in Geiger, ed., *American Colleges*, 115–26. Nutt and Simpson were light on credentials, not ability; both had distinguished careers.

exemplified them. Below the colleges were numerous academies, institutes, and coeducational and female seminaries, which, along with Asbury's precollege instruction, prepared teachers and provided general education to a far-larger population. Asbury formed tentative links with some of these schools, in keeping with its own aspirations to become a true university. It developed fledgling programs in medicine, law, theology, and a scientific course, all before the Civil War. In this respect, it evolved into a quintessential "multipurpose college." [52]

The Baptists were similar latecomers to collegiate education, but the middle-class educational values of the Methodists were less widespread and, in places, still scorned. They ministered to the common people and were originally more concerned with educating clergy, resulting in the early "literary and theological institutions" (Colby, Colgate, Denison, Shurtleff). Local boosters and benefactors, often non-Baptists, played important roles in launching many Baptist colleges. Eleven were founded before the denomination split in 1844 into Northern and Southern churches. Five of these were in the South, where state associations took the initiative to found most colleges (Mercer, Wake Forest, Richmond, and later Furman, but also Denison in Ohio). In the North, colleges more often reflected the combined initiatives of churchmen and laymen. Except for New York, Baptists established single antebellum colleges in most states, thereby concentrating potential enrollments, at least for students who could travel to them.[53]

All the reformed, evangelical Protestant churches had more in common than they had differences, though they increasingly emphasized the latter. In 1801 the Presbyterians and Congregationalists had signed the Plan of Union, an agreement to cooperate in Christianizing the Northwest. (Early Presbyterian missionaries were by far the most active in the South Central region.) The Presbyterians had more adherents in the West, although they were a shrinking and embattled minority. Presbyterian ministers were thus prominent in the extension of colleges, including state schools. The result was many colleges dominated by Presbyterians but not controlled by the Church (e.g., Dickinson and Allegheny). As its official position stressed orthodoxy and conformity and was doctrinally opposed to the predominant evangelicalism, the Church became increasingly dissatisfied with this situation. It felt that colleges founded with Congregationalists were doctrinally unsound, tainted by the New Haven theology. It soon opposed cooperative benevolent ventures like the American Home Mission and American Education societies. Relations grew increasingly acrimonious even before the Presbyterian schism of 1837. Congregational professors at Illinois College, for example, were subjected to a heresy trial and, although exonerated, experienced

52 Duvall, *Methodist Episcopal Church*, 66–72, 93–99; Manhart, *DePauw*, 40–60, 88–110.
53 Potts, *Baptist Colleges*; Tewksbury, *Founding*, 111–19.

intermittent harassment. These efforts to enforce orthodoxy proved counter-productive, especially when conducted by the Old School. Of seven coopera-tively founded colleges, initially partly Presbyterian, all but Illinois reverted to Congregationalism.[54] Pure Presbyterian colleges in the North, like Wabash in Indiana, opted for the New School and disapproved of slavery. But the schism caused Presbyterian communities to divide into two separate congregations, and support for colleges was split as well. Presbyterians, ironically the most aggres-sive college founders of the Early Republic, managed the transition to denomi-national colleges poorly, at least before the Civil War, by overemphasizing doc-trinal orthodoxy and ministerial preparation rather than education for a wider constituency.

Congregationalism was the religion of New England, and Amherst College clearly fit the denominational model, launched to promote piety and educa-tion for a regional community. The spread of Congregationalism in the West was confined to those regions settled by New Englanders, the so-called Yankee Belt. The largest impact in the West was made by Oberlin Collegiate Institute (Oberlin College in 1850), which evolved from the revivalist movement.[55] The Oberlin colony was a Christian perfectionist community created in the Ohio wilderness by John Shipherd. Only slightly less radical than coeval utopian com-munities, members signed the Oberlin compact pledging to lead ascetic Chris-tian lives and to advance missionary education.[56] The Institute, at the center of the colony, was the means for spreading Christianity in the greater Mississippi Valley. It encompassed all educational levels, from grammar school to the theol-ogy department, and embraced the contemporary fad for manual labor. In the hope of training as many teachers as possible, it was entirely coeducational.

Soon after Oberlin was founded in 1834, an upheaval in Cincinnati's Lane Theological Seminary had a decisive impact. Students there debated the morality of slavery and became active abolitionists. When the Seminary forbade such activi-ties, they withdrew en masse. Shipherd invited them to join his inchoate Institute. Agreed in principle, they insisted that their allies, trustee Asa Mahan and professor John Morgen, join them. To finance such a move, Shipherd traveled to New York

54 Namely, Knox, Beloit, Grinnell, Rockford, Ripon, Pacific, and Western Reserve; Illinois re-mained predominantly Presbyterian: Tewksbury, *Founding*, 91–103; Johnson, *Puritan Power*, 114–40; Charles E. Frank, *Pioneer's Progress: Illinois College, 1829–1979* (Southern Illinois University Press, 1979), 1–46.

55 Robert S. Fletcher, *A History of Oberlin College from Its Foundation through the Civil War* (Ober-lin College, 1943): the Oneida Institute (f. 1827) was a precursor that conflated revivalism, abolition, manual labor, vegetarianism, temperance, and ministerial education: 1–101.

56 Christian perfectionism is associated with the revivalist preaching of Charles Grandison Finney and postulated the possibility of overcoming original sin by leading an exemplary life: Sidney Ahlstrom, *A Religious History of the American People* (New Haven: Yale University Press, 1972), 460–61, 476–78.

to appeal to the antislavery philanthropists, Arthur and Lewis Tappan. The Tappans offered generous support but stipulated that the famous revivalist preacher Charles Grandison Finney (who had not attended college) should also be added to the theology faculty. Finney made stipulations too: that African Americans would be admitted as students on equal terms and that the faculty would control the internal management of the Institute. The trustees had grave misgivings, especially over racial integration, but Shipherd prevailed. Oberlin gained immediate fame, with the country's foremost revivalist preacher, and notoriety, for admitting women and African Americans—and also students. It became the largest college and educational institution in Ohio for the rest of the century and probably the largest single source of missionaries and educators for the West.[57]

The other principal concentration of Congregational settlement and educational initiative was in northern Illinois and adjacent areas of Wisconsin and Iowa. Illinois, Knox, Beloit, Ripon, and Grinnell colleges were cofounded with Presbyterians but assumed a distinctly Congregational character. Yale and Andover were the dominant influences, and these colleges aspired to uphold a high standard of classical education. Like Oberlin, they were assisted by maintaining financial ties with donors in the East. Congregational colleges thus tended to be the more academically rigorous western colleges.[58]

The major denominations played the leading role in the extension of advanced education in the West, but these efforts were only the beginning of the story of denominational colleges. The elaboration process that became paramount in the three decades after 1840 produced a far greater proliferation of colleges, reflecting college formation by smaller denominations but also the fragmentation of the major denominations. Prior to 1840, significant colleges were founded by other denominations, often as necessary complements to theological seminaries. Pennsylvania College (later Gettysburg) was felt to be a needed companion to the Lutheran Seminary, and Marshall College similarly emerged from the German Reformed Seminary in Mercersburg. Ohio Episcopalians also tried to sustain a seminary first before quickly adding Kenyon College. Roman Catholics were first to cross the Mississippi by founding Saint Louis University in 1832. The sponsors of denominational colleges continued to grow, but in other ways they were much alike.

Many denominational colleges initially felt some ambivalence toward the classical course, although such misgivings were manifest in diverse approaches.

57   Geoffrey Blodgett, *Oberlin History: Essays and Impressions* (Oberlin College, 2006), 5–28; Lawrence Thomas Lesick, *The Lane Rebels: Evangelicalism and Antislavery in Antebellum America* (Metuchen, NJ: Scarecrow Press, 1980).

58   Tewksbury, *Founding*, 119–29.

In this respect, the controversial scientific course attempted at Amherst was unusual for its publicity, not its intent. Early denominational colleges in the West often taught Latin and Greek in the freshman year but little afterward. Baptist colleges, as noted, sought to balance both theological and liberal arts courses. At Columbian (later George Washington), entrance requirements were set high for the classical course but kept flexible for theology. Shurtleff College took years to institute the classical course and still maintained an English language alternative. Among the Methodists the attention to lay education encouraged some initial experiments. Randolph-Macon College's initial course mimicked the University of Virginia. At Wesleyan, Wilbur Fisk opened the college by grouping students according to ability and including a scientific course, as did McKendree College in Illinois, another Methodist pioneer. Oberlin voiced overt hostility to the "heathen classics" and substituted "Hebrew and sacred classics for the most objectionable pagan authors" (Seneca, Livy, and Horace).[59] However, in all these cases the classical course was soon strengthened, and alternatives were either dropped or minimized. Doubters and critics never disappeared, but the classical course had powerful winds at its back.

First and foremost, the classical course defined the American college. That is, Latin, Greek, and mathematics were the core of a liberal education and the AB degree that colleges were chartered to award. Only with difficulty were they able over time to offer other types of degrees, but institutions that did not offer the classical course were something other than colleges. (This fact was a conundrum for female colleges, as will be seen.) The Yale *Reports* of 1828 bolstered these perceptions, providing cogent arguments for the superiority of the classical course. The American Education Society provided more tangible support with its insistence on and financial support for a "thorough education." Soon, the western colleges asserted their own interpretation of quality by aspiring or claiming to offer an education "equivalent to that offered by the best eastern colleges," an ideal endlessly paraphrased. This meant not just offering the classical course but extending the teaching of Latin and Greek to all 4 years.

Why, one might ask, did the old adage that bad money drives out good money in the marketplace not apply to colleges? Why did a college education that was shorter, cheaper, and less recondite fail to outcompete the longer, more arduous classical course? The behavior of currencies depends on their ability to purchase goods and services, but a college degree in the mid-nineteenth century had almost no purchasing power in labor markets. Rather, a degree represented the acquisition of a certain culture, as the Yale *Reports* claimed. And, more prestigious cultural goods trumped less prestigious ones. Thus, the denominational

---

59 Fletcher, *Oberlin*, 366–67.

colleges found themselves pulled in two directions: the wish to serve their local and denominational constituencies by offering "useful" education and involvement in a tacit competition to emulate the standard of the eastern colleges. Their direction was largely determined by how and how well they managed to finance themselves.

★ ★ ★

Perhaps the greatest misconception about denominational colleges is that their finances depended on student tuition and that the need to bolster enrollments shaped their actions. The true situation was summarized by the Baptist college in Lewisburg (later Bucknell):

> The receipts from tuition in the Collegiate Department cannot under the most favorable circumstances be expected to meet more than one-third of the cost of instruction. Taking all the colleges in the United States into account, . . . it is estimated the cost of instruction for each collegian per annum is not less than from $125 to $150. The usual charges are from $25 to $50 per annum. In the Theological Department tuition is free.[60]

Covering the gap between receipts from tuition and the costs of instruction was the continual challenge of the colleges and the source of their chronic penury. The two principal sources were endowments and fund raising. Colleges also resorted to loans and occasionally to nonpayment of salaries. The conventional wisdom, ca. 1840, was that an endowment of $100,000 was needed to operate a college on a sound foundation, and this figure was invoked as the goal of numerous campaigns. That amount might provide annual income of $6,000—not quite two-thirds of the $10,000 assumed as the typical annual budget. In fact, only a few antebellum colleges reached that figure, and almost none of the western colleges did. Rather, the quest itself made the situation worse.

New colleges typically received generous support from the towns that enticed them: a good piece of land and often funds for an initial building. They received a different reception when they sought repeated donations from the same townspeople to meet their ongoing needs. In addition, all the colleges founded in the 1820s and 1830s were severely tested by the depression that followed, which lowered donations of all sorts. In order to cast a wider net, colleges retained agents

---

60 *Report of the Board of Trustees of the University at Lewisburg* (July 27, 1858), University Archives, Bucknell University. Tuition tended to be higher in the South (Randolph-Macon, $70, vs. Wesleyan, $36) and the proportion of tuition revenues was probably higher as well.

for fund-raising, as they had since early in the eighteenth century. The agents of the denominational colleges tended to be trained ministers, but many assumed the role of professional fund-raisers. Coreligionists were the most likely donors, and college agents traveled tirelessly to regional churches. They usually preached sermons and took collections as well as soliciting larger gifts from wealthier parishioners. As they extolled the virtues of their colleges, they elicited interest among potential students and promoted the college image. In addition, agents from the western colleges made periodic trips to the "money frontier" in the East, the only likely source of significant gifts. College agents were indispensable but also inefficient. Their incessant travels could consume half of the funds they raised. Many of the gifts took the form of pledges and promises that sometimes proved uncollectable. Still, colleges depended on their agents to pursue the holy grail of building an endowment.[61]

Nearly all the new colleges resorted to the dubious practice of selling future tuition scholarships. Initially these were offered at seemingly sound prices: the going rates seemed to be $100 for 5 years of tuition and $500 for a perpetual scholarship. Colleges apparently found few takers at those prices, especially during the depression. Following these difficult years, scholarship rates were drastically reduced in increasingly desperate fund-raising efforts. Wesleyan eventually offered 15 years of tuition (at $36) for $50; Ohio Wesleyan offered 8 years for $30. By 1860 both schools were receiving virtually no tuition income. Moreover, little of these funds ever reached endowments. Besides the agents' cut and uncollectable pledges, the funds were more often used for expenses or to pay down debt.[62] The denominational colleges were truly eleemosynary institutions, to use the language of the Dartmouth College case, sustained by Christian charity. Yet, the implicit competition to emulate the "best eastern colleges" required that they continually augment their faculty and facilities.

Another dubious practice of the early colleges was the adoption of manual labor, particularly in the 1830s. Originating in Europe and popularized by the radical Oneida Institute, it appealed to American evangelicals by promising healthful exercise (games, of course, were anathema), promotion of an egalitarian spirit, and a means for preministerial students, in particular, to support their education. In 1826 a Mechanical Association was established by enthusiasts at Andover Seminary, and a mechanical workshop was created. In 1829 Elias Cornelius of the American Education society made a lengthy address to this group praising the health benefits of manual labor and describing numerous examples

---

61   James Findlay, "Agency, Denomination"; Potts, *Baptist Colleges*, 196–206.

62   Potts, *Wesleyan*, 13, 58; Charles A. Dominick, *Ohio's Antebellum Colleges*, PhD Diss., University of Michigan, 1987, 206–7.

of its successful implementation. Blessed from the summit of the Benevolent Empire, manual labor schemes were tried everywhere poor scholars sought a college education. The basic scheme called for students to work in shops or on farms, usually 4 hours a day, and thus defray their living expenses—the largest cost of college. Newer eastern colleges established shops for those students who wished to work. Western colleges generally incorporated more comprehensive arrangements but principally used farms. Oberlin, strongly influenced by Oneida, made manual labor a mandatory part of the fabric of the college, and almost all Baptist colleges signed on. However, disillusionment soon set in. Not all collegians were fit for prolonged labor, and time devoted to work definitely detracted from studies. Worse, these arrangements were inherently unprofitable. Collegians were not productive laborers, and the supervisors they required were an additional expense. Eastern colleges soon dropped their tentative commitments, and hard-pressed western college found manual labor unaffordable. Even at Oberlin, where it had powerful ideological support, manual labor disappeared in a decade. Beyond the perverse economics, the culture supporting evangelical egalitarianism was on the wane as well. By the early 1840s, Baptist educators concluded that "the system has become extensively unpopular."[63]

The denominational colleges founded in the 1820s and 1830s were beset by the inherent difficulties of neophyte institutions. Their nature and their circumstances made these initial weaknesses hard to overcome. Chronic poverty was exacerbated by financial folly. Moreover, poverty interacted with their commitment to the classical course to diminish their educational effectiveness. The classical course, taught through recitations, could be offered with minimal personnel, both in numbers and qualifications, but it could not be taught well. The problems began with the students, many of whom by all accounts were woefully underprepared. In fact, their efforts to meet bare admission requirements in Latin and Greek often left them incompetent in their native English. Presiding over recitations did not require much academic preparation, nor did most college teachers have such. Professors of math and science might have MD degrees from proprietary medical schools; professors of languages and philosophy usually had attended a theological seminary. Instructors or tutors knew little more than what the students recited. Latin and Greek occupied two-thirds of the freshman year and half of the second year, at the least. These studies were followed by a variety of subjects taught briefly from textbooks for one or two

---

63   E. Cornelius, "Union of Study with Useful Labour," *Quarterly Register* (Nov. 1829), 57–70: the American Education Society turned negative sooner: "Manual Labor Schools," *Quarterly Register* (Aug. 1833), 31–33; Kenneth H. Wheeler, *The Antebellum College in the Old Northwest*, PhD Diss., Ohio State University, 1999, 111–25; Potts, *Baptist Colleges*, 215–24, quote p. 224.

terms. The result was anything but the "thorough" education promised in the Yale *Reports*. Students at best became barely competent in the ancient languages and acquired a smattering of knowledge from their textbooks. Colleges eagerly sought to raise the quality of their education and their reputations as well, but here they were locked into the paradigm of the classical course. College reputations depended principally on the rigor and mastery of Latin and Greek, on the number of professors, and on their professional stature. Thus, raising the prestige of a college meant extending the most problematic features: spending even more class time on the ancient languages and professing additional subjects superficially in the remaining time. The 1820s and 1830s saw an accelerating expansion of American colleges; however, while it was fairly easy to launch a college, these institutions faced inherent limitations to their development. Thus, the United States was on a path to being a land of *small* colleges.

HIGHER EDUCATION FOR WOMEN

In the mid-1830s, three separate initiatives brought women into the realm of higher education. In 1834 Mary Lyon began raising the funds that would launch Mount Holyoke Female Seminary 3 years later. When collegiate classes began at Oberlin that same fall, women from the female department joined male students in some classrooms—the first coeducational collegiate instruction. The following year an interdenominational revival in Macon, Georgia, produced a resolution to found an educational institution for girls, subsequently called Georgia Female College. Each of these initiatives presaged quite different efforts to raise the level of education available to women. Each was also a by-product of the ongoing spirit of the Second Great Awakening. And each was shaped by the increasingly distinct culture of its respective region—the Northeast, the West, and the South.

Female education had been sporadically available since the late colonial era. Timothy Dwight had introduced coeducation at his Greenfield Academy, for example, and many academies continued to teach both boys and girls. However, except for a few urban schools, like the Young Ladies Academy in Philadelphia, this education was rudimentary and poorly taught. Girls were taught domestic skills—sewing and needlework—and the little substantive content was conveyed through memorization. This situation improved markedly in the 1820s. Emma Willard opened the Troy Female Seminary in 1822 to provide an academic education for future teachers. Although it firmly upheld the prevailing belief in separate spheres, it soon attracted several hundred students and became the center for a network of female educators. Female seminaries appeared in most American cities. The prevalence of the doctrine of separate spheres promoted this development but left much room for interpreting the proper education for the female sphere. Urban seminaries were expensive and offered a full menu of ornamental subjects—music, art, and, usually, French. But many also advertised an ambitious curriculum that included many subjects and textbooks taught at male colleges. Some aimed to instill mental discipline through mathematics and, in a few cases, Latin. These seminaries clearly strengthened their courses over time, driven by local competition or rising expectations.[64] They presented a stark contrast to contemporary denominational colleges, being urban, proprietary, relatively expensive, and impermanent. Regardless of their educational philosophy or interpretation of the female sphere, they existed because increasing numbers of professional and middle-class families sought education for their daughters, and providing it could furnish a good living for proprietors. This pattern would continue to predominate in the South, but in New England the evangelical movement provided a different constituency.

Mary Lyon came from an impoverished rural background in central Massachusetts. She began teaching to support herself at age 17 but also sought further schooling whenever she could. In 1821 she committed all her savings to attend Byfield Seminary, conducted by Joseph Emerson. A Harvard graduate (1798) and ordained minister, Emerson was an inspiring teacher and religious mentor who treated his female students with complete equality. He instructed them in a liberal arts curriculum without Latin or Greek. He also eschewed ornamental subjects. Lyon's one term at Byfield inspired her both spiritually and intellectually. She also found a soul mate in Zilpa Grant, Emerson's talented assistant, whose background was similar to Lyon's. They soon began teaching together, a cooperation that became full time in 1830 at Grant's Ipswich Female Seminary. Ipswich proved an important precursor of Mount Holyoke. The women taught an academic curriculum like that of Byfield but fashioned it into a 3-year course and endeavored to steadily increase its rigor. They lived together with many of the students in a boarding house in which they instilled the discipline of daily duties with moral and spiritual guidance. Despite these achievements, Lyon regretted that the high cost (ca. $180/year) prevented women with backgrounds like her own from attending, but efforts to remedy this by obtaining an endowment failed. In 1834 Mary Lyon resolved to launch a school for women in central Massachusetts that would improve upon the Ipswich model.[65]

64   Anne Firor Scott, "The Diffusion of Feminist Values from the Troy Female Seminary, 1822–1872," *History of Education* Quarterly, 19, 1 (Spring 1979): 3–26; Margaret A. Nash, *Women's Education in the United States, 1780–1840* (New York: Palgrave, 2005), 82–93 et passim; Doris J. Malkmus, *'We Were Ambitious for Ourselves:' The Coeducation of Rural Women, 1790 to 1861*, PhD Diss., University of Iowa, 2001.

65   Elizabeth Alden Green, *Mary Lyon and Mount Holyoke: Opening the Gates* (Hanover, NH: University Press of New England, 1979); Helen Lefkowitz Horowitz, *Alma Mater: Design and Experience in*

Mary Lyon had four objectives: first, to provide an evangelical setting in which religious conversion would be encouraged; second, to keep costs low so that serious, mature, middle-class women could acquire an education to become teachers; third, to create a permanent institution for women's education by acquiring an endowment; and fourth, to teach "an elevated standard of science, literature, and refinement," as had been offered at Byfield and Ipswich.[66]

She set out to raise the funds for the institution by soliciting donations in and around Amherst, seeking numerous small gifts rather than soliciting wealthy patrons. She dismissed criticism that this was unladylike behavior and was well received in the evangelical community, by friends at Amherst College, and among educated women. She also employed a male agent, though fundraising still proved to be an ongoing personal chore. By 1836 she had gathered funds to begin construction in South Hadley of what proved to be the most distinctive feature of her seminary. A single large building was designed as an enormous household to accommodate 90 women, soon enlarged to 200, in a semicloistered existence. To keep costs down she instituted a "domestic system" in which all the students performed the chores of cooking, cleaning, and washing. Lyon insisted that this was not a manual labor system, and indeed it proved highly effective in reducing costs and instilling esprit de corps. Teachers were paid a barely living wage, considering themselves volunteers in a great moral enterprise.

The seminary sought above all to educate women to assist in the evangelical mission of spreading Christianity and achieving conversions. As wives of ministers and missionaries or as teachers, Holyoke women could broaden and strengthen the evangelical cause. The religious atmosphere at Mount Holyoke was intense. Besides Sabbath worship, students heard a daily scriptural lesson from Mary Lyon, had two half-hour sessions of private devotion, and had additional "social prayer" circles. All students were classified as converted, "hopefully pious," or (for a small minority) "without hope." Every effort was made to bring about conversions, and annual revivals were the norm.

Mary Lyon fully embraced the prevailing notion of separate spheres and envisioned the role of educated women as complementing and expanding the mission of evangelical Christianity. However she scorned the norms of gentility cultivated in female academies and opposed ornamental subjects. She believed that the better the academic education of women, the more effectively

---

the Women's Colleges from Their Nineteenth-Century Beginnings to the 1930s (Boston: Beacon Press, 1984), 9–27; Andrea L. Turpin, "The Ideological Origins of the Women's College: Religion, Class, and Curriculum in the Educational Visions of Catherine Beecher and Mary Lyon," History of Education Quarterly, 50, 2 (May 2010): 133–58.

66   Quote from Mount Holyoke Prospectus, 1835; the following draws on Green, Mary Lyon, passim.

they could fulfill their roles. Thus, Mount Holyoke sought to approximate the content of male colleges while foregoing degree-granting status. The original curriculum at Mount Holyoke was a 3-year English course, but Mary Lyon was committed from the outset to extending its content and rigor. Subjects were not divided by terms but rather taught in intensive 6- to 10-week "series." Each session concluded with an extended period of examinations. Early on, Lyon envisioned incorporating Latin, first as an extra subject and, finally, in 1846 as a 1-year requirement. A 4-year course including Latin was established in 1861.

Comparing the content of male and female colleges is inherently frustrating.[67] Women's colleges, by continual upgrading, were a moving target, and men's colleges covered the gamut from Yale to dreadful. For gauging the relative merits of a Holyoke education, the following points seem salient. Many female students were poorly prepared, but here the goal of setting high standards becomes evident. The school's entrance exams were challenging, and many matriculates had to undertake extra studies to meet the standards of the junior (first-year) class. Four of the school year's 40 weeks were devoted to examinations, which by all accounts were rigorous. The 3-year female English course approximated the subject matter of the third and fourth years of men's colleges. For these subjects, roughly half of the textbooks used at Holyoke were the same as those used at Amherst College. The 7- to 10-week "series" or modules in which they were taught seem inherently superficial, but then so was collegiate instruction of boys. Perhaps the largest difference was in the faculty. Mary Lyon retained her most promising graduates as instructors, and although several made careers there, they obtained no further qualifications. In all likelihood, their lessons remained at a textbook level, although thoroughly taught.[68]

From 1837 to 1850 Holyoke enrolled nearly 1,400 students and graduated one-quarter of them. Mary Lyon served her intended constituency: relatively mature students from the rural middle class of family-owned farms. Poverty no doubt forced many to attend for only short intervals; indeed, getting students to commit for a full year was a challenge early on. For most, education at Mount Holyoke was a career strategy of education and teaching to fill the interval between family home and marriage. More than 80 percent of graduates became teachers but most of them, not for long. A similar proportion married, and very

67   Compare Thomas Woody, *A History of Women's Education in the United States*, 2 vol. (New York: Science Press, 1929), esp. I: 552–62, II: 160–84; Roger L. Geiger, "The 'Superior Instruction of Women'" in Geiger, *The American College in the Nineteenth Century*, 183–95.

68   Mary Lyon, who had received instruction from Amos Eaton, taught a 9-week series on chemistry to second-year students: Carole B. Shmurak and Bonnie S. Handler, "'Castle of Science': Mount Holyoke College and the Preparation of Women in Chemistry, 1837–1941," *History of Education Quarterly* 32, 3 (Fall 1992): 315–42.

few women taught after marriage. But many Holyoke women married ministers or missionaries, a virtual career that Mary Lyon had envisioned. The career pattern of Holyoke graduates (and nongraduates as well) paralleled that of Troy graduates; and their backgrounds are similar to the women who attended Massachusetts's pioneer normal schools beginning in 1839. However, Mount Holyoke provided a more advanced education than those institutions, and the experience profoundly shaped at least some of its graduates. Holyoke women who did become educators carried this model to a number of "sister schools" that meticulously replicated the Mount Holyoke plan. The mystique of Mary Lyon's vision was so strong in South Hadley that the seminary resisted calling itself a women's college until the 1880s.[69]

★ ★ ★

Views on evangelism and women's education form a direct connection between Mount Holyoke and Oberlin. The first two directors of the Oberlin female department had studied at Byfield with Emerson and Ipswich with Grant and Lyon. Within the Oberlin colony, however, these notions produced quite different results. In its perfectionist theology, the "elevation of female character" by provision of "all the instructive privileges which hitherto have distinguished the leading sex from theirs," was integral to the elevation of humankind. Still, the Institute proceeded pragmatically. After 2 years of shared classes, the faculty and trustees reviewed the experience. They resolved that the "mutual influence of the sexes upon each other is decidedly happy in the cultivation of both mind and manners." In 1837 four women were admitted to the classical course, and in 1841 three of them were awarded AB degrees, the first such degrees earned by women. This step was controversial even within the Oberlin colony. A committee evaluating the practice in 1845 found certain "Evils"—namely, that both genders seemed too fond of each other's company and liable to premature engagements. But coeducation gained increasing support, becoming in fact a matter of institutional pride.

The social norms of separate spheres were attenuated in the Oberlin colony, which had social norms of its own. Its ideal for the relationship between male and female students was that of a Christian family. Dining together, for

---

69   David F. Allmendinger Jr., "Mount Holyoke Students Encounter the Need for Life-Planning, 1837–1850," *History of Education Quarterly*, 19, 1 (Spring 1979): 27–46; Margaret A. Nash, "'A Salutary Rivalry': The Growth of Higher Education for Women in Oxford, Ohio, 1850–1875," in Geiger, ed., *The American College in the Nineteenth Century*, 183–95; Andrea L. Turpin, "Memories of Mary: Changing Interpretations of the Founder in the Secularization Process at Mount Holyoke Seminary and College, 1837–1937," *Perspectives on the History of Higher Education*, vol. 28 (2011): 33–61.

example, improved male behavior by precluding "all the grossness and vulgarity so often witnessed in college commons." Divergent social roles were recognized in the exclusion of women from "preparation for public speaking and for public life." Otherwise, the Institute stridently affirmed "the first and greatest right of women—the right to be educated, as being endowed with the intelligence equally as man—is fundamental to the system." As the single American college proclaiming this right, Oberlin soon attracted women who sought to expand such rights.[70]

Virtually all Oberlinites supported the movements for abolition and temperance, but women were particularly active for "moral reform." This widespread movement of the 1830s and 1840s sought to combat "licentiousness" by condemning premarital physical contact, immodest dress, dancing, reading novels, and the theater. The Oberlin Female Moral Reform Society was one of the largest and most active in the country and included those students most committed to women's rights. Drawn to Oberlin in the mid-1840s were Lucy Stone, determined to make her mark as a public lecturer, and precocious Antoinette Brown, who aspired to the ministry. Both challenged the liberal limits of female behavior, especially the taboo against public speaking. After several skirmishes, Stone made a concerted effort to read her essay at the male commencement ceremonies. Although she failed, Oberlin would concede this point in the next decade. Brown was allowed to study theology after graduation—but not to enroll! In 1853 she was ordained as a Congregational minister in South Butler, New York, the first woman minister of a major denomination. Oberlin found that its support of coeducation rapidly encouraged feminism, of which it disapproved. Nonetheless, Oberlin graduates played leading roles in the radical women's rights movement that coalesced with the 1848 convention in Seneca Falls.[71]

★　★　★

Both Holyoke and Oberlin attracted a self-selected minority of women to their halls. The female colleges of the South, in contrast, were mainstream institutions accommodating the daughters of planter and professional families. Although Georgia Female College was the first to obtain a charter, it was but one of a host of similar institutions. Previous attempts at collegiate status had fallen short. As early as 1821, plans for the University of Alabama called for establishing a female

---

70 Fletcher, *History of Oberlin*, 373–85.

71 Antoinette Brown was not enrolled in order to keep her name off the public matriculation list: Ibid., 290–315.

branch, and soon after a state institution of higher education for women was proposed in the Georgia legislature. These early gambits failed, but they reveal a sentiment that not only was the time ripe, but female higher education was worthy of state support. The private establishment of the South Carolina Female Collegiate Institute in 1828 brought southern women to the threshold of higher education. Compared with these tentative steps, the initiative in Macon stands out for its decisiveness. Prominent citizens led the effort to raise funds for an endowed institution, and the Georgia Methodist Conference backed the effort. They acquired land and commenced construction on an enormous college building with a columned facade that resembled a state capitol. Classes began in 1839, and 168 students enrolled for the first term. However, raising the funds needed to expunge the debt proved difficult during the depression, and by 1841 the college faced bankruptcy. Local backers and the Methodists came to the rescue. In 1844 it was rechartered as Wesleyan Female College under the control of the Georgia Methodist Conference.

A coeval institution found similar sponsorship. The Judson Female Institute in Marion, Alabama, was founded in 1839 by Baptists and wealthy local patrons who sought a quality institution. It recruited Milo P. Jewett, who had been a professor at Marietta, to lead the institution and constructed a school building almost as impressive as Macon's. In 1843 the trustees deeded the school to the Alabama Baptist Convention. As denominational female colleges, these two institutions were unusual. Outside of Quakers and Moravians, few denominations owned or operated institutions for women, although in the South a few other female schools were associated with churches. Some form of sponsorship was generally needed in order to raise funds for the faculty and building required for an effective college. Nonetheless, the majority of female schools were proprietary ventures.[72]

Early Southern female schools straddled the ill-defined boundary between seminaries and colleges and deliberately muddled their mission by adopting ambiguous names, like institute, academy, or high school. Frequently, the first 2 years offered college preparatory material and the last 2, college subjects. Although the level of offerings rose over time, it was not driven, as it was in the North, by the wish to provide a solid academic preparation to future teachers. In the South, higher education aimed to develop literary and artistic refinement in women who expected to marry at a young age but not work. This situation

---

72   Shirley A. Hickson, *The Development of Higher Education for Women in the Antebellum South*, PhD Diss., University of South Carolina, 1985, 33–43; Christie Anne Farnham, *The Education of the Southern Belle: Higher Education and Student Socialization in the Antebellum South* (New York: New York University Press, 57–60.

made the South particularly receptive to female education since it posed no challenge to the social order. Southern colleges offered an abundance of supplementary instruction in "feminine accomplishments"—music, art, and embroidery. Foreign languages were also taught as extra subjects for extra fees. Virtually all aspects of these schools were intended to contribute to the exalted conception of southern womanhood.[73] Students entered young, often at 14 or 15 years of age. They generally attended close to home, which encouraged the proliferation of schools. Whether church related or not, attendance was expensive. The numerous extra courses made fees quite variable, but one reliable estimate put a year's average cost at $230. This price in itself would have limited higher education to the wealthy. It was also one reason that few students remained long enough to graduate. Most students matriculated for a single year and many more, for only two. At four major antebellum female colleges the graduation rate was 15 percent. Not surprisingly, most of these girls were indifferent students, more invested in their futures as southern belles than in academic learning. In fact, the South offered no careers open to women of that class. The female teachers at these many schools often came from the North and seldom remained for long or else were wives of proprietors. The female colleges of the South and kindred institutions educated a large number of women, even if briefly. While these opportunities were no doubt squandered on some, for others this experience helped to prepare them for the unanticipated challenges of life after the Civil War.[74]

★   ★   ★

The 1820s and 1830s marked the takeoff years for the American college. A contested model at the outset, its putative rivals failed the test of experience no matter how seemingly cogent their rationales. The Yale *Reports* and the American Education Society buttressed the traditional model of the classical course, but its implacable momentum derived as much from the proliferation of denominational colleges that were scarcely equipped to offer anything else. The depression following the panic of 1837 was a hiatus of sorts, as widespread financial hardship caused a lull in college growth. But once the economy had stabilized, American higher education developed at an accelerating pace, only temporarily slowed by the crisis of the Civil War. However, this development took distinctive paths that had become evident even before the financial panic. The established colleges in the Northeast augmented their wealth, their faculties, and their

---

73   Hickson, *Higher Education for Women*, 123–77; Farnham, *Southern Belle*, 33–67, 120–45.
74   Hickson, *Higher Education for Women*, 66, 259–60; Farnham, *Southern Belle*, 97–119.

academic breadth. At the same time, their students found the freedom to begin developing an extracurricular life of their own invention. The state universities of the South formed ever closer bonds with the region's dominant political and economic class. In the West, denominational colleges multiplied in varied but similar patterns. In the mid-nineteenth century, the monolithic classical college gave rise to a more diverse array of institutions.

✶ 6 ✶

REGIONAL DIVERGENCE AND
SCIENTIFIC ADVANCEMENT,
1840–1860

THE EARLY COLLEGIATE ERA IN THE NORTHEAST

IN 1830 PRESIDENT JEREMIAH DAY INSTITUTED A NEW system of discipline at Yale. Instead of admonitions and fines, students would be assessed marks for missing chapel or recitations or other "improprieties of conduct": Sixteen marks brought a disciplinary warning and a letter to parents; thirty-two marks meant another letter; and forty-eight marks usually meant suspension for a term. However, twelve marks were forgiven at the end of each term and thirty-two, at the conclusion of the school year. Earlier that year Yale students had rebelled against an increase in the rigor of math recitations, resulting in the expulsion of almost half of the class of 1832. But that proved to be the last of the old-style student rebellions. Riots and riotous behavior persisted, but they were more often directed toward the citizens of New Haven. The new system of marks signaled the end of the old philosophy of submission and control. Instead of trying to control all aspects of their lives, Yale now held students accountable for obeying the college regimen, and they were able to calculate their improprieties.[1] Students took advantage of their greater freedom, progressively expanding their college experiences through organized and unorganized activities.

Throughout the Northeast, colleges generally followed this same path, each in its own way and at its own pace. The era of submission and control and student rebellions was superseded by one of expanding collegiate activities—the *early collegiate era*.[2] Most college regulations remained on the books, but enforcement

---

1 Brooks Mather Kelley, *Yale: A History* (New Haven: Yale University Press, 1974), 168–69, 216–17; [Lyman H. Bagg] *Four Years at Yale, by a Graduate of '69* (New Haven: Chatfield, 1871), 568–78, quote p. 575.

2 Roger L. Geiger, "Introduction: New Themes in the History of Nineteenth-Century Colleges," in Geiger, ed., *The American College in the Nineteenth Century* (Nashville: Vanderbilt University Press, 2000), 1–36.

became less vigilant. Greater student freedom did not degrade academic performance because classroom demands rose during these years. Sources of turmoil like the dining commons were often abolished, providing another dimension of freedom, and religious observances tended to become more relaxed. Methodists and Baptists, including Francis Wayland at Brown, considered games and amusements to be frivolous, if not wicked, and strongly resisted this trend for some time.

Students' primary allegiance and reference group continued to be the college class. Class suppers, elections, rituals, and ceremonies marking class milestones became more elaborate and absorbing. The literary societies, which flourished at the beginning of this era, were a partial exception to class organization, as were fraternities, whose subsequent growth undermined the role and influence of the societies. The momentum behind collegiate activities accelerated in the 1840s and 1850s, producing student literary publications, secular musical groups, and more. As students devoted increasing discretionary time to physical activity, games and athletics developed into intramural contests organized by class and, soon, the beginnings of intercollegiate athletic competition. Eventually, the collegiate extracurriculum would spread throughout American higher education, but in the antebellum years its initial manifestations largely served to transform college life in the Northeast.

Eliphalet Nott, the long-serving president of Union College (1804–1866), was among the first to conclude that the draconian approach to student discipline was counterproductive. A turning point occurred in 1809 when the trustees repudiated the most zealous faculty disciplinarian and confided this authority to Nott alone. The president advocated the parental approach, which sought to lead students through moral suasion, and he became the parental figurehead, handling all cases of discipline personally and privately.[3] Nott was adamantly opposed to rebellion and vice. But rebellion receded as an issue under a more tolerant regime. To combat vice, he had the New York State legislature pass laws suppressing sources of temptation in Schenectady, in addition to a formidable list of prohibitions in the College Laws. New laws issued in 1821 still forbade all vice or potential temptations but allowed more latitude, including the right to take meals outside. From 1825 to 1827, the first three secret Greek-letter fraternities were founded at Union. Nott was heavily involved in matters far more pressing than student misbehavior—legislation in Albany, manipulations of lottery funds, and promoting his own inventions. He became increasingly tolerant of, or

---

3 Nott's parental approach mirrors that of Timothy Dwight in some respects (chapter 4); however, the two men were antagonists, and Nott's practice of this approach was far more casual, given his numerous other activities.

preferred to ignore, student peccadilloes. In 1832 he forbade any student to join a fraternity, but the next year he was talked out of the ban. Union acquired a reputation for admitting students who had been dismissed from other colleges and was nicknamed "Botany Bay" after the original Australian penal colony. Nott personally warned such students that they would be closely watched, but in fact they seem to have been treated no differently. More by circumstance than by design, Union College offered increasing space for extracurricular activities, but Botany Bay was scarcely a model for other colleges to follow.[4]

Williams College under its amiable president Mark Hopkins (1836–1872) exemplified the transformation of antebellum college life. The year before his arrival, a senior had used his commencement address to refuse his diploma as a protest against the stifling discipline. But in 1842, a graduate wrote, "I love the college grounds, and the college buildings ... the faculty and the students and the members of our dear church." A native of Western Massachusetts and a Williams graduate (1824), Hopkins taught school to fund his own education and acquired an MD before becoming a professor at his alma mater in 1830. He understood and sympathized with the boys and believed that a school master should "know when to see things and when not." Hopkins found disciplining students distasteful, and the few students he expelled committed audacious transgressions. As long as students attended chapel and class, the college did little to restrain their behavior—nor did it do anything to meet their individual aspirations and interests. Students were on their own to shape their personal development, and their preferences were diverse. [5]

Fraternities were imported to Williams from Union in 1833 and quickly multiplied. Still, until 1848 membership in an antifraternity organization exceeded the Greeks, but afterward fraternity members comprised the largest block of students. The piety that had long characterized Williams slowly ebbed. The college still managed a revival about every 3 years, but fewer than half the students were converted, and the two religious societies had to merge in 1849 to remain viable. Students also promoted intellectual development beyond the college's cramped classical course. Although the literary societies were losing ground, their libraries provided antebellum students with contemporary literature, including best sellers. After several attempts, the *Williams Quarterly* in 1853 became a permanent outlet for student writing and was soon joined by additional publications. The most intellectually ambitious effort of students was the Lyceum of Natural

---

4   Wayne Somers, *Encyclopedia of Union College History* (Schenectady: Union College Press, 2003), 120–21, 304–6, 512–13, 529–31; Codman Hislop, *Eliphalet Nott*, 129–32, 389–90. Yale reverted to submission and control after Dwight's death in 1817.

5   Frederick Rudolph, *Mark Hopkins and the Log: Williams College, 1836–1872* (New Haven: Yale University Press, 1956), 19–85, quote p. 59.

History. Although led by faculty, it was a purely voluntary scientific association that nearly one-quarter of students joined. Its enthusiastic members collected and classified specimens, sponsored talks, established a library, erected the Lyceum's building, and led students on scientific expeditions.[6]

The emancipated students of the early collegiate era fashioned their own education according to their perceptions of culture and society, and in the process they altered the nature of their colleges. Mark Hopkins considered the college mission to be producing independent and self-disciplined young men, something the classical course alone could scarcely accomplish. Instead, neglect by the college motivated students to apply their skills and ingenuity to organize and manage extracurricular activities. These experiences generated the kind of feelings expressed by the sentimental Williams grad quoted above, which translated into alumni loyalties, financial support, and, before long, active involvement in the affairs of the colleges.[7]

In one significant sign of the changing atmosphere, students began writing about their college experiences. Rather formal depictions of Yale and Williams appeared in the 1840s, and in 1851 a Harvard student informed the world of *College Words and Customs* in a 300-page glossary. Two Princeton seniors in 1853 composed, for their own amusement, an exuberant and candid account of *College As It Is*. At the end of the decade, Yale students organized an enormous intercollege periodical in which 28 colleges participated from Bowdoin to Beloit. Originally entitled *Undergraduate* and then *University Quarterly*, it published 1,600 pages of essays and news of different campuses in 1860 and 1861. As an officially recognized publication, the essays were rather formal, but campus accounts were more spontaneous. This tradition culminated in 1871 with perhaps the most complete depiction of undergraduate life ever written—Lyman H. Bagg's 700-page account, *Four Years at Yale, by a Graduate of '69*. These writings document how midcentury students in the Northeast experienced college life.[8]

The Princeton writers describe a regime in which classroom assignments were modest and manageable, control was sufficiently authoritarian to challenge students' rebellious instincts, and free time was available for an abundant social life. The day was still structured around three recitations—at 7 a.m.,

---

6 Ibid., 101–32, 144–55.

7 Ibid., 85, 201–14.

8 Discussed in Roger L. Geiger and Julie Ann Bubolz, "College As It Was in the Mid-Nineteenth Century," in *American College in the Nineteenth Century*, 80–90; the Princeton memoir was not published until 1996: James Buchanan Henry and Christian Schaarff, *College As It Is, or, the Collegian's Manual in 1853*, J. Jefferson Looney, ed. (Princeton: Princeton University Libraries, 1996); Bagg was paid by publisher Charles H. Chatfield to write *Four Years at Yale*, Yale University Archives, Lyman H. Bagg Papers, box 3. The following draws upon these three works.

11 a.m., and 4 p.m., with the two preceding hours and the previous evening designated for preparation. However, a half-hour was usually sufficient study for those who chose to prepare, and various stratagems were possible for those who did not. At Yale the verb "to skin"—"the idea of deceiving or cheating the faculty"—was, according to Bagg, "the commonest word in the Yale dialect."[9] Latin and Greek seemed to present little difficulty, probably because eastern students were well prepared by this time—in fact, most Princeton students entered as sophomores. Math was a different story, with junior calculus being the most difficult subject in the college course. The Princeton writers complained that math was weighted too heavily in calculating class rank. They also felt that science was shortchanged, being crammed into the senior terms, and that modern languages were taught poorly by unqualified adjunct instructors. In general, collegians respected academic achievement but had nothing except disdain for anyone who tried too hard for a high rank. They never held a low class rank against a person. Students were relentlessly judged by their peers, chiefly on their personal qualities.

Every college memoir describes the college experience in terms of the 4 class years. All academic work was done by class, as were most other meaningful aspects of college life. But class solidarity assumed a larger significance because it was there that individual reputation was established or not. A Williams' senior wrote in 1859,

> The *esprit de corps* by which classes are united . . . is full of noble meaning. It is one of the great animating forces of college life, and serves an important purpose, both in stimulating to labor and in restraining from transgression. No man who is not faithful to the honor and interests of his class is fit to be trusted under any circumstances.[10]

Indeed, the psychological impact of a student's progression through the 4 years of the college course was the key to the collegiate experience. Freshmen were expected to run the gauntlet of relentless and ingenious harassment, principally by sophomores, without betraying weakness of character. Both Lyman Bagg and the Princeton writers warned against "newies" coming to college too young, or "green," because their futile efforts at acceptance ("bumming") only produced the opposite effect. Sophomores were regarded by themselves and others as the most rowdy class. Brimming with confidence for having survived the freshman

9 Bagg, *Four Years*, 620.
10 [S. Washington Gladden], "College Life in America," *The Williams Quarterly*, VI, 3 (February, 1859): 193–97, quote p. 197.

year and delighting in the persecution of the new freshmen, they also were the principal perpetrators of pranks and "sprees" against the college authorities. Typical of sophomore mentality, Princeton sophomores published the *Nassau Rake* to ridicule any and all vulnerable targets. The junior class represented a transition to greater seriousness. Coursework now included lectures, and juniors faced the dreaded higher mathematics that few could comprehend; as Bagg put it, "mathematics and other exact sciences . . . can *not* be pounded into a man's head by any number of repetitions."[11] Juniors ignored underclassmen, being preoccupied with increasingly portentous class activities. In addition, they had to survive junior examinations in order to attain the pinnacle of college life. "Dignity" is the word consistently invoked to describe seniors as they assumed the role of gentlemen for which their college experience had prepared them. Seniors were taught principally through lectures, and they could choose for themselves how much to study. Senior examinations, covering the entire college course, were a hurdle, although no one seemed to fail; but the greatest energy was directed toward senior orations and parts for commencement. As students completed this progressive transformation, they took immense satisfaction from their memories, the bonds formed with classmates, and their personal arrival as educated and polished gentlemen.

The formation of gentlemen had been an implicit outcome of colonial colleges and certainly the aspiration of their students. Later, it reflected a Federalist conception of society. College graduates expected to be natural leaders by virtue of their knowledge of history and philosophy and their public speaking skills. While many aspects of the college experience endured, this notion of the social role of graduates was overshadowed during the first third of the nineteenth century, largely due to the Awakening and the proliferation of country colleges. Its reemergence in Jacksonian America required a reformulation for a wealthier society with an egalitarian political structure. Gentility now characterized the social class that dominated the urban culture and economy but not the polity. Their culture flourished in this private sphere, which encompassed principally voluntary organizations. Student life reflected these conditions in ways that transformed the colleges.

Lyman Bagg and the Princeton authors are most forthcoming about student mores. They regard the college culture as basically democratic, where students succeed or not on the basis of intellectual and social accomplishments. While describing some types that did not partake of "the full glory of student life" ("green" freshmen; "religs," or pious students at Princeton), their samples are smaller and more homogeneous than they realized. In fact, both memoirs

11   Bagg, *Four Years,* 696.

advocated greater homogeneity: Bagg recommended that students first attend a boarding school in order to have a successful career at Yale, and the Princeton authors offered similar advice. By midcentury both schools catered to an increasingly uniform youth culture drawn from the upper reaches of society. For them the content of the college course—the furniture of the mind—was even less consequential than for Jeremiah Day. Bagg was explicit:

> The chief value of a college course lies not in the scholarship or absolute knowledge with which it supplies a man, but rather in that intangible thing called culture, or discipline, or mental balance, which only its possessors can appreciate.

This intangible thing was largely the result of "the peculiar life and customs which the students themselves adopt"; however, at Yale it was also a continual test. The ultimate end was "the making of good *men,*" which involved a continual judgment of "personal character . . . the thing by which a man stands or falls in college." For Bagg, a successful career at Yale was an end in itself but also a solid preparation for life.[12] This culture and these ideals were fully formed in the student writings of the early collegiate era, but they had begun to crystallize at other northeastern colleges, particularly in the fraternity movement.

College students had long indulged in exclusive clubs with Greek or English names and secret rituals. Phi Beta Kappa was created at William & Mary in 1776, originally as a social society, and many more or less transitory groupings were formally constituted over the next half-century. Kappa Alpha at Union College in 1825 continued these practices but with a difference. By recruiting additional students from other classes and initiating them into the secret rites, the fraternity became an ongoing institution. When Union's second fraternity, Sigma Phi (f. 1827), chartered a chapter at Hamilton College in 1831, fraternities became an intercollegiate phenomenon. By 1840 they had been introduced to most eastern colleges, and by the Civil War, 22 national fraternities sponsored 299 chapters at 71 colleges, throughout the country.[13] Greek-letter secret societies obviously struck the fancy of antebellum collegians; they were purely a creation of students for their own satisfaction. Not that all students approved: at Union, Williams, and elsewhere, opponents organized nonsecret societies as hostile alternatives. Presidents initially opposed them as well for being exclusive and secret and

12   Bagg, *Four Years*, 702, 703, 691.
13   Somers, *Union College*, 304–8; Craig L. Torbenson, *College Fraternities and Sororities: A Historical Geography, 1776–1989*, PhD Diss., University of Oklahoma, 1992; Nicholas L. Syrett, *The Company He Keeps: A History of White College Fraternities* (Chapel Hill: University of North Carolina Press, 2010), 26.

introducing divisive competition for college positions. For these same qualities, many students loved them.

The initial motivation for forming fraternities was at bottom a *"yearning . . . for fellowship of kindred souls."* The original fraternities were quite small—essentially organized cliques of men who sought a closer and more enduring bond of friendship. Hence, membership first grew through the formation of additional fraternities and chapters, not by enlarging existing ones. The secrecy, hocus-pocus, exclusivity, and competitive spirit made it all more fun and, perhaps, more psychologically gratifying. The added dimension of intercollegiate brotherhood no doubt exaggerated the presumed significance. Antebellum fraternities usually met in off-campus rented rooms, conducted secret meetings, and engaged in the kind of camaraderie little different from that described in the collegiate memoirs. Fraternity loyalties coexisted with those of class and literary societies, but as they became more firmly entrenched after 1840, they became more disruptive. Fraternities competed with one another to woo new members, and their rivalries often corrupted electioneering for class offices. The resulting kerfuffles could embroil a college for months and in some cases resulted in cancellation of the honors at issue. Fraternities were widely held responsible for the decline and demise of the literary societies. They elicited a deeper sense of loyalty, and their rivalries disrupted society activities. Eliphalet Nott regarded fraternities as an "evil," but one "inseparable from an assembly of young men." Mark Hopkins would have preferred to abolish them if it were possible, but every Williams trustee who graduated in the fraternity era had been a member. Princeton rooted out fraternities on two occasions but eventually tolerated their functional equivalent in the ultrasnobbish eating clubs.[14]

The unspoken reality of fraternities was that they attracted students concerned with worldly success and social status. The tensions these values generated were particularly visible at Williams. Although not necessarily hostile to religion, fraternity members rarely shared the piety that produced revivals and religious conversions. As half of the classes after 1850 joined fraternities, religious values no longer dominated this former bastion of Congregationalism. Evangelical colleges in general recognized the inherent threat of secret secular societies and sought to ban them, but at many colleges, like Williams and Amherst, the students established fraternities before the authorities took notice and could act. Above all, fraternity members cherished the values of worldly success—"good

14 Somers, *Union College*; Rudolph, *Mark Hopkins*; Alexander Leitch, *A Princeton Companion* (Princeton: Princeton University Press, 1978), 228–29, 146–49. For a litany of objections to fraternities, prompted in part by the 1873 death of a Cornell student in an initiation ceremony: H. L. Kellogg, ed., *College Secret Societies: Their Customs, Character, and the Efforts for Their Suppression* (Chicago: 1874).

friendship, good looks, good clothes, good family, and good income," as Williams historian Frederick Rudolph put it.[15] Nor were these tastes acquired entirely on campus: they reflected the changing social base of the college.

For the first four decades of its existence, Williams had been a country college that largely served pious youth from humble backgrounds—students like Mark Hopkins. From the start of his presidency in 1836, college enrollment swelled with increasing numbers of students from New York City and the Albany area. After the mid-1840s, they outnumbered students from Massachusetts. Social backgrounds for Williams students are not recorded, but Rudolph reports that the fraternities attracted "the most urbane young men on the campus." Other evidence suggests a growing association with urban wealth.[16]

The first Society of Alumni was organized at Williams in 1821, originally to avert the demise of the college. By Mark Hopkins's tenure, it actively memorialized college history with statues and plaques meant to foster symbolic identity. Gifts of increasing size and frequency followed as loyal graduates prospered. By 1850, old grads were building summer homes in Williamstown to reconnect with alma mater and its rustic charm. Connections with urban wealth affected attitudes on campus. When Boston philanthropist Amos Lawrence became a benefactor of the college, he and President Hopkins shared a prejudice against "an unbalanced and irresponsible power in the hands of the masses." Lawrence at one point donated copies for each student of a book of lectures extolling a Christian imperative for work and material success, which the college endorsed by holding Sunday discussion groups.[17] At Williams and other New England schools, the lure of worldly success had a palpable effect on student careers. Ministerial vocations declined, lawyering increased, and the trickle entering commercial pursuits grew larger. For all these tendencies, the 1850s was prelude to more emphatic trends in the postbellum Gilded Age. Finally, in one telling development, students showed growing enthusiasm for gymnastics and athletics—a need for exercise that earlier farmers' sons had scarcely felt. In 1859 Williams and Amherst played the first intercollegiate "base ball" game. No casual affair, this exhibition was also the first sports weekend, with trainloads of students on reduced fares traveling to Pittsfield for the game, a chess match, and concert.[18]

15   Rudolph, *Mark Hopkins*, 114.

16   The "hearth" of fraternities in the Midwest was Miami University, which had a similar mix of urbane students from nearby Cincinnati and pious rural students: Torbenson, *College Fraternities*; Walter Havinghurst, *The Miami Years, 1809–1959* (New York: Putnam's Sons, 1958), 90–102.

17   James Hamilton, *Life in Earnest. Six Lectures on Christian Activity and Ardor* (New York, 1851 [1845]); Rudolph, *Mark Hopkins,* 178.

18   Rudolph, *Mark Hopkins*, quotes pp. 108, 184; Graduate careers from Bailey B. Burritt, *Professional Distribution of College and University Graduates*, U.S. Bureau of Education Bulletin, 1912, No. 19.

The increasing wealth and social standing of northeastern college students, manifest in student culture and graduate careers, affected the character of the colleges. Generalizations on the social status of students are limited by the small proportion of students attending college (ca. 2 percent), the difficulty of relating such small numbers to specific social groups, and the ambiguity of occupational categories. Instead, a dichotomy is apparent among northeastern students between rural and urban origins.[19] How this affected student aspirations can be seen in the culture of the urban upper class. During the antebellum decades, Boston, New York, and Philadelphia were dominated socially and economically by remarkably stable groups of very wealthy families. Whereas earlier, "self-made" men occasionally acquired (and lost) fortunes, almost all the antebellum elite had inherited wealth, often across several generations. They still retained active economic interests, seldom in manufacturing but largely in a secure mix of real estate, trade, finance, and insurance. They associated and married largely among themselves. These associations included membership in and support for a panoply of voluntary societies and cultural organizations, including colleges, through which they promoted and controlled nonfinancial interests. Economically such self-dealing worked hugely to their advantage. Through good times and bad, they augmented their wealth and fortified their social positions. The few students who pursued careers in business were likely to come from elite backgrounds.[20]

According to a contemporary who should know, Charles Astor Bristed (of the Astor clan), membership in New York City's social elite required "fair natural abilities, add to these the advantages of inherited wealth, a liberal education, and foreign travel." Hence, by 1850 a college education was an expected accoutrement of these scions of wealth. Many also acquired law degrees, although their large fortunes often "precluded the drudgery of a practice." Such students were present at Yale and Princeton, where they sometimes attended social functions with local elites. They were more prominent at Harvard, Columbia, and the University of Pennsylvania, where kinsmen were trustees and where involvement with nearby families generally overshadowed their collegiate experience.[21] Far more important for the eastern colleges were the multitude of boys who lacked an inheritance and a Grand Tour but hoped to leverage natural abilities and a liberal education into entrée to genteel bourgeois society. The elites of the great cities

19   Colin B. Burke, *American Collegiate Populations: A Test of the Traditional View* (New York: New York University Press, 1982).

20   Edward Pessen, *Riches, Class, and Power before the Civil War* (Lexington, MA: D. C. Heath, 1973); Burke, *Collegiate Populations*, 135.

21   Ibid., 154, 56. For the experience of a wealthy student, for example: William Lawrence (Harvard '71), *Memories of a Happy Life* (Boston: Houghton Mifflin, 1926).

might be beyond reach, but the smaller cities and larger towns that dotted the region possessed an analogous—and accessible—bourgeoisie that mimicked the fashions and pretentions of the plutocracy. These collegians sought at least the patina of a liberal education but also wanted to learn how to dine, dress, drink, dance, play, and impress social superiors—in short, they wished to acquire the manners of gentlemen. The colleges allowed them to pursue such socialization through the extracurriculum. What had formerly been colleges of the Awakening became, in the early collegiate era, nurseries for grooming gentlemen.

This development occurred earliest and most thoroughly at Harvard under the Brahmin aristocracy. The university was a hub for the networks that controlled the cultural and medical institutions and were closely linked with the city's financial complex. In 1829, the Brahmins elevated one of their own to the Harvard presidency. Josiah Quincy (1829–1845), who replaced Reverend Kirkland, was the former mayor of Boston and a wealthy and successful businessman, active in banking, insurance, and real estate. With this background he became the "Great Organizer of the University."[22] He was assisted by a succession of wealthy and dedicated businessmen on the Corporation. Brahmin sons increasingly dominated the student body as the college became less hospitable to outsiders. Unitarianism presented one filter, but admissions and cost presented more formidable barriers. Harvard's entrance requirements were continually raised during the antebellum years, comprising a 3-day exam in the 1850s. By then, three-quarters of students were prepared at local Latin schools or private boarding academies. Harvard tuition rose from $20 in 1820 to $104 in 1860, but the average annual spending by students jumped from $225 to $700. Little wonder that enrollments slumped from 1820 to 1850, provoking public criticism. But Quincy dismissed "numbers in literary institutions" as "by no means an unqualified blessing."

Harvard students and their families above all sought refinement in the college. Harvard's numerous social clubs established nuances of social distinction without recourse to fraternities (which were banned in 1859). Harvard, and the Brahmins generally, had close ties with England, and their notions of gentility drew inspiration from Oxbridge. This ideal seemed to include a haughty disdain for the lower classes, but some borrowing was more positive. Harvard embraced the Oxbridge love of sports, particularly boating, cricket, and rugby. In 1852 Harvard crews raced Yale in the first intercollegiate athletic contest. The Oxbridge ideal of a "gentleman and a scholar" was also imbibed by at least some students, who utilized the university's incomparable resources to pursue learning on their

22 The following draws upon Ronald Story, *The Forging of an Aristocracy: Boston and the Harvard Upper Class, 1800–1870* (Middletown, CT: Wesleyan University Press, 1980), 45 et passim.

own terms. No doubt the sons of Harvard were gratified when an Englishman in 1862 declared the university an analogue to Oxford and Cambridge: the "University which gives the highest education to be attained by the highest classes in that country."[23]

The recruitment pattern at Yale was national compared with Harvard's regionalism, but social developments were parallel. The Yale student body was fed by the efforts of its far-flung alumni and retained a greater, although diminishing, clerical presence. However, Yale not only spearheaded the early collegiate era, but its student culture seemed to affect its students more profoundly than anywhere else. Its gauntlet of separate secret societies for each class year took form in the 1830s, reflecting an evolving student culture that valued refinement and savoir faire. By the 1840s, more Yale students came from urban backgrounds and undoubtedly were wealthier as well. Clerical careers declined as graduates were drawn to the business world. The best available evidence suggests that this same pattern extended across New England colleges.[24] Exceptions existed, like Methodist Wesleyan, but at most of the smaller colleges, and particularly those in or near cities, clerical careers for graduates fell by 50 percent, while a larger proportion of urban students supported the fraternity culture and gravitated toward secular careers. Other factors may have played a role. By the 1840s New England was saturated with ministers; and stiffer admission standards (raised from exceeding leniency) may have discouraged rural prospects. After about 1840, northeastern colleges were increasingly patronized by the sons of professionals seeking material and social success. However, just as was the case at Harvard, such prospective collegians were in limited supply.

College enrollment growth slowed notably in the 1840s, except perhaps in the prosperous South. In New England the number of students actually dropped by 5 percent from 1840 to 1850. Even this figure masks substantial declines at individual colleges—graduates in these years fell by one-quarter at Bowdoin and Brown, more than a third at Dartmouth, one-half at Amherst, and two-thirds at Middlebury.[25] Circumstances at each college naturally differed, and governors were often puzzled about the cause. The role and culture of colleges in New England was evolving. Whether an institution was in the forefront, raising admission requirements and cost of attendance like Harvard, or in the rear, clinging to traditional practices and clientele like Middlebury, could affect who and how

---

23   Morison, *Three Centuries of Harvard*, 253; Story, *Forging of an Aristocracy*, 133.

24   Burke, *American Collegiate Populations*, 11–150.

25   Burke, *American Collegiate Populations*, 57. Graduates numbers based on 5-year totals, from Burritt, *Professional Distribution*; also, Claude M. Fuess, *Amherst: The Story of a New England College* (Boston: Little, Brown, 1935),124; Walter C. Bronson, *A History of Brown University, 1764–1914* (Providence, 1914), 258.

many might attend. However, college critics blamed declining attendance on the classical course.

Foremost among these critics was Francis Wayland, president of Brown since 1826. Wayland had a knack for articulating the conventional pieties of the age. His textbook on moral philosophy, *Elements of Moral Science* (1835), was widely adopted and reflected his signature approach of reasoning from metaphysics to everyday affairs to Christian homilies. Utterly lacking Mark Hopkins's tolerance for human foibles, Wayland tried to make life conform to his own rigid ideals and principles. Characteristically, he killed the Brown medical school upon taking office by insisting that its practicing doctors reside in the dormitories and enforce student discipline. In 1837 he published another successful text, *Elements of Political Economy*, which inveighed against any and all interference with free markets. Soon afterward, a visit to Oxford and Cambridge set him pondering the deficiencies of American colleges. He applied political economy to higher education in *Thoughts on the Present Collegiate System in the United States* (1842). He was dismayed both by falling enrollments and by the fact that college was underpriced—not covering its cost of production. He attributed these failings to the classical course, and here his observations rang true. The subjects covered in the course had greatly expanded, but the 4 years allotted to them remained the same: "instead of learning *many* things *imperfectly*, we should learn a *smaller* number of things *well*." Further, "our colleges . . . are at present scarcely . . . more than schools for the education of young men for the professions. . . . [And] while we have been restricting our Collegiate education to one class, its value by that class is less and less appreciated." Instead, Wayland advocated establishing "courses of lectures on all the subjects . . . to which men of all classes may resort."[26]

The illogic of the colleges obviously weighed on Wayland. In 1849 he abruptly resigned his presidency but then was persuaded to remain. He set forth his terms in a *Report to the Corporation of Brown University*, subsequently published and widely read.[27] Wayland proposed to break the monopoly of the classical course by offering a broad slate of practical subjects that students might choose in various combinations. By offering more freedom, he hoped to attract a new class

26   William J. Barber, ed., *Economists and Higher Learning in the Nineteenth Century* (New Brunswick: Transaction Publishers, 1993), 72–94; Francis Wayland, *Thoughts on the Present Collegiate System in the United States* (New York: Arno Press, 1969 [1842]), 80–108, 152–55; Morison considered this "a tract probably productive of more mischief than any other in the history of American education . . . [it] gave the politicians a high-class stick with which to beat the colleges": *Three Centuries of Harvard*, 286.

27   Francis Wayland, *Report to the Corporation of Brown University, on Changes in the System of Collegiate Education, Read March 28, 1850* (Providence, RI, 1850), in Richard Hofstadter and Wilson Smith, eds., *American Higher Education: A Documentary History* (Chicago: University of Chicago Press, 1961), II, 478–87; for an account of the New System, Bronson, *History of Brown*, 258–326.

of students and motivate some traditional students to more serious study. The traditional subjects were still offered, with additions of Application of Chemistry to the Arts, Application of Science to the Arts, and several others that were never organized (teaching, agriculture, law). Most revolutionary was the change in the degree structure: The bachelor of arts (AB) became a 3-year course with variable amounts of Latin, Greek, and modern languages; the bachelor of philosophy (PhB), also 3 years, was awarded for practical subjects and required no classical languages; and the master of arts (AM) was a 4-year degree, similar to the old AB of the classical course but, hopefully, with more independent study. The corporation accepted the New System, provided that a $125,000 endowment could be raised to support it. Enthusiasm surrounding Wayland's plan, which reflected public discontent with the classical course, was sufficient to meet this goal, and the New System was implemented in 1851.

The New System got off to an auspicious start. Enrollments rose from 174 classical students (1850–1851) to 283 combined (1853–1854), with all the growth accounted for by PhB and nondegree students. The chemistry professor drew more than 300 auditors from the local jewelry industry for lectures on the chemistry of precious metals. But problems were also soon apparent. Wayland was oblivious to the emerging collegiate culture, and his efforts to enforce strict rules in the dormitories provoked a revolt in 1851. In the aftermath, two talented scientists hired to teach the applied curriculum were dismissed for their refusal to enforce the repressive disciplinary regime—and were eagerly hired by the new Yale scientific school. Nor did students use the greater flexibility and freedom of the New System to pursue their studies in greater depth, as Wayland had hoped. Instead they performed the minimum needed to meet quite permissive standards. And, after peaking in 1853, enrollments began to dwindle as well. The number of classical students was less than before the New System, and fewer graduated. The number of PhB students fell as well, and only one in six took a degree. Wayland's contention that he was supplying "The Education Demanded by the People of the United States"—the title of an 1854 speech—rang hollow. He retired in 1855, beloved, honored, and exhausted.[28]

Brown's new president, Barnas Sears, was both a true scholar and a practical administrator. To him fell the delicate task of justifying the scuttling of the New System to the same trustees who had originally approved it. After his first year, he delivered a scathing indictment: "the character & reputation of the University are injuriously affected by the low standard of scholarship required for the

---

28   Bronson, *History of Brown*, 300–16; Francis Wayland and H. L. Wayland, *A Memoir of the Life and Labor of Francis Wayland, D.D., LL.D., Late President of Brown University*, 2 vol. (New York, 1867), II, 102–5.

degrees of A.M. and A.B." These low standards are seen as "an open act of underbidding other colleges, & as a scramble for an increased number of students." As a result, "the best students of preparatory schools . . . now go elsewhere." Instead, Brown "is flooded by a class of young men of little solidity or earnestness of character." Unlike Wayland, Sears understood the gentleman's college of the early collegiate era. He quickly moved to restore the traditional degree structure, while still offering the applied courses for those who were interested. Sears also relaxed the rigid rules and stringent enforcement of the Wayland era, allowing students the extracurricular freedoms enjoyed elsewhere. An announcement soon followed: "in the order and the course of study, Brown University does not now differ essentially from her sister Colleges of the United States."[29]

SECTIONALISM AND HIGHER EDUCATION IN THE SOUTH

After the death of University of North Carolina president Joseph Caldwell in 1835, Governor David Swain informed a key trustee that he wished to become the next president of the university. Admired by all but the faculty, he was duly elected and served for the remainder of his life (1836–1868).[30] The state universities of the South had exceptional political prominence, symbolized by the three former presidents of the United States who served as Visitors to the University of Virginia. By the 1830s, populist hostility toward these "aristocratic" institutions was tempered by a growing identification with the governing class. Many men of wealth and prominence had passed through these institutions, and many more of their sons would do the same. By the 1850s the links between the state universities and the region's burgeoning upper class would become closer still. The new states of the lower South reflexively adopted this pattern, founding state universities of the same type.

The 1830s also marked a turning point in the dominant attitudes of that governing class on two vital issues—slavery and religion. In the wake of the 1831 Nat Turner Uprising, the Virginia Legislature conducted a lengthy debate over the possibility of abolishing slavery in the Commonwealth. The final resolution took the long-standing Jeffersonian position, recognizing its "great evils" but leaving the remedy to future generations. William & Mary professor and later president Thomas Dew (1836–1846) wrote an influential summary of the debate in which

---

29   Bronson, *History of Brown*, 321–23.

30   William D. Snyder, *Light on the Hill: A History of the University of North Carolina at Chapel Hill* (Chapel Hill: University of North Carolina Press, 1992), 54–55; Kemp P. Battle, *History of the University of North Carolina*, vol. I (Raleigh: 1907), 423–26.

he marshaled economic arguments to reason that emancipation would cause an unacceptable loss of capital. This was probably the last time that the subject of abolishing slavery could be publicly and honestly discussed in the South. Henceforth, the Jeffersonian apologia would be replaced by strident claims that slavery was a "positive good," justified by the Bible to boot. Dissenters were vilified and ostracized. University leaders like Dew lent prestige, sophistication, and sometimes vehemence to these rationalizations and helped to assure the silence of doubters.[31] Religion contributed as well. The Awakening had had a huge impact on the common people of the South, while the upper class perpetuated a genteel version of Enlightenment rationalism, or at least toleration, and distrusted evangelicals in particular. After 1830, the upper class embraced evangelical religion, and the churches became supportive of the social hierarchy. Early in the century the evangelical sects had largely disapproved of slavery. However, in 1844–1845 southern Methodists and Baptists withdrew from their national churches over the issue. Southern Presbyterians were the mainstay of the conservative Old School, which had no quarrel with slavery.[32] As the region's social elite found religion, the denominations founded colleges—nine from Virginia to Georgia in the 1830s alone, with more to come. However, the state universities dominated antebellum higher education in the South, none more so than South Carolina College.

South Carolina College fulfilled the ambitions of its founders to unify the state's ruling class by imbuing its sons with loyalty to the state and its distinctive culture.[33] The state, in turn, rewarded the college with generous appropriations and sympathetic governance. In 1820 it made a distinguished appointment in Thomas Cooper as professor of chemistry. President Maxcy died soon afterward, and the governors demonstrated a liberality that would later disappear by elevating Cooper, a complete outsider, to the presidency. Cooper possessed an extraordinary range of learning for his day, but he was also an inveterate controversialist. A political exile from his native England because of his revolutionary

---

31   Daniel Walker Howe, *What Hath God Wrought? The Transformation of America, 1815–1848* (New York: Oxford University Press, 2007), 475–82; Susan H. Godson et al., *The College of William & Mary: A History*, 2 vol. (Williamsburg: College of William & Mary, 1993), 247–49; Dew wrote an extensive history of the world for his classes which rationalized slavery and southern society: Denise Ann Riley, *Masters of the Blue Room: An Investigation of the Relationship between the Environment and the Ideology of the Faculty of the College of William & Mary, 1836–1846,* PhD Diss., Ohio State University, 1997.

32   Sidney Ahlstrom, *The Religious History of the American People* (New Haven: Yale University Press, 1972), 658–69.

33   The following draws on Daniel Walker Hollis, *South Carolina College* (Columbia: University of South Carolina Press, 1951), 74–211; and Michael Sugrue, "'We Desire Our Future Rulers to Be Educated Men': South Carolina College, the Defense of Slavery, and the Development of Secessionist Politics," in *American College in the Nineteenth Century*, 91–114.

views, he eventually joined fellow chemist and exile Joseph Priestley in Pennsylvania (1793). While working in both law and chemistry, he managed to be jailed by Federalists under the sedition law and later fired from his Pennsylvania post for political differences. He then concentrated on chemistry, teaching briefly at Dickinson and the University of Pennsylvania, while publishing studies promoting practical applications. Jefferson recruited him for the University of Virginia, in spite of clerical opposition (1819), but he opted instead for the security of South Carolina. Sixty years old when he arrived, Cooper may have been the most erudite man in the state, but he was also a relic of the Revolutionary Enlightenment. However, many of Cooper's convictions harmonized with those prevailing in his new home. Having a Jeffersonian aversion to federal power, he opposed tariffs and the Missouri Compromise, while championing states' rights and slavery. In a shuffle of teaching positions, Cooper was allowed to offer perhaps the first American course in political economy (1825), where he professed these doctrines to South Carolina students.

Cooper's initial years went smoothly. He expanded the faculty and subjects taught, but his basic inclination was to bolster standards. The minimum age was raised to 15, and entrance examinations were stiffened. He also increased recitations in Latin and Greek. Most students actually entered as sophomores or juniors after being prepared by tutors. All these factors kept enrollments modest—fluctuating around one hundred. Student unruliness was as bad as ever, but no worse. In his own course Cooper taught uncompromising doctrines of laissez faire, free trade, justification of slavery, and opposition to federalism, and he soon began sharing these views outside the college. As the controversy over federal tariffs heated up, he ominously advised an 1827 protest meeting, "We shall, before long, be compelled to calculate the value of our union." This veiled threat was widely publicized, and Cooper became a spokesman for the radical opposition to the hated 1828 tariff. He openly spoke of secession even before John C. Calhoun provoked the nullification crisis (1831–1833) by claiming the right of states to reject federal laws. Cooper ingratiated himself with the governing class of South Carolina, who predominately supported nullification—and, soon, secession.[34]

Perhaps intoxicated by this success, Cooper in 1829 unleashed his venom against the Presbyterians, who had earlier opposed his appointment. For the next 2 years, a pamphlet war ensued, including Cooper's derogatory (anonymous) *Exposition of the Doctrines of Calvinism* (1830). Cooper was either an atheist or a deist, depending on who asked, but he carried a Voltairian hatred for all clergy, whom he characterized as acting solely in their own grasping self-interest.

---

34   Hollis, *South Carolina College*, 97–118; Michael Sugrue, "We Desire"; Howe, *What Has God Wrought*, 395–410.

These attacks prompted his religious enemies to unite with his political foes, and they almost succeeded in having the legislature remove him from office. Instead, the matter was referred to the trustees, who tried Cooper on charges that his anti-religious writings had harmed the public standing of the college and that he had possibly indoctrinated students. The trustees delayed a full year before conducting the trial in December 1832. Cooper mustered all his talents as a jurist to mount what Richard Hofstadter called "the most elaborate justification of academic freedom in the ante-bellum period." Actually, Cooper largely defended his own views by stating that materialism, Deism, and so on, were articulated by many respectable Americans, and the Constitution guaranteed his rights to voice them as well. He struck a modern note in asserting that the teacher's obligation was to "treat those questions only that are connected with the subject of his lecture, and . . . treat them fairly and impartially." According to his students, Cooper had not attacked Christianity in class. The trustees, mostly Cooper supporters, declared that the charges were not proved.[35]

There is considerable irony in the opinionated president championing academic freedom. He and his cronies on the faculty dogmatically taught the ideology of states' rights. Different sides of political issues were debated in the literary societies, out of public view, but students received only the South Carolina creed from the faculty. Cooper himself subsequently asserted, "The political doctrines prevalent in this college are decidedly those of the majority of the State. We therefore have few students from the minority." The distinguished political scientist Francis Lieber found it necessary to conceal his Unitarian religion and repugnance of slavery for the 21 years he was at the college (1835–1855). If Cooper was not alone in planting the seeds of political extremism in South Carolina, he certainly helped to cultivated them. They became a constant in the subsequent antebellum years but shorn of Cooper's anticlericalism. In fact, the 1830s represented a shift in the religious sentiments of the South Carolina elite. Cooper's vindication, with its public airing of his anticlerical views, apparently alienated many of them. Enrollments at the college plunged to just 40 in 1834. The trustees concluded that citizens had lost confidence in the college and asked for the resignation of the entire faculty, Cooper included.[36]

For the rest of the antebellum years, South Carolina College had short-term presidents. The most successful incumbents were prominent planter-politicians

---

35   Richard Hofstadter, *Academic Freedom in the Age of the College* (New Brunswick: Transaction Publishers, 1996 [1955]), 264–69; *Dr. Cooper's Defense before the Board of Trustees*, from the *Columbia Times and Gazette* (December 14, 1832), in Hofstadter and Wilson, eds., *American Higher Education*, I, 396–417.

36   Hollis, *South Carolina College*, 116. Cooper resigned the presidency in 1833 but continued to teach chemistry; Sugrue makes the strongest case for Cooper's malign influence on secessionist politics: "We Desire."

whose stature warranted respect from both the polity and the students. Least successful were faculty members elevated to the presidency, who apparently lacked gravitas. Through all, the dominant figure was James H. Thornwell, an 1831 graduate and militant Presbyterian divine, who served as professor of sacred literature and evidence of Christianity, president (1852–1854), and trustee. Thornwell lent a strong Christian presence to the college, even while arguing explicitly that a state university must not be identified with any single denomination. He had studied briefly at Andover and Harvard, departing with a deep aversion to all things Yankee. He referred to abolitionists as "atheists, socialists, communists, red republicans, [and] jacobins" while slaveholders were "the friends of order and regulated freedom . . . . In one word, the world is the battle ground—Christianity and atheism the combatants; and the progress of humanity the stake." Curricular conservatism accompanied political extremism. As all other major universities expanded offerings by the 1850s, South Carolina College proudly defended a purely classical course and, in fact, idealized ancient Athens and its slave-based economy as an analogue to embattled South Carolina. The curriculum embellished the state ideology, but culture was the true end of education; and South Carolina College spread its doctrines of slavery and states' rights throughout the lower South.[37]

The University of Alabama opened in 1831 under nearly frontier conditions, although Tuscaloosa was then the capital of the state. Northern Baptist Alva Woods struggled ineffectually for 6 difficult years to control woefully underprepared, rebellious students. His replacement was far better suited for this challenge. Basil Manly (1837–1855), minister of the First Baptist Church in Charleston, was an 1821 graduate of South Carolina College. He made notable progress in organizing the college course and stabilizing its operations while enduring student misconduct that was severe even by southern standards. He also conveyed his own extreme version of Southern ideology. Manly was instrumental in leading the Southern Baptist Convention out of the national church, and he perceived before most compatriots that secession was unavoidable if the Southern way of life and its peculiar institution were to be preserved. Manly was a prominent proponent of the position that the Bible-sanctioned slavery. He projected an idealized Christian interpretation of southern society, epitomized in a sermon on "Duties of Masters and Servants." Christian masters were benevolent stewards of their slaves' bodies and souls, and slaves in turn would happily fulfill

---

37   Hollis, *South Carolina College*, 164–65; David W. Bratt, *Southern Souls and State Schools: Religion and Public Higher Education in the Southeast, 1776–1900*, PhD Diss., Yale University, 1999, 124–33; Sugrue, "We Desire"; Wayne K. Durrill, "The Power of Ancient Words: Classical Teaching and Social Change at South Carolina College, 1804–1860," *Journal of Southern History*, 65, 3 (August 1999): 469–98.

their Christian duty in their proper place in society—better off, in fact, than industrial laborers or native Africans. This dissociation of Christian society as he imagined it and the realities of slavery was typical of the southern mentality and in keeping with the prevailing fixations with honor and external appearance. In Manly's case, his deep Baptist faith underpinned the fantasy of social harmony. Manly embodied the fusion between evangelical religion and the southern upper class that took place in the 1830s and made the southern ideology a fixture of the universities.[38]

Manly's romantic depiction of the South contrasted with his acute grasp of conditions in higher education. In the summer of 1851 he and professor Landon Cabell Garland made a tour to investigate northern colleges at the behest of the Alabama trustees, who had asked what changes might be made "to extend the benefits of the Institution to a greater number of the citizens of the State?" Manly's subsequent *Report on Collegiate Education* provided a factual and perceptive interpretation of recent reforms.[39] Southern universities, despite their social conservatism, were affected by this reforming spirit for several reasons. The issue of internal improvements assumed increasing significance as manufacturing and railroad construction raced ahead in the North. Although often ambivalent about the implications of such developments, many believed that the South could not persist as a backward, agrarian society. However, advances in higher education also had an impact. Francis Wayland's widely publicized 1850 *Report* addressed precisely the issue that the Alabama trustees had raised. Engineering and agricultural chemistry were now being taught at northern colleges, particularly Union, Harvard, and Yale. Moreover, numerous variations on the traditional course of study provided a natural experiment in the organization of higher education.

Manly's document echoed the Yale *Reports* of 1828 in endorsing the foundational nature of the classical course. He pointedly showed that where electives were offered, the large majority of students still chose the traditional course. The numerous efforts to attract a wider clientele had not achieved that end. "The *'partial course,'* which does not lead to a degree, is an acknowledged failure everywhere." Scientific courses, with little or no ancient languages, were "expedients . . . too recent and too limited to show the effect on numbers or mental culture." An elective system, like the University of Virginia's, required a scale of

---

38 Stephen Tomlinson and Kevin Windham, "Northern Piety and Southern Honor: Alva Woods and the Problem of Discipline at the University of Alabama, 1831–1837," *Perspectives on the History of Higher Education*, 25 (2006): 1–42. A. James Fuller, *Chaplain to the Confederacy: Basil Manly and Baptist Life in the Old South* (Baton Rouge: Louisiana State University Press, 2000).

39 Basil Manly, *Report on Collegiate Instruction Made to the Trustees of the University of Alabama, July, 1852* (Tuskaloosa [sic.], 1852), 5.

operation far beyond that of most colleges in order to offer meaningful choice of courses. Nor could lectures substitute for "the faithful personal drill of class examinations" (i.e., recitations). Manly's *Report* presented a conservative assessment of the curriculum but one largely justified by contemporary evidence, circa 1850.[40] As for Alabama, he recommended establishing a separate scientific course, like Yale's and Harvard's. He hoped that entrance requirements could be elevated, and that freshmen studies could be isolated in a separate unit.

Rather than heed Manly's sensible suggestions, the Alabama trustees did the opposite. In their zeal to open the university more widely, and against faculty opposition, they opted to emulate the Virginia model. Beginning in 1854, students could determine their own "select" course of study from among the college offerings, and the minimum age for admission was lowered to 14. For the next few years the university operated a kind of hybrid system, while Manly was replaced by his former traveling companion, Landon Garland, a proponent of the Virginia model. In 1859 the trustees fully implemented a Virginia-style system that eliminated the college classes and established eight separate departments. Little can be said of this experiment because it lasted a year at most. President Garland, who was traumatized by student misbehavior, considered the existing university a failure that corrupted more students than it benefited. He embarked on another academic fact-finding tour, this time to the Citadel, Virginia Military Institute, and West Point. His recommendation that a military system be adopted was overwhelmingly endorsed by the Alabama legislatures, and the university imposed military discipline and training on all students in September 1860. If the reactions of contemporaries can be believed, which is doubtful, this truncated experiment was a great success.[41]

Alabama's erstwhile model, the University of Virginia, was by 1850 both the largest and most renowned southern university, with enrollments soon exceeding 600 drawn from all over the South. Since its founding, Jefferson's university had been sui generis, but after 1850 its version of departmental courses began to be considered as an alternative to the fixed classical course. By this time the university had evolved into three divisions: the "schools" (actually departments or chairs) of literature and science, two chairs of law, and four chairs of medicine, similar to the medical schools of the day. Although the university sought to create additional chairs, its students showed little interest in applied subjects. An

40 Ibid., passim. Manly regards Wayland's reforms at Brown as "a gratifying exception" (p. 43); however, their subsequent failure would have buttressed his case.

41 James B. Sellers, *History of the University of Alabama*, vol. I, 1818–1902 (Tuscaloosa: University of Alabama Press, 1953), 150–56, 258–63. Garland later attempted to emulate the Virginia model as founding president of Vanderbilt University in 1875: Paul K. Conkin, *Gone with the Ivy: A Biography of Vanderbilt University* (Knoxville: University of Tennessee Press, 1985), 39–46.

effort to offer engineering in the 1850s failed, as did an attempt to found a school of agriculture. The single addition of this nature was a position in applied chemistry in 1858. The BA degree adopted in 1848 found few takers; nor did many students persist to earn a master's degree. Manly calculated that the average student stay was 1.4 years. However, the faculty was highly qualified and the examinations rigorous; a high level of instruction could be had by a rare dedicated scholar. Functioning at once as a finishing school for southern aristocrats and the academic beacon of the South, the university felt no compulsion to reform.[42] This was not the case with the oldest universities of the South.

The universities of Georgia and North Carolina made concerted efforts to modernize in the 1850s. Georgia had been led since 1829 by Alonzo Church, a rather rigid Presbyterian minister who had made the school a respectable classical college. By the 1850s, however, the loss of faculty and decline in enrollments prompted the appointment of a faculty-trustee committee to suggest reforms. Its 1855 report envisioned a more comprehensive university with new schools for engineering, agriculture, teacher training, and law. The legislature completely ignored this vision, but it apparently inflamed internal discontents to such an extent that in 1857 the trustees demanded the resignation of the entire faculty. When President Church finally retired in 1859, the trustees implemented as much of the modernization plan as was possible without state assistance, namely, a separate "institute" for the instruction of freshmen and sophomores and a law school. As had been the case throughout its history, the academic ambitions of the university found little or no support among Georgia's elected politicians.[43]

North Carolina was the only southern university to implement a practical curriculum. President Swain had advocated internal improvements from his time as governor, but initiatives to establish instruction in engineering and agriculture had faltered. In 1851, it too had sent an informal delegation northward to observe academic and industrial developments. Their subsequent efforts at reform were supported by trustees connected with the state's railroad industry, which sought home-grown engineers. The School for the Application of Science to the Arts was launched in 1854. Two UNC honors grads were hired as professors of civil engineering and agricultural chemistry. The unique feature of the school was that students entered in their senior year—after previous work in the classical course. This model was an apparent success. Enrollments in the college rose above 400, and 80 to 90 percent of seniors took the scientific course,

42   Philip A. Bruce, *History of the University of Virginia, 1819–1919*, 5 vol. (New York: Macmillan, 1921), III, 1–15, 27–52; Manly, *Report*, 28–29.

43   Thomas G. Dyer, *The University of Georgia: A Bicentennial History, 1785–1985* (Athens: University of Georgia Press, 1985), 82–98.

although few of them subsequently pursued careers in these fields. But science and politics could not be kept apart in the antebellum South. When it became known in 1856 that Benjamin Hedrick, the professor of applied chemistry, favored a free-soil candidate, he was relentlessly harassed. He sealed his fate by trying to defend himself in a letter to a local newspaper. To deflect local criticism, the university solemnly fired him for becoming an "agitator."[44]

The southern state universities were in many ways responsive to academic developments occurring in the Northeast. They invested in science and sometimes seemed eager to entice larger numbers of youth to attend. However, they ultimately served the wealthy planters, politicians, and urban professionals who dominated southern society. With that dependence came the obligation, eagerly accepted, to defend the peculiar institution and its many ramifications. That commitment in turn imposed an intellectual intolerance and dishonesty that was at odds with the values of learning and science. The universities had to serve southern society in another important sense. Although they manifested a certain degree of resistance, they had to come to terms with southern students.

The dichotomy between the era of submission and control and the early collegiate era of northern colleges does not fit the South. From the eighteenth century to the Civil War, efforts to achieve student submission to college laws were frustrated, and a consistent degree of control was unattainable. Southern colleges and universities simply had fewer and less effective levers with which to discipline students. Where graduation was not valued, the threat of dismissal or expulsion inspired little fear. Routine punishments became a ritual that concluded with outward expressions of repentance followed by official forgiveness. Southern parents offered little assistance in supporting college discipline—often just the opposite, expecting special treatment due their social status. Moreover, students themselves presented real resistance. To start, they were armed and dangerous; opposing miscreants often meant physical confrontations. They also formed a united front when one of their numbers was, in their biased view, unjustly punished. They had an exaggerated sense of entitlement, which excused crimes or outrages committed against social inferiors. No southern student, for example, ever seems to have been disciplined for harming a slave.[45]

The histories of every southern university are filled with stories of student mayhem, wanton vandalism, and defiance of college authority. In the North, the colleges ultimately prevailed in major student rebellions but not so in the

44   Thomas Kevin B. Cherry, "Bringing Science to the South: the School for the Application of Science to the Arts of the University of North Carolina," *History of Higher Education Annual*, 14 (1994): 73–99; Snider, *Light on the Hill*, 64–66; Battle, *North Carolina*, 654–57.

45   Robert F. Pace, *Halls of Honor: College Men in the Old South* (Baton Rouge: Louisiana State University Press, 2004).

South. A student revolt at Alabama drove president Alva Woods from office. At Virginia, after the militia had to be called in to suppress the armed riot of 1836, students henceforth celebrated each year's anniversary of that heroic event. It was during the 1840 celebration that professor John Davis was shot to death by a student. Academics could be affected by an implicit student veto over unpopular faculty. Virginia students relentlessly insulted the brilliant mathematics professor James Sylvester for being English and Jewish, forcing his departure after just 6 months (1842). Students also led the attacks on Benjamin Hedrick. In these and other cases, student intolerance was backed by local opinion, which further inhibited any college response.[46]

Antebellum southern students showed less interest in the more constructive extracurricular activities that increasingly preoccupied northern students.[47] Literary societies remained vibrant, as students continued to value eloquence and debate. Students generally entered with advanced standing and often departed without graduating, so that class solidarity was diminished. However, the solidarity of the entire student body was correspondingly greater. Southern universities lacked a leavening of pious, preministerial students, creating greater conformity of outlook and behavior. Southern students possessed a good deal more freedom than their northern counterparts given the weakness of college control. They regularly engaged in ostensibly illegal activities like smoking, drinking, gambling, card playing, and worse.[48] Fraternities emerged later and were weaker in the antebellum era, perhaps because students felt less need for what they could offer. They already indulged in illicit activities, and the social distinctions that fraternities accentuated were overshadowed by social status largely determined by family.

A good portion of northern students looked to their colleges or their classmates to acquire the manners and mantle of a gentleman. In the South, the gentleman's code of honor was a powerful social norm that students brought with them to college. As adolescents, they still had to refine the details of the code during their collegiate years. Thus, the annals of southern colleges are filled with confrontations with faculty, presidents, townspeople, and fellow students, ostensibly to uphold honor. In fact, personal honor or reputation was of greater value in southern society than a college degree. Hence, students readily accepted expulsion rather than submit to "dishonorable" treatment. Student culture

---

46   Tomlinson and Windham, "Northern Piety"; Bruce, *University of Virginia*, III, 111–31; A. J. Angulo, "William Barton Rogers and the Southern Sieve: Revisiting Science, Slavery, and Higher Learning in the Old South," *History of Education Quarterly*, 45, 1 (Spring 2005): 18–37.

47   For the following, see Bruce, *University of Virginia*, II & III; Hollis, *South Carolina College*; Dyer, *University of Georgia*, 46–70; Sellers, *University of Alabama*.

48   Timothy J. Williams, "Confronting a 'Wilderness of Sin': Student Writing, Sex, and Manhood in the Antebellum South," *Perspectives on the History of Higher Education*, 27 (2008): 1–31.

powerfully reinforced the code, usually in opposition to the authority and purpose of the colleges.[49]

Despite all, Southern colleges and universities educated and graduated large numbers of students, often with distinction. Kemp Battle reported that one third of his classmates at UNC in the 1840s took their studies seriously— probably as good an estimate as any.[50] Governing or teaching these students was a delicate task. Effective presidents possessed an intuitive sense of how to handle Southern youth with a combination of firmness and toleration. They also had to command respect as gentlemen themselves, something that teachers sometimes found difficult. The universities functioned well enough to serve the purposes of their respective states. Although some were ambitious to accomplish more by the 1850s, populist state legislatures rarely shared those ambitions. This situation arose in part because the state universities did not alone speak for higher education. Different approaches to higher education for different clienteles were offered by different institutions—church colleges and military academies.

Denominational colleges emerged in the Old South in the 1830s through the efforts of Methodists, Baptists, and Presbyterians. Randolph-Macon (M. 1830) was the pioneer in Virginia, where Hampton-Sydney and Washington were long led but not controlled by Presbyterians. Later in the decade Georgia chartered Oglethorpe (P. 1835), Emory (M. 1836), and Mercer (B. 1837). North Carolina followed with Wake Forest (B. 1838), Davidson (P. 1838), and Greensboro (M. 1839). Virginia then added Emory and Henry (M. 1839) and Richmond (B. 1840). South Carolina delayed until 1850 to charter Erskine (P.), Furman (B.), and Wofford (M. 1851). Later in the decade Episcopalians and Lutherans joined this trend, and a succession of Methodist schools in North Carolina evolved into Trinity College (1859, later Duke University). The surge of foundings in the 1830s reflected the reversal of attitudes toward college education among Baptists and Methodists, while Presbyterians preferred institutions under direct church control.[51] As in the North, southern Baptists and Methodists sought to educate the laity of their churches. Theological training for ministers remained controversial, and most colleges explicitly renounced it; yet recruiting more and better-educated ministers and missionaries was indispensible. Still, the chief

---

49 Pace, *Halls of Honor*, 82–97; Sugrue, "We Desire."

50 Kemp Plumer Battle, *Memories of an Old-Time Tar Heel* (Chapel Hill: University of North Carolina Press, 1945), 80: Battle, a faculty son and 1849 graduate, is considered the second founder of the university for his postwar presidency.

51 President Philip Lindsley of the University of Nashville blamed the proliferation of denominational colleges for the decline of his institution—an unaffiliated college that sought to uphold fairly high standards. After some initial success, Nashville declined after 1840, largely from lack of support, and ceased operations in the early 1850s: Paul K. Conkin, *Peabody College: From a Frontier Academy to the Frontiers of Teaching and Learning* (Nashville: Vanderbilt University Press, 2002), 24–88.

motivation was to protect the flock—to provide moral education and keep the faithful away from the state universities or schools of other churches. The clientele they sought to serve came heavily from the rural middle class, sufficiently prosperous to provide sons with a bare-bones collegiate education. Every one of the 1830s' colleges adopted the manual labor system to reduce expenses, and in every case it failed miserably. Even so, costs at the church colleges were roughly one-half to three-quarters those of state universities.[52]

Each of these colleges was sponsored by a regional church organization, and both governors and teachers were likely to be fervently evangelical. The Awakening in the South showed no attenuation in the antebellum years. Some of the colleges opened the school year with a camp meeting revival. Most expected to experience a revival each school year, whether spontaneous or planned. Compared with other colleges, students were subjected to more formal religious activities and strict observance of the Sabbath. The colleges tended to have a good number of sincerely pious and converted students who organized activities such as prayer groups and missionary societies. Still, students as a whole were probably less pious than their parents or the faculty. Perhaps 20 to 30 percent became ministers, but student diaries attest that nearly half of the students were not very religious. Proximity was more important than denomination for many, so that a majority of students might not share the religion of the college. Nor were these colleges immune to disruptive student behavior, although never as violent and destructive as the extremes at state universities.[53]

The clientele of the church colleges in general were poorly prepared, and colleges regularly spoke of the need to elevate the low standards. One consequence was graduation rates generally below 50 percent. However, coming from middling circumstances, many of these students felt that college was their chance for a successful career as a professional, and they applied themselves accordingly. In contrast to UNC, one student estimated that two-thirds of his Randolph-Macon classmates were serious about their studies. Literary societies assumed an important role as a free space in which students could polish their skills. Church colleges were as adamant in defending slavery as the universities. Presidents James C. Furman of Furman and A. B. Longstreet of Emory had played prominent roles in the schisms of their respective churches. President William A. Smith taught Randolph-Macon juniors a course in "Political Economy and Domestic Slavery" using his own text, *The Philosophy and Practice of Slavery*. Along

---

52 Albea Godbold, *The Church College of the Old South* (Durham, NC: Duke University Press, 1944), 3–77. For the southern middle class: Jennifer R. Green, *Military Education and the Emerging Middle Class in the Old South* (New York: Cambridge University Press, 2008), chapter 8.

53 Godbold, *Church College*, 78–144, 196–97; James Edward Scanlon, *Randolph-Macon College: A Southern History, 1825–1967* (Charlottesville: University of Virginia, 1985), 58–92.

with Thomas Dew of William & Mary, these presidents lent respectability to the southern apologia.[54]

The military academies and institutes of the South straddled the boundary between college and preparatory schooling. The first and foremost exemplar was the Virginia Military Institute established at the state arsenal in Lexington in 1839. Alden Partridge's proselytizing had advocated such institutions to improve the sad condition of the state militia, but the chief proponent wished to create the West Point of the South. VMI was established on this basis as a 4-year, state-supported military school. Its first 2 years concentrated on math, French, and English; the last two introduced chemistry, advanced collegiate subjects, and engineering. The little military subject matter was confined to the senior year. However, the Institute operated according to military discipline and the chain of command. Cadets squeezed three recitations per day between hours of military drill. Virginia not only supported VMI but also created fifty state scholarships. These state cadets paid about $100 per year, compared to more than $200 for private cadets. In return, state cadets were required to teach in Virginia schools for 2 years following graduation. In 1842, the South Carolina Military Academy was established at the Citadel on this same basis. Elsewhere throughout the South private military schools were formed and soon received state assistance for scholarships or equipment. When the Georgia Military Institute appeared to be failing, the state took it over in 1857. Similarly, the Western Military Institute displaced the University of Nashville. Some 96 military schools or cadet corps were organized in the South prior to 1861. Although many were no more than private secondary schools, others were formed at colleges, like the University of Alabama. Nevertheless, all these states, save Texas, supported military education, while only Virginia and South Carolina provided regular appropriations to colleges.[55]

One appeal of military schools for parents and legislatures was as a solution to the problem of student misconduct. Discipline and hierarchy seemed to take precedence among cadets over the kinds of dissipation and misbehavior that roiled universities. For students, the military schools offered an alternative form of educational opportunity. The schools were largely patronized by the southern middle class, on balance mostly professional families who were less agricultural and less religious than those who looked to church colleges. The

---

54 Godbold, *Church College*, 78–93; Scanlon, *Randolph-Macon*, 69–84.

55 Rod Andrew Jr., *Long Gray Lines: The Southern Military School Tradition, 1839–1915* (Chapel Hill: University of North Carolina Press, 2001), 8–25; Jennifer R. Green, *Military Education and the Emerging Middle Class in the Old South* (New York: Cambridge University Press, 2008); Bruce Allardice, "West Points of the Confederacy: Southern Military Schools and the Confederate Army," *Civil War History*, 43, 4 (1997): 310–31.

military academies promised a practical education and specifically eschewed the ancient languages and the lengthy preparation they required. Almost none of the cadets came from clerical families, and virtually none later became ministers. The military academies represent the southern approach to practical higher education. Of known occupations, 12 percent of cadets became engineers, and 27 percent became teachers. Another quarter became lawyers and doctors. The schools represented opportunities for social advancement in the professional middle class but not the upper class. However, practical education faced the same impediments in the South as elsewhere. The realities of the military schools were that students entered very young, often 12 to 14, and very few graduated. VMI was the outstanding success, graduating 45 percent of its cadets and supplying a large number of the South's engineers and military instructors. The Citadel graduated only 14 percent, and the others, under 10 percent. Thus, relatively few of the 12,000 antebellum cadets ever reached the third- and fourth-year courses in science and engineering. They all acquired extensive training in military drill, however, and virtually all served as officers in the Confederate Army.[56]

By 1860 the Southeast had the highest enrollment rates in the country—2.8 percent of 16- to 19-year-old white males, compared with 2.5 in New England and 1.8 nationally.[57] If the 1,500 cadets in military academies in 1860 are added to the 3,300 college and university students, the South could claim an enrollment rate of 4 percent.[58] This high rate of enrollment was buoyed by the booming economy of the 1850s, but it also reflected the region's hierarchical structure of society and schooling. The southeastern state universities, especially the University of Virginia and South Carolina College, catered to the upper class of the region and nurtured an elite culture. The denominational colleges served a largely middle-class population that was more socially, religiously, and geographically homogeneous than their northern counterparts. The military academies, the South's unique concession to practical higher education, served a mixed group of less prepared, middle-class students. While the first group of students depended on wealth to maintain their social status and universities for cultural finishing, the latter two looked specifically to their schooling as the grounding for future careers. All, nevertheless, strongly supported the social order and an economy

56 Green, *Military Education*, 151–81, 265–72; Allardice, "West Points," 317–26.

57 Burke, *American Collegiate Populations*, 54–83: I have converted Burke's 6-year cohorts to 4-year cohorts, which still overestimates average time in college. The percentage of males receiving some college could have been somewhat higher.

58 Estimate from Allardice, "West Points," 322: Southeastern enrollments in 1860 can be roughly estimated as 1,400 in state universities, 1,900 in denominational colleges, and 1,500 in military schools; cf. Burke, *American Collegiate Populations*.

predicated on involuntary servitude. Intellectually, the accomplishments of the South are much less impressive. Relatively few of these students earned bachelor's degrees. Distinguished academics like Francis Lieber and William B. Rogers fled the region in the 1850s. The apologists referred to above only confirm the judgment of Richard Hofstadter: "By the 1850s the South had lost its ability to take realistic stock of social issues. While the absence of freedom in its halls of learning was only one symptom of this loss, it was a token of a severe general intellectual paralysis."[59]

DENOMINATIONAL COLLEGES II: PROLIFERATION IN THE UPPER MIDWEST

In 1860, the states of the upper Midwest, stretching from Ohio to Minnesota and Iowa, contained 31 percent of American colleges. They enrolled just 24 percent of students but accounted for 36 percent of enrollment growth in the previous two decades.[60] Aside from a few state universities, this was a land of denominational colleges. Some had colonized new lands on the real estate frontier, but many more provided education in settled and developed communities for the faithful and locals under the aegis of their respective churches. The hallmark of these 65 to 70 colleges was variety; meaningful generalizations about them are largely negative. The sharp social distinctions that affected higher education in the Northeast and South were considerably muted in the dynamic, egalitarian society of the rural Midwest. The status of gentleman was cultivated by some students within colleges but had a limited currency outside. The dearth of schooling required these colleges to assume responsibility for precollegiate education as well. And, the region lacked leading institutions for others to emulate. The two largest institutions—Oberlin and the University of Michigan—were polar opposites; wealthy families concerned with social status would likely send sons to eastern schools. In fact, most denominational colleges could be located on a continuum that stretched from the traditional classical college to multipurpose, coeducational colleges. Where each would fall was largely determined by circumstances and constituencies—especially by their level of resources and how they were acquired.

---

59 Richard Hofstadter, *Academic Freedom*, 259; Angulo, "William Barton Rogers"; Paul Finkelman, "Lieber, Slavery, and the Problem of Free thought in Antebellum South Carolina," in Charles R. Mack and Henry H. Lesesne, eds., *Francis Lieber and the Culture of the Mind* (Columbia: University of South Carolina Press, 2005), 11–22. Robert V. Bruce offers a judgment like Hofstadter's regarding the incomprehension of science in Southern culture: *The Launching of Modern American Science* (Ithaca: Cornell University Press, 1987), 61–62.

60 Burke, *American Collegiate Populations*, 19, 57.

The denominational colleges in these decades developed along the lines described in chapter 5. That is, they all offered the classical course, the defining feature of the American college. It was also all that many could offer given the available personnel and financial limitations. However, while newer colleges repeated the tribulations of their predecessors, more mature institutions managed by the 1850s to expand their faculties and offerings. Amidst this rich natural experiment in educational survival, three overlapping tendencies can be distinguished. A few colleges sought to elevate the classical curriculum in emulation of the "best" colleges in the East; most adopted additional educational programs and degrees to serve local constituencies; and a third group molded their offerings to serve close-knit religious communities.

In 1843 the Plan of Union colleges that had been founded in the West by Presbyterians and Congregationalists received some badly needed assistance. The depression had made their financial situations direr than usual, with budgets in deficit and large debts to repay. Their annual sojourns to the eastern money frontier were becoming less lucrative and less welcome. To address this problem, a new organization was created by college supporters of the Benevolent Empire—the Society for the Promotion of Collegiate and Theological Education at the West— better known as SPCTEW, or the Western College Society. The society became a collective fund-raiser chiefly for the Plan of Union colleges, but its intentions were larger than finance. The inspiration was basically evangelical, coming straight out of the Awakening. The founders deplored the "unorganized state of society" in the West, the result of rapid growth and "recent immigration," especially of Roman Catholics. The Christian society they sought to foster required solid colleges that would educate future ministers in the New England way. SPCTEW's head was Theron Baldwin, one of the original Yale Band of missionaries to frontier Illinois, who believed "*an educated and evangelical ministry constitutes, of God, the great central instrumentality for the evangelization of the west.*"[61]

Five institutions participated in organizing the Western Society, and they were its first beneficiaries: Illinois, Marietta, Wabash, and Western Reserve colleges and the Lane Theological Seminary. The society hired agents to canvas the churches for donations in given regions of the East. Thus, it looked to the broad base of the faithful rather than philanthropists (who generally gave to specific institutions). In its first year, the society raised $17,000, which was distributed on a pro rata basis, with Western Reserve receiving $6,000 and Lane, more than $1,000. Knox College, founded, like Oberlin, in the Christian perfectionist tradition, requested entrée into this charmed circle in 1844 but was assisted in 1848

61 James Findlay, "The SPCTEW and Western Colleges: Religion and Higher Education in Mid-Nineteenth Century America," *History of Education Quarterly*, 17, 1 (Spring 1977): 31–62, quotes pp. 53n, 36.

only after being examined by a visiting committee. The expectation of support from the Society also encouraged the founding of Beloit College in 1847. The society provided two Lutheran colleges, Heidelberg and Wittenberg, with small awards, but it chiefly aimed support toward the expanding frontier, adding Grinnell College in Iowa and three colleges on the west coast. The society's contributions were intended to support current budgets. Western Reserve in 1844 had expenses of $8,000 and tuition revenues of just $2,000. Perhaps more typical, Beloit's grant for 1855 covered 18 percent of its $7,400 budget. The society provided badly needed income for these colleges, especially during the hard times of the 1840s. Western Reserve was essentially bankrupt, and Knox probably was too. The society made the greatest effort to save Western Reserve, which stubbornly maintained a theological department it could not afford. Besides large grants, it assisted with an endowment drive that provided some financial breathing room. However, the next colleges in line for endowment drives, Marietta and Wabash, received little from the society's overworked donors.[62]

The resources of the Society gave it a great deal of influence over the colleges, although their leaders shared the same goals. Revivals were regarded as indications of active evangelical fervor. In 1848 the Society reported that six major revivals had occurred at Illinois College, seven at Wabash and Marietta, and more at Knox. The other criteria valued by the society were upholding high standards in the classical course and producing ministerial candidates. In keeping with the New England way, coeducation was frowned upon. Theron Baldwin informed the Knox president, who favored coeducation, "union on the part of males & females as exist at Oberlin . . . would be an insuperable barrier to the reception of an institution by [the Western Society] Board." Congregationalist and New School Presbyterians supported only colleges with no direct church affiliation. By the 1850s, however, this was a small universe in the West. Hence, college leaders of both churches sought to stay connected with their denomination's strength in the East. The colleges provided the Society with detailed annual reports of their finances and operations, and presidents made regular eastern visits. This eastern orientation could cause resentment. A local paper attacked the Wabash president for telling Easterners of the sad state of education in the Mississippi Valley (part of his pitch), accusing him of snobbery and disloyalty to the West.[63]

62   Ibid., 57; Daniel T. Johnson, *Puritan Power in Illinois: Higher Education Prior to 1870*, PhD Diss., University of Wisconsin, 1974, 62–76; C. H. Cramer, *Case Western Reserve: A History of the University, 1826–1976* (Boston: Little, Brown, 1976), 27–45.

63   Johnson, *Puritan Power*, 75; Findlay, "SPCTEW"; James Insley Osborne and Theodore Gregory Gronert, *Wabash: The First Hundred Years, 1832–1932* (Crawfordsville, IN.: Banta, 1932), 66; Doris Malkmus, "Small Towns, Small Sects, and Coeducation in Midwestern Colleges, 1853–1861," *History of Higher Education Annual*, 22 (2002): 33–66, quote p. 47.

The Plan of Union was formally dissolved in 1852 amid a rising spirit of denominational defensiveness and contention that affected all the churches. The Western Society became basically a Congregational organization but did not revise its strategy or mission. It persisted in raising and distributing support until 1874, when it merged with its charitable rival, the American Education Society. The eastern orientation of the society's wards ultimately worked to their advantage. By maintaining standards and building prestige, they subsequently appealed to a wealthier and better educated clientele that provided a more reliable base of support. However, nearly all western antebellum colleges felt the need to offer additional forms of education for their diverse communities.

The antebellum western colleges all faced the problem of ill-prepared students. From their opening, they were compelled to offer preparatory instruction, which became permanent departments. Years often lapsed before a college charter was sought and college classes begun. The western colleges were inherently "multi-level, multi-purpose" institutions that provided "educational upgrading" where it was sorely needed. Many began or passed through a phase as academies or seminaries, which were general-purpose schools and usually coeducational as well. Marietta College, for example, evolved from an academy into the Marietta Collegiate Institute and Western Teachers' Seminary (1832–1835) before receiving a college charter. It then completely divested the female department.[64] Knox College also separated its Ladies' Seminary under pressure from the Western Society. Colleges that retained their original academies, however, were able to educate diverse kinds of students and also maintain an important stream of income. At Oberlin, for example, the preparatory and ladies' departments produced a profit, while the collegiate and theological departments were in deficit.

Several factors shaped the organization of the western colleges. First, by obtaining a college charter, the schools were committed to offering the classical course for the AB degree. The second defining element was the relationship to a church. The Plan of Union colleges, as was just seen, preserved important ties with the eastern base of their churches. For Methodists and Baptists, regional conferences sponsored colleges directly, which then conformed to their conception of college roles. But individuals or groups from those denominations also founded colleges that identified with, but were not formally linked to, those churches. A third factor shaping these colleges was their relationship with the local and/or denominational communities. Sometimes they were one and the same; other times the college community might be defined locally or religiously. David Potts concluded that the Baptist colleges he studied were shaped more by

---

64   Burke, *American Collegiate Populations*, 38; Arthur G. Beach, *A Pioneer College: The Story of Marietta* (Private printing, 1935), 27–52.

local conditions than the denomination.[65] In either case, the educational needs of the populations served by the antebellum western colleges were predominately precollegiate. Hence, the ubiquitous preparatory departments existed, but there was also considerable demand for other kinds of advanced instruction.

After 1850, these three factors interacted to yield a profusion of approaches pursuing multiple purposes. Some more or less traditional colleges differentiated by offering additional degrees and courses.

Illinois College was typical in harboring ambitions of adding professional schools. It never ventured into theology or law, but in 1843 it launched a medical school, the first in Illinois. The school soon attracted thirty-some students, and was apparently part of the college rather than proprietary. The school abruptly terminated in 1848, allegedly because the instructors were paid in promissory notes with an indefinite payment date. In 1852 the college created a bachelor of science course, which was largely the traditional course stripped of Latin and Greek, leaving less than 3 years of study. Like many other such courses, it provided an English-language college degree for a class of young men "believed to be very numerous," not serious study of science.[66] Indiana Asbury had similar aspirations to expand into a full university, the capstone of the Methodist educational empire in Indiana. In the 1840s, with approximately fifty college students and three times that number of preparatory, irregular, and scientific students, it explored schemes to establish schools or professorships in law, agriculture, Bible studies, and, finally, medicine. Only the latter succeeded, temporarily, with the 1848 establishment of the Indiana Central Medical College in Indianapolis. Apparently a respectable school, it enrolled 100 students in its 3-year existence, before folding for financial reasons. Asbury did not forsake this goal and did succeed in establishing a law course in the 1850s—again temporarily. In 1859 it upgraded the scientific course to 4 years, although still inferior to the classical course. It considered the possibility of admitting women but was reluctant to take that step until after the Civil War.[67]

In the 1840s and 1850s, midwestern colleges augmented their offerings from a menu of possible courses. A scientific course was adopted almost everywhere, and it was accompanied by the acceptance of irregular students. These approaches fared poorly in the East, where they seemed incompatible with powerful loyalties to college classes, but they suited conditions in the West. Preparation in

---

65   David B. Potts, "American Colleges in the Nineteenth Century: From Localism to Denominationalism," *History of Education Quarterly*, 11 (1971): 363–80.

66   Charles E. Frank, *Pioneer's Progress: Illinois College, 1829–1979* (Carbondale: Southern Illinois University Press, 1979), 35–36, 55–56.

67   George B. Manhart, *DePauw through the Years*, 2 vol. (Greencastle, IN: DePauw University, 1962), I, 40–60.

Latin and Greek was weak, making an English alternative more attractive; and only a minority of students graduated from any course, making partial studies the norm. Later in the century, the bachelor of science courses came to be disdained as "less discipline, less work, less culture, and inferior in contents." However, antebellum conditions often attracted more such students than the classical course. Since the early science courses contained little science, a 3-year English or modern languages course was sometimes also offered, with similar results. Many colleges offered a teacher's course as well, since a good number of graduates normally became teachers. What changed in the 1840s was acceptance of a shorter course without classical languages as suitable training. Denison and Oberlin established such courses in the 1840s, and soon many others followed. The ever-present need for teachers could attract substantial enrollments. There was recurrent interest in establishing agricultural courses, centered on teaching agricultural chemistry. However, only a few colleges made short-lived attempts, and only that of the Farmer's College endured. Initiatives in engineering had even shorter lives. There was an apparent interest in commercial studies, principally bookkeeping, which colleges generally offered as a separate course, much the same as music or art. Catholic Saint Louis University and St. Xavier College in Cincinnati both offered a commercial course to their urban clientele but not to their academic students.[68]

The most diverse offerings were found in colleges that evolved from academies. This common path of development was facilitated by the overlap between academy and college subjects. In the absence of developed secondary education and ambiguity about the extent of preparation needed for college, academy subjects could approximate those of colleges. Some adopted a halfway posture as a "collegiate institute," like Marietta or the Western Reserve Eclectic Institute (later Hiram College). Ohio produced three unique exemplars. Freeman Cary, a Miami graduate (1832), aimed to provide practical education "for the industrial pursuits of life." He founded a successful academy just north of Cincinnati and in 1846 elevated it into Farmer's College—named for the local farmers who subscribed to the stock offering that bankrolled the venture. It originally offered a 3-year BS course with multiple options in addition to a 3-year preparatory department. The college soon offered a 2-year normal course and commercial instruction and was chartered to offer a 4-year AB. In 1854 it developed and launched what became the most fully developed antebellum agricultural course. Cary himself became an avid promoter as well. In the late 1850s Farmer's College

68   Roger L. Geiger, "The Era of Multipurpose Colleges in American Higher Education, 1850–1890," in *American Colleges in the Nineteenth Century*, 127–52; Charles A. Dominick, *Ohio's Antebellum Colleges*, PhD Diss., University of Michigan, 1987, 221–51.quote, 238.

enrolled more than 300 students, roughly one-quarter in the college course. However, Cary's strategy of offering practical education to the sons of farmers and mechanics was ultimately its Achilles heel. Most attended for only 1 or 2 years, and about 10 percent took degrees. The college ceased to be financially viable during the war and never recovered afterward.[69]

Mount Union grew from a seminary to a college (1849–1858), while remaining committed to offering "any person . . . thorough, illustrative, integral instruction in any needed studies." It aspired to be a "college for the masses," offering elective courses and practical subjects. It was particularly attractive for teachers and later added a summer term to accommodate them—anticipating an innovation later credited to the University of Chicago but frowned upon by coeval colleges. Baldwin College, also in northeastern Ohio, followed a similar path to collegiate status (1854). Its diverse studies featured an extensive commercial course that, unlike others, was a permanent offering. At the end of the 1850s, Baldwin enrolled more than 400 students—23 in the college and the rest in preparatory, scientific, German, commercial, and ladies' departments. Baldwin and Mount Union admitted women from the outset, and Farmer's, belatedly, as well. Multipurpose colleges generally provided female education, although under different arrangements. In the 1850s a number of them followed Oberlin's example and practiced full coeducation.[70]

Demand for women's education in the Midwest probably grew more rapidly than colleges after about 1850. In Evanston, Illinois, for example, newly opened Northwestern University enrolled ten students in 1855, while neighboring Northwestern Female College founded that same year attracted eighty-four students. Multipurpose colleges incorporated women in a variety of ways. They were welcomed into ladies' courses, teachers' courses and preparatory departments, even while colleges were reluctant to admit women to the AB course.[71] After 1850, the smaller evangelical churches chartered colleges that were fully coeducational. From Alfred in southwestern New York across the Midwest to Iowa, more than twenty such colleges were begun before 1861 (and more afterward). Most stemmed from coeducational academies or seminaries (an all-purpose term). Coeducation required no debate or new commitment; it was a continuation of

---

69 Julianna Chaszar, "Leading and Losing in the Agricultural Education Movement: Freeman G. Cary and Farmer's College, 1846–1886," *History of Higher Education Annual*, 18 (1998): 25–46; Dominick, *Ohio's Antebellum Colleges*, 238.

70 Dominick, *Ohio's Antebellum Colleges*, 227; Geiger, "Multipurpose Colleges."

71 Harold F. Williamson and Payson S. Wild, *Northwestern University: A History, 1850–1975* (Evanston: Northwestern University: 1976), 23–24. The adoption of coeducation by radical Oberlin in 1837 may have discouraged, rather than encouraged, other colleges to do the same, which would account for the hiatus until coeducation found supporters in the 1850s.

existing practices of these denominations. These churches had previously been distrustful of higher education, especially for preachers, and had few college graduates among their followers. But by the 1840s they felt compelled to establish schools to preserve and uplift the community of the faithful. Coeducation mirrored social customs and denominational beliefs. Financially, it lowered the costs of operations and attendance—a virtual necessity for these rural communities, especially the new communities founded on the real estate frontier. Over time, these schools offered college-level material, particularly in their teachers' course; after 1850 they applied for college charters. The Methodists, in particular, created coeducational institutions for all levels, including 3-year college degrees. In general, most new foundings began with precollege classes.[72]

In a paradigmatic example, the Seventh Day Baptists in and around Alfred established a school in 1839 especially to train teachers of their faith. Incorporated as an academy in 1843, its principal teacher-training course provided elective subjects for those not planning to teach. In 1852 it began offering the first 2 years of a college course, along with numerous possibilities for partial courses. In 1856 collegiate offerings were extended to 4 years, and the following year Alfred University was chartered. It then offered three 4-year degree courses—ladies', classical, and scientific—and two 3-year courses—teachers' and English. The first six graduating classes received sixty-nine teachers' degrees (forty to women), nineteen ladies', seven classical, and thirteen scientific degrees.[73] Typically, students at such colleges heavily favored the shorter and/or English courses. Similar tales could be told for the Freewill Baptists who founded Hillsdale College (1853) with a prohibition of discrimination on the basis of race, religion, or sex; the United Brethren who founded Otterbein College (1856); the Quakers who established Earlham College (1856); and others.[74]

Variations on this pattern also existed. Antioch College (1853) was founded by "Christians" with financial and moral support from eastern Unitarians. It opened with a freshman class of 4 men and 2 women but more than 200 in its preparatory department. Northwestern Christian University (1855: later Butler University) organized by the Disciples of Christ had a similar profile. Philanthropist Amos Lawrence provided funds for the Methodists to establish an eponymous all-male college (1853) in rural Wisconsin. Since this

---

72 Malkmus, "Small Towns."

73 Kathryn M. Kerns, *Antebellum Higher Education for Women in Western New York State*, PhD Diss., University of Pennsylvania, 1993; Susan Rumsey Strong, *Thought Knows No Sex: Women's Rights at Alfred University* (Albany: SUNY Press, 2008). Because a "bachelor's degree" seemed inappropriate for women, they were given an equivalent *laureate's* degree; 3-year courses awarded bachelor's/laureate's of philosophy.

74 Malkmus, "Small Towns," esp. 55–63.

stipulation was impractical for a new, isolated institution needing the support of local Methodists, they concealed the women students from the benefactor. Lawrence University graduated its first class of 4 men and 3 women in 1857, but Amos Lawrence was sent a picture of only the men. As at Lawrence, coeducation was a virtual necessity on the western frontier. All 5 of the Iowa colleges chartered in the 1850s were coeducational, and the State University of Iowa (1855) opened as the first public institution to admit men and women on equal terms. It was more difficult before the Civil War for established male colleges to accept women. Muskingum and Franklin colleges in Ohio, both serving splinter Scotch-Irish Presbyterian churches, committed to admitting women in 1851 and 1857, respectively, but no other male colleges took this step until the next decade.[75]

Data on 17 antebellum coeducational colleges reveal a paucity of male or female students at the highest level of study and a preference of women for English courses. Around 1860, the average enrollment was 363 students: 59 percent in preparatory departments (one-third women); 19 percent in the ladies' course, 12 percent in the classical, and 10 percent in the scientific. Men outnumbered women 8 to 1 in the classical course.[76] This distribution was consistent with multipurpose colleges across the Midwest. Ohio colleges were the most mature by 1860, and they enrolled 1,800 students in collegiate courses and 2,100 below that level. Farther west, the balance tilted further toward preparatory classes. For multipurpose colleges generally, more students enrolled in 3- or 4-year ladies', teachers', or scientific courses, based largely on college-level subjects, than took the classical course. Moreover, the basic multipurpose pattern persisted through and beyond the Civil War to the 1880s, including numerous postwar conversions to coeducation.[77] However, midwestern higher education contained one additional distinction—state commitments to nurture broad-based public universities.

The three original state-sponsored institutions in Ohio and Indiana never transcended the status of denominational colleges in the antebellum era.[78] However, by the 1850s, the next three public foundings in Michigan, Wisconsin, and

---

75 Dominick, *Ohio's Antebellum Colleges*, 229, Malkmus, "Small Towns," 43–48; Erving E. Beauregard, *Old Franklin, the Eternal Touch: A History of Franklin College, New Athens, Ohio* (Lanham, MD: University Press of America, 1983), 74: Franklin had considered admitting women in the 1830s but rejected it in an acrimonious dispute.

76 Malkmus, "Small Towns," 64–65.

77 Dominick, *Ohio's Antebellum Colleges*, 221; Geiger, "Multipurpose Colleges": in 1890 one-third of enrollments at Ohio colleges were collegiate (146).

78 Ohio University suspended collegiate operations (1845–1848), and Miami University closed temporarily in 1873. Thomas D. Clark, *Indiana University: Midwestern Pioneer. Volume I/The Early Years* (Bloomington: Indiana University Press, 1970), 49–98.

Iowa all aspired to become secular universities. Only the University of Michigan progressed toward that goal before the Civil War. The bane of all public universities of this era was legislative interference, usually compounded with fiscal caprice and opposition from denominations favoring their own colleges. The latter factor was particularly acute in the Midwest, given the proliferation of denominational colleges. Michigan was unique in minimizing these conditions, at least for a time. An influx of Yankee settlers via the Erie Canal brought a population comparatively supportive of education. A fledgling college was attempted at Detroit in 1817. The legacy of this gambit was to implant the Napoleonic notion that a public university should be responsible for all levels of education. State responsibility for education was also inspired by the Prussian model and embodied in the Michigan Constitution of 1835. A state university governed by a Board of Regents was established in Ann Arbor, with "university branches" supposedly providing secondary education at six towns. Private academies and colleges were not welcome. The University of Michigan opened a traditional literary course in 1841 with intentions of adding departments for medicine and law. Michigan quickly grew into a thriving traditional college, a rare example of centralization rather than fragmentation in American higher education. It was strongly Christian, although nonsectarian, and managed to organize a well-attended medical department by the end of the decade. In the absence of a president, the Regents exerted heavy and disruptive influence. Michigan's new constitution in 1851 gave the Regents, now popularly elected, full control of the university and also created a president. After several candidates declined the position, the new Regents chose Henry Tappan as the university's first president.[79]

Tappan was nurtured in reform-minded pockets of American higher education. A graduate of Union College (1825) and Auburn Theological Seminary (1827), he became professor of philosophy in 1832 at the new University of the City of New York, which had been founded with great fanfare to expand the traditional college course.[80] Fired in 1838 for protesting as that experiment foundered, Tappan wrote and traveled extensively in Europe. His *University Education* (1851) issued a challenge to the American status quo. Tappan disparaged the existing classical course as mere preparation for advanced study, equivalent to

---

79   Howard H. Peckham, *The Making of the University of Michigan, 1817–1992*, edited and updated by Margaret L. Steneck and Nicholas H. Steneck (Ann Arbor: University of Michigan, 1994), 1–34. The 1850 Michigan Constitution prohibited the chartering of denominational colleges, but this was rescinded in 1855.

80   The ambitions of the University of the City of New York (now New York University) to initiate scientific and graduate education were undermined through maladministration without proving or disproving their feasibility: Richard J. Storr, *The Beginnings of Graduate Education in America* (Chicago: University of Chicago Press, 1953), 33–43.

German *Gymnasia*, and he dismissed Wayland's approach to practical studies, although not his critique of the colleges. Instead, Tappan argued, "The establishment of Universities . . . alone can reform our educational system." By Universities he meant,

> *Cyclopaedias* of education: where, in libraries, cabinets, apparatus, and professors, provision is made for studying every branch of knowledge in full, for carrying forward all scientific investigation; where study may be extended without limit; where the mind may be cultivated . . . in the lofty enthusiasm of growing knowledge and ripening scholarship. . . . [68]

This university ideal was based on Tappan's observations of universities in Paris and the German states. He offered a plausible plan of how an American university might be launched for a mere $450,000 and concluded that New York City was the only locale with the human and financial resources to do this. Instead, in 1852 he inherited a midwestern college, albeit one least encumbered with fossilized practices. His inaugural discourse addressed precisely this challenge.[81]

Tappan realistically proposed to build upon the existing college toward the university ideal. He identified highly ambitious goals: to hire distinguished scholars for new professorships, to augment the library and all scientific apparatus, to displace recitations with lectures, to invite graduates to return for further studies, and to cultivate a separate course in science—and he soon accomplished them all. He rapidly assembled by far the most competent faculty in the region. Andrew Dickson White revolutionized the teaching of history, and Henry Simmons Frieze became a distinguished Latinist and philologist (later, acting president). He bolstered the sciences by hiring a physicist and civil engineer. The university created bachelor's degree courses in science and, later, engineering based on these augmented scientific studies, not a watered-down English course. Tappan raised money for an observatory and hired astronomer Franz Brünnow, a Berlin PhD. From his time in Germany, Tappan acquired the belief that university professors should engage in research and scholarship, and he did all he could to instill this in Ann Arbor. Adopting another European practice, he moved students out of the dormitory to room and board in the town. At the end of the decade, the university opened a law department that attracted

---

81   Henry P. Tappan, *University Education* (New York: Arno Press, 1969 [1851]), 68 et passim; Tappen, "A Discourse Delivered by Henry P. Tappan at Ann Arbor, Mich., on the Occasion of His Inauguration as Chancellor of the University of Michigan, December 21, 1852." Tappan continued to advocate the American university in New York while at Michigan: Storr, *Beginnings*, 82–93.

ninety initial students, and he created the first earned master's degrees—a step toward the university ideal of graduate education. In his first 5 years, university enrollments more than doubled to 460, with the entire increase in the literary department. The Board of Regents, whose terms all ended in 1857, gave him a vote of confidence, "believing that his views of a proper University Education are liberal, progressive, and adapted to the present age."[82]

The new set of regents felt quite differently; several opposed Tappan for personal and political reasons and sought to shift control of the university to their own hands. Although popular with students, Tappan's European manners alienated some locals and probably exacerbated the usual town-gown tensions. Although an ordained minister, he tried to be religiously neutral by attending each Ann Arbor church in turn but ended by alienating all of them. He flouted the growing temperance movement as well—although scarcely alone: Ann Arbor sported six breweries and forty-nine saloons. In 1863 a new slate of regents was elected, but before relinquishing office the outgoing regents conspired together and abruptly fired Tappan. They tied the hands of their successors by electing as president Erastus Haven, a pious Methodist and former Michigan professor. Haven was resented by Tappan admirers, both contemporaries and historians. However, he was an able administrator and sustained the momentum of university development, adding degree courses in mining engineering and pharmacy. After the war, Michigan became the largest university in the country, with more than 1,200 students—two-thirds from outside the state. Tappan had predicted in his inaugural that development of a true university "would enable it to attract students from the surrounding, and even from more distant states . . . but only the quality of the education" could accomplish this.[83]

Unlike Michigan, the universities created in Wisconsin and Iowa felt constant political pressure to expand downward from the traditional college—to offer "practical" subjects and provide the broadest possible access. The University of Wisconsin was born in 1849 with the appointment of John H. Lathrop as Chancellor and President of the Board of Regents. A graduate of Yale who had previously presided over the University of Missouri, his grandiose rhetoric mirrored the exalted expectations for higher education in the new state, but his gaze was on pleasing his patrons, not the realities of his institution. The first college class was organized in 1850, and faculty were slowly added to reach a full complement of five professors in 1856, one of whom also instructed in the normal department. Despite the modest resources, Lathrop announced a succession of measures to provide more practical instruction: departments of science applied to the arts and

82   Peckham, *University of Michigan*, 35–58, quote p. 43.
83   Ibid., 51–67; Tappan, "Discourse," 46.

engineering were announced, and a proprietary commercial college was attached (temporarily) to the university. The university could scarcely teach all these subjects but admitted students to study any subjects they chose. Discontent with the university provoked the intervention of the legislature, which chiefly valued wider access and greater practicality. Two years of discord produced a reorganization of the university into six departments of engineering, natural science, philosophy, philology, polity, and a projected department of agriculture—and the resignation of Lathrop. Despite a decade of political machinations and timid leadership, the University of Wisconsin emerged at this juncture as essentially a multipurpose college. In 1865 (before a more meaningful reorganization), it enrolled 331 students: 41 in regular college classes, 110 in the preparatory department, 80 in the normal department, and 100 special students.[84]

The distance between aspirations and attainments was wider at the State University of Iowa. It opened in 1855 with a plan for nine departments, five in philosophy and four in science. This so-called departmental system, loosely modeled after the University of Virginia, gained currency in the 1850s. Its purported advantage was to avoid the rigidities of the traditional "class system" and to accommodate students with uneven preparation. Iowa students could study any subjects they wished for a short degree (BPhil, BSc) or a longer one (BA) or none at all. The university also included preparatory and normal departments. However, with four professors, the university actually offered only four standard subjects. Little matter; 105 of the 124 students were in the preparatory and normal departments. In 1858 lack of students and funds led to the closing of the college departments. For 2 years, the university operated as a normal school, before the college was reopened in 1860. Like Wisconsin, a postwar reorganization was required before progress toward a true university could begin.[85]

The halting development of these two universities was typical of fledgling multipurpose colleges. They appear disappointing only in relation to grand expectations as state universities and unrealistic demands from elected politicians. In contrast, the accomplishments of Henry Tappan appear all the more impressive. He possessed a deep understanding of higher education in Europe and the United States, which he used to formulate and implement a vision for moving toward the university ideal. As a result, the University of Michigan was the only institution of higher education in the West that made academic quality

---

84   Merle Curti and Vernon Carstensen, *The University of Wisconsin: A History, 1848–1925*, 2 vol. (Madison: University of Wisconsin Press, 1949), I, 70–119, 185.

85   L. F. Parker, *History of Education in Iowa*, U.S. Bureau of Education, Circulars of Information, 1893–1896, #17, 79–89.

its foremost value. But Tappan was not entirely alone. By 1850 aspirations for greater quality and advancement were becoming goals within the inchoate community of American science.

SCIENCE AND THE ANTEBELLUM COLLEGE

Science assumed three guises in antebellum America. First, it had enormous cultural popularity for purposes of self-improvement and the enlightenment of common citizens. Second, science had been associated with useful knowledge since the Enlightenment—especially the belief that scientific knowledge could make ordinary workers more useful and productive in their labors. Third, and most problematic, was professional science dedicated to the advancement of knowledge, for this required cultivation of specialized fields of study, communication among active investigators, and replication of expertise through advanced study and training. For contemporaries, there were no clear distinctions among these spheres, and early practitioners typically participated in them all. However, by the 1840s, separate developments brought each of these facets of American science to a crucial juncture in relation to higher education.

Nineteenth-century Americans held generally favorable views toward science, regarding it as a manifestation of progress, a form of entertainment, compensation for deficient education, and a hallmark of civic virtue. One-fifth of the popular lectures of the Lyceum movement that blossomed in the 1830s addressed scientific topics. Many well-known scientists relished the podium and gave lectures to support their inquiries and themselves. Benjamin Silliman and Amos Eaton together delivered some 3,000 lectures outside their classrooms. The Lowell Lectures by celebrated Swiss naturalist Louis Agassiz attracted an overflow crowd of more than 5,000. Ohio astronomer Ormsby Mitchel translated his lecturing skill into a successful campaign that raised funds for the Cincinnati Observatory (1845). A decade later Henry Tappan mobilized the civic pride of Detroiters to fund the Michigan observatory. Every town of any size had a scientific society that enlisted upstanding citizens with some interest and variable degrees of knowledge of science. Popular science had to be considerably diluted for public consumption, but the effort was justified by the resources it garnered, not to mention good will. However, scientists who came of age after 1830 tended to be more comfortable in laboratories than lecture halls, and their chief locus was most likely to be the classroom.[86]

---

86   Robert V. Bruce, *The Launching of Modern American Science, 1846–1876* (Ithaca: Cornell University Press, 1987), 115–34; Sally Gregory Kohlstedt, *The Formation of the American Scientific Community* (Urbana: University of Illinois Press, 1976), 1–24.

Since Newton, science had occupied a secure place in the American college curriculum, an inherent part of liberal arts culture. Natural philosophy, or physics, was taught to the higher classes, accompanied by demonstrations using philosophical apparatus, and astronomy was a continual preoccupation. The eighteenth-century revolution in chemistry was assimilated into the colleges with some difficulty but became a fixture by the 1820s. Until then, colleges could readily add subjects in the effort to fill out and offer a 4-year course. In that decade or shortly thereafter, all the northeastern colleges stabilized their courses with a generous amount of science. A typical faculty of seven would include a professor of mathematics, who might also teach astronomy and optics; a professor of natural philosophy; and one of chemistry, including mineralogy and geology. By 1850, a typical faculty of nine included four professors of mathematics and science. However, the change was more than incremental; it represented a transformation of the teaching and role of science in the colleges.[87]

Science, then and since, possesses an inherent dynamic of cumulative advancement that any institution of higher learning had to accommodate. In the 1830s and 1840s, colleges hired more qualified science teachers, paid them more, purchased the apparatus they required, and permitted greater specialization in their subjects. These were gradual, piecemeal steps, but underlying them was an increasing respect for scientific expertise. Individuals distinguished themselves by studying with one of the few renowned professors, by publishing papers with scientific societies, or through supplemental studies in Europe. A new generation spread their learning by publishing up-to-date textbooks that advanced instruction of these subjects across colleges. Science subjects were taught to juniors and seniors chiefly through lectures, which required greater knowledge than recitations. They also required props—equipment, supplies, and collections—not just for demonstrations but to further the teachers' learning as well. Considering the desperate finances of most colleges, it was remarkable that they found funds to purchase materials for chemical laboratories, apparatus for physics, mineral cabinets for geology, and—before long—collections of specimens for natural history. Most remarkable were the exertions to fund observatories. North Carolina mounted a telescope in 1831, and the coeval Yale telescope was the first to detect the return of Halley's Comet in 1835. Still better observatories were constructed in the 1830s at Williams and Western Reserve colleges and West Point. The country's largest telescopes were built in Cincinnati (initially linked with the college, 1845), Harvard (1847), and the Naval Observatory (1846). In

---

87　Stanley M. Guralnick, *Science and the Ante-Bellum American College* (Philadelphia: American Philosophical Society, 1975), 18–46, 116.

the 1850s the United State boasted twenty-five astronomical observatories, most connected with colleges.[88]

Still, chemistry was the subject that led the transformation of academic science or, rather, chemistry and its applications to mineralogy and geology. Initial professors of chemistry were supported by medical schools, and the first college chairs optimistically included applications to the arts in their titles. Bowdoin professor of mathematics and natural philosophy, Parker Cleaveland, turned to chemistry to study minerals, publishing the first volume on mineralogy in 1816. By that date, Benjamin Silliman's teaching and research had also taken the same direction. His *American Journal of Science and the Arts* from 1818 published especially on mineralogy, geology, and natural history; Yale, defender of the classical languages, became the foremost locus of American science. Chemistry and its associated fields took off in the years 1825 to 1835 with the influx of a new generation of scientists. Their careers were enhanced by participation in state geological surveys. Among the most eminent, Edward Hitchcock had studied with Silliman while earning a divinity degree from Yale. He then spent his entire career at Amherst teaching science, serving as president (1845–1854), and leading the Massachusetts geological survey. Henry Darwin Rogers taught geology at the University of Pennsylvania for a decade while leading the geological surveys of New Jersey and Pennsylvania; his brother William taught at the University of Virginia and led that state's survey. One historian estimated that "most chemistry (etc.) professors prior to 1860" worked on state surveys or as consultants.[89]

The importance of this work earned it a rightful place in the college course. The same was true of the life sciences, which as latecomers grew out of developments in geology and natural history, primarily after 1840. Until 1850, these subjects were wedged into the classical course during the junior and senior years. Given three terms per year, geology, mineralogy, and natural history could be accorded a term or less of recitations from now-plentiful textbooks. In 1840, one course review found biological subjects receiving 2 to 3 weeks of study. When college critics complained of superficiality, they were not exaggerating. No room remained in the classical course for additional subjects—hence, the turmoil over curricular issues that ensued from that date.[90] However, the problem was not simply one of accommodating the proliferation of science; the loudest demands were for useful knowledge.

The ideal of Useful Knowledge was dear to the American Enlightenment, where it seemed that self-educated individuals like Benjamin Franklin and

88 Ibid., 85–90 et passim.
89 Ibid., 107n.
90 Ibid., 94–118.

David Rittenhouse could advance science, just as scientific knowledge could make farmers and artisans more productive.[91] This doctrine persisted as conventional wisdom in the nineteenth century and, in fact, grew more compelling as the pace of technological change quickened. The difficulty was finding an educational formula that could join the progress of theoretical science with applications to the practical arts. The frustration was not for want of trying. The two great areas of application were agriculture on one side and civil engineering or the mechanical arts on the other. The two principal educational strategies were through the agency of the colleges or other types of institution.

Noncollege alternatives emerged in the 1820s. Mechanics institutes were formed in many cities to provide lectures, libraries, and fellowship for artisans. Of hundreds of such initiatives, the Franklin Institute of Pennsylvania for the Promotion of the Mechanic Arts (f. 1824) was the most elaborate—establishing classes, a journal, and a museum, as well as conducting research. It was also the only such creation to endure. In 1823 the Gardiner Lyceum opened in Maine, offering a 3-year course in which year 2 was devoted to practical applications in engineering or agriculture. It closed in 1832 after its state appropriation was discontinued. This same era saw Amos Eaton's tireless efforts to unite science and practical arts in his Rensselaer school.[92] West Point still set the standard for engineering education, producing not only graduates who became practicing engineers but science leaders like Alexander Dallas Bache (1825), great-grandson of Benjamin Franklin. However, after 1840 the Academy's increased emphasis on military training diminished its contribution to engineering. Although colleges were eager to duplicate the West Point formula, the numerous initiatives to hire engineering instructors and offer an engineering alternative in the 1830s were all short lived. But the clamor for useful knowledge grew through the next decade.[93]

By the 1840s the railroad boom in the United States was in full swing, and the scarcity of civil engineers was increasingly felt. Realization of the need for scientific expertise in agriculture was heightened by the appearance in 1840 of a volume by Justus von Liebig, professor at the University of Giessen: *Organic Chemistry in Its Application to Agriculture and Physiology*. Liebig summarized

91   Joseph F. Kett, *The Pursuit of Knowledge under Difficulties* (Stanford: Stanford University Press, 1994), xv, 21; Roger L. Geiger, "The Rise and Fall of Useful Knowledge," in *American College in the Nineteenth Century*, 153–68.

92   Kett, *Pursuit*, 110–25; Bruce Sinclair, *Philadelphia's Philosopher Mechanics: A History of the Franklin Institute, 1824–1865* (Baltimore: Johns Hopkins University Press, 1974); Julius A. Stratton and Loretta H. Mannix, *Mind and Hand: The Birth of MIT* (Cambridge: MIT Press, 2005), 39–45: Alden Partridge's early efforts at Norwich belong with this group.

93   Bruce, *Launching*, 160–62; Terry S. Reynolds, "The Education of Engineers in America before the Morrill Act of 1862," *History of Education Quarterly* 32, 4 (Winter 1992): 459–82.

previous findings and identified the key roles of nitrogen and minerals in plants. He opened a whole new field for the application of chemistry, promising the key to effective fertilizers and potential remedies for the problem of worn-out soils.[94] Agricultural chemistry thus became a necessary addition to useful knowledge, one that rested on sophisticated understanding of organic chemistry. It became paired with civil engineering as subjects that many thought colleges ought to teach, but the challenge was how.

Francis Wayland's advocacy of agricultural chemistry and engineering in the 1850 *Report* to the Brown Corporation was scarcely original in light of practices already adopted at Union, Yale, and Harvard. However, it was read throughout the country and, together with his critique of the classical course, galvanized support for introducing useful knowledge in the colleges. Reactions varied according to the institutional possibilities in each of the three regions of higher education. In the South, as just seen, most state universities made gestures in this direction in the 1850s, but only the University of North Carolina succeeded in establishing a specific course of study with dedicated faculty. The multipurpose colleges of the Midwest might include some agriculture or engineering in the BS course, but these superficial treatments did little to build professional competence. Only the University of Michigan established engineering upon a scientific foundation in its BS course—and was precluded from adding agriculture by the chartering of the Michigan College of Agriculture in 1855.

In the Northeast, the most significant departures were the formation of separate schools of science at Yale and Harvard, which will be considered below. Elsewhere, engineering and agriculture tended to develop separately. In 1845 Eliphalet Nott resigned as president of the struggling Rensselaer Institute and appointed a European-trained professor of engineering at Union. This first college course in civil engineering could be taken as either part of a 4-year bachelor's or a 2-year diploma. In nearby Troy, instead of expiring, Rensselaer was rehabilitated by its new head, Benjamin Greene. He instituted a 3-year engineering course on the plan of the École Polytechnique, and the school was reborn as Rensselaer Polytechnic Institute (1851). It soon inspired a host of polytechnic imitators in eastern cities offering 2- or 3-year bachelor of engineering courses.[95] Engineering in various guises, but usually as a diploma course, was

94 Margaret W. Rossiter, *The Emergence of Agricultural Science: Justus Liebig and the Americans, 1840–1880* (New Haven: Yale University Press, 1975), 3–46.

95 Amos Eaton died in 1842: Codman Hislop, *Eliphalet Nott* (Middletown, CT: Wesleyan University Press, 1971), 429–32; V. Ennis Pilcher, *Early Science and the First Century of Physics at Union College, 1795–1895* (Schenectady: Union College, 1994), 48–49. Reynolds, "Education of Engineers," 466–75. Polytechnic College of Pennsylvania (1853), Brooklyn Polytechnic Institute (1855): Geiger, "Useful Knowledge," 156–59.

offered in the 1850s at Brown, Pennsylvania, and New York universities, among others, but found few takers. Union and RPI accounted for nearly two-thirds of civilian engineers graduated before 1865, all in civil engineering.[96]

Agriculture established only a toehold in the East before the Civil War. The Pennsylvania State Agricultural Society chartered the Farmer's High School (now Penn State University) in 1855 and managed to begin classes in 1859. The Michigan Agricultural College (now Michigan State University) had a similar origin and opened 2 years earlier. Clearly, by the 1850s widespread expectations and institutional backing existed for the higher study and teaching of useful knowledge. What American science needed was institutions to support its advancement.

The United States in the first half of the nineteenth century was a provincial outpost of the world of science, and American scientists knew it. They also were aware of the principal means of improving that situation. Interaction and communication among scientists required the internal organization of science and its specialties, as European models demonstrated. Educational institutions obviously had an important role to play, although European models could scarcely be replicated. But there was always the alternative of studying directly at European centers of learning. Benjamin Silliman embarked on the first of these paths when he launched his journal in 1818 to render "service not only to science and the arts, but to the reputation of the country." "In every enlightened country," he reminded readers, "the labors and discoveries [of natural science are] communicated to the world through the medium of Scientific Journals." He also implied that North America presented unique opportunities for the descriptive sciences of mineralogy and geology. Looking back a generation later (1847), Silliman was gratified that the journal was fulfilling its original purposes, facilitating the growth of American science: "The cultivators of science . . . were then few—now they are numerous"; "societies and associations . . . for the cultivation of natural history have been instituted in many of our cities and towns"; "and our discoveries— illustrated by treasures of facts drawn from this country—are eagerly sought for and published abroad."[97] But American science still had a long way to go.

The scientific activity that Silliman celebrated was chiefly located in the Northeast. The country at that time had thirty-two scientific societies, and a triangle drawn from the vicinity of Boston to Albany to Philadelphia would encompass twenty-five of them. Boston was the most vibrant center of science, followed by Philadelphia, New York, and New Haven. Scientists very

96 Thomas N. Bonner, "The Beginnings of Engineering Education in the United States: The Curious Role of Eliphalet Nott," *New York History* (Jan . 1988): 35–54.

97 Benjamin Silliman, "Preface," *American Journal of Science and the Arts*, 50 (1845): iii–xviii.

far removed from this imaginary triangle suffered from isolation—a lack of informed colleagues, recent literature, and the appurtenances of scientific work. By 1860, scientific societies had begun to appear in the West as well—Cleveland, Cincinnati, Saint Louis, and Chicago. While all of them served science by supporting libraries and collections, they were largely dominated by amateur members, and at this juncture belonged more with popular than professional science.[98]

The first true professional organization was the American Association of Geologists and Naturalists, created in 1840 to bring together the leaders of state geological surveys. Membership was limited to persons "devoted to Geological research with scientific views and objects." Its annual meetings were led by patriarchal figures, Edward Hitchcock and Benjamin Silliman, but the association was soon dominated by younger scientists with specialized training. Isolated college science professors especially found the meetings "of precious value," providing a forum for sharing research findings and clarifying issues. However, both geologists and related scientists yearned for a more encompassing organization, and at the 1847 meeting they voted to become the American Association for the Advancement of Science [AAAS]. Inspired in part by the British forerunner (f. 1831), the AAAS was a hybrid of popular and professional science. Linked organizationally with local science societies and basically open to all interested parties, it enrolled more than 2,000 members at various times before the war, and its rotating meetings prompted gala local celebrations. But direction of the association was in the hands of the country's most distinguished scientists. The AAAS represented a coming of age for American science, but it also reflected dismal conditions in the colleges.[99]

The number of college professors of math and science had grown from around 60 in 1828 to more than 300 in 1850. Moreover, an analysis of the most productive scientists found that 41 of 56 had held college posts. However, except for those at Harvard or Yale, the leaders of the AAAS had largely abandoned college teaching. Bache found work with the Franklin Institute more absorbing and soon abandoned his professorship at the University of Pennsylvania; Joseph Henry left Princeton to head the Smithsonian Institution; Henry Darwin Rogers also left Pennsylvania for Boston, and later brother William departed the University of Virginia to join him. In his 1851 presidential address to the AAAS, surveying the state of American science, Bache discounted the contributions of college professors. Given the weakness of the colleges, most were overworked, were professionally isolated, and lacked the time or equipment for research. He

98   Bruce, *Launching*, 31–36.
99   Ibid., 251–65; Kohlstedt, *Formation*, 59–99.

called instead for a superior organization for the scientific elite.[100] At that same Albany meeting, such an organization appeared to be a real possibility. Earlier that year the New York state legislature had chartered the University of Albany. The university trustees had high hopes for this paper creation, seconded by the AAAS leaders. Bache saw "a great and growing demand in our country for something higher than college instruction; and one great University, if fairly set in motion, would thrive." Bache's colleagues—"the leading scientific men of this country"—supported this notion and at least contemplated moving to Albany "to make one very brilliant institution." For the next year, these same men offered a succession of speeches and testimonials intended to convince the New York legislators to fund a graduate university of science. When the legislature declined, the vision of financial largesse disappeared and so did the leading scientific men. The University of Albany chimera, the same year as the appearance of Tappan's *University Education*, signaled a realization of the need for an American equivalent of a European university, along with the hopes of the scientific elite that this could be achieved with a single dramatic creation. During the campaign, one writer dismissed the scientific schools recently established at Yale and Harvard as capable of offering little "more than a mere commencement of . . . education in many of the sciences." But at this juncture they were the best that American higher education could offer.[101]

In the 1840s Yale and Harvard were the outstanding centers for American science. Silliman had led the initial dominance of Yale with his contributions to chemistry and geology, his *Journal*, and the resident graduates he attracted. His son and namesake remained in New Haven and also became an active scientist. When joined in 1836 by former student, James Dwight Dana, Yale was the undisputed leader of American chemistry and geology. At Harvard, the presence of Benjamin Pierce, the country's most celebrated mathematician and astronomer, soon gave it precedence in the physical sciences. When Asa Gray was appointed professor of natural history in 1842, Harvard established itself in this field as well. It also possessed chairs in chemistry and "the application of science to the useful arts" but had difficulty making distinguished appointments in those fields. Nearly one-third of the leaders of the AAAS attended one or the other institution.[102]

---

100   Guralnik, *Science*, 142; George H. Daniels, *American Science in the Age of Jackson* (New York: Columbia University Press, 1968), 27; Bruce, *Launching*, 136–38; Alexander Dallas Bache, "Address," AAAS, *Proceedings*, V (1851): xli–lx; Axel Jansen, *Alexander Dallas Bache: Building an American Nation through Science and Education in the Nineteenth Century* (Frankfurt: Campus Verlag, 2011).

101   Storr, *Beginnings of Graduate Education*, 68–74.

102   Kohlstedt, *Formation*, 211. Chemistry professor John Webster is notorious for the macabre murder of Dr. George Parkman, for which he was hanged in 1851: Simon Schama, *Dead Certainties: Unwarranted Speculations* (New York: Knopf, 1991).

Both institutions independently and virtually simultaneously resolved to expand and elevate their teaching in this area. Vague plans crystallized into concrete steps in 1846 and institutional commitments the following year. Interestingly, both linked the wish to offer formal instruction beyond the baccalaureate level with plans to teach practical applications of science. But, despite similar origins, the two scientific schools followed divergent paths.

In 1846 the Yale Corporation appointed John Pitkin Norton, a Silliman protégé who had studied agricultural chemistry in Europe, professor in that field, and Benjamin Silliman Jr., professor of practical chemistry, a subject he had been teaching informally. The new professors were to teach "graduates and others not members of the undergraduate classes," and these unpaid positions were to have no claim on college funds. The next year, to regularize this situation, the Corporation created a fourth professional school—the Department of Philosophy and the Arts. The new department opened with eleven courses—Yale professors offering advanced study in their specialties, including Greek and Sanskrit, and Norton and Silliman Jr. teaching eleven students in the "school of applied chemistry." Although a handful of students followed the graduate courses, the applied offerings drew increasing numbers. In 1852, after Norton's untimely death, the two defectors from Wayland's experiment at Brown became the new professors of civil engineering and agricultural chemistry, bringing their students with them. From this point the "Yale Scientific School" (1854) continued to develop as a vigorous teaching institution. At the end of the decade, the gifts of industrialist Joseph Sheffield finally put the school on a sound financial basis, and the name was changed to the Sheffield Scientific School. The school then offered a common first year of studies, followed by seven special 2-year courses, leading to a bachelor's of philosophy degree. Graduate studies were not forgotten. In 1861 the Department of Philosophy and the Arts awarded the first American PhDs to three students for work in philosophy, philology, and physics.[103]

When Edward Everett was elected president of Harvard in 1845 he envisioned establishing advanced university studies of the kind he had known as a student at Göttingen. He had Benjamin Pierce draw up a preliminary plan and called in his 1846 inaugural address for the creation of a "School of Theoretical and Practical Science." After due consultation, the Corporation announced the "Scientific School" the next year. As at Yale, the students were to be graduates or otherwise qualified and were not subject to college discipline. Unlike Yale, the Harvard school would be taught by regular Harvard professors, and, contrary to Everett's wishes, graduate teaching in nonscientific subjects would not be included. At

---

[103] Kelley, *Yale*, 182–89; Yale College, *First Annual Report of the Board of Visitors of the Sheffield Scientific School of Yale College* (New Haven, 1866).

this point, the industrialist Abbott Lawrence offered a $50,000 donation with strings attached: he wanted the school to train "engineers or chemists, or ... men of science, applying their attainments to practical purposes." Specifically, he envisioned courses in engineering, mining, metallurgy, and "manufacture of machinery"; and his gift provided partial support for professorships in engineering, chemistry, and geology. The entire project was then altered by the possibility of hiring Louis Agassiz, a Swiss naturalist and scientific superstar who was on an extended visit to the United States. Both Everett and Lawrence subordinated their previous visions in a successful effort to crown the Lawrence Scientific School with this spectacular hire. Agassiz brought enormous prestige, but his overbearing presence also dominated the direction of the new school. Totally dedicated to research, he had little interest in classroom teaching and insisted on establishing a museum where he and his students could perform hands-on research. The Lawrence Scientific School largely conformed to Agassiz's image.

Lawrence's restricted gifts did not save the school from chronic underfunding. It lacked the resources to expand the faculty or provide adequately for their scientific needs. It operated as a group of uncoordinated departments, each admitting and graduating students, instructing them or not as professors saw fit. There was no entrance examination and no common curriculum. Enrollment averaged about fifty students—less than one-third of the anticipated level. Just 20 percent were college graduates, and many of the rest were clearly unqualified. More than half of students matriculated for 1 year or less, and fewer than one-quarter bothered to obtain a BS degree. Still, this being Harvard, some students had illustrious careers, and the scientific achievements of Pierce, Gray, and others were a credit as well—but not Agassiz. In 1860 he finally opened his museum, just as Charles Darwin's *Origin of Species* (1859) exposed the error of many of his theories. Scientifically, the Lawrence School was a disappointment, like its most famous professor. It failed to point the way toward graduate education, as Everett had wished, or educate practitioners, as Lawrence had hoped. Rather, in the opinion of Charles W. Eliot, who had tried to impose a common curriculum at Lawrence, the 3-year course at Sheffield provided the most effective model for undergraduate scientific education.[104]

By the 1850s, the American scientific community had come of age and connected with wider currents of international (European) science. However, scientists were frustrated that America had so little to contribute, outside, perhaps,

---

104   Richard Yanikoski, *Edward Everett and the Advancement of Higher Education and Adult Learning in Ante-Bellum Massachusetts*, PhD Diss., University of Chicago, 1987, 185–234; Stratton and Maddox, *Mind and Hand*, 113–38; Charles W. Eliot, "The New Education," *Atlantic Monthly*, XXIII (Feb.–Mar. 1869); 202–10, 365–66.

of geology. They seemed to agree that the best hope for embedding advanced learning and scholarship would be a single American university that could bring together the few leading men of science. They failed to perceive at this juncture that the scientific prowess of German universities derived from their numbers—that institutional competition elevated standards of attainment. Instead, the compulsive desire for knowledge and scientific careers drove increasing numbers of Americans to those same German universities. An earlier generation of scientists had sought access to European learning at Edinburgh, Paris, or London, but by the 1840s this traffic increasingly sought out German professors. Would-be agricultural chemists flocked to Giessen to study with Liebig; The Royal School of Mines in Freiburg became the haven for American mining engineers. In the 1850s more than 300 Americans studied at the three largest German universities, and many more would follow.[105] In 1860 it was not yet evident to the leaders of the AAAS or the governors of colleges that American universities would be needed to bring the country abreast of international science.

★   ★   ★

In the two decades before the Civil War, the major crosscurrents of American higher education emerged with enhanced clarity. And the contradictions among these purposes were clearly exposed. The predominant value of culture in a college education had been cogently argued in the 1828 Yale *Reports*. In these years, the connection between curriculum and content was occasionally questioned but not challenged in practice. Instead, the *experience* of college assumed precedence over content in the formation of culture. This was evident in the rise of the extracurriculum in the Northeast, in the pervasive and binding social norms of southern universities, and especially in the rise of fraternities. The inexorable expansion of knowledge, epitomized by but not limited to the natural sciences, put a different kind of pressure on the classical curriculum. A liberal education required acquaintance with up-to-date scientific knowledge, but the advancement and proliferation of scientific fields made this increasingly problematic. For cultural purposes, the superficial coverage of even the strongest colleges would suffice, but it was manifestly inadequate to prepare for careers in applied fields or participate in the advancement of science. With the need for scientific practitioners so obvious, why did attempts to offer such instruction draw so few

105   Rossiter, *Emergence of Agricultural Science*; Bruce, *Launching*, 160; Daniels, *American Science*, 31; Robert McCaughey, "The Transformation of American Academic Life: Harvard University 1821–1892," *Perspectives in American History*, VIII (1974): 239–332, esp. 264–65; Anja Werner, *The Transatlantic World of Higher Education: Americans at German Universities, 1776–1914* (New York: Berghahn, 2013).

students? Many of those who sought careers in such fields lacked the educational and cultural preparation needed for college studies; and those who acquired such preparation in the classical languages chiefly sought bourgeois respectability in the professions. This dilemma handicapped attempts to provide applied courses of studies in all three regions of the country and would do so for another generation. Even the multipurpose colleges of the West, with a broader palette of offerings, promised a passport to the fluid livelihoods of the emerging market economy, not preparation for specific careers.

The colleges of this era are universally accused of ossification, but this was far from the case. As they attempted to adapt to changing conditions, they were successful in meeting only one of the three challenges—the formation of what is now called cultural capital. Ironically, students themselves were responsible in large measure for creating the vehicles for this process, but the college implicitly understood and acquiesced in this role. Attempts to prepare students for careers in the commercial economy or for participation in the advancement of science achieved only partial and fleeting success: antebellum higher education found no *institutional* solutions for these challenges. Instead, thousands of individuals found their own solutions in the interstices of these institutions by surviving in one of the new engineering courses, by independent study with active scientists, or by studying at European universities. American higher education had not yet assumed its modern forms. Instead, it evolved a set of premodern institutions that were adapted to the conditions of the mid-nineteenth century.

* 7 *

LAND GRANT COLLEGES AND
THE PRACTICAL ARTS

HE CIVIL WAR ERA BROUGHT FAR-REACHING CHANGE. Economic development accelerated in the North; devastation and dislocation plagued the South; and the trans-Mississippi West was opened for settlement and exploitation. These years marked the transition from a predominantly preindustrial to an industrializing economy. The war is conventionally regarded as an inflection point in higher education as well, heralding the inception of characteristically modern institutions. However, this view misrepresents the actual conditions and the pace of change during the midcentury decades, from the 1850s to the 1880s. The educational institutions that arose and flourished during this era are more accurately described as premodern. They emerged for the most part in the decades before the War and proliferated in the years afterward. But the academic revolution that occurred after 1885 rendered them obsolete, either sooner or later.

"During the ten years after 1865," historian Laurence Veysey has written, "almost every visible change in the pattern of American higher education lay in the direction of concessions to the utilitarian type of demand for reform."[1] Indeed, the belief that colleges could foster useful knowledge and the practical arts lay behind the creation and the distinctively premodern character of land grant universities and institutes of technology. Their appearance helped to make the years from 1865 to 1873 one of the most fecund periods for founding institutions of higher education. But the Panic of 1873 and the long depression that followed subdued the development of higher education for at least a decade. Widely publicized advances like the founding of Johns Hopkins University and the reforms of Charles Eliot at Harvard obscured the persistence of premodern institutions throughout most of the educational system.

---

1 Laurence Veysey, *The Emergence of the American University* (Chicago: University of Chicago Press, 1965), 60.

CHAPTER 7

PREMODERN INSTITUTIONS

The liberal arts college, possessing the legal authority to grant BA degrees, was one of the few fixed points among American educational institutions. Another was the system of common schools that emerged by midcentury as an educational base throughout much of the country, a base that varied widely in the extent of schooling available but less so in its nature. In between the bottom and the top lay a host of institutions that provided intermediate and advanced education, inside and outside of the colleges. Academies had long filled that role and continued to do so, sometimes under the auspices of individual teacher-proprietors but increasingly incorporated and community based.[2] But now they were supplemented by high schools in cities, by private and state normal schools, by "female" colleges and seminaries, and by polytechnic institutes. On a somewhat higher level, schools of science sponsored by colleges may have preferred college graduates for students but actually catered to students with varying amounts of educational preparation. This situation was worse for law and especially medical schools, which were wholly proprietary and inadequate whether connected with a college or not. What this menagerie of institutions shared were permissive standards of admission, heterogeneous bodies of students, intermittent enrollments, and low rates of completion. Like multipurpose colleges, which also belong here, they provided varying degrees of educational upgrading and, to some extent, preparation for life and livelihoods. They were by no means static during these years. Rather they either evolved into quite different animals, often without changing names, or became extinct.[3] What follows is an overview of these sectors, which were sometimes rivals of and sometimes affiliated with American colleges.

HIGH SCHOOLS, OR THE PEOPLE'S COLLEGES. Just as the Boston Latin School was the first educational institution in British America (1635), the Boston English High School was the first of that genre to be established in the United States (1821). The school taught an academic curriculum that extended beyond academy subjects (English, geography, history) to mathematics, science and modern languages—"branches of great practical importance which have usually been taught only at the Colleges." The high school thus offered a

2 Nancy Beadie and Kim Tolley, *Chartered Schools: Two Hundred Years of Independent Academies in the United States, 1727–1925* (New York: Routledge Falmer, 2002): incorporated academies often converted to high schools or normal schools.

3 Roger L. Geiger, "The Era of Multipurpose Colleges in American Higher Education," in Geiger, ed., *The American College in the Nineteenth Century* (Nashville: Vanderbilt University Press, 2000), 127–52.

terminal course—a "people's college." Boy's High was an immediate success, attracting sons of white-collar and artisan families for the most part, who were then readily hired by the city's commercial establishments. Since the same vocational connection could not be made for girls, the city governors saw no reason to spend tax money on advanced education for them. In 1854, the link with preparing teachers justified founding the Boston Girl's High and Normal School.[4]

Philadelphia opened Central High School in 1838 to provide "a liberal education for those intended for business life." Its first principal, Alexander Dallas Bache (1838–1842), left his Penn professorship to take the position. It was the realization of the vision of his great grandfather, Benjamin Franklin, a century before. It taught a practical curriculum that was particularly strong in science, supported with philosophical apparatus and an observatory. Highly selective, a rigorous entrance examination kept enrollments relatively stable at 500 to 600 from the 1840s to the 1890s. In 1849, the Pennsylvania Legislature granted Central the right to award college degrees, although this had little effect on the school or its clientele. The school credentialed sons of the commercial middle class to enter the world of Philadelphia business. In the 1880s it enlarged its offerings with vocational and college preparatory tracks.[5]

In New York City, an initiative to establish a public high school in the 1820s was thwarted by opposition from private academies. Only in 1847 was the Free Academy of the City of New York chartered to serve the large population unable to attend the two private colleges. In this case, the people's college became an actual college when it was reincorporated in 1866 as the College of the City of New York. Elsewhere, urban high schools largely followed the people's college model of providing a terminal academic course that prepared students for the "business of life"—actually, a life in the city's business community. These schools were created following the formal organization of the common school system. They thus developed from below and reflected the desires of middle-class taxpayers for immediately useful education.[6]

An alternative role for public high schools was to serve as the "connecting link" between the common schools and colleges. The several states that attempted to organize education from the top down, most notably Michigan, sought to institutionalize this approach, which required teaching classical

4 Jurgen Herbst, *The Once and Future School: Three-hundred and Fifty Years of American Secondary Education* (New York: Routledge, 1996), 42–45, quote p. 43.

5 Ibid., 45–46, quote p. 45; David F. Labaree, *The Making of an American High School: The Credential Market and the Central High School of Philadelphia, 1838–1939* (New Haven: Yale University Press, 1988).

6 Herbst, *Once and Future School*, 46–52. CCNY is discussed in chapter 10.

languages. However, states proved unable to fund local high schools, and city taxpayers often balked at the cost of preparing students for college. High schools tended to offer Latin, at least, and patterns of enrollment varied across cities; but in most high schools a large majority of students sought only preparation for the business of life and immediate employment. Even Michigan had difficulty forging the connecting link. In the 1870s, the Kalamazoo decision by the Michigan Supreme Court validated the authority of public school districts to fund high schools with tax revenues. The University of Michigan then pioneered a system of certifying high schools so that their graduates were admitted without examination. Still, before 1881 only 4 percent of the state's high school graduates planned to attend college. However, the decade of the 1880s saw the transformation of American high schools. The number of public high schools grew tenfold as they became the advanced level of common schooling. College prep and preparation for life ceased to be opposing models as the schools embraced both roles as well as vocational education. In doing so, the high schools came to define secondary education and shed the premodern role as an alternative to higher education.[7]

NORMAL SCHOOLS. The model for separate schools for the training of elementary teachers originated in Prussia, and the term *normal* was copied from the French adaptation of that pattern (*écoles normales*). The first American version appeared in Massachusetts in 1839. The three state normal schools were humble affairs, offering a course of up to 3 years (which few completed) of professional training for teachers of rural primary schools. Their accomplishments were modest, too. Rural boys and girls attended them as the only available education beyond common schools. Most became teachers, as promised, in order to receive free tuition—but not for long, given the miserable pay and working conditions in rural school districts. The movement to establish normal schools was led by educational reformers, who advocated systems of public education to advance and unify the nation while deploring the hodgepodge of private schools. They addressed, on one hand, a crying need for trained teachers for the nation's mushrooming schoolrooms. On the other hand, potential students like those in Massachusetts sought any form of further education and were scarcely content to remain elementary school teachers. Normal schools developed slowly before the Civil War, as only a few states yielded to the entreaties of educational reformers. Those states established single, central normal schools, unlike Massachusetts's

---

7 Ibid., 53–66; Marc A. VanOverbeke, *The Standardization of American Schooling: Linking Secondary and Higher Education, 1870–1910* (New York: Palgrave Macmillan, 2008); William J. Reese, *The Origins of the American High School* (New Haven: Yale University Press, 1995).

rural strategy. The New York State Normal School at Albany was founded in 1844, followed by schools in Connecticut and Michigan chartered in 1849. In Illinois, agitation for an agricultural college resulted instead in the substantial Illinois State Normal University (1857). That same year a Pennsylvania law created twelve normal school districts but left it to private stockholders to actually establish the schools. After the war, normal schools grew rapidly in numbers and in scope.[8]

At the end of the 1860s, 35 state normal schools were operating, and in the next decade that figure doubled. The largest number of normal schools was opened in the 1890s (42 schools, 10 new states), producing a total of 139 in 1900. The overriding issue during the early stages of this development was the tension between instilling professional teaching skills versus providing teachers with a broader academic culture. Over time, most normal schools succumbed to academic drift, offering a 2-year elementary course and a 4-year advanced course. The former represented secondary studies, while the final 2 years of the advanced course contained college-level material. The late nineteenth-century normal school thus straddled secondary and higher education. However, students increasingly identified with the collegians by imitating the growing range of extracurricular activities, beginning with literary societies and elaborate class functions and proceeding to fraternities, sororities, and athletic teams. Such activities provided women in particular with opportunities for participation and leadership that were seldom available in coeducational colleges. Who attended the normal schools depended heavily on the availability of local alternatives. Most normal schools enrolled a majority of women, given the emphasis on teaching, and those majorities grew over time. They tended to draw predominantly from the middle and working classes, including some representation of recent immigrant groups. Thus, the normal schools too sometimes adopted the mantle of "people's colleges."[9]

FEMALE COLLEGES. The women's colleges of the South and Midwest described in chapter 5 represent a single type. Although often named institutes or seminaries as well as colleges, almost all included *female* in their titles. They

---

8 Jurgen Herbst, *And Sadly Teach: Teacher Education and Professionalization in American Culture* (Madison: University of Wisconsin Press, 1989); Christine A. Ogren, *The American State Normal School: 'An Institution of Great Good'* (New York: Palgrave Macmillan, 2005); Elizabeth T. Bugaighis, *Liberating Potential: Women and the Pennsylvania State Normal Schools, 1890–1930*, PhD Diss., Pennsylvania State University, 2000, 56–67. Pennsylvania purchased the private normal schools from 1913 through 1921.

9 Ogren, *American State Normal School*, 65–119, 201–9. Most normal schools in New England and in the South were all female; normal departments were often the largest units of historically black colleges. See chapter 10.

taught an English course that was weighted toward science and composition and also offered ornamental electives. Most began as 3-year courses but added an optional 4-year course by the 1860s that included a smattering of Latin. Their students tended to be relatively young, needed work in preparatory departments, and seldom persisted through to graduation. This approach to women's education was paralleled in coeducational colleges by a "ladies' course," omitting Latin and Greek and usually occupying 3 years. At Oberlin, for example, most women took the ladies' course, even though they were allowed in the classical course. At most female colleges the ladies' course was also more popular than the 4-year course. In 1880, 155 female colleges granted college degrees; 59 of them had been founded in the 1850s and 58, in the following 2 decades; 107 were located in southern and south-central states.[10]

Contemporaries regarded the female colleges as inferior to men's colleges, although they compared them with the stronger rather than the weaker ones. Consequently, efforts began in the 1850s to provide young women with a true collegiate—that is, classical—course. Mary Sharp College for Young Ladies in Tennessee and Elmira Female College in New York were the first to offer such courses and conferred their first AB degrees in 1855 and 1859, respectively. Matthew Vassar, Sophia Smith, and William Durant soon aimed even higher, founding Vassar, Smith, and Wellesley colleges to be analogues of Harvard and Yale. The high aspirations of these institutions encountered early difficulties, but they easily projected an identity separate from the female colleges. In 1887 the Bureau of Education made this distinction official by classifying this group as Division A Colleges and the female colleges as Division B. In effect, it labeled these premodern schools as anachronisms. Given their attempt to offer preparatory, ornamental, basic education, and "mental discipline and culture," the Bureau of Education opined, "it is obvious that some part of the scheme must fail of satisfactory results." From 1880 to 1900, Division A college enrollments grew from 800 to 5,000; women in coeducational colleges increased from 4,000 to 22,000; but Division B stagnated at 11,000 students.[11]

This class of colleges proved incapable of adapting to the modern era. Lacking endowments, patrons, or effective leaders, even long-established female colleges succumbed. Mary Sharp (1853–1895), Wesleyan Female College in Delaware (1841–1885), and Pittsburgh Female College (1854–1896) all closed after 40+ years of operation. Ingham University (1857–1892) had its property foreclosed by one of its trustees. The educational space that the female colleges

10   Roger L. Geiger, "The 'Superior Instruction of Women,' 1836–1890," in *American College in the Nineteenth Century*, 183–95. See for further references.
11   Ibid., 187–94; *Report of the Commissioner of Education*, 1888, 596.

had occupied from the 1840s to the 1890s was gradually claimed by high schools, normal schools, and modern women's and coeducational colleges.[12]

MULTIPURPOSE COLLEGES. Described in the previous chapter, they were the modal institution of American higher education from the 1840s to the 1890s. Ninety-two such colleges were opened in the 1860s, and sixty-one and sixty-nine in the following 2 decades. These numbers dwarf the new land grant colleges, institutes of technology, or endowed universities. Multipurpose colleges all had religious sponsorship or links. At their core was the classical AB course, organized into four separate classes, each performing fifteen recitations a week. In addition, they all offered a preparatory department and less demanding bachelor's degrees labeled science, philosophy, or literature. This curriculum could be offered by a relatively small and unspecialized faculty. The average number of college students was seventy-eight in 1840 and eighty-eight in 1880, but most institutions enrolled a larger number in preparatory and special classes. They thus served the eclectic educational needs of the island communities of rural America, untouched by high schools or normal schools. They were also entirely unsuited for the educational system of modern America that emerged at the end of the century.[13]

By then this fact was apparent to contemporaries. University of Chicago president William Rainey Harper offered a dour assessment of *The Prospects of the Small College*:

Each college is a duplicate of its nearest neighbors. A terrible monotony presents itself to the eye. . . . All alike try to cover too much ground, and worse than this, all alike practically cover the same ground.

Harper explained how the organizational plan of 30 years previous had worked, "so long as the curriculum could be restricted in large measure to the study of Latin, Greek, and mathematics," but it was now inadequate to cover advanced subjects in the third and fourth years. Of some 400 small (multipurpose) colleges, he recommended that 100 revert to private academies, 200 would function best as "junior colleges"—a term he coined—able to teach a secondary curriculum and the first 2, unspecialized years of college. The other one-quarter of small colleges, he predicted, would endure as "the survival of the fittest . . . stronger

12 Geiger, "Superior Instruction of Women," 194–95; Richard L. Wing, "Requiem for a Pioneer in Women's Higher Education: The Ingham University of Le Roy, New York, 1857–1892," *History of Higher Education Annual*, 11 (1991): 61–79. Division B was discontinued in 1910.

13 Geiger, "The Era of Multipurpose Colleges," 127–52.

and heartier because of the difficulties through which [they] passed."[14] Their travails in this process will be examined in a subsequent chapter. However, compared to female colleges, the multipurpose colleges proved far more resilient and resourceful. The large majority adapted and updated the multipurpose legacy to persist as liberal arts colleges.

SCHOOLS OF SCIENCE. When Yale and Harvard established their scientific schools, they mimicked the pattern of professional schools with which they were familiar. Yale emphasized that its school was open to all but students of Yale College, and the original teachers received income only from student fees. This approach solved the problem of introducing new studies without disturbing the prestigious classical college. They envisioned the teaching of applied sciences to rise above what passed for bachelor of science courses in other colleges and linked it explicitly with postgraduate studies. In theory, they would have preferred college graduates for students, as would university law and medical schools; but the realities of mid-nineteenth century America were otherwise for all professional schools.[15]

A booklet published just after the war expressed the ideology behind scientific or polytechnic schools. The author expressed two widely shared contemporary beliefs. First, two distinct realms of human knowledge existed: the "*subjective*, relating to man himself," which provides "the foundation of the ancient professions of Medicine, Law, Divinity, and Polite Literature"; and the "*objective*, relating to all external nature," wherein "lies the foundations for the distinctively modern technological professions." Second, another clear distinction existed between education for general culture and the scientific professions:

> Civil, Mechanical, Topographical, and Mining Engineering, Physical and Chemical Technology, and Architecture, are not taught . . . merely to discipline the mind, or to qualify one to participate in the intercourse of polite society. . . . These great subjects are taught, principally, as elevated scientific practical *professions*.

The problem with this model was the absence "of preceding institutions bearing the same relation to [scientific schools] that a classical education does for

14   William Rainey Harper, *The Prospects of the Small College* (Chicago: University of Chicago Press, 1900), quotes pp. 39–40, 30, 34, 31. Harper described the economic model: "money paid by students of the first six years has been used for instruction of a few men who are working in the last two years, in order that the college may continue to be known as a college" (36).

15   Roger L. Geiger, "The Rise and Fall of Useful Knowledge: Higher Education for Science, Agriculture, and the Mechanic Arts, 1850–1875," in *American College in the Nineteenth Century*, 153–68.

example to a theological school." In the mid-1860s the author found only one student in eight to be a college graduate.[16]

Writing on this "new education" only 3 years later (1869), Charles W. Eliot declared the professional school model to have failed, but he still upheld the "incompatibility of the practical spirit with the literary spirit." Instead, the schools had largely reverted to an undergraduate model of instruction, in which the schools themselves provided foundational instruction. From the 1850s to the 1870s the separation of scientific-technical education from the humanistic predominated, at least in the East. Six scientific schools were established at prominent colleges, and the fact that five of them were named for their donors attests the social support for these innovations.[17] The integration of science and technology only remained problematic for as long as the classical course dominated the colleges. When that domination began to wane in the 1880s, the scientific schools became undergraduate units rather than separate alternatives.

The 1880s, then, were a turning point for institutions in the higher education space. High schools became committed to their role of preparing students for college rather than serving as people's colleges. Normal schools planted one foot in higher education and increasingly adopted collegiate practices. The obsolescence of female colleges became apparent to the Bureau of Education and to a majority of women students. Technical education in engineering developed effective educational curricula and began a dramatic expansion. These developments did not bring clarity to American education but confusion, conflict, and intense debate. Only in the 1890s would the new directions of higher education become evident.

THE COLLEGES AND THE CIVIL WAR

The American Civil War was the bloodiest conflict in the nation's history and the largest military conflict between the Napoleonic Wars and World War I. History seemed compressed in those 4 fateful years as momentous issues hung in the balance of political and military developments.[18] The experience of higher education from 1861 to 1865 was nearly the opposite, as coping with the exigencies of wartime largely superseded institutional initiatives. The most significant breakthrough of these years, the Morrill Land Grant Act of 1862, affected higher

16   S. Edward Warren, *Notes on Polytechnic or Scientific Schools in the United States: Their Nature, Position, Aims, and Wants* (New York, 1866), quotes pp. 14–15, 39.

17   Charles W. Eliot, "The New Education," *Atlantic Monthly*, XXIII (February and March 1869): 202–20, 365–66; Geiger, "Rise and Fall of Useful Knowledge," 156, 164–66.

18   For background, James M. McPherson, *Battle Cry of Freedom: The Civil War Era* (New York: Oxford University Press, 1988).

education after 1865, as will be seen in the next section. The wartime experiences of the colleges varied by region. In the South colleges for men virtually ceased to operate as the enormous sacrifice of human, physical, and financial resources mounted. In the North, subtle differences existed between the experiences of colleges in the East and the West.

Southern college students were eager to fight even before the war began. The University of Alabama had already converted to a military institute in 1860. Students at South Carolina College organized a cadet corps in 1860 and paid their own train fare to Charleston to be present at the battle of Fort Sumter. Two companies of University of Virginia student volunteers departed immediately for an imaginary front. Some colleges did their best to keep students enrolled, but large numbers melted away to join state militias. Those remaining on campus, faculty and students, organized militia units and began drilling. These units were subject to state governors, and despite persistent pleas to allow students to finish their studies, most were soon mobilized. By 1862 state universities had probably lost three-quarters of their students, nine-tenths at the University of Virginia. Private colleges were, if anything, affected more severely, and most were forced to close. The universities of Georgia, Virginia, and North Carolina managed to remain open throughout the war, chiefly by teaching preparatory or underage students and maimed veterans.[19]

In the North, the shock of Fort Sumter ignited a wave of patriotic fervor across all colleges, but this enthusiasm produced fewer volunteers than in the South, in part because of confusing terms of enlistment. President Lincoln had initially called for 75,000 volunteers to enlist for ninety days, eliciting respondents from almost every college. Students also organized campus companies and began some form of regular drill. When enlistment terms were lengthened to 3 years, many students had second thoughts, preferring to continue their schooling. Thereafter, reactions in colleges were rather different in the East and West. Support for the Union and volunteers for the Army were particularly strong in the Protestant island communities of the Midwest, which also sustained the multipurpose colleges. At Kenyon College, president Loren Andrews intentionally set an example by being the first person in Ohio to respond to Lincoln's call for volunteers—and he was also one of the first to lose his life several months

19 Wartime developments are described in the principal institutional histories: Daniel Walker Hollis, *University of South Carolina: Vol. I, South Carolina College* (Columbia: University of South Carolina Press, 1951), 212–29; Thomas G. Dyer, *The University of Georgia: A Bicentennial History, 1785–1985* (Athens: University of Georgia Press, 1985), 99–122; Philip Alexander Bruce, *History of the University of Virginia, 1819–1919*, 5 vol. (New York: Macmillan, 1921), III, 256–340. Also, Michael David Cohen, *Reconstructing the Campus: Higher Education and the American Civil War* (Charlottesville: University of Virginia Press, 2012), 19–51.

later. Indiana Asbury, like many other colleges, encouraged students to enlist rather than trying to hold them back. Abolitionist colleges were almost as eager to fight as their southern counterparts. Oberlin organized a corps of 90-day volunteers, which instead saw almost continuous action for 3 years. When mustered out in 1864, only 9 of 151 emerged unscathed. At tiny Franklin College in New Athens, Ohio, not only did most male students enlist, but so did almost all eligible males in the town. Still, after the ardor of Fort Sumter cooled, most midwestern colleges lost only a small portion of their students over the course of the war. Instead, students organized military companies on campus, hopefully ready to defend their states or be mobilized for the major theaters. Many of these units were, in fact, mobilized later in the war but wisely used only for guard duties that freed regular troops.[20]

In the northeastern colleges post-Sumter patriotism produced a handful of volunteers, but college life soon reverted to normal. Although Boston was a bastion of support for the Union and abolition, there was no expectation that Harvard students would or should serve in the army. Bowdoin refused to release professor Joshua Chamberlain, a subsequent war hero, who had to fake a study leave in order to enlist. Student news reports in 1861 from other campuses reflected aloofness more than commitment.[21] Columbia students affected a wry detachment in describing the patriotic extravagance surrounding the campus. At Yale, five companies of faculty and students were initially formed, but by summer they had "gradually subsided into neglect." Similarly at Dartmouth, early enthusiasm had led to an unprecedented cooperation with the gung-ho cadets of nearby Norwich University, but the volunteer company lasted only 3 months. Student reporting from both Yale and Dartmouth devoted more attention to athletics than war-related developments. "If it were not for the daily papers," Hamilton students wrote, "we would almost forget there was a war." The situation seems to have been similar at Williams, where just twenty-nine students withdrew to enlist throughout the war.

However, if most (but not all) northeastern students were reluctant to participate in the conflict, the same was not true of the graduates of these colleges. They seem to have volunteered (since the draft was easily avoided) in significant numbers, and each college possessed its Honor Role of the fallen. From Harvard, 1,568 graduates served in uniform, from Yale, 932, and from Union, 568,

---

20 George B. Manhart, *DePauw Through the Years*, 2 vol. (Greencastle, IN: DePauw University, 1962), I, 61–74; Fletcher, *History of Oberlin College*, 843–66; Erving E. Beauregard, *Old Franklin: The Eternal Touch* (New York: University Press of America, 1983), 79–88.

21 *University Quarterly*, published in 1860–1861 by students at Yale with contributions from more than thirty other campuses, contained News Reports from these colleges: the following reports are from Vol. 4 (July–October, 1861), quotes pp. 164, 303.

although one-sixth of Harvard and Yale grads fought for the Confederacy. For Yale classes from 1851 to 1863, 35 percent of graduates entered active service in the war, mostly as officers. These gentlemen no doubt felt a greater social obligation to serve and to lead than the would-be gentlemen still in college.[22]

The direct impact of the war on southern universities was debilitating and long lasting, but it cannot be separated from the turmoil of Reconstruction. The experiences of the principal universities varied widely. Perhaps worst, the University of Alabama had to rebuild a destroyed campus and could not reopen until 1871. The University of South Carolina underwent several reorganizations before closing completely from 1877 to 1880. More positively, there was a widespread postwar sentiment to resuscitate the universities, institute modernizing reforms, and provide opportunities for wounded veterans to prepare for productive careers. The University of Virginia was most successful in these respects, adding chairs in engineering and applied chemistry and attaining three-quarters of its prewar enrollment of 600 by 1870. The University of Georgia, too, made initial progress in reforming courses of study with helpful support from the state. But these efforts stalled in 1873 on all fronts, forcing the university into survival mode. The University of North Carolina launched ambitious postwar reforms, but they were soon undermined by the Reconstruction regime. The institution was compelled to close from 1870 to 1874 before beginning a more determined effort. After some hopeful postwar efforts, the longer-lasting effects of regional impoverishment and increasingly reactionary political regimes tended to diminish both attendance and support for higher education.[23]

In the North, the short-term impact of the war upon the colleges was minor or negligible. Enrollments at Harvard and Yale barely dipped and quickly returned to normal. From 1865 to 1870, sixty-two new institutions of higher education opened, forty-nine of them denominational colleges and almost all of these in the North and West. A few colleges blamed the war for falling enrollments, among them Union, Williams, and Illinois colleges. But enrollments at these schools continued to fall after the war as well—a reflection of longer-term rigidities in the institutions and their clienteles. The end of the Civil War, in fact, marked the onset of dynamic new forces affecting higher education, and colleges that failed to adapt were soon left behind.

22   Samuel Eliot Morison, *Three Centuries of Harvard* (Cambridge: Harvard University Press, 1936), 303n; Brooks Mather Kelley, *Yale: A History* (New Haven: Yale University Press, 1974), 198; Wayne Somers, *Encyclopedia of Union College*, 165. See also Kanisorn Wongsrichanalai, "Leadership Class: College-Educated New Englanders in the Civil War," *Massachusetts Historical Review* 13 (2011): 67–96.

23   See note 20; James B. Sellers, *History of the University of Alabama*, 2 vol. (University of Alabama Press, 1953), I, 281–313; James L. Leloudis, *Schooling the New South* (Chapel Hill: University of North Carolina Press, 1996), 52–60.

THE MORRILL LAND GRANT ACT OF 1862

On July 2, 1862, President Lincoln signed the Land Grant Act, giving each state that accepted its terms 30,000 acres of federal land for each representative and senator in Congress, to be used to establish an endowment to support:

> at least one college where the leading object shall be, without excluding other scientific and classical studies, and including military tactics, to teach such branches of learning as are related to agriculture and the mechanic arts, in such manner as the legislatures of the States may respectively prescribe, in order to promote the liberal and practical education of the industrial classes on the several pursuits and professions in life.[24]

These clauses conveyed far-reaching aims to institutionalize practical fields of study, meld them with liberal education, open them to a new class of students, and charge the states with finding the means to accomplish it all. The act immediately affected the expansion and structure of higher education and, eventually, the productivity of the American economy.

At the time, it was a minor piece of work by a Congressional session that historian James McPherson has called "one of the most productive in American history." In the absence of southern obstruction, the 37th Congress passed a host of measures that drove a Whig-Republican agenda for aggressive socioeconomic development that has been called "the blueprint for modern America." Besides stabilizing federal finances with the Internal Revenue Act, the 37th Congress gave away far larger swaths of federal lands under the Homestead Act and the Pacific Railroad Act (for building the transcontinental railroad), which together laid the basis for the huge westward expansion following the war, and it created the Department of Agriculture as well. The educational consequences of the Morrill Act were far less evident and scarcely discussed at the time. The Congressmen who passed or opposed the legislation viewed it chiefly in terms of federal lands policy. However, though the public lands loomed large in the sponsor's calculations, education was his primary concern.[25]

---

24 "An Act Donating Public Lands to the several States and Territories which may provide Colleges for the Benefit of Agriculture and Mechanic Arts": Act of July 2, 1862, ch. 130, 12 Stat.503, 7 U.S.C. 301–8, quote Sec.4.

25 McPherson, *Battle Cry of Freedom*, 450–53; Leonard P. Curry, *Blueprint for Modern America: Nonmilitary Legislation of the First Civil War Congress* (Nashville: Vanderbilt University Press, 1968); Carl L. Becker, *Cornell University: Founders and the Founding* (Ithaca: Cornell University Press, 1943), 34–36.

Vermont Representative Justin Smith Morrill had sought national sponsorship for agricultural colleges from the time he was elected in 1854. He had shepherded a similar bill through Congress against southern opposition in 1859, only to have it vetoed by President Buchanan. The fundamental ideas behind the act were scarcely original and later spawned claims of at least partial paternity. Land grants had been used to support education since the beginning of the Republic; practical education for useful knowledge had been seriously pursued since the 1840s; and agricultural colleges were already operating in Ohio, Michigan, Maryland, and Pennsylvania, as Morrill himself noted. Morrill's formula, however, was unique, as were his skills as a parliamentarian in designing and sponsoring the act.[26] By weighting the size of the land grants by population, he made the act more attractive to large eastern states. By stipulating that the proceeds were to be used only as endowment, the act induced states to make a permanent commitment to these colleges. Rather than specifying the nature of these institutions, the act indicated only "the leading object," leaving interpretation and implementation to states. And most consequential for higher education, it specified an integration of agriculture and the mechanic arts with "other scientific and classical studies" to promote "liberal and practical education." Yet, within these parameters, Morrill sought to achieve quite definite aims, which he stressed in his justification to Congress.

First, he intended to open educational opportunity for the "industrial classes." Since colleges largely prepared students for the professions and were patronized by that same class, Morrill envisioned a college in each state, "accessible to all, but especially to the sons of toil"—the "thousand willing and expecting to work their way through the world by the sweat of their brow." Second, to provide instruction in the "practical avocations of life," the act specifically mentioned agriculture and the mechanic arts as the leading object. The third aim was to teach the practical arts alongside "other scientific and classical studies." Morrill's purpose was at once cultural—to elevate these studies and students to the same social standing as AB degrees—and functional—to advance these subjects through connection with the higher learning. The fourth goal was to encourage what today would be called economic development through research. A large part of Morrill's speech advocating his bill described the declining productivity of American agriculture, in contrast to European countries, where agriculture was studied scientifically. Modern sciences, he presciently argued, "are more or less related to agriculture or the mechanic arts," He envisioned professors of

---

26   Earle D. Ross, "The 'Father' of the Land Grant Colleges," *Agricultural History*, 12, 2 (April, 1938): 151–86; William Belmont Parker, *The Life and Public Services of Justin Smith Morrill* (Boston: Houghton Mifflin, 1924), 262–71.

agriculture at the land grant colleges who would apply scientific knowledge to reverse the curse of falling farm productivity.[27]

The four objectives of the Land Grant Act had personal meaning for Justin Morrill. The son of a blacksmith in Strafford, Vermont, his formal education ended with two terms in local academies before he began working in retail trade. He became a voracious reader and collector of books, becoming broadly self-educated, but he deeply regretted his own limited schooling. He also resented the "monopoly" of education and higher careers by "the thoroughly educated," who sent their sons to classical colleges. Morrill rose, through his own efforts, from bookkeeper to successful business proprietor, and he retired at age 38 to become a gentleman farmer. He was knowledgeable and well read about farming issues, including the agricultural schools of Europe, but he rejected that specialized model for the United States. The growing industrial prowess of the nation required that these schools serve the industrial classes in the mechanic arts, too. But further, he wanted agriculture connected with science and liberal education, which could occur only as a full partner with traditional colleges.[28]

The general ideas behind the Morrill Act were rooted in the burgeoning agricultural societies of the country. By 1860 more than 800 local societies had been formed, the majority in the previous decade. In New England and elsewhere, agricultural societies and agricultural journals were patronized chiefly by educated, gentleman farmers who believed that scientific education would translate into useful knowledge for farmers and greater productivity. Justin Morrill was a prominent member of his local Orange County Agricultural Society. State agricultural societies had already founded agricultural colleges in Michigan, Pennsylvania, and Maryland. The United States Agricultural Society (1852–1860), the most eminent of this type, assisted in the creation of the Department of Agriculture. This constituency, along with a smattering of university-trained agricultural scientists, would be core supporters of land grant colleges.[29]

Morrill's four objectives defined the Land Grant movement or tradition. These protean and evolving ideals, continually invoked by institutions and their champions, were: access to college for the industrial classes, meaning all

---

27 "Speech of Hon. Justin S. Morrill of Vermont in the House of Representatives, June 6, 1862."

28 Nathan M. Sorber and Roger L. Geiger, "The Welding of Opposite Views: Land-Grant Historiography at 150 Years," *Handbook of Higher Education Theory and Research* (forthcoming: 2014).

29 Parker, *Justin Smith Morrill*, 48–50; Lyman Carrier, "The United States Agricultural Society, 1852–1860: Its Relation to the Origin of the United States Department of Agriculture and the Land Grant Colleges," *Agricultural History*, 11, 4 (Oct. 1937): 278–88; Nathan M. Sorber, *Farmers, Scientists, and Officers of Industry: The Formation and Reformation of Land-Grant Colleges in the Northeastern United States, 1862–1906*, PhD Diss., Pennsylvania State University, 2011, chapter 3.

nonprofessionals who worked in the productive economy; education in the practical arts, meaning the applied fields of knowledge; the social and intellectual equivalence of practical and literary fields; and the useful application of scientific findings to stimulate economic development. Realizing these intentions within the context of the Morrill Act was another matter.

Three broad issues were problematic from the outset and would spawn conflicts and complications for the remainder of the century. First, although the objectives could be stated in general terms, the act, its sponsor, and its supporters were indelibly linked with agriculture. A large majority of the American population was engaged in agriculture, but they by no means agreed about farming, science, or education. Yet agricultural interests in every state at one time or another would claim ownership over the "agricultural colleges," with varying results. Second, the intellectual base for technological improvement in agriculture or the mechanic arts was rudimentary at best. While improving this condition was a compelling justification for creating land grant colleges, the meager initial results invited criticism that undermined this very effort. Third, the educational approach written into the act thrust the land grant movement into the amorphous realm of pre-modern educational institutions. Whether practical and liberal education were complementary or contradictory was hotly debated, as seen above. How and where students from the industrial classes would be prepared for land grant colleges would determine not only who might attend, but also what they could be taught. The land grant colleges, like other premodern schools, had to navigate the ill-defined channels between secondary and higher education before they could decisively opt for the latter. For the next generation, bitter conflicts arose in each of these areas, as states tried to organize, operate, and pay for the designated recipients of the land grant funds. But after 1862, the states had immediate choices to make.

States were given 2 years, later extended, to accept the terms of the land grant and 5 additional years to create a college. They thus faced two challenging tasks—determining what institution(s) would fulfill the terms of the act and be beneficiaries of the funds and transforming grants of public land into funds for endowment. Claiming land was somewhat easier for those western states that contained public lands. Eastern states were issued land scrip instead, good for obtaining federal lands in western states or territories. This meant identifying parcels of land, securing title, and finding a buyer (states could not hold land in other states). The alternative was to sell the land scrip to speculators. These brokers were reviled by contemporaries for reputed sharp dealing and because western states feared having large blocks of their territory monopolized by profiteers. Making markets for desperate sellers is a timeless economic function, seldom honored but often quite profitable. Brown University, for example, sent its president West with the school's agent to claim land but found the process too complicated. Instead it sold the scrip to the agent for 42 cents per acre—the lowest price realized by any state. In Pennsylvania, legislative quarrels delayed selling the scrip until the market was glutted, and it also received a low price for its large allotment. States that managed to hold onto their land grants for a number of years achieved the best returns—Illinois, Michigan, and, especially, Cornell University.[30]

Since land grant funds provided only income, the states were responsible for supplying a college. Doing so created little difficulty if an existing institution could fulfill the terms of the act, but this was seldom the case. Not that they lacked for volunteers; in most states existing colleges petitioned for all or part of this bounty, usually without any pretense of educational programs in agriculture or mechanic arts. Here the agricultural societies played a positive role by insisting that this resource be concentrated in a single institution, but these squabbles caused delays in designating and opening land grant colleges.

Each state found a unique solution to creating a land grant college, and the initial results fell into four basic patterns. Some states awarded the land grant to an existing state university, such as Wisconsin and most southern states when they returned to the Union. Some states that lacked a university created one as the land grant designee such as Cornell and the University of California but also some that bore original land grant names, like Illinois Industrial University and Ohio Agriculture & Mechanical [A&M] College. In these cases, locating the new institution presented an additional fractious issue, but these new institutions ultimately proved to be one of the most valuable fruits of the Land Grant Act. Together, these state universities would seem to best fulfill Morrill's intention of integrating practical and liberal education, but in fact many states merely attached "A&M" units to universities. Some states chose to bypass their public universities and establish a separate A&M college. This course reflected a lack of confidence that existing universities—largely classical colleges—could accommodate applied subjects. A fourth pattern was to award the land grant to an agricultural college, either already chartered (Michigan, Pennsylvania, Maryland, Iowa) or newly created (Massachusetts, Kansas, and, later, others). In addition, three colleges for African Americans were given land grant designations by southern states, the consequence of Reconstruction politics and the intent to keep African Americans away from all-white state universities.[31] The different

---

30   Roger L. Williams, *The Origins of Federal Support for Higher Education: George W. Atherton and the Land-Grant College Movement* (University Park: Pennsylvania State University Press, 1991), 46–49; Peter L. Moran and Roger L. Williams, "Saving the Land Grant for the Agricultural College of Pennsylvania," in Roger L. Geiger and Nathan M. Sorber, eds., *The Land-Grant Colleges and the Reshaping of American Higher Education* (New Brunswick: Transaction Publishers, 2013), 105–30.

31   Mississippi, South Carolina, and Virginia; Geiger, "The Rise and Fall of Useful Knowledge," 162–64.

forms taken by land grant colleges reflected the different interpretations of the Morrill Act.

In 1867 Daniel Coit Gilman of the Sheffield Scientific School published an article explaining and justifying the new land grant colleges. Sheffield had been one of the first designees, signing a contract with Connecticut in 1862 to use the land grant revenues to enhance studies of agriculture and mechanic arts and subsequently adding three new professors in these fields. Gilman was familiar with agricultural and technical education in Europe and understood the fault lines in the land grant movement. For him, Sheffield embodied the intention of the act to marry technological advancement through research and scientific training with the instruction of educated practitioners. He proposed that the new institutions be called "our National Schools of Science," stressing that the gift of federal lands made them a national project and that they were dedicated above all to "natural science in its applications to human industry." He objected to the already prevalent term "agricultural colleges": "the mechanical arts . . . are placed on the same footing as agriculture, and the *liberal education* of the industrial classes is as much an object of the grant as their practical training." Gilman saw nothing but problems with expectations that agricultural colleges were intended to train farmers. Educated young men could not be expected "to go back and labor with the hoe or the anvil." For that, the country needed to develop "industrial schools of a lower grade." The national schools of science should rather aim to train scientists, who were badly needed to fill the faculties of the new schools, so that they might train people for "the higher avocations of Life, and especially to take charge of mines, manufactories, the construction of public works." Gilman's national schools of science articulated the position of the university party of the land grant movement and foreshadowed a good deal of the struggles ahead.[32]

By 1871 the battle lines were clearly drawn. All thirty-seven states had accepted the terms of the land grant, but only nineteen institutions were actually teaching students. There was widespread interest in these inchoate institutions, and that year the Commissioner of Education asked Gilman to survey and report on their condition. He expressed disappointed that only one institution (obviously Sheffield) regarded "post-graduate students, studying science for its own sake . . . as of the highest value." He found the predominate emphasis to be to "train up men who shall lead in the applications of science to industry." However, he also noted that some institutions catered to "those who are to labor

32   Daniel Coit Gilman, "Our National Schools of Science," *North American Review* (Oct. 1867): 495–520.

with their hands upon the farm and in the workshop."[33] This last position, the mission of educating farmers, had been called the "Michigan plan," referring to the Michigan Agricultural College. When land grant college representatives met in Chicago to discuss agricultural education, these views were "sharply contested" by advocates for the "university grade of agricultural education." Michigan representatives defended manual labor, in particular, as the only approach that would not "educate the students away from the farm." Gilman defended the university position that the institutions should pursue "experimental work bearing directly upon each state's practical problems," and he was supported by the delegates from the universities of Mississippi, Illinois, Minnesota, and Wisconsin.[34] Going forward, the land grant movement would mean different things for universities, agricultural colleges, and, belatedly, the mechanic arts.

LAND GRANT UNIVERSITIES

In 1868 Cornell University opened as the land grant institution of New York State. The following year Charles W. Eliot began his 40-year presidency of Harvard. And, in 1876 Johns Hopkins University opened, with Daniel Coit Gilman as president. In less than a decade, these three institutions consciously exemplified what would prove to be the principal facets of the American university. Cornell's melding of academic and practical studies would characterize American state universities. Eliot oversaw the transformation of undergraduate and professional education at Harvard. And John Hopkins stood for research, graduate education, and the American PhD. The latter two developments will be the subject of the next chapter. State universities emerged from the land grant movement, but only after struggling to impose their definition of its meaning. Cornell, a product of the New York State Legislature but governed by a self-perpetuating Board of Trustees, would become the exemplar for land grant universities.[35]

Cornell University was both a direct product of the Morrill Act and the first American university to be dedicated to the new principles of advanced and

---

33 Daniel Coit Gilman, "Report on the National Schools of Science," *Reports of the Commissioner of Education, 1871* (Washington, DC, 1872), 427–43, quotes p. 435.

34 Alfred C. True, *A History of Agricultural Education in the United States, 1785–1925* (Washington, D.C., 1929), 118, 192–93. The representative from Mississippi was Eugene Hilgard, who later pioneered agricultural education and research at the University of California.

35 An indispensable overview: Laurence R. Veysey, *The Emergence of the American University* (Chicago: University of Chicago Press, 1965). Cornell University later evolved a unique dual governance structure of private "endowed colleges" and public "statutory colleges."

practical knowledge.[36] It became a unique amalgam of the ideas of its founders, Ezra Cornell and Andrew Dickson White. This unlikely pair was brought together in the New York State Senate over the disposition of the Land Grant designation, originally directed toward two weak and suspect claimants. Instead Cornell and White collaborated to found a university endowed with Cornell's fortune and shaped by White's educational ideals. Ezra Cornell, a Quaker with little formal education, followed diverse occupations before participating in the early telegraph industry, which eventually brought him a fortune in Western Union stock. He became a gentleman farmer and state senator, active in the agricultural societies, and he resolved to devote most of his wealth to promote agricultural education. Andrew D. White graduated from Yale after acquiring an abiding disdain for classical colleges and a dream of an American university like Oxford and Cambridge. These ideas were honed by a European grand tour and the experience of professing history under Henry Tappan at Michigan. His university ideal was both aesthetic and intellectual but also completely open to the inclusion of practical subjects. Ezra Cornell made the university possible by donating his large farm in Ithaca and $500,000. Further, he multiplied the value of the land grant by purchasing the university's land scrip, locating valuable timberlands in Wisconsin and holding the lands in pledge to the university as they appreciated in value. The university ultimately realized more than $5 million, almost ten times the average price per acre received by land grant schools. He was famously alleged to have said, "I would found an institution where any person can find instruction in any study."[37] White's vision of a university included history, political science, modern literature, and high academic standards. Cornell University was wealthy enough to fulfill both visions.

The new university was predicated on the equivalence of agriculture, mechanic arts, and other professional studies with the liberal arts. White devised two broad divisions, one for the academic departments and the other, the Division of Special Science and Arts, for nine applied or professional fields. He included history and political science in the latter, intending that department for the education of statesmen. White was adamantly opposed to prevailing notions of mental discipline, arguing that knowledge was paramount and mental discipline was achieved only when student interests were engaged. He thus asserted student choice as a fundamental principle. Students were originally offered several distinct courses, which consisted of groups of subjects, or the option of

36 For the early history of Cornell: Carl L. Becker, *Cornell University: Founders and Foundings* (Ithaca: Cornell University Press, 1944); Morris Bishop, *Cornell, a History* (Ithaca: Cornell University Press, 1962); Andrew Dickson White, *Autobiography of Andrew Dickson White*, 2 vol. (New York, 1905).

37 The motto of Cornell University, it expresses Ezra Cornell's sentiments but not his diction: Bishop, *Cornell*, 74.

studying any subjects taught in the university. This soon evolved into a set of required classes in the first 2 years and virtually free electives afterwards. White would have liked to hire renowned professors and achieved a coup of sorts by attracting Oxford historian Goldwin Smith for a time, but he realized the institution's limitations. Instead, he consulted widely to identify and hire promising young scholars. In addition, he lured some academic stars like Louis Agassiz to teach as visiting professors. This policy immediately established academic credibility while the regular faculty was maturing. Cornell conferred graduate degrees, although in the absence of formal studies, what they meant was open to interpretation. In 1872 it awarded its first PhD as well as a master's degree to David Starr Jordan, whose 4 years of study apparently merited more than a bachelor's. During the university's first years, Ezra Cornell exerted a counterbalancing influence. He insisted on the manual labor requirement, which worked as badly at Cornell as elsewhere, and advocated for a student shoe factory. He regarded the institution as partly a manual labor school and was particularly supportive of poor country students with backgrounds like his own. Ezra Cornell's attention soon drifted to other projects, and both his influence and his pet schemes waned in the years before his death in 1874.

Before the university opened, Ezra Cornell had written a letter to the New York *Tribune* promising that students could work their way through the college. President White received more than 2,000 letters of inquiry. Three years of publicity for the "Cornell idea" and the promise that any person could study any subject—and support himself too—elicited this avalanche of interested persons, most with dubious preparation. On October 8, 1868, the faculty enrolled 412 students who had passed the entrance examination—the largest entering class in the history of American higher education. It was also a class that would have pleased Justin Morrill: "young farmers and mechanics for the most part ... rough outside and inside," drawn largely from New York's rural towns and countryside with the aid of annual scholarships for each assembly district. Only about 10 percent of these students would earn a Cornell degree, but some, like David Starr Jordan, in fact worked their way through. Both White and Cornell favored the equal education of women—in theory. Women were not included in the original plan for lack of accommodation and reluctance to upset the trustees with such a controversial issue. They arrived nonetheless, beginning in 1869, and their awkward presence was institutionalized when trustee Henry Sage donated a large building to accommodate them (opened 1875). Enrollments at Cornell rose to 561 in 1876 but then began to shrink, bottoming at 384 in 1881. These were years of financial hardship for the country and the university, and it was no help that President White was abroad on diplomatic missions almost continuously during this period. However, the character of the university was changing as well. Enthusiasm for the practical arts waned along with career opportunities in a stagnant economy. Students from the industrial classes became less numerous on campus, discouraged by high costs, diminishing opportunities for work, and rising standards of admission. Cornell students increasingly came from higher social strata, were better prepared for college studies, and were more likely to graduate. Socially, these students compared themselves with peers at the eastern universities and, academically, so did the faculty.[38]

With forty-seven professors in 1880, Cornell had one of the largest faculties in the country and wide coverage of subjects. Such scale was needed to achieve the integration of pure and applied science ideally sought by land grant universities. The Cornell culture seemed to encourage cross-fertilization as well. Chemistry, where Cornell would emerge as a national leader, established an early course in industrial chemistry, which later developed into chemical engineering (1891). The professor of physics contrived several electrical devices before starting the first program in electrical engineering (1881). Cornell's initial agriculture department was a disaster, not rectified until 1874, but it compensated somewhat with professors in botany and zoology. Cornell also established the first department of veterinary science. It followed MIT in establishing the country's second department of architecture. President White's devotion to history and literature assured that those subjects would be nurtured as well. White assembled a highly competent faculty devoted to the transmission and application of knowledge—teaching and practice—but not yet committed to research. Still, due to White's high standards and discerning judgment—and relatively ample resources—Cornell was poised to be in the forefront of the impending academic revolution. The most rapid academic development occurred after White retired in 1885, bringing distinction in the liberal arts, the natural and physical sciences, agriculture, and engineering.

The ideal of a land grant university was more difficult to achieve where institutions had to contend with rough-and-tumble statehouse politics. When the land grant was awarded to an established university, as it was throughout the South, agriculture and mechanic arts were generally isolated in separate units that had little interaction with traditional colleges. The premier state university and largest in the country, the University of Michigan, attempted to join the land grant club through a hostile takeover of Michigan Agricultural College but was thwarted by the legislature. It nevertheless included public service and practical instruction in engineering in its mission but was spared the confrontation with agricultural interests that land grants faced. Otherwise, states that chose to

38 Bishop, *Cornell*; Edwin E. Slosson, *Great American Universities* (New York: Macmillan, 1910), 312–43.

create new universities for the land grant or those that awarded it to recent creations were best able to embrace the university ideal—but not without a struggle. California was most successful in this respect, while the upper midwestern states of Illinois, Minnesota, Wisconsin, and Ohio traveled rougher roads.

The University of California was founded in 1868 through the amalgamation of the College of California (f. 1860) and the land grant institution.[39] The state had originally opted to create an "Agricultural, Mining, and Mechanical Arts College," but some still advocated a university. In 1867, Yale's Benjamin Silliman Jr. had extolled the virtues of a full university as a visiting speaker and warned that creating a technical college would preclude such benefits. The governor found these arguments persuasive and pushed through new legislation founding the university. The university vision was reinforced in 1872 when Daniel Coit Gilman was persuaded to accept the presidency. Gilman brought the spirit of the national schools of science to California—an ardent endorsement of universities and science, now adapted to the people of the state: "to their public and private schools, to their peculiar geographical position, to the requirements of their new society and their undeveloped resources." Gilman was an immediate success, an inspiration to faculty and students and well received by the Bay Area community. The atmosphere changed abruptly in his second year when the unscrupulous professor of agriculture launched a campaign to secure the land grant revenues for his own college. He mobilized agricultural interests and the Grange to condemn the university for neglecting agriculture. They proposed creating a separate agricultural college, abolishing the Board of Regents, and establishing a new board chosen by popular election (and hence beholden to agriculture). The legislature responded by conducting a formal investigation into the management of the university. The university ably defended itself and was exonerated, but the ordeal disillusioned Gilman. Dissuaded from resigning in the aftermath, later in 1874 he accepted the presidency of the projected Johns Hopkins University.

The battle between the university and agricultural interests persisted for another 4 years. Bills were repeatedly introduced to alter the governance of the university to gain greater political control. These efforts were related to widespread popular discontent, fanned by economic hard times, and prompted a Constitutional Convention in 1878. There the university narrowly achieved a signal victory by obtaining autonomy from the political maelstrom. It had argued, in words that were relevant to all state universities:

39   Verne A. Stadtman, *The University of California, 1868–1968* (New York: McGraw-Hill, 1970); John Aubrey Douglass, *The California Idea and American Higher Education: 1850 to the 1960 Master Plan* (Stanford: Stanford University Press, 2000).

In the history of all institutions of higher education, it has been found that they owe their prosperity, and the valuable endowments they receive, to the commanding fact . . . that they are organically exempt from the disturbing effects of political intervention.

The new California Constitution identified the university as a "public trust"—"entirely independent of all political and sectarian influence, and kept free therefrom in the appointment of its Regents and in the administration of its affairs." The university clause also included the exact language of the Morrill Act and added that "no person shall be debarred admission . . . on account of sex."[40]

The independence of the University of California for the remainder of the century was enjoyed primarily by the regents. Through the tenures of several weak and pliable presidents, the regents not only decided large issues but micromanaged the institution as well. Their role may have produced unwelcome interventions, but they supported the growth and development of the university. In fact, the Cal Regents in some ways resembled the Cornell trustees. Ezra Cornell had named people like himself to the Cornell board—self-made industrialists who believed in an institution that complemented their view of the new industrial economy. They readily contributed when the university faced financial embarrassment, and their major gifts advanced its strategic development. The Cal Regents were similar types—the new plutocracy of the gilded age. Their philanthropy expanded the university's assets well beyond what was available from the public fisc. They were motivated by regional pride, compounded by an innate California compulsion to overcome any alleged cultural inferiority to the East. The governors of both universities valued the prestige of academic distinction as well as contributions to the economy.

The four midwestern land grant universities followed somewhat similar patterns of development but in different time frames and with different results. All had early presidents with university outlooks who were frustrated by domineering boards and hostile or indifferent legislators. All also endured confrontations with agriculture. Initial progress was consequently grudging, and enrollments were stagnant through the mid-eighties. This phase was followed by dynamic growth and emergence as inchoate universities. The presidents who guided these later developments tended to be conciliators more than intellectual leaders, achieving institutional expansion, peace with agriculture, harmony with trustees, and appropriations from legislators.[41] After 1900, these factors undergirded

---

40   Stadtman, *University of California*, 82–83.
41   A point emphasized by Laurence Veysey in *Emergence of the American University*.

the transformation of Illinois, Minnesota, and especially Wisconsin, but Ohio State's inability to transcend the old obstacles retarded its development.

The University of Wisconsin was reorganized in 1866 to accommodate the Morrill Act, but it continued to envision more units than its meager resources could sustain. It sought national figures to lead the university, but they did not remain in Madison for long.[42] A degree of stability was achieved only with the presidency of John Bascom (1874–1887), whose vision for a state university far transcended land grant notions of utility. Previously a professor at Williams, Bascom had developed a distinctive philosophy combining a "new theology" that incorporated evolutionary science, a moral philosophy applied to government, and a theory of an activist state to provide moral leadership and actions. The state university played a key role in Bascom's worldview; it epitomized the moral authority of the state and stood at the pinnacle of a comprehensive system of public education. Bascom thus gave an entirely new meaning to the prevailing conceptions of practical education—the university was to be handmaiden to the state for the attainment of the moral organization of society. He could scarcely impose this philosophy on the University of Wisconsin, but he did teach it to the seniors as moral philosophy, which, given its predominant social emphasis, he likened to the new field of "sociology." This partnership of university and state is credited as the germ of the "Wisconsin Idea" of the early twentieth century—a university mission to supply intellectual services to the entire state. In fact, Robert LaFollette, the state's progressive governor, and university president Charles Van Hise were classmates and students of Bascom.[43]

Enrollment grew little during Bascom's tenure, but the university changed in character. Bascom strengthened the liberal arts and scientific teaching, in particular, and laid the foundation for Wisconsin's subsequent leadership in the social sciences. As for practical studies, the agriculture department had no students, forcing the university to fend off protests from state farmers. Bascom held that students should be treated like responsible adults and ended faculty supervision of student discipline. In 1880 he was able to dispense with the preparatory department. The equal rights of women were a pillar of his moral philosophy. He immediately ended the segregation of women students and established full coeducation. Despite these contributions and his popularity with students and faculty, moral philosophers can be difficult managers. Bascom held strong,

42   Education journalist Henry Barnard was Chancellor (1859–1861) and naturalist Paul Ansel Chadbourne was president (1866–1870): see Merle Curti and Vernon Carstensen, *The University of Wisconsin, a History, 1848–1925*, 2 vol. (Madison: University of Wisconsin Press, 1949), I, 163–235.

43   J. David Hoeveler Jr., "The University and the Social Gospel: The Intellectual Origins of the 'Wisconsin Idea,'" *Wisconsin Magazine of History*, 59, 4 (Summer 1976): 282–98; Veysey, *Emergence*, 105–9, 217–20; John Bascom, *Sociology* (New York, 1887).

rationalized convictions, and he never hesitated to speak his mind. Neither trait helped relations with the Wisconsin Board of Regents. The division of responsibilities was not clear, and before long Bascom became embroiled in recurrent quarrels with regents, both trivial and substantive. The board possessed ultimate authority, of course, but Bascom felt that they intervened far more than was prudent. He objected with good reason that the president was not a member of the board, a common arrangement in early land grant schools that distanced trustees from campus realities. A number of trustees were overtly hostile toward the president. Bascom, in turn, castigated the trustees as businessmen and politicians who were concerned primarily with power, not with the best interests of the university. Eventually, the trustees used Bascom's active participation in the Prohibition Party as an excuse to force his resignation. By 1887, however, Wisconsin was poised to join the ranks of the new American universities.[44]

The University of Minnesota was chartered in 1851, before the territory became a state, but it could not open for collegiate instruction until 1869.[45] The new president was William Watts Folwell (1869–1884), an academic jack-of-all-trades who had taught math and classical languages, briefly studied philology at Berlin, built bridges for the Union Army, and fervently believed in the "new education." He quoted Ezra Cornell in his inaugural address but had a higher conception of the university as a "federation of professional schools." The first 2 years of college, including the classical languages, belonged with preparatory education, not with what he called "proper University work." This "Minnesota Plan" was an ambitious vision for a university that had few persons qualified to be freshmen, let alone more advanced professional students. His tentative steps toward realizing such a structure were consequently resented. Folwell was completely focused on his educational mission, and he engaged in extensive correspondence with other university leaders. He was instrumental in the development of Minnesota high schools and connecting them with the university. He doggedly supported agriculture, which failed to attract any students in the 1870s, and found an effective formula for enrollment growth and extension in the 1880s. Folwell's insistence that admission to professional studies required 2 years of college actually delayed the establishment of law and medical schools until after his presidency.

The state university at Minneapolis, like its counterpart in Madison, Wisconsin, at times appeared to be the university of the state capital, where educated and professional families were concentrated. Students from such backgrounds

44   Curti and Carstensen, *University of Wisconsin*, I, 246–95 et passim.

45   James Gray, *The University of Minnesota, 1851–1951* (Minneapolis: University of Minnesota Press, 1951).

tended to favor more traditional collegiate education. Thus, Folwell faced a protest from one group (he called them the "Bourbons") who wanted more offerings in Greek and Latin (1879). These conflicts were compounded by the domination of the university by the Board of Regents. The impractical nature of Folwell's Minnesota Plan and the conservatism of the regents led to his resignation in 1884, although the precipitating issue was the resistance of students to (in their minds) excessive college discipline. Folwell's vision of the American university was clearly ahead of his times, and the friction between a dogmatic visionary and autocratic regents may have been inevitable. However, like Bascom at Wisconsin, Folwell's lofty aspirations laid a foundation for the subsequent development of the university.

Illinois Industrial University opened in 1868 after prolonged haggling over structure and location.[46] Agitation for agricultural education had earlier been led by Jonathan Baldwin Turner, who is locally credited with inspiring the Morrill Act and did help found the Illinois State Normal University in 1857. Selected to lead the new land grant university was John Milton Gregory (1868–1880), who had a conventional ministerial background but had also been Superintendent of Public Instruction in Michigan. The Illinois charter established a "regent" to lead the university who had somewhat more authority than most presidents. Gregory placed liberal ahead of practical instruction of the industrial classes. Still, he aimed for a middle course between the arts and sciences and the applied departments, and students were allowed considerable choice. The paucity of students in agriculture elicited a steady stream of criticism, but his undoing, like Folwell's, was student resistance to an authoritarian approach to campus discipline, despite national trends toward greater freedom. His successor, Selim Peabody (1880–1891), although professor of engineering, was more traditional, stressing mental training as the paramount objective of college. His efforts to raise academic standards were perhaps needed, but higher admission requirements depressed enrollments, and the elimination of electives within courses of study was unpopular. Enrollments in the arts and sciences stagnated, and by the end of his tenure, the majority of students studied engineering. Peabody's most fateful misstep was attempting to stanch the tide of fraternities and athletics. A more assertive Board of Trustees, now largely representing alumni interests, forced Peabody to resign in 1891. By this date the "University of Illinois" (the name was changed in 1885 at the behest of alumni) had established a foundation somewhat different from that intended by its first two regents but was on the verge of rapid advance in enrollments, offerings, and college spirit.

46 Winton U. Solberg, *The University of Illinois, 1867–1894: An Intellectual and Cultural History* (Urbana: University of Illinois Press, 1968).

With a plethora of denominational colleges and two struggling state-affiliated universities, Ohio endured a protracted process to organize and locate its land grant institution.[47] However, when the Ohio Agricultural and Mechanical College opened outside the state capital in 1873, it appeared to have a clear mandate. Its president, geologist Edward Orton, the influential secretary of the Board of Trustees, and outgoing governor Rutherford B. Hayes all envisioned an institution like Cornell that would unite science, scholarship, and utilitarian studies for the industrial classes. Instead, the institution was dominated by a politicized Board of Trustees and the nearby state legislature, with little regard for academic considerations. Three times in the 1870s, changes in legislative majorities were followed by reconstitution of the board. The trustees had little understanding or sympathy for university values and, worse, sought to regulate rather than develop the institution. The secretary of the board was a permanent official on campus, more powerful than the titular head, who was often called the "president of the faculty." Other land grant universities had carefully presented themselves as "nonsectarian Christian institutions," and Orton, too, maintained this stance despite trustee pressures to become less "Godless." When the Board finally accepted Orton's resignation in 1881, it appointed a minister as his replacement. But he turned out to be a strident proponent of the social gospel, with far less intellectual sophistication than Wisconsin's Bascom. He also advocated a much larger role for the state university, which frightened the legions of denominational colleges. His popularity with students was probably a further negative, and the Trustees fired him after 2 years. A more pliable successor finally gave the Board what it wanted—compulsory daily chapel.

As the student extracurriculum expanded at OSU, as elsewhere, the administration responded with a growing list of prohibitions: no dancing parties, restrictions on visiting other campuses, and censorship and control of student publications. The president regarded fraternities, clubs, and athletics as "evils" that diverted students from their studies. With the passage of the Hatch Act in 1887, agricultural interests launched a concerted effort to seize federal funding for a separate agricultural college. The return of Rutherford Hayes, now as head of the Board of Trustees, saved the university through a negotiated compromise and, until his death in 1893, a more benign trustee hegemony. The next president, James Canfield (1895–1899), had been a popular chancellor of the University of Nebraska. Egalitarian and assertive, he was quickly fired for claiming too large an educational role for the state university. Support for a land grant university in Ohio was limited, and opposition was considerable, making it difficult to attract

47 William A. Kinnison, *Building Sullivant's Pyramid: An Administrative History of the Ohio State University, 1870–1907* (Columbus: Ohio State University Press, 1970).

or retain strong academic leadership. Ohio State University was consequently stunted in enrollments, finance, and offerings well into the twentieth century.

The development of state land grant institutions into genuine universities was a long and arduous process with many pitfalls, and it was a route initially chosen by few states. These six universities represent the principal attempts to implement a broad and inclusive interpretation of the land grant mandate. Beyond these institutions, Missouri, Nebraska, and Maine created land grant universities on a more limited scale.[48] Other states that attached the land grant to the flagship state university did so by creating a separate unit that would later have to be integrated or made independent.

There was no obvious formula for implementing Justin Morrill's vague mandate, which seemed to call for an amalgamation of disparate and seemingly incompatible activities.[49] Hence, the first requirement was an idea—a vision—combining the high academic standards expected of university work, the application of science to practical fields, teaching liberal and practical subjects on several levels, and recruitment of both traditional and industrial-class students. The first two institutions to incorporate these elements were difficult to replicate: Cornell was a private institution with a substantial endowment; the University of Michigan lacked agriculture and the land grant. Most essential for a university was that early land grant presidents possess some such vision in order to guide or cajole their institutions in the right directions. Doing this, above all, meant securing a highly qualified faculty, competent in the new and emerging fields. Hence, the ability to identify and attract such people was indispensable, as were the resources to support and expand such a faculty. The original land grant revenues were inadequate for developing such a university, so that additional funding had to be sought from the state or private individuals. Here the early boards of trustees could play a positive role by supporting the development of their universities. Trustee contributions to Cornell and California have been remarked, and the boards for Wisconsin and Minnesota ultimately backed a dynamic and modern university, too. Finally, the new land grant universities needed students—to legitimize their existence and to justify expanding their scope. Building a clientele was a slow process of accommodating admissions and programs to the desires and capabilities of potential students, inhibited further

48   The University of Nebraska was consciously modeled after the University of Michigan and in the 1890s was considered among the top four public universities (after Michigan, California and Wisconsin): Robert E. Knoll, *Prairie University* (Lincoln: University of Nebraska Press, 1995); at Missouri, the university vision of the president and governor prevailed after a 4-year struggle against local politics: Frank E. Stephens, *A History of the University of Missouri* (Columbia: University of Missouri Press, 1962), 194–216; in Maine, the state university had few resources for academic development.

49   Sorber and Geiger, "Welding of Opposite Views."

by the economic depression after 1873. The special conditions in agriculture and engineering will be considered below. In general, conditions began to favor the state universities with the expansion of high schools in the 1880s. What was clear by 1890 was that the integrated model of the land grant university possessed greater vitality and dynamism than the truncated models created in the majority of states that placed agriculture and mechanic arts in their own institutions.

AGRICULTURE COLLEGES AND A&Ms

By the twentieth century, the majority of states had chosen not to establish universities with the land grant endowment but separate colleges of agriculture or agriculture and mechanic arts (A&Ms). These colleges assumed three basic patterns. First, a group of agricultural colleges established or planned before the Morrill Act were designated land grant recipients. Second, most of the institutions established specifically to meet the terms of the act initially adopted its exact language and the title "agricultural and mechanical," or "mechanic arts." Third, units that were incorporated into universities later faced removal campaigns, and in six cases the land grant designation was moved—along with federal monies—to newly created agricultural or A&M schools. In general, politics took precedence over educational considerations in producing these outcomes. In the first case, agricultural societies pressed and were granted their wish to establish schools to teach a subject that they felt could not be accommodated in traditional colleges. In the second case, the longer the disposition of the land grant festered in legislatures, the greater the influence of statehouse politics and local interests in defining the institution. And in the third case, the political power of the Grange was decisive in wresting the land grants away from universities in favor of agricultural colleges.

The separate, specialized nature of A&M institutions handicapped their development. Given the limited funds that states were prepared to devote to higher education, maintaining both a land grant college and a state university diminished the resources available to either. The need to attract students primarily interested in the practical arts required a lower standard of admission and a more basic level of instruction. Finally, the focus on applied science and the weakness of basic science departments long retarded the fruitful interactions that propelled advances in agricultural and engineering sciences at universities. Whereas the challenge for land grant universities was to accommodate the mechanic arts and, particularly, agriculture, the persistent problem at agricultural colleges and A&Ms was whether or how much to include "scientific and classical studies."

Indiana provides one example of dual public universities. Indiana University initially presented the most solid plan for meeting the terms of the Morrill

Act, but the legislature dithered over several fanciful schemes. A rival plan was offered by Northwestern Christian University (later, Butler University), but the real problem was that IU had few friends in the state and more than a few enemies among the denominational colleges and in the state capital (home of Northwestern Christian). The legislature finally accepted the terms of the Morrill Act in 1865 by incorporating the "Trustees of the Indiana Agricultural College," leaving its character and location open. The placement of the institution became a matter of local-interest politics, the numerous claimants making it impossible for any one to obtain majority backing. After 4 years, the logjam was broken by John Purdue, who offered to donate $150,000 to the institution on conditions (1) that it be located near his home town of Lafayette; (2) that it be named "by an irrepealable law 'Purdue University'"; and (3) that he be named a trustee for life. A successful merchant whose ample wealth came from selling pork to the Union Army, Purdue was a generous but vain local booster. He had taught school as a young man, like many others, and strongly supported education, despite having few strong convictions about it. However, he was dogmatic and proprietary about the building of "his" university, which no doubt delayed its opening (1874). His death 2 years later liberated the university from its sometimes-difficult lifetime trustee.

The university's maturation began with the appointment of its third president, Emerson White (1876–1883). A schoolman and previous president of the National Education Association, White stridently proclaimed the distinctive role of scientific and technical education. Land grant universities, he believed, spread themselves too thin by attempting to cover all academic fields. He considered a primary emphasis on science as good a foundation of a liberal education as languages and preparation for technological careers as well. White gave a direction to the university's mission that would become its permanent signature. Specifically, he focused on establishing a strong general science course and laid the groundwork for special science courses in agriculture and mechanical engineering. He inherited one of the best-furbished public land grant institutions: Purdue possessed an endowment of $300,000, modern buildings, and an annual appropriation from the state. However, it lacked students. Most were recruited locally and needed years of work in the preparatory department.

White did little to make the campus a more inviting place. Like many leaders of these schools, he carried a deep animus against the traditional classical colleges, which he characterized as dominated by the "aristocracies" of caste, capital, and culture that blocked the rise of the industrial classes. In his zeal to surmount these obstacles, he envisioned his scientific university as a solemn, Spartan cloister. He feared that any contact with the classical colleges would corrupt "a central, vigorous, all-controlling industrial life and spirit." To this end, he withdrew the university from the Indiana Oratorical Association and eliminated teaching of Latin. However, he overreached when he banned fraternities, which in his mind were linked with traditional colleges. The fraternities fought back and succeeded in having the Indiana Supreme Court abrogate the suspension of fraternity members. The legislature, in sympathy, used the fraternity ban as an excuse to withhold Purdue's appropriation. Doubly repudiated, White had little recourse but to resign. His interpretation of a scientific and technical university nonetheless became Purdue's hallmark—but in an atmosphere more favorable for student life.[50]

Purdue was fortunate to have effective and stable leadership from its next two presidents. By the twentieth century, Purdue was the strongest of the public A&Ms in terms of students, budgets, and programs, but it was above all an engineering school. It boasted four schools of engineering, schools of agriculture and pharmacy, and a school of science that included all other subjects, including home economics.[51]

Two state agricultural colleges were operating before the Morrill Act, but each developed differently.[52] The Agricultural College of Pennsylvania opened in 1859, led by Evan Pugh. The son of a Pennsylvania blacksmith, Pugh earned a PhD in agricultural chemistry at Göttingen and distinction for his experimental work in plant nutrition at Rothamstead experiment station in England. One of the few American agricultural scientists, Pugh strongly supported separate institutions for the practical arts. The land grant act was intended, he argued, "not simply to found Industrial Chairs in Literary Colleges, but to endow Industrial Colleges." His vision of agricultural progress informed by science was a sophisticated utilitarian interpretation of the Morrill Act, for which he had lobbied. Ultimately, he envisioned a faculty of twenty-nine offering six courses of study in scientific and practical agriculture and industry. But he had established only the agricultural course when he died suddenly in 1864. Unable to find a replacement of Pugh's stature, the school stagnated for two decades, a barely viable multipurpose college, until President George W. Atherton (1882–1906) sparked its renewal.[53]

50   Robert W. Topping, *A Century and Beyond: The History of Purdue University* (West Lafayette. IN: Purdue University Press, 1988), 21–111, quote p. 99.

51   H. B. Knoll, *The Story of Purdue Engineering* (West Lafayette, IN: Purdue University Studies, 1963). Purdue took the title university but fulfilled the role of an A&M with a rival state flagship university.

52   The Maryland Agricultural College was chartered in 1856 and opened in 1859. Essentially a private effort by aristocratic planters, it adopted the southern pattern of high tuition for planters' sons—a disastrous formula for postwar conditions: George H. Callcott, *A History of the University of Maryland* (Baltimore: Maryland Historical Society, 1966), 131–52.

53   Peter Moran and Roger L. Williams, "Saving the Land Grant for the Agricultural College of Pennsylvania," in Roger L. Geiger and Nathan M. Sorber, eds., *The Land-Grant Colleges and the Reshaping*

The development of Michigan Agricultural College (open in 1857) was nearly the inverse of its Pennsylvania counterpart. Its early years were difficult indeed as a handful of students and a few faculty labored to fashion a campus and farm out of a forest swamp. The early faculty had few credentials for their mission and often recruited the school's graduates to teach, but for the most part they proved dedicated and effective. Professor Manly Miles, for example, possessing only an MD, achieved recognition as professor of agriculture and director of the experimental farm. MAC professors apparently learned on the job because Manly and others were later recruited by other agricultural colleges, including Cornell. Admission requirements were minimal, and most students still needed preparatory classes. The curriculum was basic and largely taught from textbooks. In "practical agriculture" students received lessons on topics such as "manures—their management and mode of application; . . . cultivation of grain crops; cultivation of root crops; . . . fattening of animals; and management of sheep." By 1871, with 141 students, mostly freshmen but now also including 8 women, MAC had weathered its difficult infancy and was beginning to prosper as a distinctive, homegrown agricultural college. In some ways MAC managed to create the agricultural college that was so elusive elsewhere: permissive admissions made it accessible, and most of its students came from farming backgrounds; it taught and practiced practical agriculture, while also providing basic scientific underpinnings; and a far larger proportion of its students remained in agriculture. In its first 30 years, the college matriculated 4,000 students and graduated 400, with at least half apparently becoming farmers. MAC developed slowly from this agricultural paradigm. It started teaching mechanic arts in 1885 and added a women's course in 1896. However, by the twentieth century it visibly lagged behind the academic revolution occurring elsewhere.[54]

Agricultural colleges varied considerably across the country. In Massachusetts, which had many colleges, the agricultural college could develop as a specialized institution. With a relatively qualified faculty, it offered a 4-year bachelor's of science course consisting of general studies and agricultural studies, including compulsory manual labor until 1883. In 15 years (1871–1886), the Massachusetts Agricultural College graduated 237 of 643 students, with just over one-quarter pursuing careers in agriculture. Although it remained small, the college was a

of American Higher Education (New Brunswick: Transaction Publishers, 2013), 105–30; Michael Bezilla, The College of Agriculture at Penn State: a Tradition of Excellence (University Park: Pennsylvania State University Press, 1987); True, Agricultural Education, 165–72.

54   True, Agricultural Education, 130–36, quote p. 132; Madison Kuhn, Michigan State: The First Hundred Years (East Lansing: Michigan State University Press, 1955); Keith R. Widder, Michigan Agricultural College: The Evolution of a Land-Grant Philosophy, 1855–1925 (East Lansing: Michigan State University Press, 2005).

significant contributor to agricultural education and research. In both Iowa and Kansas, agricultural colleges were established before the state universities were well organized, largely due to local politics. Iowa State Agricultural College consisted of a plot of open prairie when it was chartered in 1858 and could not open until 1869. Kansas State Agricultural College inherited a defunct Methodist college in 1863. It opened immediately but had few students for the first two decades. Kansas State began by offering a literary course, but after a decade it was reconfigured under pressure from the Grange into an agricultural model. The majority of students came from farms and attended for a single year before returning to the farming community. To 1890, Kansas State enrolled more than 2,500 students but graduated just 232; by the 1880s it had a larger enrollment than the University of Kansas but fewer graduates. Iowa State began with fairly robust enrollments of 200+, but it grew little over its first two decades. It still managed to rival the State University of Iowa in student numbers. When enrollments mushroomed after 1890, both Kansas State and Iowa State developed with few liberal subjects and heavy emphases on agriculture.[55]

★ ★ ★

Agricultural education faced fundamental difficulties, whether offered in a university, an A&M, or an agricultural college. Agriculture departments had little to teach that could yield practical benefits to farmers; rural students generally lacked schooling to prepare for college work; and they scarcely needed the subject material that colleges were able to teach. This situation was aggravated by the financial panic of 1873, which ushered in a long agricultural depression characterized by rising production and falling prices. Farmer's claimed that the "agricultural colleges" should serve their needs, and with the spread of grange organizations, they gained a louder voice and more potent political influence. Agricultural science made steady progress, but a large gap persisted between theoretical findings and practical applications. When Isaac Roberts began teaching agriculture at Iowa State, for example, he found nothing on the subject in the library: "thus [in his words] I was driven to take the class to the field and farm, there to study plants, animals, and tillage at first hand." Roberts soon took this empirical approach to Cornell (1874), where he invigorated the school of agriculture. This hands-on approach inspired practical training at Michigan Agricultural College too; however, the scarcity of able exponents not only slowed

55   True, *Agricultural Education*, 137–58; Earl D. Ross, *A History of Iowa State College* (Ames: Iowa State College Press, 1942); Scott M. Gelber, *The University and the People: Envisioning American Higher Education in an Era of Populist Protest* (Madison: University of Wisconsin Press, 2011).

adoption but also exacerbated the frustration of farmers. The original fixation with model farms and compulsory manual labor also handicapped agricultural education. Such farms demonstrated few exemplary practices, and manual labor continued to be inefficient and resented until it was finally phased out. Gradually and unevenly, solutions to at least some of these difficulties evolved over the first 3 decades of land grant education.[56]

From an early date, the colleges tried to reach farmers directly through farmer's institutes or traveling lectures. By the 1880s, the realization began to sink in that alterations in the curriculum were imperative to reach and accommodate their target constituency. In Wisconsin, where the university's agriculture course had almost no students, the Grange agitated for a separate agricultural college. A trustee committee instead proposed establishing short courses for farmers during the winter and forced the reluctant agriculture professors to offer them (1885). Short courses gradually gained acceptance and were widely adopted. Wisconsin followed this step by organizing a special dairy school to serve creameries and cheese factories, another popular innovation. The University of Minnesota, under similar pressure from agricultural secessionists, established a 2-year School of Agriculture, essentially a high school open to students with only a common school education.[57] Similar schemes became common across agriculture departments, producing a two-tier system of admissions but populating these departments with students for the first time. While model farms were failures, useful knowledge could be gained by well-run experimental farms. Often, as at Wisconsin, the absence of students allowed agricultural professors to devote their time to the farms. States were sympathetic to such activities, and by 1885 agricultural experiment stations were operating in seventeen states with some degree of state support.[58]

In Pennsylvania, legislation to fund an experiment station at Pennsylvania State College was twice vetoed by the governor, in 1883 and 1885. President Atherton turned to Washington, mobilizing land grant college leaders to support the passage of the Hatch Act (1887). This legislation gave each state a $15,000 annual appropriation to operate an agricultural experiment station, which in almost all cases was connected with the land grant college. That same year,

56   True, *Agricultural Education,* quote p. 155 et passim. Voluntary paid labor was a welcome substitute for compulsory manual labor schemes.

57   Curti and Carstensen, *University of Wisconsin,* I, 470–75; Gray, *University of Minnesota,* 94–98. In 1900 the College of Agriculture had 27 students and the Agriculture School, 517.

58   The first agricultural experiment station was established in Connecticut in 1875. Their popularity derived from testing fertilizers, not scientific research: Alan I. Marcus, *Agricultural Science and the Quest for Legitimacy: Farmers, Agricultural Colleges, and Experiment Stations, 1870–1890* (Ames: Iowa State University Press, 1985), 71–77, et passim.

Atherton convened a meeting that transformed the periodic gatherings of land grant leaders into a permanent organization—the Association of American Agricultural Colleges and Experiment Stations. This organization allowed successful practices to be communicated and facilitated cooperation in establishing common standards for admissions and degrees. It also served as a potent lobbyist. These years marked the high tide of agriculture's influence in Congress. In 1890, Atherton mobilized the association presidents and worked tirelessly himself to assist Justin Morrill in passing the Second Morrill Act, which provided annual subsidies to land grant universities of $15,000, rising to $25,000, for general operations. The land grant colleges were no longer struggling institutions.[59]

The Hatch Act not only funded but also legitimized agricultural research as a core function of land grant colleges. However, at the same time it reenergized agricultural critics of the colleges who were incensed that additional funds were directed to institutions that, in their view, neglected farming and farmers. In states where a land grant unit had been appended to a traditional university, they had reason to complain. The University of Mississippi, for example, lacked resources and students to teach agriculture and was not displeased to see this burden moved to a new A&M college in Starkville (1880: later, Mississippi State University). In North and (especially) South Carolina, removal resulted from bitter campaigns against the universities. Although the University of North Carolina attempted to support agriculture with its meager resources, agricultural interests mounted a determined campaign to establish their own land grant institution. In 1887 they were joined by North Carolina populists and succeeded in removing land grant revenues to an A&M college (later, North Carolina State University). UNC president Kemp Plumer Battle regretted the loss of income but not "the constant demand to build stables and work shops." In South Carolina, demagogue Ben "Pitchfork" Tillman opposed the University of South Carolina as much for its association with the old ruling class as for its glaring neglect of agriculture. The university appeared to emerge from its tumultuous postwar struggles when it was reorganized in 1888, the same year that Thomas Clemson bequeathed his fortune and estate to establish an agricultural college. As soon as he was elected governor in 1890, Tillman transferred the land grant and federal appropriations to the new Clemson Agricultural College.[60]

59   Appropriations under the Second Morrill Act rose by $1,000 per year: Williams, *Origins of Federal Support*, 87–173.

60   Gelber, *University and the People*, 35–38, quote p. 37; Kemp Plumer Battle, *Memories of an Old-Time Tar Heel* (Chapel Hill: University of North Carolina Press, 1945), 247–54; Jerome V. Reel, *High Seminary: A History of the Clemson Agricultural College of South Carolina* (Clemson University: Clemson University Digital Press, 2011); Daniel Walker Hollis, *University of South Carolina: Volume II, College to University* (Columbia: University of South Carolina Press, 1956), 128–58.

This same drama played in New England at a slower tempo. Yale's Sheffield Scientific School, Connecticut's land grant designee, epitomized the national school of science approach. It had few students in agriculture, although many were in engineering, but no farm. But it possessed Samuel Johnson, the foremost agricultural scientist, and was a leader in research. In 1875 the state had established the Connecticut Agricultural Experiment Station, which worked closely with Johnson and Sheffield. In 1881 the state chartered the Storrs Agricultural School, which offered a 2-year course in basic science and practical agriculture to students with common school backgrounds. Thus, the state possessed a full range of basic and applied research and a school for teaching farmers to farm. The Sheffield School nevertheless became a target of grange attacks for its high admission standards and few agricultural graduates. The Hatch Act bounty touched off a campaign to wrest the land grant monies from Yale, and the Second Morrill Act raised the stakes. Given Yale's elite image, its case was not easily defended in the state political arena. In 1893 the land grant designation and revenues were transferred to Storrs. However, to be eligible, what had been a high school for practical farming now had to be elevated to an agricultural college (later, the University of Connecticut). In this higher incarnation, it soon incurred the same grange criticism for inaccessibility, teaching "book farming," and diverting farm boys away from farming. As for Yale, Sheffield was scarcely affected, and the university was ultimately awarded $154,000 in damages. A parallel scenario unfolded in Rhode Island, where an agricultural school was first established in Kingston, and its backers soon challenged Brown for the land grant. Brown had never been given resources for agricultural education, and in 1887 it was ready to concede the piddling endowment revenues to the new school. It reversed itself when funding from the Second Morrill Act was on the table. But, as in Connecticut, state politicians sided with organized agriculture and the Kingston school, which also had to be elevated to college status (later, the University of Rhode Island).[61]

Although these new agricultural colleges would one day become full universities, they were relatively weak institutions for decades. The grangers who hijacked the land grant revenues were the educational Luddites of the era, defying

---

61 Sorber, *Farmers, Scientists*, chapter 4. Ironically, a parallel campaign by the Vermont Grange to wrest the land grant from the University of Vermont was countered by Justin Morrill himself, who was a trustee. Addressing the Vermont legislature in 1890, the 80-year-old Morrill left no doubt that the intent of the land grants was quite opposite what was claimed by the Grange. "The fundamental idea," he explained, was to provide a liberal education to "those needing higher instruction for the world's business, for industrial pursuits." "Not manual, but intellectual instruction was the central object." Moreover, the advancement of science and highly trained graduates were essential for the economic competitiveness of the country: Ibid., 251.

the academic and industrial revolutions taking place around them and, in the name of farmers, imposing regimes with low standards of admission and instruction, vocational instead of professional studies, intended to keep students down on the farm.[62] Of the eleven agricultural and A&M colleges named above, only Purdue and Iowa State could claim parity with their state university counterpart. By 1906, they required a full high school course for admission, had near 1,000 college students and at least 50 faculty. These dimensions made them about two-fifths the size of the land grant universities discussed in the previous section. The other nine colleges all required less than a high school course for admission, still had students below college level, and had enrollments ranging from 49 to 686 and faculties ranging from 11 to 38.[63]

Most of these colleges were handicapped by the control exercised by agricultural interests. Paradoxically, the agricultural nexus provided an enormous stimulus for the land grant institutions that were positioned to exploit it. Hatch Act funds for agricultural experiment stations supplied badly needed dollars to a starved enterprise. More important, the stations established the foundation for sustained advance of agricultural science and practice. For many of these institutions, agriculture became the locus for the first institutionalized academic research, especially after the Adams Act (1906) increased funding and more closely targeted research. The second Morrill Act, too, was largely an achievement of the agricultural interests. It gave significant amounts of funding to these institutions at a critical juncture—the cusp of the academic revolution—a time when expansion was imperative for success. Still, for some, attachment to the grange interpretation of agricultural education remained an incubus that muffled these other benefits. Ironically, the peak of agriculture's influence over the land grant colleges occurred as they began to fulfill their promise as industrial universities—not yet in agriculture but rather in engineering.

ENGINEERING AND THE LAND GRANT COLLEGES

Justin Morrill gave a personal rationale for according the mechanic arts equal billing in the Land Grant Act: "Being myself the son of a hard-handed blacksmith . . . I could not overlook mechanics in any measure intended to aid the industrial classes in the procurement of an education that might exalt their usefulness." Contemporaries would have understood the class of workers to whom

---

62   Scott Gelber presents a more positive portrayal of the Populists' impact on higher education, a political movement that overlapped with the Grange (*University and the People*), but Nathan Sorber portrays the backward-looking motives of the New England agricultural movement (*Farmers, Scientists*).

63   *Bulletin of the Carnegie Foundation for the Advancement of Teaching*, no. 1 (March 1907), 22, 34.

Morrill was referring, but how they might be schooled was no less uncertain than educating farmers. "Mechanics" were associated with the machine shops that complemented the proliferation of textile mills and factories, especially in the Northeast. Essentially skilled artisans, many operated, or aspired to, independent shops. They learned the mechanic arts through immersion in a common shop culture, well removed from colleges or engineering.[64]

It seems doubtful that Morrill was concerned about engineers per se. Civil engineering had become established in the colleges by 1860. In the years surrounding the Civil War, two thirds of prominent civil engineers were college graduates. The different fields of engineering, in fact, developed according to their own internal dynamics. By the 1850s, the needs of the Navy and the railroads for better and more powerful steam engines had spawned the development of "steam engineering," and a few individuals assumed the title of mechanical engineer. However, the field was inchoate at the time of the Land Grant Act, as was its relation to the mechanic arts.[65]

The larger issue was how to join the needs of industrializing America with the capabilities of the colleges and the potential contributions of science. The issue had been addressed in multiple ways before the Civil War, as already seen. However, the models that emerged all bore the limitations of premodern institutions. Following the war, these efforts were expanded and intensified along numerous fronts. The Morrill Act's endorsement of the mechanic arts touched only obliquely on the central issue, but it committed most land grant colleges to finding ways to address the challenge. In the East, schools of science, all dedicated to the practical arts, were appended to Columbia (1864), Lafayette (1866), Dartmouth (1871), Penn (1872), and Princeton (1873). And, new ideas for technological colleges were embodied in Lehigh University (1866), Worcester County Free Institute of Industrial Science (1868, later Worcester Polytechnic Institute), and Stevens Institute of Technology (1871).[66] The school that addressed the challenge most directly and successfully was the Massachusetts Institute of Technology (MIT, 1865), a product of the singular vision and energy of William Barton Rogers.

Rogers was one of four sons of William & Mary science professor Patrick Rogers, all of whom became scientists. He and brother Henry were renowned both for practical geological surveys and theoretical contributions to the field. They also shared a dedication to teaching practical applications of science. As

64   Parker, *Justin Smith Morrill*, 262; Monte A. Calvert, *The Mechanical Engineer in America, 1880–1910: Professional Cultures in Conflict* (Baltimore: Johns Hopkins University Press, 1967), 29–40.

65   Robert V. Bruce, *The Launching of Modern American Science, 1846–1876* (Ithaca: Cornell University Press, 1987), 150–55.

66   Geiger, "Rise and Fall of Useful Knowledge," 153–68.

early as 1846, William had devised "A Plan for a Polytechnic School in Boston." He then married into a wealthy Boston family and left his University of Virginia professorship in 1853. He was by this juncture a leading American scientist, prominent in the principal scientific societies, and now connected with the Brahmin society. He soon utilized these advantages to pursue his dream of bringing "industrial science" to bear on the "useful arts." In 1859 the governor included "educational improvements" in the plans for the new land created by draining Boston's Back Bay. The following year, Rogers formulated a proposal, "*Objects and Plan of an Institute of Technology, including a Society of Arts, a Museum of Arts, and a School of Industrial Science, Proposed to be Established in Boston.*" This comprehensive plan sought to address all facets of elevating the useful arts. The Society of Arts was conceived as a learned society with regular meetings and presentations of expert papers. The Museum was a typical nineteenth-century device for the collection and display of, in this case, examples of current technology for the edification of scientists and practitioners. The School of Industrial Science and Arts was intended to provide advanced scientific instruction for the useful arts. Rogers actually envisioned two schools: a regular day school for qualified students and open evening lectures to provide working people with useful knowledge. Rogers used his social network in 1861 to obtain a charter for the Massachusetts Institute of Technology and a plot of Back Bay land to put it on, subject to raising $100,000 in endowment. [67]

Rogers made little initial progress in obtaining the necessary funds but then received a second break from the Morrill Act. The land grant designation was coveted by Harvard and the Lawrence Scientific School, but when rural interests succeeded in designating the proposed Massachusetts Agricultural College in Amherst, Rogers captured one-third of the endowment for MIT—the only case in which land grant funds were divided between separate institutions of agriculture and the mechanic arts. When he finally secured the requisite private funds in 1863, the Institute became possible. However, the land grant designation shifted the emphasis to the college-level School of Industrial Science. The Society of Arts was actually launched in 1862 (at no cost). It held regular meetings for years and undoubtedly solidified relations with Boston's industrial-scientific community. With funding scarce, the museum had to be deferred, indefinitely as it turned out. Some evening lectures were initially offered for workers, with disappointing results. When MIT opened its Back Bay building in 1866, it was above all a college devoted to advanced scientific instruction applied to technology.

---

67 Julius A. Stratton and Loretta H. Mannix, *Mind and Hand: The Birth of MIT* (Cambridge: MIT Press, 2005); A. J. Angulo, *William Barton Rogers and the Idea of MIT* (Baltimore: Johns Hopkins University Press, 2009).

MIT offered a 4-year course consisting of 2 years of common grounding in math, drawing, physical science, English, and modern languages, followed by 2 years' study in one of six specialized courses: mechanical engineering, civil and topographical engineering, practical chemistry, geology and mining, building and architecture, and general science and literature. The course in architecture was a new departure; the other departments resembled subjects taught elsewhere but with a difference. The MIT curriculum most closely resembled that of the Sheffield School. However, Sheffield offered only 1 year of basic education before specializations. MIT was also distinctive in emphasizing laboratory instruction, a central feature of Rogers' approach. Sheffield utilized a chemical laboratory but relied more heavily on theoretical lectures. Sheffield and MIT were largely alone in considering research to be an integral component of technological education. Charles W. Eliot, former instructor at the Lawrence School and future president of Harvard, joined the original faculty and helped shape the curriculum. Having failed to introduce general education at Lawrence, he strongly supported the 2-year common program at MIT. For advanced studies, he helped organize the chemistry laboratory and, with a colleague, authored a widely adopted text.[68] MIT emerged as a complete and effective embodiment of technological education at a time when other land grant universities were still being organized. Enrollments passed 200 in 1870 and 350 three years later. MIT graduates fanned out across the country, working for railroads, building urban water and sewage systems, and spreading the gospel of technological education. Rogers was debilitated by a stroke in 1868 and ceded direction of the Institute to a colleague, John D. Runkle, who proved a diffident leader. MIT progressed nonetheless on the strong foundation that Rogers had established.[69]

The most ambiguous practical field, at MIT and elsewhere, was mechanical engineering. MIT was unable initially to establish an instructional laboratory. The difficulty was linking formal collegiate instruction with the shop culture of decentralized machine shops. Different approaches were tried, particularly at new institutions. The Worcester Free Institute was organized around a commercial machine shop. Students began by working in the shop and were subsequently given classroom instruction. Fully one-quarter of their time was spent in the shops, which produced and sold commercial products. The Worcester

---

68 Hugh Hawkins, *Between Harvard and America: The Educational Leadership of Charles W. Eliot* (New York: Oxford University Press, 1972), 33–38. By 1884 the School of Industrial Science offered ten courses (majors) with some specialization in the first 2 years: Massachusetts Institute of Technology, *Twentieth Annual Catalogue, 1884–1885* (Boston: 1884).

69 Stratton and Mannix, *Mind and Hand*, 450–51, 523–29, 533–76; Angulo, *William Barton Rogers*, 124–52; Philip N. Alexander, *A Widening Sphere: Evolving Cultures at MIT* (Cambridge: MIT Press, 2011), 47–99.

approach retained its admirers into the 1880s, when the new Georgia Institute of Technology (f. 1885) sought to duplicate it exactly. Worcester established a regular engineering course by the end of the decade but still retained the commercial shops.[70]

Cornell had the opportunity to define this discipline when Hiram Sibley's gift established the Sibley College of Mechanic Arts (1871). It hired John Edson Sweet, an outspoken proponent of shop culture. The school offered a robust hands-on immersion in the mechanic arts, though for instructional rather than commercial purposes. Its graduates received a bachelor's of mechanical engineering. After the mercurial Sweet resigned in 1878, the department drifted amidst student unhappiness with slack standards and teaching. This situation was rectified in 1885 with another Sibley donation and the hiring of Robert Thurston.[71]

At the 1876 Centennial Exposition in Philadelphia, the Russian exhibition presented a curriculum for teaching generic skills employed in all mechanical trades. Besides drawing, students successively learned carpentry, wood turning, the use of forges, and, finally, machine shop operations. MIT's Runkle regarded this approach as the inspiration for mechanical laboratories that he had been seeking and established the School of Mechanic Arts on this basis. An engineering course at Washington University in Saint Louis was established on the same basis. In 1883, latecomer Pennsylvania State College sent a young instructor to MIT to learn this system and in 1886 implemented it with a new mechanic arts building. By this date, however, its limitations were becoming evident. At MIT the mechanic arts school did not rise to Rogers' standard of industrial science. It was offered to younger students as a nonacademic secondary course, and the school was closed in 1887. But the shops endured. Penn State soon did the same. These basic mechanic arts, woodworking and metal shop, remained in the engineering curriculum. A report in 1918 found "mechanic arts . . . work itself is seldom recognized as being of 'university grade.' Yet no one denies that it is an essential element in the equipment of every engineer."[72]

What soon emerged as a superior course in mechanical engineering was devised by Robert H. Thurston at Stevens Institute of Technology in the 1870s. Thurston, a civil engineering graduate of Brown (1859), learned mechanical engineering first in industry and then in the Navy, becoming an instructor at Annapolis after the Civil War. When Stevens Tech was founded in 1871, dedicated

---

70 Calvert, *Mechanical Engineer*, 57, 78–80.
71 Ibid., 87–96.
72 Solberg, *University of Illinois*, 140–42; Alexander, *Widening Sphere*, 73–74; Michael Bezilla, *Engineering at Penn State* (University Park: Pennsylvania State University Press, 1981), 15–18; Charles Riborg Mann, *A Study of Engineering Education*, Carnegie Foundation for the Advancement of Teaching, Bulletin 11 (New York: 1918), 75.

to advancing instruction and research in mechanical engineering, Thurston was hired and given the resources to achieve these goals.[73] He reviewed engineering schools in France and Germany, but he ultimately fashioned a system based on engineering practice in the United States. His 4-year curriculum began with basic concepts like strength, elasticity, and friction and then advanced to machinery and power, prime movers like steam engines, and, finally, applications to railroads, ships, and factories. Basic courses in math and science accompanied this progression, and teaching was rooted in instructional laboratories. Thurston exemplified the mechanical engineering elite, an organizer and first president of the American Society of Mechanical Engineers (1880–1883). He broadcast his views in extensive writings on engineering education and projected the image of a high-status engineering profession in partnership with captains of industry. Students trained purely in mechanic arts, on the other hand, would at best supervise shops. In 1885, Thurston felt constrained by limited resources at Stevens, and Andrew White sought to resolve the malaise of Cornell engineering. With additional resources from the Sibley family, Thurston installed his system of engineering laboratories and raised academic standards, soon making Cornell the foremost school of mechanical engineering. Renowned nationally and internationally, Thurston proselytized the gospel of engineering laboratories and research to other land grant engineering schools.[74]

Thurston's combination of science and instructional laboratories gradually prevailed in American engineering schools, but it did not entirely displace the shop culture. Thurston's approach managed to incorporate the socialization process that was at the heart of shop culture. More science and mathematics were taught, but the shops and forges of the mechanic arts remained a part of the curriculum well into the twentieth century. Mechanical engineering brought hands-on laboratory instruction into the heart of the college curriculum in ways that distant agricultural farms could not. Still, the pull of academic science continued to require increasing academic rigor, led by the engineering demands of industry.

Mining became the first branch of engineering to draw extensively on emerging scientific fields. Thomas Eggleston Jr., a wealthy New Yorker and Yale graduate (1855), spent 5 years in Paris studying at the École des Mines and, upon his return, convinced the Columbia trustees in 1864 to open the School of Mines as a separate,

---

73   Edwin A. Stevens bequeathed $600,000 to endow an institution of learning, which the trustees determined would be an institute of technology. As president they appointed Henry Morton of the Franklin Institute, who chose to devote the institute to mechanical engineering: William Frederick Durand, *Robert Henry Thurston: A Biography* (New York: American Society of Mechanical Engineers, 1929), 61–64.

74   Gregory Zieren, "Robert H. Thurston, Modern Engineering Education, and Its Diffusion through Land-Grant Universities," in Geiger and Sorber, eds., *Land-Grant Colleges*, 195–214; Calvert, *Mechanical Engineer*, 97–105.

proprietary venture. Launched on a shoestring, the school tapped the needs of a booming mining industry for expertise in geology, chemistry, and mineralogy. Led by an outstanding chemist and academic entrepreneur, Charles Frederick Chandler, and committed to rigorous academic standards, the school's enrollments soon exceeded those of Columbia College, and it was quickly incorporated into the university. Although mining engineering was offered widely, demand was sparse, and the Columbia School of Mines dominated the field. As of 1892, the school had awarded 402 of 871 mining degrees, with MIT a distant second.[75]

Electricity had long been taught as part of physics, but in the 1880s it was redefined as a course in electrical engineering. That decade witnessed a revolution in electrical technologies, as the telephone, electric lighting, and electric power generation all came of age. Thomas Edison, famous for his nonacademic approach to invention, led the latter two developments, but Alexander Graham Bell worked closely with scientists at MIT. Behind these technologies, however, lay earlier scientific breakthroughs; and their further development required additional scientific progress. University departments of physics and engineering were actively experimenting in the 1870s. In the next decade these individual investigations were organized into courses for electrical engineers and then departments of electrical engineering, with varying chronologies. MIT organized the first EE course in 1882 but did not form a department until 1902. Earlier departments were formed at the University of Missouri (1886), Purdue (Applied Electricity, 1887), Cornell (1889), and Wisconsin (1891). Unlike mechanical engineering, the objectives, opportunities, and technology were readily apparent, and academic development was, accordingly, swift. Moreover, academic requirements in physics and mathematics also escalated, especially with the onset of alternating current systems. MIT led all other universities in science and application, soon establishing active relationships with American Bell Telephone Company and General Electric (f. 1892).[76]

Engineering students appeared serious and dedicated to their studies—a marked contrast to the growing fixation on extracurricular activities of contemporary collegians. Math and science courses required more application than traditional recitations and more readily exposed slackers. Engineering students also spent considerable time in laboratory work (Thurston recommended 40 percent). They were treated differently as well, with no parietal rules or compulsory chapel, even in the scientific schools of colleges. At the Columbia School of Mines,

75   Robert A. McCaughey, *Stand Columbia* (New York: Columbia University Press, 2003), 152–55; Bruce, *Launching*, 331–32.

76   Karl L. Wildes and Nilo A. Lindgren, *A Century of Electrical Engineering and Computer Science at MIT, 1882–1982* (Cambridge: MIT Press, 1985), 16–30; Knoll, *Story of Purdue Engineering*, 262–72.

students apparently relished 8 straight hours of labs and classes. For its first three decades, MIT enrolled a large minority of older, special students who sought particular skills rather than the full course. In this sense, the institute served Morrill's industrial classes or, as one Harvardian put it, "a class of students who rarely find their way to Cambridge."[77] Whether obtaining a degree or not, its students manifested deep loyalties to the institute and an eagerness to assist it as alums.

The depression that struck in 1873 dampened postbellum enthusiasm for utilitarian higher education. Engineering colleges and courses struggled for a decade with curricular uncertainty and low enrollments. By the middle of the 1880s, however, engineering entered a period of accelerating growth—in enrollments, faculty, facilities, and offerings. Engineering graduates rose from fewer than 4,000 in the 1880s to more than 10,000 in the 1890s and double that number in the following decade. Land grant universities experienced a surge of engineering students in the 1890s. Ironically, many "agricultural colleges" became predominantly engineering schools. At middecade, the majority of students at Illinois and Cornell were in engineering; two-thirds at Penn State and four-fifths at Purdue. Enrollments continued to boom through the next decade, rising to 30 percent of students at California and Michigan in 1909, for example. At this point, growth slowed. Engineering educators speculated that potential students were drawn instead to agriculture and commerce, that rising admissions standards were thinning enrollees, or that students feared engineering had become overcrowded.[78] However, other conditions may have affected the rising tide of aspiring engineers.

Large enrollments in engineering did not translate directly into graduates. Only 40 percent of enrolled students were graduating, circa 1915, an improvement over an estimate of 25 percent before 1900. Almost half of this attrition occurred in the first year, and one-quarter occurred in the second, that is, before students experienced real engineering courses. Moreover, the status of graduates was equivocal as well. Before 1900 it was widely held that graduates had to enter the shops and work their way up like anyone else, and skepticism about the value of school culture persisted into the twentieth century. Surveys found no correlation between high grades in engineering courses and ratings in the workplace. In a survey of 120 employers, just one-half preferred college graduates to men trained through practical experience—and one-third preferred the latter. As late as 1916, 43 percent of the "technical men" in U.S. manufacturing industries were graduate engineers.

77   Hawkins, *Between Harvard*, 35.
78   Mann, *Engineering Education*, 7; Slosson, *Great American Universities*; "Is Attendance at Engineering Schools Falling Off?" *Bulletin of the Society for the Promotion of Engineering Education*, IV, 3 (Nov. 1913): 18–24.

However, a finer-grained look at this situation presents a different picture. Engineers were clearly more vital to "high-tech" industries, led by 87 percent graduate employees in metal refining. Conversely, the proportion of engineers was lowest in mechanical industries like automobiles and the still-decentralized machine tool shops. Engineering leaders testified that "younger men with theoretical training" were far superior to those with older and weaker educations and would soon displace them. They also noted that firms were now actively recruiting students from graduating classes, disproving the belief that graduates were worthless before acquiring practical experience.[79] Engineering schools established close relationships with American industry that strengthened over time.

Unlike agriculture, engineering always had a presence and drew support from the private sector. The first large-scale philanthropy for American higher education was directed toward furthering education in the practical arts. The donations of industrialist Abbott Lawrence, Joseph Sheffield, Ezra Cornell, and Hiram Sibley have already been described, as well as later scientific schools named for their donors. In 1866 Asa Packer, a successful entrepreneur in coal and railroads, founded Lehigh University as a "polytechnic college" with a $500,000 gift, and Stevens Institute of Technology was founded with a bequest of $600,000 from the estate of Edwin A. Stevens. Later in the decade, Leonard Case Jr. made the gift that founded the Case School of Applied Science (now Case Western Reserve University). For the most part these were acts of faith, no less than the Morrill Act, in future contributions to industrial development. Once established, engineering schools benefited from gifts of machinery and material from firms that took increasing interest in their work and the research that Thurston-style laboratories could perform. MIT established the earliest and closest ties with industry, receiving support for courses and research from AT&T and founding the Research Laboratory for Applied Chemistry to perform industrial research (1908). The engineering departments of state and private universities created the earliest nexus between higher education and the American industrial revolution. A slender thread at first, it grew selectively among emerging high-tech industries and the infrastructure of a burgeoning urban economy. By the end of the 1910s, these bonds would be celebrated in American society, vindicating the nineteenth-century prophets who sought to join the colleges with industry and the industrial classes.[80]

79   Mann, *Engineering Education*, 19–20, 32–36; "Attendance at Engineering Schools," 22–23.

80   W. Ross Yates, *Lehigh University: A History of Education in Engineering, Business, and the Human Condition* (Bethlehem: Lehigh University Press, 1992); David F. Noble, *America by Design* (New York: Oxford University Press, 1977), 137–41 et passim.

THE CREATION OF AMERICAN
UNIVERSITIES

"A" UNIVERSITY, IN ANY WORTHY SENSE OF THE TERM, must grow from seed. It cannot be transplanted from England or Germany," wrote Charles W. Eliot in 1869.[1] The United States in the 1860s had many institutions that bore the name of university, including the one over which Eliot was about to preside, but he was right in asserting that none merited the term and more prescient in sensing that the country would have to evolve its own version of that ideal. Notions of universities dated from the dawn of the Republic; however, by this date they encompassed breadth and depth of knowledge—the study of all significant realms of learning to the most advanced level of current understanding. This had four implications for American institutions—a commitment to the advancement of knowledge through original investigations, a corresponding capacity for training advanced scholars, broad coverage of academic fields, including the professions, and incorporation with collegiate education. Initiatives in all these areas were present in the United States but, despite occasional links, largely existed independently.

Roughly half of antebellum scientists were employed in colleges, but most of the scientific community looked to government bureaus as the setting most suitable for research. A handful of aspiring scholars had long sought out academic mentors for individual study, but attempts to systematize graduate education produced "a wealth of inconsistent precedents."[2] The dominant pattern was advanced study in Europe, increasingly in Germany. Professional education, with the partial exception of theology, grew progressively estranged from the colleges during most of the nineteenth century and similarly distanced from the frontiers of knowledge. Finally, the American college loomed as the most awkward piece of the university puzzle. Undergraduate education was the overwhelming

---

1 Charles W. Eliot, "The New Education: Its Organization," *Atlantic Monthly*, XXIII (Feb. and Mar. 1869): 203–20, 358–67.

2 Richard J. Storr, *The Beginnings of Graduate Education in America* (Chicago: University of Chicago Press, 1953), 132.

mission of the colleges, and their students lacked both preparation for and interest in advanced learning. Those familiar with German universities likened the American college course to the last 3 years of the Gymnasium (classical secondary school), broaching academic subjects only in the upper classes. As long as higher education was defined by the collegiate course, the university ideal was indeed remote. Conversely, any approach that ignored the undergraduate college was doomed to failure. For an American university to "grow out of the soil" would mean knitting together research, graduate education, advanced knowledge, and the college.

THE FIRST PHASE

Aspects of the university ideal had stirred the imaginations of academic reformers at least since the 1850s. The initiatives described in chapter 6 aimed to broaden the curriculum and overcome the rigidities of the classical course. Henry Tappan articulated a clear notion of a university and implemented practical measures to move the University of Michigan in that direction. By the end of the 1860s, however, the issue had become more urgent. The Morrill Act had forced the incorporation of new subjects, albeit in ways that were still contested. The prowess of German universities in advancing academic scholarship was increasingly evident, as was the inadequacy of American efforts. These circumstances inspired the first principal university architects—Andrew Dickson White, Charles W. Eliot, and Daniel Coit Gilman. Each was connected with a land grant institution. Each had first-hand experience of European universities. None was an original scholar himself, but each had deep appreciation for scholarship and similar determination that it should inform undergraduate education. Most significant, each formulated and implemented a distinctive conception of the American university.

White's founding of Cornell has been described as part of the land grant movement. With the stimulus of the Morrill Act, White shaped the first new model for collegiate education since Thomas Jefferson opened the University of Virginia. White's guiding principles were the equivalence of practical and theoretical studies and the freedom for students to choose their courses of study. The first of these was embedded in the Morrill Act and was the overriding aim of Ezra Cornell, too, but White managed the most complete and successful integration of the different courses of study. He had a broad view of what Laurence Veysey has called "utility," including modern literature and history.[3] The academic structure

---

3   Laurence Veysey's concept of utility encompasses the broadening of curriculum to include practical subjects as well as a wider range of elective academic subjects: *The Emergence of the American University* (Chicago: University of Chicago Press, 1965), 81–98.

of Cornell also permitted the ready incorporation of additional fields, such as veterinary science, electrical engineering, and pharmacy. Cornell pioneered one version of an elective system, variously called the group or major system. Believing strongly in student choice of studies, White held that the university was responsible for structuring classes only within a chosen field. In practice, most courses were prescribed for at least the first 2 years. White elevated the mandate of the Morrill Act to the "Cornell Idea," but his conception of the American university was largely about undergraduate education.[4]

White had dreamed of an American university since his college days. He admired the inspiring architecture and the intense social life fostered in Oxbridge residential colleges. In Paris he discovered the "clearness, breadth, [and] wealth of illustration" of the French university-lecture system. And at the University of Berlin, he found his "ideal of a university not only realized, but extended and glorified." This ideal, however, reflected the lecture halls and not the seminars: White apparently failed to appreciate the imperative to discover new knowledge that inspired the entire enterprise. His formative experience came instead from the University of Michigan, where he taught history from 1857 to 1864. He credited Tappan with "the real beginning of a university in the United States, in the modern sense." But it was a truncated beginning, cut short when Tappan was fired by political foes. From Michigan, and also from the Yale Scientific School, he grasped the effectiveness of allowing students to choose among different courses of study. Negatively, he concluded from the Michigan example that the American university must be privately controlled and from the stodgy Congregationalism of Yale that it must be resolutely nonsectarian.[5]

White's apparent unconcern for research or graduate education no doubt reflected the unsettled state of midcentury academic opinion. His primary objective was to educate men of character, the future leaders of government and society. In his inaugural address he declared that the university had no place for pedants. He later supported reviving the idea of a national university as a locus for advanced academic scholarship. White possessed, nonetheless, a deep respect for learning and admiration for the leading academic figures of his time. He instinctively committed to bringing the world's knowledge to the university in preference to creating new knowledge. A lifelong bibliophile, White assiduously built Cornell's library collections. Inviting distinguished nonresident professors

4   Morris Bishop, *A History of Cornell* (Ithaca: Cornell University Press, 1962), 153–79.

5   Andrew Dickson White, *Autobiography*, 2 vol. (New York: Century, 1905), I, 289–93. White had sought an appointment at Yale before taking the Michigan position but was apparently rejected because of his liberal religious views. He was offered a Yale position in 1866 but chose to lead Cornell: Glenn C. Altschuler, *Andrew D. White—Educator, Historian, Diplomat* (Ithaca: Cornell University Press, 1979), 36–65.

to campus served the same purpose. These esteemed American academics rec-reated the magic of Berlin and Paris lecture halls in bucolic Ithaca. The atten-dant social occasions allowed the Cornell community to bask in the intellec-tual ambience of the great men. Beyond major subjects and technical courses, White fashioned a university engaged with contemporary scientific and literary thought.[6]

In May 1869, Charles W. Eliot was confirmed as the new president of Har-vard University. At 34 years of age, Eliot was the university's youngest president, and his 40-year tenure would make him the longest serving as well. The most influential educator of his era, the evolution of his views and his subsequent ac-complishments tend to obscure his initial intentions and the prospects for re-form at the end of the 1860s.[7]

The Eliot family had served Harvard since before the Revolution, Charles's father as treasurer (1843–1854). Charles (H.1853) became a tutor, then assistant professor of chemistry (1854–1863), but when passed over for the chair in chem-istry, he forfeited his university position. He had sought in vain to establish a foundational curriculum in the Lawrence School and admirably organized its chemical laboratory, but he was undistinguished as a chemist and was displaced by Wolcott Gibbs, America's most accomplished research chemist. Eliot took his family to Europe for the next 2 years. Instead of studying chemistry, however, he examined the educational system of France and then the operations of German universities. He admired the depth and breadth of learning he found in Paris and Germany but considered the institutions quite inappropriate as models for America. A professorship in chemistry at MIT brought Eliot back to Boston. Impressed by the effectiveness of technical institutes in Europe, he devoted him-self to shaping technical education in the institute. He also remained connected with his Harvard associates and was named to the Board of Overseers in 1868.

The following year he published a two-part overview of the "New Educa-tion" in the *Atlantic Monthly* that solidified his credentials as a reformer—New England style. He asserted the legitimacy of the new education "based chiefly upon the pure and applied sciences, the living European languages, and mathe-matics"; however, he dismissed the land grant institutions (and, by implication, Cornell) as too young to merit consideration.[8] Much like White, Eliot denied

6   Bishop, *Cornell*, 89 et passim; Altschuler, *Andrew D. White*, 181–84.

7   Samuel Eliot Morison, *Three Centuries of Harvard* (Cambridge: Harvard University Press, 1936), 322–99; Hugh Hawkins, *Between Harvard and America: The Educational Leadership of Charles W. Eliot* (New York: Oxford University Press, 1972); Henry James, *Charles W. Eliot, President of Harvard Univer-sity, 1869–1909*, 2 vol. (Boston: Houghton Mifflin, 1930).

8   Eliot praised Connecticut and New Hampshire for awarding the land grant to Yale and Dart-mouth, respectively, but otherwise was a severe critic of publicly supported higher education, most

that "mental training afforded by a good polytechnic school is necessarily inferior in any respect to that of a good college." But unlike White, he insisted that
"the practical spirit and the literary or scholastic spirit are . . . incompatible. If
comingled, they are both spoiled." He specifically charged that was the case at
the University of Michigan. Hence, he saved the most fulsome praise for a 4-year
technical course of the sort he had advocated at Lawrence and helped to create
at MIT. Throughout Eliot's tone was prophetic, envisaging an American system
of higher education in rapid evolution toward a "real university," where "every
subject should be taught . . . on a higher plane than elsewhere."

The Harvard Corporation's election of Eliot reflected their frustration with
more than 2 decades of ineffectual leadership and recognition that modernization was now imperative. Their choice was vindicated by the vision of the university portrayed in Eliot's magisterial inaugural address. He began by sweeping
aside the long-running controversies over practical and liberal subjects, saying
"we would have them all, and at their best." The challenge "is not what to teach,
but how to teach." His survey of the educational system identified need for improvement at every level. For Harvard College, Eliot's dominant emphasis on
teaching had three implications. First, he believed that students should have the
freedom to choose those subjects that best fit their interests and abilities. Second, this belief led to an unequivocal endorsement of the elective system. Eliot
noted that Harvard students could choose some of their subjects in their last 3
years, but, in fact, these were limited to options specific to each of those classes
(sophomores, etc.). He now committed the college to "persevere in its efforts to
establish, improve, and extend the elective system." Third, Eliot recognized that
"the University as a place of study and instruction is, at any moment, what the
Faculties make of it." Hence, the necessity of improving the quality of the faculty despite the difficulty of finding and attracting highly qualified individuals.
Eliot promised to increase professorial stipends and, in a huge understatement,
make "the professors' labors more agreeable" by offering a greater variety of elective courses. However, Eliot also revealed the limits of his purview; he noted
that although "the strongest and most devoted professors" might "contribute
something to the patrimony of knowledge," or more likely "do something toward
defending, interpreting, or diffusing the contributions of others. Nevertheless,
the prime business of American professors in this generation must be regular
and assiduous class teaching." Harvard possessed no endowments "intended to
secure to men of learning the leisure and means to prosecute original researches."

notoriously at the 1873 meeting of the National Education Association: Roger L. Williams, *The Origins of Federal Support for Higher Education: George W. Atherton and the Land-Grant College Movement* (University Park: Pennsylvania State University Press, 1991), 64–74.

Eliot was determined to strengthen teaching at the university, and he began the process immediately with the professional schools.

Eliot remarked in the "New Education" that "the term 'learned profession' was getting to have a sarcastic flavor." Professional degrees in law and medicine, in fact, represented "decidedly less culture" than did the AB. In Eliot's conception of a university, professional and utilitarian subjects should follow a general, liberal education. Making a bachelor's degree a prerequisite for professional schools was clearly a long-range goal in 1870, and Eliot was virtually alone among reformers in advocating it. But first it was necessary to address the abominable conditions in existing professional schools. None of Harvard's autonomous professional schools had requirements for admission. A degree in divinity could be obtained by 3 years' residence without an examination; a law degree by three terms (18 months), also without examination; and an MD by two terms of attendance and passing five of nine 10-minute oral examinations. The crying need was for admission standards to ensure competent students, a graded system of courses, enforced with examinations, and professional instructors to replace the practitioner-professors.

Early in 1870, the university statutes were revised to establish deans in each of the professional schools and to require examinations for degrees. Eliot succeeded in installing his supporters as deans, and revolutions ensued. In law the new professor and dean was Christopher Columbus Langdell, who believed that the law should be a science constructed from the analysis of decisions in previous cases. Langdell and other new appointees successfully implemented the case method, which gradually became the foundation of law school pedagogy. More immediately, they established a graded structure of courses with examinations required for advancement. Admissions were tightened in 1875 to require either a college degree or passing an entrance examination. The Harvard law school thus moved toward Eliot's model of professional education long before other institutions.[9]

Reforming the larger medical school was a more difficult undertaking, with higher stakes. "The ignorance and general incompetency of the average graduate of American Medical Schools," Eliot wrote, "is something horrible to contemplate," and Harvard products were no exception. Eliot soon convinced the Overseers of the necessity of reform. The school was incorporated into the university, placing the professors on salary and ending its proprietary nature. A 3-year graded course was established, accompanied by examinations, and admissions standards were gradually raised. Enrollments suffered but only in the short term. Harvard would lead the ongoing modernization of American medical schools

9   Bruce A. Kimball, *The Inception of Modern Professional Education: C. C. Langdell, 1826–1906* (Chapel Hill: University of North Carolina Press, 2009).

for the next 4 decades. At the end of his career, Eliot named the reformation of the professional schools as among the most significant achievements of his 40-year presidency.[10]

He moved with similar decisiveness to establish the elective system. Throughout American colleges, subjects were identified by the class year and usually by the texts to be covered. Eliot transformed the subjects into courses identified by department, number, and instructor, and he opened the courses to qualified students from any class. This was the distinctive feature of Eliot's system of "free electives," compared with course options offered elsewhere.[11] Beginning in 1872, Eliot abolished the curricular walls that had separated each of the classes—a radical change in the traditional fabric of college life. A second jarring break with tradition had to wait until 1884, when the freshman year was opened to electives by eliminating compulsory Latin and Greek. This was the most controversial step in establishing the free elective system, generating criticism among the governing boards and alumni and from other New England colleges. But once he had weathered this storm, Eliot emerged as a patriarchal leader. The last required subjects were eliminated in the 1890s. To graduate from Harvard College, a student need take only eighteen courses of his own choosing but all of a liberal nature. Eliot now believed that this should be done in 3 rather than 4 years. He reasoned that with college becoming a precursor to professional education, formal schooling took too long. His advocacy of a 3-year degree, however, found few sympathizers. Roughly 30 percent of Harvard graduates nevertheless followed this pattern in the final 2 decades of Eliot's presidency, before the practice was repudiated by his successor.

The greatest benefit of the elective system stemmed from granting professors opportunities to teach their subjects on an advanced level, which allowed them to develop and convey their specialized expertise. Eliot recognized this from the outset but had difficulty connecting this insight with graduate education and research. His initial attempt to offer lecture series on advanced subjects failed. He adapted by establishing the graduate department, which resembled arrangements at Yale that he had praised in the "New Education." Harvard discontinued awarding the AM "in course" (to Harvard graduates after 3 years and payment of $5) and instituted earned graduate degrees. However, at first graduate students merely took additional college courses or studied special topics on their own. In 1875 courses "primarily for graduates" appeared in the catalogue, and a decade

10   Morison, *Three Centuries*, 338–41; Frederick C. Shattuck and J. Lewis Bremer, "The Medical School, 1869–1929," in Samuel Eliot Morison, ed., *Development of Harvard University since the Inauguration of President Eliot, 1869–1929* (Cambridge: Harvard University Press, 1930), 555–94, quote p. 556; James, *Eliot*, II, 170–71.

11   Hawkins, *Between Harvard*, 80–119; Morison, *Three Centuries*, 341–47: Andrew D. White strongly resented that Eliot claimed (and was generally accorded) credit for establishing the elective system.

later "special instruction" by professors appeared. Harvard averaged just five doctorates per year until 1890, when the inadequacy of graduate study caused further reorganization. That year the Lawrence School was, for all practical purposes, folded into a new Faculty of Arts and Sciences, with a parallel Graduate School of Arts and Sciences. Courses were now designated as being for undergraduates, for both undergraduates and graduates, or for graduates; for the first time instruction in research was recognized.

Before 1880 Eliot, as he had in his inaugural speech, subordinated research in his plan for Harvard University. Harvard possessed greater infrastructure for scientific research than any other American university, with special collections, museums, and the Harvard Observatory. However, the faculty Eliot inherited was a combination of eminent scientists and scholars and timeserving alumni pedagogues. During his first decade, Eliot did nothing to change this. Faithful to his focus on teaching, he largely ignored professional credentials in expanding the faculty. He favored personal acquaintances, like Langdell and his cousin Charles Eliot Norton, both of whom succeeded brilliantly; but such an approach was a step backward toward the Brahmin era. Although the elective system demanded a large faculty, Eliot was constrained by a limited budget to hire mostly junior faculty. These hires inadvertently bolstered the professional credentials of the faculty, since increasing numbers of young Americans had studied in Germany and wished to pursue academic careers, especially at Harvard.

Eliot's disregard for academic research changed abruptly in 1879, when he suddenly found himself competing for faculty with the new Johns Hopkins University—the first glimmer of an academic market. Eliot had to offer promotions and opportunities for research to retain several outstanding faculty members. He lured Sanskrit scholar Charles Lanman from Hopkins in 1880 with the promise of sabbatical leaves—another first. To uphold the assumed academic preeminence of Harvard University, he now looked to recruit academic stars, especially from Europe. Although few Europeans were actually hired, Eliot had to utilize the expertise of his faculty to identify the talents he sought. In the 1880s, he began a concerted effort to terminate those faculty members of the old sort who had not achieved professional distinction. Although this was done on an individual basis, and exceptions were numerous, it amounted to an implicit policy of "up or out." The impact of Eliot's new approach was soon evident: whereas one-half of the faculty held PhDs in 1880, two-thirds did so in 1892, and most of them had received at least part of their training elsewhere.[12] That same

---

12   Robert A. McCaughey, "The Transformation of American Academic Life: Harvard University, 1821–1892," *Perspectives in American History*, VIII (1974): 239–332.

year, Eliot announced that Harvard was "now well on the way to the complete organization of a university in a true sense."[13] Indeed it was—but chiefly because Johns Hopkins and the academic revolution had forced him to recognize the imperative role of research.

★ ★ ★

The Johns Hopkins University was made possible by the bequest of its bachelor Quaker benefactor, given its orientation by the trustees' determination to establish a new departure in American higher education, and realized by Daniel Coit Gilman's inspired leadership. Hopkins's will gave $7 million to be divided evenly between a university and a hospital, joined by a medical department. The will's trustees were expected to devise a university but were given no guidance and lacked any experience in this area. They felt that the largest gift in the history of American higher education deserved an institution of comparable significance. They recognized the absence of an institution at the highest level, with teachers capable of adding "something by their writings and discoveries to the world's stock of literature and science." For guidance they consulted with presidents White, Eliot, and Michigan's James B. Angell. White made encouraging suggestions from his experience at Cornell, Angell was skeptical, and Eliot could not imagine more than a fledgling regional college in Baltimore. But all agreed that the best person to lead such a venture was Gilman.[14]

The presidency of Johns Hopkins was Gilman's third attempt to define an American university. At Yale, Gilman had filled a variety of positions, but he identified chiefly with the Sheffield School, where he served as secretary of the governing board. He had promoted Sheffield's integration of the practical arts with research and graduate study as a template for "national schools of science" under the Morrill Act. He was the choice of reform-minded alumni for the Yale presidency in 1871 but, unlike Harvard, the Yale governing board chose an outspoken traditionalist in Noah Porter. With national schools of science on the defensive in the land grant movement and now out of favor at Yale, Gilman accepted the call to California. There he envisioned building a modern university, encompassing all practical and liberal arts, extending through advanced studies and research and especially tailored to the unique attributes of the state.

---

13   Morison, *Three Centuries*, 361.

14   Hugh Hawkins, *Pioneer: A History of the Johns Hopkins University, 1874–1889* (Ithaca: Cornell University Press, 1960), 3–20, quote from trustee George William Brown (1869), p. 6. Eliot had advised against both graduate education and the elective system; Gilman had written to White, his Yale classmate, in 1874 to signal his willingness to leave the University of California, and White recommended him in particularly strong terms.

Disillusioned by populist attacks, Gilman gladly accepted the offer of the Hopkins trustees. Initially, he envisioned a national institution limited to graduate education and advanced scholarship. This notion provoked a storm of criticism in Baltimore (endowed institutions are not immune to popular opinion). He and the trustees consequently included undergraduates in this graduate university. Research and graduate education had been central to all three of Gilman's conceptions of an American university. Johns Hopkins opened in 1876 as a unique experiment in which they would be the chief focus.[15]

Active scientists and scholars greeted the prospect of the new university enthusiastically, but few senior figures could be induced to join. Instead, the Hopkins faculty was filled with promising younger academics eager for the opportunity to advance their fields.[16] To attract advanced students, the university created graduate fellowships for promising candidates intending to pursue academic careers. The response demonstrated that Hopkins filled a lacuna in American higher education. More than a hundred qualified candidates applied, prompting the trustees to increase the number of fellows from ten to twenty. Four fellows were already PhD and thus became the country's first postdocs. They soon joined the faculty as associates, which was one of the aims of the fellowships. All but Charles Lanman spent their careers on the Hopkins faculty. Other fellows had successful university careers. The fellowships contributed significantly to the initial success of graduate education at Hopkins, creating a critical mass of scholars and a distinctive culture of learning.

Talented aspiring academics flocked to Hopkins as the only university promoting advanced scholarship. A handful of other universities offered graduate work mainly to their own graduates, and none offered fellowships to outsiders. Hopkins fellows like Lanman, who refused a tutorship at Yale, sought an alternative to the drudgery of teaching recitations to unruly collegians. Gilman, for his part, provided all possible assistance for faculty and students. He funded scientists to purchase the latest equipment for their laboratories and aggressively built library collections for literary scholars. He far outdid White by bringing in guest lecturers on a regular basis for varying stays. He also accorded scholars and departments complete freedom to organize their activities—an approach unprecedented for its time. Hopkins opened in 1876 with 54 graduate students and 12 undergraduates. Departmental autonomy produced a disorganized curriculum

15   Hawkins, *Pioneer*, 21–37; Daniel Coit Gilman, "The University of California in Its Infancy" in *University Problems in the United States* (New York: Century, 1897), 153–88; Francesco Cordasco, *The Shaping of American Graduate Education: Daniel Coit Gilman and the Protean Ph.D.* (Totawa, NJ: Rowman and Littlefield, 1973), 35–53.

16   Exceptions were J. J. Sylvester, a leading British mathematician, and Virginia classics professor Basil Gildersleeve, both of whom provided leadership in their fields.

at first, but professors, associates, fellows, and students mixed in and out of class-rooms to share and pursue knowledge.

Hopkins graduated its first 4 PhDs in 1878, and by 1889 graduated a total of 151—more than Harvard and Yale combined. Hopkins PhDs were soon sought by ambitious universities throughout the country. The university did much to standardize and bolster the prestige of the American PhD. After some tinkering, the degree could be awarded 3 years after the AB to students who had studied one main subject and two subsidiary subjects, could read French and German, and wrote a substantial thesis during most of an academic year. Other universities employed variants of these elements, but the Hopkins formula largely prevailed, especially the emphasis on the thesis.[17] Doctoral education persisted as the institution's chief focus. Undergraduate student numbers rose to 130 in 1890 but comprised only one-third of the student body. Hopkins set a high standard for undergraduates and expected them to graduate in 3 years. It established the group system that Gilman had employed at Sheffield and California, with courses prescribed for seven fields. Given the small numbers, however, actual studies were fairly flexible. While graduate students were drawn from the entire country, undergraduates were largely local. Still, they made an important contribution. Of the first decade of ABs, more than half continued as graduate students, and 52 earned Hopkins PhDs.[18]

Hopkins embodied a spirit of scholarly engagement that other universities were soon compelled to emulate. This meant encouraging as best they could graduate education and faculty research. After its initial rise, however, the limitations of the Hopkins model became evident. By the wishes of its benefactor, the endowment was largely invested in the stock of his beloved B&O Railroad. When the company suspended its dividend in 1887, the university plunged into a fiscal crisis. Hopkins benefited from the gifts of wealthy Baltimoreans, but its tiny undergraduate population generated little tuition income and few alumni. Going forward, Hopkins would maintain high academic standards while struggling to keep pace with the scale and scope of developing American universities.[19]

In 1876 the Johns Hopkins University, with it concentration on research and graduate studies, was revolutionary. After 1880, though, acceptance and

17   Cordasco, *Shaping of American Graduate Education*, 110–13. In German universities, the chief emphasis of the PhD was the final examination before the doctoral committee: James Morgan Hart, *German Universities: A Narrative of Personal Experience* (New York, 1874).

18   Hawkins, *Pioneer*, 240.

19   Throughout the 1880s, activity slowly progressed toward fulfilling the other half of the founder's bequest. The hospital was opened in 1889 and the medical school in 1893. Together, they influenced the modernization of medical education as profoundly as the Hopkins PhD affected graduate education (below, chapter 9). By the twentieth century, Hopkins had more medical students than graduates and undergraduates.

cultivation of these elements spread at an accelerating pace. Eliot's conversion may have been most consequential, but by the end of the decade, research had become the foremost preoccupation among emerging universities, new and old.[20] Cornell, Harvard, and Johns Hopkins, each in its own way, established the foundations of the American university. Their presidents each developed important pieces of its structure, if not the whole. Most significant, they established institutional frameworks in which a growing multitude of dedicated scholars and scientists could pursue specialized knowledge in their respective fields. White, Eliot, and Gilman above all had the acumen to recognize academic ability and the means to provide conditions for its development. They nurtured the real revolutionaries who shaped the American university—faculty scholars who developed the academic disciplines.

THE ACADEMIC REVOLUTION

In the last years of the nineteenth century, education in colleges and universities was transformed. The pillars of the traditional college—the curricular separation of the classes, the fixed course for the AB, required Latin and Greek, and routines structured around three daily recitations—were all superseded by a curriculum based on academic disciplines and student choice. The universities pioneered this revolution, led by the three just discussed but soon joined by the major flagship and private universities and especially the new philanthropic creations. The true revolutionaries were the faculty whose scholarly and scientific endeavors provided the basis for academic disciplines. A discipline is an intellectual community that exercises authority based on expertise over a delimited, esoteric body of knowledge. Historically, disciplines crystallized in the 1880s and 1890s in the United States. Scholarly and scientific advances produced bodies of specialized knowledge comprehended solely by trained practitioners. They exercised social control over their respective communities by establishing associations and journals under expert authority. These disciplines gained legitimacy and permanence through institutionalization in universities. Academic disciplines and universities each have a separate but complementary existence; the latter depend on disciplines for the validation of knowledge, and scholars depend on universities for most professional roles. This symbiotic relationship evolved in a decentralized, uncoordinated process in the core of the American university.[21]

20   Veysey, *Emergence*, 164–65.
21   Roger L. Geiger, *To Advance Knowledge: The Growth of American Research Universities, 1900–1940* (New Brunswick: Transaction, 2004, 1986), 20–39; Veysey, *Emergence*, 121–79.

The organization of knowledge in America had been characterized by premodern forms analogous to the premodern institutions described in chapter 7. The American Association for the Advancement of Science had elite intellectual leadership but opted for social distinction as well by including prominent amateurs from local societies. These same leaders organized the National Academy of Science in 1863—a deliberately exclusive organization but one that did nothing to promote the sciences it represented.[22] For another decade the scientific community would depend on a single learned publication, the *American Journal of Science*.

The AAAS was preceded by the American Oriental Society (f. 1842), an eclectic grouping of mostly linguistic scholars whose interest extended from ancient Greece and Egypt to missionary work in the South Pacific. Its founder, Edward Salisbury, returned from 5 years' study in Europe to become the country's first professor of Arabic and Sanskrit at Yale (unpaid). For Salisbury's protégé, William Dwight Whitney, unlocking the mysteries of Sanskrit and the new field of comparative philology constituted "as great a revolution . . . in the study of language & of languages as has been effected in the departments of science." The Oriental Society gave birth to the more scholarly American Philological Association (APA) in 1869. Philology, as then understood, encompassed a broad intellectual territory from English spelling reform to the languages of antiquity. The historical study of languages invoked literature, history, and several branches of linguistics. Over time, philology evolved into an academic discipline focused on classics and archeology.[23]

The American Social Science Association traced a similar pattern, although for different reasons. It brought together prominent educators, professionals, and men of affairs in a quest to address social issues like poor relief, crime, prisons, and the treatment of the insane. It aimed to dispense useful knowledge on these pressing concerns and to enhance standards of scientific inquiry. The disciplines of history, economics, and sociology had to break away from the genteel reformism of the ASSA by forming their own organizations.[24]

---

22   A. Hunter Dupree, "The National Academy of Sciences and the American Definition of Science," in Alexandra Oleson and John Voss, eds., *The Organization of Knowledge in Modern America, 1860–1920* (Baltimore: Johns Hopkins University Press, 1979), 342–63. The AAAS began to adapt to disciplinary specialization in 1874, when it created sections for physical and natural sciences; by 1895 it had eleven disciplinary sections.

23   Whitney quoted in Carl Diehl, *Americans and German Scholarship, 1770–1870* (New Haven: Yale University Press, 1979), 124; Frank Gardner Moore, "A History of the American Philological Association," *Transactions and Proceedings of the American Philological Association*, 50 (1919): 5–32; James Turner argues convincingly in a forthcoming study that philology provided gestation for the disciplines of the modern humanities. My thanks to him for sharing this work.

24   The ASSA was closely associated with the new universities; Daniel C. Gilman served as president (1878–1880) but rejected a merger with JHU, recognizing that social reform and investigation were

These premodern associations helped to modernize learning. They brought together the most accomplished American scholars, allowed them to exchange views and findings, and nurtured aspiring scholars. However, while the intellectual elite of these fields provided leadership, they also welcomed "literary gentlemen" and local dignitaries who graced their annual meetings. They consequently resisted specialization, sought to make their erudition relevant to current events, and were reluctant to exert intellectual authority. Their gatherings thus heard a mixture of general topics along with the specialized papers of scholars. Over time, however, the preponderance of specialization grew. This development was inherently linked with the growing influence of German universities.

★　★　★

Americans had studied at German universities since Edward Everett and George Ticknor prepared for the Harvard faculty following the Napoleonic Wars. Some, like Andrew D. White, mimicked a grand tour; others, like aspiring Biblical scholars or chemists, sought the expertise of famous German professors. The excellence of German universities stemmed from several unique conditions. The multitude of institutions sponsored by individual states and principalities interacted as a decentralized system. They shared a unifying ideology that idealized *Wissenschaft*, or systematic inquiry in theoretical bodies of knowledge. Accordingly, a German professor's sole obligation was to pursue, master, and extend knowledge of his subject and then to profess it to students as he saw fit. This principle was honored as *Lehrfreiheit*, or freedom to teach. The corresponding principle for students was *Lernfreiheit*. That is, students were expected to learn their subjects as they saw fit—from the lectures of professors and unpaid private docents, from reading, or from matriculating at different universities. The dynamic element animating this structure was merit-based competition among universities for the most accomplished academic talents—scholars who advanced their fields. Aspiring academics studied for years beyond their doctorate (the only degree granted) to produce original research and qualify to be *privatdozenten*; assistant professors were chosen from the most able docents; and professorial chairs were filled by the most able candidates from any university. Full professors, the elect of this winnowing process, were furnished with ample resources to advance their research. Scientists had institutes or laboratories and humanists had seminars in which to work with advanced students, junior faculty, and, often, foreign acolytes.

---

incompatible: Thomas L. Haskell, *The Emergence of Professional Social Science: the American Social Science Association and the Nineteenth-Century Crisis of Authority* (Urbana: University of Illinois Press, 1977).

During the first half of the nineteenth century, the growing intellectual prowess of German universities outpaced all other countries.[25] Universities grew in size, state support, and professors. The latter, driven by dedication to *Wissenschaft* (or career advancement), pursued their investigations with increasingly greater specialization and expertise. Crucially important, achievement in learning was supported by the state in university appointments. After 1850, the superiority of German scholarship became more obvious and, for the ensuing decades, virtually unrivaled. During the peak years of academic prestige, German scholarship was characterized above all by close empirical investigation. Historians minutely examined and interpreted documents; philologists focused painstaking erudition on ancient near-eastern languages; even philosophy acquired an empirical dimension by measuring physiological reactions in psychological laboratories. To master these fields meant catching up with German scholars, usually by studying with them in their universities. In the 1850s more than 100 Americans matriculated in German universities, and their numbers continued to rise. Early in the century many studied theology and, later, medical science, but overall about two-thirds of Americans studied in the faculties of philosophy—the home of the arts and sciences—and slightly more studied humanities than science.[26] What they brought back with them was a dedication to pure science and, particularly, the German style of research.

Johns Hopkins was the first American university to embody this Germanic approach and, hence, to create a home for dedicated young scholars who had embraced the "religion of research." Hopkins consequently became identified with German universities. Its fellows, for example, organized a German Club for regular beer and fellowship. However, the most significant linkage was the emphasis on rigorous, empirical (*wissenschaftlich*) research. The opening of Johns Hopkins advertised the prestige and accomplishments of German universities, and their influence persisted at its height through the 1880s. American students were no doubt further encouraged by an admiring account by James Morgan Hart, *German Universities: a Narrative of Personal Experience* (1874), which was widely read during these years. American matriculations in German universities peaked at 517 in 1895, although by then developments in both countries were beginning to weaken this relationship. American assimilation of the ideals of German scholarship nevertheless stimulated the development of academic disciplines, led principally by the initiatives of Johns Hopkins.[27]

25   R. Steven Turner, "The Growth of Professorial Research in Prussia, 1818 to 1848—Causes and Context," *Historical Studies in the Physical Sciences*, 3 (1971), 137–82.

26   Diehl, *Americans and German Scholarship*; Anja Werner, *The Transatlantic World of Higher Education: Americans at German Universities, 1776–1914* (New York: Berghahn, 2013).

27   James Morgan Hart, *German Universities: A Narrative of Personal Experience* (New York, 1874).

President Gilman realized that an institution dedicated to advancing knowledge required more than professors and students—it had to be part of a vital intellectual community. He promoted this locally with the fellows program and a visiting lecturer series; nationally he encouraged journals and associations. Above all, Gilman wanted Hopkins faculty to play central roles in developing their fields.[28] Mathematics professor J. J. Sylvester, who had edited a leading journal in England, reported that Gilman had badgered him almost from his arrival to found an American journal. Hopkins became the first university to subsidize academic publications when the trustees voted to provide $500 per volume. The first issue of the *American Journal of Mathematics* appeared early in 1878, and the high quality of Sylvester's journal is credited with advancing theoretical mathematics in the United States. Chemistry professor Ira Remson (PhD Göttingen, 1870) needed no prompting, informing Gilman of the need for an outlet for the research findings of his laboratory. With the university's blessing, Remson began publishing the forerunner of the *American Chemical Journal* in 1877.

The natural sciences generally made halting progress toward disciplinary organization before 1890. Few universities had meaningful doctoral programs, and productive researchers were scattered in colleges, universities, and government agencies. Local societies for chemistry, for example, existed in New York and Washington, and publications, including Remson's journal, tended to have a narrow focus. After 1890, the natural science disciplines coalesced. The American Chemical Society unified that discipline in 1892, and the smaller community of physicists formed a society in 1899. Underlying these milestones was a more important convergence of graduate education and disciplinary leadership in the major universities.[29]

In other fields the Germany-JHU-discipline nexus was more evident. Greek professor Basil Gildersleeve (PhD Göttingen, 1853) declared his indebtedness "to Germany and the Germans . . . for everything professionally, in the way of apparatus and method, and . . . inspiration." He hosted the American Philological Association in Baltimore (1877), served as its president, and founded the *American Journal of Philology* in 1880. During the four decades of his editorship, the journal became the centerpiece for American classical scholarship and the professionalization of classics as a discipline.[30]

Herbert Baxter Adams (PhD Heidelberg, 1876) came to Hopkins as a fellow and soon became head of the department of history, politics, and economics. He

28   For activities at JHU: Hawkins, *Pioneer*, passim; founding dates for journals and associations are listed in Geiger, *To Advance Knowledge*, 23–24.

29   Daniel Kevles, "The Physics, Mathematics, and Chemistry Communities: A Comparative Analysis," in Oleson and Voss, *Organization of Knowledge*, 139–72.

30   "Basil Lanneau Gildersleeve," *American National Biography Online*; Hawkins, *Pioneer*.

brought the Germanic method of close documentary analysis to American historiography and had his seminar students apply it to researching Anglo-Saxon roots of early American local government. Woodrow Wilson, an early Hopkins fellow (PhD 1886), found such minutia repugnant, but he recognized Adams as an historical "captain in the field of systematic and organized scholarship." Adams's signal achievement was founding the American Historical Association in 1884. The AHA looked a good deal like a premodern association: Andrew D. White was named the first of many celebrity presidents, and two-thirds of the membership came from local historical societies. However, it was a professionalizing project from the outset, first suggested by Gilman, dominated by university historians, and having Adams as a permanent secretary. The AHA was only one of three Hopkins-inspired associations. A. Marshall Elliott[31] launched the Modern Language Association in 1883, and Richard T. Ely (PhD Heidelberg, 1879) organized the American Economic Association in 1885. Like Adams, both men guided the associations as secretary. These associations were intended to establish separate professional identities for their respective subjects. Historians who employed German scientific methods sought to control the professional field. Professors of modern languages were ill served by the philology establishment and sought recognition for scholarship on French and German in particular. Economists took inspiration from the German historical and institutional school, seeking a scientific identity separate from the ASSA reformers.[32]

The creation of disciplinary associations was only one important step in the process of discipline formation. More significant, this process reflected growing commitments to research among university faculty. One manifestation of this trend was the appearance of publication series sponsored by individual university units. Hopkins naturally led this trend. Remson's journal was originally *Notes from the Chemical Laboratory* (1877–1879), and *Studies from the Biological Laboratory* appeared the same year. Adams and Elliott launched JHU series (1883 and 1886), and Hopkins subsidized a German language series known as "Contributions to Assyriology" (1890). The imitation of this practice by other universities marked both the significant presence of disciplinary scholarship and institutional recognition of a research mission. Only a handful of institutions made such commitments during the 1880s: Harvard's publications in economics (1886), law (1887), and mathematics (1889); Cornell's in classical philology

---

31 Elliott studied in France, Italy, Spain, and finally Germany (1868–1876) but did not take a PhD: *American National Biography Online*.

32 Hawkins, *Pioneer*, passim. Possibly the most self-consciously *wissenschaftlich* subject was experimental psychology, where Harvard led, awarding the first PhD in that subject to G. Stanley Hall (see below), who was then hired by Johns Hopkins: James H. Capshew, *Psychologists on the March: Science, Practice, and Professional Identity in America, 1929–1969* (New York: Cambridge University Press, 1999), 9–14.

(1887); Pennsylvania's in political economy (1885); Columbia's *Political Science Quarterly* (1886); and MIT's *Technology Quarterly* (1887). The 1890s saw an explosion of such publications by these same universities, now joined by Yale and others. All were surpassed by the new University of Chicago, which opened in 1892 with a university press and soon sponsored a dozen academic publications, most of which became national journals. Public universities were slower to embrace research publications. However, Wisconsin launched three series in the 1890s, and California joined the parade after 1900.[33] For some universities, at least, the reluctance to endorse an explicit role for research was gradually overcome in the 1880s. At most institutions, however, the academic revolution still confronted stubborn obstacles.

★   ★   ★

The foremost impediment to academic modernization was the undergraduate college. Where the care and nurture of collegians was the principal concern, opportunities for advanced studies were difficult to justify or implement. Most college students were neither prepared nor interested. The burdens of student discipline and recitations in the classical course consumed the time and energy of the faculty, and student discipline preoccupied governors as well. The religious foundations of most colleges dated from their founding and remained inherent to the moral stewardship of collegians. Through midcentury most American academics considered religion and scholarship to be compatible and complementary. However, this outlook proved increasingly irrelevant to advancing disciplinary knowledge. Finally, the attitudes of the governors of academic institutions—presidents and particularly trustees—determined the extent to which these first two considerations would predominate over pressures to incorporate new knowledge. Before 1890, these factors impeded the academic revolution in different ways at Yale and Princeton.

Yale College's difficulty in adapting to the academic revolution stemmed from its previous success. The largest and most national antebellum college, it was also a national leader in literary and scientific scholarship. It epitomized the premodern characteristics of midcentury higher education. Historian Louise Stevenson described Yale from the 1840s to the 1880s as a Christian college, a distinctive type that stood between the early classical college and the modern university. Most notable was the ideological consensus that reigned there during these years: the faculty agreed fundamentally and axiomatically about

33 Hawkins, *Pioneer*, 107–13; the principal university journals are listed in Geiger, *To Advance Knowledge*, 32–33, but there were additional short-lived series as well.

education, religion, and scholarship. They believed that the purpose of Yale College was to instill culture and character and that this could be accomplished only through the study of classical antiquity. They still subscribed to the hoary notion of mental discipline but now also emphasized the furniture of the mind. The idealization of ancient Greece accorded the study of literature and history a special formative power, while also contributing to philosophy and politics. Only the fixed curriculum could instill the virtues inherent in all these subjects, thus forming truly cultured graduates. In religion, the Yale community subscribed to an inclusive Congregationalism that respected all Reformed Protestantism. Given this consensus, they were more interested in Biblical scholarship than theological dogma. This tacit religiosity pervaded their views of scholarship. Underlying and unifying their different fields was a common search for divine truth—for scientists no less than philologists. The unity of these "New Haven Scholars" was physical as well as spiritual. Up to one-third of the Yale faculty belonged to a discussion group known simply as "The Club" that dined together twice a month and presented papers evincing liberal evangelical Protestant perspectives. The Club included most of Yale's distinguished scholars. Gilman was a member, as was the next president of Yale, Noah Porter (1871–1886).[34]

For historians, Porter has symbolized Yale's resistance to the coming of the university. More accurately, he sought to defend and uphold the college of the New Haven Scholars. Porter left his ministerial calling to become Yale professor of moral philosophy in 1847. An active scholar, he studied philosophy at Berlin (1853–1854) and chaired one of the first three Yale PhD dissertations. In his mind, the four professional departments of Yale (including philosophy and the arts) comprised a university, but the mission of Yale College was to precede university studies.[35] In explicit rejoinders to Eliot, Porter attacked the "serious evils" of the elective system, contrasting it with Yale's goal of educating "men who are elevated and refined by a culture which is truly liberal." Professors, he believed, could be committed to both instilling culture in their students and "the organized and persistent pursuit of science and learning." But not the wrong kind of learning: Porter ruled out "atheistic materialism . . . fatalistic theory . . . and the ignoble tendencies of a godless and frivolous literature." Rather, he would have "the influence of Christ and Christianity . . . distinctly, emphatically, and

34   Louise L. Stevenson, *Scholarly Means to Evangelical Ends: The New Haven Scholars and the Transformation of Higher Learning in America, 1830–1890* (Baltimore: Johns Hopkins University Press, 1986), 62–63 et passim.

35   In 1872 the Yale Corporation resolved: "that [Yale] be recognized as comprising the four departments of which a university is commonly understood to consist, viz., the Department of Theology, of Law, of Medicine, and of Philosophy and the Arts": James L. (New York: Henry Holt, 1879), 2 vol. (New Haven, 1879), I, 161.

reverentially recognized."[36] The Yale Corporation knew what they were getting in President Porter. His candidacy had been opposed by alumni of the "Young Yale" movement, who had vociferously protested clerical domination of the Corporation and curricular conservatism. In consolation, they were accorded representation on the Corporation but no real influence. Unlike the frustrated members of the Harvard Corporation who elected Eliot, the governors of Yale were pleased with the state of their institution.[37]

The national press also noted Yale's disregard for the new currents sweeping through higher education. Yale received particularly unflattering publicity when Porter objected to professor William Graham Sumner assigning Herbert Spencer's *Principles of Sociology*. In fact, Porter's determination to preserve mid-century Yale appeared increasingly anachronistic as the academic revolution progressed. Reform sentiment among the faculty became difficult to ignore. A concession to electives was implemented in 1876 when juniors and seniors were offered optional language studies. Still, pressure to open the curriculum continued to build. In 1883–1884 a faculty committee devised a still-conservative revision that allowed greater choice for juniors and especially seniors. When the reform reached the Corporation, Porter reverted to his bedrock convictions and withdrew his approval. Faculty indignation was intense, and Porter was ultimately compelled to acquiesce.[38] The following year he announced his retirement. By no means was Yale a failure during Porter's tenure (see chapter 9), but the resistance to change during these dynamic years impeded its academic development. Young research-minded scholars like Charles Lanman shunned Yale in order to teach on a higher level. Yale had been the leader in doctoral education in 1871, but by the mid-1880s, PhD graduates had dropped from five to three per year. Symbolically, the Corporation adopted the name Yale University in 1886, following Porter's departure, and undertook in its own conservative fashion to live up to the name by assimilating the academic revolution.[39]

36   Porter's 1869 articles in the *New Englander* (the unofficial journal of the New Haven Scholars) were published in *The American Colleges and the American Public* (New York, 1870); quotes from "Inaugural Address": Stevenson, *Scholarly Means*, 62; Veysey, *Emergence*, 46; and George Levesque, "Noah Porter Revisited," *Perspectives on the History of Higher Education*, 26 (2007): 29–66.

37   Peter Dobkin Hall, "Noah Porter Writ Large? Reflections on the Modernization of American Higher Education and Its Critics, 1866–1916," in Roger L. Geiger, ed., *The American College in the Nineteenth Century* (Nashville: Vanderbilt University Press, 2000), 196–220.

38   George Wilson Pierson, *Yale College, an Educational History, 1871–1921* (New Haven: Yale University Press, 1952), 66–94.

39   Levesque, "Noah Porter"; Brooks Mather Kelley, *Yale: A History* (New Haven: Yale University Press, 1974), 267–73. Porter was succeeded by Timothy Dwight (the Younger, 1886–1899), grandson of Yale's inspirational president of the same name, who was a moderate reformer; his successor, Arthur Twining Hadley (1899–1918), a railroad economist, is credited with being Yale's first modern president: Pierson, *Yale College*, 95–128.

In contrast to Yale, Princeton felt the need for change in 1868 when it appointed as president the Reverend James McCosh, a Scot then teaching at the University of Belfast.[40] Exactly 100 years after Witherspoon, the trustees consciously hoped to again rejuvenate the college from its prevailing torpor with a Scottish divine. The college enrolled only 264 students, drawn principally from Scottish Presbyterian families in the mid-Atlantic region. The 17 faculty members were mostly Princeton graduates. The Princeton Theological Seminary was a bastion of Old School orthodoxy. Its influence pervaded the board of trustees, who had no intention of diluting the religious foundation of the institution. McCosh was an ardent Presbyterian, if a bit too evangelical for Old School tastes, but acceptable to both sides of the newly reunited church. He was also an accomplished scholar with strong convictions and abundant energy—if not a reincarnation of Witherspoon, then the next best thing.

McCosh envisioned erecting a university on a foundation not just religious but Presbyterian. This required preserving the denominational context of campus life, modernizing the curriculum, and enhancing the size and standing of the institution. For the first, McCosh enforced compulsory chapel twice a day and multiple services on the Sabbath. Despite the competition of collegiate activities, religiosity was evident among many students, including campus revivals. Unlike most religious leaders, McCosh strongly supported science, even endorsing evolution. His clinching argument against the elective system was that all students needed to learn modern science. He regarded classical studies as essential but felt they needed to be reinvigorated in America by stressing cultural rather than grammatical lessons. He also advocated the inclusion of English and other modern subjects. McCosh differed from other university leaders in arguing that only a fixed course could guarantee that students learned all these essential subjects. He advocated a set course for the first 2 years but (unlike Porter) considerable choice for juniors and seniors. Inheriting an inbred faculty, McCosh first looked outside for scholars to teach modern subjects. Later, he granted fellowships to outstanding Princeton graduates for study in Europe and then appointed them to the faculty. Still, faculty beliefs had to be compatible with Presbyterianism, and alumni were generally the safest in this respect.

McCosh kept Yale and Harvard in view, aiming to make Princeton a university of comparable national stature. He pursued a modernizing strategy with great energy and skill. He was an effective fund-raiser, tapping into the generosity

---

40 J. David Hoeveler Jr., *James McCosh and the Scottish Intellectual Tradition* (Princeton: Princeton University Press, 1981), 215–349; P. C. Kemeny, *Princeton in the Nation's Service: Religious Ideals and Educational Practice, 1868–1928* (New York: Oxford University Press, 1998), 17–86; Thomas Jefferson Wertenbaker, *Princeton, 1746–1896* (Princeton: Princeton University Press, 1996 [1946]), 290–343.

of sympathetic Scottish Presbyterians. Large donations were essential to create professorships in modern fields and recruit distinguished scholars. Too, McCosh looked beyond the college's immediate building needs and sought funds to create a serene, Oxbridge-type campus that would be conducive to reflection and learning. The college's greatest benefactor, John C. Green, endowed the School of Science, which McCosh saw as necessary "to keep up with the other great Colleges of the country." McCosh personally endeavored to give the college a national presence. He made several long midwestern trips to establish alumni associations and encourage their members to send students and donations. He supported intramural athletics and was also tolerant, if occasionally alarmed, by the growing role of intercollegiate athletics—well aware of the favorable publicity for the college. However, McCosh's greatest interest was in intellectual life. He expanded the college library from a pitiful condition to one of the country's largest. He established graduate studies, arguing that they would be the conduit for new knowledge to enter the curriculum. (Princeton conferred its first PhD in 1879.) Especially noteworthy, he established biweekly "library meetings" in which students and faculty gathered to hear and discuss learned papers on a variety of subjects. Over the two decades of the McCosh presidency, enrollments more than doubled, the faculty and the number of courses tripled. He elevated Princeton into the institution of his vision—a vital college abreast of contemporary intellectual currents, built upon a denominational foundation, and also a rival of Yale and Harvard.[41]

This idiosyncratic vision—and his dogmatic nature—also made McCosh the champion of lost, or losing, causes. He was hostile to publicly supported higher education and the land grant institutions in particular. At the 1873 convention of the National Education Association, he joined Eliot in a gratuitous and distorted attack on the latter. Considering only the number of agriculture graduates, he condemned them as a huge waste of the public lands. Later, McCosh engaged in two famous debates with Eliot (1885 and 1886). The first addressed the elective system, and McCosh cogently charged that the Harvard system of free electives allowed students to graduate without taking any math, science, or other challenging subjects. The second debate addressed religion in higher education, and there Eliot outflanked McCosh's simple dichotomy between religious and irreligious colleges, arguing that an "unsectarian" university could better promote religion through scientific study, like any other subject.[42] However, by the 1880s McCosh faced more serious opposition at home in Princeton.

41   Kemeny, *Princeton*, quote p. 69.

42   Williams, *Origins of Federal Support*, 66–75; Hoeveler, *James McCosh*, 235–37, 252–53; Julie A. Reuben, *The Making of the Modern University: Intellectual Transformation and the Marginalization of Morality* (Chicago: University of Chicago Press, 1996), 80–83.

Cracks were increasingly evident in the edifice McCosh had built. Although the students greatly respected him personally, the piety and decorum that he expected of them eroded in growing misbehavior and collegiate license. The professional faculty that he had recruited found the task of student discipline irksome. They eschewed responsibility for student moral behavior, and many no longer attended chapel. McCosh had remarkable success in organizing and mobilizing the alumni, but he was rebuffed when he sought to obtain their representation on the board of trustees. Indeed, the board remained a bastion of Presbyterian orthodoxy and distrustful of much of the McCosh project. These tensions came to a head in the mid-1880s when McCosh embarked on his "University Campaign." Feeling that the College of New Jersey had, in fact, become a true university and that it needed the tonic of an official designation to rekindle enthusiasm for further development, McCosh asked the trustees to declare Princeton a university and create graduate fellowships like those at Hopkins. Despite his advocacy, the trustees in 1886 found such measures "inexpedient." The trustees represented the Presbyterian community but also McCosh's own ideals for collegiate education, while the alumni tended to support McCosh's university aspirations. Although the board would succumb to alumni control and reverse its decision a decade later, Princeton would continue to be characterized by the split personality of being both a college and university.

The frustrations encountered by Porter and McCosh in coming to terms with the academic revolution affected all traditional colleges. Porter hoped to segregate the new knowledge in the department of philosophy and the arts; McCosh attempted to reserve it for juniors and seniors. However, the specialization ushered in by academic disciplines undermined the old college in numerous ways. The ideal of wholeness and balance in the AB course became chimerical. The capstone course in moral philosophy that united the natural world with the divine was moribund. Fundamental aspects of human behavior were parceled off to the human sciences, and the natural sciences proceeded without any need for epistemological moorings. Moreover, all these subjects had now become *wissenschaftlich*—they admitted explanation based only on evidence and experiment. The Christian foundations of these institutions were now invoked by presidents on ceremonial occasions, but God no longer had a place in the classrooms.[43] In the decade of the 1880s, these issues were inchoate and institutional adaptations were diverse. By the end of that decade, however, the coalescence of the academic disciplines and the ascendancy of the research ideal clearly marked a transformation that would engulf the entirety of American higher education.

43 Reuben, *Making of the Modern University*; John H. Roberts and James Turner, *The Sacred and the Secular University* (Princeton: Princeton University Press, 2000).

CHAPTER 8

RESEARCH, GRADUATE EDUCATION, AND THE NEW UNIVERSITIES

In January 1887, Jonas Clark announced his intention to endow and found Clark University in his home city of Worcester, Massachusetts. In May, Leland Stanford and his wife laid the cornerstone for a university dedicated to their late son, Leland Jr. The same year, John D. Rockefeller resolved to employ some of his burgeoning wealth to endow another new university. None of these men had ever attended a college or university: Clark began his several successful business ventures after a common school education; Rockefeller attended high school and a commercial college; and Stanford read law after an academy education.[44] Their ideas about higher education were ambitious but relatively unformed. Nevertheless, all proceeded judiciously. The Stanfords had visited Cornell, Harvard, and MIT, which particularly impressed them. They envisioned a practical institution but also "a university of high degree," employing "men of the very highest attainments." However, they constructed a campus before having a president, faculty, or academic plan. Clark was inspired in part by his friend Leland Stanford, but he had visited European universities and clearly intended an institution similar to Cornell or Johns Hopkins. Rockefeller was the most cautious, rejecting requests to single-handedly launch a "great graduate university" and instead waiting for a plan to germinate among fellow Baptists in Chicago and a trusted academic visionary, William Rainey Harper. The nature of the resulting universities would be determined not by the founders, but by the founding presidents, all accomplished scholars whose conception of a university emphasized graduate education and research.[45]

Clark's choice for president in 1888 was G. Stanley Hall, a Harvard PhD who had also studied in Germany. Hall had been professor of psychology at Johns Hopkins for only 4 years and was founder of the *American Journal of Psychology*. Hopkins was clearly his model for a research university, but he sought to better it by eliminating undergraduates entirely. He convinced Jonas Clark that by beginning

---

44 Jonas Clark (1815–1902) retired in 1878 to Worcester, near his birthplace, after acquiring a respectable fortune as a merchant in California and investor in New York City real estate; Leland Stanford (1824–1893), from upstate New York, made his fortune building the transcontinental railroad and served as governor of California, U.S. senator, and president of the Southern Pacific Railroad. John D. Rockefeller (1839–1937), raised in Ohio, organized the Standard Oil Company.

45 William A. Koelsch, *Clark University, 1887–1987* (Worcester: Clark University Press, 1987), 1–42; Richard J. Storr, *Harper's University: The Beginnings* (Chicago: University of Chicago Press, 1966), 7–34; Ron Chernow, *Titan: The Life of John D. Rockefeller* (New York: Random House, 1998), 301–23; Willard J. Pugh, "A 'Curious Working of Cross Purposes' in the Founding of the University of Chicago," in Geiger, ed., *American College in the Nineteenth Century*, 242–63; Orrin J. Elliott, *Stanford University: The First Twenty-five Years* (Stanford: Stanford University Press, 1937).

as a graduate university, it could achieve immediate standing as a leading institution. The Stanfords aimed high but were unable to persuade Andrew White or MIT president Francis A. Walker to move to Palo Alto. As time grew short, they acted on White's suggestion to appoint the young president of Indiana University, David Starr Jordan. A dedicated scientist (ichthyology), Jordan had used the Cornell model to move Indiana toward becoming a true university and would have the opportunity to do far more as president of Stanford. Before accepting the position, he received assurance that the new university would blend the liberal arts and sciences and the applied sciences, that faculty would be furnished with materials for instruction and research, and that the university would publish "the results of any important research on the part of professors or advanced students." Rockefeller, in contrast, refused to take the lead in founding the University of Chicago, holding back to ensure that the venture had backing in the community. Nevertheless, he wisely placed confidence only in Harper as its head. The country's foremost Hebrew and Biblical scholar, Harper needed considerable wooing to leave his scholarship and Yale professorship. At the critical moment, when the nature of the institution was not yet settled, Harper wrote to Rockefeller:

> The denomination and indeed the whole country are expecting the University of Chicago to be from the very beginning an institution of the highest rank and character. Already it is talked of in connection with Yale, Harvard, Princeton, Johns Hopkins, the University of Michigan, and Cornell. . . . with the example of Johns Hopkins before our eyes, it seems a great pity to wait for growth when we might be born full-fledged."

Rockefeller added $1 million to the endowment, 80 percent of it for graduate education, and Harper soon accepted the presidency.[46]

Why did two of the wealthiest men in the United States and a third multimillionaire almost simultaneously and independently decide to found universities committed to research? Quite simply, the academic revolution had redefined the prestige structure of American higher education. When these plutocrats sought the very best for their universities—"men of the very highest attainments"—this now meant disciplinary scholars, exemplars of Germanic research, distinguished by postgraduate study and academic publications. Thus, Hall convinced Jonas Clark that a graduate university was the surest route to academic distinction; Stanford had no qualms that his faculty would engage in research and publication; and Rockefeller gave Harper the means to build an "institution of the highest rank and character." These Christian philanthropists readily accepted

46   Elliott, *Stanford*, 41–52; Storr, *Harper's University*, 47.

that their universities would be entirely secular, faithful to the new academic mores rather than the old faiths, which is especially notable in light of the Baptist origins of Chicago.

If any single development had shifted the values in American higher education, it was the remarkable success of Johns Hopkins. The 1880s marked the peak influence of German universities, but Hopkins more importantly demonstrated how Germanic research could be incorporated into an American university. In 1890, after just 14 years, Gilman's radical experiment represented the leading edge of graduate education and the academic revolution.[47] That same year, Eliot restructured Harvard to form the Graduate School and the Faculty of Arts and Sciences. Yale had finally declared itself to be a university, and Michigan and Columbia were fashioning their own distinctive versions of graduate education. These universities had institutionalized the values and practices of graduate education and academic research. Before 1890, however, there was no clear consensus on how this was best done.

G. Stanley Hall's conception of a graduate university hardly seemed fanciful in the late 1880s at the height of enthusiasm for research and PhDs. Contemporary supplicants of Rockefeller proposed to establish "great graduate universities" without college students. Numerous academic leaders, including Gilman, felt that the natural divide between preparatory and advanced work lay between the sophomore and junior years. Catholic University opened in 1889 as a graduate university and did not admit undergraduates until 1904, but the Catholic hierarchy was not yet in step with the academic revolution, having little conception of research.[48] However, the Clark University that Hall opened in 1889 foundered for a number of reasons. Personal factors overshadowed a distinctive academic experiment.[49]

Jonas Clark was by nature cautious and secretive, keeping council only with his inseparable wife Susan. These traits no doubt served him well in his business dealings but were not conducive to rallying supporters for an institution with as many interested parties as a university. He envisioned his university as a gift to Worcester: the trustees were drawn from the city's business elite, and Clark invited local gifts with promises of matching funds. The trustees, however, felt no obligation to Clark or his eponymous university, nor did they ever donate. Many had attended Harvard, and encouraged Hall's graduate university because it would offer no competition to

47 Hawkins, *Pioneer*, 316–26.

48 Pugh, "Curious Working"; Roger L. Geiger, "The Crisis of the Old Order: The Colleges in the 1890s," in Geiger, *American College in the Nineteenth Century*, 264–76; C. Joseph Nuesse, *The Catholic University of America: A Centennial History* (Washington, D.C.: Catholic University of America Press, 1990), 67–70.

49 The following draws on Koelsch, *Clark University*.

their alma mater. Financial arrangements complicated this situation: Clark used his own funds to support the founding and first years, with a promised endowment and the hoped-for contributions to follow. Hall and the trustees quickly assumed that they could humor the 74-year-old founder and obtain his fortune when he passed away. They underestimated his intelligence and his health.

G. Stanley Hall succeeded initially in founding a science university focused entirely on research and graduate education. He recruited an outstanding faculty to the five departments—mathematics, physics, chemistry, biology, and Hall's own field of psychology, writ large to encompass anthropology and education. *Lehrfreiheit* and *Lernfreiheit* made it the closest American analogue to a German university. Professors gave two lectures a week on topics of their own choosing; students attended or not as they saw fit; and the only examination was the 4-hour PhD oral. But Hall proved to be an unstable leader. A brilliant intellect in some ways, he had a knack for seizing upon new ideas and extrapolating implications, but he lacked the scientific temperament to verify his theories. Worse for the university, he was both authoritarian and duplicitous. Hall had initially agreed to launch the undergraduate college after 3 years, in 1892, but he had no intention of honoring that commitment, nor did the trustees. As relations with Jonas Clark became more strained, the financial position of the university was unsustainable without an infusion of additional funds. Hall misled the faculty with promises that could not be met, and by the third year their growing suspicions erupted into an open revolt. In 1892 it also became clear to Clark that Hall did not intend to open a college. Several professors had begun looking for other positions. When William Rainey Harper visited to recruit for the new University of Chicago, there was a rush for the exits. Two-thirds of the faculty and three-quarters of the junior members resigned, half of them for positions at Chicago.

Jonas Clark, too, was disillusioned. He turned over the promised endowment of $700,000 and essentially withdrew from involvement with "his" university. Hall was able to sustain a faculty of ten, mostly in psychology, and this rump continued to function as a graduate center of idealistic researchers and doctoral students. With Clark's fortune still uncommitted, Hall and the trustees, in the words of the university historian, "adopted a deliberate strategy of trying to bamboozle the founder into thinking they would follow his wishes without actually moving to implement them." Clark knew better, however, and drafted a will that left the bulk of his assets for the establishment of a "Collegiate Department." When he died in 1902, the trustees had no recourse but to finally establish what became known as Clark College, but this unit was united with Clark University only after Hall retired in 1920.[50]

50   Koelsch, *Clark University*, 82–92, quote p. 85.

It cannot be known whether more sincere and forthright individuals could have succeeded in establishing a full modern university in Worcester. Certainly Hall placed his ego and public persona ahead of the interests of the university. But Worcester proved in many ways an uncongenial setting. The local muckraking newspaper attacked the university with scurrilous and largely baseless charges, and the community offered no financial support. Hall's graduate university, unlike the college that Clark had wanted, had few educational benefits to offer Worcester. On a deeper level, Hall's conception of an endowed graduate university was almost self-defeating. While his original creation pushed the academic frontiers of 1889, it lacked the capacity to expand in scale and scope—the hallmark of the major universities of the era. After 1892 Hall's university, even in truncated form, enjoyed academic prestige far out of proportion to its size. The intense intellectual dedication of its few faculty and students produced a cadre of distinguished academics. Perhaps its last hurrah was the Twentieth Anniversary Conference in 1909, where Hall introduced Sigmund Freud to American audiences. But after this occasion the university's parlous finances weakened further, and Hall's band of aging psychologists faded from the academic mainstream.

★　★　★

Stanford had several traits in common with Clark University—an autocratic president, financial dependence on a devoted but often inscrutable founder, and the constraint of relying on endowment income alone. However, combined with Stanford's unique bad luck, the initial results were disappointing in quite different ways.

In the fall of 1891, David Starr Jordan welcomed faculty and students to the enormous Palo Alto ranch that now contained the nearly finished Leland Stanford Junior University.[51] He had hastily recruited a faculty of thirty-three. Scarcely able to attract established scholars to this remote experiment, he hired well-qualified, relatively young academics who shared his academic vision. Most were chosen through his Cornell contacts and from the Indiana faculty. They met a class of 559 students, 25 percent female, drawn to the new enterprise by a spirit of adventure, by a modern disciplinary curriculum, or by free tuition. Students, teachers, and administrators soon bonded with a pioneering esprit de corps, a curious amalgam of elegant architecture, rural isolation, and academic idealism. Manifesting the latter was the major-subject system, the distinctive feature of the curriculum, largely inspired by Jordan's alma mater. At Cornell,

---

51　The following draws on Elliott, *Stanford University*.

students chose a structured course in one of several areas, which focused chiefly on the major subject for the third and fourth years. At Indiana, Jordan had retained only the fixed freshman year, allowing students to pursue a major field for the remainder of the course and also making all studies lead to a BA degree. At Stanford, students chose a major subject upon entrance and were then guided in their studies by the professor of that subject. The major-subject system allowed Jordan's young faculty to teach their fields of expertise, but they began with a freshman class of uncertain preparation. About half of the regular students in the pioneer class graduated in 1895. Stanford University would long remain predominantly an undergraduate college.

While still formulating their plans, the Stanfords had asked President Eliot the cost of endowing a modern university. When he answered not less than $5 million, Leland Stanford reportedly said to his wife, "Well, Jane, we could manage that, couldn't we."[52] The university, in fact, had the largest endowment on paper for much of its first two decades—about $20 million. However, a succession of developments kept the university underfunded throughout Jordan's presidency (1891–1913). The first misfortune was the death of Leland Stanford in 1893, exacerbated by the devastating financial panic of that year. His complicated assets, which provided the entire income of the university, were tied up in probate for the next 5 years. His death also left Jane Lothrop Stanford as the sole trustee. Despite being advised to close the university temporarily, she sustained it out of her household allowance on a bare-bones budget. Faculty salaries were reduced by 12 percent, and all hopes of academic expansion were put on hold. When the endowment was finally secured in 1899, Mrs. Stanford kept the operating budget to a minimum in order to devote nearly two-thirds of endowment income to completing the building program. This strategy was continued after her death in 1904 by the trustees who now governed the university. Jordan dubbed this period "the stone age." By the spring of 1906, construction was almost completed when the great San Francisco earthquake destroyed $3 million worth of buildings. Essential structures were rapidly rebuilt, but limitations continued on student enrollments, faculty salaries, appointments, and curricula. Fiscal stringency was only part of the reason that Jordan was never able to shape Stanford into the research university he had envisioned.

Stanford opened with 37 graduate students, most of whom had followed their professors west. But graduate education never took root during Jordan's

---

52   Elliott, *Stanford*, 15–16. The source is a letter from Eliot to Jordan more than 30 years afterward (June 26, 1919). A spurious and entirely implausible version of this encounter has circulated on the Internet, attributed falsely to Malcolm Forbes.

tenure. The university averaged fewer than two annual PhDs, and faculty repeat-edly dithered over establishing a graduate school. Palo Alto was hardly a conge-nial place for advanced research, especially during the lean years when any extra expenditures were prohibitive. But the university lacked faculty leadership in terms of distinguished scientists or scholars. For the first decade, there was no money for such hires, and then the Ross affair cast a pall across the university. Sociologist E. A. Ross became active in Democratic politics, much to the annoy-ance of Mrs. Stanford. She considered his inflammatory speech against Asian immigration in 1900 as the last straw and insisted that Jordan fire him. As this crisis brewed, Eliot warned Jordan against such a step: "Indeed, I can imagine no greater calamity; for nothing would so effectually deter men of strong character and good abilities from accepting places in the University." Poor Jordan had to choose between a certain calamity and the wishes of the woman who controlled the university endowment. Predictably, the firing of Ross was followed by the resignations of seven faculty and widespread opprobrium across the academic community. Scholars at Stanford would have to be homegrown.[53]

The Ross affair was followed by general dissatisfaction with the lack of aca-demic progress at Stanford. President Jordan concluded that "to make a univer-sity, in the world sense, of Stanford University" would require "the elimination as soon as possible . . . of the junior college, by the addition of two years to the entrance requirement." The basic idea of dividing the undergraduate course at this point had already been proposed in several versions, and it would have a long life in American higher education. In Stanford's case, its appeal and its im-practicality stemmed from the same source. Stanford suffered egregiously from the incompatibility between the "university spirit" and the student mentality of the *high collegiate era*. Jordan was disheartened by increasing drinking and mis-behavior in student residences, especially among freshmen and sophomores. His advocacy of a junior-senior university can be seen as a fairly desperate attempt to resuscitate his original university ideal. He accurately described the institution he had shaped as "a large college, well ordered for the most part, giving good in-struction and with the highest collegiate standards. Its university work, though not extensive, has commanded respect." Truncating the college had no appeal to alumni, who now dominated the board and were devoted to this large college. When Jordan was eased out of the presidency, it was clear that Stanford Univer-sity would have to build on that foundation, not the ideal of 1890.

53   Elliott, *Stanford University*, 524; Veysey, *Emergence*, 397–416; Slosson, *Great American Univer-sities*, 110–47. Stanford ranked twelfth among universities in the number of scientists listed in *American Men of Science* in 1906 and again in 1927: Geiger, *To Advance Knowledge*, 39. *American Men of Science*, 1927, 1127.

★ ★ ★

William Rainey Harper graduated from hometown Muskingum College at age 14 and 4 years later earned a Yale PhD (1875) in ancient languages. The founding president of the University of Chicago was no less precocious as an administrator. While filling several teaching posts, Harper made a mission of popularizing the study of Hebrew and, later, Bible studies. He founded a general journal (*Hebrew Student*, later *Biblical World*), a scholarly journal (*Hebraica*), and a correspondence course. He began teaching Hebrew at the renowned Chautauqua Institution, an evangelical adult education summer institute in southwestern New York, and soon became director of its entire education program.[54] After he assumed a Yale professorship in semitic languages (1886), Harper was teaching popular audiences, Yale College students, and divinity and graduate students. In a sense, he sought to shape the University of Chicago after his own portfolio. This orientation dovetailed with the goals of the Baptists who thought of the university as the pinnacle of Baptist education. However, Harper's zeal and energy and Rockefeller's millions carried the institution far beyond their purview.

The combination of genius and hyperactivity make Harper's abundant plans for the university almost impossible to recount. His memoranda often contained more than one hundred subpoints. He essentially invented the entire organization de novo rather than relying on past precedent. Many of his innovations, like a 3-year degree beyond the PhD, came to nothing; others, like the Chicago summer term, altered American higher education. Moreover, his commitments were fluid—constantly evolving during the 15 years of his presidency. Nonetheless, two relatively fixed convictions characterized the University of Chicago. Harper held that the highest purpose of a university was original investigation; and he pursued this ideal by hiring the most outstanding research faculty, by providing them, despite difficulties, with the infrastructure and means for research, and by emphasizing the graduate training of future scholars. However, unlike the cloistered Germanic approach of Hall and Gilman, Harper sought to make university learning as inclusive of subject matter and as widely dispersed as possible. In this quest he went well beyond state universities and introduced a new dynamic into higher education.[55]

54 Joseph E. Gould, *The Chautauqua Movement* (Albany: SUNY Press, 1972).

55 Thomas Wakefield Goodspeed, *A History of the University of Chicago: The First Quarter-Century* (Chicago: University of Chicago Press, [1916], 1972); Storr, *Harper's University*. Harper was critical of the influence of German training on American academics, charging that it made them, at least temporarily, unsuited for teaching in American universities: Willard J. Pugh, *The Beginnings of Research at the University of Chicago*, 3 vol., PhD Diss., University of Chicago, 1990, I, 240–41.

In *Official Bulletin No. 1*, Harper announced that "the work of the University shall be arranged under three general divisions, viz., the University Proper, The University Extension, and the University Publication Work." He soon added divisions for the "University Libraries, Laboratories, and Museums [and] the University Affiliations." The University Proper was to be comprehensive, with undergraduate colleges, graduate and professional schools, schools for engineering (never created), pedagogy, fine arts, and music. The university press, the first, was intended to print university publications, scholarly journals, and books by instructors. Extension provided lectures and courses around Chicago and correspondence courses, including Harper's own enterprise. By affiliations Harper envisioned an entire educational system controlled by the University of Chicago, which would raise standards among smaller colleges and prepare students for college work in academies. Although he consistently sought to implement affiliations, such arrangements lacked funding and remained tenuous. They were abandoned after his death. Extension, too, implied a new mode of delivering instruction through an autonomous unit with its own faculty. It quickly developed into a substantial operation having an ambiguous relation to the University Proper. Research-minded faculty, then as now, had little enthusiasm for Extension or affiliations.[56]

The university opened in 1892 with a Faculty of Arts, Literature, and Science teaching undergraduate and graduate courses and a School of Divinity. Here, too, Harper's academic vision was inclusive. Fourteen autonomous departments included the country's first in sociology, under Albion Small. In 1894 John Dewey joined the philosophy department but soon focused on education, later founding the Laboratory School and a College of Education. In 1898 Chicago opened the second (after the University of Pennsylvania) College of Commerce and Administration. Although personally uncomfortable with coeducation, Harper recruited former Wellesley president Alice Freeman Palmer to be part-time dean of women, and she brought Marion Talbot, who succeeded her. An MIT graduate in sanitary science, Talbot was appointed assistant professor in that subject and later head professor of a new department of household administration. Amos Alonzo Stagg, famous for his exploits in baseball and football, was given a faculty appointment to lead the Department of Physical Culture, but in effect he also became the first football coach when told by Harper "to develop teams we can send around the country and knock out all the colleges."[57]

The distinctive feature of the university organization was the quarter system, which allowed for a regular term during summers. Students were expected to

---

56   Goodspeed, *History of the University*, 130–57, quote p. 134; Storr, *Harper's University*, 196–222.
57   Ibid., 179.

attend and faculty, to teach during any three quarters of the year. Originally the quarter system complemented Harper's objective that students should concentrate on fewer subjects at a time. However, its greatest virtue was to open the university to a multitude of students desiring advanced studies. Teachers were especially numerous among summer students. Many enrolled as unclassified students, and some of those remained to pursue graduate degrees. With an abundance of serious, advanced students, the summer quarter became more attractive for professors. Summer sessions were adopted by most other universities within a decade, but none had as full offerings as Chicago. In 1909 the summer quarter had almost one thousand students more than in the fall and a higher proportion of graduate students. The flexibility of the quarter system also furthered Harper's aim to supersede class loyalties. Like others, he perceived a difference in the character of work in the first 2 and last 2 years of college, but, being Harper, he also did something about it by dividing undergraduate studies into junior and senior colleges. He repeatedly suggested that the preparatory mission of the junior college might be outsourced to other institutions but never seriously attempted this.[58] In later years, Harper tried to encourage greater collegiate spirit through residence halls but also by segregating the sexes in the junior college—an unpopular initiative that was soon dropped. However, the junior-senior college split became a permanent feature of the university.[59]

Through all these machinations, Harper never wavered in his commitment to a faculty dedicated to advancing knowledge and graduate education. He employed the persuasive force of his personality as much as attractive salaries to appoint distinguished heads of each department. Given these aspirations, there was never enough money, and the budget was perpetually in deficit. The chief patron, John D. Rockefeller, had an almost fatherly affection for Harper and took great pride in the accomplishments of the faculty, but he was offended by Harper's unbusinesslike stewardship of the university and annoyed by his continual importuning. He also expected Chicagoans to provide more support, although they did donate numerous buildings. The financial history of the university thus consists of deficits, requests for more funds, demands to control expenditures and raise funds in Chicago, and, eventually, further gifts. Rockefeller gave $24 million to the university before he finally cut Harper off ($35 million with subsequent gifts). The result, despite the drama, was an astounding success. In a decade Harper created an institution that stood with Harvard

---

58   Harper has been called the "father of the junior college": he coined this term first for the lower division of the University of Chicago and later (1900) used junior college, for lack of a better term, to cover the work of the freshman and sophomore years: Walter Crosby Eells, ed., *American Junior Colleges* (Washington, D.C.: American Council on Education, 1940), 11–15. See chapter 10.

59   Goodspeed, *History of the University*, 141–43; Slosson, *Great American Universities*, 405–41.

and Columbia as the nation's finest research universities. Chicago, in fact, led in graduate studies, with the largest number of graduate students and the most PhDs. But, above all, it possessed a distinguished faculty in all its departments. Going forward, after Harper's untimely death in 1906, it would be the research-minded faculty that would determine the course of the university.[60]

By 1900 Chicago symbolized the new American research university. Having neither the social biases of the Eastern universities nor the remoteness of esoteric Germanic research, it combined intellectual distinction with democratic openness and a spirit of innovation. Chicago's Americanization of the research ideal set a standard that other major universities could scarcely ignore. On the cusp of the twentieth century, the *Great American Universities*, each in its own fashion, embraced that same ideal.

THE GREAT AMERICAN UNIVERSITIES

In 1910 science journalist Edwin E. Slosson published a volume depicting fourteen *Great American Universities*. He had spent time on each campus and provided rich description of administration, faculty, and student cultures, along with insightful comments and comparative statistics. The greatness of these institutions was owed, by his working definition, to their size: Slosson chose universities with the largest instructional budgets—those having the most resources to spend on their faculties. Johns Hopkins, with a slightly smaller budget, was grandfathered in. If MIT, whose budget qualified, were included, these institutions would form oddly symmetrical groups.[61] Five were founded as colonial colleges—Columbia, Harvard, Pennsylvania, Princeton, and Yale. Five were western state universities—California, Illinois, Michigan, Minnesota, and Wisconsin. And, five were postbellum new universities—Chicago, Cornell, Johns Hopkins, MIT, and Stanford. They were what would later be called research universities—the leaders of the academic revolution, able to cover the largest number of disciplines, nurture the most expertise, and institutionalize graduate education and research.[62]

---

60 On departments: Pugh, *Beginnings of Research*; on finance and philanthropy: Goodspeed, *History of the University*; on Rockefeller: Chernow, *Titan*, 493–97.

61 Instructional budgets ranged from $1,145,000 at Columbia to $263,000 at Minnesota, with Johns Hopkins at $211,000 and MIT at $301,000. Ohio State, Nebraska, and Missouri just missed the cut with budgets near $240,000; all other public universities had budgets less than $200,000: Carnegie Foundation for the Advancement of Teaching, "The Financial Status of the Professor in America and in Germany," Bulletin No. 2 (New York: 1908), 10–19.

62 Edwin E. Slosson, *Great American Universities* (New York: Macmillan, 1910), ix–x. Laurence Veysey includes Clark in *The Emergence of the American University*, but not Penn, Illinois, or Minnesota.

These universities were characterized, above all, by their size, resources, and commitment to academic quality. Previous sections have described how several of them developed. For the others, large enrollments, commensurate income, and a mission of academic advancement emerged in various ways. Students were clearly attracted by academic distinction and proliferating programs or both. Eleven of these institutions were the largest in the country, while Stanford, Princeton, and MIT were of moderate size. Together, the share of total U.S. enrollments at these fifteen universities reached 22 percent in the mid-1900s, before the rest of higher education began to catch up. As early as 1900 the "leading universities" organized as the Association of American Universities (AAU). The immediate motive was to bolster the prestige of the American PhD in the eyes of European universities and distinguish their degrees from dubious doctorates being awarded by unqualified colleges. The original members were the principal doctoral granting universities—Slosson's "Great Universities" without Illinois and Minnesota (admitted in 1908) but including the two graduate universities, Clark and Catholic. The AAU was immediately recognized as an exclusive club of those institutions best embodying academic values. The attainments of these institutions stand out. Most of the Great Universities had 200 or more regular faculty outside of professional schools; only three other universities even barely exceeded 100. Budgetary comparisons are similar.[63] In part, these universities grew better by simply growing—by adding new units to teach modern subjects and hiring new faculty with PhDs. However, at some point aggressive and inspired leadership was also required to force essential reforms upon existing units, upgrade standards, and secure resources essential for academic progress.

The circumstances of the transition to research universities varied widely among these institutions. At one extreme, epitomized by Princeton and Yale, collegiate values were paramount and a continuing obstacle to incorporating the academic revolution into the curriculum. Even after Porter and McCosh, tampering with the 4-year AB course was never contemplated, as it was elsewhere.[64] Both schools embraced, or succumbed to, the academic revolution after 1900 without threatening the preeminence of their colleges, as will be seen in chapter 9. At the other extreme, the colleges of the old city universities remained small

---

Roger L. Geiger adds MIT and (later) Caltech to Slosson's list in *To Advance Knowledge* and provides data on these sixteen universities, 270–78.

63   Geiger, *To Advance Knowledge*, 12–20, 270–71; Hugh Hawkins, *Banding Together: The Rise of National Associations in American Higher Education, 1887–1950* (Baltimore: Johns Hopkins University Press, 1992), 10–15, 37–41; Carnegie Foundation for the Advancement of Teaching, "The Financial Status of the Professor in America and in Germany," Bulletin No. 2 (New York: 1908), 10–19.

64   Yale offered a 3-year degree in the Sheffield School but resisted any change in the Yale College AB: Pierson, *Yale College*, 203–7.

and weak entering the new era, and they were overshadowed in the process of university building by more powerful professional schools.

COLUMBIA COLLEGE AND THE UNIVERSITY OF PENNSYLVANIA

An enduring symmetry exists in the development of Columbia and Penn, from their colonial incarnations to their emergence as modern universities. Both stagnated during the first two-thirds of the nineteenth century under the domination of trustees drawn from a narrow circle of eminent families. In the 1850s, Columbia famously refused to appoint the country's finest chemist because he was Unitarian. In the 1860s, the Penn provost believed that only about 100 young men in Philadelphia had an interest in a college education, and that number was not likely to increase.[65] Both institutions soon began a long process of developing into universities under determined modernizing leaders. Both moved to new campuses; expanded the university mission by establishing new units in unprecedented subjects; modernized and upgraded professional schools; and appointed wealthy local businessmen to lead their development. Both finally emerged as collections of loosely connected schools. However, Columbia emerged as the stronger university, benefiting from more effective leadership, greater wealth, support from local elites, and a stronger commitment to academic excellence.

In 1864 the trustees of Columbia College in the City of New York named Frederick A. P. Barnard as the tenth president, a seemingly unlikely reformer. Although from New England and a Yale grad, Barnard had spent the previous 25 years at the universities of Alabama and Mississippi before crossing the battle line and declaring his allegiance to the Union. Barnard was talented in all his endeavors and attuned to contemporary currents in higher education. He recognized the anachronistic character of the classical AB course and marshaled statistics to demonstrate its declining popularity. In his first years, he tripled official enrollments to 446 (1868) by incorporating the recently created School of Mines and a Law School. Barnard soon concluded that the growth of academic knowledge made the elective system imperative, but only a limited number of institutions could support the large faculty needed for such offerings. Joining that number became his goal for Columbia. He insisted on Columbia's destiny to become a great university. He was supported by a key trustee against a predominantly

---

65   Robert A. McCaughey, *Stand Columbia: A History of Columbia University in the City of New York, 1754–2004* (New York: Columbia University Press, 2004), 120–30; Edward Potts Cheney, *History of the University of Pennsylvania, 1740–1940* (New York: Arno Press, 1977 [1940]), 260. The following account draws largely from these histories.

conservative board. Barnard became the first Columbia president to assert authority over the institution rather than acting merely as an agent of the trustees. The School of Political Science was established to offer graduate degrees in 1880, and the graduate school in 1882. In the years before his death in 1889—amid the enthusiasm for graduate universities—he advocated dropping the college entirely. Barnard was also a consistent advocate of coeducation, but this innovation had too many strategic opponents. Instead, a separate women's college was created at the time of his death (1889), which ironically bore his name.[66]

Barnard's counterpart at Penn was Charles Stillé (1868–1880), whose title was provost, not president, and who presided only over the faculty of arts. With 100 students, the college was overshadowed by the 500 students in the autonomous schools of law and medicine. Conservative trustees ruled the university. The provost could not even attend their meetings, but the powerful medical school always had their ear. Although he had taught for only 2 years, Stillé caught the university spirit. He managed the university's move to West Philadelphia and the erection of the new campus. He also arranged the creation of a scientific school and electives for juniors and seniors. During his tenure Penn established a dental school, although, typically, this was accomplished by the medical school without the knowledge of the provost. Stillé was increasingly frustrated by the absence of leadership by the trustees and, particularly, their refusal to make him the university's president. His distemper undermined his effectiveness and finally provoked his resignation. His successor, William Pepper (1881–1894), was a medical aristocrat, following his father's affluent footsteps as a professor of medicine. With this pedigree, he was given what had been denied to Stillé: chairmanship of the board of trustees and oversight of the entire university. With competence and foresight, Pepper presided over the elevation of the university on all fronts. Prominent Philadelphians began donating to the university for the first time. Thirteen departments were added during his administration, including the country's first university schools for business and veterinary science. Particularly important was the establishment of a graduate school with a select faculty and earned graduate degrees. The university roughly doubled in size during his 14 years to more than 2,000, with three-quarters of students in graduate or professional departments, and it remained larger than Columbia.[67]

Both universities next turned to independently wealthy trustees for leadership. Seth Low (1890–1901) transformed Columbia into a true university, so named in 1896. A trustee since 1881, Low assumed the presidency dedicated

---

66   McCaughey, *Stand Columbia*, 146–70; John Fulton, *Memoirs of Frederick A. P. Barnard, 10th President of Columbia College in the City of New York* (New York: Macmillan, 1896).

67   Cheney, *University of Pennsylvania*, 257–84.

both to making Columbia a top institution academically and integrating it with the life of its dynamic and expanding city. He began by reorganizing the separate units into five faculties—Columbia College, philosophy, political science, applied science, and law—soon joined by medicine and pure science. Each faculty was led by an elected dean, and a University Council was formed to coordinate the colleges and inform the president. The scope of Columbia was further widened by affiliations with three theological seminaries, Barnard College (opened 1894), Teachers College (1898), and an extension division (1899). Low deferred to faculty ambitions in elevating Columbia to preeminent academic status. The number of full-time faculty grew from 45 to 250 in his 11 years. Departments recruited young PhDs and also senior scholars with established reputations, including several from Princeton and Penn. Low also initiated and managed the move of the entire university to its uptown Morningside Heights campus. He induced wealthy fellow trustees to make substantial donations to construct the new buildings and gave more than $1 million himself. Low resigned in 1901 to run (successfully) for mayor of New York City. He was succeeded by Nicholas Murray Butler (1902–1945), a brilliant local wunderkind who had been groomed by Barnard and Low. Butler was even more driven to make Columbia the biggest and best university in the country. He largely sustained the momentum in faculty building, civic engagement, and philanthropy. When Slosson visited the Great Universities, Columbia had the largest enrollment, the biggest budget, and the most graduate students.[68]

Penn's new provost was retired businessman Charles C. Harrison (1895–1910). As chair of the trustee budget committee, he had directed the university's finances for the previous 15 years, and he was also the largest donor. His tenure is noted chiefly for the numerous buildings he added to Penn's campus, partly with his own funds but also by relentlessly tapping his wealthy friends. But his educational imprint was diffuse, with academic matters left largely to his vice provost. He clearly had the greatest interest in extracurricular matters, although not just in the arts college. He erected Houston Hall, the first all-purpose student union in the country (1896) and perhaps the most unifying agent in this fragmented institution. He also built several student dormitories, a gymnasium, and Franklin Field for football. At the same time, he supported research by endowing the Harrison Foundation for the support of full time graduate students and generally encouraged the expansion of research, particularly in fields related to the

68   McCaughey, *Stand Columbia*, 177–233; Joby Topper, "College Presidents, Public Image, and the Popular Press: Francis L. Patton of Princeton and Seth Low of Columbia, 1888–1902," *Perspectives on the History of Higher Education*, 28 (2011): 63–114; Michael Rosenthal, *Nicholas Miraculous: The Amazing Career of the Redoubtable Dr. Nicholas Murray Butler* (New York: Farrar, Straus and Giroux, 2006); Slosson, *Great American Universities*, 442–73.

medical school. As a businessman, he appreciated the practical curricula of the Wharton School and allowed it to expand without interference (with one exception) or help. Penn, in fact, drifted toward a service role by offering night school, weekend, and extension courses in certificate subjects while also seeking and receiving support from the state. These developments, however, did not form a coherent strategy and certainly nothing like Columbia's lust for academic glory. Rather than providing direction for the collection of uncoordinated schools, Slosson found that "nobody seems to worry in the University of Pennsylvania about anything."[69]

The contrast between Columbia and Penn is particularly telling in the social sciences, where each made important but different contributions. Their original initiatives, however, had much in common. Before the Wharton School opened in 1883, John Burgess had established the School of Political Science at Columbia in a conscious effort at university building. Burgess was a German trained academic entrepreneur who left his alma mater Amherst when it would not let him teach graduate students. At Columbia he pioneered a distinctive approach to the American PhD. Seniors from Columbia or other colleges could take their senior year in his school to earn an AB and then earn a PhD (or law degree) with 2 years of additional work. The school, which taught history and social sciences, was thus superimposed on the college and became the locus for graduate education. With a like-minded faculty, Burgess followed the Hopkins formula for discipline formation by establishing the Academy of Political Science and a journal, *Political Science Quarterly*. Under Low, the faculty was greatly expanded, and Burgess served as the university's senior dean. Under Butler, the faculties of philosophy and pure science were folded into political science to become the graduate faculty, the core of Columbia's academic eminence. Burgess is credited with engineering the predominance of graduate and professional studies that became the hallmark of Columbia University.[70]

The Wharton School at Penn was originally designed to be elected for the third and fourth years of the college course. It, too, taught a history and social science curriculum along with finance and the protectionist economics favored by the Philadelphia business community. In 1883 Edmund James joined the faculty, a research-minded Halle PhD whose major field was public administration. The dynamic James soon dominated the school. He fully endorsed Joseph Wharton's basic aims and, in fact, sought to expand the school's influence through extension courses. But his chief goals were academic and mirrored those

69 Ibid., 356.
70 John W. Burgess, *Reminiscences of an American Scholar: The Beginning of Columbia University* (New York: Columbia University Press, 1934), 191–244; McCaughy, *Stand Columbia*, 160–63, 236–37.

of Burgess. James, too, established an association and a journal for his field, and he sought in vain to create a School of Political and Social Science. He hired like-minded scholars, mostly Halle PhDs, and led the establishment of doctoral education. By the early 1890s, James had academicized the faculty and graduate students of the Wharton School, if not the undergraduates, and the school bore some resemblance to Burgess's. However, in 1895, in his first day as provost, Harrison demanded James's resignation. His reasons, which remain undocumented, were probably both personal and ideological. James left quietly, but the Wharton School soon developed a dual personality.

One of James's last achievements was to gain approval for extending the Wharton course to all 4 years. Enrollments immediately grew, and they grew more rapidly in the next decade. With more-lenient admissions criteria, Wharton attracted a mixed clientele of future family business owners, nonwealthy students seeking job credentials, and those with few interests at all. At the same time, the 4-year curriculum allowed for greater concentration and specialization of business subjects. As the legacy faculty of the James regime busied themselves with graduate education and progressive causes, the growing numbers of regular and night school students were offered a functional business curriculum. However, politics, practical studies, and socially diverse students caused the Wharton School to lose favor with an increasingly conservative administration. In 1915 the trustees fired professor Scott Nearing for his outspoken progressive views. The firing prompted an uproar and one of the first academic freedom investigations by the new American Association of University Professors. For Penn, it signaled the end of the James legacy and pointed toward Wharton's next quarter century as a practical business school.[71]

STATE UNIVERSITIES

A number of state universities were well suited to join the academic revolution. Relatively large by the 1890s, they were adept at expanding horizontally by adding new schools, departments, and degrees. Hiring young faculty brought the new learning to campuses. They faced less trauma in superseding traditional curricula or accommodating disciplinary mitosis. On the other hand, they faced some limitations in embracing or fulfilling university aspirations, particularly for graduate education and research. State universities were typically dominated

---

71 Steven A. Sass, *The Pragmatic Imagination: A History of the Wharton School, 1881–1981* (Philadelphia: University of Pennsylvania Press, 1982); "Report of the Committee of Inquiry on the Case of Professor Scott Nearing of the University of Pennsylvania," *Bulletin of the American Association of University Professors*, II, 3, Part 2 (May, 1916): 5–57.

by boards of trustees and/or legislatures, neither of which was disposed toward academic distinction. These bodies, not unreasonably, judged the colleges largely in terms of the numbers of students educated and their fitness for careers. Presidents with academic ambitions, as seen in chapter 7, may have nudged their institutions forward but tended not to last long in office. The governance of these institutions thus fostered an insular outlook, bounded by the state borders, and a preference for leaders who could pacify the Grange, mitigate student mayhem, and keep faculty indiscretions out of newspapers. The states, to their credit, provided increasing funds for buildings and, for the fortunate, regular appropriations. However, state universities remained relatively poor compared with private universities.

These conditions improved markedly after 1900 in most states. General prosperity brought full treasuries, and university growth and prominence tapped into civic pride. Still, only five state universities qualified as Slosson's "Greats," and, except for Michigan, this achievement largely reflected progress since 1900. Before then, these universities had been held back by several factors. Relative poverty restrained faculty salaries and university resources, making it difficult for them to compete. Although they paid lip service to academic aspirations, they were unable or unwilling to seek out or retain top scholars: the top five private universities, for example, had three times as many "leading men of science" as these five publics. Finally, they graduated very few PhDs before 1900. Doctoral education increased after that date, but from 1898 to 1909 these public universities *together* conferred fewer PhDs than *each* of the top five privates. But by that date the public universities were improving rapidly. In the decade, state appropriations increased from two to five times, and although enrollments grew, the number of faculty grew faster.[72] Perhaps more important, California, Illinois, and Wisconsin installed new presidents who were dedicated to raising their institutions to the highest level of academic distinction.

Still, the University of Michigan was the unrivaled dean of state institutions. In 1890 it boasted the largest student body in the country, the majority of whom came to Ann Arbor from other states and enrolled in the professional schools. It had acquired the aspect of a university under Henry Tappan, establishing electives, abolishing parietal rules, and acquiring a reputation for spirited teaching. Since 1871 it had been presided over by James Burrill Angell (1871–1909), who guided the gradual accretion and modernization of the university and who is generally considered one of the era's university builders. He had taught languages

---

72 Slosson, *Great American Universities*, 485; Geiger, *To Advance Knowledge*, 39 and appendix. State universities tended to be preoccupied with local responsibilities and seldom adopted a national perspective.

at his alma mater, Brown (1853–1860), but Angell antedated the academic revolution, as did Eliot and White. Like them, he understood the challenges it raised. Indeed, Angell was a national leader, frequently consulted in university matters, but he was personally responsible for few reforms at Michigan. The university pioneered the admission of students by graduation from "certified" high schools—an approach soon copied by other state universities—but this was initiated by Acting President Henry Frieze before Angell arrived.[73] Similarly, vital state support in the form of a mill tax was passed in 1869. The boldest initiative in graduate education was also launched by Frieze, again as acting president: the School of Political Science (1881), an arrangement like Columbia's, allowed students to start working toward advanced degrees in their junior year. Unlike Columbia and Penn, however, the Michigan School was short lived. It produced small numbers of master's degrees in the 1880s but no PhDs. Michigan, which had awarded its first PhD in 1876, continued to graduate a handful of PhDs of the traditional kind (an average of eight per year in the 1900s), hindered by lack of support for advanced students or faculty research.[74]

University presidents receive the lion's share of credit for academic advancement, but Michigan professors attempted to take matters into their own hands by organizing a Research Club in 1900.[75] Led by senior professors, chiefly from chemistry and the medical school, it aimed to promote research, make original investigation a factor in faculty promotion, and organize a university-wide graduate school. Clearly the active scholars and scientists at Michigan felt that the university had not sufficiently institutionalized academic values, and they were seconded by younger colleagues, who formed a Junior Research Club and a Women's Research Club. President Angell was sympathetic, but the Regents were not. Angell's annual reports for the 1890s and 1900s repeatedly warned that additional support was imperative for research, for graduate students, and for advanced seminars—"if we are not to fall behind . . ." was his repeated refrain. However, the complaints of the Research Club indicate that the problem was

---

73 Mark A. Van Overbeke, *The Standardization of American Schooling: Linking Secondary and Higher Education, 1870–1910* (New York: Palgrave Macmillan, 2008); Mark R. Nemec, *Ivory Towers and Nationalist Minds: Universities, Leadership, and the Development of the American State* (Ann Arbor: University of Michigan Press, 2006).

74 James Turner and Paul Bernard, "The German Model and the Graduate School: The University of Michigan and the Origin Myth of the American University," in Geiger, *The American College in the Nineteenth Century*, 221–41; Howard H. Peckham, *The Making of the University of Michigan, 1817–1992*, edited and updated by Margaret L. Steneck and Nicholas H. Steneck (Ann Arbor: University of Michigan Bentley Historical Library, [1967], 1994), 77–126.

75 Originally, the "Society for the Promotion of Research at the University of Michigan": "The Research Club of the University of Michigan," *The University of Michigan, an Encyclopedic Survey*, Wilfred B. Shaw, ed. 6 vol., II, 399–406; "The Horace H. Rackham School of Graduate Studies," loc. cit. 1037–51: http://quod.lib.umich.edu/u/survey/.

administrative as well as financial. The Club particularly pressed the point that scholarly work should be the basis for faculty appointments and promotion. Michigan hired excellent young scholars but then lost many of them to more aggressive universities. John Dewey left Michigan twice, for Minnesota (1888) and Chicago (1894), and members of the Research Club were subsequently recruited to Stanford, Penn, Hopkins, and the University of Toronto. An administrative commitment to improve conditions only followed Angell's retirement in 1909. A scathing report by the Research Club (initially suppressed by President Harry Hutchins to avoid demoralizing alumni) prompted long-requested reforms. The Graduate School was created in 1912, led by members of the Research Club, and a more sympathetic Board of Regents voted funds for graduate fellowships. Michigan remained a Great American University, but it was no longer the undisputed leader of public higher education.

That mantle passed to the University of Wisconsin, which President Eliot in 1908 anointed as the country's leading state university.[76] The occasion was the conferral of an honorary degree on the university's president, Charles Van Hise (1903–1918), a distinguished geologist who earned all his degrees at Wisconsin, including the university's first PhD (1892). Van Hise's career included important contributions in both pure and applied science (geological surveys and economic geology), and he carried that perspective to his stewardship of the university. He emphasized that the chief tasks of the university were to prepare undergraduates for careers and citizenship, to advance knowledge through research and creative work, and to make the expertise of the university available to the state for addressing economic, social, and political issues. However, research was the lynchpin of the university mission, since discovery and expertise were necessary to inspire collegians and to assist the state. Van Hise governed the university with calm but unshakable confidence in these views. Within the state, he presented these views forcefully and persistently in the belief that if citizens understood its contributions, they would provide the resources it needed to become a great university.

The promotion of the utilitarian role by Van Hise struck a new note for public universities. Perceptions of the usefulness of university expertise were largely confined to agriculture and were still contested. Van Hise envisioned the university contributing to the governance of the entire state (the capitol was conveniently located up the street from the Madison campus) as well as providing educational services widely through extension. Van Hise's advocacy of this role soon

---

76 Slosson, *Great American Universities*, 219. The following draws on Merle Curti and Vernon Carstensen, *The University of Wisconsin: A History, 1848–1925*, 2 vol. (Madison: University of Wisconsin Press, 1949).

caught the fancy of the national press and was dubbed the "Wisconsin Idea." In 1909 investigative journalist Lincoln Steffens lauded these efforts in a popular article, "Sending a State to College"; and Slosson also embellished this role in his account. He reported that forty Wisconsin professors were advising state or federal bodies and described the inchoate extension system as "rural free delivery" of education.[77] The realities of the university largely matched the image, giving Wisconsin a distinctive profile that was more pronounced, but consistent with, the service orientation pioneered by Harper at Chicago and evident at Columbia and Penn.

Van Hise became president under Progressive governor Robert La Follette (1900–1906); both had absorbed the social morality of President John Bascom. Utilizing university expertise for intelligent administration dovetailed with the Progressive impulse to expand and rationalize state government. These efforts were specifically assisted by eminent social science departments that taught courses on current social issues. However, "nonpartisan expertise" for one party can be political bias for their opponents. When "Stalwart" Republicans returned to power, they were critical of the university's emphasis on research and extension, and they harassed it with dubious investigations of "efficiency." Throughout this running battle, Van Hise defended the university. Perhaps the provision of university services actually did win over the citizens of the state. The university had offered a variety of extension courses in the 1890s, but outside of agriculture they had largely lapsed. Van Hise was persuaded to revive extension only in 1906, but he soon became a fervent champion. With agricultural short courses as a model, he took the controversial position that no subject was too rudimentary for university extension if there was a public need. The legislature provided financial support, and Wisconsin developed the largest system of university extension in the country.

Most important, Van Hise was able to link the Wisconsin Idea with the bolstering of research, graduate education, and faculty quality. He inherited a strong academic base when he assumed the presidency, largely due to the earlier efforts of President Thomas Chamberlin (1887–1893). During Van Hise's tenure, state support quadrupled while enrollments did not quite triple, making Wisconsin the best-funded state university. These funds were employed to maintain an accomplished faculty of active scholars and scientists. The social sciences benefited from the Hopkins spirit brought by frontier historian Frederick Jackson Turner and economist Richard Ely, both of whom built their respective departments. Powerful deans with solid academic values also helped

77   Lincoln Steffens, "Sending a State to College," *American Magazine*, 68 (1909): 350–63; Slosson, *Great American Universities*, 214–15, 241.

to shape the faculty. Wisconsin, for example, tried to match the offers made to its faculty: Turner's suitors were thwarted on several occasions with generous raises before he decamped to Harvard for other reasons (1910). Efforts by President Chamberlin to emulate Johns Hopkins committed Wisconsin to doctoral education well in advance of any other state university. Under Van Hise it became the first to award significant numbers of PhDs. The university organized the graduate school in 1904 and supported students with graduate fellowships and teaching assistantships, buoyed by growing numbers of undergraduates. It led all state universities in awarding PhDs (1898–1909) and retained that distinction until World War II. Wisconsin's amalgam of democracy, service, growth, and academic research in many ways mirrored the prewar zeitgeist of the progressive era, but it also signified a new ambition among state universities to attain academic distinction.

Unlike Wisconsin, the University of Illinois embarked on a new direction when it joined this movement under President Edmund James (1904–1920). The university had expanded its scope and scale dramatically under the presidency of Andrew S. Draper (1894–1904). Undergraduate enrollments tripled; five professional schools were added; and the state appropriation, including capital, almost quadrupled. Illinois advanced from the fourteenth to the seventh largest university, but its academic standing was far lower. Draper was a schoolman who had attended law school but not college. With little appreciation for academic values, he functioned as an agent of the trustees. His treatment of faculty was particularly heavy handed, and he was dismissive toward research. The university advanced along several fronts during his decade in the presidency, but Edmund James inherited an institution of huge unrealized potential.[78]

James attacked the presidency with the zeal he had previously shown as director of the Wharton School. A progressive Republican, he shared the core tenets of the Wisconsin idea—the university contribution to public administration and governance, the expansion of its impact through extension and teacher education, and its democratic connection with the people of the state. In his inaugural address, "The Function of the State University," he asserted that the institution should train the state's youth for all careers requiring liberal preparation and scientific training. The latter emphasis reflected his German training: that all the undertakings of the university should be scientific in character. In a sense, James was committed to imposing the character of a German university while preserving the mission of a land grant college. He succeeded in large measure by winning the support of state legislators, establishing and expanding doctoral

---

78 Winton U. Solberg, *The University of Illinois, 1894–1904: The Shaping of the University* (Urbana: University of Illinois Press, 2000).

programs, and imposing a more liberal and scientific outlook on a largely professional university.[79]

To gain favor with the legislature, James undertook a grassroots letter-writing campaign to enlist the support of educators throughout the state for advanced education in the university. He also dealt openly and honestly with legislators, telling them that graduate education would cost a great deal. Apparently it worked. In 1908 the legislature appropriated $50,000 for graduate work in the arts and sciences. Moreover, it passed a remarkable joint resolution endorsing the university's aspirations: to provide all forms of quality higher education needed by the sons and daughters of Illinois; to undertake "extensive and important investigations of vital interest to the agriculture, industry, and education of the State"; and "to compete [on salaries] on equal grounds with other State and private universities" to prevent other institutions from "drawing away the members of the faculties."[80] The legislature delivered as well: while enrollments doubled during James's presidency, per-student spending doubled as well. The progress of doctoral education was one tangible result of James's efforts. Illinois did not grant its first PhD until 1903. Three years later James organized a graduate school and in 1908 was invited to join the AAU. Graduate enrollments quickly doubled and doubled again in the next decade. In the early 1920s, after James retired, Illinois ranked ninth in PhDs awarded. He endeavored to develop a university character in an institution where less than one-fifth of students studied arts and sciences (1904), which meant imposing a research culture on the professional schools. An Engineering Research Station was established in 1905, for example. His efforts to reform medical education were more protracted but eventually successful. For the liberal arts, his obsession was to build a great library. And here, too, his persistent efforts set it on a path to become the third-largest university library in the United States.[81] The times may have been propitious, but James provided the vision and cultivated the support that made this transformation possible.

The third transformational president of this era was Benjamin Ide Wheeler of the University of California (1899–1919). Wheeler had taken a German PhD (Heidelberg, 1885) in comparative philology before becoming a classics professor at Cornell. Although a scholar, he had been immensely popular with students at Ithaca, as he would be at Berkeley. Perhaps he got on well with students because he had enjoyed being one himself, playing baseball and rowing

---

79 Winton U. Solberg, "President Edmund James and the University of Illinois, 1904–1920: Redeeming the Promise of the Morrill Act," *Perspectives on the History of Higher Education*, 30 (2013): 225–46.

80 Slosson, *Great American Universities*, 277–311, quote p. 285.

81 Solberg, "President Edmund J. James"; Lori Thurgood et al., *U.S. Doctorates in the 20th Century* (National Science Foundation: June 2006), 104; Winton U. Solberg, *Reforming Medical Education: The University of Illinois College of Medicine, 1880–1920* (Urbana: University of Illinois Press, 2009).

crew at Brown and remaining a sports fan throughout his life. The university he joined was already accustomed to research. A tradition of philanthropy that was unique for public universities before 1900 had yielded the Lick Observatory, a research institute supported by continuing private contributions. The University of California Press was created in 1893 to facilitate faculty publications. The problem seemingly plaguing the university was trustee governance: it was widely recognized in academic circles that Regent domination of the university was responsible for a succession of short-lived presidencies. Wheeler made rectifying this situation a condition for accepting the presidency. The Regents agreed that the president would be the sole channel of communication with the board; that he would have complete control over appointments, removals, and salaries; and that he would direct all other employees and officers of the university. If Wheeler sounded autocratic in his demands, he was. But he moved the immediate governance of the university to the campus.[82]

Wheeler's firm rule was facilitated by a dignified, yet affable, personality. He accorded the students greater self-government, which they exercised responsibly. He exerted moral authority through regular meetings with students and exhorted them to be loyal to the university. He frequently took to the road, making speeches around the state to generate support for the university. He was especially adept at charming legislators into generous appropriations. Reputed to be the best-dressed university president, he moved comfortably in the social circles of the Regents. In sum, Wheeler translated his personal popularity into support for the university from both the public fisc and private donors. Only faculty, it seems, resented his authoritarian tendencies. The entire administration consisted of his appointees, and he made all decisions on salaries and promotions without consultation. On the other hand, Wheeler possessed a keen academic judgment and actively sought to recruit senior scientists and scholars. Wheeler personally vetted candidates on eastern trips, and his hires built a strong faculty. California, in fact, had the largest number of "leading men of science" among state universities. During Wheeler's first decade, in particular, the university made great strides materially and academically. After 1910, he confronted leaner budgets and growing faculty resistance. The latter unleashed a faculty revolt in his final years that achieved a large measure of self-government through the Academic Senate (1920). Subsequently, faculty authority over academic matters further enhanced a supportive political and social climate for cultivating academic quality.[83]

82   Verne A. Stadtman, *The University of California, 1868–1968* (New York: McGraw-Hill, 1970), 179–201.

83   Ibid., 191–213; Slosson, *Great American Universities*, 148–81; J. McKeen Cattell and Jacques Cattell, eds., *American Men of Science: A Biographical Dictionary*, 4th ed. (New York: Science Press, 1927), 1127.

The Great American Universities described by Edwin Slosson in 1909 were a far cry from the institutions that, circa 1890, had pondered how graduate and undergraduate education should be structured. Twice as large, on average, they had grown far more in their faculties, administration, and budgets. For example, Angell's first two decades have been called his "personal presidency," when he knew each faculty member and most students. But after 1890, Michigan, like other universities, gradually assembled a nonteaching administration to manage its multiplying parts. William Rainey Harper brought a new level of administrative complexity as he elaborated the structure of the University of Chicago. Nicholas Murray Butler advanced central administration another degree with a large presidential staff to handle his voluminous communications. Charles Eliot, who presided over a vast expansion of Harvard, summarized these lessons in *University Administration* (1908). Universities had changed not only in growing an internal bureaucracy, but also in becoming more dependent on external relations.[84]

Major universities now consisted of a hierarchy that extended downward from president to deans of multiple colleges to heads of departments and, finally, to faculty. The existence of this administrative core tended to distance both trustees and faculty from decision making. Trustees retained ultimate authority, of course, and still made important decisions; but the cases just reviewed indicate that they were no longer in positions to comprehend, let alone dominate, everyday management. Faculty largely lost the personal interactions they formerly had with presidents as well as many unpleasant chores toward students. They could now attend to their academic specialties with departmental colleagues having similar interests. Moreover, the pervasive concern for prestige now made (some of) them valuable property. More than ever, presidents were the key figures, exercising much broader responsibilities within the administration. "Everywhere," Laurence Veysey concludes, "the trend was toward increased presidential vigor"—and institutions where this was lacking suffered. Eliot described the essential tasks as supervision: presidents had to consult and negotiate before reaching decisions, while at all times seeking to control situations. History tends to feature presidential success stories, but many failed these prescriptions. In the cases above, Angell's loss of effectiveness in his final years was apparent; Harrison's administration became isolated and incoherent; and Wheeler's autocratic ways eventually provoked a backlash.[85]

84   Peckham, *University of Michigan*, 99; Charles W. Eliot, *University Administration* (Boston: Houghton Mifflin, 1908).

85   Veysey, *Emergence*, 302–17, quote p. 304; Eliot, *University Administration*, 235–39.

A president's external relations became more crucial as universities grew dependent on different constituencies for the resources on which they depended. Eliot's advice for state university leaders mirrored the strategies of Van Hise, James, and Wheeler: demonstrate the value of the university to the people of the state as well as the legislators in order to acquire the resources needed for growth and improvement. The advice for presidents of endowed institutions was more nuanced. They, too, had to demonstrate value but also project a positive image of their university to alumni, potential benefactors, and the popular press: "realization of the service a strong university renders to the country, and to mankind, is the great inducement to education benefactions; and it is therefore an important function of the president." Thus, private research universities, as well as public ones, embrace service to society as a fundamental mission, and this view accounts for the great expansion in their scope of activities. State universities, Eliot instructed, ought "to meet every appropriate demand for the services of the university," but private universities, too, acted in this manner. Besides mushrooming enrollments in engineering and agriculture, these universities added schools or departments for dentistry, pharmacy, commerce, education, home economics, music, forestry, and architecture; and nearly all operated extension divisions.[86] By broadening their scope the universities addressed the career interests of far more students, even as student interests in college became increasingly preoccupied by extracurricular activities.

86   Geiger, *To Advance Knowledge*, 39–57; Eliot, *University Administration*, 235, 231.

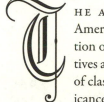

THE COLLEGIATE REVOLUTION

HE ACADEMIC TRANSFORMATION THAT PRODUCED American universities was accompanied by a parallel transformation of the undergraduate experience. Beyond the triumph of electives and academic disciplines in the classroom, student life outside of class assumed a richness and intensity that imparted new significance to the meaning of college. Any connection between these two developments would appear to be circumstantial. Campuses that clung to the old regime—Dartmouth, Princeton, Yale—in fact were the leaders of the collegiate revolution. Although the timing of the two revolutions was remarkably similar, the transformation of collegiate life had a dynamic all its own. The trend toward greater student autonomy and activities that was evident before the Civil War strengthened markedly in the 1870s. Just as the next decade was the tipping point for the academic revolution, it was the same for collegiate life.[1] The years around 1890 marked an indelible change, most noticeable in the burgeoning popularity of intercollegiate football, but encompassing all aspects of college life. Most remarkable was the rapid spread of the chief forms of collegiate activities geographically and institutionally. After 1900, idealization of the collegiate experience was further enhanced—cherished by graduates and celebrated in the middle-class media. Research had become an end in itself at a handful of universities; now collegiate life was for many an end in itself. Whereas research and PhDs were the hallmarks of the academic revolution, football and fraternities were hallmarks of the collegiate revolution.

THE HIGH COLLEGIATE ERA

A generation separated Lyman Bagg (Yale 1869), introduced in chapter 6 as the author of *Four Years at Yale*, from Henry Seidel Canby (Yale 1899), whose recollections in *Alma Mater* idealize undergraduate life at the zenith of the *high collegiate era*. On no campus was college life pursued with more intensity and ostensible joy than the Yale that each author described, a distinction recognized

---

[1]   Cornelius Howard Patton and Walter Taylor Field, *Eight O'clock Chapel: A Study of New England College Life in the Eighties* (Boston: Houghton Mifflin, 1927).

by contemporaries. A curious Harvard instructor, George Santayana, paid a visit in 1892 to investigate. "Nothing could be more American," he concluded, than the Yale Spirit, by which "young men are trained and made eager for the keen struggles of American life." Compared to Harvard, Yale exhibited "more unity, more energy, and greater fitness to our present condition."[2] These qualities were not unique to Yale, of course, but they were concentrated there by insularity, competition, and a pervasive moral code. Canby described the college as "a state within a state. . . . [A] student body, aware really of only themselves, their own life, their own ideals." The mainspring of this spirit was competition for achievement, for success and recognition outside the classroom. Seemingly, every student internalized an expectation to "do something for Yale" and to be judged by those contributions, whether "heeling" for the *Yale Daily News*, volunteering in the YMCA, joining athletic teams, or any of the other myriad organizations that students formed and ran: "the immediate goal was to be regarded as a success by your friends"; the ultimate goal was election to one of the three senior secret societies. A belief in "Yale democracy" was an article of faith—that success resulted from personal effort and character, not wealth or family status. A second article of faith was that education occurred outside the classroom. Canby described Yale's retrograde curriculum as "a rotted house about to fall in and in parts already fallen" and any ideas or intellectual stirrings as "mere byproducts." It was collegiate experience that achieved "a moulding [*sic*] of character and intellect, and a complete shaping of behavior." And this formation, all believed, was the best preparation for the competitive struggles of American life.[3]

Several factors helped make Yale's unity and moral code so powerful. Yale was the most national of colleges in recruitment of students, but geographical diversity produced social homogeneity. Like Canby, whose father was a banker, most students came from well-to-do families and had attended private prep schools. Students from humble backgrounds who became big men on campus, like baseball prodigy Amos Alonzo Stagg, were cited as proof of Yale democracy, but backgrounds like Canby's were almost de rigueur for possessing the social skills and wardrobe needed to fit in. In Canby's time each class of 300+ competed for 51 positions in sophomore societies, 120 in junior fraternities, and 45 in the three senior societies. The pressure to achieve and impress was thus continual for those who aspired to these honors. Other colleges had their own forms of distinction. Harvard was dominated socially by Boston Brahmins, and its hierarchy of clubs

2 Lyman H. Bagg, *Four Years at Yale: By a Graduate of '69* (New Haven: Chatfield, 1871); Henry Seidel Canby, *Alma Mater: The Gothic Age of the American College* (Murray Hill, NY: Farrar & Rinehart, 1936); George W. Pierson, *Yale College: An Educational History, 1871–1921* (New Haven: Yale University Press, 1952), Santayana quote, pp. 6–7.

3 Canby, *Alma Mater*, 23–80; quotes pp. 28, 37, 62, 78, 68.

reflected both social status and merit, and members of Princeton's exclusive eating clubs were chosen largely on social criteria, sometimes before matriculation.[4] At most colleges, social standing was refracted through the fraternity system, and such arrangements encouraged tribal competitions instead of Yale's individual strivings. Colleges varied as well in the proportion of students who identified with the collegiate ethos.[5] Here Yale's structure was unique. During Canby's time, Yale College comprised just under half of enrollments in Yale University. Even in the college, Canby dismissed some students as "socially impossible," others as "grinds." The professional schools were "attended by hard-working meager creatures with the fun drained out of them," many of whom were not college graduates.[6] And the nearly 600 students in the Sheffield Scientific School were literally beyond the pale. They may have enjoyed their college experiences too, despite having to learn math and science, but not in the company of Yale College students.[7] Taken together, Yale University may have had a similar proportion of ardent collegians as the universities of Michigan or California.

Still, Yale College exaggerated characteristic features of the high collegiate era, for good and for ill. A less sentimental nonalum provided some perspective. Edwin Slosson noted in 1909 that the first requirement for success at Yale was conformity—fulfilling the local definition of a gentleman, being clubbable, and piously observing student traditions and customs. Conformity also extended to opinions; heterodox views were entertained at one's peril. Combined with the dismissive attitude toward classes, the result was decidedly anti-intellectual. Honors students were underrepresented by almost 50 percent in the senior societies. Slosson reported that senior society members were twice as likely as other graduates to achieve prominence after graduation—but the same was true of honors students. As sons of wealth and privilege increasingly patronized the college, social discrimination increased as well. This was most evident in attitudes toward Jewish students. In the 1880s it could be reported that there were no ill feelings toward Jewish students, but in the next decade anti-Semitism began to be evident.

---

4   Jerome Karabel, *The Chosen: The Hidden History of Admission and Exclusion at Harvard, Yale, and Princeton* (Boston: Houghton Mifflin, 2005), 39–76. Edwin Slosson noted: "There are so many kinds of democracy . . . every university boasts the purest brand"; regarding Yale democracy amidst Yale affluence, he found it "distinctly encouraging to find that the democratic spirit is still regarded as a desirable thing to have in a university": *Great American Universities*, 362, 71.

5   Helen Lefkowitz Horowitz, *Campus Life: Undergraduate Cultures from the End of the Eighteenth Century to the Present* (New York: Knopf, 1987).

6   Canby, *Alma Mater*, 48–49, 60. Canby would include himself among the "meager creatures," having earned a PhD in English in 1905. He taught at Yale until 1916 before pursuing a literary career in publishing.

7   Pierson, *Yale College*, 36. Like the heroine of *The Scarlet Letter*, Sheffield graduates had to bear the letter *S* after their class numerals for the sin of attending the scientific school.

By 1911, the newest senior society unanimously voted "That Jews should be denied recognition at Yale."[8] Such attitudes reflected a national trend in Yale's social base but apparently did not affect classroom treatment. However, it signaled the hardening of social lines at colleges and universities, especially after 1900. This also distinguished the high collegiate era from the late collegiate era.

The transformation of college life from the 1870s to the 1890s was a reciprocal process. On one side, colleges gradually relaxed the rules and discipline governing student behavior, though in some places this was a protracted and contested affair. On the other side, once allowed greater freedom, student activities and customs spontaneously proliferated. Colleges approved of some of this new behavior and opposed other aspects but over time became less able to affect either. Once students broke free from the anachronistic disciplinary regime, they found themselves in a virtual vacuum of authority, where their organizations need conform to few rules. Only in the twentieth century would universities develop administrative offices to reassert some measure of control.

The old regime sought to preserve the discipline of recitations and the piety of compulsory chapel. It persisted into the postbellum years at virtually every college but with a crumbling foundation. Where church ties remained strong, so did the will to uphold the old regime. But colleges drew their students and financial support not from organized churches but from the lay membership that included successful urban alumni. Student piety on campus rejected compulsory church services in favor of student chapters of the Young Men's Christian Association. Faculty had long chafed under the burdens of enforcing student discipline, but postbellum professionals largely avoided this task. Moreover, lectures and the elective system lessened the need for recitation discipline. Presidents, of course, were the ultimate authority, and the colleges long remained small enough for them to exercise this oversight. But growth forced university presidents to delegate. Charles Eliot appointed a dean for students in 1890; in 1901 the University of Illinois created the first official dean of undergraduates, later dean of men. These officials, though charged with enforcing rules and curbing excess, were generally warm supporters of collegiate activities. Finally, colleges and universities had only tenuous control over students because most no longer lived on campus. Henry Tappan initiated this change when he turned Michigan students out of university buildings to find lodgings in the town. In fact, most nineteenth-century colleges were too poor to build dormitories, and growing universities had other priorities.

8 Edwin E. Slosson, *Great American Universities*, 34–74; Karabel, *The Chosen*, 74–76; Dan A. Oren, *Joining the Club: A History of Jews and Yale* (New Haven: Yale University Press, 1985), 24–37. Jewish students at Yale College rose from near 2 percent (1900) to near 6 percent (1916), with perhaps one-third coming from wealthy, assimilated homes and two-thirds (ca. fifteen) from the New Haven ghetto.

Students living in rooming houses (sanctioned or not) and procuring their own meals had considerable freedom in how they used their time.[9]

Organizing and choosing their own activities, students wedged open these cracks in college authority. College glee clubs were first established for the pleasure of their members but soon serenaded nearby towns as well as the campus. By the early 1880s, glee clubs regularly embarked on lengthy tours. Belonging to the glee club thus offered the pleasures of singing and camaraderie but also the excitement of such excursions.[10] Theater was long forbidden to collegians by the descendants of the Puritans, but such restrictions were overcome in the 1880s. The first plays may have been serious renditions of Sophocles, but Gilbert and Sullivan quickly followed. College journalism had a longer history, but its forms began to multiply as literary journals, yearbooks, newspapers, and humor magazines appeared. Newspapers originally tended to follow an official line, supporting college policies, scholarship, and piety. However, by the 1880s they largely assumed a purely collegiate focus, preoccupied with the full range of student activities but especially promoting athletic chauvinism. The proliferation of such activities had some benign effects for colleges. Student preoccupation with their organizations may have distracted them from pranks and other forms of mayhem. Appeals to avoid sullying the honor of the college or a student's particular organization were often effective. Class loyalties still remained powerful, especially in the East, and class rituals represented an entire category of activities. But collegewide organizations tended to break down the isolation of the classes. On some campuses various forms of "rushes" in which freshmen and sophomores fought bloody battles for possession of some symbolic token were abandoned or suppressed. At Dartmouth, for example, the last "cane rush" was held in 1883.[11] New students came to be perceived as potential members of fraternities, the YMCA, or athletic teams. This was only one way in which these organizations placed a distinctive stamp on the high collegiate era.

Organizations of religious students existed at many midcentury colleges, but in 1877 the YMCA organized some forty of them into chapters of a college division. The intercollegiate Y grew like wildfire: by 1900, 559 chapters claimed 32,000 members, 31 percent of all male college students. Members had to belong

9 W. Bruce Leslie, *Gentlemen and Scholars: Colleges and Community in the 'Age of the University'* (New Brunswick: Transaction, 2005 [1986]), 95–114; David P. Setran, *The College 'Y': Student Religion in the Era of Secularization* (New York: Palgrave Macmillan, 2007); Robert Schwartz, *Deans of Men and the Shaping of Modern College Culture* (New York: Palgrave Macmillan, 2011).

10 Singing well represented the collegiate spirit: J. Lloyd Winstead, *When Colleges Sang: The Story of Singing in American College Life* (Tuscaloosa: University of Alabama Press, 2013).

11 Leslie, *Gentlemen and Scholars*, 110–11, 195–209; Patton and Field, *Eight O'clock Chapel*, 236–302. Rushes persisted at many campuses well into the twentieth century.

to an evangelical church, but associate members could also be voted in. The Y found members in all regions and types of institutions. More than half of the men at historically black colleges belonged.[12] The Christian leadership of the Y sought to address a dual college problem: first, too many college students—the future leaders of the country—were not observant Christians; second, college men were surrounded by constant temptation. To address the first, the college Y was consciously evangelical, sponsoring periodic revivals and weekly prayer and Bible-study meetings. For the second, Ys competed with less wholesome campus gatherings by sponsoring their own activities. Dedicated social centers were erected at Princeton (1879), Yale (1887), and Cornell (1890). By 1915 thirty-six Y chapters had their own campus buildings.

The college Ys enhanced their presence by providing a multitude of student services, beginning with newly arriving freshmen. The Y chapters printed handbooks, financed by local advertisements, that gave students information on college history, customs, organizations, churches, directories, and much else. They also maintained housing and employment bureaus. Y members would meet arriving students at the railroad station, transport them to campus, and help them find lodging. A substantial portion of college students made use of these services to find rooms or part-time jobs. The vigor of the college Y, despite the secularization of the college curriculum, the declining influence of established churches, and student resistance to compulsory religious observance, represented a melding of traditional religiosity with the collegiate revolution. The Y, above all, sought to be fully engaged with school spirit and campus life but to bolster moral and religious values at the same time. This was a potent combination that buoyed membership. The religious influence of the Y peaked at campuses like Illinois before 1910, although membership grew nationally until circa 1920.[13]

★ ★ ★

Fraternities were in many ways emblematic of the high collegiate era, but this period was actually one phase in their long evolution. The early fraternities described in chapter 6 were relatively small and tended to congregate in rented

12   The leadership of the Y was steadfastly committed to gender separation, even though some campus Christian Associations were originally coed. Michigan, for one, was expelled in 1886 for remaining coed after the Young Women's Christian Association was formed, primarily as a student organization: Setran, *College 'Y,'* 33–35; David P. Setran, "Student Religious Life in the 'Era of Secularization': The Intercollegiate YMCA, 1877–1940," *History of Higher Education Annual,* 21 (2001): 7–45.

13   Setran, *College 'Y'*; Scott J. Peters, *The Promise of Association: A History of the Mission and Work of the YMCA at the University of Illinois, 1873–1997* (Champaign, IL: University YMCA, 1997), 18–52; Lewis Sheldon Welch and Walter Camp, *Yale: Her Campus, Class Rooms, and Athletics* (Boston: Page, 1900), 50–65.

rooms. They changed dramatically beginning in the 1870s as they acquired their own residential chapter houses. After 1890, some fraternities entered a more opulent age, characterized by impressive, custom-built houses and larger memberships. To their critics, fraternities were inherently unlikable for their secrecy, exclusiveness, snobbery, hedonism, and disregard of academics. They nonetheless became campus fixtures for the ensuing decades, especially at men's colleges, where membership sometimes reached 90 percent. The large role of fraternities (and their mirror images, sororities) affected four different facets of college life.

First, secret Greek-letter fraternities were a unique cultural construct for dealing with basic needs for food, shelter, and companionship. Most colleges had abandoned the responsibility of feeding and housing some of or all their students. Fraternities often formed when students in boarding houses created a fraternal organization, with or without national affiliation. Colleges and universities without dormitories recognized the inevitability of the fraternity system and generally considered them superior to the arrangements that students could make independently.

Second, a clear social bias determined which young men hived together. Students from wealthy, urban families sought each other's company and reinforced their social mores. How this worked depended on the social composition of the student body. As wealthier students flooded campuses at the end of the century, some fraternities mimicked the style and pretentions of urban gentlemen's clubs. At Cornell, where affluent students set the tone, such houses topped a steep prestige hierarchy of fraternities. At Wesleyan, with a more middle-class student body, a 90 percent rate of fraternity membership undoubtedly diluted elitism. As was the case at Yale, social selection became more rigid after 1900. Jewish students at the larger schools countered by establishing their own fraternities.

Third, fraternity men played a central role in supporting "school spirit" and the entire menu of collegiate activities. Students joined fraternities for entrée into these kinds of activities; fraternities, for their part, sought to dominate such endeavors as part of the ubiquitous competition for campus prestige.

Fourth, and most controversial, were the positive and/or negative effects fraternities had on their members. On the negative side, fraternity men on average had inferior academic records; they were variously accused of monopolizing competitions for student offices; and their proclivities for drink and dissipation were notorious. Positively, membership brought immediate companionship and psychological support as well as enduring relationships, including useful networks; it clearly served the manifest purpose of socializing members into the refined culture of the haut bourgeoisie, and it was praised by students and college leaders as a fitting preparation for careers in the business world. Although the overall trend might be similar, these factors had different effects across different types of institutions.

At the New England men's colleges, fraternities dominated both social functions and quotidian life. Where nearly everyone belonged, a certain amount of differentiation existed among fraternities, even given the relative social homogeneity of students. Fraternities were integral to the college ethos, supported and often praised by presidents, who themselves were graduates and brothers. These arrangements amounted to student self-government, with the colleges exerting some leverage through the granting of recognition and campus privileges.[14]

Conditions differed in the western public universities. Where the social origins of students were more diverse, greater social stratification existed between Greeks and non-Greeks. Fraternities were more controversial under these conditions, with ongoing tensions between Greeks and "Barbarians" over student offices, newspaper positions, and the organization of social events. Wisconsin and Michigan were typical in offering no university housing for men until well into the interwar years, making fraternities attractive simply for room and board. Fraternities intentionally emphasized social distinctions but were not entirely exclusive. A faculty inquiry at Wisconsin reported that one-third of fraternity members were partly or wholly self-supporting. These growing universities were largely middle-class institutions in which Greek membership reflected social aspirations as well as social distinctions. Fraternity membership peaked in the 1920s, when about one-third of male students at western public universities belonged to fraternities, and perhaps 20 to 25 percent of women were in sororities.[15]

In Southern universities fraternities tended to develop more unevenly, often facing religious or political opposition. At the University of Virginia, where student housing was provided, almost half of students joined for purely social reasons by the end of the century, even though fraternities were overlain by more socially exclusive "ribbon societies" that largely dominated campus offices. After

14 Wayne Somers, *Encyclopedia of Union College History* (Schenectady: Union College Press, 2003), 304–15; Claude M. Fuess, *Amherst: The Story of a New England College* (Boston: Little, Brown, 1935), 287–90, 346–48.

15 Fraternity members at the University of California grew from 10 percent in 1900 to 37 percent in the 1920s: Laurie A. Wilkie, *The Lost Boys of Zeta Psi* (Berkeley: University of California Press, 2010), 222; at Michigan in 1924, 32 percent of men and 22 percent of women belonged to more than one hundred fraternities and sororities: Howard H. Peckham, *The Making of the University of Michigan, 1817–1992*, edited and updated by Margaret L. Steneck and Nicholas H. Steneck, (University of Michigan, Bentley Historical Library, 1994), 168; at Wisconsin, more than one-quarter of students in 1930 lived in fraternity or sorority houses: Merle Curti and Vernon Carstensen, *The University of Wisconsin: A History, 1848–1925*, 2 vol. (Madison: University of Wisconsin Press, 1949), II, 503; at Illinois, which had banned fraternities until 1889, the dean of men held office in ATθ, and the University had the largest number of Greek-letter organizations in 1930: Schwartz, *Deans of Men*, 32–36.

1900, sumptuous chapter houses were erected, and a majority of students joined fraternities. At Duke, on the other hand, no chapter houses were permitted until 1930. In Mississippi, opposition to fraternal organizations as undemocratic led to their legal proscription until 1926, but students at Mississippi State invested military companies with exclusive selection and initiation rites, much like fraternities.[16]

Across the landscape of American colleges, conditions for Greek organizations varied enormously. Traditional church-related campuses were likely to remain opposed, and acceptance of fraternities sometimes became a part of the battle over modernization. At Indiana-Asbury, renamed DePauw University in 1884, three-quarters of the men belonged to fraternities by that date. Earlier, in 1870, women who had been turned down for membership organized what is recognized as the first women's fraternity (as they were then called)—Kappa Alpha Theta.[17] At Carleton College, petitions to form fraternities were denied by the faculty in the 1880s. Instead, campus literary societies long thrived. By 1923, the college had nine societies for men and seven for women, and they operated a great deal like . . . fraternities. They elected members, leaving many excluded, had elaborate initiations, and engaged more in social than literary activities. It could be difficult to avoid the drawbacks of fraternities even in their absence.[18] Above all, fraternities exaggerated features that were inherent to the high collegiate era.

★　★　★

Athletics, in contrast, added a whole new dimension to the college experience. The antecedents were laid in the early collegiate era when eastern colleges established rowing clubs, an import that had first become popular in England. In 1852 a railroad seeking to promote the resort on Lake Winnipesaukee, New Hampshire, invited Yale and Harvard crews to stage a boat race. Thus the first intercollegiate athletic contest was a product of commercial sponsorship. But the experience soon inspired a succession of ad hoc races in the 1850s involving

16　Philip Alexander Bruce, *History of the University of Virginia, 1819–1919*, 5 vol. (New York: Macmillan, 1921), IV, 97–101, 335–40; V, 271–79; John K. Bettersworth, *People's College: A History of Mississippi State* (n.p.: University of Alabama Press, 1953), 373–78.

17　George B. Manhart, *DePauw through the Years*, 2 vol. (Greencastle, IN: DePauw University, 1962), I, 133–37; Diana B. Turk, *Bound by a Mighty Vow: Sisterhood and Women's Fraternities, 1870–1920* (New York: New York University Press, 2004). Several colleges claim the first sororities; they were originally formed for mutual support in a hostile environment at recently coeducational institutions, like Asbury, only later becoming the female counterpart of a Greek system.

18　Leal A. Headley and Merrill E. Jarchow, *Carleton: The First Century* (Northfield, MN: Carleton College, 1966), 372–77.

Yale, Harvard, and other schools. Over the next two decades, college athletics grew significantly but haphazardly, led by crew and baseball. The euphoric effects of winning—on classmates as much as athletes—inspired teams to improve skills, training, personnel, and strategies. In this process, the several class teams were superseded by a "university club," thus rallying the support of the entire student body. Faculties were often alarmed by these activities, but the limitations they imposed slowed developments only slightly. A greater impediment was the confused state of competition. Only at the end of the 1870s did it become fairly clear who would play whom under what conditions. For crew, the most popular sport of the 1870s, multischool regattas lost their appeal when Harvard and Yale dropped out. They were principally interested in competing against each other and avoided contests that they could not dominate. In baseball, well-organized teams like Harvard played mostly professional teams in the 1870s. At the end of the decade, the American College Base Ball Association was formed to structure competition among Eastern schools. It lasted 7 years before Harvard, Yale, and Princeton broke away to compete against each other. Baseball was the most popular college sport through most of the 1880s, until it was eclipsed by football.[19]

Although the first intercollegiate football game was played between Princeton and Rutgers in 1869, the game developed only after a team from McGill University taught Harvard to play a rugby-style game in which players ran with the ball. Harvard and Yale first played this game in 1875, but it took a decade of rule adjustments before the basic game of American football stabilized in the mid-1880s. The person most responsible for devising common rules was Walter Camp, who had played for Yale from 1876 to 1882 and served thereafter as an unofficial coach until 1909. Under Camp's tutelage, Yale dominated eastern football, winning 95 percent of its games over 34 years. Still, the games that really counted were against rivals Princeton and Harvard. The unique stature of the Big Three lent prestige and popularity to the game of football, and football in turn gilded the reputations of the three schools. Annual Thanksgiving Day games in the New York City Polo Grounds between (usually) Yale and Princeton drew huge crowds of socially prominent spectators—23,000 in 1886 and soon more.[20]

After 1890 American football spread across the country. The University of Michigan, for example, had experimented earlier, playing the first 'western'

---

19   Ronald A. Smith, *Sports and Freedom: The Rise of Big-Time College Athletics* (New York: Oxford University Press, 1988).

20   Ibid., 67–82. Thanksgiving Day games between traditional rivals in major cities quickly spread across the country, not least for the revenues they raised.

intercollegiate game against Racine College in 1878. Despite eastern trips to battle the Big Three in 1881 and 1883, athletics did not become formally organized there until 1891. As elsewhere, "missionaries" from Yale and Princeton helped to teach the basics of the game. In 1895, the major public universities of the region organized the Western Conference (later, the Big Nine), bringing a common set of rules and regularly scheduled games. William Rainey Harper may have drawn on his Yale experience in using football to speed the recognition of his new university. Under coach Amos Alonzo Stagg, Chicago became a powerhouse in the Western Conference. Only 2 years after the university opened, he led the football team on a 6,200-mile trip to the West Coast, where Stanford and California had begun play in 1892. In 1902, Michigan played Stanford in the first Rose Bowl on New Year's Day. Southern universities embraced football at about the same time as the Midwest. The University of Virginia began tentatively in the late 1880s before enthusiastically committing to the sport after 1890. By the end of the century, football had assumed an iconic status throughout American higher education, too important, in fact, to be left to students.

Like other activities in this era, athletic teams were organized and run by students. Team manager was a prestigious position responsible for logistics and finances; the elected captain was in charge of practices and games. While no doubt encouraging student initiative, responsibility, and spirit, student management hampered the establishment of common rules or the formation of stable leagues. In baseball, the perennial problem was professionalism—ringers hired by college teams or collegians playing professionally in the summer. Teams largely refused to accept eligibility rules that worked to their disadvantage. Football, too, was plagued with "tramp athletes," but the overriding problem was brutality, caused by increasingly aggressive mass plays, like the flying wedge, and blatantly unethical conduct. Football had a rules committee, but it was long dominated by Walter Camp, whose Yale team benefited most from the status quo. This issue rose to a crisis in 1894, but Walter Camp quieted public outrage by publishing a deceptively benign evaluation of the game, *Football Facts and Figures* (1894). Numerous gridiron deaths caused public concern to rise to another crescendo in 1905, prompting an ineffectual intervention by President Theodore Roosevelt, an admirer of the game. This time, a consensus of universities was able to overcome Camp and the Big Three to organize the National Collegiate Athletic Association and impose more sensible rules. After 1900, in fact, universities gradually asserted authority over athletics, hiring coaches and athletic directors. College athletics largely embarked on a history of its own. However, the influence of college athletics, and especially football, went to the heart of American higher education. Achievement on athletic fields overshadowed not just other collegiate activities, but all manner of academic work. Athletics thus validated the anti-intellectual bias of the collegiate revolution and projected a powerful image of the college life, especially to alumni.[21]

★   ★   ★

The high collegiate era stimulated closer involvement of alumni with their colleges and universities. Earlier alumni groups formed social clubs in major cities, but now younger alumni sought to stay connected with campus activities. Walter Camp was not the only graduate to maintain a relationship with a college team. More obviously, athletic contests created a sentimental link between graduates and alma mater, as well as an excuse to return to campus. Fraternities also provided a tangible link. Each house would typically have some alumni members who maintained ongoing relations with the chapter. Donations from devoted alumni built the sumptuous chapter houses that burnished pride and prestige for both students and graduates.

Alumni served as agents of change, applying pressure to accelerate collegiate activities and atmosphere, especially where these things were resisted. As in the Young Yale movement, described previously, the younger alumni identified most strongly with the collegiate spirit. On several occasions, alumni sought to force modernization by deposing old-style presidents. Most notorious was the "trial" of Dartmouth president Samuel Colcord Bartlett (1877–1892). A conservative Congregational minister, Bartlett was a throwback to the era of submission and control. He valued only the "old college" and regarded Dartmouth's schools of science, engineering, and agriculture as "parasites, who were eating her life out." In 1881 the New York Alumni Association expressed the general unhappiness by asking the trustees to investigate Bartlett's governance of the college. This quickly escalated into petitions for his removal from alumni, faculty, and graduating seniors. The alumni were led by a writer for *The New York Times*, so the controversy and the resulting formal hearing received blanket press coverage. Each of the twenty-five charges against Bartlett was, in isolation, somewhat trivial; what his accusers found most objectionable was the entire reactionary regime. Focusing only on the specific charges, the trustees failed to find sufficient grounds for his dismissal. Stubborn by nature, he remained another decade but with little authority to enforce his views. Similar trials occurred at Union (1882) and Hamilton (1884) colleges.[22] However, in the long run alumni found more effective ways to exert their influence.

---

21   Ibid., 147–208; John S. Watterson, *College Football: History, Spectacle, Controversy* (Baltimore: Johns Hopkins University Press, 2000), 26–98.

22   George E. Peterson, *The New England College in the Age of the University* (Amherst, MA: Amherst College Press, 1964), 80–112; Marilyn Tobias, *Old Dartmouth on Trial: The Transformation of the Academic Community in Nineteenth-Century America* (New York: New York University Press, 1982).

Historian W. Bruce Leslie has depicted how church-related colleges (including Princeton) were weaned from their denominational moorings by financial dependence on their younger alumni. In the last decades of the century, neither church organizations, older clerical alumni, nor the denominational faithful could provide the funds needed to hire more faculty and erect new buildings. Rather, younger, more secular alums with successful business careers were the most likely source for large donations. They naturally advanced a collegiate agenda as the price of their support. William Bucknell, for example, a prosperous Philadelphia Baptist, used his fortune to induce a reorganization of the University of Lewisburg in 1882. The institution then acquired fraternities, intercollegiate athletics, support from Philadelphia alumni, and, in 1886, the name of its benefactor.[23] The influence of alumni nonetheless had the most consequential impact on Harvard, Yale, and Princeton—the Big Three.

The collegiate revolution was connected with the consolidation of a Protestant upper class at the end of the nineteenth century. The 1880s saw the creation of the Social Register, gentlemen's clubs, country clubs, and exclusive summer resorts, all of which flaunted cultural superiority by excluding Jews and most other non-Protestants. In education, the most significant innovation was the establishment of seven new elite boarding schools between 1883 and 1906. These schools immediately joined the principal feeders of the Big Three. They also espoused the Victorian notion of "muscular Christianity." This vague doctrine combined evangelical Christianity with the idea that physical vigor, and particularly sports, had an independent moral value. This viewpoint harmonized with social Darwinism to uphold a Christianity for the strong, rather than the weak, which had an obvious appeal for wealthy Americans. This image supplemented rather than replaced the previous ideal of a cultivated, Christian gentleman. Together, these notions formed an ideology that conjoined Christianity, physical vigor, service, achievement, and character—frequently united under the rubric of "manliness." These were precisely the virtues claimed for the collegiate ideal.[24]

Manly virtues had long been claimed for a college education. Such claims rationalized the cultural value of college since the Yale *Reports* of 1828. After the Civil War, the New England colleges increasingly invoked masculinity as a defense against the new education, practical or academic. Mark Hopkins in 1868 defined a liberal education as "the cultivation of man as man," and college presidents increasingly defended their purpose as forming the "whole man." This sentiment was, by 1900, a rationalization that disguised the bankruptcy

23   Leslie, *Gentlemen and Scholars*, 43–45 et passim.
24   Karabel, *The Chosen*, 13–38; Kim Townsend, *Manhood at Harvard: William James and the Others* (Cambridge: Harvard University Press, 1996).

of their educational mission, a surrender of intellect to the ascendant values of the high collegiate era, which enthroned the principal features of manliness. [25] The Y represented respectable Protestantism without the distraction of theology; fraternities provided manly brotherhood with the exclusion of social and religious deviants; the competition for campus distinction supplied symbolic achievement; and athletics, especially football, demonstrated manly courage. By 1900 this collegiate ideal had spread across most of the country's colleges and universities, with nuances of interpretation everywhere. However, its earliest and strongest expression occurred at the Big Three, where it bonded with upper-class culture. The boarding schools that set the tone literally prepped students for this role. The schools emphasized strenuous athletic programs, nondenominational Protestantism, Spartan living conditions, and, above all, an emphasis on the development of manly Christian character—all in anticipation of attending Harvard, Yale, or Princeton. By the 1890s, 74 percent of upperclass Boston and 65 percent of upperclass New York sent their sons to one of these three schools. [26]

Harvard was the country's most distinguished university, and Yale, the preeminent college, but Princeton's rise reversed a dismal nineteenth-century record. While President McCosh did much to rehabilitate Princeton's academic life, the great leap in public image occurred during the presidency of Francis L. Patton (1888–1902). A conservative theologian and incompetent administrator, Patton is generally considered to have retarded the institution's development into a university (although it assumed that title in 1896). However, Patton had a knack for public relations. He expanded support for the university by extolling athletics and pandering to wealthy alumni. Princeton's success on the gridiron was second only to Yale's, and Patton played up the virtues of sports for instilling "lessons of manliness," even mental discipline. He was especially adept at charming the New York alumni with such rhetoric, which also brought favorable publicity in the city's newspapers. Alumni responded with growing donations—and by enrolling their sons. During his presidency, Patton allowed the exclusive eating clubs to proliferate, from two to eleven, and in the process they came to dominate the social life of the university. He consoled the faculty: "Whether we like it or not, we shall have to recognize that Princeton is a rich man's college and that rich men frequently do not come to college to study." This complacency toward student learning damaged the university's academic

25   The president of Amherst stated in 1905: "The aim of the college is not to make scholars. The aim is to make broad, cultivated men . . . not athletes simply, not scholars simply, not dilettantes, not society men, not pietists, but all-round men," Peterson, *New England College*, 30–43, quotes 31, 39.

26   Karabel, *The Chosen*, 25.

reputation and ultimately led to Patton's downfall. However, it did little to harm Princeton's collegiate image and support from alumni. Princeton assumed its status as one of the Big Three during Patton's tenure largely through its athletic ties with Harvard and Yale, the national publicity they generated, and the support provided from loyal alumni.[27]

Athletics made the activities of college students of compelling interest to wider audiences—first alumni, then readers of metropolitan newspapers and, by the turn of the century, of national middle-class magazines. The exploits of teams from Harvard, Yale, and Princeton no doubt ignited this process, not only stimulating school spirit but also advancing an image of the college man widely covered in major newspapers. The heroes of the gridiron or crew projected the manliness admired by that age onto the entire student body. In the last decades of the century, the popular image of a college student as an effete, studious character, memorizing Greek and Latin to prepare for teaching or the ministry, was displaced by one explicitly joining manliness, athletic prowess, Christian character, and worldly success.

After 1900 the collegiate ideal was equated with the qualities required to succeed in business. Nor was this association fanciful, as the number of graduates of the Big Three pursuing business careers surged at the end of the century. At this juncture, historian Daniel Clark has shown, the themes belabored by college presidents at alumni dinners were adopted by middle-class magazines with circulations in the hundred thousands. The collegiate ideal, in fact, harmonized with the zeitgeist: Theodore Roosevelt gave his famous speech advocating the strenuous life in 1899, and the Spanish-American War linked manliness with war and imperialism. American colleges, so it seemed, were shaping the type of men needed by the country and the economy. *The Saturday Evening Post* (circulation reaching 1,000,000 in 1909) published a "College Man's" issue in 1899, with a cover depicting two collegians, one in football gear and the other in academic robe carrying books. The picture was emblematic of the interpretation of the collegiate ideal that these mass-circulation publications conveyed to the middle class through articles and fiction: college students could be manly men and the extracurricular life was at least as important as the classroom and more likely to prepare one for success in the world of business. This message no doubt found a receptive audience, since publishers and advertisers knew their readers. But it also had serious implications: college was now perceived as the appropriate

---

27   Patton's failures are depicted by P. C. Kemeny, *Princeton in the Nation's Service: Religious Ideals and Educational Practice, 1868–1928* (New York: Oxford University Press, 1998), 87–126; his success with alumni by Joby Topper, "College Presidents, Public Image, and the Popular Press: A Comparative Study of Francis L. Patton of Princeton and Seth Low of Columbia, 1888–1902," *Perspectives on the History of Higher Education*, 28 (2011): 63–114, quote p. 69.

training ground for business, something that had scarcely been true before the end of the nineteenth century.[28]

After 1900, the impact of the collegiate revolution produced paradoxical results, simultaneously reinforcing privilege and offering democratic opportunity. Harvard, Yale, and Princeton became dominated socially by the eastern upper class. Sons of the most privileged families attended these schools to gain further advantages of cultural refinement, elite socialization, potentially valuable connections, and, if they chose to make the effort, superior intellectual training. These schools, of course, were more or less open to students from more humble circumstances: Harvard more, Princeton less, and Yale somewhere in between. But their upper-class constituency would reward these schools bounteously for generations to come for honoring this contract.[29]

The collegiate revolution sent a different signal to middle-class America. It depicted an institution that was open to talent, where any hardworking son (for daughters, see below) could achieve success on campus and acquire the skills and judgment to succeed in America. These rewards were sweetened by the possibility of acquiring some degree of culture and socialization as well, the attributes to achieve respectability in the upper middle class. College was open to all who qualified for admission, not simply members of the professional class or students who had studied Latin and Greek. These students too came to college in increasing numbers as the twentieth century progressed. Mass magazines no doubt helped to spark this development through the turn of the century, reinterpreting the cultural meaning of college studenthood. However, this opening of American higher education could not have occurred without a fundamental restructuring of the college's role.

HIGH SCHOOLS, COLLEGES, AND PROFESSIONAL SCHOOLS

An American college education was assumed to take 4 years ever since Henry Dunster extended the Harvard course in 1650, though this standard was often clipped. Colleges of the Early Republic sometimes failed to form four classes, and everywhere students entered with advanced standing. However, in the years around 1890, this venerable pattern was challenged more seriously than ever before or since. Johns Hopkins had introduced a 3-year AB, and Eliot advocated the

---

28   Daniel A. Clark, *Creating the College Man: American Mass Magazines and Middle-Class Manhood, 1890–1915* (Madison: University of Wisconsin Press, 2010).

29   Karabel, *The Chosen*; Joseph A. Soares, *The Power of Privilege: Yale and America's Elite Colleges* (Stanford: Stanford University Press, 2007).

same for Harvard. Many BS courses were also just 3 years, including Yale's Shef-field School. Critics who emphasized the preparatory function contemplated shortening it further. The transition from sophomore to junior years was seen as a natural break point between foundational and advanced subjects. Daniel Coit Gilman and Andrew D. White recommended starting collegiate training 2 years earlier, with university work to follow. John Burgess at Columbia appropriated the senior year to begin graduate or legal study, and similar schemes were introduced at Michigan and elsewhere. William Rainey Harper defined the freshman and sophomore years as junior college, and both he and David Starr Jordan contemplated dropping it from their universities. A reconfiguration of the 4-year college course seemed in these years to be an appropriate response to the academic revolution. However, the college course not only survived these challenges intact, it emerged stronger after 1900.

This outcome was the result of three separate developments. The first was the collegiate revolution, just described. Given the prominence assumed by collegiate life, institutions could scarcely truncate its duration merely for curricular reasons, and college proponents after 1900 advocated strengthening instead, as will be seen. Second was the gradual emergence of high schools as the principal form of preparation for college. With the recognition of a threshold between secondary and higher education, their respective roles became more clearly defined. Third, the elevation of professional education, by requiring first some college and, eventually, a college degree, restored the foundational role that had atrophied in the nineteenth century. What emerged was the modern American pattern of high school–college–graduate/professional school, but these developments evolved slowly after about 1880.

Serious consideration of altering the college course was largely an Eastern phenomenon. In the West, Michigan's experiment fizzled, the pragmatic Harper abandoned the notion of affiliated junior colleges after a poor response, and Jordan's disdain for underclassmen helped ease him into a ceremonial chancellorship. Similarly, the problem of preparation for college assumed different forms in the East and the West. The East possessed a rich array of private schools, academies, and boarding schools, all of which provided preparation in Latin, Greek, mathematics, and English—the subjects of college entrance examinations. Eastern high schools before the 1880s were known as "people's colleges," teaching modern subjects to students intending commercial careers. In the West, preparation for college was more difficult to obtain. Outside of cities, private schools were few and far between, and nearly every college was compelled to maintain a preparatory department to ensure its own enrollments. As urban high schools were established, although poorly staffed and furnished in the smaller cities, the larger schools gradually assumed a dual role of serving local educational needs and providing a possible path to college. Hence, the first initiatives for linking secondary and higher education occurred in the West.[30]

COLLEGE ADMISSIONS. In 1871 faculty from the University of Michigan began visiting high schools in the state to determine if their graduates were qualified for admission without examination. The faculty's interest in assuming this onerous task was not simply student recruitment but rather bolstering the quality of the high schools and the students they graduated. Throughout the country, colleges were saddled with the burden of poorly prepared students who depressed the level of teaching. Would-be universities, in particular, needed more qualified students if they were to raise instruction to a university level. James B. Angell, who became Michigan's president that year, strongly supported school certification as part of the university strategy, but also to build a unified educational system with the university at the pinnacle. In the first year, 6 high schools were approved, and 50 students were admitted on the basis of their diplomas or certificates. By 1890, 82 schools were on the approved list, about half of Michigan's high schools. That year, 164 students were admitted by certificate, compared to 131 by examination. Faculty inspectors could be severe in their written judgments of high schools, but they were lenient in granting approvals. In fact, they had limited leverage with local school boards. Outside of the 6 principal feeder schools that produced 80 percent of certificate students, the remaining 82 high schools were sending few students to any college. But the certificate program had other attractions. Localities valued the seal of approval from the state university, and it also relieved high schools of reviewing old material for college entrance examinations. For universities, it simplified the process of admission, was thought to bring more students (although here opinions differed), and defined a systemic relationship between high schools and colleges that had not hitherto existed.

Michigan's certificate system spread throughout the Midwest and West and, soon, the entire country. The University of Wisconsin adopted it in 1876, although some thought it incompatible with maintaining a preparatory department. President Bascom was able to close that department in 1880 with no ill effects, a step repeated at other state universities in the ensuing decades. The University of California established its certification system in 1884, the same year Michigan began inspecting and certifying schools outside the state. The

---

30 The following draws on Marc A. VanOverbeke, *The Standardization of American Schooling: Linking Secondary and Higher Education, 1870–1910* (New York: Macmillan, 2008); and Harold S. Wechsler, *The Qualified Student: A History of Selective Admissions in America* (New York: Wiley, 1977), 16–130.

certificate system was also adopted in the Northeast, although the principal private universities stood apart, preferring to admit students only through examinations. And, a watered-down certificate system was adopted in the South. By 1890 the practice was so widespread that universities and even private colleges accepted students from schools that were on the approved lists of major universities. Such arrangements were not a system, however, but rather the beginnings of one that required further elaboration.

These developments reflected rapid change in public high schools. In the 1880s, high school enrollments almost doubled, and the number preparing for college grew from a trickle to about one-third of graduates. In 1890, 6,500 high school graduates were prepared to enter college, compared with 5,000 private school graduates and about 8,000 products of college preparatory departments. A decade later, these last two sources of potential students had grown by 20 percent, but the high school number tripled, now supplying the majority of college students.[31] High schools did not displace the traditional sources, at least not immediately, but rather grew from an independent dynamic. High school enrollments and graduates roughly doubled in each of the next three decades— and proved to be the growth engine for American higher education. But first, relations between the two sectors had to be regularized.

In 1885, the need for greater cooperation led to the formation of the New England Association of Colleges and Preparatory Schools, and 2 years later to a similar association for the Middle States and Maryland. The schools were frustrated by the different books and authors covered in each college's examination. Some progress was made standardizing these matters and bolstering the certificate system, but individual colleges largely clung to their idiosyncratic requirements. It was clear that a more comprehensive approach was needed. Such an effort was launched when the National Education Association created the Committee of Ten in 1892. Led by Charles Eliot, the committee sponsored extensive research on secondary school curricula and proposed model courses of study as a national standard. The committee's recommendations mirrored the academic offerings of the stronger schools. It was nonetheless heavily criticized for "college domination" by secondary educators, who were under pressure at this time to increase vocational offerings as well. The committee's chief impact was in forwarding an issue that could not be avoided. A Committee on College Entrance Requirements followed in 1895, and it offered the fruitful suggestion for a unit of measure for high school coursework. By the end of the century, an organizational superstructure existed for at least addressing the admissions problem.

31   Roger L. Geiger, "The Crisis of the Old Order: The Colleges in the 1890s," in Geiger, *American College in the Nineteenth Century*, 264–76.

For years, reformers had called for the establishment of separate, independent examinations that any college might use for admissions. In 1899, Nicholas Murray Butler persuaded the Middle States Association to establish such a body to organize examinations on the subjects identified by the Committee of Ten. The resulting College Entrance Examination Board was a private organization that offered its first examinations in 1901. Although begun with few members, Harvard joined in 1904, and Yale and Princeton joined in 1909–1910. Despite a small membership, the College Board removed a huge obstacle for these institutions, which refused to participate in any admissions scheme that would limit their independence but also sought to widen recruitment. Institutions were free to specify which exams prospective students would take and what scores were acceptable.

Still to be resolved for the majority of institutions were the larger issues of standardizing high school offerings and moving from certificates to regional accreditation. The North Central Association (f. 1895) addressed these goals by defining the "unit course of study" for high school subjects in terms of class hours and subject requirements. Students needed fifteen yearlong units to graduate, and colleges were advised to demand the same for admission. It specified that three units should be in English and two in mathematics, but otherwise high schools were free to offer, and colleges to require, what courses best suited them. The Carnegie Foundation for the Advancement of Teaching (CFAT, f. 1905) adopted and popularized the unit system, which became known as Carnegie units, helping to spread it nationwide.[32]

Acceptance of the unit system finally established a definitive threshold between secondary and higher education. It greatly simplified both college admissions and high school accreditation, but its impact extended far beyond administrative convenience. Standardization efforts in the 1900s were intended above all to raise the level of teaching in both high schools and colleges—to raise high schools to the level of fifteen qualified units and to allow colleges to focus exclusively on advanced instruction. Abysmal conditions persisted in many parts of the country, where secondary and higher education remained blurred. In the South, many high schools offered only 2 or 3 years, and colleges competed with secondary schools for students, bringing down standards for both. Conditions were little better elsewhere in rural areas that lacked or had just established high schools. Many of the country's "colleges" functioned more as secondary schools, as William Rainey Harper had noted in "The Prospects of the Small College" (1900). Of some 400 institutions, he judged that one-quarter were little more than academies and should assume

32   VanOverbeke, *Standardization*, 156.

that role.[33] The CFAT set stringent criteria for colleges: absence of denominational control, fourteen Carnegie units for admission, and no preparatory department. The College Board too barred colleges with preparatory departments, and the number of Carnegie units required for admission became a benchmark of college quality. By 1910 a clear separation from secondary education had become a hallmark of the American college and university.

This last development was gratifying to Charles Eliot, who labored more than 20 years to achieve this result. Eliot helped form the New England Association in the 1880s, led the Committee of Ten, worked for the establishment of the College Board, served as a reforming president of the National Education Association, and chaired the CFAT board of trustees. These activities were intended not simply to resolve the incoherence of college admissions; rather, they stemmed from a comprehensive view of the place of the college in the proper ordering of American education. That order, Eliot felt, had to include high schools capable of preparing students to continue on to college. The fundamental aim of college, then, was mental training acquired through the study of liberal, or academic, subjects. A college degree, Eliot strongly believed, should, therefore, be a prerequisite for the mastering of practical bodies of knowledge in professional schools. However, as with secondary education, this required that existing patterns be reshaped. Restructuring professional education was a challenge that Eliot tackled from the first years of his presidency. Harvard consequently played a leading role in the long process of upgrading professional schools.[34]

"Higher" education at the end of the nineteenth century appears in a different light when professional schools are included. In 1890 roughly 41,000 students were enrolled in schools of theology, law, and medicine, compared with 64,000 college students of all types. Yet, more professional degrees were awarded than bachelor's degrees and more medical degrees than ABs. Moreover, fewer than 10 percent of medical students and one-quarter of students in theology and law had graduated from college. Professional studies and degrees were, in fact, alternatives to college, not a sequential stage of education.[35] This condition was a general liability for professional schools, which with few exceptions lagged well behind the academic revolution, not the least because of unprepared students. But the winds of reform were being felt, particularly in medical education.

---

33 William Rainey Harper, *The Prospects of the Small College* (Chicago: University of Chicago Press, 1900).

34 Hugh Hawkins, *Between Harvard and America: The Educational Leadership of Charles W. Eliot* (New York: Oxford University Press, 1972), 224–62; VanOverbeke, *Standardization of American Schooling*, 115–42.

35 Geiger, "Crisis of the Old Order," 268–75.

MEDICAL SCHOOLS. Eliot broke the mold of the autonomous proprietary medical school in 1870–1871 by incorporating Harvard's school into the university. It subsequently established salaried, professional professors in place of practitioners and imposed a 3-year graded course with meaningful examinations and laboratory teaching of basic sciences.[36] However, progress elsewhere was grudging for the next two decades. Predictably, Harvard suffered lower enrollments for the next decade, as did Yale when it set a 3-year course in 1879. In 1880, the fledgling American Medical College Association attempted to require a 3-year course for its members, but 2 years later it suspended the rule as impracticable and subsequently dissolved. Only the universities of Pennsylvania and Michigan were able to approximate the Harvard reforms by 1880. Yet, the 1880s witnessed accelerating advances of medical science, including European discovery of the bacterial basis of diseases. Reforming medical education on a scientific basis became imperative, but only Michigan and Harvard incorporated the beginnings of research by German trained professors and, in 1890, expansion to a 4-year course.

After 1890, though, the pace of reform accelerated. The American Association of Medical Colleges was reconstituted in that year and now was able to demand a 3-year graded course of all members. In 1893, the opening of the Johns Hopkins Hospital and Medical School presented a new and higher model. Hopkins offered a 4-year course and required a college degree for admission. In addition to offering laboratory-based scientific instruction for the first 2 years, it elevated clinical teaching to a scientific and observational basis for the final 2 years. Momentum shifted from resistance to reform to proactive efforts by the leading universities to strengthen medical education. University-based medical schools now emerged as a distinct sector that was advancing both the training of doctors and, to a lesser extent, the treatment of disease. Some of the more reputable private medical schools saw the advantage, if not necessity, of affiliating with universities. The College of Physicians and Surgeons united with Columbia in 1891, and similar mergers occurred at Western Reserve, Chicago, Illinois, and Pittsburg. Cornell opened an endowed medical school in 1898, and Wisconsin founded its school in 1907. The modernizing trend was bolstered in 1904 when the American Medical Association created the Council on Medical Education, consisting

---

36 Chicago Medical College, affiliated with Northwestern (1870) offered a 3-year graded course, and Michigan employed salaried medical professors since 1851. The following draws on Kenneth M. Ludmerer, *Learning to Heal: The Development of American Medical Education* (New York: Basic Books, 1985); a comprehensive overview is provided in Abraham Flexner, *Medical Education in the United States and Canada: A Report to the Carnegie Foundation for the Advancement of Teaching*, Bulletin No. 4 (New York: CFAT, 1910); for a panorama of medical education in Chicago, the city with the most medical schools, Winton U. Solberg, *Reforming Medical Education: The University of Illinois College of Medicine, 1880–1920* (Chicago: University of Illinois Press, 2009).

of five distinguished university professors. In advancing the university agenda of continual upgrading, the Council conducted an evaluation of the entire sector.

The reform of university medical schools alone could not resolve the failings of American medical education. Some 50 of the country's 160 medical schools had university affiliations. This group was led by strong schools at Johns Hopkins, Harvard, Columbia, Michigan, and Minnesota, among others, but it also included woeful proprietary schools with only nominal university affiliations. Among the rest, the situation was far worse. The number of medical schools and the number of graduates continued to swell until the mid-1900s, when 162 schools disgorged about 5,500 graduates. Lax licensing laws that allowed these graduates to practice medicine kept proprietary schools operating and profitable up to that point. They also flooded the country with poorly educated physicians, almost four times as many per capita as Germany. When the Council on Medical Education inspected the nation's medical schools, it found one-half to be "acceptable," 30 percent might be improved to an acceptable level, and 20 percent were "worthless" and should have state recognition withdrawn. Even these ratings would prove generous. The council did not publish its findings because of scruples about criticizing fellow doctors, but it did ask Henry Pritchett if the CFAT would conduct an independent evaluation of medical schools. The request fit with Pritchett's goal of raising standards in American higher education, and in 1909 he commissioned Abraham Flexner to examine the state of American medical schools.

Although possessing no medical training, Flexner was a dedicated educator with independent views.[37] A classics graduate of the early Hopkins, he went first to the Hopkins Medical School to learn how medical education ought to be organized. Flexner held, above all, that medicine was a scientific undertaking—but one with two dimensions. Medical science rested on the physical laws of nature, which had to be taught in laboratories of the basic sciences; but medical art depended on acquiring an ingrained scientific approach to clinical practice through direct observation and hands-on learning. The ideal medical school required ample facilities of laboratories, teaching hospitals, and endowments; its teachers should be full-time professionals engaged in original investigations; and its students must possess at least 2 years of prior college science. Outside of Johns Hopkins, few medical schools could meet Flexner's exacting standards. His 1910 *Report* was, consequently, a bombshell. Its two parts consisted of a lengthy overview of all aspects of medical education, followed by descriptions and evaluations

---

37 Flexner's emphasis on learning by doing placed him among progressive educators: Ludmerer, *Learning to Heal*, 166–90; Thomas Neville Bonner, *Iconoclast: Abraham Flexner and a Life in Learning* (Baltimore: Johns Hopkins University Press, 2002), 69–90. Flexner's brother Simon was one of the country's leading medical scientists and educators.

of the 155 schools he had visited in the United States and Canada. His acerbic depictions of the worst proprietary schools rivaled the muckraking journalism of the era. Just 31 strong medical schools, he concluded, would suffice for the physician needs of the United States.

The Flexner Report is credited with delivering the coup de grâce to the proprietary schools. The total number of medical schools declined to eighty-five by 1920, but in fact the commercial schools were doomed by the tightening standards of state licensing boards. Twenty had already suspended operations from 1907 to 1910. As Flexner pointed out, it had "become virtually impossible for a medical school to comply even in a perfunctory manner with statutory, not to say scientific, requirements and show a profit." Medical educators reacted to the negative tone of the report somewhat defensively, reminding that medical education was stronger than ever before. However, this criticism worked to their advantage. The better schools thanked Flexner and Pritchett for exposing their shortcomings. Flexner had provided a blueprint for improvements that they promptly used to raise the money for the expanded facilities that his model demanded. Yale and Washington University launched major fund-raising efforts; President James appealed to the Illinois legislature, which provided support for the first time for medical education; similar efforts occurred nationwide. Medical schools, even at leading universities, were heavily, often entirely, dependent on student tuition. The Flexner Report, by exposing glaring deficiencies, helped to usher in a new financial era for medical education characterized by philanthropy and state support.

Tuition dependency was also the reason why entrance requirements were the slowest element to change in medical school reform. Only Harvard in 1901 followed Hopkins in requiring a college degree for admission. Before that date, most schools had no entrance requirements at all, and those that did felt unable to ask for more than a high school diploma. Entrance examinations, where they existed, were notoriously lenient. In the first decade of the century, the main thrust among university medical schools was to require entering students to have studied college chemistry, physics, and biology. Medical educators were uninterested in bachelor's degrees per se; in fact, they refused to honor them if the course lacked science. Before 1910, these schools were moving to embrace the 2 years of college science advocated by Flexner. In the years following the report, this became the accepted standard.[38]

Was the Flexner Report the turning point in the reform of American medical education? More accurately, the years from 1905 to 1915 marked a revolutionary

38   Flexner, *Medical Education*, 11; William G. Rothstein, *American Physicians in the Nineteenth Century* (Baltimore: Johns Hopkins University Press, 1985), 287–94; Solberg, *Reforming Medical Education*, 139–74; Ludmerer, *Learning to Heal*, 139–206.

transformation in which the best practices of the leading schools spread among university medical schools. The Flexner Report contributed enormously as stimulus and guide for these schools to institute improvements they had long sought in any case but had been unable to afford or accomplish. The assimilation of American medical schools into universities was a triumph of the university movement. The universities essentially imposed the institutionalization of the academic revolution on medical faculty and the integration of medical students with at least part of the college course. Medical schools, with an overriding preoccupation with health care, evolved as special enclaves, loosely linked with their universities, but academic science and collegiate preparation remained two firm points of attachment.

LAW SCHOOLS. By the twentieth century, Eliot could bask in the stature of the Harvard Law School. He told alumni, "If there be a more successful school in our country or in the world for any profession, I can only say that I do not know where it is."[39] Such effusive praise was backed by real accomplishment: Harvard Law fulfilled Eliot's vision for the proper role of professional schools; it stood foremost and unchallenged among the nation's law schools; and, most extraordinary, it transformed the content and pedagogy of its field.

Harvard founded the first true law school and, with two endowed professors and the redoubtable Justice Joseph Story (1828–1845), it was easily the most prestigious. But otherwise it differed little from the other twenty-one law schools operating in 1860. Practitioner-professors, dependent on student fees, lectured to a floating population of students, who derived most of their training in law office clerkships. Law school was an alternative form of undergraduate education for the minority of aspiring lawyers who cared to attend. This was the situation that Eliot sought to reform in 1870 by appointing Christopher Columbus Langdell as professor and dean. Described by a classmate as "a bookworm if there ever was one," the impecunious Langdell had worked his way through the Law School, impressing both students and teachers with his learning and diligence. He then practiced for 16 years in Manhattan before Eliot's call. He believed that students should learn the law much as he had, by studying the decisions of appellate courts in individual cases. This was the genesis of the case method that revolutionized the teaching of university law schools.[40]

39 Quoted in Arthur E. Sutherland, *The Law at Harvard: A History of Ideas and Men, 1817–1967* (Cambridge: Harvard University Press, 1967), vii.

40 Bruce A. Kimball, *The Inception of Modern Professional Education: C. C. Langdell, 1826–1906* (Chapel Hill: University of North Carolina Press, 2009); Robert Stevens, *Law School: Legal Education in America from the 1850s to the 1980s* (Chapel Hill: University of North Carolina Press, 1983).

Law school pedagogy had relied on the presentation of fully formed legal principles through professorial lectures and textbooks. Langdell regarded this approach as superficial and unreliable. He wished to derive the essence of legal principles from their original sources—the reasoning and decisions of actual judges. He made students read and study the cases and then subjected them to rigorous questioning in class—the so-called Socratic method. Langdell consistently emphasized "first that law is a science; secondly, that all available materials of that science are contained in printed books." Hence, "the library is the proper workshop of professors and students alike," akin to the laboratories of natural scientists. And students could be properly taught only by "teachers who have traveled the same road" in learning the law. Langdell concluded: "then a university, and a university alone, can furnish every possible facility for teaching and learning law." Langdell's case method thus taught the law as a theoretical subject with an empirical scientific foundation (books, cases) that belonged in the American university alongside other *wissenschaftlich* subjects.[41]

This approach required a different kind of law school. The intellectual demands of interpreting judicial decisions presupposed mature students with some liberal education. Part-time students could scarcely accommodate such a regimen, so the case method also required full-time students. Full-time professional teachers were needed who themselves had analyzed the sources of the law. Langdell immediately lengthened the Harvard course of study to 2 years and imposed examinations for advancement. In 1875 it was decreed that "the course of instruction in the School is designed for persons who have received a college education," the first such stipulation in American legal education.[42] The following year the course was extended to 3 years. As a professor, Langdell himself set an example of undistracted devotion to scholarship. Eliot signaled that this was the new criterion for faculty in 1873 when he hired Langdell's protégé, the scholarly James Barr Ames, only 1 year after his graduation—a startling departure from the usual hiring of eminent practitioners. Ames later succeeded Langdell as dean (1895–1910) and chief advocate for the case method.

The demands of the Harvard model on students and professors hardly commended it to other law schools. Furthermore, the theoretical approach of the case method failed to train students in the practical aspects of lawyering. Enrollments

---

41   Quoted in Sutherland, *Law at Harvard*, 175.

42   Ibid., 168; Alfred Z. Reed, *The Training for the Public Profession of the Law* (New York: CFAT, 1921). Virtually all requirements of professional schools in this era contained loopholes or exemptions, which tended to be tightened over time. Harvard Law offered nongraduates the option of taking a rather stiff entrance examination from 1875 to 1909 (Sutherland, *Law at Harvard*, 168–70). The difficulties of achieving these reforms against opposition within and outside the Law School is detailed by Kimball, *Inception*, 193–232.

at Harvard remained fairly steady, but as late as 1882, it had fewer students (138) than had enrolled under Justice Story. But then the superior quality of Harvard law graduates became evident. Proponents of the case method defended it as teaching students to "think like a lawyer." However, Harvard Law was unique in more fundamental ways. It enrolled well-prepared college graduates; forced them to prepare for class; examined them in class on their understanding of the material; and subjected them to annual examinations.[43] In short, it supplied the elements of a rigorous education that would be effective anywhere. Perhaps more important, it created conditions for what historian Bruce Kimball has labeled "academic meritocracy." In 1885 Eliot reported that the school was "unable to fill all the places in lawyers' offices which have been offered . . . for third-year students just graduating." By the end of the decade, a leading Boston firm wrote Langdell that it preferred "young lawyers from the Harvard Law School" who rank "among the leaders of their respective classes." Success in Harvard Law School was directly linked to successful careers in the commercial economy— the first solid exemplar of this phenomenon in American higher education.[44] As recognition spread, enrollment shot upward, exceeding 450 by the time of Langdell's retirement in 1895 and, 15 years later, topping 800.

The success of academic meritocracy forced the Law School to confront an issue that had never before arisen in American higher education: selecting candidates for a limited number of places. The difficulty of the entrance examination was ratcheted upward until it was eliminated in 1909, but this affected fewer and fewer applicants. In 1893 the faculty limited admission to graduates of a select list of sixty-five colleges, a not unreasonable approach considering the enormous variation in standards across American colleges. Rather than rating individual colleges, however, the list was based on institutions that had previously sent students to the Law School or Harvard College. No Catholic institutions were included, which enraged Catholic educators. In reaction, Eliot added Georgetown, Boston College, and the College of Holy Cross; but the last two were subsequently removed. Eliot, who was directly involved with this policy, had a deep aversion to Catholic colleges because, he felt, they did not teach sufficient science and because they presented philosophy as dogmatic truth instead of open inquiry. Langdell apparently concurred. Although deeply offensive to Catholic educators, this tempest raised deeper questions about academic meritocracy. Merit in the Harvard Law School was assumed to result from, first, the

---

43 Kimball, *Inception*, 210–29, quotes pp. 224, 266; the pass rate on Harvard examinations appeared to be 70 to 80 percent, but a substantial number of students chose not to sit the exams: Reed, *Training*, 356–68.

44 Kimball, *Inception*, 264–70.

high requirements for admission and, second, from relative achievement in the classroom. However, selective admission, has been affected from its inception by the assumptions embedded in the process.[45]

After 1890, the case method began to be adopted by other leading universities, despite legitimate criticism that it was ill suited for average law students.[46] The lure of academic meritocracy made these institutions aspire to join the circle of elite law schools favored by corporate firms. Events at Columbia in 1891 signaled the onset of a new era. Theodore W. Dwight was founder (1858) and autocratic dean of the Columbia Law School. He located the school downtown amid the courts and law offices, easily accessible to their employees. Splitting the school's revenues with Columbia, he maximized enrollments and minimized teachers. During the 1870s he graduated more students than Harvard enrolled. But Dwight also resisted reforms that might threaten this model. He opposed entrance requirements, especially a bachelor's degree, and held off adding a third year until 1888. When Seth Low became president in 1890, he immediately sought to raise the stature of the law school. He brought in a professor from Harvard and forced Dwight to retire. Dwight, along with his faculty, returned downtown to found the New York Law School on the old model, while the new faculty "Harvardized" the Columbia Law School. By the mid-1890s high admission standards, a 3-year course, and the case method could be found at Cornell, Stanford, and Northwestern as well. When William Rainey Harper launched the Chicago Law School in 1900, he consulted Eliot and Dean Ames before hiring a Harvard professor to be dean. By that date a distinct sector of reformed university law schools had emerged. These schools, and others hoping to move in that direction, organized the Association of American Law Schools (AALS) to raise standards in legal education.[47] However, the tide was moving very much in the opposite direction.

Legal education mushroomed around the turn of the century. From 1890 to 1910, the number of operating law schools roughly doubled, graduates tripled, and enrolled students quadrupled. While a handful of university law schools focused on full-time students and strengthened admissions and coursework, the most rapid growth occurred in schools with low or no entrance requirements

45   Kathleen a. Mahoney, *Catholic Higher Education in Protestant America: The Jesuits and Harvard in the Age of the University* (Baltimore: Johns Hopkins University Press, 2003); Kimball, *Inception*, 295–308, 341–42.

46   Bruce A. Kimball depicts this complex process extending 25 years, to 1915: "The Proliferation of the Case Method in American Law Schools: Mr. Langdell's Emblematic 'Abomination,' 1890–1915," *History of Education Quarterly*, 46, 2 (Summer 2006): 192–247.

47   Robert A. McCaughey, *Stand Columbia* (New York: Columbia University Press, 2003), 138–40, 182–84; Stevens, *Law School*, 51–72, 96–98.

that catered largely to part time students. Although these two opposite types are distinct, there were multiple possible patterns. Some universities, like Georgetown, expanded their regular law course into evening classes to tap this burgeoning market. Numerous universities, like Southern California, took over commercial law schools to do the same. Such units attracted large numbers of part-time students and served as cash cows for the institution. New York University, for example, served every market segment with regular, late afternoon, and evening courses. Many of the part-time schools were purely commercial undertakings, like Dwight's New York Law School and Chicago Kent. However, the YMCA was also a large participant in this market. Quite separate from the Campus Y, urban YMCAs sought to provide young, working men opportunities for self-improvement through education. In 1920 nine operating law schools were outgrowths of these efforts. In 1915, five of the six largest law schools (Harvard being the outlier) served the part-time evening market—Georgetown, New York University, Chicago Kent, Southern California, and New York Law School. A classification in 1920 found 21 percent of law schools to be "high-entrance, full-time schools"; 29 percent "low-entrance schools" with full-time courses; 39 percent "part-time" schools; and 11 percent "short-course schools."[48]

This distribution reveals a curricular stratification of law schools, with the first category representing primarily university law schools employing the case method. However, it also indicated social stratification between college-educated students studying full time and those who could not afford college attending in late afternoons or evenings. After 1900, the elite of the legal profession, represented in the American Bar Association and the AALS, became increasingly alarmed by the influx into the profession of less-well-educated lawyers from urban proprietary schools, especially the large numbers of immigrants and Jews. The remedy they advocated was to raise intellectual standards to those of the AALS schools, particularly the requirement of some college for admission. Such reforms would, of course, address their social concerns as well. However, states would not raise requirements for the bar by mandating study in law schools, and most schools were averse to limiting their clientele by raising admission requirements. The situation in legal education was similar to that in medicine, but without the external pressure exerted by state medical boards. Nevertheless, the Flexner Report inspired a legal counterpart, and in 1913 Alfred Z. Reed of the CFAT embarked on a protracted evaluation of legal education, not published

48   Stevens, *Law School*, 73–91; Reed, *Training*, 434–52; Dorothy E. Finnegan, "Raising and Leveling the Bar: Standards, Access, and the YMCA Evening Law Schools, 1890–1940," *Journal of Legal Education*, 55, 1–2 (Mar./June 2005): 208–33; Joseph E. Kett, *The Pursuit of Knowledge under Difficulties: From Self-Improvement to Adult Education in America, 1750–1990* (Stanford: Stanford University Press, 1994), 261–69.

until 1921. By that date, the rise of nativism after World War I emboldened the impatient legal elite to seek to marginalize the part-time schools. A separate report engineered by the AALS claimed that only law schools provided valid legal education, that 2 years of college should be required for attendance, and that part-time programs should be lengthened to 4 years.[49]

Reed's report appeared just 1 month later, with a radically different message:

> Humanitarian and political considerations unite in leading us to approve of efforts to widen the circle of those who are able to study the law. The organization of educational machinery especially designed to abolish economic handicaps—intended to place the poor boy, so far as possible, on an equal footing with the rich—constitutes one of America's fundamental ideals. . . . Inherently . . . the night school movement in legal education is sound. It provides a necessary corrective to the monopolistic tendencies that are likely to appear in every professional class . . . [and] constitute a genuine element of danger.[50]

Educationally, Reed found features to praise in the case method while criticizing its neglect of the practical aspects of a lawyer's work. He also found the part-time approach to be deficient when it was not complemented by work in a legal office. However, his defense of the social opportunities presented by these wide-open night schools struck to the core of American belief in the democratic potential of higher education. Reed continued to champion the broad social access provided by part-time legal education through the 1920s. Enrollments in these institutions peaked in 1929. Ironically, legal education, which had been only tenuously linked with colleges and universities before 1870, pioneered three of the distinctive features of twentieth-century American higher education—academic meritocracy, selective admissions, and, with open, part-time evening schools, the first vestiges of mass higher education.

HIGHER EDUCATION FOR WOMEN, 1880–1915

What the Commissioner of Education called "the superior instruction of women" marked a milestone around 1890. That year, a slight majority of female enrollments were found in modern women's colleges (Division A: 2,000) or coeducational colleges (9,000) rather than "premodern" Division B female colleges (10,000). This last category was already in terminal decline, with nearly

---

49 Stevens, *Law School*, 92–115; Kett, *Pursuit of Knowledge*, 264–67.
50 Reed, *Training*, 398–99; Finnegan, "Raising and Leveling the Bar," 231–33.

half of institutions closing from 1880 to 1900 and enrollments stagnant. But enrollments accelerated at Division A and coeducational schools, rising by about 150 percent in the 1890s. However, these patterns were far from uniform. The remaining Division B schools were concentrated in the South, where they were not yet challenged by high schools and normal schools. Division A schools clung to the eastern seaboard, with two exceptions. Coeducation was the dominant pattern for the public universities of the Midwest and West. These last two regions had the highest enrollments of women in modern institutions, especially the West. There are several stories within the expansion of higher education for women.[51]

The two great innovations after the Civil War were coeducation in universities and the creation of endowed women's colleges. Women's educational experiences in these two domains were initially rather different. Antebellum coeducation had been confined to small evangelical colleges and, in Oberlin, one very large one. The decade following the Civil War saw a surge in coeducation in new or formerly male institutions and serious consideration of admitting women in others. Coeducation was largely imposed on the new western land grants by legislators in their original charters. Among private institutions, Methodist colleges were quick to adopt coeducation as well, including Wesleyan and the new Boston University in the East.[52] By 1880, roughly 4,000 women attended regular colleges and universities (most of which remained all male), more than 10 percent of the total. These enrollments would grow, but few institutions joined this group after that date. Enthusiasm for coeducation diminished greatly, and a backlash later developed.

In 1865, Matthew Vassar's eponymous college opened with the intention to "build a college in the proper sense of the word, an institution which should be to women what Yale and Harvard are to young men." His sentiments were seconded by Sophia Smith and William Durant, whose creations, Smith and Wellesley colleges, opened in 1875. These three became the core of what would be known in the twentieth century as the Seven Sisters, the most prestigious women's colleges, analogous to what would later become the Ivy League. Bryn Mawr joined this endowed elite in 1885, followed by the "coordinate colleges"

---

51 Roger L. Geiger, "The 'Superior Instruction of Women,'" in Geiger, *American Colleges in the Nineteenth Century*, 183–95; Nancy E. Durbin and Lori Kent, "Postsecondary Education of White Women in 1900," *Sociology of Education*, 62 (Jan. 1989): 1–13.

52 Methodists had always supported women's education, and Asbury (1867), Northwestern (1869), and Ohio Wesleyan became coeducational, as did new foundings Syracuse and Vanderbilt; Bates (f. 1863) was the first coeducational New England college, followed by Colby and the University of Vermont (1871). Coeducation was specifically rejected by Amherst, Brown, Williams, and Middlebury (until 1883): David B. Potts, *Wesleyan University, 1831–1910* (New Haven: Yale University Press, 1992), 98–105.

of Radcliffe (Harvard) and Barnard (Columbia). Mount Holyoke, despite historical pride of place, required prolonged upgrading after it became a college in 1893. The success of these privileged colleges buttressed the residual hostility to coeducation in the East.[53]

The women who attended these institutions before 1890 are often referred to as the first generation of collegiate women. These pioneers endured psychological pressures from Victorian culture, which upheld mutually exclusive sex roles, with women occupying a separate sphere of domesticity. A stereotypical idealization of womanhood paralleled the coeval fixation with manliness and was conventionally interpreted as precluding the masculine regimen of traditional colleges. Besides this impediment, women faced hostile environments in formerly male colleges and a profound ambiguity surrounding the role of an educated woman in Victorian society.[54]

Prejudice against coeducation was endemic in the East, where the infamous Dr. Edward Clarke published his best-selling *Sex in Education* in 1873. Arguing that women were biologically unfit for the "brain work" required by a standard college course, Clarke detailed the baneful effects that such "identical education" could produce. Critics echoed these misconceptions for a decade, and they planted doubts in the minds of prospective students and their parents. But Clarke's "science" was belied by contemporary experience. At Cornell, Andrew D. White sought to resolve the coeducation issue with a fact-finding tour of Oberlin, Antioch, Michigan, and Northwestern. His report to the trustees answered every objection: most important for his male audience, he found that the presence of ladies did not harm male students and might even have a positive impact. He found no evidence for a deleterious influence on the health of women students, and he defended their capacity to benefit from the identical course of studies as men.[55] Despite proponents like White, nearly ubiquitous suspicion or disapproval placed a heavy psychological burden on the first generation of women students. They typically devoted themselves to their studies in part to prove the legitimacy of female higher education to a skeptical public—and to themselves.

Such efforts were probably reinforced by the hostile environment they entered. Presidents and faculty had nearly all been educated in all-male settings, mostly in the East (or in Germany), and were predominantly opposed to coeducation. The

53   Helen Lefkowitz Horowitz, *Alma Mater: Design and Experience in the Women's Colleges from Their Nineteenth-Century Beginnings to the 1930s* (Boston: Beacon Press, 1984).

54   Barbara Miller Solomon, *In the Company of Educated Women: A History of Women and Higher Education in America* (New Haven: Yale University Press, 1985).

55   Sue Zschoche, "Dr. Clarke Revisited: Science, True Womanhood, and Female Collegiate Education," *History of Education Quarterly*, 29, 4 (Winter 1989): 545–69; Charlotte Williams Conable, *Women at Cornell: The Myth of Equal Education* (Ithaca: Cornell University Press, 1977), 66–74.

decision to admit women at public institutions was usually imposed from outside by legislators or, at Michigan and California, regents, out of vaguely democratic sentiments. At private schools, donors sometimes forced the issue. Henry Sage made Cornell truly coeducational by donating the first women's dormitory at a coeducational university; Washington Duke made an endowment gift to Trinity College (later Duke University) contingent on admitting women; and Mary Garrett's conditional donation forced the Hopkins Medical School to accept women. President Eliot, however, refused an offer by women to buy their way into Harvard. Male students were almost always opposed. They feared that coeducation would tarnish a college's status but were probably most disturbed by the disruption to the social cohesion and camaraderie of the class. Young men were accustomed to dealing with females as sisters, as servants, or through the formal protocols of courtship, and they seemed unable to relate to them as fellow students. Resenting their presence, college men treated coeds condescendingly, when not ignoring them entirely. The first women students were often restricted from participating in college ceremonies and activities and segregated in classrooms, but otherwise they had a remarkable degree of freedom. Public universities were too poor to provide separate facilities or residence for women. Left to fend for themselves, ostracized from much of campus life, the first generation of college women had all the more reason to focus on their studies. But these psychological hardships also produced a high rate of attrition.

A further negative was the absence of careers for women outside of teaching. The universities of Wisconsin and Missouri created normal departments to accommodate their first women, but such units resembled inferior normal schools. Most collegiate women who worked did, in fact, become teachers at all levels of education, including women's colleges. However, Victorian norms frowned upon paid work for genteel women, and work after marriage was taboo. First-generation women graduates who fashioned careers for themselves were thus exceptional, socially and psychologically. Most telling, they sacrificed marriage and family for careers. Roughly one-half of first-generation women graduates married, compared to a 90 percent national rate, and those that did had fewer children.[56]

The patrons of the new endowed women's colleges and their advisors aimed, above all, to provide a liberal education identical to Harvard's and Yale's but at the same time to respect and protect the unique qualities of womanhood. They consequently sought to create a carefully controlled environment—quite the opposite of women's experience at coeducational universities. Both Vassar's original advisor and Wellesley founder William Durant looked to Mount Holyoke for inspiration. They resolved to immure their students in a single building, where

56 Solomon, *Company of Educated Women*, 115–40.

communal activities, solitary study, and devotion could be fully programmed. Both patrons commissioned monumental, luxurious structures for this purpose, where students could be closely supervised by "lady principals." Smith College sought to nurture femininity by housing its students in cottages, each with a "lady-in-charge" and a faculty member, to create a natural, family atmosphere. All three founders, especially William Durant, hoped to promote an evangelical spirit, but their charges proved resistant. In the absence of the evangelicalism that animated Mount Holyoke, they developed independent student cultures instead. The cloistered nature of Vassar and Wellesley, in particular, fostered intense personal relationships among students and rebelliousness against rules and their agents. Descriptions of their early years document an overwhelming student preoccupation with extracurricular activities. With the advent of the hypothecated second generation of students after 1890, the experience of women at both the endowed and coeducational institutions was transformed by the female version of the collegiate revolution.[57]

Women of the second generation at coeducational universities were more numerous, more confident, and more open to a fuller collegiate experience. Like their male counterparts, they organized a growing number of activities outside the classroom. The University of California, with almost 40 percent women, was in the forefront of these developments. In 1894 Cal coeds organized a governing body to coordinate and articulate women's interests. At first it focused on mundane issues—bathrooms, lunchrooms—but it soon began to organize women's clubs for sports, debating, drama, and music. It sponsored a "Woman's Day" on campus with multiple activities, and it became the female arm of President Wheeler's promotion of student government. A YWCA chapter also contributed to the organizational mix at Cal and elsewhere. In 1901 Cal women founded their own honor society, since they were not eligible for the men's society, and in 1912 they staged a pageant like those performed at eastern women's colleges. The 1890s also saw the establishment of the first four sororities at Berkeley. Like fraternities, they emphasized social distinctions but also channeled their members into campus activities. By offering superior room and board, they resolved that difficult issue for some women students. Women in these decades threw themselves into campus activities as fervently as men. As a precaution against overcommitment, several schools devised a point system to limit the offices one woman could hold.[58]

---

57   Horowitz, *Alma Mater*, 28–81.
58   Lynn D. Gordon, *Gender and Higher Education in the Progressive Era* (New Haven: Yale University Press, 1990), 55–70. Point systems for women's activities were used at Smith, California, and Minnesota and no doubt, at other schools; Turk, *Bound by a Mighty Vow*.

Universities had few funds available to invest in the needs of women students.[59] The appointment of deans of women by major universities at least showed recognition of such needs. William Rainey Harper characteristically invented this post in organizing the University of Chicago, but these positions became widespread only after 1900. They were often filled by graduates of the Seven Sisters, who apparently brought the requisite femininity to the task. Deans of women were not disciplinarians—although always concerned with upholding standards—but rather served as advocates for women on male-dominated campuses and built consensus for the common weal among the different groups of women. In 1903 the deans of midwestern state universities began meeting as a group to discuss their responsibilities. Of greatest concern was housing. With few dormitories, most women lived in boardinghouses. Deans of women worked vigorously to impose reasonable standards upon the private proprietors. The proper regulation of social activities was another common concern. And, at the first meeting, the deans unanimously opposed intercollegiate athletics for women.[60]

The second generation of women adapted to the high collegiate era with a flurry of activities and organizations. However, women's activities were largely segregated and everywhere subordinate to those of the men. Male students were especially covetous of prestigious positions. Women were denied academic honors, excluded from campus government, and denied newspaper posts. Even football games were a "distinctively masculine event," where women fans were segregated and expected to watch passively. Prevailing cultural preconceptions of femininity imposed confusing expectations. Cal president Wheeler advised women to prepare for a future of marriage and motherhood; male students believed that study was harmful to femininity and produced schoolmarms; and the dean of women sought to identify careers for graduates other than teaching. And women themselves? Second-generation women tended to go to college for their own personal reasons, including intellectual fulfillment. A significantly larger percentage eventually did marry but still had fewer children than average. They also pursued a growing variety of still circumscribed careers. The collegiate revolution made their college experience more natural and fulfilling, despite a hostile environment, but aspirations for greater equality had to wait.[61]

---

59   California was fortunate to receive the benefactions of Phoebe Apperson Hearst, who took a direct interest in Cal women. She donated scholarships and athletic facilities and, for a time, supported a female physician: Gordon, *Gender and Higher Education*, 56–60.

60   Jana Nidiffer, *Pioneering Deans of Women: More than Wise and Pious Matrons* (New York: Teachers College Press, 2000).

61   Gordon, *Gender and Higher Education*, 66–71; Ruth Bordin, *Women at Michigan* (Ann Arbor: University of Michigan Press, 1999); Claudia Goldin, "The Meaning of College in the Lives of American Women: The Past One-hundred Years," National Bureau of Economic Research, Working Paper No. 4099 (June 1992).

All three endowed women's colleges started slowly. In striving to emulate Harvard and Yale, they set entrance requirements in Latin and Greek well beyond the schooling then available to women. Vassar and Wellesley had to establish preparatory departments, and Smith's first two entering classes had only 14 students. Smith then opened its doors to "specials" (nondegree students), as had the others, and its enrollments soared. Secondary education for women rapidly adapted to the stringent entrance requirements, and by the late 1880s, such growing pains were largely behind them. Wellesley enrolled 660 students in 1890—more than Johns Hopkins or the University of Illinois—and Smith and Vassar were not far behind. With large faculties, they were better equipped than most colleges to offer the elective curriculum demanded by the academic revolution. In 1906, Vassar had a larger income than Princeton and Wellesley, almost equal. Smith's 1,500 undergraduates ranked fifteenth in the country. These colleges largely achieved the academic stature to which they aspired, but that was not what shaped their reputations.

The endowed colleges fostered an all-encompassing collegiate culture more intense than Princeton's or Yale's. They generated more than their share of the usual class and campus organizations and activities, and students engaged in them with unmitigated zeal. Intramural athletics flourished on these campuses, producing fiercely competitive interclass contests. Students delighted in ceremonies, both in planning and execution. Student dramas, all-female dances, and pageants embellished student life. Student energies were further absorbed with complex social relationships, both among cliques and social groups, as well as the "crushes" and "smashes" students developed toward one another. Students were completely immersed in "the life" that swirled within these campuses, or at least that was the image. Of course, not every girl had the money, talents, personality, or inclination to thrive in this environment.[62]

The most obvious fact about student life at these schools was the increasing predominance of wealthy students. Smith president L. Clark Seelye remarked in 1896 that "each year [the wealthy] are more largely represented." Tuition, room, and board cost $450 in 1907, the ceiling for American higher education, but 80 percent of Wellesley students spent at least as much on personal expenses. Society on these campuses was dominated by the "swells" who came from affluent families and had attended the same schools. The swells dominated campus organizations and also formed exclusive clubs, societies, and "snobby cliques." One Wellesley student lamented in 1896: "a person counts for *absolutely nothing* unless she is a Society girl." Posh societies were allowed to erect their own houses on the Wellesley campus. Poorer students were given the opportunity to save

---

62   Horowitz, *Alma Mater*, 147–68.

money by living in an annex and joining a club for nonsociety members. Social cleavages could hardly be starker. High prestige also was accorded to "all-around girls," who became leaders in campus activities by force of personality. Historian Helen Horowitz reveals "the most closely guarded secret of the women's colleges, that in a college composed only of women, students did not remain feminine." All-around girls, in particular, were admired for assuming masculine leadership roles, excelling in athletics, and playing male roles in dramas.[63]

Much the same could be said of these schools as of the Big Three: dominated socially by the eastern upper class, they specifically conveyed cultural refinement and elite socialization and—for those who chose this path—intellectual enrichment and leadership skills. But for women, too, as social exclusiveness rose, so did disdain for academic achievement and the stigmatization of "grinds." Unlike the Big Three, however, success on campus had no analogue in successful business careers. The modal graduate of the endowed women's colleges was expected to marry according to her social station, raise a family, and possibly assume a prominent role in voluntary organizations. Only Bryn Mawr adopted more ambitious ideals, despite being originally intended as an Orthodox Quaker female college, a counterpart to nearby Haverford College.

In the closed circles of Orthodox Quakers, members of the Haverford and Johns Hopkins boards of trustees overlapped. When these gentlemen met to discuss Quaker education in 1877, Joseph Taylor lamented the absence of a Quaker college for women. He then wrote a bequest that allocated his fortune of $800,000 to founding Bryn Mawr as a Christian college for Quaker women but admitting others "of high moral and religious character" and from "the higher and more refined classes of society."[64] Its all-Quaker board contained mostly pious Haverford trustees. However, the institution was virtually hijacked by the redoubtable M. Carey Thomas to fashion the most academically ambitious college for women.

The daughter of a Quaker trustee of Hopkins and (later) Bryn Mawr, the precocious Thomas completed a Cornell AB in 2 years. Unable to pursue graduate study at Johns Hopkins, she studied at Leipzig and was awarded a PhD in philology (1883) by the University of Zurich (which, unlike Leipzig, granted degrees to women). She then presented herself as a candidate for the presidency of Bryn Mawr. With educational and family credentials that could scarcely be ignored, she was instead appointed Dean of the College at the age of 26. In this position

---

63   Ibid., quotes pp. 148, 163; Patricia Ann Palmieri, *In Adamless Eden: The Community of Women Faculty at Wellesley* (New Haven: Yale University Press, 1995), 199–211, quote p. 203.

64   Katherine Sedgwick, "An Ambiguous Purpose: Religion and Academics in the Bryn Mawr College Curriculum, 1885–1915," *Perspectives on the History of Higher Education*, 27 (2008): 65–104. The liberal Hicksite Quakers established Swarthmore as a coeducational college in 1864.

(the first of its kind) she seized the authority to shape the academic life of the new college. Visiting all the endowed colleges, she was disappointed by their lack of academic rigor. She resolved to model Bryn Mawr after Johns Hopkins, embracing the new academic spirit. Thomas's academic aspirations were supported by the trustees, who thus conceded initiative to her, despite frequently disagreeing. But in one respect she remained true to the donor's wishes: she, too, sought to educate the more refined classes of society.[65]

Thomas was able to set a high standard from the outset. She informed the board that "a college is ranked among other colleges by the difficulty of its entrance examination" and accordingly took Harvard's as a model. She hired male professors for their scholarly abilities and established a graduate school. She opposed trustee suggestions to establish fellowships for poor students as wasteful, advocating instead graduate fellowships that would bolster prestige. In 1894 she was elevated to the presidency (1894–1922).[66] She had made Bryn Mawr a conspicuous success, but it was still a tiny college. In 1898 she began a concerted effort to raise funds for more dormitories, a library, and expansion to a great college. She mobilized the support that she enjoyed among alumnae and obtained vital Rockefeller gifts by charming John D. Rockefeller Jr. Bryn Mawr became recognized as the academic leader of women's higher education. Socially, however, it mirrored college life at the other three endowed colleges. Thomas fused both academic and social distinction in the ideal of a "Bryn Mawr woman," who would add "scholarship and character [to] gentle breeding." Bryn Mawr graduates did emerge as a distinctive type, characterized by genteel culture, achievement in learning, and unapologetic championing of women's rights. When alumnae were added to the trustees in 1906, M. Carey Thomas's domination of her college was complete.[67]

In 1899, a Charles Eliot speech advocating a distinctively female curriculum for women enraged Thomas. In a widely publicized rejoinder, she mocked the president of Harvard for implying the world of knowledge "existed only for men" and saying he might as well have proposed for women "a new Christian religion . . . new symphonies and operas . . . in short, a new intellectual heaven and earth." She emerged as the most prominent and most forceful advocate for offering women the same higher education as men. She made a more comprehensive

65   For the most thorough treatment of Thomas, including her lifelong attachments to women: Helen Lefkowitz Horowitz, *The Power and the Passion of M. Carey Thomas* (New York: Knopf, 1994).

66   Thomas was, by 1894, acting as president; she had the support of the outgoing president and her trustee father; her companion, Mary Garrett, pledged to give $10,000 (ca. 10 percent of the college budget!) each year that Thomas was president. Yet, trustees were reluctant to name a woman, and many wanted to assert the Quaker character of the college. She was elected president on a 7 to 5 vote: Horowitz, *Power and Passion*, 257–64.

67   Ibid., p. 318. After 1910, Thomas experienced internal resistance to her autocracy from students and faculty.

statement when asked by Nicholas Murray Butler to write a description of women's higher education.

In *Education of Women* (1900), she ignored most institutions for women, discussing only those providing modern academic courses and emphasizing how past limitations had been overcome. Coeducation predominated as the most widespread and economical form and was now standard for publicly funded universities. But in the East, where separate women's colleges could be supported, the four endowed "great colleges" provided a superior residential educational experience. Bryn Mawr was the smallest of them with 269 undergraduates, but it exceeded the others academically with 61 graduate students and 19 PhD graduates. Thomas paid special attention to graduate education, where she reported that only four reputable universities still excluded women (Catholic, Clark, Princeton, and Johns Hopkins universities). She looked forward to a similar acceptance of women into professional schools. This factual account concluded with an affirmation of equality: "an inferior education shall not be offered to them in women's colleges, or elsewhere, under the name of a modified curriculum." By the turn of the century, M. Carey Thomas had become the foremost spokesperson for women's higher education and defender of unqualified equal opportunity.[68] However, the trend in American higher education, at least in the short run, was moving in the opposite direction.

Male students by and large had not tempered their hostility to coeducation. On the contrary, the nature of the collegiate revolution tended to magnify their resentment. To disentangle rationalizations of prejudice from deeper motivations may be pointless, but several issues clearly bothered the boys. Fears of diluting athletics and manliness were prominent in complaints against coeducation. These were invariably linked with school prestige and, hence, the reputations not just of students but of younger alumni as well. On campus, the persistent steps to monopolize prominent extracurricular activities and class ceremonies testify to the value men placed on maintaining campus dominance. Psychologically, males appeared to have difficulty reconciling female cultural stereotypes with actual female classmates, who often outperformed them academically. However, this dissonance was rooted in social class. Refined, genteel women—suitable for marriage—prepped at exclusive academies and attended the Seven Sisters; coeds were predominately graduates of nearby high schools who would probably become teachers. That the most mean-spirited opposition to women was usually found in fraternities underlines the class-based nature of male hostility.

---

68   Ibid., 315–23, quote p. 318; M. Carey Thomas, *Education of Women*, Monographs on Education in the United States, Nicholas Murray Butler, ed. (Washington, D.C.: U.S. Department of Education, 1900), quote p. 40.

Among coeducational universities, Cornell was notorious for male disdain toward women, even coining the ugly term (and concept), "anticoedism." Women were only 14 percent of Cornell students in 1900 but one-third of Letters and Sciences. By that date, most male students in professional schools hailed from wealthy urban families and were part of an extensive fraternity system. Cornell coeds were judged by no less than the *New York Herald* to be "out of place in fashionable college society," and fraternities forbade their members from having any social contact with them. The forerunner to the dean of women reported in 1912 that the university had refused to commit to coeducation, was fearful that it diminished Cornell's stature vis-à-vis Harvard and Yale, and was determined to be, "in curriculum and atmosphere, as distinctly a man's institution as possible." The plight of women was even worse at Wesleyan, where Methodists apparently no longer championed the education of women. Women had been admitted in 1872, but by the 1890s the chief preoccupation of Wesleyan students and alumni was status anxiety toward Amherst and Williams. The school's difficulties were facilely blamed on coeducation. The customary activities of women were progressively circumscribed, and after 1900 women were virtually ostracized on campus. Far more than Cornell, Wesleyan coeds were locals seeking a relatively inexpensive education, and they were accordingly treated contemptuously. The university made a pretense of considering a coordinate women's college, but, lacking funds, trustees voted to cease admitting women in 1909. Connecticut College was founded for women in nearby New London in 1911, in part to accommodate the Wesleyan coeds.[69]

The rapid growth of women students in the 1890s caused a different kind of reaction among university leaders. Both William Rainey Harper and Charles Van Hise suggested establishing segregated classes, at least for the first 2 years. Their anxieties, which were widely shared, stemmed from fears that women were driving men away from literary courses, and they imagined a threat to the masculine character of the campus. Harper's initiatives faltered, and Van Hise provoked a barrage of intemperate criticism by merely raising the subject.[70] Both gynephobes and women's advocates wished for curricula specifically tailored to acceptable feminine roles. Early "domestic courses" teaching household skills, pioneered at Iowa State and Kansas State, had poor enrollments and reputations. Only much later, a movement to found a science-based field of home economics

---

69   Conable, *Women at Cornell*, quote p. 117; Morris Bishop, *A History of Cornell* (Ithaca: Cornell University Press, 1962), quote p. 420; Potts, *Wesleyan*, 212–20.

70   Gordon, *Gender and Higher Education*, 113–15; Thomas Woody, *A History of Women's Education in the United States*, 2 vol. (New York: Octagon, 1966, [1929]), II, 290–94. For Penn's aversion to women, see Sarah Manekin, "Gender, Markets, and the Expansion of Women's Education at the University of Pennsylvania, 1913–1940," *History of Education Quarterly*, 50 (Aug. 2010): 298–323.

was initiated by Ellen Swallow Richards, the first female graduate and faculty member of MIT. In annual conferences at Lake Placid (1899–1907), she laid the foundation for applying chemistry (her field) to household economy. Home economics was readily incorporated into state universities (Wisconsin, Illinois, California) as an applied science promising careers for women. However, Carey Thomas essentially blackballed home economics as a "women's subject" in liberal arts colleges.[71]

The same aversion to coeducation lay behind a number of efforts to establish coordinate colleges. These creations were motivated by contradictory aims: either to establish women's education where all-male colleges would not tolerate coeducation or to solve the woman problem at coeducational schools through segregation. Carey Thomas identified five coordinate colleges in *Education of Women*. Four were of the first kind: Radcliffe, Barnard, Sophie Newcomb, and the Women's College of Brown (Princeton's feeble entry, Evelyn College, 1887–1897, had closed). Radcliffe had begun as the "Annex" in 1879, where women were taught by Harvard faculty volunteers, and it was incorporated at but not of Harvard University in 1894. Sophie Newcomb Memorial College for Women became a coordinate college of Tulane University when it was endowed by its namesake in 1885. The others were supported by the respective presidents, especially Benjamin Andrews of Brown, and combined separate women's classes with some upper-level coeducation. Radcliffe and Barnard were quickly recognized as "Sisters." Sophie Newcomb had no academic links with Tulane but aspired to bring the model of the Seven Sisters to the South.[72]

The other coordinate college was established by Western Reserve in order to eject its women. President Carroll Cutler (1872–1887) was a vigorous proponent of women's education and had opened the college to them when he assumed office. But the men were never reconciled. In 1884 the entire faculty petitioned to end coeducation, and male students boycotted classes when Cutler convinced the board otherwise. His successor, however, wished to restore the college's image as the Yale of the West. He feared that coeducation was discouraging wealthy Clevelanders from supporting the college. In 1888 the girls were exiled to the College for Women, which was launched with almost no resources.

71 R. D. Apple, "Liberal Arts or Vocational Training? Home Economics Education for Girls," in S. Stage and V. Vincenti, eds., *Rethinking Home Economics: Women and the History of a Profession* (New York: Cornell University Press, 2004); Sarah Stage. "Richards, Ellen Henrietta Swallow," *American National Biography Online* Feb. 2000, http://www.anb.org/articles/13/13-01382.html (Nov. 5, 2013); Maresi Nerad, *The Academic Kitchen: A Social History of Gender Stratification at the University of California, Berkeley* (Albany, NY: SUNY Press, 1999). Home economics received a huge boost when it was included in the Smith-Lever Act (1914) for cooperative extension and the Smith–Hughes Act (1917) for teachers.

72 Woody, *History*, II, 304–20.

But the strategy apparently appealed to Cleveland's moneyed elite, who began to support both the men's and the women's colleges with a stream of gifts. Cooperation developed between the two colleges. Coeducation, it seemed, was tolerable academically when each gender had its own separate social base and extracurricular life. A similar scenario occurred later at Tufts College, which had admitted women in 1892. In 1907, however, the president declared, "the average young man will not go to a coeducational institution if other things are anywhere near equal." Jackson College was established for women in 1910 to banish the stigma of coeducation. Here, too, after a decade the colleges became increasingly integrated. Coordinate colleges were contemplated at many institutions (as at Wesleyan) as a solution to the supposed liabilities of coeducation but in most cases proved infeasible financially or politically.[73]

Of course, coeducation was anathema among more conservative constituencies, especially Catholics and Southerners. In both cases, support for women's higher education came belatedly, for calculated reasons, and was tolerable only in protected all-female institutions. Catholics were motivated by the realization that large numbers of Catholic girls were attending secular colleges. The first Catholic college for women, The College of Notre Dame, was chartered in Maryland in 1896 and graduated its first class in 1899. Eighteen more colleges were established by religious orders by 1915 and another fifty-six, by 1930. These colleges were organized much like cloisters, seeking to shield their charges from the outside world and protect their faith. The destiny of students was marriage and motherhood, with the possibility of teaching. Academically, their offerings were limited, since the religious who taught generally had not themselves attended college.[74]

In the South, female colleges took three forms. An abundance of weak institutions that the Bureau of Education classified in "Division B" operated in the twilight zone between secondary and higher education. Only the strongest of these schools survived as women's colleges, but even then they retained legacies of ornamental and vocational courses. In the 1890s, southern states became conscious of their enormous educational deficit and consequent need for teachers. They responded by establishing "normal and industrial colleges for white girls." Tuition was remitted for students promising to teach for 2 years, and most students took this option. Private women's colleges comparable to those in the North were few and late to appear. Sophie Newcomb Memorial College was the result of a windfall bequest, and Agnes Scott College in Georgia was raised from

---

73   Ibid., 318–20; C. H. Cramer, *Case Western Reserve: A History of the University, 1826–1976* (Boston: Little, Brown, 1976), 89–105.

74   Tracy Schier and Cynthia Russett, eds., *Catholic Women's Colleges in America* (Baltimore: Johns Hopkins University Press, 2002), 25–60; Edward J. Power, *A History of Catholic Higher Education in the United States* (Milwaukee: Bruce, 1958), 183–97.

a traditional seminary only by the philanthropy of the Scott family, becoming a college in 1906. As late as 1903, Randolph-Macon Women's College, an endowed institution opened in 1893, alone offered a 4-year course, although most students stayed for only 2. That year the Southern Association of College Women formed to raise standards in the region's colleges. However, its first survey more than a decade later identified 7 "standard colleges" out of 140. Most women's colleges remained largely finishing schools with inadequate resources spread thinly over several levels of programs.[75]

In 1915, a half-century after the opening of Vassar, advocates of women's higher education had many reasons to be disappointed. By their record, women had refuted every argument that had been raised against their access to advanced education, only to be accused of fomenting "race suicide" because of the low fecundity of intelligent, Anglo-Saxon graduates.[76] Women now possessed richly resourced liberal arts colleges, but their educational efficacy was clearly diminished by the frivolous preoccupations of their students. Women now formed the majority of literary college students, or close to it, at major state universities, but their experience was still circumscribed by male dominance of the campus. Women had proved their intellectual mettle in PhD programs but were given few chances to advance as scientists and scholars in coeducational universities. When normal schools are included, an equal number of men and women were obtaining advanced education in 1910, but 60 percent of the women were in normal schools or Division B schools, institutions inferior to colleges.[77] The Association of Collegiate Alumnae recognized only twenty-four institutions as meeting its standards. Perhaps most galling, discussions of higher education still characterized all women by a single, undifferentiated, cultural stereotype.[78] Above all, this stereotype impeded women from using higher education for economic or social advancement. Of college-educated women who worked in this era, a large majority became teachers, and the rest were mostly librarians, nurses, or social workers.[79]

In one sense, women were granted access to the world of academic knowledge through admission to graduate and professional schools. Women gained admission to doctoral programs in the early 1890s, led by Yale, Columbia, and

75 Amy Thompson McCandless, *The Past in the Present: Women's Higher Education in the Twentieth-Century South* (Tuscaloosa: University of Alabama Press, 1999), 18–38; Gordon, *Gender and Higher Education*, 165–88; Woody, *History*, 187.

76 Woody, *History*, 295–302; Palmieri, *Adamless Eden*, 217–31.

77 In 1909–1910, 158,620 women were enrolled in colleges and universities (43,441), Division A women's colleges (8,874), Division B (11,690), and normal schools (94,615); 157,401 men were enrolled in colleges and universities (119,578) and normal schools (37,823): Bureau of Education, *Biennial Survey of Education, 1916–1918*, 4 vol. (Washington, D.C.: GPO, 1921), III, 686; IV, 10.

78 Woody, *History*, 189–92, 290–303; Palmieri, *Adamless Eden*, 211–16.

79 Goldin, "Meaning of College in the Lives of American Women."

Chicago. In that decade, 204 women earned doctorates. However, women scientists were relegated to marginal positions in the world of science—professorships at women's colleges at best—or were segregated in women's fields of home economics and hygiene. These occupational patterns hardened after 1910.[80] Law and medicine were more difficult to enter, despite the unsettled state of professional education already described. Flexner declared, "No woman desiring an education in medicine is under any disability in finding a school to which she may gain admittance," including Johns Hopkins, Cornell, or Michigan. Nevertheless, he found the number of female students and graduates to be declining. In 1920 women received 6 percent of MDs and comprised 6 percent of physicians and surgeons. The rise of law schools opened legal training to women, since preparation in a law office was impossible. Women increased from 1 to 6 percent of law graduates from 1900 to 1920, but in the latter year they comprised barely over 1 percent of lawyers, and many apparently did not practice.[81] American society did not allow knowledge alone to provide access to careers. Some determined women naturally overcame these odds, but as long as the linkage between schooling and careers was tenuous, their numbers remained small. After World War I, the status of women would change markedly. They obtained the right to vote, greater personal freedom, relaxed codes of behavior, and greater participation in the labor force. And they also attended colleges and universities in ever-rising numbers. However, the cultural barriers that kept women from realizing comparable economic and professional rewards from investments in higher education would persist until well after World War II.

LIBERAL CULTURE

The academic revolution and the collegiate revolution were far-reaching transformations in the history of American higher education. That they occurred simultaneously made the fin de siècle era both pathbreaking and exhilarating. Both revolutions were implacable and irreversible, yet they drew universities and colleges in opposite directions.[82] The consequent tensions were felt most acutely in undergraduate education, and by the turn of the century they could no longer be ignored. Critics of Germanic erudition attacked specialization, arguing that increasingly esoteric expertise had little to offer most college students. The

80   Margaret W. Rossiter, *Women Scientists in America: Struggles and Strategies to 1940* (Baltimore: Johns Hopkins University Press, 1982). Women earned 10 percent of PhDs in 1901 and 20 percent in 1921.

81   Flexner, *Medical Education*, 178–79; Woody, *History*, 333–81. For women in Chicago medical schools: Solberg, *Reforming Medical Education*, 86–94.

82   These disparities are treated in somewhat different form by Laurence R. Veysey, *The Emergence of the American University* (Chicago: University of Chicago Press, 1965).

proliferation of courses combined with the elective system, they charged, had produced "curricular incoherence." An emerging body of humanists had a particular grievance, that the narrowly empirical approaches to philology and history had drained aesthetic sensibility from literary studies. Before 1890, a liberal education had meant the classical course; now there was no consensus on what studies should take its place, or why. On the collegiate side, the negative effects were all too apparent. The numerous extracurricular activities, particularly athletics, had become absorbing preoccupations and too often the source of boorish behavior. The supposed social benefits of college were curtailed for many by residential and social stratification. Too many students took advantage of lecture courses and electives to minimize effort. Most discouraging, disdain for study and learning was increasingly evident. But there was no turning back. Disciplinary knowledge had enriched the curriculum, and institutions now hired only teachers with advanced training. Collegiate life had infused enormous vitality into the student experience. Moreover, it had made college attractive to a far larger population by promising social advancement and productive careers. How could institutions reconcile scholarly, liberal, and collegiate values?

One model was at hand, if impossible to replicate: Oxford and Cambridge. Anglophilia was thoroughly embedded in the American upper class in the late nineteenth century, and educators were familiar with Oxbridge from an adulatory literature and occasional visits. There they imagined a harmonious blending of liberal learning, sport, student socialization, and academic community. These effects were produced in the residential colleges. The universities employed learned professors, but students were taught by fellows in their colleges. They could choose to study for a pass or an honors degree, with the latter requiring close work with tutors to prepare for rigorously graded general examinations. The colleges nurtured frequent interactions among students and fellows, fostering both cultural and intellectual socialization. And for honors students, at least, genuine learning was demanded. Much as German PhDs had for the previous generation, Oxbridge provided inspiration for reforming American universities.[83]

The conflict caused by the two revolutions was felt acutely by the Big Three, accustomed to lead in both academic excellence and collegiate endeavors and committed to nonvocational education in the liberal arts. Each faced somewhat

---

83   Alex Duke, *Importing Oxbridge: English Residential Colleges and American Universities* (New Haven: Yale University Press, 1996), 39–64; W. Bruce Leslie, "Dreaming Spires in New Jersey: Anglophilia in Wilson's Princeton," in James Axtell, ed., *The Educational Legacy of Woodrow Wilson: From College to Nation* (Charlottesville: University of Virginia Press, 2012), 97–121. Oxbridge had critics in Britain: "Down to 1914, aristocratic idleness and hearty philistinism cohabited at Oxbridge with serious scholarship and academic competition": Robert D. Anderson, *European Universities from the Enlightenment to 1914* (Oxford: Oxford University Press, 2004), 198.

different manifestations of the same root problem. At Harvard, students exploited the elective system to take easy courses and avoid serious study. At Yale, students were casually dismissive toward the retrograde curriculum and boastful about cheating. Princeton's academic laxity under president Patton was a tacit scandal in academic circles. After 1900, each school felt compelled to address the abject state of student learning. In 1902 Harvard appointed the Committee on Improving Instruction and Yale an unnamed committee for the same purpose.[84] Harvard discovered that students spent only half the expected time on their studies; the Yale committee concluded that "hard study has become *unfashionable* at Yale."

The guiding hand of the Harvard committee was Abbott Lawrence Lowell, a critic of Eliot's elective system and soon to become his successor. The committee report was a turning point toward a more structured curriculum and presaged Lowell's dedication as president to greater student achievement. Yale too instituted piecemeal reforms to stiffen the course of study. Its new president, Arthur Twining Hadley (1899–1920), favored strengthening undergraduate education, but any actions had to come from the conservative Yale faculty, who in this case were motivated to act. As reforms were made, student scholarship appeared to improve from its nadir in the classes of 1904 and 1905. The class of 1904 claimed in its yearbook "more gentlemen and fewer scholars than any other class in the memory of man," while the next class boasted that never had the Heavens witnessed "a class whose scholarship approached so close to naught."[85] At Princeton, in contrast, the new president not only acted decisively to raise the academic performance of students, he also promoted a new vision of the goals of undergraduate education.

Woodrow Wilson was associated with Princeton for 24 years as a student (1875–1879), a professor (1890–1902), and president (1902–1910). In this last position he sought to implement a vision for college education known as "liberal culture." Largely formed by his earlier experience, aspects of liberal culture garnered growing sympathy, but Wilson molded them into a compelling set of ideas that he articulated with force and persistence as a new ideal for American colleges.[86] Wilson possessed extraordinary gifts of intellect and magnetism, which

84   The year 1902 marked heightened awareness of the Oxbridge model as inspiration for liberal culture in American higher education with publication of John Corbin's *An American at Oxford* (Boston: Houghton Mifflin, 1902) and the creation of the Rhodes Trust to fund study at Oxford by college graduates of English-speaking nations: Duke, *Importing Oxbridge*, 54–63.

85   Samuel Eliot Morison, *Three Centuries of Harvard* (Cambridge: Harvard University Press, 1936), 385–87; Pierson, *Yale College*, 232–57, quotes pp. 240, 629, 241n.

86   Laurence R. Veysey, "The Academic Mind of Woodrow Wilson," *Mississippi Valley Historical Review*, 49, 4 (March 1963): 613–34; James Axtell, "The Educational Vision of Woodrow Wilson," in Axtell, *Educational Legacy*, 9–48.

were evident throughout his career. His student days at Princeton coincided with the blossoming of the high collegiate era, including intellectual pursuits like debating. Wilson indulged in them all, being elected to two of the most prestigious posts, editor of the newspaper and secretary of the football association. Wilson cherished this close-knit community and the formative experiences it offered. After Princeton, he studied law at the University of Virginia and was a student leader there as well. But he found legal practice distasteful, and in 1883 he decided to pursue an intellectual career by enrolling at Johns Hopkins in the department of history, politics, and economics. There he found the "minute examination of particulars" under Herbert Baxter Adams insufferable and worked instead on his own comparison of congressional and parliamentary government. Wilson impressed faculty and fellow students despite his aversion to German-style erudition and later became a regular visiting lecturer on government (1888–1898). In 1885 he was hired as a founding faculty member at Bryn Mawr on Adams's recommendation. Although this post allowed him to advance his own scholarly work, his aversion to teaching women made this a trying time. An offer from Wesleyan provided a 2-year interlude and a chance to informally coach the football team while waiting for a call to his alma mater.[87]

Wilson emerged from these years with powerful convictions about American higher education. Remarkably, he opposed the dominant trends of the day—empirical research in the Germanic tradition, all forms of practical college training, coeducation, and the elective system. Instead, he affirmed the goal of *liberal culture* in various iterations over the remainder of his academic career. *Liberal* meant that the focus was entirely on the liberal arts, or what Wilson once called pure literature, pure philosophy, pure science, and his own specialty, history and politics. *Culture* meant that the object was to instill "the intimate and sensitive appreciation of moral, intellectual, and aesthetic values." But such training was "not for the majority who carry forward the common labor of the world. . . . It is for the minority who plan, who conceive, who superintend, who mediate between group and group and must see the wide stage as a whole." Thus, the end purpose was preparation for leadership and national service, and Wilson emphasized these ends as the goal for both Princeton University and its graduates. Finally, these effects could be gained only by a full 4 years in a "compact and homogeneous" residential college—"you cannot go to college on a streetcar and know what college means."[88] Liberal culture might, in theory, be open to all, but

---

87   On Wilson's academic life: Henry W. Bragdon, *Woodrow Wilson: The Academic Years* (Cambridge: Harvard University Press, 1967); John M. Mulder, *Woodrow Wilson: The Years of Preparation* (Princeton: Princeton University Press, 1978).

88   Veysey, "Academic Mind," 632, 633; Axtell, "Educational Vision," 28.

practically it was the province of those who could afford to reside for 4 years at a liberal arts college.

By the time Wilson rejoined Princeton, he had perfected the skills that made him one of the most effective orators of the era—not just in style but in substance. He easily became a popular professor at Princeton and lectured constantly to alumni, civic, and educational groups. In these speeches, he played to audience distrust of universities by disparaging pedantry, "narrow particularistic technical training," the scientific method of investigation, or the "chaos" of unchecked electives. His audiences understood him perfectly when he lauded the kind of elite, liberal training that he envisaged for Princeton. His most spectacular triumph occurred at the gala celebration of Princeton's sesquicentennial, where he addressed an audience of national and international celebrities on "Princeton in the Nation's Service" (1896). The speech extolled the crucial role of Princetonians in the Revolution and the Early Republic, but particularly "the generous union then established in the college between the life of philosophy and the life of the state." To rekindle that spirit, he explicitly rejected science as a method and instead advocated "full, explicit instruction in history and politics, in the experiences of peoples and the fortunes of governments," so long as it was undertaken "like a man and not like a pedant." Wilson's message was greeted with thunderous applause. His combination of iconoclasm and idealism obviously struck a responsive chord, and Wilson emerged as the person who could realize the vision.[89]

Wilson assumed the presidency of Princeton in 1902 with a mandate to transform rhetoric into reality. His overriding goal was to enhance student learning and mold it to his conception of liberal culture. Given the neglect of the Patton administration, this required reorganizing faculty and courses. Wilson replaced the single Academic Department with eleven disciplinary departments in four divisions. He fired some of the most inept professors, making clear that rigorous teaching was now demanded of all instructors. He then worked with the faculty to require all students to major in an academic department for their junior and senior years. Although scarcely a novel concept, the Princeton curriculum established a balance between breadth and depth—concentration and electives—that served as a model for other colleges. With the academic house now put in order, Wilson sought to bolster this system with his most original innovation. He hired young scholars to work closely with students in small groups to guide and enhance their learning. Wilson called them "preceptors"—an

---

89 Veysey, "Academic Mind," 618–21; Bragdon, *Woodrow Wilson*, 284–86; Woodrow Wilson, "Princeton in the Nation's Service," in Woodrow Wilson, ed., *College and State: Educational, Literary and Political Papers (1875–1913)*, 2 vol. (New York: Harper & Brothers, 1925), 259–85, quotes pp. 275, 280. Key alumni considered Wilson to be indispensable and in 1898 executed a secret contract promising him $2,500 per year to remain at Princeton for the next 5 years: Bragdon, *Woodrow Wilson*, 227.

English term, although the obvious inspiration was Oxbridge tutors. Enlisting the support of wealthy trustees and alumni, Wilson hired forty-five preceptors in 1905, augmenting the faculty by more than 40 percent with young, engaged scholars. With this audacious step, Wilson recruited emerging academic talents who served as productive faculty for decades afterward. It also placed the crown of success on Wilson as an academic visionary, locally and nationally.[90]

Wilson's objectives then escalated from ambitious to utopian, and his leadership from consensual to dogmatic.[91] He felt that his ideal of liberal culture for Princeton was frustrated by disunity in the college, chiefly caused by the domination of social life by the exclusive junior-senior eating clubs. Intense social competition for club membership and the priority accorded to wealth and social status, Wilson now charged, had undermined what he considered the democratic foundations of the college. At the end of 1906, Wilson launched a campaign to achieve the social "coordination of the undergraduate life with the teaching of the university" by proposing residential quadrangles to supersede the clubs. Wilson's rhetoric initially convinced the trustees to endorse his Quad Plan, but it soon faced mounting opposition from wealthy younger alumni—largely former club members. Although there was never a concrete plan to finance such a scheme, Wilson adamantly fought this opposition, inflating the plan's significance by invoking a national mission—"because Princeton is the national leader among all the Universities of America." His intransigence only eroded support until the Quad Plan was decisively rejected by the board.

This struggle complicated a longstanding effort to build a residential graduate college. His antagonist in this dispute was Graduate Dean Andrew F. West, a more extreme Anglophile than Wilson. West had already placed his stamp on a temporary graduate residence, where he sought to cultivate gentlemen scholars with all the trappings of an Oxbridge college. Although Wilson and West held fairly similar views, they fell out over the location of the college but more fundamentally over who would set university policy. In this acrimonious conflict, Wilson further alienated his former backers among trustees and alumni, all to West's pointed advantage. When he was decisively repudiated on this issue, Wilson opted to accept the Democratic nomination for governor of New Jersey. Humbled in Princeton largely due to his own ill-advised campaigns, Wilson's academic reputation nonetheless remained untarnished. In defending his positions, he articulated an interpretation of liberal culture that was more inclusive

---

90   Axtell, "Educational Vision"; Mulder, *Woodrow Wilson,* 157–86; Bragdon, *Woodrow Wilson,* 287–311.

91   Wilson scholars have speculated that a severe stroke he suffered in 1906 affected his personality, leaving him more single minded and authoritarian: Axtell, "Educational Vision," 35–36; Mulder, *Woodrow Wilson,* 225–28.

in stressing campus unity and less elitist in condemning the undue influence of wealth and social status.[92] By 1910, his chief and certainly most important academic admirer was now president of Harvard.

Forty years after the installation of Charles W. Eliot, Abbott Lawrence Lowell announced a new orientation for Harvard by devoting his entire inaugural address to his vision for the undergraduate college. Lowell tacitly accepted the achievements of Eliot's reign but asserted "we must go forward and develop the elective system," which meant structuring student choice and retaining students for 4 years. The contemporary college had lost the solidarity that had formerly been an important part of student learning, and he cited Wilson on the "chasm that has opened between college studies and college life." Like Wilson, his aim was to reshape and invigorate student scholarship and to restore some measure of social integration. His approach was essentially the same, but his temperament was not. Lowell was a Boston Brahmin and Harvard aristocrat with supreme confidence in his own judgments, but he also understood the virtues of patience and process.[93]

Lowell immediately established a system of "concentration and distribution," much like Princeton's, since "the best type of liberal education in our complex modern world aims at producing men who know a little of everything and something well." This was followed by provision for divisional examinations, although the faculty took several years to implement them. They were complemented by the addition of tutors to work individually with students and particularly help them prepare for divisional exams. Finally, Harvard established honors degrees, distinguished by an honors thesis. Perhaps learning from Wilson's missteps, Lowell sought the reintegration of social life incrementally by establishing residences for freshmen very much on the Oxbridge model: "dormitories and dining halls, under the comradeship of older men, who appreciated the possibilities of a college life, and took a keen interest in [students'] work and their pleasures." While falling short of the "social coordination" envisaged by Wilson, this was still a significant step toward democratization of college life. And it was feasible, being accomplished by 1914. Under Lowell,

---

92 Mulder, *Woodrow Wilson*, 185–225, quote p. 199. During this last campaign (1909), Wilson made his famous complaint: "the side shows are so numerous, so diverting—so important, if you will—that they have swallowed up the circus": quoted in Leslie, *Gentlemen and Scholars*, 189n. Wilson's departure was a victory for social elitism at Princeton (Bragdon, *Woodrow Wilson*, 384–409), but not a defeat for his academic reforms: see James Axtell, *The Making of Princeton University* (Princeton: Princeton University Press, 2006).

93 Morison, *Three Centuries of Harvard*, 439–49; Abbott Lawrence Lowell, "Inaugural Address (October 6, 1909)," in Samuel Eliot Morison, ed., *The Development of Harvard University Since the Inauguration of President Eliot, 1869–1929* (Cambridge: Harvard University Press, 1930), lxxvii–lxxxviii, quote p. lxxvii.

Harvard realized the essential features of liberal culture or at least realistic approximations: raising the bar for everyone by eliminating easy options and requiring some measure of achievement; providing real incentives to motivate ambitious students to excel; and recognizing collegiate life as an integral feature of student learning. Most emphatically, in practice and in rhetoric, Lowell upheld 4 years of liberal studies as the ideal course for intellectual development and subsequent careers or professional study. Thus, he seconded Wilson in reasserting the value of a liberal arts education.[94]

★   ★   ★

This last affirmation was badly needed by the country's hundreds of private colleges. For them, the demise of the classical AB course had created a curricular Purgatory, uncertainty over what direction they should, or could, take. They faced the daunting challenge of adapting to the disciplinary coursework demanded by the academic revolution. This required a different scale of operation. In 1880, when the average college had 88 students, a proper college was deemed to need 10 faculty. In 1900, 25 faculty were recommended to teach the expanded curriculum. However, in 1915 an "efficient college" called for 400 students and 40 faculty. At the time, one-half of private colleges had fewer than 300 students and not close to adequate faculties. William Rainey Harper in 1900 had estimated that only one-quarter of the colleges could remain viable. Most of them doggedly hung on, but their ambiguous status was known as the plight of the colleges. They badly needed more students, more teachers, and more money, but perhaps the greatest need was a refurbished, positive image. It was difficult to claim superiority of teaching given the demonstrable inferiority of faculty qualifications, course offerings, and laboratory facilities. Church sponsorship proved to be a two-edged sword, tapping a dependable (often shrinking) clientele, but alienating those preferring nondenominational settings. During the zenith of popularity for graduate programs, circa 1890, many colleges joined the doctoral lists. Twelve Ohio colleges granted PhDs before 1900, but only the program at Ohio State endured. Dickinson College in Pennsylvania was typical of these efforts, awarding four doctorates in the 1890s before abandoning the program as hopeless. In the tradition of multipurpose colleges, colleges were tempted to increase vocational offerings, even though it became evident that they might bring enrollments but not prestige. Bucknell, for example, sought additional students by turning away from the liberal arts and establishing vocational programs in education, law, premed, engineering, and home economics. After 1900, it became

94   Ibid., lxxxiv, lxxxvii.

increasingly apparent that colleges could not compete with universities on the latter's terms but rather had to find their own turf.[95]

The growing consensus favoring liberal culture was encouraging for the colleges, though they could not yet identify with Yale or Princeton. The need to strengthen undergraduate education was pervasive in the 1900s and had powerful allies. Both the CFAT and the Rockefeller General Education Board placed their influence and their dollars behind this movement. The increasing use of rankings to distinguish standard colleges from their weaker brethren forced institutions to be mindful of measures of quality.[96] Abraham Flexner, who would work for both foundations, published a volume in 1908 articulating contemporary criticisms of the colleges, particularly the incoherence of the curriculum. Anglophilia was given a tangible boost in 1902 by creation of the Rhodes Scholarships for study at Oxford. Intended to strengthen ties between Britain and English-speaking nations, a Rhodes clearly had the desired effect on Frank Aydelotte, whose years at Brasenose College (1905–1907) burnished admiration for thorough study, residential community, amateur sports, and the cultural value of literary study. He sought to inculcate these values as a teacher at Indiana University and MIT and founded the *American Oxonian* to popularize them more widely by mobilizing the Rhodes alumni. Given these intellectual currents, possible remedies for the predicament of the college soon appeared.[97]

The founding of new institutions often reflects or even exaggerates the fresh ideas of the times, as was the case with Cornell, Johns Hopkins, Bryn Mawr, and Clark universities. This was also the case in Portland, Oregon, where Simeon and Amanda Reed dedicated their $3 million estate to the establishment of an institution of higher education. The implementation of their vague wishes was placed in the hands of the local Unitarian minister and leading citizen, Thomas Lamb Eliot, who conscientiously explored all possibilities. The Reeds had specifically mentioned "practical knowledge," but when he queried educators around the country, they responded that a technical institute was expensive and would probably duplicate offerings of the state universities. Founding

---

95   Geiger, "The Crisis of the Old Order"; Charles Coleman Sellers, *Dickinson College: A History* (Middletown, CT: Wesleyan University Press, 1973), 290; W. Bruce Leslie, *Gentlemen and Scholars*, 177–88.

96   After 1900, efforts to classify institutions according to the quality of education proliferated. The CFAT was compelled to make such judgments for eligibility for pensions. In 1908 the AAU began an ongoing effort to classify colleges on the basis of the fitness of their graduates for graduate study. In 1910–1911 the Bureau of Education made a comprehensive classification of colleges on the same basis, which was suppressed as too controversial to publish: David S. Webster, *Academic Quality Rankings of American Colleges and Universities* (Springfield, IL: Charles C. Thomas, 1986).

97   Abraham Flexner, *The American College* (1908); Frances Blanchard, *Frank Aydelotte of Swarthmore* (Midddletown, CT: Wesleyan University Press, 1970).

a university with professional schools was also deemed too expensive. Eliot was then advised by the secretary of the General Education Board, Wallace Buttrick, that "a strong, high grade college of the arts" would fill a lacuna for the region. Buttrick further recommended for president of such a college a young professor at Bowdoin with bold ideas about college education, William Trufant Foster. He accepted the presidency of Reed College (1910–1919) on the condition that it be dedicated exclusively to the liberal arts and sciences and offer "as high grade of scholarship as any in the country."

Foster visited about one hundred colleges, discovering widespread unrest over lack of student interest in their studies, exacerbated by devotion to athletics and social affairs. In response, he formulated a model for what he called the "ideal college." It had to be private to resist outside influence; it should be small to promote interaction and community; the content of courses was less important than the thoroughness with which they were taught; and it would avoid the distractions of intercollegiate athletics and fraternities. These characteristics were preconditions for its two essential purposes: "to become a Johns Hopkins for undergraduates, the Balliol of America," in the quality of education and to be "broadly cultural and ultimately practical" by applying knowledge to socially useful purposes. With a concentration on rigor and relevance, Reed set a new model for liberal education. It quickly gained widespread recognition for academic seriousness and became an exemplar of new possibilities.[98]

The year after Reed opened, Alexander Meiklejohn was named president of Amherst College (1912–1923). Son of a Scottish immigrant, he attended Brown on a scholarship, followed by a PhD in philosophy at Cornell (1897). Returning to Brown to teach philosophy, Meiklejohn became a favorite with students in the classroom and on athletic fields. Named the first dean of the college in 1901, he combined an idealistic commitment to student moral and intellectual development with excellent rapport with students in extracurricular affairs. Elevated to the presidency of Amherst, Meiklejohn inspired his inaugural audience with an idealistic depiction of the "Liberal College." Its purpose was to lead students "into the life intellectual. The college is not a place of the body, nor of the feelings, nor even of the will; it is first of all, a place of the mind." He condemned prevailing notions that college should prepare students for practical careers, and he castigated the elective system for producing "intellectual agnosticism, a kind of intellectual bankruptcy, into which, in spite of our wealth of information, the spirit of the time has fallen." Rather, the liberal college should provide the

---

98 Dorothy Johansen, "History of Reed College to 1920," ms. (1984), Reed Digital Archives, quotes, pp. 17, 52, 64–65; "Comrades of the Quest: The Story of Reed College" (adapted from the *New York Times* of April 15, 1917), Reed Digital Archives.

kind of enduring mental formation needed for long-term leadership and success. More tangibly, he asserted that a liberal education consisted of just five elements: "the contributions of philosophy, of humanistic science, of natural science, of history and of literature." Meiklejohn thus asserted that the basic liberal arts provided a college education that was superior to the professional and specialized disciplinary offerings of universities. The Liberal College address was widely publicized and struck a responsive chord by offering a seemingly plausible ideal, given the colleges' limitations.[99]

Foster and Meiklejohn both saw the enhancement of student learning as the essence of the problem, but they differed on strategies. For Foster, academic rigor was the solution, and he institutionalized it by the selective admission of motivated students, elimination of "distractions" (athletics and fraternities), and thoroughness of instruction, reinforced with senior theses and oral examinations. Meiklejohn focused on the content of the curriculum, believing that challenging material, well taught, could stimulate greater student interest and effort. At Amherst he soon proposed a core curriculum centered on social and economic institutions to provide a unifying focus for the five elements of the liberal arts. Only one such course was created, but Meiklejohn would persist in believing that the essence of liberal education could be captured with the right curricular formulas. Both men were idealists in positing the intellectual autonomy of their colleges, but Foster sought to aggressively address social problems and enlighten the community, while Meiklejohn advocated more aloof cultural criticism. Both men also shared the fate of being more successful in devising ideal colleges than administering them. Foster's self-righteousness and political radicalism cost the college potential support, and he resigned in 1919 after falling out with the trustees. Meiklejohn injected new life into staid Amherst with young faculty and the new course, but his governance of the college was a disaster. He failed to put the interests of the institution ahead of his own preoccupations, and he was dramatically and inevitably fired in 1923. However, in the prewar years, both men accomplished much of their respective visions and helped to lay a foundation for the rehabilitation of the liberal arts college.[100]

The organization of the Association of American Colleges (AAC, 1915) was a concrete step in this direction. The last sector to develop a national association,

99 Alexander Meiklejohn, "What the Liberal College Is," *The Liberal College* (Boston: 1920), 21–50; Adam R. Nelson, *Education and Democracy: The Meaning of Alexander Meiklejohn, 1872–1964* (Madison: University of Wisconsin Press, 2001), 33–96.

100 Johansen, "Reed College"; Burton R. Clark, *The Distinctive College* (New Brunswick: Transaction, 1992 [1970]), 91–150; John P. Sheehy, "What's So Funny 'Bout Communism, Atheism, and Free Love? The Radical Legacy of William Trufant Foster," *Reed Magazine* (Summer 2007): 25–32; Nelson, *Education and Democracy*, 97–129.

the colleges lagged in defining their role in the emerging system of higher education. As a spokesman at the inaugural conference asserted, "The present-day college must show that it is doing a work that is not done and cannot be done by the university." They were threatened from below as well by the ongoing expansion of high schools, junior colleges, and normal schools/teachers colleges. Their defensiveness was heightened by the nature of the original membership—predominantly denominational colleges from the Midwest. By bringing its rather isolated members together, the AAC served a number of purposes: it provided quality control by adopting the Carnegie standards and setting requirements for membership; its meetings and publications provided a valuable forum for comparing practices; and a permanent central office focused particularly on aiding members to strengthen administration. For example, an extensive survey was conducted to define "the efficient college," which produced data that allowed any college to compare student/faculty ratios or expenditures per student with peers.[101]

Most important, the AAC gradually embraced a liberal arts education as the signature mission for its membership. Not all of its original members were classical liberal arts colleges, by any means. But as the AAC elaborated this ideal, colleges such as Bucknell and Dickinson adopted it as a distinctive and defensible mission. Foster and Meiklejohn participated in AAC meetings and helped to articulate this mission. In 1915 the country's 400+ private colleges were still arrayed at all stages of development. The commissioner of education addressing the AAC in 1916 repeated Harper's observation that half of the nation's colleges, those with incomes under $40,000, would better serve as junior colleges. The AAC represented the stronger half of colleges, but there were still large gaps between the average college, the efficient college, the liberal college, or the ideal college. The organization of the AAC and its subsequent work sought to define the nature of a liberal arts college and offer practical guidance for attaining it.[102]

★ ★ ★

Liberal culture in the prewar years was too diffuse to be a movement, yet too widespread to be ignored. On one hand, it was a protest against the dominant quantitative trends of the era: the predominant vocational emphasis of most institutions; the inexorable specialization of disciplinary knowledge in

---

101 "The Efficient College: Read before the Association of American Colleges" (Jan. 21, 1916), *American Association of Colleges Bulletin*, 2, 1 (1916); Hugh Hawkins, *Banding Together: The Rise of National Associations in American Higher Education, 1887–1950* (Baltimore: Johns Hopkins University Press, 1992), 16–20, quote p. 41.

102 Philander P. Claxton, "The Junior College," *Association of American Colleges Bulletin*, 2, 3 (1916): 104–12; Hawkins, *Banding Together*, 41–44.

universities; the fragmentation of the curriculum through the elective system; and the disdain for intellect of the high collegiate era. On the other hand, it advocated a menu of educational ideals: an overriding desire to enhance the learning of undergraduates, specifically in the arts and sciences; an admiration for the educational model of Oxbridge colleges; a recognition of the learning benefits of a residential community; a similar appreciation of the developmental contributions of extracurricular activities, including (sometimes) athletics; and, above all, a belief in the value, articulated with various phrases, of a liberal education. The history of virtually every college during these years shows them wrestling with some combination of these issues.[103] The negative complaints of liberal culture were principally early twentieth-century reactions to aspects of the academic revolution and the rise of applied fields. The positive aspects would have continued repercussions after World War I. Members of the AAC tended to converge toward the liberal arts model; the residential component of liberal education assumed paramount influence among private universities; Frank Aydelotte implemented a true honors curriculum as president of Swarthmore College; and Meiklejohn and others proposed new curricular formulas for capturing the essence of the liberal college.

Liberal culture was but one of the enduring legacies of the collegiate revolution. Between 1875 and 1915, the American college had been transformed for students, for the American public, and for the educational system. Where students had formerly experienced most of college life within a formal institutional structure, they now were socialized in fraternities or sororities, at football games, with the Campus Y, or in other organized student activities. Moreover, these activities were fundamentally democratic. They may have originated at eastern private schools, but by the twentieth century they were common at colleges everywhere, including normal schools and historically black colleges. They may have been most liberating for women, who created their own collegiate space on male-dominated campuses and an extraordinarily rich slate of activities at their own colleges. However, the collegiate revolution also had a huge impact on the American public. The colleges no longer appeared to be reserved for a narrow population aiming for professional careers but rather appeared open to all qualified aspirants, even if that was still a small slice of an age cohort. Colleges were portrayed as promoting the manliness and savoir faire needed for success in the business world. This image was reinforced by alumni, who, in turn, took pride in their alma maters and made donations for their improvement. In short, colleges had emerged as a clear route to middle-class careers and life styles. Colleges

---

103   For example. Nancy Jane Cable, *The Search for Mission in Ohio Liberal Arts Colleges: Denison, Kenyon, Marietta, Oberlin, 1870–1914*, PhD Diss., University of Virginia, 1984, 279–339.

also assumed an unambiguous place in the educational structure. By 1915 a clear separation of secondary and higher education existed in most of the country, and blurring was stigmatized in places where separation was not yet complete. Similarly, college, or at least the first 2 years, had now become the gateway to professional schools. Liberal culture offered a theoretical justification for a changing reality, idealizing an institution whose structural position had now become fixed. It was also, sub rosa, an effort to recapture the elite character that a college education had formerly represented. The elaboration of the virtues of a liberal arts education was thus a premonition of the emergence of greater differentiation in the realm of higher education—the herald of mass higher education.

★ 10 ★

MASS HIGHER EDUCATION,
1915–1940

WORLD WAR I

THE UNITED STATES WAS AT WAR WITH THE CENTRAL Powers for just 19 months, but the experience precipitated far-reaching changes in America's economy, society, culture, and higher education. The wartime boom in production and profits evolved, after a postwar recession, into the consolidation of corporate oligopolies and the prosperity of the Roaring Twenties. The superficial wartime unity of American society began to unravel soon after the Armistice, but the industrial economy enhanced the standard and style of living of most Americans. America's genteel Victorian idealism sustained the nation through the "war to end all wars" and provided moralistic support for two great postwar experiments, Prohibition and women's suffrage. But moral certainties, progress, and high culture would all be called into question in the ensuing years. These changes affected higher education. Colleges and universities adapted to instructing new kinds of students in new types of institutions for careers in the new economy while also seeking to preserve the traditional social and cultural order.

In 1917 American students, faculty, and administrators experienced the euphoria of war, as had their counterparts in other belligerent nations 3 years before. Universities immediately proffered their services for training, research, and morale building but ended by abandoning their academic mission almost entirely. Academic freedom, let alone freedom of speech, fared no better. Both these aberrations were temporary. More lasting were the new organizations that testified to the enlarged national role that higher education assumed.

When the European war commenced, Americans were largely sympathetic to the Western Allies, but substantial numbers favored pacifism or noninvolvement, and a small minority sympathized with Germany.[1] Active support for

---

[1] Carol S. Gruber, *Mars and Minerva: World War I and the Uses of Higher Learning in America* (Baton Rouge: Louisiana State University, 1975), 46–80.

the Allies was evident at anglophile eastern colleges, where ambulance units were organized and students volunteered for military drill. After preparedness became the official policy in 1916, support for the Allies became more strident and hostility toward dissenters more overt. The first measure affecting universities that year created the Reserve Officers' Training Corps, which was voluntary for institutions and students. Patriotic fervor intensified in anticipation of the declaration of war in April 1917 and soon was heated by government stoking. American entry touched off a frenzy of patriotism, which only intensified during the next 2 years. In terms of indoctrination through crude propaganda and suppression of civil liberties, World War I surpassed all other American wars. The federal Committee on Public Information was partly responsible, training, for example, 75,000 "four-minute men," charged with whipping up war fever with patriotic rants to any and all assembled groups. Extreme expressions of devotion to the war effort were prominent among the upper reaches of American society, including educators. American war fever was an amalgam of hate and hope: ceaseless loathing of the Kaiser, the Hun, and other symbolic enemies and a moral crusade to end war and make the world safe for democracy. Above all, super patriots demanded national unity—100 percent Americanism—which targeted immigrants from eastern and southern Europe, radicals (identified with same), pacifists, and German-Americans. The zeal of 100 percent Americanism persisted after the war in the persecution of radicals known as the Red Scare. Universities figured prominently in this *trahison des clercs*.[2]

University spokesmen identified with the idealistic aims of prowar Progressives, including President Wilson, but readily stooped to purveying propaganda. The publications section of the Committee on Public Instruction was led by Guy Stanton Ford, head of the history department and dean of the graduate school at the University of Minnesota. Ford recruited eager academics to write, among other things, the *War Cyclopedia*—a one-sided reference handbook with such entries as "atrocities," "Edith Cavell" (a British nurse executed by the German Army in Belgium) "Belgian Violation," and so on. Campuses endured successive patriotic rallies, all repeating the same refrain. A lack of sufficient enthusiasm at such rallies could provoke charges of disloyalty, as happened at the University of Wisconsin. At Illinois, faculty were investigated for not buying Liberty Bonds. In 1918, all universities were compelled to offer a mandatory "War Issues Course" intended to enhance the morale of future

---

2   David M. Kennedy, *Over Here: The First World War and American Society* (New York: Oxford University Press, 1980), 45–92; *trahison des clercs* was the phrase used by Julian Benda to condemn intellectuals who served power instead of truth: Gruber, *Mars and Minerva*, 253–59 et passim.

soldiers by explicating how the fate of civilization depended on the struggle between democracy and autocracy.[3]

Faculty members readily set aside the ethics of their profession. The American Association of University Professors (AAUP) had been formed in 1915 principally to safeguard academic freedom. Its "Declaration of Principles" explicitly forewarned that the conclusions of men of learning should be determined by the "quest for truth" and "not echoes of the opinions of the lay public." This eloquent defense of freedom of speech and thought in the academy was repudiated by the end of 1917, when new wartime grounds for dismissal were approved. Universities were deemed justified in firing professors without due process for conviction or indictment of any offense relating to the war; for "*tending* to cause others to resist or evade the compulsory service law"; or for seeking "to dissuade others from rendering voluntary assistance to the efforts of the government." Professors of German or Austrian birth or parentage were held to stricter scrutiny, "not to give, by their *utterances* or *associations*, reasonable grounds for the belief that they *contemplate* [disloyal] acts." The AAUP wartime policy allowed professors less freedom than even the draconian Espionage and Sedition Acts. Numerous dismissals occurred, often of war skeptics who were also disliked for holding radical views or for personal eccentricities. A German-born professor at the University of Wisconsin was fired for sarcastically suggesting that a patriotic colleague should wear his Liberty Button on the seat of his pants so that his patriotism would still be displayed when he wrote on the blackboard. The distinguished Columbia psychologist, James McKeen Cattell, long a thorn in the side of trustees and President Butler, was dismissed ostensibly for writing a critical letter to members of Congress. This action prompted the resignation of renowned historian Charles Beard, but such principled protest against war hysteria—and those who exploited it—was costly and rare.[4]

The organization of the Students' Army Training Corps in 1918 transformed colleges and universities into preinduction camps—in two stages. The first version had male students enlist in the army but remain on furlough status while completing their education and receiving on-campus military training. When the final German offensive caused the draft age to be lowered to 18, the SATC

---

3 Ibid., 138–52, 238–44; Merle Curti and Vernon Carstensen, *The University of Wisconsin: A History, 1848–1925*, 2 vol. (Madison: University of Wisconsin Press, 1949), II, 111–20; Karl Max Grisso, *David Kinley, 1861–1944: The Career of the Fifth President of the University of Illinois*, PhD Thesis, University of Illinois, 1980, 325–50.

4 American Association of University Professors, *Report of the Committee on Academic Freedom and Tenure* (December, 1915); Gruber, *Mars and Minerva*, 164–72, quotes pp. 167–69; Curti and Carstensen, *Wisconsin*, II, 114n; Michael Rosenthal, *Nicholas Miraculous: The Amazing Career of the Redoubtable Dr. Nicholas Murray Butler* (New York: Farrar, Straus and Giroux, 2006), 226–39.

was reformulated to place colleges and universities under military control. On October 1, 1918, 140,000 college men on 516 campuses were inducted into active duty in the Army. Colleges and universities became units of the SATC, accommodating student-soldiers as well as qualified volunteers, who thus became students too. Under military discipline, students wore uniforms, had regimented schedules, and marched to and from their assignments. Education was to be determined by the needs of the Army. Students divided their time between drill and classes, but, in fact, academic standards were virtually abandoned: regular classes were foreshortened and adapted to military purposes, and students had little time for study. All campuses converted to the quarter system so that the oldest quartile of students could be transferred to active units at the end of each term. Thus, the SATC would have drained the entire male population in 1 year. However, the Armistice was signed on November 11, and the SATC was one of the first military units to be disbanded.

University leaders had originally welcomed the SATC. They had already pledged their institutions' resources to the war effort, and government revenues promised to avert an impending budgetary disaster. Although it lasted for fewer than 3 months, the SATC was a daunting experiment. Confusion reigned over the respective roles of faculty and military, and all pretenses of academic standards were disregarded. Nonetheless, under the lingering wartime euphoria, it was generally praised by educators for displacing the former collegiate distractions with discipline, purpose, and unity.[5]

The one area in which the war experience set positive precedents was the utilization of university expertise. This was largely accomplished through the National Research Council (NRC), inspired and chaired by George Ellery Hale. America's foremost astrophysicist and solar astronomer, Hale founded and directed the Yerkes Observatory at the University of Chicago and then the Carnegie Institution's Mount Wilson Observatory near Pasadena. Elected to the National Academy of Sciences in 1902, he sought to make that moribund body into an active scientific organization, like its European counterparts. The impending scientific needs of the war finally prompted President Wilson to create the NRC in 1916, with Hale as chairman. The NRC acted as the executive arm of the academy. It soon began to organize the employment of scientific talent for the war. The NRC was able to tap the scientific leadership of universities, industry, and

5   Roger L. Geiger, *To Advance Knowledge: The Growth of American Research Universities, 1900– 1940* (New Brunswick: Transaction, 2004 [1986]), 101–5; Gruber, *Mars and Minerva*, 213–48. The SATC fiasco was marred further by the worldwide influenza epidemic: crowded quarters, outdoor marching, and fatigue made student-soldiers vulnerable. At the University of Michigan 1,200 were stricken and 57 students died: Howard H. Peckham, *The Making of the Universityof Michigan, 1817–1992*, edited and updated by Margaret L. Steneck and Nicholas H. Steneck (Ann Arbor: University of Michigan, 1994), 149.

government, as well as the academy. It operated through committees of experts who were familiar with scientists in their fields and recommended appropriate personnel for government laboratories, where war research was conducted. University scientists made notable contributions to submarine detection, sound ranging, and communications, among other areas. The NRC also worked directly with industry to achieve large-scale production of essential materials. The Psychology Committee of the NRC was responsible for administering intelligence tests to new recruits, the first such large-scale application.[6] As valuable as the individual projects were, they were far outweighed for universities by the experience of working with other sectors of science.

University scientists played a leading role in the NRC. Robert Millikan of Chicago and Arthur Noyes of MIT filled key positions. They interacted with research chiefs of the country's principal science-based industries—AT&T, General Electric, Western Electric, and DuPont—and strategic organizations like the Carnegie Institution of Washington and the Engineering Foundation. The projects of the NRC integrated basic and applied research, university and industrial science. Leaders from all sectors not only considered those efforts highly fruitful, they believed such cooperation should be perpetuated in peacetime. Robert Millikan exulted, "For the first time in history the world has been waked up by the war to an appreciation of what science can do." This consensus has been labeled the "ideology of national science"—the conviction that coordination of basic and applied science would multiply the rich benefits of discovery and innovation for American society. This ideology shaped the development of postwar academic science.[7]

In the aftermath of the war, there was widespread enthusiasm in higher education for the kind of centralization and coordination that had been imposed to win the war. University of Akron President Parke Kolbe was typical in praising the SATC, advocating a permanent version of compulsory military training on campus, and foreseeing coordination of colleges and universities by a federal department of education.[8] However, legislation to establish such a cabinet-level

---

6 Daniel J. Kevles, *The Physicists: The History of a Scientific Community in Modern America* (New York: Random House, 1979 [1971]), 102–38; Daniel J. Kevles, "Testing the Army's Intelligence: Psychologists and the Military in World War I," *Journal of American History*, 55, 3 (Dec. 1968): 565–81. University personnel also largely staffed 'The Inquiry'—a White House effort throughout the war to assemble intelligence for the postwar peace settlement. The Inquiry employed 63 scholars in May 1918 and twice that number at year's end, the largest numbers recruited from Harvard, Columbia, Yale, and Princeton: Lawrence E. Gelfand, *The Inquiry: American Preparations for Peace, 1917–1919* (New Haven: Yale University Press, 1963).

7 Geiger, *To Advance Knowledge*, 94–101, quote p. 98; Ronald C. Tobey, *The American Ideology of National Science, 1919–1930* (Pittsburgh: University of Pittsburgh Press, 1971), 20–61.

8 Parke Rexford Kolbe, *The Colleges in Wartime and After* (New York: Appleton, 1919), 183–206; Geiger, *To Advance Knowledge*, 105–7.

department failed to pass Congress. Similarly, the NRC initially envisioned a postwar role in coordinating the many spheres of government science but never obtained such authority. Instead, leaders of American science and of major universities soon rejected any involvement with the federal government, preferring to coordinate activities privately among independent entities. Such cooperation soon became a reality. Not only were universities and industry inclined to collaborate and the NRC to coordinate and guide such interactions, but the great American philanthropic foundations were poised to provide the resources for a privately funded system of university research. Before these developments occurred, however, colleges and universities faced a more immediate challenge. Wartime inflation had eroded their resources and escalated their expenses, and peacetime now brought an unexpected influx of students.

MASS HIGHER EDUCATION

During the interwar years, American higher education grew into what came to be called mass higher education. In 1915, 5.5 percent of 18- to 21-year-olds attended some form of college, and 1.7 percent of 21-year-olds received first degrees. In 1940, 15.5 percent of the age group attended, and 7.7 percent were awarded first degrees. Although participation in 1940 does not appear massive by twenty-first-century standards, it was far greater than any other country. More significant, expansion of higher education brought new relationships with culture, careers, and knowledge. It would be another generation before sociologist Martin Trow explicated distinctive ideal types of elite and mass higher education, but contemporaries in the 1920s and 1930s were sensitive to these differences and reacted to them.

The differences can be presented as appositions.[9] Elite higher education is ostensibly intended for students of privileged social backgrounds or extraordinary talent; access to mass institutions is a *right* for all who meet the qualifications. Elite institutions emphasize culture—the formation of character and preparation for leadership; mass institutions transmit instrumental knowledge for a broad range of technical and economic roles. Elite curricula are structured by academic or professional conceptions of knowledge and proclaim meritocratic standards; mass curricula emphasize practical content and can be variously structured, leading institutions to serve as "holding companies for quite different kinds of academic enterprises." Elite institutions prefer small residential communities with

---

9   Enrollments and degrees from the *Biennial Survey of Education*, published by the Department of the Interior, Office of Education; the following paragraph paraphrases Martin Trow, "Reflections on the Transition from Elite to Mass to Universal Access," in Michael Burrage, ed., *Martin Trow: Twentieth-Century Higher Education: Elite to Mass to Universal* (Baltimore: Johns Hopkins University Press, 2010), 556–610, esp. pp. 558–59.

"impermeable boundaries"; mass institutions include commuting and part-time students and value links with external constituencies.

American higher education never conformed fully to Trow's elite typology, nor are elite and mass traits mutually exclusive. Since the Civil War, though, the movement had been away from elite modes. This caused advocates of liberal culture to react against this tide. In the interwar years, developments toward mass higher education exemplified those characteristics identified by Trow, and the countermovement resisting those changes reflected an effort to preserve or enhance elite forms. This section will analyze the former, the next section, the latter.

Higher-education enrollments surged after 1915, despite wartime dislocations, doubling by 1924. Enrollments rose more slowly into the Depression years, stalled for a short time, and then resumed growth in the last half of the 1930s. The proximate cause was the increase in high school graduates. Numbering 95,000 in 1900 and 200,000 in 1913, high school graduates reached 500,000 in 1924 before growth tapered off. Much of this growth came from the expansion of high school education in smaller towns and cities, where graduates tended to continue on to college. Economic returns to education were high in such locales, which helps to account for the high school movement and high rates of continuation. In manufacturing centers, conversely, the opportunity for early employment lured many away from high school completion. Economists Claudia Goldin and Lawrence Katz estimated college-going rates near 50 percent for high school graduates (1910–1924), largely because the "economic return to a year of high school or college around 1915 was enormously high." After 1924, the number of high school graduates continued to grow, but more of them took vocational courses and did not go on to college. Still, high school graduates had ample reason to pursue higher education, and they found institutions eager to accept them.[10]

The increased supply of higher education resulted from the expansion of traditional institutions, especially universities, and the appearance of new kinds of institutions characteristic of mass systems. Underlying this expansion were two distinctive features of the United States. First, although the higher-education system was crystallizing into a definite structure, considerable flexibility—or ambiguity—still existed. High schools could extend upward to offer the first 2 years of college work, and normal schools could stake a claim in the tertiary sector as teachers colleges. Second, the broad scope of higher education in the United States already encompassed technical and commercial subjects eschewed

---

10   Claudia Goldin and Lawrence F. Katz, *The Race between Education and Technology* (Cambridge: Harvard University Press, 2008), 72–85, 194–246, quote pp. 287–88.

by universities elsewhere—agriculture, engineering, commerce, home economics, and, especially, education. Mass institutions were thus able to adapt these curricula according to institutional capacity and student needs, occasionally drawing the disdain of the elite sector but seldom facing actual barriers. Above all, the independent adaptations of myriad institutions created virtually unlimited places for burgeoning cohorts of high school graduates.

JUNIOR COLLEGES. The term "junior college" was coined by William Rainey Harper in 1896 to distinguish the first 2 years at the University of Chicago, which were then recognized with an Associate in Arts degree. Harper also foresaw the development of feeder institutions that could send their graduates to Chicago's "senior college." Only the school board of Joliet, Illinois, responded, opening a junior college department in its high school in 1902. More significant than this often-told tale, the first 2 years of college were regarded by many as basically foundational for the university-level studies of the junior and senior years. In the early twentieth century, for example, this segment of college was practically institutionalized in efforts to require 2 years of college for admission to professional schools. Once the idea gained currency that freshman and sophomore studies could be offered separately from degree-granting colleges, the spread of junior colleges became a grassroots phenomenon. Junior colleges were practical and cheap. Specialized faculty were not needed to offer introductory subjects, and facility requirements were minimal (usually space in existing high schools). Students were long accustomed to following diverse paths to college, including preparatory classes (which faded away in the 1920s) and normal schools. Where alternatives were not locally available, junior colleges offered educational upgrading at minimal cost and possible entrée to a full college course.

Many early junior colleges were private, "decapitated" colleges that shed their upper classes, as Harper had recommended. Some were new or upgraded foundings by Catholics or other denominations taking advantage of the minimal initial investment. Public junior colleges soon eclipsed the private sector in enrollments and significance, led by California.[11] David Starr Jordan became a convert to the junior college model in 1906 but was rebuffed by Stanford trustees. Alexis Lange, Dean of Letters and then head of the Education Department at University of California, became the principal advocate. Having experienced the 1880s curricular experiments at the University of Michigan, Lange became convinced that freshman and sophomore studies belonged naturally with secondary education. As dean, he organized the Berkeley undergraduate course into lower

---

11 Basic information can be found in Walter Crosby Eells, ed., *American Junior Colleges* (Washington, D.C.: American Council on Education, 1940).

and upper divisions, with a junior certificate awarded to students completing the sophomore year. As head of Education, he advocated "six-year high schools." He was instrumental in passage of the 1907 law permitting high schools to offer the first 2 years of university coursework. The city of Fresno, with the nearest college more than 200 miles distant, was the first to act on this provision in 1910, and other school districts soon followed. By 1917, 21 such junior colleges enrolled almost 1,600 students. Succeeding laws furthered the development of junior colleges, including provision for state and county funding. Vocational courses, which Lange had long supported, were also approved.[12]

Modern scholars have interpreted Lange's motives (and Jordan's) as anti-democratic—intended to divert students away from more prestigious universities. Such views confound a later controversy with original motives. An educational progressive and admirer of John Dewey, Lange sought an overall expansion of educational opportunities, which was badly needed in California given great distances and the poverty of many school districts. He also, following Dewey, believed that students should be able to choose studies that best suited them, including vocational curricula. Occupational courses at this juncture had the potential to enlarge the clientele of junior colleges while still offering an educational advantage for social and economic betterment.[13]

While the advocacy of Lange and Jordan helped to establish junior colleges, local boosters who wanted their children to have access to advanced education were the driving force behind their growth. In this respect, junior colleges were one part of a general scramble for normal schools and (later) state colleges, with which they sometimes merged. The junior college movement mushroomed after World War I: 74 institutions in 1915; 207 in 1922; and 408 in 1928. Enrollments increased more steadily, passing 50,000 in 1928 and quadrupling to nearly 200,000 in 1940, 13 percent of total higher-education enrollments. Michigan and Kansas were first to follow California with enabling legislation in 1917. Public junior colleges, with 70 percent of enrollments in 1940, were densest (after California) in the Midwest, especially Iowa, Kansas, and Oklahoma. Most were organized locally, but Utah and Georgia sponsored state institutions. Private junior colleges were concentrated along the Atlantic Seaboard. Overall, the safest generalization about junior colleges is their extreme heterogeneity, including

12   John Aubrey Douglass, *The California Idea and American Higher Education: 1850 to the Master Plan* (Stanford: Stanford University Press, 2000), 114–34; Edward A. Gallagher, "Jordan and Lange: The California Junior College's role as Protector of Teaching," *Michigan Academician*, 27 (1994): 1–12; Gallagher, "Alexis Lange and the Origin of the Occupational Education Function in California Junior Colleges," *Michigan Academician*, 22 (1990): 241–57.

13   Edward A. Gallagher, "Revisionist Nonsense and the Junior College: Early California Development," *Michigan Academician*, 24 (1995): 215–28; Douglass, *California Idea*, 124–26.

Bible colleges, urban institutions, branch campuses of universities, secretarial schools, military academies, and historically black colleges in the South. More than one-half of junior colleges had fewer than 200 students, and most public colleges operated in high school classrooms, often taught by high school teachers. In contrast, Los Angeles City [junior] College, with 6,700 students, possessed a 27-acre campus and 209 full-time instructors, most with advanced degrees.[14]

The appeal of these institutions is apparent. A survey of more than 3,000 students in the late 1920s gave the following reasons for attending junior colleges: to save money (57 percent); to prepare for the university (55 percent); unable to meet university admissions requirements (36 percent); and to prepare for a vocation (30 percent). Students were happy with their instruction (93 percent) and pleased to live at home (74 percent) but were disappointed with "the spirit, traditions, and the general college atmosphere" (26 percent approving). Clearly, junior colleges made higher education a realistic possibility for a substantial segment of the population, especially in California, which enrolled 37 percent of all junior college students in 1940.[15]

Despite the variety and grassroots origins of junior colleges, educators quickly sought to mold the dominant public sector. The chief issue animating discussion of junior colleges was the role of vocational versus academic transfer courses. During the burgeoning growth through the 1920s, there was little doubt that students sought, and the colleges provided, an academic course approximating college studies. However, leaders of the junior college movement and the American Association of Junior Colleges (AAJC, f. 1920) soon began to promote the mission of providing practical training for semiprofessional occupations. This message gained strength in the 1930s in the face of terrible youth unemployment and was advanced as the signature mission of the colleges. For the institutional leaders of junior colleges, the attraction of what they called terminal education lay in carving out a distinctive and socially valued role. In the academic world, junior colleges entered at the bottom of the status hierarchy—in curricula, faculty, students, and collegiate atmosphere. Nor were they very successful in producing college transfers. Preparation for the semiprofessions, on the other hand, was a role they could claim for their own. These aspirations dovetailed with widespread concern among college and university leaders that the expansion of enrollments had brought too many students into higher education—substantial numbers who were intellectually unfit for advanced study. A survey conducted in 1940 found 40 percent of public

14   Eells, *American Junior Colleges*, passim. Eells reported junior college enrollments of 196,710 in 575 colleges in 1939 (p. 27); *Biennial Survey, 1938–40 and 1940–42* reported 149,854 students in 456 colleges (II, 4, p. 6): apparently the AAJC had contact with more institutions.
15   Eells, *American Junior Colleges*, 20.

university presidents agreeing that "too many youth [were] in universities," and perhaps one-half of educators felt the same. Or, as Harvard's President Lowell put it, "one of the merits of [junior colleges] will be keeping out of college, rather than leading into it, young people who have no taste for higher education."[16]

In 1939 the General Education Board supported an extended project by the AAJC's Commission on Terminal Education intended to bolster its previous advocacy. The AAJC executive secretary, Walter Crosby Eells, reported some disconcerting facts to build this case. A study of student attrition at 25 representative universities by the Office of Education found one-third of freshmen failing to advance to sophomores. The junior class retained only 49 percent of the original cohort, but three-quarters of them managed to graduate—or three of eight original freshmen. These figures appeared to validate the concerns of educators and suggest a need for a more efficient alternative. As for junior colleges, the Terminal Study surveyed 400 institutions and found 40 percent attrition the first year and another 20 percent in the second. Overall, no more than one-quarter continued their education after graduation, leading Eells to conclude emphatically, "*the junior college is terminal . . . for three-quarters of its students who enter as freshmen.*"

Given that reality, proponents foresaw a more grandiose mission for the junior college in embracing terminal education. The sympathetic director of the American Council on Education, George Zook, asserted that junior colleges should address "the educational needs of the entire youth population, particularly those 18 and 19 years of age," for whom academic programs will be "only a small part," far exceeded by "terminal curricula in various vocations, including homemaking, and in general education as a preparation for social life." Eells calculated that the semiprofessions targeted by terminal programs comprised 49 percent of employment opportunities and were growing, compared with 6 percent for college graduates. But the junior college movement would not limit itself to vocational tracks: "terminal education in the junior college should prepare young people . . . for civic responsibility, social understanding, home duties and responsibilities, law observance, and the devotion to democracy." Eells conceded that universities selected "young people of superior native ability and intelligence," leaving junior colleges to prepare "the citizen of moderate or inferior native ability" for "educated followership."[17]

---

16 Steven Brint and Jerome Karabel, *The Diverted Dream: Community Colleges and the Promise of Educational Opportunity in America, 1900–1985* (New York: Oxford University Press, 1991), 30–61; Walter Crosby Eells, *Why Junior College Terminal Education?* (Washington, D.C.: American Association of Junior Colleges, 1941), quotes pp. 76, 288.

17 Eells, *Why Junior College*, 29, 60, 280; Brint and Karabel, *Diverted Dream*, 61–66; Joseph F. Kett, *The Pursuit of Knowledge under Difficulties: From Self-Improvement to Adult Education in America, 1750–1990* (Stanford: Stanford University Press, 1994), 409–15.

This condescending image of junior college clientele reflected a contemporary conception of the social order as a rigid intellectual hierarchy in which the position and social role of individuals could be determined by intelligence tests. Given belief in a natural distribution of talent, the junior college's overriding purpose was to expand access to higher education ("postsecondary" had not yet been coined) by ministering to the rungs of the intelligence ladder just below university students. This theory of stratification dominated thinking about who should attend college in the interwar years. Of course, intelligence is fundamental, but its relation to success in college remains fiercely contentious, even in the twenty-first century, after research found it to be more malleable and multidimensional than pre-1940 intelligence testers could have imagined.

During the interwar years, this fixation on the natural distribution of talent produced misguided educational policies. Despite strenuous promotion of terminal education, students and parents predominately wanted academic courses leading to a possible college degree. At best, one-third of junior college students chose vocational subjects, and a large number of these were various forms of business education intended for office work—forms of education that had long existed in a variety of settings. Although relatively few junior college entrants reached universities, those who did performed well, tending in one study to outperform students entering as freshman. A huge gap existed between the education sought by students and that thought best for them by junior college leaders, such as civic education for followership. The University of Minnesota, in fact, established a General College in 1932 for just such a purpose—to divert inferior students away from the university with a terminal education in life skills. This approach was inspired by John Dewey's ideas about educating for life and social efficiency, but it promised little more than elevating to grades 13 and 14 subjects being taught with dubious effectiveness in the high schools. Most students wanted college courses; some preferred vocational subjects; but none wished to spend 2 years learning to be, as Eells put it, "more efficient homemakers, better buyers, better consumers, better parents."[18]

The rise and spread of junior colleges in the interwar years broadened access to higher education. The leaders of the junior college movement by 1940 envisioned far more, and national leaders in the public sector such as Zook shared this vision. After the hiatus of World War II, this conception of a radically larger incidence of higher education would be advanced by some of the same

18   Eells, *Why Junior College*, 29; Kett, *Pursuit of Knowledge*, 411–12; Roland L. Guyotte, III, *Liberal Education and the American Dream: Public Attitudes and the Emergence of Mass Higher Education, 1920–1952*, PhD Diss., Northwestern University, 1980, 111–48.

individuals, but without the limiting assumptions of terminal education. Despite originating as a marginal form of higher education, junior colleges became central to issues of the size and scope of mass higher education.

FROM NORMAL SCHOOLS TO TEACHERS COLLEGES. The elevation of institutions for teacher training into the ranks of colleges and universities was a drawn-out process. Most normal schools in the late nineteenth century offered a 2- or 3-year elementary course and 2 more years of advanced study. By 1900, the elementary course corresponded to the last 2 years of high school and certified graduates to teach in primary or rural schools. The advanced courses approximated the first 2 years of college and earned a higher diploma. The normal school curriculum included general education and pedagogical subjects and in some locales offered the most accessible form of advanced education, including preparation for college. As high school graduates became more prevalent among normal students, depending on the region, normal schools sought to dispense with the elementary course and focus on a 4-year curriculum of more advanced studies. But many students still preferred the elementary course. Early twentieth-century normal schools thus straddled the line between secondary and higher education. In order to become colleges, they had to eliminate their secondary offerings, offer a 4-year college course, require a high school diploma for admission, rename the principal as president, and legally change the name of the institution to teachers college. Such steps tended to occur incrementally and separately as normal schools adjusted curricula to student demand, overcame internal resistance, negotiated with state boards of education, and secured legislative changes to their names and missions.[19]

The Albany State Normal College assumed its new title in 1890 but could not dispense with its last secondary offerings until 1908; in Ypsilanti, the sixth-oldest normal school became Michigan State Normal College in 1899 and offered the first 4-year degree program. During the century's first two decades, many more normal schools were founded than were converted to colleges; but in the 1920s the majority of state normal schools made this transition. Enrollments doubled in the teacher-training sector from 1919 to 1925, with teachers colleges garnering two-thirds of students. Beneath the surface, however, change was less apparent. In 1928, teachers colleges certified 38,000 teachers, the majority with 2-year certificates and only 8,000 with bachelor's degrees. Apparently, most students took the minimum required to secure appointment as an elementary school teacher. The growing demand for high school teachers was largely met by graduates of

---

19 Christine A. Ogren, *The American State Normal School: "An Instrument of Great Good"* (New York: Palgrave, 2005).

university departments of education, which resisted encroachment on this task from teachers colleges.[20]

Animating the movement for teachers colleges was a concerted effort among educational professionals (schoolmen) to make institutions for teacher education more narrowly specialized and vocational. This view foreshadowed somewhat later developments in the junior college movement. Increasingly after 1900, state educational leaders and university professors objected to the academic offerings of normal schools. Some of this content was high school–level coursework that compensated for weak student preparation; some allowed rural students to prepare for universities, and in a few states normal courses could be transferred for university credit. To educationists, however, the road to higher professional status required an exclusive focus on educating teachers. This position was advanced most prominently by the Carnegie Foundation in a 1920 study of the normal schools of Missouri. This massively detailed study was conducted by education professors who shared the CFAT's commitment to professionalization. It emphatically concluded that the preparation of teachers should be the "sole purpose and concern" of Missouri normal schools. The study criticized the democratic influence of school boards and parents, which caused the normals to include liberal arts subjects, and it advised the schools to purge students who attended chiefly to obtain a general education. Championing efficiency and prudent use of taxpayer money, the report, in fact, placed professionalization ahead of democracy. To promote the professionalizing agenda, the report defined teacher education as part of higher education, encouraging schools to excise the stigma of secondary offerings and embrace greater specialization.[21]

Although it analyzed a single state, the Missouri Report placed the prestige of the Carnegie Foundation behind the professionalizing agenda of schoolmen and undoubtedly eased the transition to teachers colleges in other states. However, the new teachers colleges produced some dubious consequences. Developments in Pennsylvania were representative. There the state Department of Public Instruction assumed control of the normal schools in 1921 and established a uniform, strictly professional curriculum: "unless each course has a functional value in terms of public school procedures, it . . . has no place in the curriculum of an institution devoted to the preparation of teachers." In 1927, the normal

20   *Biennial Survey of Education, 1926–1928*, 885–93; Jurgen Herbst, *And Sadly Teach: Teacher Education and Professionalization in American Culture* (Madison: University of Wisconsin Press, 1989), 140–60.

21   William S. Larned et al., *The Professional Preparation of Teachers for American Public Schools: A Study Based upon an Examination of Tax-Supported Normal Schools in the State of Missouri* (New York: Carnegie Foundation for the Advancement of Teaching, 1920), 75–79, quote p. 78; Herbst, *Sadly Teach*, 165–71.

schools were renamed teachers colleges, awarding bachelor's degrees in education and gradually eliminating secondary offerings. The Missouri Report had documented the low educational attainments of normal schools—conditions not confined to that state. The schools were nonselective in admissions, granted college credits for "very elementary" work, and had ridiculously low failure rates—about 1 percent in education courses. Nationally, teachers of liberal arts subjects were more highly regarded than those teaching education, who now dominated the institutions. As intended, students seeking a general education were driven away, which feminized the student body. In Pennsylvania, male and female students were roughly equal in 1890, but women outnumbered men four to one by 1928. Unlike junior colleges, which obtained a toehold in higher education, interwar teachers colleges were in some cases more narrow and marginal than the normal schools they replaced.[22]

Not all teachers colleges endorsed the schoolmen's prescriptions for narrow professionalism. A 1922 survey found thirty-nine colleges that discouraged attendance by nonteachers and twenty-four that welcomed them. Many educators aspired to offer a liberal arts curriculum befitting a university level institution.[23] California was the first state to confront this predicament. Normal schools there had been converted to teachers colleges in 1921 with the same professionalizing intentions and against community desires for academic education. As local and legislative pressure for liberal arts rose, several colleges began to offer such courses despite their mandate for teacher training. This alarmed University of California President Robert Gordon Sproul (1929–1958). The university had already agreed to the establishment of a southern branch in Los Angeles but was determined to keep academic studies under its control.

In 1931, Sproul arranged an external examination of higher education in California by the sympathetic CFAT. This inquiry was the first systematic consideration of how the new sectors of higher education should be integrated with traditional institutions. The Commission appointed by CFAT President Henry Suzzalo included George Zook and other proponents of a clear differentiation of sectors in the name of social efficiency and limiting taxpayer expenditures. Their report relegated the junior colleges to a vocational role as part of secondary education and recommended that the teachers colleges be limited to professional teacher training. The Suzzalo Report gave Sproul all he could hope for in terms of university domination of the heights of higher education, but it

22   Elizabeth Tyler Bugaighis, *Liberating Potential: Women and the Pennsylvania State Normal Schools, 1890–1930*, PhD Diss., Pennsylvania State University, 2000, quote p. 132; Larned et al., *Professional Preparation*, 321–36, quote p. 332.

23   National Council of Education Committee, "The Teachers College Movement," *American Association of Teachers Colleges Year Book* (October, 1922), 29–50.

also fomented opposition in the other sectors and in the legislature. The Coordinating Council recommended by the report, instead of keeping the sectors in harness, succumbed to internecine bickering. The State Board of Education ignored the report and the council in approving additional liberal arts degrees in teachers colleges. In 1935, the legislature bowed to popular demands by elevating the teachers colleges to California state colleges. By 1940, one-half of their enrollments were in liberal arts.[24] California's experience should have exposed the myopia of interwar schoolmen in focusing teachers colleges on a single occupation, thereby frustrating local demand for access to higher education. However, other states failed to follow California's lead until after the surge of postwar veterans under the GI Bill forced teachers colleges to expand enrollments and offerings.[25]

URBAN COLLEGES AND UNIVERSITIES. In November 1914, formation of the Association of Urban Universities postulated a new identity and distinctive mission for institutions located in cities. Mirroring the preoccupations of the Progressive Era, the charter members addressed "the need for universities maintained as parts of the systems of public education in cities . . . and the forms of service to the cities which they and the privately endowed universities of urban location should undertake." Private universities predominated in cities and comprised one-half of the sixteen original members, including Reed College and Johns Hopkins; and the seventeen institutions that joined the next year included eleven private schools, including Chicago and Harvard.[26] Beyond urban locations and a desire to improve civic government, these institutions had a variety of identities and missions. However, as enrollments in city schools mushroomed after the war, urban institutions faced market demands to offer professional and vocational courses to nontraditional students.

Most American colleges located in or near cities originally served particular groups rather than regional populations. Catholic institutions exemplified this pattern, since many were placed among concentrations of the faithful. While serving these populations, Catholic colleges tended to cling to the traditional classical course for undergraduates and resist accommodating demand for other subjects. By 1900 Catholic universities existed in all the major eastern and midwestern cities. Otherwise, cities had been graveyards for antebellum colleges,

24   Douglass, *California Idea*, 137–57; Carnegie Foundation for the Advancement of Teaching, *State Higher Education in California* (Sacramento: California State Printing Office, 1932).

25   Names, dates, and name changes are given in Ogren, *American State Normal School*, appendix.

26   Association of Urban Universities, *University Training for Public Service: A Report of the Meeting of the Association of Urban Universities, 15–17 November, 1915*, Bureau of Education Bulletin, No. 30 (1916), 5–7.

largely due to the abundance of other premodern types of education. Municipal efforts long focused on providing high schools; public institutions for higher studies were the exception. In Cincinnati, an 1858 bequest from Charles Mc-Micken provided the seed for a true municipal university. However, the University of Cincinnati opened only in 1874 and gradually consolidated many of the city's professional schools under its aegis by the 1890s. Still, the original and unique municipal experiment was launched in New York City.[27]

The College of the City of New York (CCNY) opened in 1849 as a "Free Academy" to provide liberal and practical education for students from the city's public schools. The proposal anticipated the language of the Morrill Act, envisioning a "College . . . in no way inferior to any of our colleges" to educate children of the "laboring class" in "chemistry, Mechanics, architecture, agriculture, Navigation, physical as well as moral or mental science, &, &." While democratic in access, the school proved conservative in form. All male—a free, female normal school opened in 1870 (later Hunter College)—it developed a unique 5-year college course in which the first, "sub-freshman" year compensated for the absence of public high schools in the city. This unique model produced a closed system where students from public schools were not qualified to attend other colleges, nor were outsiders likely to attend CCNY. Nonetheless, rigorous, traditional standards were imposed to uphold respectability: as of 1902, 30,000 students had matriculated but the college had graduated only 2,730 with bachelor's degrees. By the 1890s the city's educational system was hopelessly anachronistic, but a series of reforms gradually brought it into conformity with the rest of secondary education. The college experienced a similar transformation when it was emancipated from the unsympathetic NYC Board of Education, given its own Board of Trustees, and moved to a new campus in Upper Manhattan (1908). Under President John Finley (1903–1913), who had studied at Johns Hopkins and taught at Princeton, CCNY eliminated the vestiges of the classical college and joined the mainstream of American higher education. Still tethered to the city's public schools, it now served burgeoning cohorts of graduates of the city's new high schools, chiefly the sons of Eastern European Jewish immigrants.[28]

In 1921 CCNY enrolled 3,000 collegiate men and Hunter College, 1,500 women, but they also counted 16,000 students in extension courses. CCNY created separate colleges for engineering, education, and Business and Civic

27   Edward J. Power, *A History of Catholic Higher Education in the United States* (Milwaukee: Bruce, 1958); Roger L. Geiger, "The Era of Multipurpose Colleges in American Higher Education, 1850–1890," in *American Colleges in the Nineteenth Century*, 127–52.

28   S. Willis Rudy, *The College of the City of New York: A History, 1847–1947* (New York: City College Press, 1949), quote p. 13; Sherry Gorelick, *City College and the Jewish Poor* (New Brunswick: Rutgers University Press, 1981), 61–86.

Administration (1919).[29] Growing demand led to extension courses in Brooklyn and Queens, which then became separate colleges in 1930 and 1937, respectively. Brooklyn College opened with 2,800 regular students and 5,000 studying part-time at night. By 1940, these colleges enrolled 52,000 students throughout the city. New York City's free municipal colleges were unique in a number of ways. They served a huge number of students in all manner of extension and evening courses, but a large proportion were full-time, traditional-age students studying arts and sciences, particularly at City College, the name adopted by CCNY's main North Manhattan campus. Its student profile between the wars was like no other: two-thirds of parents were foreign born; 80 percent of students were Jewish; 90 percent graduated from New York public schools; and 97 percent lived at home. As these students flocked to the overcrowded City College campus, standards of admission were repeatedly tightened. In the early 1920s a 60 percent high school average guaranteed admission, but by 1940 an average of 88 percent was required, giving City College, with 27,500 students perhaps the most stringent admission standard in the nation.[30]

Twentieth-century municipal universities either grew out of public systems of higher education or were created by the conversion of struggling private colleges. The first conversion occurred in Akron, where Buchtel College was transformed into the Municipal University of Akron in 1913. Founded by the Universalist Church in 1870, over time the denomination ceased to supply financial support or students. Serving local students and with little endowment, the college's survival was at stake. The thriving University of Cincinnati was repeatedly invoked as an attractive model. The new president, Parke Kolbe (1913–1925), spearheaded the transfer of the college's assets to the city, which accepted responsibility for maintaining the new institution. Akron thus preserved a community asset, and its citizens obtained access to college with free tuition. The university committed to serve the community from the outset. A college of engineering was formed with one of the first cooperative education programs and a School of Household Arts was established, both in the first year. Subsequently, evening classes were offered and a school of education was created. Such offerings found students. Buchtel in its last year had 180 students; 15 years later the University of

---

29   The latter opened two decades after NYU's hugely successful School of Commerce, Accounts, and Finance (1900: see below): this delay (despite several previous efforts) and the high initial academic and admission standards reveal a bureaucracy less responsive to market demands than private universities: cf. Selma C. Berrol, *Getting Down to Business: Baruch College in the City of New York, 1847–1987* (New York: Greenwood Press, 1989), 1–26.

30   Rudy, *College of the City of New York*, 396–98; Gorelick, *City College*, 195; David O. Levine, *The American College and the Culture of Aspiration, 1915–1940* (Ithaca: Cornell University Press, 1986), 85–87; *Biennial Survey of Education*, 1938–40, 1940–42, II, 131. CCNY stands out in the history of American higher education for providing substantial access to students from lower-class origins.

Akron (newly named) enrolled 1,200 in regular classes (500 in arts and sciences) and 1,600 in evening sessions.[31]

In 1933 the city of Detroit consolidated the institutions of higher education under its authority into Wayne University, which with 6,500 students became one of the larger municipal universities. That this step occurred so belatedly testifies to the haphazard nature of urban public higher education. Detroit established a Normal School in 1881 that developed into Detroit Teachers College (1924). The proprietary Detroit Medical College (f. 1868) was rescued by the city from post-Flexner oblivion in 1913. Rehabilitation of the medical school required that entering students have some college preparation, which prompted a 1-year premedical course in 1914, located in Central High School. This course was extended to 2 years in 1917 and became the Detroit Junior College. Inexorably, it advanced to become the College of the City of Detroit in 1923, still sharing a building with the high school. The city also embraced a College of Pharmacy (1924) and the self-supporting Detroit City School of Law (1927). These were the units that formed Wayne University in 1933.

Many aspects of the Wayne saga typified public urban education. Its expansion was driven largely by the demand for professional education and accomplished by creating new schools or taking over existing ones. It provided education not otherwise affordable for most of its students. The mere existence of these opportunities generated demand: Wayne doubled its enrollments from 1933 to 1939. For these students, some college education was preferable to none, as one-third were not in a degree course, and two-thirds of regular students were freshmen and sophomores. This was higher education on a shoestring: all these units except medicine occupied the same building, "Old Main," that had included Central High School until 1926. Longer term, the burgeoning university presented an impossible burden for the Detroit Board of Education, even without Depression austerity. Student tuition provided roughly half of revenues, and in 1937 Wayne County initiated appropriations; but total revenues per student in the 1930s were roughly $150, compared with four times that amount at the University of Michigan. Inevitably, the state assumed this burden but not until the 1950s.[32]

In the interwar years, mass higher education in American cities was offered chiefly by private universities. For private institutions, accommodating mass

---

31   P. R. Kolbe, *A History of the Establishment of the Municipal University of Akron* (Akron: Municipal University of Akron, 1914); *Biennial Survey of Education*, 1926–1928, 752. Akron's next president, George F. Zook (1925–1933), moved on to play a large role in higher-education policy as director of the American Council on Education.

32   Leslie L. Hanawalt, *A Place of Light: The History of Wayne State University, a Centennial Publication* (Detroit: Wayne State University Press, 1968). Per-student revenues at the University of Michigan in the 1930s were about $600: Geiger, *To Advance Knowledge*, appendix C.

higher education presented a dilemma. They struggled to meet the expectations of both the academic and the collegiate revolutions—upholding the rising standards of the academic disciplines and cultivating the social and cultural accoutrements of a liberal education. But providing vocational or professional training to irregular, nonresident students was antithetical to these aims, which were held dear by administrators, faculty, and, especially, alumni. Nonetheless, although urban research universities generally took the high road, other urban private universities found ways to do both.

The dilemma was first addressed by New York University under Chancellor Henry M. MacCracken (1891–1910).[33] A staunch Presbyterian who had studied in Germany, MacCracken seemed to comprehend the several conflicting trends of the era. He established the university's first PhD programs, sought to enlist the university in service to the city, and thought liberal arts were better nurtured in a residential setting, along with social activities and athletics. To accomplish the latter, MacCracken felt it necessary to move the liberal arts college out of downtown Manhattan. He purchased a large estate in the still-rural Bronx, overlooking the Harlem River, and raised the funds to construct the University Heights campus by 1894. Arts and sciences students, soon joined by engineering, could enjoy amenities of collegiate life amidst splendid classical architecture. However, University Heights had only 233 students in 1900 and a mountain of debt for its stately campus, while professional students crowded into the facilities around Washington Square. MacCracken believed that the future of New York University lay with University Heights but added units downtown nonetheless. In addition to schools of law and medicine, he established a School of Pedagogy in 1890 and a 2-year School of Commerce, Accounts, and Finance in 1900. All together, NYU enrolled almost 1,800 students at the turn of the century.[34]

New York City added 1.3 million inhabitants in the first decade of the century, and their children generated an insatiable demand for both liberal and career education (as seen at CCNY). Enrollment pressures confounded the separation of liberal arts and professional studies on NYU's two campuses. University Heights added premedical students to boost its enrollments (1911), but they allegedly spoiled the collegiate atmosphere. After World War I, students complained of too many Jewish students, and the adoption of selective admissions reduced their numbers from 50 to 31 percent (1921). The financial deficits at the Heights were covered by burgeoning enrollments at Washington

---

33 The following draws on Thomas J. Frusciano and Marilyn H. Pettit, *New York University and the City: An Illustrated History* (New Brunswick: Rutgers University Press, 1997), 119–84.

34 Abraham L. Gitlow, *New York University's Stern School of Business: A Centennial Retrospective* (New York: New York University Press, 1995), 5.

Square, where any and all were welcome. There, demand for liberal arts courses arose from students in education, commerce, and prelaw. A Collegiate Division was established in 1903, which soon had twice as many students as the Heights and became a separate college in 1914. NYU neared 13,000 students in 1921, 8,000 in the School of Commerce. By 1930 NYU counted more than 40,000 students, becoming the largest private university in the country. Although liberal arts flourished at Washington Square, this explosive growth reflected the multiple forms of career education. Besides Commerce and Education, NYU added a Graduate School of Business near Wall Street (1919), Dentistry, Fine Arts, Extension, and the first School of Retailing (1921). Selective admissions were abandoned too, so that both the Heights and Washington Square reflected and served the population of the city.

Urban Catholic universities also reflexively sought to separate the collegiate from the professional. DePaul University, near Lincoln Park in Chicago, for example, was originally a commuter school for mostly Irish Catholics. In 1912 it moved commercial programs downtown as a separate college and affiliated with the proprietary Chicago College of Law. It soon added more downtown units to take advantage of market opportunities—an education course for teachers, a secretarial school, and the Downtown College of Liberal Arts. These programs educated a diverse clientele that for the most part worked full or part time, and they generated income that supported the entire enterprise. The university's expansion seemed to combine entrepreneurship with traditional service. However, financial calculations inspired the erection of a debt-financed seventeen-story office building (1928) to house all its downtown units, with additional rental space for income. In contrast, the liberal arts college at Lincoln Park, with 600 commuting students, nurtured a collegiate culture, including coeducation, dances, football, and Greek life. Catholic universities never achieved the gargantuan size of NYU or CCNY. DePaul enrolled 4,500 students in the late 1920s, most of them downtown, with 2,000 in summer school and extension. The Depression upset the DePaul business plan, especially when renters could not be found for its heavily indebted downtown building. Painful cutbacks occurred throughout the decade, including ending the football program in 1939. DePaul's Catholic mission was never completely absent but was essentially nurtured on the Lincoln Park campus. Chicago's Catholic teachers filled the downtown classrooms in education and liberal arts, but law and commerce were patronized by Chicagoans of all backgrounds.[35]

35 John L. Rury, "The Urban Catholic University in the Early Twentieth Century: A Social Profile of DePaul, 1898–1940," *History of Higher Education Annual*, 17 (1997): 5–32; John L. Rury and Charles S. Suchar, eds., *DePaul University: Centennial Essays and Images* (DePaul University, 1998).

An additional, "bottom-up" pattern of urban university development was traced by the schools founded by city YMCAs. From the 1890s to the 1920s, at least twenty-six YMCA schools elevated their studies to the collegiate level in cities from Boston (Northeastern) to San Francisco (Golden Gate). The original mission of the urban YMCAs was to encourage the spiritual, cultural, and vocational betterment of young males employed in cities. The Ys originally offered educational evening lectures but soon offered evening courses intended to enhance employment skills. The Ys were exceedingly adaptive to local conditions. Early courses, for example, bolstered student competence for office work, and later offerings included insurance and sales. After 1900, the Ys joined the national trend of establishing part-time evening legal education, eventually establishing nineteen such law schools. The Ys initially offered courses but not degrees, including law. As they matured, they sought degree-granting authority, which generally required cutting ties with the parent YMCA. Many Y schools remained small or marginal institutions, later closing or being absorbed by other universities. The Y colleges in Cleveland, Youngstown, and Houston were transformed into public universities after World War II. The most robust Y school was Northeastern College/University, which began as law courses in 1898. It added an automobile school in 1903 as well as engineering, commerce, and liberal arts in 1925. Northeastern also founded satellite campuses in New Haven, Providence, Springfield, and Worcester, which all became independent colleges. In 1927, the Boston campus enrolled 1,700 students in law and engineering and 1,400 in commerce. Like other urban schools, Northeastern sought to serve the immigrant population of the city, who were largely ignored by existing colleges and universities.[36]

★　★　★

Mass higher education embraced unprecedented numbers of students, many from groups that had virtually no previous access to colleges. It also incorporated different kinds of studies and institutions into the collegiate sphere. Premodern institutions evolved into more modern configurations. High schools, which had once provided terminal precollegiate education, now offered the first two years of college. Normal schools were consigned to the dustbin of history by teachers colleges. And urban universities, in particular, achieved their enormous expansion by assimilating proprietary professional schools, launching teacher

36　Dorothy E. Finnegan and Brian Cullaty, "Origins of the YMCA Universities: Organizational Adaptations in Urban Education," *History of Higher Education Annual*, 21 (2001): 47–79; Dorothy E. Finnegan, "Raising and Leveling the Bar: Standards, Access, and the YMCA Evening Law Schools, 1890–1940," *Journal of Legal Education*, 55, 1–2 (Mar./June 2005): 208–33; Everett C. Marston, *Origin and Development of Northeastern University, 1898–1960* (Boston: Northeastern University Press, 1961).

education programs, and experimenting with novel fields of professional preparation. However, the dynamics were rather different for traditional and aspiring professions.

Law schools played a key role in the development of urban universities. Part-time evening law schools after 1900 already verged on mass institutions. They benefited from exploding demand, the promise of respectable careers, and the latent prestige of the legal profession. Besides the urban Y schools that offered law classes, DePaul, Wayne, and others readily annexed law schools. The University of Toledo, for example, took over the Y law school 2 years after it opened (1909). These moves were self-supporting, probably income generating too, and they enhanced service to a school's constituency. They did not in themselves contribute greatly to access, since proprietary law schools continued to take all comers until enrollments peaked in 1929. Rather, newly affiliated law schools eventually joined in raising standards of legal education as they emulated practices of more prestigious schools. Longer term, this trend actually reversed the momentum toward mass higher education. Medical education, for example, was for all practical purposes open to mass enrollment in the first decade of the century, but reforms following the Flexner Report reduced access and caused the number of students and institutions to contract. The same process occurred somewhat less dramatically in legal education after 1930. In both cases, mass access was a passing phase in an evolution toward postgraduate status.[37]

The situation was quite different for emerging professions or semiprofessions. The outstanding success here was schools of commerce or business. These subjects had long been taught in high schools and commercial schools. Offering them at the university level implied a higher level of study and content. Penn's Wharton School had pioneered making business a learned profession, as discussed above, but it conspicuously lacked imitators before 1900. What altered business education after that date was the rise of accountancy as a necessary tool of modern corporations. Here was a technical skill in short supply that was needed for career advancement by legions of business employees. As states created licensing examinations for certified public accountants (1896–1923), aspirants filled the evening commerce classrooms of urban universities. These evening classes provided the foundation for full-time colleges of business. Still, at the end of the 1920s, 70 percent of business students were enrolled in evening classes.[38] This phenomenon constituted both a new constituency and a new technical field for higher education, an exemplar of Trow's model of mass higher education. But other initiatives

37   Finnegan and Cullaty, "Origins of the YMCA," 55–59, 77; Finnegan, "Raising and Leveling the Bar"; Kett, *Pursuit of Knowledge*, 261–69.
38   Kett, *Pursuit of Knowledge*, 269–77.

to elevate semiprofessions were not so fortunate. Automobile schools sponsored by the Y proved ephemeral, and more business-related specialties like insurance, sales, or advertising failed as separate schools. The concerted effort to implant education for semiprofessions into junior colleges, as described above, was disappointing. These institutions were too small and localized to support specialized curricula, and their target fields were largely misdirected.

Mass higher education was not confined to technical and professional courses. Colleges were still associated with liberal learning, and a large portion of the new clientele tapped by mass institutions sought those cultural and intellectual rewards. The majority of junior college students aspired to a full college education. Many students at teachers colleges sought intellectual substance rather than pedagogy, as developments in California showed. And the growth of urban universities gave a whole new population access to the liberal arts. Students at City College were perhaps most notorious for the pursuit of arts and sciences, and NYU found it impossible to separate these subjects from professional studies. Elsewhere, substantial numbers enrolled in liberal arts colleges. One large constituency was teachers who had graduated from high schools or normal schools, but now sought the liberal learning that they had missed. Thus, mass higher education supplemented rather than undermined the nexus between collegiate education and liberal culture. However, many traditional institutions found these developments threatening and sought instead to distance themselves from mass higher education.

SHAPING ELITE HIGHER EDUCATION

The years following the Great War were tumultuous for colleges and universities, mixing financial crisis, popular notoriety, surging enrollments, and unsettling changes in student mores. Wartime inflation of 79 percent (1915–1920), followed by a deep postwar recession, severely cramped both endowed and public institutions. However, the most difficult period, immediately after the war, turned out to be a temporary interlude in a decade of expanding resources. In 1919 John D. Rockefeller gave $50 million to the General Education Board to bolster faculty salaries at private colleges and universities. As was their practice, the GEB offered matching grants, forcing recipients to organize their own fundraising campaigns. Major public universities of the Midwest also conducted million-dollar campaigns in the early 1920s. Once the economy improved, many public universities received substantial increases in state appropriations.[39] The

39　Geiger, *To Advance Knowledge*, 42–43; 122–29.

liberality of state legislators reflected growing public fascination with youth and especially college life, mirrored in the magazines and media of the day.

Historian Paula Fass noted how in the 1920s "two institutions—the school and the peer group—came to define the social world of middle class youth." In particular, "the structure and mores of peer life on the campus helped to create the first modern American youth culture." This campus peer culture was, in some ways, an extension—indeed, intensification—of the prewar collegiate culture, but in other ways it brought marked changes. Foremost was the magnified prominence of the peer culture that students themselves created, as distinct from organized extracurricular activities. Activities remained central to collegiate life, but now class loyalties and rituals were overshadowed by school spirit, fanned by football, and allegiance to social groups, notably fraternities and sororities. Social cleavages increasingly characterized the peer culture, reflecting in part postwar tensions among social classes in American society. The increased affluence of some students was displayed in the conspicuous consumption admired in the youth culture—automobiles, expensive clothes, jazz, speakeasies, and raccoon coats. The ascendancy of the peer culture heightened the underlying anti-intellectualism among students. Fraternities boomed in the 1920s, followed closely by sororities, and the campus prestige hierarchy became more pronounced. Relations between the sexes changed in important ways. Socializing became the norm at coeducational universities with the rise of dating, dances, and parties, and even at the eastern single-sex colleges, men invited dates from the women's colleges to weekend functions. These trends were accompanied by a marked decline in religion among students and the eclipse of the Campus Y.[40] This *late collegiate era* differed from the preceding era in these respects, especially in the growing social stratification of campus life. The peer culture of the 1920s placed greater value on one's associates than what one learned.

The institutions that these students attended would, to different degrees, have preferred to invert this valuation. That is, they ostensibly wished to enhance student learning but accepted that the social context of campus life was an important, if not inseparable, factor in the kind of learning they wished to instill. This outlook was strongest in eastern colleges and universities where the prewar notion of liberal culture had taken root. Liberal culture was articulated forcefully and explicitly as an alternative to the trend toward professional training and practical courses—against mass higher education. As such, it postulated the essential features that Martin Trow labeled elite higher education:

40   Paula Fass, *The Damned and the Beautiful: American Youth in the 1920s* (New York: Oxford University Press, 1977), 121–22; Setran, *Campus Y.*

Elite forms of higher education are marked by attempts to infuse a general moral and cultural outlook, by efforts to shape qualities of mind and feeling, attitudes and character, and not merely to train or inform students; ... [it] intends to convey to students that they can accomplish large and important things in the world.... In this sense, institutions of elite higher education are arrangements for raising ambition and for providing social support and intellectual resources for the achievement of ambition.[41]

These purposes posed two kinds of challenges for institutions: managing settings that provided such social support and offering curricula that provided the needed intellectual resources. The former meant adapting to conditions facing all institutions, while the latter spawned a profusion of curricular experiments.

The colleges of Harvard, Yale, and Princeton consciously committed to elite higher education in two respects. First, they publicly and repeatedly espoused an ideology by which the ideal student exhibited outstanding character, personality, and social breeding. Athleticism was an admired trait, but scholastic achievement was not. They disdained mere academic achievement, which was disparaged as gained by "grinds" through excessive study. Rather, the character of the ideal student was nurtured, enhanced, and sanctified outside the classroom in college activities and the peer culture. Second, the foremost enrollment objective for these schools was to retain the patronage of eastern upper-class families. These were the families of the *Social Register,* who sent their sons to one of the top dozen New England boarding schools to socialize them for life at the Big Three and to prepare them to pass the unique entrance examinations. This constituency was crucially important to the colleges as alumni-donors, as networks for future graduates, and for students who set the social tone of collegiate life— inspiring the emulation of others. Boarding school graduates constituted from one-fifth to one-third of students at the Big Three in the 1920s and 1930s. This elite ideology was embraced by other private colleges, particularly in the Northeast, combining as it did features of the late collegiate era and rationalizations of liberal culture. However, the pipeline from *Social Register* families was nearly monopolized by the Big Three, and their admissions policies were designed to preserve that connection.[42]

---

41 Martin Trow, "Elite Higher Education: an Endangered Species?" in Michael Burrage, ed., *Martin Trow: Twentieth-Century Higher Education, Elite to Mass to Universal* (Baltimore: Johns Hopkins University Press, 2010), 143–73, quote p. 150.

42 This subject is treated most thoroughly in Jerome Karabel, *The Chosen: The Hidden History of Admission and Exclusion at Harvard, Yale, and Princeton* (Boston: Houghton Mifflin, 2005), 77–109; and Marcia Graham Synnott, *The Half-Opened Door: Discrimination and Admissions at Harvard, Yale, and Princeton, 1900–1970* (Westport, CT: Greenwood, 1979).

Before 1920, H-Y-P each required a battery of examinations for admission but then accepted everyone who was academically qualified. As they opened alternative routes like the College Board examinations in order to reach a wider clientele, enrollments grew by about 50 percent from 1914 to 1924. In the postwar enrollment surge, institutions that were accessible to high school graduates found themselves inundated by applications. Dartmouth, which admitted high school graduates by certificates, had 1,600 more applicants than it could accommodate in 1921 and promptly adopted a "Selective Process for Admission." Cornell and Stanford did the same. The Big Three were somewhat more sheltered by their arcane examinations, but they too felt the need to limit enrollments in order to preserve the quality and character of the educational experience.[43]

For the first time, these schools had to select their students from a surfeit of qualified applicants. How they chose to do this was conditioned from the outset by the fear of increasing numbers of Jewish students graduating from nearby urban high schools. Largely the sons of immigrants from Eastern Europe, these students were bright, industrious, and ambitious—all in the wrong ways. According to stereotypes, they devoted all their energy to the classroom ("greasy grinds"), contributed nothing to the college through activities, and lacked qualities of character and personality valued by the peer society. Behind this caricature (and more demeaning ethnic slurs) lay a rising tide of anti-Semitism. To the exclusion practiced by the upper class since the 1880s were added claims for the superiority of the "Nordic race" (i.e., WASPs) by Madison Grant, among others (in *The Passing of the Great Race,* 1916), and allegations of anti-Americanism stemming from the postwar Red Scare and union agitation—all part of a postwar tide of nativism that culminated in the restrictive Immigration Act of 1924. While doctrinaire anti-Semitism was rare in the academic community, a tacit aversion to Jews was endemic and underpinned discriminatory practices, including the virtual exclusion of Jews from faculty positions.

Events at Columbia provided an object lesson for private colleges and universities. Despite the great strides the university had made in graduate and professional studies, Columbia College had long been losing the patronage of New York's elite families. As early as 1914, Columbia, in the midst of the city's burgeoning Jewish population, recognized that it had a "Jewish problem." The college dean, Frederick Keppel, explicitly denied in his book, *Columbia,* that the college was "overrun with European Jews, who are most unpleasant persons socially." But to President Butler he warned that although most Jewish students were "excellent and desirable students . . . the danger of their preponderating

43 Geiger, *To Advance Knowledge,* 129–39; Levine, *American College and the Culture of Aspiration,* 138–44.

over the students of the older American stock is not an imaginary one. This has already happened at NYU and CCNY."[44] Thus, regardless of whether Jewish students were excellent and desirable or unpleasant persons, the social composition of the college required careful management.

In 1919 Columbia established an elaborate system of selective admission, administered by the country's first Office of Admissions. The entering class was capped at 550 students; applicants had to supply extensive information on family background and submit to a personal interview with a member of the admissions board. For a number of years, city applicants also had to take an intelligence test in the belief that it would expose grinds, whose academic achievements exceeded their natural intelligence by dint of excessive study. All this gave the admissions board more than enough information to make subjective judgments on, in Butler's words, "their record, their personality and their promise."[45] Jewish students at Columbia exceeded 20 percent in the early 1920s and declined thereafter. Under selective admissions, one-half of non-Jewish applicants and one-sixth of Jewish applicants were admitted to Columbia College.

Harvard, Yale, and Princeton each feared a "Jewish problem" like Columbia's. As they implemented selective admissions, Harvard President Lowell's maladroit direct approach provided a second object lesson. In 1920, when Jewish enrollments may have reached 20 percent, Lowell became concerned that Harvard too might face a tipping point that would alienate its Brahmin constituency, who sent 85 percent of their sons to Cambridge.[46] Lowell, who had served as vice president of the Immigration Restriction League, was certainly no friend of Jews, but he believed that the necessity of preserving the social character of Harvard College by restricting Jewish enrollments was blatantly obvious. However, his suggestion in 1922 that Jewish enrollments be limited was attacked in the press and initially rejected by the faculty. Instead, a committee was appointed to study the admissions question and specifically to address the "Jewish problem." Now a heated public controversy, Lowell's notion of a quota was generally condemned

44   Robert A. McCaughey, *Stand, Columbia: A History of Columbia University in the City of New York, 1754–2004* (New York: Columbia University Press, 2003), 265, 263: the following draws on this volume and Harold S. Wechsler, *The Qualified Student: A History of Selective College Admission in America* (New York: Wiley, 155), 131–85.

45   Wechsler, *Qualified Student*, 155.

46   Jerome Karabel, *Chosen*, 77–109; Synnott, *Half-Opened Door*. Percentages of Jewish students should be considered approximations, sometimes reported for the college and other times for the entire university; a survey by the Bureau of Jewish Social Research in 1918–1919 reported the following figures: Columbia University, 21.2%, University of Pennsylvania, 14.5%, Harvard, 10%, Cornell, 9.1%, Brown, Dartmouth, Princeton < 3 percent; Amherst, Bowdoin, Williams < 2 percent: Synnott, *Half-Opened Door*, 16. The number of Jewish high school graduates seeking college admission increased significantly after that date.

by alumni, led by 88-year-old Charles Eliot, as a violation of Harvard's liberal tradition and, indeed, a violation of a historic norm against religious discrimination. Despite the prevalence of anti-Semitic prejudice throughout the Harvard community, the faculty committee reported that the record of Jewish students provided no basis for discrimination. In the aftermath, Harvard adopted a policy of admitting students who graduated in the top one-seventh of their class. It also imposed a cap of 1,000 students on entering classes and began gathering personal information on applicants.

In 1922 Princeton capped its entering class at 600, and the next year Yale set its limit at 850. As they developed procedures for selecting students, they learned from Harvard's example that measures to restrict Jewish students would have to be concealed from public scrutiny. In 1926, Harvard, too, implemented a quota through the admissions process, hidden from public view. To manage the social character of their respective colleges, each school adopted the same four elements. First was the establishment of a separate office of admissions, headed by an old grad strongly committed to preserving the social character of the college. Second came the gathering of personal information, including a picture and an interview, so that judgments of character, personality, and appearance could be factored into admissions. Third was the capping of enrollments so that selection was imperative. The final element was a de facto quota—15 percent for Harvard, 10 percent for Yale, and just 3 percent for Princeton.[47]

Directors of admissions were the key figures in this system, often assisted by committees of like-minded faculty. They interpreted the information about applicants and made decisions that would produce the results expected by presidents. Quotas were a minor part of this task; of paramount importance was recruiting elite students. They had clear conceptions of the desired intangible qualities of character, personality, and leadership and even devised methods for measuring them. Each director proceeded by his own cloaked approach. At Princeton, the director first classified applicants into four social categories, ranging from (1) automatic admits to (4) automatic rejections, and *then* considered academic qualifications. Yale was most concerned about bringing objectivity to this subjective process, apparently in the belief (or hope) that the students they favored were truly superior. Through elaborate institutional research on student records, Yale calculated "Predicted Grade" formulas, adjusted for types of high school, that were first applied in 1930. Yale explicitly embraced the mission of

---

47 Karabel, *Chosen*, 130 et passim. African American students, although rare, were not discriminated against in admissions at Harvard and Yale but were completely excluded from Princeton. They were barred from the Harvard dormitories by Lowell but distinguished themselves in extracurricular activities at Yale and Harvard: Synnott, *Hal-Opened Door*, 47–53, 80–84, 133–35.

providing elite higher education, which implied future leaders with sufficient academic fitness to pass courses. This system actually improved the academic profile of Yale students, not by recognizing academic merit but by eliminating those likely to fail.

These schools sought merit only within their preferred clientele. To this end both Princeton and Yale requested the College Board to develop an IQ test to measure raw intelligence, which led to the launching of the Scholastic Aptitude Test (SAT) in 1926. Yale became the test's principal user in its early years. Above all, these schools sought to preserve their core clientele, who were largely private school graduates from New England and the Middle States and who were also paying customers. They assured their alumni that selective admissions would not be used against their sons; in fact, the sons of graduates increased during the first decade of selective admissions at Yale from 15 to 30 percent. For additional students of the right sort, they counted on alumni in other regions to recruit and screen applicants. This system was severely pressed during the Depression, when the number of applicants plunged, but anti-Semitism was never compromised. True to convictions, Yale lowered academic standards, admittedly "scraping the bottom of the admissions barrel," to enroll additional WASPs and then intensified recruitment efforts at boarding schools, with some success. Princeton, where standards were already fairly low, began admitting high school graduates without a College Board exam, attracting upper-middle-class Protestants from other regions. Lowell's successor at Harvard, James Conant (1933–1953), reputedly tilted the admissions process in the direction of merit by establishing national scholarships. However, he too sought above all to preserve the privileged admissions of Harvard's traditional clientele rather than challenge the discriminatory practices that were now institutionalized.[48]

As growing numbers of Jewish applicants "overflowed" to the smaller eastern colleges, the same discriminatory practices were replicated. In instituting selective admissions at Dartmouth in 1922, President Ernest Hopkins had claimed to seek an "aristocracy of brains," but in practice he preferred the "well-rounded boy" who was anything but a top scholar. Dartmouth had no "Jewish problem" until 1931, when the number of Jewish matriculates in the incoming class more than doubled, to 75. At Hopkins' explicit direction, the usual steps were taken. The number of Jewish admits was halved for the rest of the decade, despite rising applications.[49] Union College imposed a quota about the same time, as did other

48   Joseph A. Soares, *The Power of Privilege: Yale and America's Elite Colleges* (Stanford: Stanford University Press, 2007); Karabel, *Chosen*, 139–247, quote p. 200.

49   Levine, *American College*, 138–58; Charles E. Widmayer, *Hopkins of Dartmouth: The Story of Ernest Martin Hopkins and His Presidency of Dartmouth College* (Hanover, NH: University Press of New England, 1977), 61–65.

New England colleges. Jewish quotas persisted unabated through World War II, but after 1945 a public clamor arose criticizing the obvious, but unacknowledged, ethnic exclusion and inspiring antidiscrimination laws in New York and Massachusetts. Institutions responded by loosening restrictions to some degree, replacing Jewish quotas with geographic quotas that worked against the New York area, for example. However, the basic system of discriminatory admissions endured into the 1960s because it produced the results that these institutions wanted.[50]

Selective admission at a single institution is a zero-sum situation, where favoring one group implies discriminating against others. The admissions process consequently requires decisions that institutions feel must be kept private, such as favoring affluent students who can pay full tuition, children of graduates and donors, athletes, or—more recently—minority beneficiaries of affirmative action.[51] The mix is intended to serve the best interests of the institution—not abstract notions of merit or worthiness. Private colleges and universities in the interwar years believed that quotas for Jewish students and favoritism for WASPs maintained a "balanced" student community that served their best interests by nurturing the peer society and supporting the education of elites. And, in the short term, they may have been correct. However, in doing so, they transgressed, deliberately and surreptitiously, bedrock values of American higher education. Prohibitions of discrimination on religious grounds were written into state charters and honored since colonial times, when Witherspoon had boasted of the openness of the College of New Jersey. The flouting of academic merit was more open and amounted to a tacit endorsement of undergraduate anti-intellectualism. These postures brought affluence, at least for the Big Three, but at the cost of social and intellectual myopia in the undergraduate college. When they finally overcame these limitations, three decades later, they became far stronger and more admirable institutions.[52]

★ ★ ★

Beyond the rarified social climate of the eastern colleges, the same tendencies of the late collegiate era—liberal culture and reaction to mass higher education— were manifest in more democratic contexts. In growing state universities, elite

---

50   Soares, *Power of Privilege*; Karabel, *Chosen*.

51   Affirmative admissions for underrepresented groups has been justified in social science literature and by the Supreme Court for the benefits of diversity, or a "balanced" student population. Thus, balance is invoked today as it was in the interwar years, only now to defend inclusion rather than exclusion.

52   Cf. James Axtell, *The Making of Princeton University: From Woodrow Wilson to the Present* (Princeton: Princeton University Press, 2006), 111–42.

behaviors were cultivated in the extracurriculum rather than by manipulating admissions. The principal flagship universities had generally been patronized by a thin but mixed slice of state populations weighted toward the professional classes. Whether land grant designees or not, they all embraced a democratic image in one form or another, even while preparing graduates for upper-middle-class careers. With the postwar hardening of social class lines and the rise of mass institutions of higher education, these universities instinctively sought to shield their preeminent status. Academically, they were scarcely challenged, but public attention focused in the 1920s on the undergraduate college. There they mimicked some aspects of elite higher education in the social stratification of the student body and in attempts to impose higher standards through restrictive policies.

The 1920s constituted the apogee and apotheosis of Greek life, as reflected in popular media and as experienced on campus.[53] In the popular press, novels, and song, fraternities were celebrated as the essence of the college experience. Given an already prominent position, fraternities and sororities filled the lacuna created as the growing size of college classes dampened class traditions and loyalties. Furthermore, Greek organizations became the agents for differentiating campus populations. In this respect, fraternities fulfilled the same basic role they had since the 1820s—uniting like-minded boys who wished to acquire and cultivate upper-middle-class culture. In the 1920s, this role was exaggerated by the desire to distinguish themselves from a more heterogeneous body of students, by the greater wealth that students now deployed, and by the virtual absence of meaningful institutional restraints on their behavior. The Universities of Michigan and California typified the new era. At Michigan, with largely upper-middle-class students, the Greeks represented the cream of the relatively affluent. To support a pleasure-seeking student lifestyle, they spent liberally for fraternity living, clothing, and entertainment. Their most serious endeavor was maintaining dominance over student organizations. The Greeks naturally provoked resentment from the "Barbs." Reflecting on his student days at Berkeley, sociologist Robert Nisbet observed, "Through the twenties the fraternities were as close to an aristocracy as one could easily conceive . . . [and] the social difference between a Greek and a Non-Org was wide and kept getting wider."[54]

The Greek system served as another means for achieving the purposes that Trow ascribed to elite higher education, namely, by social isolation within a

53   Paula Fass, *The Damned and the Beautiful: American Youth in the 1920s* (New York: Oxford University Press, 1977); Helen Lefkowitz Horowitz, *Campus Life: Undergraduate Cultures from the End of the Eighteenth Century to the Present* (New York: Knopf, 1987).

54   Fass, *Damned and Beautiful*, 147; Robert Cooley Angell, *The Campus: A Study of Contemporary Undergraduate Life in the American University* (New York: Appleton, 1928); Robert Nisbet, *Teachers and Scholars: A Memoir of Berkeley in Depression and War* (New Brunswick: Transaction, 1992), 93–95.

larger student body. Chapter houses achieved residential seclusion in which distinctive culture and values could be instilled and reinforced. The Greeks practiced social and ethnic exclusion more rigorously than did selective admissions at eastern private colleges, although Jews and African Americans compensated with fraternities of their own (which sometimes had difficulty gaining recognition). Fraternities, in particular, disdained academic achievement and thus hardly shaped what Trow called mature qualities of mind, but they did enforce a rigid culture of conformity and consumerism. Whether this model was conducive to the raising and achieving of ambition is more problematic. Cultural conformity and participation in college activities may have groomed fraternity members for assimilation into the corporate world, but hardly for intellectual achievement.

LIBERAL CULTURE AND THE CURRICULUM

Universities, too, reacted to the advent of mass higher education. As the faculty became more academically focused, institutions pondered how better to educate their primary population of undergraduate students. The university knowledge base was becoming more advanced and specialized, while the burgeoning ranks of college students were seemingly less motivated (or more distracted) and more varied in aptitudes and preparation. This thinking was tinged with elitist nostalgia for an idealized past but also sought earnestly to grapple with the new conditions of the age. In keeping with the impulse toward liberal culture, universities felt the need to either raise academic standards or to devise more effective curricula or both.[55]

Mass higher education brought students with different aptitudes, aspirations, and motivations to traditional colleges and universities. Students in the 1920s were certainly no more diverse in academic preparation than their nineteenth-century predecessors, who were variously fitted for classical colleges with a modicum of Latin and Greek. Now, the vast majority of matriculates arrived with fourteen or more Carnegie units, but such units were of variable quality, both within and across the nation's high schools. Most state universities were obliged, by charter or by political pressure, to accept all graduates of public high schools. But who went to college was determined as much by social class as by intellect. College for many had become a badge of social status, "a natural sequel to

---

55 Laurence Veysey discerns three orientations of interwar reformers: followers of John Dewey who emphasized life skills; intellectual elitists who sought higher attainments for select students; and those in the liberal culture tradition who advocated new curricula for the first two years of college: "Stability and Experiment in the American Undergraduate Curriculum," in Carl Kaysen, ed., *Content and Context: Essays on College Education* (New York: McGraw-Hill, 1973), 1–64, esp. 9–14.

secondary education." As enrollment swelled, educators expressed concern for the detrimental influence of inferior or below-average students. Frank Aydelotte spoke for many when he warned, "The variation in levels of ability of our undergraduates is the most serious problem confronting American higher education today."[56] This problem was manifest in the low rates of completion of bachelor's degrees, as has been noted. State universities, in particular, dropped a significant portion of students for academic reasons. Certainly not all were lacking in intelligence; some, no doubt, were attracted solely by the collegiate image and then consumed by extracurricular activities; others were unable to relate to academic curricula; and still others may have left early for professional schools. Both college and university educators felt an imperative need to strengthen the college course. The interwar years witnessed an efflorescence of curricular experiments, most of which confronted an increasingly entrenched academic and collegiate system. Institutional initiatives tended to take one of three approaches: culling the herd by inserting a radical break between the second and third years of undergraduate study; enhancing the achievements of superior students through honors; and adding curricular innovations designed to rekindle that will-o'-the-wisp, liberal education.

The idea of separating the preparatory grounding of the freshman-sophomore years from the advanced studies of juniors and seniors had been endemic to higher education since the academic revolution, but the junior college movement supplied fresh impetus. A prominent attempt to implement this distinction on a university scale was made at the University of Michigan by its new president, Clarence Cook Little (1925–1929). An accomplished cancer researcher, his high standard for the collegiate experience was shaped by his Brahmin background and three Harvard degrees. He immediately proposed to establish a "University College" for the first 2 years. With its own dean and faculty, students would be given a common core education, consistent with their preparation and foundational for advanced studies. To continue as juniors, they would have to pass a comprehensive examination. The University College would provide general education for all and the basis for selective admission to the upper division. Although faculty posed sensible objections—leery of an internal junior college with a less-qualified faculty and inadequate grounding for professional colleges like engineering—a series of committees did the president's bidding, approving its implementation for fall 1929. However, Little resigned early that year for personal reasons. His successor, Alexander Ruthven (1930–1951), was a practical, homegrown administrator,

56   Guyotte, *Liberal Education and the American Dream*, 65; Frank Aydelotte, *Breaking the Academic Lock Step: The Development of Honors Work in American Colleges and Universities* (New York: Harper & Bros., 1944), 18.

steeped in Michigan's university tradition. Without support from faculty or president, the University College was quietly forgotten.[57]

The University of Minnesota established an internal junior college explicitly designed for the academically unfit. President Lotus D. Coffman (1920–1938) was the antithesis of Little—a midwesterner who had worked his way through college as an adult student and subsequently become a national spokesman for public universities. Coffman's abiding goal was to extend public higher education to all who sought it. In 1930 Coffman challenged his deans to devise fundamental changes in the academic structure. Their principal response was to propose an essentially terminal "Junior College," soon rechristened the "General College," to provide general education for academically marginal students. This unit opened in 1932 with 500 students led by an entrepreneurial director, Malcolm MacLean.[58]

The General College eschewed both academic and vocational courses; it proposed instead to teach life skills and adjustment in order to form solid, contented citizens. Inspired by the doctrines of John Dewey, which now dominated educationist circles, the College offered survey courses with standardized examinations in "socio-civic competence," home and family life, and an evolving menu of like subjects. In one sense, this approach was consistent with the zeitgeist of the Depression, when vocational training appeared futile in the absence of jobs and academic specialization was relentlessly deprecated. Coffman championed the college, and MacLean made a career of advocating this model in countrywide speaking tours. Both men found receptive audiences, since their message dovetailed with the terminal junior college movement and the generally elitist thinking of foundations. Support from the General Education Board and the Carnegie Corporation helped sustain the college through the 1930s. However, the college was less successful at home. Although enrollments quickly surpassed 1,000, only 1 of 5 students chose it voluntarily; the rest, having failed to gain admission to a regular college course, likely would have preferred either academic preparation or vocational training for work. The General College nonetheless persisted somewhat awkwardly as a terminal junior college within a research university.[59]

57　Peckham, *Making of the University of Michigan*, 177–92. The University of Wisconsin too passed, but never implemented, a similar measure in 1930 that would have required better than a C average to continue beyond the sophomore year and awarded consolation certificates to those who were dropped: E. David Cronin and John W. Jenkins, *The University of Wisconsin: A History, 1925–1945*, vol. III (Madison: University of Wisconsin Press, 1994), 750–52.

58　Guyotte, *Liberal Education*, 111–47.

59　Ibid. An honors program was established at the same time the General College was created but had little impact.

At the opposite end of the spectrum, colleges reacted to the late collegiate era on campus by encouraging intellectually serious students, most notably by establishing honors programs. Honors work long had a nominal status at many colleges, but actual programs had virtually disappeared before President Lowell resuscitated honors at Harvard.[60] Inspiration came from Oxbridge, where students could opt for a perfunctory "Pass" degree or study for "Honours" through individual study, tutorials, and comprehensive examinations. Thus, the Oxbridge model served not merely to challenge serious students while tolerating slackers but also to give public recognition of intellectual accomplishment. The postwar popularity of honors was spearheaded by Frank Aydelotte, who created a distinctive new approach as president of Swarthmore (1922–1938) and tirelessly promoted the honors movement. A midwestern graduate of Indiana University, Aydelotte's experience at Oxford as a Rhodes Scholar (1905–1907) shaped a commitment to liberal education and especial admiration for the pass/honours system. Returning to teach English at Indiana, he made a significant contribution to the pedagogy of that subject with *College English*, which united the teaching of literature and composition. Recruited to MIT in 1915 by President R. C. Maclaurin, who believed that humanities should be incorporated into technical education, he performed a similar feat with *English and Engineering* (1917), long a standard text. Aydelotte burnished his attachment to Oxford by organizing and editing a journal for Rhodes scholars, *American Oxonian*, by becoming an administrator of the Rhodes Trust and by publishing *The Oxford Stamp: Articles from the Educational Creed of an American Oxonian* (1917). He thus became a public advocate for an English style of education that put the onus on students to shape their intellectual development through individual work. Above all, he sought to raise "the standard of achievement required by the best American colleges for the AB degree." When offered the leadership of Swarthmore, he received assurances from faculty and trustees that they shared this goal and then set out to achieve it.[61]

The honors program at Swarthmore began in 1922 with eleven students in the divisions of English Literature and Social Science. They were given complete

60　Frank Aydelotte, ed., *Honors Courses in American Colleges and Universities* (Washington, D.C.: National Research Council, 1925). Arthur Hadley had suggested an honors course for Yale, but alumni summarily rejected any notion of special treatment: George W. Pierson, *Yale: College and University, 1871–1937*, 2 vol. (New Haven: Yale University Press, 1952), I, 329.

61　Frances Blanchard, *Frank Aydelotte of Swarthmore* (Middletown, CT: Wesleyan University Press, 1970); Burton R. Clark, *The Distinctive College* (New Brunswick: Transaction, 1992 [1970]), 184–208, quote p. 186.

freedom to pursue their intellectual development during their junior and senior years, attending classes as they chose and foregoing examinations. Special seminars were organized for the honors students, and at the conclusion of studies they sat for comprehensive examinations by outside examiners (as at Oxbridge). By 1927, 40 percent of Swarthmore students were in honors, now extended to every subject. Aydelotte had indeed raised the level of undergraduate education and provided a model of sorts for liberal education. But the model was not easily replicated. Abraham Flexner at the General Education Board had supplied extra funds in the 1920s for this costly approach, and he helped build the Swarthmore endowment in the 1930s. An alumni donation for five annual "Open Scholarships" not only funded a handful of bright students but also attracted an avalanche of applications from students interested in honors. As the quality of Swarthmore students rose, the president gradually reduced the glamour of collegiate activities, exiting from big-time football (vs. Princeton and Penn) and abolishing sororities (1934).

Unlike the honors programs introduced in the 1950s, which placed superior entering students in separate classes, interwar programs focused on upperclassmen who had demonstrated their mettle during their first 2 years. Roughly one hundred honors programs were identified in the late 1920s and one hundred fifty by the late 1930s.[62] A variety of practices were included under this rubric. Most of these programs allowed juniors and/or seniors to substitute advanced honors work for one or more courses under special supervision, often requiring a senior thesis. At a few colleges (e.g., Bowdoin, Colgate, Wabash, Reed), general examinations were required of all students to raise the level of scholarship, as Lowell had done at Harvard. Only a few institutions attempted to implement a full-time honors plan like Swarthmore's, and these generally affected small numbers of students. Aydelotte noted that more than twenty state universities had established honors, chiefly at the end of this period. Most were limited to departmental honors, as was the case at many privates as well, which negated one ostensible goal of integrating knowledge across disciplines. Nonetheless, the interwar honors movement attests to a widespread desire to combat collegiate anti-intellectualism, to raise the level of achievement for serious students, and to rehabilitate liberal education. Swarthmore was most successful in this endeavor due to Aydelotte's deft leadership, which included attracting outside support, but also because he advocated a realistic goal of elevating the better students at

---

62   Frank Aydelotte, *Breaking the Academic Lock Step: The Development of Honors Work in American Colleges and Universities* (New York: Harper & Bros., 1944); National Society for the Study of Education, *Change and Experiments in Liberal Arts Education*, 31st Yearbook, Part 2 (Bloomington, IN: Public School Publishing, 1932); Julianna K. Chaszar, *The Reinvention of Honors Programs in American Higher Education, 1955–1965*, PhD Diss. Pennsylvania State University, 2008, 10–38.

the better colleges. Reformers who envisioned radically new curricula for the liberal arts foundered on just this last factor.

The dizzying pace of social and economic change after the Great War, continuing through the Roaring Twenties, seemed to engender a spirit of experiment among traditional colleges and universities. The principal motivation was the perceived need to rehabilitate liberal education, now justified more than ever in reaction to mass higher education and collegiate hedonism. Piecemeal reforms were widespread in the twenties, especially for the freshman year. The American Association of University Professors formed a "Committee on Methods of Increasing the Intellectual Interest and Raising the Intellectual Standards of Undergraduates." And a 1931 survey listed 128 "Outstanding Changes and Experiments."[63] The spirit of the times encouraged trustees and donors to back young, enterprising presidents committed to revolutionizing the undergraduate curriculum. Arthur E. Morgan assumed the presidency of Antioch College in 1921 and introduced a radical plan of alternating work and study, not for vocational purposes but rather to provide a "more symmetrical" liberal education. Rollins College was transformed in 1925 when President Hamilton Holt replaced regular classes with two hour "conferences" and eliminated lectures and examinations. In 1925 Pomona president James Blaisdell incorporated the Claremont Colleges as a cluster of colleges in hopeful imitation of Oxford and Cambridge. In 1924 Bennington College was chartered (opened, 1932) to integrate the visual and performing arts into a liberal education for women. Such experiments continued into the thirties, including John Andrew Rice's founding of Black Mountain College (1933) and the conversion of St. John's College to a great books curriculum (1937).[64] Still, the two most notorious challenges to the standard college course occurred at leading research universities—Wisconsin and Chicago.

When Alexander Meiklejohn was fired by Amherst in 1923, Walter Lippmann observed that "he could inspire, but he could not manage." However, he was popularly regarded as a martyr to the ideal of the "liberal college" that he had described in his inaugural address and which retained a certain currency through the interwar years. Readily assuming that role, Meiklejohn elaborated the failings of collegiate education in articles for *Century* magazine, encouraged by its dynamic editor, Glenn Frank. His 1925 article, "A New College: Notes on a Next Step in Higher Education," proposed a course that would transcend the anarchy of the elective system and establish closer relationships between students

---

63   Guyotte, *Liberal Education*, 56–61; National Society, *Change and Experiments*, 43–156.

64   Guyotte, *Liberal Education*, 46–50; Clark, *Distinctive College*, 13–88; Alex Duke, *Importing Oxbridge: English Residential Colleges and American Universities* (New Haven: Yale University Press, 1996), 125–43; Katherine Chaddock [Reynolds], *Visions and Vanities: John Andrew Rice of Black Mountain College* (Baton Rouge: Louisiana State University Press, 1998).

and teachers. The first year of such a college would endeavor to comprehend the Athens of Pericles and Plato as a total civilization, and the second would apply the same approach to modern America. Students and teachers would reside together; teaching would be through tutorials with students responsible for readings; and there would be no examinations. Later that year, after a deadlocked search, Glenn Frank was named the surprising choice for president of the University of Wisconsin. Eager to confirm his image as a reformer, he recruited Meiklejohn to implement what became the Experimental College (1927–1932).[65]

The Experimental College opened in the fall of 1927 with eleven "Advisers" (faculty, mostly old supporters from Amherst) and 119 young men (everyone who had applied) in one-half of a new dormitory. Initially, the college generated a powerful esprit in its insular setting and was praised in glowing terms by Meiklejohn, Frank, and a credulous press. However, the college was conceived and founded as a rebuke to existing higher education, and the Wisconsin faculty soon resented this implicit insult. Moreover, the college itself increasingly appeared as an alien implant on the Wisconsin campus. Two-thirds of the students were from out of state, and many chose to emphasize their differentness in dress and demeanor; a few outspoken communists among them fanned an exaggerated reputation for radicalism, scandalizing the locals; and intellectual freedom seemed to extend to license in crude behavior, which Meiklejohn chose to ignore. The Depression exacerbated all these tensions while making the college's extra resources more difficult to justify. Nonetheless, the Experimental College failed on its own terms: entering students declined each year to just 74 for 1930–1931, the year Meiklejohn resolved to terminate his experiment. Many of the students—and advisers—found the college an exhilarating intellectual adventure and long honored its memory, often becoming educators themselves. But whatever an uncertain future might have held, Meiklejohn hastened its demise by refusing to compromise his original conception by adapting to the realities of a large midwestern university.[66]

The University of Chicago was the only major university to restructure undergraduate education. Two developments roiled the institution, one implemented and one advocated: Chicago achieved the most radical separation of lower- and upper-division education, but the efforts to install a Great Books

65   Adam R. Nelson, *Education and Democracy: The Meaning of Alexander Meiklejohn* (Madison: University of Wisconsin Press, 2001), 119–42, quote p. 120; Lawrence H. Larson, *The President Wore Spats: A Biography of Glenn Frank* (Madison: State Historical Society of Wisconsin, 1965).

66   Nelson, *Education and Democracy*, 133–196; Cronin and Jenkins, *University of Wisconsin*, III, 13–211. Meiklejohn's exculpatory account was written during the college's last year and depicted it as an educational experiment that needed to be free from "interferences" from the rest of the university: *The Experimental College* (Madison: University of Wisconsin Press, 2001 [1932]), esp. 278–94.

curriculum never advanced beyond pilot efforts. However, these two initiatives were united in the person of Robert Maynard Hutchins, the wunderkind who presided over the university from 1929 to 1951. Hutchins had graduated from the Yale Law School in 1925 (while serving as secretary to the Yale Corporation) and became an instructor in the school that year, acting dean in 1927, dean in 1928, and president of the University of Chicago at age 30. His meteoric rise was owed to personal attributes—a tall imposing presence, striking good looks, a keen intellect, and a gift for speaking, made all the more captivating by an acerbic wit.[67] In keeping with the spirit of the times, his early career was notable for brash challenges to the status quo, which were rewarded by recognition and advancement. He attempted no less at Chicago, with some initial success.[68]

Hutchins assumed the presidency of an institution that challenged Harvard as the country's preeminent research university but was less distinguished for undergraduate education. The majority of the faculty seemed to regard what Harper had designated the junior college as "an unwanted, ill-begotten brat that should be disinherited"—or at least altered so that they would not have to teach in it. Such a plan was developed by Dean Chauncey Boucher but left in limbo when President Max Mason resigned in 1928. Hutchins not only endorsed this reform but used it to rationalize the university structure. The New Plan transformed the junior college curriculum into a series of survey courses in humanities, social science, biological science, and physical science. Rejecting the measurement of learning by the accumulation of credits (a practice often assailed by contemporary critics), each course was capped with a comprehensive multiple-choice examination designed to assess mastery of the subject matter. Entry into advanced work required passing these examinations, which students could take at any time. Besides reconstituting the College, the reform created four divisions of upper class and graduate studies in those same areas, each with a dean and a budget. The New Plan for the college was popular with students, no doubt due to the dedicated efforts of mostly younger faculty in designing and teaching the survey courses. Departmental faculty in the divisions could focus on advanced studies and research, activities for which Hutchins expressed increasing disdain.[69]

67   Hutchins is the most quoted figure in Robert Birnbaum's collection of higher-education quotations with 50 percent more entrees than second-place Charles Eliot: *Speaking of Higher Education: The Academic's Book of Quotations* (Westport, CT: Praeger, 2004).

68   William H. McNeill, *Hutchins' University: A Memoir of the University of Chicago, 1929–1950* (Chicago: University of Chicago Press, 1991); Mary Ann Dzuback, *Robert M. Hutchins: Portrait of an Educator* (Chicago: University of Chicago Press, 1991).

69   The University of Chicago departments were rated as prestigious as Harvard's in 1925: Raymond M. Hughes, *A Study of Graduate Schools of America* (Oxford, OH: Miami University Press, 1925); Chauncey Samuel Boucher, *The Chicago Plan* (Chicago: University of Chicago Press, 1940 [1935]), 1.

Not content with his accomplishment, Hutchins sought a larger impact on American higher education. Given his rather narrow training in law, he lacked the vision that such a project called for, but he found inspiration instead from Mortimer Adler, whom he brought to Chicago. Essentially an autodidact, Adler had been enthralled by the Great Books course at Columbia, described below. His advocacy of the liberal arts based solely on Great Books and of a rigid neo-Aristotelian philosophy lay completely outside accepted academic practice; but this posture, buttressed by Adler's dogmatic certainty, appealed to Hutchins' iconoclasm. Hutchins' first confrontation with the faculty occurred when he attempted to impose Adler on the philosophy department. Appointed to law instead, where Hutchins had quite good relations, Adler functioned more as a free agent and gadfly, exasperating faculty by propounding doctrines of metaphysical "truth" against the alleged shallowness of academic disciplines. In 1936 Hutchins articulated this vision in *The Higher Learning in America*. The volume gained some plausibility from Hutchins' pithy condemnation of some well-worn half-truths: the fragmentation of learning from disciplinary specialization, the distortion of university policies by "the love of money," vocationalism, and anti-intellectualism. To rectify these failings, he proposed that universities be guided by a higher metaphysic and devoted to "the search for truth," which Hutchins asserted could be done only through metaphysics.[70]

More concretely, he now argued for a 4-year liberal arts course, beginning after the tenth grade and based largely on survey courses emphasizing readings of Great Books. Hutchins was able to launch this experiment the following year with special classes carved out of the University High School. The "Hutchins College" was perfected during and after World War II as a 4-year prescribed curriculum consisting of fourteen survey courses. Additional discussion sections were added to the previous surveys, and each concluded with a standardized multiple-choice examination. The Hutchins College came closest to the president's ideal in teaching what he believed was general knowledge needed by all educated Americans and having dedicated instructors unconnected with the academic departments of the upper-level divisions. Hutchins' aspiration to impose this plan on all of American education illustrates the primacy of his idiosyncratic logic over reality. Enrollments were weak and attrition high. Worse, universities, including Chicago's upper divisions, refused to recognized BAs from the Hutchins College for graduate or professional studies without additional work.

70   Robert Maynard Hutchins, *The Higher Learning in America* (New Haven: Yale University Press, 1936): "If we can revitalize metaphysics and restore it to its place in the higher learning, we may be able to establish rational order in the modern world as well as in the universities" (105). "The departmental system, which has done so much to obstruct the advancement of education and the advancement of knowledge, will vanish" (111). Edward Shils, "Robert Maynard Hutchins," *American Scholar*, 59 (1990): 211–35.

After Hutchins' departure, the college began requiring high school graduation for admission and its courses became elective in 1957.[71]

As the basis for a liberal arts education, the great works of the Western intellectual tradition had a convoluted history in the twentieth century. Hutchins and Chicago played a key role in this odyssey. This notion was originally developed by the multitalented John Erskine when teaching English at Columbia. In 1916 he proposed a 2-year sequence for juniors and seniors in which one Great Book would be read and discussed each week. He feared that under the elective system, students had less learning in common and less acquaintance with great literature: above all he sought to give students "the advantage of knowing the contents of great books and discussing them intimately and the advantage . . . of knowing the same books and reading them at the same time." The turmoil of the war years delayed implementation until 1920, when the faculty only approved it as a "general honors" course. The distinctive Socratic pedagogy was as much a hallmark of the Great Books idea as the books themselves.[72]

Erskine's course became a striking success, soon requiring more sections and recruiting enthusiastic teachers, including Mortimer Adler, a former student. Adler introduced this model to Scott Buchanan, whose educational idealism had been honed by Meiklejohn's Amherst and a Rhodes scholarship and was undiminished by a Harvard PhD. Buchanan employed this same approach in extension courses for adults in New York City, often taught by Columbia converts. When Buchanan took a position at the University of Virginia in 1929, he was disheartened to find uninspired students and an uninspiring undergraduate curriculum. He teamed with fellow Rhodes scholar, Stringfellow Barr, whom he converted to the Great Books idea, to develop an honors curriculum in which the first 2 years were devoted to Great Books. They were disappointed, however, when the university failed to implement the honors program. But Adler promised a more congenial setting at Chicago.[73]

With Hutchins's blessing, Adler sought to engraft the Great Books onto the University of Chicago, but circumstance and faculty resistance kept it on the periphery. Adler and Hutchins taught a 2-year Great Books seminar to undergraduates, and Adler taught a 1-year course to third-year law students. Adler's friend and ally, Thomist philosopher Richard McKeon, was brought from

71   MacNeill, *Hutchins' University*, 133–65; Dzubak, *Robert M. Hutchins*, 146–59.

72   Katherine Chaddock, "A Canon of Democratic Intent: Reinterpreting the Roots of the Great Books Movement," *History of Higher Education Annual*, 22 (2002): 5–32; Katherine Chaddock, *The Multi-Talented Mr.Erskine: Shaping Mass Culture through Great Books and Fine Music* (New York: Palgrave Macmillan, 2012), 81–100, quote p. 87.

73   William N. Haarlow, *Great Books, Honors Programs, and Hidden Origins: The Virginia Plan and the University of Virginia in the Liberal Arts Movement* (New York: Routledge Farmer, 2003).

Columbia in 1934 and made Dean of Humanities the next year. This set the stage for a Great Books offensive to be orchestrated by the new Committee on the Liberal Arts. The committee was Hutchins' vehicle for bypassing the academic departments. Besides Adler and McKeon, Scott Buchanan and Stringfellow Barr were recruited in 1936 to join this effort. However, the faculty saw the committee and the backdoor appointments for what they were—an end run around faculty prerogatives and university procedures. McKeon had to resign from the committee to avoid compromising the Division of Humanities. The committee soon self-destructed in vehement disagreements over book choices, interpretations, and teaching methods. Frustrated in Chicago, Buchanan and Barr found another opportunity when the failing St. John's College in Annapolis hired them to renovate and, hopefully, save the college. With Barr as president and Buchanan as dean in charge of curriculum, St. John's established the first 4-year undergraduate course based mainly on Great Books.[74]

The diverse experiments and innovations of the interwar years had several traits in common. Foremost, they all regarded the liberal education of undergraduates as the overriding mission of higher education and considered the first 2 years particularly problematic. This view was a reaction to the dominant features of contemporary universities. Collegiate reformers condemned the fragmentation of knowledge in the academic disciplines, its increasing specialization as knowledge advanced, and its curricular embodiment in the elective system. They further rejected the many practices grouped under the rubric of vocationalism, which would encompass most of the land grant tradition as well as the schools for the minor professions and much more. In this respect, these reforms echoed the prewar liberal culture movement, though these similarities faded with time. But the two chief aims—to raise the intellectual level of undergraduates and to devise a new formulation for liberal education—had different results. Efforts to impose greater academic rigor on some or all students advanced where they were consistent with the hegemony of academic disciplines. Thus, Aydelotte wanted Swarthmore honors students to excel in learning no matter what field they studied, and Lowell established honors and divisional examinations without disturbing the disciplines. Foundations, whose support for university research will be examined in the next chapter, supported aspirations for excellence that were consistent with academic knowledge growth but apparently ignored the University of Chicago after Hutchins' endorsement of metaphysics in *Higher Learning*. Innovations that separated liberal education from

---

74   Chaddock, "Canon of Democratic Intent," 18–32; Dzuback, *Robert M. Hutchins*, 127–28, 189; MacNeill, *Hutchins' University*, 70–71. After the fiasco of the committee, Adler began to emphasize Great Books for adults, outside the university. One result was *Great Books of the Western World*, compiled by Adler and Hutchins and published in 54 volumes by *Encyclopaedia Britannica* (1952).

academic knowledge faced inherent difficulties. Formerly, the distinctive mark of a liberal education was some knowledge of Latin and Greek. Twentieth-century formulations sought in vain to define a suitable replacement but managed only to perpetuate variations of genteel Western culture, tinged with Anglophilia. Ironically, this essentially elite notion of inculcating Western culture through Great Books migrated to the general public through adult education, first advocated by Buchanan in New York City and later by Meiklejohn, Adler, and Hutchins. In higher education, these aspirations either failed or had little impact. Instead, they were transmogrified into a more prosaic movement called general education—or at least one interpretation of that amorphous phenomenon.

At Columbia, the general honors course that Erskine launched evolved into a humanities course for all students while retaining much of its original flavor. It was paired with a course incorporating history and social science that originated in 1918 as "War Aims." After the war, the course was continued as "Contemporary Civilization," an overview of current events for freshmen. This course was broadened historically and culturally into a 2-year sequence in 1929. Great Books was dropped that same year, despite its popularity and multiple sections, when Erskine resigned to become president of the Juilliard Conservatory. It was revived in 1932 by two young and rising scholars, Lionel Trilling and Jacques Barzun, keeping the same format of intensive discussion of important books. The course was later expanded to a 2-year sequence, with the second devoted to fine arts. These two courses embodied Columbia's core of general education and became the enduring signature of a Columbia College education.

At Chicago, the Hutchins College curriculum embodied a doctrinaire commitment to general education, and it, too, persisted in modified form after the demise of the original scheme. Although the Hutchins' presidency weakened the University of Chicago, it achieved his aim of raising the intellectual level of undergraduate education. Despite falling enrollments and substantial attrition, the Hutchins College was noted for intellectual intensity among students and among the teachers who collectively designed these unique courses. The relative success of general education at Columbia and Chicago owed much to the talents and dedication of the instructors. The leaders of Great Books at Columbia's core have been described as placing "higher value . . . on the 'good life' over the 'successful career'" (although they exemplified the latter). The postwar Hutchins College assembled a phalanx of future academic luminaries, including Daniel Bell, David Riesman, and Edward Shils. However, none remained with the college.[75]

75   McCaughey, *Stand Columbia*, 285–99, quote p. 295; Daniel Bell, *The Reforming of General Education: The Columbia College Experience in Its National Setting* (New York: Columbia University Press, 1966), 12–53.

Despite the uniqueness of their interpretations of general education, Columbia and Chicago were in the vanguard of this movement. By the late 1930s, general education became the accepted rubric for addressing the discontents associated with undergraduate education under conditions of relentless disciplinary specialization. Specifically, it aimed at unifying knowledge across disciplines and providing a fundamental (or general) basis of knowledge prior to specialization. It recognized that giving priority to undergraduate learning required specially designed courses, and it sought, perhaps vainly, a common intellectual foundation for educated citizens in a democracy. These concerns would become dominant themes of American higher education after World War II, when they were popularized by the "Harvard Redbook," *General Education in a Free Society*. Even then, the popularity of general education owed not to the cogency of the arguments or compelling content, but rather to the dearth of common learning and cultural distinction in undergraduate education.[76]

ADVANCED EDUCATION OF AFRICAN AMERICANS

The Union victory in the Civil War emancipated roughly four million slaves in sixteen southern and border states, launching them into an uncertain future as free citizens. Many, together with abolitionist supporters in the North, saw education as a means to distance the freedmen from their former bondage and to equip them for life's new possibilities. Schools of all title and description were started with help from the Freedman's Bureau, the American Missionary Association, northern churches, and Reconstruction governments. They sought to meet the overwhelming needs for literacy and elementary education. Advanced education for African Americans was necessarily slow to develop, retarded by a dearth of prepared students and the crushing poverty of much of that population. By 1890, a pitifully small number of African Americans were enrolled beyond primary courses:[77]

---

76 Harvard University Committee on the Objectives of a General Education in a Free Society, *General Education in a Free Society: Report of the Harvard Committee* (Cambridge: Harvard University, 1945). The Harvard Redbook was preceded by a 1939 study and report of the Harvard Student Council's Committee on Education, which criticized "the penetration into the liberal college of the university function" and recommended establishment of introductory courses of general education: Nathan M. Sorber and Jordan R. Humphrey, "The Era of Student Bureaucracy and the Contested Road to the Harvard Redbook, 1925–1945," *Higher Education in Review*, 8 (2011): 13–40, quote p. 28.

77 *Report of the Commissioner of Education for the Year 1890–91* (Washington, GPO, 1894), 1469–73; James D. Anderson, *The Education of Blacks in the South, 1860–1935* (Chapel Hill, University of North Carolina Press, 1988); Bobby L. Lovett, *America's Historically Black Colleges and Universities: a Narrative History* (Macon, GA: Mercer University Press, 2011).

Secondary instruction	2,602
Normal and industrial schools	7,189
Schools of theology	755
Law and medical departments	427
Colleges and universities (HBCUs)	808

Behind these figures from the Bureau of Education, the meagerness of educational opportunity can be glimpsed. Elementary students were of necessity accommodated anywhere feasible; more than 10,000 in secondary schools and 6,500 in colleges. These students also predominated at some normal schools. Many "collegiate" students were in "industrial" courses, and 20 percent attended northern institutions. Colleges also accounted for 40 percent of secondary, or preparatory, students. These are paltry numbers of future teachers, preachers, and medics for a southern black population of nearly 7 million, who by that date were increasingly abandoned to their own resources.

The decade of the 1890s marked the decisive onset of Jim Crow in the South. Blacks were systematically deprived of civil and political rights; de facto segregation was given legal sanction by the Supreme Court, as was blatantly unequal provision of education; and white supremacy was enforced through terrorism by lynch law.[78] With state governments monopolized by increasingly racist white politicians, Blacks were given few opportunities for publicly supported education, leaving them dependent on private initiatives for anything beyond rudimentary instruction. While the mere provision of education was problematic, a fundamental question loomed as to its purpose. How could education address the "Negro Question"—how should the education of African Americans be related to the role they would fulfill in white-dominated society? All discussion of black education in this era was premised on this issue. Booker T. Washington emerged as the foremost black spokesman by articulating and exemplifying a strategy for industrial education that was compatible with white supremacy in the Jim Crow South.

Washington's well-known autobiography, *Up from Slavery* (1901), credits his experience at Hampton Normal and Agricultural Institute (f. 1868) and its founder Samuel Chapman Armstrong with forming his philosophy. A former general of black troops, Armstrong established Hampton in the belief that Blacks above all required work discipline and moral uplift. As a student and later staff member, Washington excelled in this milieu and was recommended by Armstrong to found a new institution in Tuskegee, Alabama. In 1881, starting with

78 *Plessy v. Ferguson* (1896) gave legal sanction to 'separate but equal' segregation, but *Cumming v. School Board of Richmond County, Georgia* (1899) rendered equal schooling meaningless.

virtually no resources, Washington established Tuskegee Normal and Industrial Institute on the Hampton model. Exemplifying the doctrine of self-help, students and staff quickly (and physically) built it into a thriving institution—31 instructors and 450 students after less than 10 years, and 1,600 students, still mostly elementary, by 1910. Washington traveled the national lecture circuit preaching the doctrine of racial advancement through industrial education and self-reliance. Most notable was his "Atlanta Compromise" speech to a national audience in 1895, in which he advocated black accommodation to the segregated status quo and economic advancement through industrial education and hard work. This was an answer to the Negro Question that Northern Whites found congenial and Southern Whites could tolerate. Washington served as the principal spokesman for African Americans on social and educational issues until his death in 1915. Moreover, northern foundations and industrialists embraced this nonconfrontational view and directed their philanthropy toward the Hampton-Tuskegee model and those institutions in particular.[79]

Washington built a thriving educational institution under conditions in which educational opportunities of all kinds were sorely needed. His optimism in the face of terrible race relations may seem Panglossian, but racial accommodation was probably the only course for accomplishing the possible under those fraught circumstances. One can scarcely begrudge his success with northern philanthropy, although these funds might have been put to better uses. However, the Hampton-Tuskegee model became increasingly anachronistic after 1900. "Industrial education" taught only basic workplace skills: the majority of women learned sewing, the men, agriculture. And the substandard character of teacher education soon had to be rectified. Perhaps more damaging, the Tuskegee model condoned a permanent subordinate status and the false hopes of economic advancement. It also undercut an alternative response to the Negro Question through academic education in colleges and universities.

In 1890 W.E.B. Du Bois graduated cum laude from Harvard University. A native of Barrington, Massachusetts, he earned an AB from Fisk University in 3 years before entering Harvard as a junior. Five more years of study, two in Germany, earned a Harvard PhD, the first awarded to an African American. After graduation he completed sociological studies of *The Philadelphia Negro* and *The Negroes of Farmville, Virginia* that were well ahead of scholarship in that discipline. He then accepted a professorship at Atlanta University in 1897. He soon challenged Washington on racial accommodation and industrial education, asserting that Blacks needed above all, "the right to vote; civic equality; and education of youth according to ability." For Du Bois the last point meant a liberal

79   Anderson, *Education of Blacks*, 33–78.

college education for the "Talented Tenth," who would become "leaders of thought and missionaries of culture among the masses." He accordingly sought to publicize the crucial role of colleges for the education of the Talented Tenth over and above industrial training. To this end, he conducted an empirical social study of *The College-Bred Negro* (1900) as one of the annual studies of "the Negro Problems" sponsored by Atlanta University.[80]

Du Bois identified nearly 2,400 black college graduates (through 1898), and that list, although an approximation, defined black opportunities for higher education before 1900. Northern institutions had graduated 390 black students, one-third of them from Oberlin. Despite that college's pioneering role in admitting black students, these students now experienced discrimination and segregation on the Oberlin campus. The same was true at the University of Kansas, which had the second-largest number of black graduates (16). Most graduates of the other 70 colleges had attended as isolated individuals, often cordially treated.[81] Almost one-third of the graduates were from Lincoln University in Pennsylvania (615) and Wilberforce University in Ohio (130), both established before the Civil War. Lincoln was a conservative Presbyterian school in which an aloof, all-white faculty taught a 4-year classical course. Modeled after Princeton, it was the most expensive HBCU with the most extensive extracurricular activities—the HBCU most like traditional white colleges. Fisk University in Nashville was the next-largest producer of black graduates (180). Founded and supported by the American Missionary Association, it escaped the penury of peer institutions through the fund-raising tours of the Fisk Jubilee Singers (1873–1878). Fisk emerged as the most respected liberal arts college among the HBCUs (followed by Atlanta University with 85 graduates), but in 1900 it still offered elementary, secondary, and normal classes.

Howard was the only true university among the HBCUs. It had received an annual federal appropriation since 1879 and benefitted from the less restrictive atmosphere of the nation's capital. Although its college produced only 96 graduates by 1898, they were dwarfed by far larger numbers of graduates in theology, medicine, law, dentistry, and pharmacy. Howard dominated the education of black professionals and would build a reputation as the "capstone of Negro education." In Nashville, Meharry Medical College rivaled the Howard Medical

---

80   David Levering Lewis, *W.E.B. Du Bois: Biography of a Race, 1868–1919* (New York: Henry Holt, 1993); W.E.B. Du Bois, *The Souls of Black Folks*, 100th Anniversary Edition (Boulder, CO: Paradigm Publishers, 2004 [1903]), 29; W.E.B. Du Bois, ed., *The College Bred Negro* (Atlanta: Atlanta University Press, 1900), 111.

81   Ibid., 14, 29–30; W.E.B. Du Bois, *The College-Bred Negro American* (Atlanta: Atlanta University Press, 1910), 34–45; Callie L. Waite, *Permission to Remain among Us: Education for Blacks in Oberlin, Ohio, 1880–1914* (Westport, CT: Praeger, 2002).

Department. Beyond these institutions, conditions were bleak. Only two other HBCUs enrolled more than 20 college students in 1898, and Du Bois regarded the collegiate status of many as dubious. This was especially true for state-sponsored institutions. Although the Second Morrill Act of 1890 had required states to share Morrill Act funds between white and black institutions, the public HBCUs were limited to normal and industrial education and did not rise to collegiate level for two more decades.[82]

Black higher education made grudging progress from this low base during the first 2 decades of the new century. Besides the burden of white racism, the lack of public secondary education impeded college attendance. Southern states began to address their educational backwardness after 1900 by creating public high schools for Whites, but a similar, and weaker, effort for Blacks was begun only after 1920. Rising enrollments in normal schools compensated somewhat, especially in the border states, providing training for the predominant career open to educated Blacks. Collegiate enrollments in HBCUs grew to only 1,131 in 1909, while secondary and elementary enrollments increased much more. Black collegians favored the stronger academic institutions: Fisk increased its college students from 59 in 1900 to 392 in 1914, and Howard claimed 30 percent of black college enrollments that year. However, even the stronger HBCUs were starved for resources as northern churches and the American Missionary Association no longer provided meaningful support. Northern colleges continued to account for about 15 percent of black graduates.[83]

Black secondary enrollments grew from 30,000 in 1915 to 100,000 in 1925, and college enrollments followed. From 3,600 college students in 1915, HBCUs expanded to 12,000 in 1925 and 44,000 in 1940. During these years, the black public land grants finally rose to collegiate status. By 1930 they officially enrolled one-quarter of HBCU college students but, in fact, were still heavily tilted toward teacher education and industrial subjects. All had large subcollegiate enrollments, including manual trades, and southern state governments regarded such instruction as their main purpose. Most had black presidents whose chief responsibility was to keep students under tight control and, above all, exclude

---

82   Joe M. Richardson, *A History of Fisk University, 1865–1946* (Tuscaloosa: University of Alabama Press, 1980); Rayford W. Logan, *Howard University: The First Hundred Years, 1867–1967* (New York: New York University Press, 1967).

83   Anderson, *Education of Blacks*, 186–237; Richardson, *History of Fisk*, 55–70; Marybeth Gasman and Roger L. Geiger, "Introduction: Higher Education for African-Americans before the Civil Rights Era, 1900–1964," in Gasman and Geiger, eds. *Higher Education for African Americans before the Civil Rights Era, 1900–1914* (New Brunswick: Transaction Publishers, 2012), 1–16; Michael Fultz, "City Normal Schools and Municipal Colleges in the Upward Expansion of Higher Education for African Americans" in ibid., 17–42. Enrollments from *Reports of the Commissioner of Education*. The data given in Du Bois's two volumes are inconsistent but representative.

politics or protest.[84] Black higher education continued to be led by private institutions, which now had to deal with growing enrollments and rising black consciousness.

W.E.B. Du Bois left Atlanta University in 1910 to join the National Association for the Advancement of Colored People (NAACP) as editor of the magazine *Crisis*. Formation of the NAACP symbolized the beginning of the struggle for equal rights. By the 1920s, resistance to white supremacy and the subjugation of African Americans emerged on HBCU campuses. Students had many grievances. They resented the strict disciplinary regimes that Whites assumed were necessary to maintain control. They also resented inferior instructional courses that limited liberal arts in favor of industrial courses. But increasingly, they protested the manifestations and consequences of white control—by presidents, boards, and donors—that enforced or implied a subordinate status. They were powerless to affect the Jim Crow conditions surrounding their campuses, but their efforts improved the racial climate and enhanced race pride at HBCUs themselves.[85] The most dramatic confrontation occurred at Fisk University.

In his 10 years as president of Fisk, Fayette McKenzie (1915–1925) updated the curriculum, expanded facilities, and gained the support of foundations and donors. He sought to advance the institution by ingratiating himself with the white elite of Nashville and northern educational philanthropists. Autocratic and inflexible (scarcely unusual attributes in university leaders), he expected unquestioning loyalty from students and staff toward his stewardship of the university. White and black faculty largely supported the president, but the minute regulation of all aspects of student behavior soon alienated Fisk students. The strict disciplinary regime prohibited all fraternization between men and women, prohibited attractive clothing with a detailed dress code, and imposed constant supervision. Originally, Fisk was no worse than other HBCUs in this respect, but in an era of expanding freedom on white campuses, McKenzie imposed more draconian rules at Fisk. Petty regulations multiplied, the student newspaper was abolished, and no student organizations were permitted. Worst of all was the atmosphere of distrust and suspicion that pervaded the campus.

In 1924 Du Bois, whose daughter was graduating from Fisk, attacked this entire regime in an excoriating commencement address. He likened the discipline to that of a reform school, entirely incompatible with university ideals of freedom and learning. Further, the Fisk tradition of interracial cooperation

---

84   Gasman and Geiger, "Introduction"; Arthur J. Klein, ed., *Survey of Land-Grant Colleges and Universities*, United States Department of the Interior, Bulletin, 1930, No. 9, 2 vol. (Washington, D.C.: GPO, 1930), 837–913; Lovett, *America's Historically Black Colleges*, 88.

85   Ibram H. Rogers, *The Black Campus Movement: Black Students and the Racial Reconstruction of Higher Education, 1965–1972* (New York: Palgrave Macmillan, 2012), 29–48.

had been replaced with a tacit acceptance of segregation and black subordination. By laying bare the pathologies afflicting Fisk, Du Bois mobilized alumni and sparked student resistance. Protests escalated, leading up to a destructive demonstration in February 1925. McKenzie called in the hated Nashville police and imposed punishments on student critics without knowing whether or not they had been involved. Students responded with a boycott of classes that lasted 10 weeks, strongly supported by Fisk alumni and the Nashville black community. Although the white establishment praised McKenzie's "firm handling" of the situation, he no longer had the confidence of the trustees. In April he resigned. An interim executive committee basically acceded to changes proposed by students: the newspaper was restored, Greek organizations were permitted, an elected student council was created, the Fisk Code of Discipline was liberalized, and alumni were added to the board of trustees. A white, Quaker president was named, Thomas Elsa Jones (1925–1946), who both accepted the reforms and reassured Fisk's traditional white supporters. He would be succeeded by the eminent black sociologist, Charles S. Johnson (1946–1956). The confrontation at Fisk was a clear repudiation of white domination and secured Fisk's standing as the leading black liberal arts college.[86]

Similar confrontations at other HBCUs also united alumni with students and succeeded in gaining Blacks greater respect and recognition. At Lincoln University, a presidential vacancy aroused the adamant opposition of alumni against white clerical domination of the institution. The board offered the presidency to three successive white ministers, all of whom were forced to decline when confronted with solid student and alumni hostility. Finally, the board appointed two longtime, respected professors as president and vice president, who accepted on condition that black alumni would be appointed to the board of trustees and black instructors, to the faculty.

Similar opposition to white clerical leadership undermined the presidency of J. Stanley Durkee (1919–1926) at Howard University. Like McKenzie, Durkee could be authoritarian, condescending, and vindictive, but he confronted distinguished black faculty and administrators, who were not easily bullied. Their opposition peaked in 1925 just as an accumulation of student grievances fomented a short-lived strike. Although officially exonerated by the trustees, Durkee resigned in the face of opposition from faculty, students, and Howard alumni, all of whom agreed that the university should appoint a black educator as its next

---

86   Richardson, *History of Fisk*, 71–100; Raymond Wolters, *The New Negro on Campus: Black College Rebellions on the 1920s* (Princeton: Princeton University Press, 1975), 29–69; Anderson, *Education of Blacks*, 262–70. For Du Bois's 1924 commencement address: W.E.B. Du Bois, "Diuturni Silenti," in Herbert Aptheker, ed., *The Education of Black People: Ten Critiques, 1906–1960* (New York: Monthly Review Press, 1975), 41–60.

president. Mordecai Johnson (1926–1960) filled that role and provided strong, sometimes controversial, leadership that solidified Howard's position as the capstone of Negro education.

Repudiation of black subordination took somewhat longer at Hampton, which continued to uphold industrial education as the solution to the Negro Question. However, state requirements that teachers have some college education forced Hampton (and Tuskegee, too) to introduce college level courses. As collegiate enrollments grew in the 1920s, these students chafed against the racism of white instructors and the incompetence of industrial teachers. Protest culminated in a student strike at Hampton in 1927 protesting racism, paternalism, and inferior education. Initially suppressed, continuing turmoil on campus finally forced the resignation of Principal James E. Gregg (1918–1929) and the closing of the industrial secondary school. Hampton abandoned the industrial ideology and committed to collegiate education, but relations between black students and white administrators remained stormy. [87]

While conditions improved for black students at many HBCUs that experienced student protest, they tended to worsen for Blacks at white institutions outside the South. The growth of racial prejudice on northern campuses in the early twentieth century is a story seldom told. However, greater numbers of black students combined with increasing public intolerance may have made the interwar years the low point for academic race relations in the North.[88] In 1927 at least 1,500 Blacks attended predominately white institutions, 115 at the University of Illinois and 114 at the University of Kansas. There and elsewhere, black students were systematically excluded from campus residences, social activities, and some facilities. They often had to find housing in the local black communities and work menial jobs to support their studies. A few played on football teams, but the usual quota was one, and coaches concluded "gentlemen's agreements" not to field black players against all-white schools. Black fraternities and sororities were organized in part to compensate for this ostracism. They provided residences and social activities, as well as the opportunity to cultivate middle-class culture. Despite surmounting considerable obstacles, they were subject to demeaning lampoons in student newspapers and ridiculed in student minstrel shows. In 1938, nearly 3,000 northern Blacks attended HBCUs in the South (and another 1,000 at HBCUs in

---

87   Wolters, *New Negro*, 278–93, 70–136, 230–75; Andrew J. Rosa, "New Negroes on Campus: St. Clair Drake and the Culture of Education, Reform, and Rebellion at Hampton Institute," *History of Education Quarterly*, 53.3 (August, 2013): 203–32; Anderson, *Education of Blacks*, 270–74.

88   Richard Breaux dates a rise in white racial intolerance on northern campuses from the 1915 release of D. W. Griffiths movie, *Birth of a Nation*; and 1915–1925 were years of greatest racial violence: "Nooses, Sheets, and Blackface: White Racial Anxiety and Black Student Presence at Six Midwest Flagship Universities, 1882–1937," in Gasman and Geiger, *Higher Education for African Americans*, 43–73.

the North). They chose these institutions in order to participate in athletics and have normal social lives, even if it meant enduring southern segregation.[89]

Most progress toward improving conditions for African Americans between the wars occurred within black institutions, not in American society, and the HBCUs were instrumental in these developments. The 1920s witnessed renewed affirmation of black identity and intellectual accomplishment. Howard professor and dean, Carter G. Woodson, pioneered the subject of Negro history as a source of racial pride, before resigning in 1919 over Durkee's refusal to allow him to teach the subject. The Harlem Renaissance of the mid-twenties publicized the accomplishments and boosted the self-esteem of black artists and writers. A pivotal event was the publication of an anthology of this work, *The New Negro* (1925), by Howard professor Alain Locke. A Harvard PhD and the first black Rhodes Scholar, Locke was fired by Durkee in 1925 but rehired by Johnson in 1927. Charles S. Johnson also contributed to the Renaissance as research director of the National Urban League and editor of its journal. He subsequently became director of the social science department at Fisk in 1928 and led sociological studies of race relations. Howard University under Mordecai Johnson quickly became the foremost center of black scholars: Charles Thompson founded the *Journal of Negro Education*, an important forum for criticizing discrimination and exposing injustice; E. Franklin Frazier, first employed at Fisk, contributed to the sociology of black families; and Ralph Bunche addressed racial issues as a political scientist. In the Howard law school, Charles Hamilton Houston and others devised the legal strategy for the NAACP campaign against racial segregation.[90]

With the election of Franklin D. Roosevelt and the coming of the New Deal, African Americans began to receive some consideration in high places. Roosevelt directed substantial building funds to Howard, wishing to elevate a national Negro university in Washington. Eleanor Roosevelt belonged to the NAACP and, along with a small but growing number of liberals, supported black civil rights.[91] The General Education Board supported Charles Johnson's

89   Ibid.; Wolters, *New Negro*, 313–38; Clifford S. Griffin, *The University of Kansas: A History* (Lawrence: University Press of Kansas, 1974), 626–32; U.S. Office of Education, *National Survey of the Higher Education of Negroes*, vol. 2 (Washington, D.C.: GPO, 1942), 77–91; Lane Demas, *Integrating the Gridiron: Black Civil Rights and American College Football* (New Brunswick: Rutgers University Press, 2011).

90   Alain Locke, ed., *The New Negro: An Interpretation* (New York: Boni, 1925); Michael R. Winston, "Through the Back Door: Academic Racism and the Negro Scholar in Historical Perspective," *Daedalus*, 100, 3 (Summer, 1971): 678–719; Wolters, *New Negro*, 82–93; Jonathan Scott Holloway, *Confronting the Veil: Abram Harris Jr., E. Franklin Frazier, and Ralph Bunche, 1919–1941* (Chapel Hill: University of North Carolina Press, 2002).

91   Further to the Left, student groups began to protest segregation and the denial of civil rights in the North and South: Robert Cohen, *When the Old Left Was Young: Student Radicals and America's First Mass Student Movement, 1929–1941* (New York: Oxford University Press, 1993), 204–25. See chapter 11.

years of research on *The Negro College Graduate* (1938), and the Carnegie Corporation in 1937 enlisted Gunner Myrdal to direct an "objective and dispassionate" study of race relations in the United States.[92] An important step for the HBCUs was the creation in 1929 of a form of accreditation by the Southern Association of Colleges and Schools (SACS). Previously, SACS had refused to consider HBCUs because accreditation brought automatic membership in the association and the right to attend meetings. Instead, special categories were created for "Class A" and "Class B" recognition of collegiate status. Although discriminatory, this recognition provided clear standards that institutions could strive to meet. With the Julius Rosenwald Fund and the General Education Board now supporting the strengthening of the most promising HBCUs, these institutions were able to improve the credentials of faculty and library holdings. By 1940, twenty-two HBCUs had achieved Class A status or equivalent and sixteen, Class B; however, another thirty HBCUs were not considered to be college grade.[93]

Such progress as occurred in black higher education was limited by segregation to the HBCUs, and the intellectual awakening was largely confined to Atlanta, Fisk, and Howard universities. These three institutions employed 80 percent of black PhDs in 1936, mostly at Howard. Although Du Bois returned to Atlanta University in 1932, that school struggled to maintain its distinction. Fisk did somewhat better, with Charles Johnson conducting annual Race Relations Institutes. Black PhDs were earned at the most prestigious universities—the majority from Chicago, Columbia, Penn, Harvard, Cornell, Ohio State, and Michigan. However, no matter how distinguished their research or scholarship, these graduates had no chance of faculty appointments at traditionally white universities. Opportunities for research were limited too, even at the best HBCUs, and black scholars in these segregated locales were denied access to resources routinely available to Whites. This situation changed only slightly after 1945. Clearly, the only real solution to the Negro Question, recognized among leading black academics but unthinkable to most of white America, was to dismantle segregation and grant equal civil rights.[94]

In 1935, in seventeen southern and border states, no black and white students occupied the same classroom, from kindergarten to graduate school.

92 Frederick Keppel, president of the Carnegie Corporation, was influenced by Alaine Locke to seek a reevaluation of Negro education and the Negro problem: Ellen Condliffe Lagemann, *The Politics of Knowledge: The Carnegie Corporation, Philanthropy, and Public Policy* (Middletown, CT: Wesleyan University Press, 1989), 123–46.

93 Lovett, *America's Historically Black Colleges*, 102–4, 112–13; Charles S. Johnson, *The Negro College Graduate* (Chapel Hill: University of North Carolina Press, 1938), 296–97.

94 Winston, "Through the Back Door," 695–707.

This pattern was pricked that same year when NAACP litigation forced the enrollment of Donald Murray in the University of Maryland Law School. The guiding hand behind this case was Charles Hamilton Houston, professor in the Howard Law School from 1924 to 1935 and chief administrative officer for the last 6 years. Houston was responsible for reorganizing the law school, making it smaller with higher standards and achieving accreditation from the ABA. He also fostered a commitment in the school to achieving racial justice and trained a cadre of civil rights lawyers, including future Supreme Court justice Thurgood Marshall, who litigated the Maryland case. Houston chose to target graduate and professional schools as a weak point in the "separate but equal" doctrine.

In segregated states, graduate and professional education for black citizens was not unequal, it was nonexistent. Most of those states sought to obviate this embarrassment by offering out-of-state scholarships to black students who demanded such studies. In 1939, nine border and upper-south states reported support for 1,250 such students.[95] The plans purported to provide the extra expenses of travel and tuition but, in fact, were hedged with restrictions and financially inadequate. These practices had already been rejected in the Murray case and in the first such case to reach the Supreme Court—*Missouri ex rel. Gaines v. Canada* (1938). The Court ruled that a law school in another state was no substitute for admitting Lloyd Gaines to the University of Missouri Law School and constituted denial of equal protection. However, it offered the state three possible remedies: close the all-white law school; admit Gaines; or create an equivalent law school for Blacks. Missouri chose the latter and immediately provided funds to establish a law school at Gaines's alma mater, Lincoln University. The NAACP sought to challenge the equivalence of the new school, but Gaines disappeared, most likely murdered, and the case could not be pursued.[96]

The legal campaign for equal access to higher education achieved important precedents in the 1930s, but the main battles remained to be fought. In the next 2 decades, Blacks achieved only token integration of selected units in public higher education in border states and the upper South.[97] In the first four decades of the twentieth century, Blacks had succeeded in fashioning their own colleges

95   *National Survey of Higher Education of Negroes*, II, 17–21.

96   Mark V. Tushnet, *The NAACP's Legal Strategy against Segregated Education, 1925–1950* (Chapel Hill: University of North Carolina Press, 1987).

97   Peter Wallenstein, ed., *Higher Education and the Civil Rights Movement: White Supremacy, Black Southerners, and College Campuses* (Gainesville: University Press of Florida, 2008); Peter Wallenstein, "Black Southerners and Non-Black Universities: Desegregating Higher Education, 1935–1967," *History of Higher Education Annual*, 19 (1999): 121–48.

and universities, establishing an indigenous tradition of scholarship, and growing a small, educated professional class—all despite the suffocating conditions of
rigid segregation and pervasive discrimination. It would take the 20 years after
World War II to unlock the opportunity to benefit from the entire system of
American higher education.

★ 11 ★

THE STANDARD AMERICAN
UNIVERSITY

PHILANTHROPIC FOUNDATIONS AND THE
STANDARDIZATION OF HIGHER EDUCATION

OUNDATIONS PLAYED A LARGE ROLE IN SHAPING
higher education in the early twentieth century due to conditions
prevailing in the American polity and society. Rapid economic and
social development seemed to call for national policies and programs, but the realities of regional politics precluded such initiatives
by the federal government. This lacuna was filled partly by voluntary
organizations, but they had limited capacity to formulate or implement national
policies. The new foundations entered this same space, with greater resources to
effect social action. In higher education, the General Education Board justified
its actions because "neither the national government nor any one of the states
has accepted the responsibility of providing adequately for higher education."[1]
Foundations were able to further the standardization of American higher education and impose a national science policy after World War I. What, in fact, were
foundations trying to accomplish?

A philanthropic foundation consists of capital held in trust for a designated
public purpose. The trustees are the keepers of the funds and guardians of the
mission; operations are delegated to a president, who appoints additional staff.
The founders tended to be the most financially successful exemplars of the burgeoning industrial economy, and here Andrew Carnegie and John D. Rockefeller tower above all others in wealth and the magnitude of their philanthropies.
Foundations acquired a reputation for conservatism, but they were established
to promote change. They embodied the outlook of the new industrial economy,
admiring and promoting stability, order, and—their favorite word—efficiency.
Carnegie and Rockefeller had imposed order and efficiency on the steel and

---

1   Barry D. Karl and Stanley N. Katz, "The American Private Philanthropic Foundation and the
Public Sphere, 1890–1930," *Minerva*, 19 (1981): 236–70; *The General Education Board: An Account of Its
Activities, 1902–1914* (New York: GEB, 1915), 103–59, quote p. 103.

petroleum industries, respectively, and they devoted a large part of their fortunes to achieve similar results in other spheres. This mission of shaping social institutions made foundations inherently controversial at their beginnings and throughout their history. Populist critics alleged that such aims subverted the democratic process and served the founders' interests. Their penchant for social stability favored established, successful institutions, distrusted popularly elected legislatures, and abhorred anything associated with organized labor. In higher education, their direction was always clear: Rockefeller charged the General Education Board with promoting "a comprehensive system of higher education in the United States," and the Carnegie Foundation was dedicated to "standardizing American education."[2]

For higher education, the philanthropy of Andrew Carnegie and John D. Rockefeller followed nearly parallel tracks. While Rockefeller bankrolled the University of Chicago, Carnegie's skepticism toward colleges led him to found a technical school in Pittsburgh (1900), soon upgraded to Carnegie Institute of Pittsburgh (1912: later Carnegie-Mellon University). He announced with great fanfare a major gift to address the weakness of American science, which, after a national debate, led to the Carnegie Institution of Washington in 1902. That same year, his counterpart also endowed a research institution, the Rockefeller Institute for Medical Research (later, Rockefeller University). In 1905, Rockefeller directed the General Education Board (GEB, f. 1902) toward higher education, the same year the Carnegie Foundation for the Advancement of Teaching (CFAT) was launched. Both men's philanthropy culminated with the dedication of a large part of their fortunes to general-purpose foundations: the Carnegie Corporation ($125 million, 1911) was pledged to "promote the advancement and diffusion of knowledge and understanding among the people of the United States," and the Rockefeller Foundation ($182 million, 1913) aspired "to promote the well-being of mankind throughout the world." By these dates, their previous creations had already had an appreciable impact on American higher education.[3]

The General Education Board, run by trusted Rockefeller advisors, first sought to shore up the finances of American private colleges. Scanning some 700 such institutions, they concluded "only a minority were rightly called college or university." The board chose to aid the stronger institutions by awarding grants that had to be matched by locally raised funds, usually several times over.

---

2   Karl and Katz, "American Private"; Roger L. Geiger, *To Advance Knowledge: The Growth of American Research Universities, 1900–1940* (New Brunswick: Transaction, 2004 [1986]), 45–47, quotes p. 143.

3   Ibid. 140–45: $100 million in 1913 would approximate $2.4 billion in 2013.

It foreswore any intention to interfere with college internal affairs but in fact coerced them—for their own good—to conduct fund-raising campaigns, adopt up-to-date financial practices, and preserve the new funds as endowment. The GEB chose well-established colleges and universities, in favorable locations, focused on arts and sciences. Special consideration was given to the educationally underdeveloped South. To 1914, some $10 million was awarded, to be matched by $40 million, spread fairly evenly between 33 institutions in the South, 39 in the Midwest and West, and 31 in the Northeast and Middle States. Wealthy institutions were asked to match far more than colleges new to fund-raising. In fact, one specific purpose was to induce colleges to appeal systematically to their alumni. These grants helped liberal arts colleges, in particular, to expand faculty in keeping with the expanding academic disciplines.[4]

The Carnegie Foundation was established to provide pensions for college professors, but President Henry S. Pritchett used his strategic position to advance the standardization of American higher education.[5] Pritchett had been appointed president of MIT in 1900 after an eclectic scientific career. He worked closely with Charles W. Eliot in exploring a merger with Harvard and also befriended Andrew Carnegie. Merger possibilities were rejected by Tech alumni, but Carnegie acted on his suggestion to provide funding for faculty pensions and then named Pritchett to lead the CFAT. The foundation's board, with Eliot as chair, included the presidents of the major research universities—the senior leaders of the university movement. Like the GEB, the CFAT had to determine which institutions to aid. It rejected state and denominational institutions but still had to define what the foundation considered a college. One strategic criterion Pritchett invoked was to demand 4 full years of high school for admission—or 14 "Carnegie units." Although scarcely a problem for the 52 prominent institutions initially admitted to Carnegie pensions, it quickly set a standard for American education. High schools were judged by their ability to deliver 14 academic units, and "true colleges" were expected to use this criterion for admissions. These standards brought the wide variation in college quality under glaring scrutiny. The Carnegie list of accepted institutions, expanded to 73 schools, including some state universities by 1911, became such a badge of prestige that the foundation felt compelled to publish a list of schools with denominational ties that otherwise met its criteria. The Bureau of Education in 1911 had classified

---

4 *General Education Board, 1902–1914*, 103–59, quote pp. 109–11; the GEB also aided African American education but largely dismissed the need for black colleges—it awarded $140,000 to seven HBCUs (one-half to Fisk), somewhat more than the average gift to a single white college, 204–9.

5 Joseph F. Kett notes: "the drive for educational standards was ubiquitous between 1905 and 1915"; Pritchett contributed significantly to this drive: *Merit: The History of a Founding Ideal from the American Revolution to the 21st Century* (Ithaca: Cornell University Press, 2013), 185.

American colleges into 4 quality tiers but was prevented by the White House from publishing the controversial list. The Association of American Universities then assumed the responsibility for judging college quality with its own classification. In these rankings, the number of Carnegie units required for admission became a telling indicator of the level of instruction.[6]

The CFAT also had an immediate impact on medical education. The effect of Abraham Flexner's 1910 Report was described in chapter 9, but it also influenced collegiate education by encouraging medical schools to require 2 years of college science for admission. This foray into professional education was a calculated part of Pritchett's drive to impose order and efficiency. Before commissioning the Flexner study, Pritchett had the board approve a "Plan for an Examination of the Status of Professional Education," which detailed the low prevailing standards, a "fluid" situation ripe for reform, and backing within the professions themselves. Such antecedents were certainly present in medical education, but the foundation was less successful elsewhere. Alfred Z. Reed dashed hopes for doing a Flexner for law when he endorsed the wide access to law schools provided by urban proprietary institutions and part-time night schools. Ironically, reaction to Reed's report united university law schools and the American Bar Association in favor of restrictive higher standards—2 years of college for admission and a full-time law degree to qualify for the bar. However, it still took two decades for these reforms to become widely accepted. The CFAT study of engineering education (1918) expressed the view of industry and the engineering associations that courses should address the technical needs of the workplace. Although its impact was muffled by the war, this stance reinforced postwar sentiment. The foundation endorsed a different approach for teacher education in the Missouri study. Elevating the principal of efficiency, it advocated a strictly vocational course of study for the emerging teachers colleges. Over all, excepting the apostasy of Reed and the low status accorded teachers, the CFAT consistently sought to upgrade and standardize professional education by concentrating it in reputable universities. It thus sought to elevate universities as pillars of the emerging social order and to make them more efficient as well.[7]

6 *Carnegie Foundation for the Advancement of Teaching, First Annual Report* (New York: CFAT, 1906); Ellen Condliffe Lagemann, *Private Power for the Public Good: A History of the Carnegie Foundation for the Advancement of Teaching* (Middletown, CT: Wesleyan University Press, 1983), 21–55; David S. Webster, *Academic Quality Rankings of American Colleges and Universities* (Springfield, IL: Charles C. Thomas, 1986), 71–89. The CFAT disallowed colleges with preparatory departments, casting a lasting stigma on that widespread practice; and several colleges removed charter language linking them to churches in order to be eligible.

7 Lagemann, *Private Power*, 59–93, quote pp. 60–61; David F. Noble, *America by Design: Science, Technology, and the Rise of Corporate Capitalism* (New York: Knopf, 1982), 202–7.

As much as Pritchett supported universities, he admired the singularity of purpose and efficient organization of corporations even more. He wrote often of university relations with business, arguing hopefully that university administration was tending "more and more to conform . . . to the methods of the business corporation." In 1909 Pritchett commissioned Morris L. Cooke, a protégé of scientific management expert Frederick Taylor, for a study of *Academic and Industrial Efficiency* (1910). In his preface, Pritchett acknowledged that the "human side" of universities differed from industry, but "the mechanical side of their organizations has not kept up with the demands and the complexities of their problems, and that they might gain . . . real help from those who conduct industrial enterprises." Cooke offered just such help by measuring faculty efficiency in terms of "student hours" of instruction, which then might be calculated to determine compensation, retention, or dismissal of instructors. Since principles of scientific management required specialization of function and division of labor, Cooke would have faculty removed from all aspects of governance, which should be the exclusive prerogative of management.[8] Cooke's study had little impact, but it exemplified a deference toward the new industrial order shared by CFAT board members, like Columbia President Nicholas Murray Butler.

The CFAT and foundations generally were on the side of progress—universities teaching more subjects at higher levels, scientific research, rationalization of administration and financial management, and integration with the economy; but they disdained other contemporary trends, such as the wider access achieved by mass higher education.[9] Further, the CFAT's elevation of management over faculty touched a particularly sensitive nerve. Columbia professor James McKeen Cattell, publisher of *Science* and *School and Society*, answered Morris Cooke with *University Control* (1913), advocating greater faculty authority to counter expanding presidential powers.[10] A controversial CFAT recommendation in *Education in Vermont* (1915) stirred additional opposition. In a typical appeal for efficiency, the foundation-sponsored report advised the state to terminate subsidies for private colleges and, since Vermont had an agricultural

---

8 Morris L. Cooke, *Academic and Industrial Efficiency*, Bulletin Number 5, Carnegie Foundation for the Advancement of Teaching (New York: 1910), v; Clyde W. Barrow, *Universities and the Capitalist State: Corporate Liberalism and the Reconstruction of American Higher Education, 1894–1928* (Madison: University of Wisconsin Press, 1990), 64–75.

9 For example, Pritchett blasted "mass production of higher education attempted at public cost" as fiscally unsustainable and contradictory to university intellectual ideals: "Preface," Howard J. Savage, *American Collegiate Athletics*, Carnegie Foundation for the Advancement of Teaching, Bulletin Number 23 (New York, 1929), xviii.

10 The larger controversy over the role of faculty prompted formation of the American Association of University Professors in 1915: Walter P. Metzger, *Academic Freedom in the Age of the University* (New York: Columbia University Press, 1961 [1955]), 139–221.

economy, concentrate all state resources in the land grant agricultural college. Harvard philosopher Josiah Royce warned that the CFAT conclusions transcended reasonable limits for both standardization and centralized administrative control.[11] The foundation would undertake more than twenty studies and reports in the next two decades, but the typical recommendations for a rigid separation of functions and managerial control over faculty governance had little effect. However, the power of American foundations soon turned more productively to strengthening science.

★ ★ ★

When World War I ended, the American experience was euphorically regarded as a vindication of American science. Scientists had indeed made appreciable contributions to submarine detection, ballistics, and other technical subjects; however, the postwar enthusiasm focused especially on the organization of the scientific effort. Scientists and engineers from industrial labs, scientific institutes, and universities had all been mobilized for the national effort. Those associated with this effort were convinced that similar measures would be needed in peacetime to make American industry competitive with European rivals. To this end, legislation was proposed to establish federally funded engineering research stations in each state, but such support was eventually scuttled after agreement could not be reached over placement of such units or federal oversight. Instead, a consensus emerged for working through the chief wartime coordinating agency, the National Research Council (NRC), assisted by the great foundations.[12]

The wartime efforts of the NRC symbolized the merging of basic and applied science, and its leaders determined even before hostilities ceased to perpetuate this kind of cooperation, chiefly for the benefit of industrial science and the science-based industries of the era. For George Ellery Hale, this was the destiny of the NRC, and early in 1919 he prevailed upon the Carnegie Corporation to donate $5 million to provide the National Academy with a permanent home and the NRC with an operating endowment. The Rockefeller Foundation also shared this enthusiasm, seeking in 1918 to advance American science by endowing a freestanding institute for the physical sciences, where scientists would be free from the distractions found in universities. This approach was opposed by NRC scientists, who favored strengthening science at a select group of

11   Josiah Royce, "The Carnegie Foundation for the Advancement of Teaching and the Case of Middlebury College," *School and Society*, I (1915): 145–50: discussed in Lagemann, *Private Power*, 89–93; Barrow, *Universities*, 98–101.

12   Daniel J. Kevles, *The Physicists: The History of a Scientific Community in Modern America* (New York: Vintage, 1979 [1971]), 117–54; Geiger, *To Advance Knowledge*, 98–101.

universities. The foundation rejected both plans and instead awarded $500,000 over 5 years for postdoctoral fellowships, to be awarded by NRC committees. This program, subsequently expanded, was enormously beneficial for developing American science. In 1919 it validated the role of the NRC and the paradigm of postwar science: control by the scientific elite was maintained through NRC committees, which, in turn, ensured that postdoctoral fellows were channeled to the principal research universities. Among the latter was the new California Institute of Technology, which Hale was intent on developing into a major locus for academic science.[13]

The NRC thus became a lynchpin for interwar science. It was firmly committed to a "best science" policy of reserving scientific choice in the hands of the most competent scientists. In practice, best science meant a repudiation of federal involvement, which to their minds posed the danger of political influence on science funding. Rather, the NRC elite envisioned a system in which foundations and industry could provide private funds to energize American science. Such collaboration was assured by an interlocking elite who encountered one another at the NRC, on corporate boards, and on the boards of the major foundations. Among others, Henry Pritchett dominated the board of the Carnegie Corporation, and Herbert Hoover was a guiding spirit, advocating public initiatives through private associations. This pattern of intermediate organizations was soon replicated in the American Council of Learned Societies, the American Council on Education, and the Social Science Research Council (SSRC). Although each was unique, they all allowed a leadership cadre to coordinate activities and allocate resources in their respective spheres. The postwar enthusiasm for science and coordination produced an organizational superstructure, tangible support, and additional possibilities for the future; however, there were limited funds for expanding university science.

Despite their enormous wealth, both the Carnegie Corporation and the Rockefeller Foundation were heavily encumbered with obligations to existing programs. Carnegie bankrolled the Food Research Institute at Stanford and the National Bureau of Economic Research at Columbia—both inspired by wartime experience. After Frederick Keppel assumed the presidency in 1923, Carnegie offered little support for science or universities except through the NRC and the Carnegie Institution.[14] The General Education Board was soon disillusioned

13   Geiger, *To Advance Knowledge*, 97–101; Robert E. Kohler, *Partners in Science: Foundations and the Natural Scientists, 1900–1945* (Chicago: University of Chicago Press, 1991), 71–129; Ronald C. Tobey, *The American Ideology of National Science, 1919–1930* (Pittsburgh: University of Pittsburgh Press, 1971), 20–61.

14   Ellen Condliffe Lagemann, *The Politics of Knowledge: The Carnegie Corporation, Philanthropy, and Public Policy* (Middletown, CT: Wesleyan University Press, 1989); Kohler, *Partners in Science*, 118–22.

with the results of its $50 million postwar effort to bolster endowments. The enrollment explosion rendered chimerical its financial goal of having endowment income provide 50 percent of operating costs. By the early 1920s, foundations largely withdrew from supporting colleges and universities directly, to focus instead on building specific areas of academic strength. Medical education was the largest target for support, followed by social and natural sciences.

Although the Flexner Report had been sponsored by the CFAT, it was the GEB that acted upon its recommendations. In his implacable opposition to proprietary arrangements, Abraham Flexner advocated that clinical instruction be organized with full-time instructors and no private, paying patients. In 1913 he convinced the GEB to adopt this position as the basis for supporting the upgrading of medical schools. This was a controversial stance that affected physician compensation, medical school finances (to pay full-time salaries), and the research/practice balance of clinical skills. Flexner joined the GEB that year and over the next 6 years shepherded an investment of some $8 million to engineer the reorganization of medical schools on the "full-time or university basis" at Johns Hopkins, Yale, Columbia, Chicago, Washington University, and Vanderbilt—the last three representing complete restructurings of the schools into first rate institutions. Then, in 1919–1921, John D. Rockefeller donated $45 million to the GEB to continue the advancement of medical education. Flexner became the most powerful figure in this realm, due to his incomparable knowledge of medical education throughout the United States and Europe, his combative advocacy, and solid backing from the GEB board. He embarked upon a campaign for the elevation of medical schools across the country, shaped by his personal vision; he encouraged the leading institutions to adopt the full-time research orientation and raised second-tier schools up to prevailing standards.

His determination to aid the University of Iowa challenged a tacit foundation rule against supporting public universities. Longtime Rockefeller advisor Frederic Gates vehemently opposed this grant, but the board voted with Flexner, opening the foundation to the public sector. The extensive grants made to Vanderbilt were part of Flexner's effort to upgrade medical education in the South, which also motivated grants to the municipal University of Cincinnati. To alleviate the dire condition of medical education for Blacks, Flexner led the rehabilitation of Meharry Medical College in Nashville, giving some $8 million in total as well as encouraging other philanthropic support. At the University of Rochester, he joined with philanthropist George Eastman to found a new, state-of-the-art medical and dental school. All told, Flexner directed GEB aid to twenty-five medical schools during his 15 years with the GEB, 40 percent of the 4-year medical schools that survived the 1920s. Each of these grants represented a "hands-on" personal effort by Flexner himself, in which he negotiated with university leaders, required reforms and matching funds to improve facilities, and imposed higher standards of education and research. He eventually tempered his dogmatic insistence on the full-time model, which was dropped by the GEB in 1925. By that date, although his fame was at its apogee, Flexner's influence was waning at the foundation, where new stars had emerged.[15]

In 1923, the Rockefeller trusts adopted new strategies for building American science. Beardsley Ruml, a Chicago psychologist and protégé of Carnegie Corporation and Yale president James Rowland Angell, was named director of the Laura Spellman Rockefeller Memorial (LSRM). Originally created to aid Mrs. Rockefeller's favorite charities, Ruml devoted the memorial to building academic social science. The same year, Wickliffe Rose, an old Rockefeller medical hand, assumed direction of the GEB, plus an international counterpart, the International Education Board (IEB). He resolved to advance the natural sciences, chiefly in universities.

Ruml began by commissioning a study of "The Status of Social Science in the United States." The immaturity of these fields was evident in the predominance of historical, a priori (if not polemical) studies and an absence of empirical research. He foresaw the possibility of a scientific breakthrough of the kind that had recently occurred in psychology and clinical medicine, but given the dearth of qualified practitioners, this could occur only through building social science in universities. He began by encouraging the creation of the SSRC, which joined representatives of the six social science disciplines. Unlike much foundation patronage, the SSRC provided a conduit for grassroots support. The $4 million it received during Ruml's tenure (1924–1928) was devoted primarily to small grants-in-aid and fellowships to train future social scientists. Ruml's alma mater, the University of Chicago, had the strongest social science faculty. In 1923 he began to fund a Local Community Research Committee, enabling it to conduct empirical research in the Chicago community. Chicago became the favored—and deserving—recipient, receiving more than $3 million from the LSRM. Other grants also tended to be targeted at specific problem areas: child development at the University of Iowa, race relations at the University of North Carolina and Fisk, and "social technologies" at some law schools and the Harvard and Penn business schools. All told, five public universities each received more than $200,000, as did six other privates, led by Columbia with $1.4 million. The LSRM was folded into the Rockefeller Foundation in 1929, but by that juncture Ruml had significantly expanded the foundations of academic social science, if not always in ways that he had intended. The greatest progress no

---

15   Thomas Neville Bonner, *Iconoclast: Abraham Flexner and a Life in Learning* (Baltimore: Johns Hopkins University Press, 2002), 144–212.

doubt occurred in the emergence of disciplines, particularly sociology and political science, building strong departments at a handful of universities and training a new generation of empirical social scientists. Little progress was achieved in addressing social problems, and even less was made toward his goal of unifying the social sciences. The most grandiose project in the latter effort, the Yale Institute for Human Relations, which aspired to unify the study of man at Yale, was a disappointment to all concerned. Ruml later complained, "We tried everything to encourage . . . unity in the social sciences." Instead, LSRM programs strengthened the social science disciplines, probably a more feasible and worthy result.[16]

Rose was as dedicated to advancing natural science as Ruml was to social science.[17] His approach, succinctly stated, was "to make the peaks higher." However, this did not imply simply favoring leading institutions but rather selectively advancing the best science wherever it was found. To accomplish this, he employed two lieutenants, one for Europe and one for the United States, to evaluate institutions and scientists. These objectives were more easily met in Europe, where support could be focused on the self-contained university institutes of leading scientists, such as Niels Bohr's Institute of Theoretical Physics at the University of Copenhagen. In the United States, it was frequently difficult to isolate exceptional programs for support. At the leading universities, strong departments and entrenched rivalries complicated efforts, as did university presidents with their own objectives. A further obstacle was created by the GEB's insistence on matching funds. The standard GEB grant endowed a group of departments to hire new faculty, acquire equipment, and conduct relatively focused lines of research. These things were not easily arranged. The most successful supplicant was Caltech, where Hale had recruited NRC insiders Alfred Noyes and Robert Millikan. These three experienced negotiators proposed large projects but always accommodated what GEB was willing to offer. They were also able to tap local Southern California boosters who believed that research would further economic development in the region. More than $3 million in grants from the GEB (and almost $1 million from the Carnegie Corporation) propelled the former Throop Institute into a major center of science and graduate education. Princeton provided another success, where two grants of $1 million anchored

16   Geiger, *To Advance Knowledge*, 149–60; Martin Bulmer, *The Chicago School of Sociology* (Chicago: University of Chicago Press, 1984); Andrew Abbott, *Department and Discipline: Chicago Sociology at One Hundred* (Chicago: University of Chicago Press, 1999); Donald Fisher, *Fundamental Development of the Social Sciences: Rockefeller Philanthropy and the United States Social Science Research Council* (Ann Arbor: University of Michigan Press, 1993): from 1925 to 1940 the SSRC awarded fellowships to 519 recipients and made 589 grants-in-aid (pp. 200–202).

17   The following draws on Kohler, *Partners in Science*, 162–232; and Geiger, *To Advance Knowledge*, 160–73, 183–89, 200–203.

leading programs in mathematics and theoretical physics. Matching funds were raised despite an alumni base oblivious to these subjects—or to academic research generally. However, similar GEB initiatives failed at Stanford and Cornell when those universities were unable to raise matching funds.

Public universities remained at a disadvantage, even after foundations began considering them for research grants. This was partly self-imposed: the Wisconsin trustees voted not to accept any "tainted money" from foundations. Rose nevertheless looked for opportunities to advance science in public universities, especially in the South. However, given the constraints of annual budgets, universities found it difficult, if not impossible, to afford matching contributions or pledge funding for future years. Although public universities had some excellent programs, their large science departments tended to be heavily inbred with many faculty who did no research, making them unattractive targets for general support. Presidents, too, were inexperienced in negotiating with foundations or respecting foundation intentions. A possible grant to Michigan's highly regarded program in quantum physics was scuttled when President Little tried to divert the funds to his own biological research. Rose finally made annual grants to the universities of Virginia and Texas under lenient terms, but overall GEB and IEB science support was given in large grants to private universities. Harvard received multiple awards, culminating in $3 million for a biology building; Chicago received almost $1.8 million. Rose climaxed his philanthropic career with two enormous pledges from the IEB: $6 million to Caltech for the Mount Palomar observatory and $8.5 million to James Breasted's Oriental Institute at Chicago—both projects admired by John D. Rockefeller Jr.

During their short tenures, Ruml awarded some $20 million for social science, and Rose, more than $13 million (1924–1928), mostly to universities. Both aimed to change the culture of American universities, the former by building a base for academic social science, the latter by fostering ongoing support for scientific excellence. Early in the decade, considerable skepticism still existed toward universities as places for research, given preoccupations with teaching, scant administrative backing for research, and departmental logrolling. By the end of the 1920s, there could no longer be any doubt that universities were the dominant institutions of American science. Foundation patronage and the direct influence of foundation officers pressured the handful of research universities to invest in and nurture productive scientists and programs. No foundation program was more valuable than fellowships. The original Rockefeller postdocs in the physical sciences were duplicated for medical science, by LSRM in the social sciences, by support for international exchanges by the IEB, and, after 1925, by Guggenheim fellowships. Postdocs emancipated promising scientists from their doctoral departments, allowed further intellectual development at a key point in their careers, and groomed them for appointments in leading departments. Americans who studied in Europe were eagerly sought by research universities, while European scientists who visited the United States often chose to remain. Large foundation grants were chiefly responsible for several strategic programs—genetics at Caltech, theoretical physics at Princeton, and the nation's most developed social science complex at Chicago. Beyond the large projects, foundation support for research made possible smaller projects (grants-in-aid) by thousands of academic researchers, thus encouraging universities to employ and nurture productive scholars.[18]

★　★　★

The impact of foundations on American higher education from the war to the Depression falls into two parts. The postwar years were dominated by visions of the coordination of industrial and academic science, midwifed by the great foundations. The NRC both symbolized and perpetuated this ideology of science: its first publication was "The National Importance of Scientific and Industrial Research." Although much lip service was paid to this ideology of science, its influence was most evident in engineering, where both university and state-sponsored engineering research stations came to perform extensive research for industry. Its signal initiative was the campaign to collect $20 million from industry for a National Research Fund dedicated to supporting university research. Inspired by Hale, chaired by Herbert Hoover, and supported by the NRC elite, the Fund was announced with great fanfare in 1925. But donors were unenthusiastic. Unable to raise half the original goal, it expired ignominiously with the onset of the Depression.[19]

Instead, the independent endeavors of Ruml and Rose overshadowed all other foundation activities for the last years of the 1920s. Their objectives were focused on universities and their respective sciences. Foundation leadership had evolved from the trusted associates of the founders with essentially industrial mindsets to professional philanthropoids who came from university backgrounds and viewed universities as key institutions for social progress. Historian Robert Kohler characterized this generation as "university handymen"—trained scientists, for the most part, who migrated into university administration,

18　Geiger, *To Advance Knowledge*, 167–73.
19　"The National Importance of Scientific and Industrial Research," *Bulletin of the National Research Council*, no. 1 (1919); Geiger, *To Advance Knowledge*, 97–98, 188–91; Bruce Seely, "Research, Engineering, and Science in American Engineering Colleges, 1900–1960," *Technology and Culture*, 34, 2 (Apr. 1993): 344–86; Lance E. Davis and Daniel J. Kevles, "The National Research Fund: A Case Study of Industrial Support of Academic Science," *Minerva* 12 (1974): 207–20.

gained experience in wartime agencies, and rose to leadership in the postwar foundations. This second phase of foundation activity extended only to 1929, when the Rockefeller Foundation was reorganized and Flexner, Ruml, and Rose retired. The reorganization was specifically intended to bring order and efficiency to the multiple Rockefeller philanthropic legacies and, henceforth, to preclude the kind of unchecked authority exercised by the three retiring barons. The 1929 Rockefeller Foundation absorbed the IEB and the LSRM into a structure with five divisions—international health, medical sciences, natural sciences, social sciences, and humanities. The new divisions were saddled for years with the commitments of their predecessors even before the Depression diminished their assets. However, a more modest and regular system emerged for supporting research, largely in American universities. [20]

The outpouring of foundation grants peaked during the most exuberant years of the Roaring Twenties. Their contributions were consequently overlain upon a university system that was experiencing its greatest period of material prosperity. The mid- to late twenties were years of extraordinary development, especially for American universities.

RESEARCH UNIVERSITIES IN THE GOLDEN AGE AND BEYOND

American universities came of age in the years between the World Wars. Considered provincial outposts in the world of science in 1914, they had become leaders in breadth and depth of scientific attainment by the time the world again descended into war. Universities tended to converge upon a common pattern in which faculty research and graduate education were institutionalized as valued and, in some cases, the most prestigious university activities. Unlike the initial formation of research universities, these developments were seldom inspired and led by visionary presidents. Rather, a combination of factors propelled an evolution toward university consolidation. Foundations contributed, as just seen. Voluntary associations of institutions and disciplines formed an organizational matrix in which academic advancement was encouraged. On campus, faculty were most responsible for undertaking the small acts of building departments, conducting research, and bolstering graduate programs. In large, decentralized universities, initiative for academic advancement passed to deans and departments, sometimes in spite of preoccupied or unsympathetic presidents. All this activity was accelerated by the extraordinary prosperity of the Roaring Twenties, especially the latter years. Philanthropy of unprecedented dimensions

20 Kohler, *Partners in Science*, 62–70, 233–62.

augmented the wealth of favored private universities, and legislators, while scarcely generous, significantly raised appropriations for at least some public universities. Who received this bounty, and how much, played a role in determining which institutions were able to advance as research universities. The distribution of the markers of academic success—highly rated departments, professors identified as "leading men of science," dollars for research, and PhDs awarded—was tremendously skewed. Edwin Slosson's "Great American Universities" of 1910, plus MIT and a single newcomer, Caltech, remained the principal universities conducting research and upholding academic quality throughout the interwar period.[21]

The postwar financial crisis quickly passed for most research universities. Fund-raising campaigns, now conducted by outside professionals, stretched into the early 1920s; enrollments and tuition revenues rose; and legislatures increased appropriations as the economy improved. Ten private research universities averaged $25 million in total annual gifts through most of the decade, although Harvard and Yale claimed half of these funds. For 1929–1930 this figure rose to $60 million, with Harvard and Yale receiving two-thirds. The five state research universities were more similar in size and finances. They ranged from 7,000 to 10,000 students in 1919 and 9,500 to 12,400 in 1929, a collective growth of 32 percent; however, their state appropriations increased on average by 127 percent. All these universities benefited from far greater resources by the end of the 1920s.

How universities got these monies affected what they did with them. Alumni were an important donor constituency for both public and private universities and hence influenced leaders and policies. Alumni proclivities leaned heavily toward students, the extracurriculum, and their own pleasures. Alumni donations helped to erect the football stadiums at California (1923), Illinois (1924), and Wisconsin and Minnesota (1925). Alumni provided funding for student unions where they could lodge and theaters where they were entertained, and they financed the building of many of the first dormitories. In addition, universities received some colossal individual gifts and bequests, the residue of Gilded Age fortunes inflated by wartime profits. William Cook financed the Law Quadrangle at Michigan, and the gifts of Edward Harkness built the residential complexes at both Harvard and his alma mater, Yale. Largest of all was the bequest of John W. Sterling (like Harkness, a Standard Oil millionaire) to Yale (1918) that provided almost $40 million for buildings and endowments over two decades.

---

21   That is, the universities of Chicago, Columbia, Cornell, Harvard, Johns Hopkins, Penn, Princeton, Stanford, Yale, California, Illinois, Michigan, Minnesota, and Wisconsin, plus the Massachusetts and California Institutes of Technology: Geiger, *To Advance Knowledge*, appendices, pp. 270–78. The following data are taken or calculated from these appendices.

The 1920s witnessed an accelerating building boom with results that can still be seen on these campuses.

Academic development, however, required greater general funds for departmental faculty. State research universities depended on legislative appropriations for roughly 80 percent of their budgets. Private research universities looked to endowment revenues, which varied more across institutions. Endowments provided between one-half and two-thirds of their revenues during the 1920s, with Columbia and Princeton slightly below that level and Penn at only half of that. The ten private "great universities" increased endowment income by an average of 140 percent from 1919 to 1929, and tuition revenue rose by 158 percent. In other words, in 1929 these universities had 29 percent more students and 2½ times more revenue. The five state universities had 32 percent more students and 2¼ times more revenue. This prosperity allowed universities to develop along multiple dimensions, with research seldom considered uppermost.

Universities valued academic achievement, but they were not yet structured to encourage it systematically. One problem was graduate education, which in the 1920s was open to all comers. A large number, particularly at state schools, were the universities' own graduates—some with genuine academic aspirations and others who had not yet found employment. Attrition was consequently high: even at Harvard, fewer than half of graduate students enrolled for a second year. The need to raise the bar for admissions became increasingly apparent but difficult to implement given departmental autonomy. Only Princeton deliberately limited the size of its graduate school (to 250) and was recognized for generally high quality. Change did not come until demand for graduate study increased at the end of the decade. Harvard in 1930 asked applicants to show some evidence of scholarly attainment but excluded few at first. Other universities soon followed this lead. In 1937, Columbia, Harvard, Princeton, and Yale joined in developing the Graduate Record Exam, which further aided selection. The steady growth of graduate fellowships bolstered this process. By the end of the 1930s, the leading graduate schools had evolved beyond eliminating the incompetent to seeking to identify and aid the most talented students. The number of PhDs awarded rose steadily in in the interwar years, doubling from 1927 to 1937 (2,709), and their quality undoubtedly rose as well. However, a national report in the late 1930s still stressed the need to raise standards in graduate admissions and doctoral education.[22]

Beyond mere finance, academic development required a stable academic profession, which scarcely existed before the war. The sparring of Pritchett

---

22 Ibid., 219–23; National Resources Committee, *Research—A National Resource* (Washington, D.C.: GPO, 1938), 184–86.

and Cattell was indicative of a larger controversy over the alleged domination of universities by conservative trustees from the business world versus the role and rights of faculty. In 1913 the principal social science associations sponsored a committee to consider the state of "liberty of thought, freedom of speech, and security of tenure for teachers." Its recommendations led to the formation of the American Association of University Professors (AAUP) in 1915. The AAUP was a moderate body led by some of the country's most distinguished academics, including Cattell and John Dewey. It sought to uphold academic freedom and assert reasonable terms of appointment. Under prevailing practice, faculty were legally appointed for a single year and could be terminated "at will." Of course, in reality appointments were automatically renewed—except on rare occasions when they were not, especially for political reasons. The AAUP's formation co-incided with two of those egregious exceptions: the University of Utah termi-nated four senior faculty for criticizing the administration; and the University of Pennsylvania dismissed Scott Nearing, whose economic teachings, politics, and eccentricities offended trustees. AAUP investigations failed to reverse these decisions, but both schools more or less promised not to do it again.

The succeeding years saw a flurry of such academic-freedom cases, as faculty rights were virtually abandoned during the war and subsequent Red Scare. These years saw Thorstein Veblen's polemic against the domination of universities by business trustees, *The Higher Learning in America* (1918, but written earlier), and Upton Sinclair's overdrawn tract, *The Goose Step* (1922). Ironically, the trustee domination they attacked was receding by these dates, and faculty power was making inroads against autocratic presidents. University issues were becoming more esoteric for lay trustees, and the matrix of higher-education organizations made arbitrary acts less tolerated. Certainly, faculty rights were respected at the research universities and soon throughout most of the system. In 1925 the Amer-ican Council on Education advocated a probationary period for new professors and due process for terminations. These measures were then endorsed by all the major institutional associations, although they were not binding on members. Thus, a tacit guarantee of academic freedom and tenure emerged for established professors, but the situation for more junior appointments was still murky.[23]

The enrollment explosion after World War I caused universities to enlist their graduate students as teachers. At Cornell in 1920, 55 percent served in this capac-ity. This practice blended graduate study and the beginning of a faculty career. Students benefited from teaching experience and welcomed the income, but in-stitutions needing teachers tended to make appointments for convenience rather than scholarly promise, first as TAs and then as instructors. This exacerbated two

---

23   Barrow, *Universities and the Capitalist State*, 166–77, 242–49, quote p. 170.

inherent problems: inbreeding and the absence of structure for promotion and tenure. The prevalence of their own graduates on the faculty was commonly 70 to 80 percent for instructors and more than 50 percent for full professors. Inbreeding fostered conservatism and complacency and lessened the receptivity to new discoveries—traits that the foundations were well aware of as they sought to seed new research. Universities consciously pursuing academic improvement typically sought to recruit recognized scholars from other institutions. Internal promotion often had to await such a call, which was not uncommon in the active academic marketplace of the 1920s. The result of this nonsystem tended to be departments containing some faculty engaged in research or scholarship and many content simply to teach. An abundance of middling instructors and assistant professors was common by the late 1920s. High-quality departments tended to endure, after a fashion, and strong departments could be built through aggressive and discerning hiring, but universities in the 1920s depended on individuals, not structures, to build or renew academic stature.[24]

★　★　★

The first rating of academic faculty—in terms of the relative standing of graduate programs—appeared in the 1920s. Lists and numbers of the "Leading Men of American Science," compiled by James McKeen Cattell from 1903 to 1943, were originally indicative of scientific strength but progressively less representative as Cattell failed to update his methodology. The first survey of academic peers was done by Raymond Hughes and Miami University in 1924. A second survey was sponsored by ACE in 1933 and also overseen by Hughes. The two studies reported results differently but are, nonetheless, indicative of conditions in doctoral education and, by implication, faculty research.[25]

What stands out is the dominance of Harvard, Chicago, and Columbia. In 1924, seven Harvard departments were rated first, and six were rated second ($N = 20$); Chicago had eight firsts and four seconds; and Columbia three firsts and six seconds; together these universities claimed thirty-four of the top forty ranks. They were clearly in a stratum by themselves, although the academic (and

24　Geiger, *To Advance Knowledge*, 219–28.

25　R. M. Hughes, *A Study of the Graduate Schools of America* (Oxford, OH: Miami University, 1925); R. H. Hughes, *American Council on Education: Report of Committee on Graduate Instruction* (Washington, D.C.: ACE, 1934): Both asked well-known scholars to evaluate graduate programs in their field, but the first employed a crude ranking while the second asked respondents to judge only "distinguished," "adequate," or "not adequate" for graduate study, where distinguished meant the top 20 percent. On Cattell: Kingsley Davis, Review of Visher, Stephen Sargent, *Scientists Starred, 1903–1943*, in '*American Men of Science*,' *Annals of the American Academy of Political and Social Science*, 257 (1948): 231–32.

financial) prowess of Harvard increasingly outdistanced the other two. In the next stratum, Yale, Princeton, Michigan, California, and Wisconsin had different combinations of superior departments. Cornell was competitive with this group, though weakening; Johns Hopkins was handicapped by the small size of its academic units but was a leader in medical science. Stanford, Penn, Minnesota, and Illinois operated on a lower stratum still but were better staffed for doctoral study than any of the rest of American universities.

By the early 1930s the most significant change suggested by the ACE study was a far greater number of departments rated as distinguished or, more accurately, considered by their peers capable of providing first-rate doctoral studies. Edwin Embree, an officer of the Rockefeller Foundation whose business it was to judge academic quality, then did what the ACE had sought to avoid—he consolidated minor fields and added ratings for medical sciences to construct a ranking of the eleven best American universities. Embree's ranks encompassed the first two strata from 1924, except that the University of California jumped to the top group; and the inclusion of medicine raised the ratings of Yale, Johns Hopkins, and number eleven, Minnesota. The methods by which departments were rated and counted affected this hierarchy, but more important than precise rankings is how each university managed academic advancement. [26]

Harvard, according to Embree, was "in a class by itself." This was an unexpected judgment on the presidency of Abbott Lawrence Lowell (1909–1933), who reigned as the anti-Eliot, placing greatest value on undergraduate education, socialization, and liberal culture. Lowell had an ambivalent attitude toward research and graduate education, accepting the preeminence of Harvard as axiomatic but often critical of mere scholarship and specialization in particular. This insular conceit, combined with control of appointments by departments and deans, meant Harvard retained many of its own graduates. Such graduates spent long years as tutors or instructors, preferring serfdom in Valhalla to citizenship in a lesser realm. Lowell was largely aloof from this process, intervening directly only in senior appointments, where he often preferred eminent foreign scholars like Alfred North Whitehead, recruited to philosophy in 1924, and Wassily Leontief and Joseph Schumpeter, who joined economics in 1931 and 1932. Still, Harvard's residual academic strength was owed largely to the bedrock academic values of its senior faculty—that, and the incomparable resources that Harvard offered in its collections, libraries, and research institutes. Harvard not only had the most members in the National Academy of Science and starred

---

26 Edwin R. Embree, "In Order of Their Eminence: An Appraisal of American Universities," *Atlantic Monthly*, 155 (June, 1935):652–64. Compare David S. Webster, "America's Highest Ranked Graduate Schools, 1925–1982," *Change* (May/June, 1983): 14–24.

faculty in *American Men of Science*, it also had awarded doctorates to the largest number so honored. However, James B. Conant (1933–1953), who succeeded Lowell, estimated that one-half of the Harvard faculty were scholars and half were "men who were not active or interested in the advancement of knowledge." Conant was selected as the anti-Lowell in order to change that.[27]

Conant was an insider but not a Brahmin. From a middle-class Boston family, he studied under Harvard's most distinguished chemist (AB 1913, PhD 1916), Theodore Richards, and followed his mentor (and father-in-law) onto the faculty and a distinguished scientific career. His criticism of Lowell's Harvard for softness in upholding meritocratic standards brought him to the attention of the corporation. He regarded Harvard's showing in the ACE rankings, for example, as "nothing to brag about . . . [T]here are four universities in this country which are running a neck and neck race and we have very little margin." As a scientist, he felt the university had a moral imperative to reserve Harvard's resources for the most capable scientists and scholars: "to fill one of these positions with a second-rate person was to betray a trust—to be guilty of almost criminal negligence." He consequently placed academic merit uppermost for students and faculty. For students, he is best known for instituting a system of national scholarships, based entirely on ability, to bring a leavening of talented students to the college from outside the Northeast. Harvard wished to compete for such students with Yale and Princeton, which recruited nationally using their dispersed alumni; but Conant raised the ante by offering more generous scholarships and selection by examination instead of interviews. For faculty, after a bruising battle, he established the principle of "up or out" for faculty appointments. That is, procedures for promotion were regularized so that junior faculty could hold a nontenured appointment for up to 8 years before they must be promoted or terminated. Conant's original challenge was to cull the large number of junior faculty who staffed Lowell's tutorial system, but the resolution went far beyond this problem. For promotion to tenure, junior faculty would now have to compete against external candidates, with an ad hoc committee of experts to determine who possessed the greatest merit, which chiefly meant recognition for research. When this system was fully implemented in 1939, Harvard was committed to appointing only the best available scholar or scientist to a tenured professorship. Conant not only reoriented Harvard toward a renewed commitment to excellence in graduate education and research, but his policies signaled

---

27   Embree, "In Order of Their Eminence," 655, 657n; Geiger, *To Advance Knowledge*, 193–96; Morton Keller and Phyllis Keller, *Making Harvard Modern: The Rise of America's University* (New York: Oxford University Press, 2001), 23; Henry A. Yeomans, *Abbott Lawrence Lowell, 1856–1943* (Cambridge: Harvard University Press, 1948), 275–90; Clark A. Elliott and Margaret W. Rossiter, eds., *Science at Harvard University: Historical Perspectives* (Bethlehem, PA: Lehigh University Press, 1992), 13–27.

to other research universities a course of action that, whether they favored it or not, would soon prove imperative.[28]

In conjunction with Harvard's Tercentenary, Conant contradicted the conventional wisdom: "It is because of specialization that knowledge advances, not in spite of it; and that cross fertilization of ideas is possible only when new ideas arise through the intense cultivation of special fields." At the University of Chicago, the nation's second-most distinguished university, President Robert Maynard Hutchins was engaged in a quixotic quest to displace specialization and empiricism, the basis of modern science, with metaphysical "truth."[29] He made a concerted effort in his first years to promote this Aristotelian/Thomist metaphysics in the university. However, his agent, Mortimer Adler, discredited the effort through arrogant contempt for and ignorance of the academic disciplines he disparaged. The philosophy department resisted Adler's appointment in an ugly fight that prompted four resignations and undermined confidence in Hutchins among the faculty. Afterward, as Hutchins focused largely on undergraduate education, metaphysics and Great Books tended to be ignored by the departments but remained ongoing preoccupations of Hutchins and Adler and thus a continual source of tension in the university.

More than any other American university, Chicago fit the image of an academic ivory tower. The multidimensional institution assembled by William Rainey Harper had, under his successors, shed much of its service mission and contracted around its academic core. During the 1920s, faculty hegemony, fortified by Rockefeller research dollars, reached its apogee. The reorganization that was in the works when Hutchins assumed the presidency reinforced this situation by grouping the departments in four divisions responsible for only upperclass and graduate instruction. Hutchins thus confronted a faculty with an outlook diametrically opposite to his own, and relations between them became increasingly strained. Hutchins was a notable defender of academic freedom. He sought the highest quality in professorial appointments, but given his disdain for academic scholarship, it was never clear what constituted the "good men" he claimed to seek. His influence was largely exerted by appointing sympathetic division heads. He failed in several attempts to undermine or bypass faculty governance. A gambit to abolish tenure for new hires was blocked, but he deferred deserved promotions for years. An AAUP investigation and report that criticized

28   Keller and Keller, *Making Harvard*, 24, 64–71; James B. Conant, *My Several Lives: Memoirs of a Social Inventor* (New York: Harper & Row, 1970), 81–179, quote p. 83; Richard F. Teichgraeber, "The Arrival of 'Up-or-out' Tenure: James B. Conant and the 'Tempest at Harvard,' 1936–1939," *Perspectives on the History of Higher Education* (forthcoming).

29   Keller and Keller, *Making Harvard*, 6; Conant's and Hutchins' views were so opposite that they engaged in humorous banter in correspondence: ibid., 27, 131.

these practices was simply ignored by Hutchins. He could be vindictive toward his many opponents on the faculty, often punishing entire departments. The philosophy department, after rejecting the Adler appointment, lost faculty, stature, and its "distinguished" rating in the ACE survey. Appointments and promotions were withheld from the history department, a subject Hutchins and Adler did not consider a discipline because it dealt with "facts." The humanities suffered most in the Hutchins years; the strong social sciences held their own; and the president largely ignored the biological and physical sciences. Law was the one field that Hutchins understood, and it was the only school that emerged as more robust. Hutchins had no interest in building academic departments because he did not value their mission of advancing knowledge. In fact, he tried several schemes to structure the university without them—the Hutchins College, the Committee on the Liberal Arts, and the Committee on Social Thought. After Hutchins' resignation, the next assessment of research universities placed Chicago sixth.[30]

The most famous university president of the interwar years was not Hutchins, but Columbia's Nicholas Murray Butler (1902–1945). He campaigned for the Republican presidential nomination in 1920, shared the Nobel Peace Prize in 1931 (for his role in the Pact of Paris outlawing war), and boasted in his memoirs of "warm friendship [with] almost every man of light and learning who has lived in the world during the past half-century." Although much of his activity in these years was devoted to building this résumé, he took great pride in presiding over a preeminent university. As a new president, Butler had declared, before Henry Pritchett, that universities ought to be run like corporations, and he centralized control over Columbia's many parts in the president's office, largely at the expense of faculty prerogatives. His initial strategy was to make Columbia the best university by becoming the biggest. By World War I, Columbia had the largest enrollments of graduate and professional students drawn from across the country and granted the most advanced degrees. Its faculty contained the leaders of numerous disciplines: Franz Boas in anthropology, Thomas Morgan in genetics, John Dewey in philosophy, Edward Thorndike in psychology, James Harvey Robinson in history, and Wesley C. Mitchell in economics. Its 56-year-old president was considered one of the most capable executives in America.

By the outbreak of World War II, Butler was still president—age 79 and much diminished in vigor and effectiveness. The schools and departments, long run on

30   Mary Ann Dzuback, *Robert M. Hutchins: Portrait of an Educator* (Chicago: University of Chicago Press, 1991); Edward Shils, "Robert Maynard Hutchins," *The American Scholar* (2001): 211–35; Philo A. Hutcheson, "In the President's Opinion: Robert Maynard Hutchins and the University of Chicago Department of History," *History of Higher Education Annual*, 17 (1997): 33–52; Geiger, *To Advance Knowledge*, 196–200.

autopilot, had not declined as much as the president, but only some managed to adapt to the more competitive conditions of the late 1930s. The signal achievements of the interwar years were not Butler's doing. The invention of general education and the revitalization of Columbia College were beneath his radar. The prolonged efforts to create a modern medical school—the Columbia-Presbyterian Medical Center—owed to Edward Harkness and incurred Butler's displeasure. Negatively, the Butler administration had a mediocre record of replacing the original generation of academic stars. Some were recruited away; some retired: however, no strategy of faculty building or rejuvenation was apparent. Columbia did not institute an "up-or-out" system until the midfifties. The cost of Butler's vanity, most egregious in his refusal to relinquish the presidency, would become more apparent after World War II.[31]

★   ★   ★

The devolution of responsibility for academic advancement from presidents to faculty is particularly evident in the five leading state universities. Presidents remain important for enabling this process—for sustaining a culture of academic excellence, for ensuring good relations with the polity, and for the structures and personnel that recognized a faculty role in university governance. The five "great" public universities were roughly similar in enrollments, faculty, and spending. They all experienced the rush of the Roaring Twenties and the pain of the Great Depression. Their relative achievements as research universities were the result of myriad conditions, but certain factors appear in each case to have retarded or furthered their development.

In 1913 John B. Johnston, anatomy professor at the University of Minnesota, published a radical critique of why "our universities . . . work so badly." He did not blame autocratic presidents, since they were "wholly at the mercy" of the deans and department heads on whom they depended "for information, advice, and executive assistance." Department heads "enjoy[ed] a remarkable liberty," often used in a self-serving, "*ir*responsible" manner. This system led presidents to mismanage university affairs and, worse, "lowers the efficiency and the moral and spiritual tone of the whole institution."[32] Johnston's candid critique is testimony that the devolution of authority in growing universities more often

31   Robert A. McCaughey, *Stand Columbia: A History of Columbia University in the City of New York, 1754–2004* (New York: Columbia University Press, 2003), 211–327, quote p. 215; Michael Rosenthal, *Nicholas Miraculous: The Amazing Career of the Redoubtable Dr. Nicholas Murray Butler* (New York: Farrar, Straus and Giroux, 2006).

32   J. B. Johnston, "University Organization," *Science*, 38, 991 (Dec. 26, 1913): 908–18: quotes pp. 909–12.

produced conservative "barons" rather than democratic faculty governance. But individuals could make a difference. After reading Johnston's article, President George Vincent appointed him dean of the College of Arts.

Indeed, Vincent shared Johnston's vision of a democratic university dedicated to teaching, research, and making "its store of knowledge practically available to its community." During his brief presidency (1911–1917), described as "the second founding of the university," Vincent revitalized the Minnesota faculty with careful appointments and gave it a voice with a University Senate. He also advanced medical education, despite opposition from medical school barons, by concluding an affiliation with the Mayo Clinic. Although he left in 1917 to become president of the Rockefeller Foundation, his influence endured through the appointment of other key deans. He recruited Guy Stanton Ford from Illinois as dean of the new Graduate School. He also raided Illinois for the dean of Education and his eventual successor, Lotus Coffman (1920–1938). All followed Johnston's dictum of opening the university to innovation, but each pulled in a different direction. Ford sought to identify productive scholars to advance the university in all its colleges. Johnston was fixated on rationalizing admissions by developing a model to predict college performance and sort students accordingly. Coffman believed that the university should offer opportunity to all who could benefit and implemented this by expanding the university offerings to fine arts, journalism, graduate business administration, and wider medical fields—as well as the General College. In his undisguised wish to monopolize all higher education in the state (and all higher education appropriations), Coffman's university sought to be all things to all people. He became a spokesperson and advocate for public universities in his home state and nationally, and both he and Ford were well connected in the associations and among foundations. However, he and his principal deans were united in the Vincent tradition of building the strongest possible academic faculty.[33]

The University of Michigan was well established as a research university, but in the 1920s it suffered from the ailment that Johnston had diagnosed—domination of schools and departments by academic barons, who often dealt directly with individual regents in budgetary and educational matters. In 1929, the university selected, Alexander Grant Ruthven (1929–1951) as president, who in 26 years had risen from accomplished zoologist, to director of the museum, to dean of administration. A dedicated research scientist himself, Ruthven was dismayed that research seemed to be optional for university faculty. He believed a university "can be no better than its faculty" and consistently sought to promote

33 James Gray, *The University of Minnesota, 1851–1951* (Minneapolis: University of Minnesota Press, 1951), 148; John B. Johnston, *The Liberal College in Changing Society* (New York: Century, 1930).

"original investigations." Acutely aware of the prevailing organizational senescence, he immediately took steps to remedy it. He severed the connection between deans and regents, removing the latter from a direct role in educational affairs and placing the former under direct scrutiny of the president. His most distinctive measure, known for a time as the Michigan System, was to establish vice presidents for buildings, university relations, and auxiliary enterprises. Although forming an additional layer of bureaucracy, these positions actually removed nonacademic tasks from the president, allowing him to devote more time to academic matters. For these, he displaced the ineffective senate (the total faculty) with a smaller university council of elected faculty and administrators. Ruthven's rationalization of the administration had the intended effect of empowering the faculty—and no doubt helped Michigan to preserve its academic standing through the two difficult decades of his presidency.[34]

At the University of Illinois, David Kinley, who practically ran the university during President James' last years, assumed the presidency in 1920 for the remainder of the decade (1920–1930). One can hardly imagine a more suitable choice; he had been a dean since 1894 and had upheld academic values for the College of Literature and Arts and the Graduate School. But some of that baggage compromised his tenure. As an autocratic dean, he had alienated many faculty and was openly contemptuous of certain academic departments (sociology, psychology). He genuinely supported 100 percent Americanism during the war, through the postwar Red Scare, and afterward. His conservatism was shared and encouraged by the trustees and the business community, whom he cultivated, but not by many of the faculty. Like other leaders of that era, he felt that students needed to be protected from radical ideas. He forced an historian with socialist leanings to resign and routinely vetted the politics of potential hires. He also held a view of the faculty typical of those times—that a few outstanding scholars were desirable but that most faculty were essentially teachers. There was a notable exodus of some of the university's best scholars, particularly in the humanities. One departing professor decried "the intolerance of independent opinion, the suppression of free speech, the everlasting paternalism . . . the failure to give democratic ideals even a hearing." There was general resentment against the absence of

---

34   Peter E. Van de Water, *Alexander Grant Ruthven: Biography of a University President* (Grand Rapids, MI: Eerdmans, 1977), quote p. 72; Alexander G. Ruthven, *Naturalist in Two Worlds: Random Recollections of a University President* (Ann Arbor: University of Michigan Press, 1963), 34–56, 117–20; Howard H. Peckham, *The Making of the University of Michigan, 1817–1992*, edited and updated by Margaret L. Steneck and Nicholas H. Steneck (Ann Arbor: University of Michigan Press, 1994), 193–243. The American Student Union's (see below) *Student Advocate* attacked Ruthven as "Academic Napoleon #1: Ruthven of Michigan" (Clifford McVeagh, Feb. 1936), largely for expelling student radicals: cited in Robert Cohen, *When the Old Left Was Young* (New York: Oxford University Press, 1993), 400, n.11.

intellectual freedom and excessive, petty regulations. Departments like engineering and chemistry operated largely in their own bubble. The latter, in fact, was the nation's largest producer of chemistry PhDs. But the pathology in the humanities and social sciences weakened those fields through the next decade.[35]

At the University of Wisconsin, the solid academic foundations established during the presidency of Charles Van Hise had to sustain the university through weak leaders and political turmoil in the interwar years. His successor, Edward Birge (1918–1925), had been dean of the College of Letters and Sciences since 1891 and belonged to an earlier generation. He saw himself as such, merely a caretaker, but that role dragged on for 7 years. The university went to the opposite extreme when it next appointed a youthful nonacademic, Glenn Frank (1925–1937). By the end of his tenure, the Wisconsin Idea began to seem like a bad idea. The notion that the university should be intimately involved in providing state services was a product of the close relationship of President Van Hise and Progressive Governor Robert La Follette. Birge endorsed this idea 20 years later, but it still carried political ties to Wisconsin Progressivism. A continuing political force in the state, Progressives felt entitled to control the university, which they largely did through the Board of Regents. When their opponents gained power in the capitol, however, the university budget tended to suffer. The impact of progressive moralism on the university was most evident in the 1925 Grady Resolution, refusing gifts to the university "from any incorporated Educational endowments or organizations of like character" (i.e., foundations). Inspiration came directly from Senator La Follette, who had written months earlier that the university's search for truth "is paralyzed by the subsidies, direct and indirect, of the Monopoly System."[36]

The same Progressive regents appointed *Century* editor Glenn Frank as president, although his candidacy was forwarded by a single regent, novelist Zona Gale. The regents' initial choice, the distinguished Harvard jurist Roscoe Pound, abruptly withdrew when he learned of "the intimate relation of university and its conduct to politics." An impartial scorecard would rate Frank a mediocre president.[37] Relatively popular at first, his shortcomings became increasingly apparent

35   Karl M. Grisso, *David Kinley, 1861–1944: The Career of the Fifth President of the University of Illinois*, PhD Diss., University of Illinois, 1980, quote p. 571. My thanks to Winton U. Solberg for insights into the interwar years at Illinois.

36   *The University of Wisconsin: A History, Vol. II, 1848–1925* by Merle Curti and Vernon Carstensen, 123–58; *Vol. III, 1925–1945* by E. David Cronin and John W. Jenkins, quotes pp. 67, 124, (Madison: University of Wisconsin Press, 1949, 1994). The Grady Resolution in practice only pertained to Rockefeller and Carnegie foundations and was rescinded in 1930.

37   The principal history of the university offers faint praise: Cronin and Jenkins, *University of Wisconsin, III*, 317–20; Frank's biographer emphasizes his personal failures: Lawrence H. Larson, *The President Wore Spats; A Biography of Glenn Frank* (Madison: State Historical Society of Wisconsin, 1965), 136–38.

with the difficulties of the Depression. He alienated faculty with the Experimental College and the public with an extravagant lifestyle. He was generally considered a poor administrator, preferring to delegate authority but failing to provide oversight. His academic ideas were derivative and not fully digested—not just the Experimental College but also a 1930 proposed reorganization of the faculty (never acted upon) into multidisciplinary "institutes"—a pipe dream apparently inspired by foundation support for such units at other universities. Addicted to self-promotion, he never connected with the university community or made the university his highest priority. These failings cost him the support of the La Follette family, and when they returned to power in Wisconsin, Frank's days were numbered. Nonetheless, his firing by the Regents was a political mugging that shamed the university. Still, the unseemly confrontation that surrounded the ultimate regent vote was prompted by Frank's own refusal to resign in a dignified manner—a final assertion of ego over duty.[38]

Given weak leadership in the interwar years, the faculty's considerable role in university governance only increased. This development was encouraged by the long stewardship of George Sellery as dean of the College of Letters and Science (1919–1942). Serving as acting president after Frank, Sellery symbolically signaled the end of the Frank era by declaring "I am a faculty man, bred in the faculty points of view and convinced of the superior wisdom of faculty conclusions in the matters entrusted to the faculty by the laws of the University." While other deans operated as barons, at least until the 1930s, Sellery worked closely with departments for most appointments. Wisconsin had the highest state appropriation of the public research universities before the war but the lowest afterward and the biggest decrease in the 1930s. It managed to recruit some new faculty to the university, but the standard approach was to find and retain promising junior faculty, often from its own departments. Agriculture was heavily inbred, but its departments and graduates were among the best; Engineering was equally inbred but with far less distinction. Economics chair John R. Commons rationalized that with Wisconsin's low salary scale, "we have to run our own seed-bed for future professors and take them when they are young." To a considerable degree, the solidarity of the scholarly community in Madison retained the loyalties of distinguished faculty. Faculty also benefited from dedicated research funds, voted by the legislature in 1919 and judiciously awarded first by the dean of the Graduate School and later by a faculty committee. These funds received a substantial boost from the Wisconsin Alumni Research Foundation, created by biochemist Harry Steenbock's selfless donation of his patent for vitamin D

38   Cronin and Jenkins, *University of Wisconsin, III*, 13–143, quote 37; G. C. Sellery, *Some Ferments at Wisconsin, 1901–1947: Memories and Reflections* (Madison: University of Wisconsin Press, 1960).

irradiation and dedicated to supporting research at the university. These funds reached $100,000 annually by the late 1930s, possibly the largest fluid research fund in the country. Wisconsin sustained its academic distinction during these trying years but was surpassed by the more dynamic University of California.[39]

California differed from other state research universities in significant ways. In the jockeying for power between president, faculty, and regents that occurred from the last years of Wheeler's presidency to the appointment of William Campbell (1923–1930), the Academic Senate emerged with predominant authority over curriculum and appointments. The longtime director of the Lick Observatory, Campbell scarcely wished to challenge faculty hegemony. As one department head told a recruit in 1928, "the conduct of this University now is really in the hands of the exact scientists." Moreover, the California faculty shared an underdog's ambition to have their far western outpost of learning challenge the eastern establishment. They recruited academic talent to Berkeley, particularly in the physical sciences. Unlike other universities, they refused to appoint their own graduates, and they hired all junior scientists from the ranks of NRC postdoctoral fellows. In 1928, a persistent recruiting effort dislodged from Yale E. O. Lawrence, a rising star and future Nobel Laureate who soon invented the cyclotron. The following year brought another prize when J. Robert Oppenheimer accepted a dual appointment with Caltech. Together they would lead what became the premier program in nuclear physics. But the university built excellent departments across the curriculum, as shown in the 1930s ratings. Academic distinction was assisted by a research fund provided by the legislature since 1915 and distributed by a faculty committee. This effort also benefited from a supportive and highly effective president.[40]

Robert Gordon Sproul (1930–1958) was a nonacademic with only a bachelor's degree, but unlike Glenn Frank he knew the university inside and out from 10 years as head of its financial office. Indeed, his mastery of detail and skill in defending the university budget before the legislature convinced the regents of his fitness. With academic governance safely confided to the senate, there was no faculty objection to a president from outside the guild. In fact, Sproul was fiercely loyal to the university and to its academic ambitions. Despite the stringency of the Depression, he attempted to support academic quality in the hiring, retention, and equipping of faculty. These efforts reinforced the loyalties of a

39   Cronin and Jenkins, *University of Wisconsin, III*, 464–515; National Resource Committee, *Research—A National Resource*, 179.

40   J. L. Heilbron and Robert W. Seidel, *Lawrence and His Laboratory: A History of the Lawrence Berkeley Laboratory*, vol. 1 (Berkeley: University of California Press, 1989), quote p. 23; Verne A. Stadtman, *The University of California, 1868–1968* (New York: McGraw-Hill, 1970), 239–57; Geiger, *To Advance Knowledge*, 211–13.

close-knit academic community. Sproul was exceedingly adept at fighting for the university. He was an eloquent speaker with a phenomenal memory. To minimize the damage of budget cuts necessitated by the Depression, Sproul spread the message of the value of the university to the state and its people. His speeches on radio and around the state were effective not just for their eloquence but also because he was perceived as a regular, middle-class, churchgoing, American—at one with his audiences. Sproul maintained this Sisyphean budgetary struggle at least as well as any of his counterparts through the Depression. The university's popularity was boosted by developing a presence throughout the state—the first multicampus state university. Most important was the southern branch in rapidly growing Los Angeles, vigorously promoted by powerful southern regents. Begun as a normal school in 1915, it offered bachelor's degrees in 1924 and graduate work after 1933. By 1936 it had 8,000 students, 600 in graduate courses. It required all of Sproul's charisma and political acumen to hold this "one great university" together, but it set a precedent for expanding the university's smaller units in Davis, Riverside, and San Diego. The University of California not only survived the Depression but emerged as a far-stronger institution—the foundation for postwar eminence.[41]

★ ★ ★

The university expansion made possible by the prosperity of the 1920s strengthened universities greatly in material and human resources without forcing significant structural adjustments. The austerity of the 1930s had the opposite effect, creating pressure to make their operations more efficient and effective by rationalizing key structural features, particularly for the faculty. For the research universities considered in this section, how well or poorly they adapted to the evolution of the academic profession was increasingly critical. Specifically, universities needed to incorporate expanding fields of knowledge, to encourage faculty research and funding from external sources, to seek active scholars in the academic marketplace, to delegate authority to departments for the democratic management of their own affairs, and to establish norms for promotion and tenure that would assure the recognition of competence and the elimination of mediocrity. This agenda for faculty development was the hidden history of universities in the 1930s and a premonition of the academic expansion that would follow World War II. Different universities fulfilled it to varying extents with different timetables. Presidents whose policies synchronized with it fared better than those that did not.

41 Stadtman, *University of California*, 257–80.

The conventional wisdom of the 1920s held academic research and scholarship to be narrow and overly specialized, as were its practitioners. Presidents who mouthed these pieties gained public approbation but set themselves against the intellectual tide. For Lowell and Butler, these sentiments echoed the previous decade's popularity of liberal culture; for Frank and Hutchins, they conveyed a facile sagacity. Presidents whose strong ideas about reforming university education contradicted the faculty agenda appear in retrospect to have retarded, if not harmed, their institutions. After the Experimental College fiasco, Frank proposed but never acted on further reforms; Hutchins pressed on with remarkable stubbornness and arrogance, founding the Hutchins College but alienating distinguished university faculty. Conversely, presidents without educational theories left the curriculum to the faculty. Sproul was deferential to the Academic Senate, took great pride in the scholarly accomplishments of the faculty, and shared that pride with fellow Californians. Only a handful of presidents, including Sproul, fully endorsed research as a primary university mission. Ruthven clarified this mission at Michigan but was wedded to an outdated suspicion of external funding. His opposition to sponsored research handicapped the postwar phase of his presidency. At universities with potentially conflicting missions, like Minnesota and Yale, graduate deans embodied and worked for academic advancement. Strident advocacy for research was displayed by only a handful of presidents besides Sproul and Conant: Isaiah Bowman at Johns Hopkins (1935–1948), a national spokesman from the NRC and the New Deal Science Advisory Board; the scientists who led Caltech; and Princeton physicist Karl Compton, who reinvigorated basic research at MIT (1930–1948). Conant, in particular, rationalized both graduate education and faculty careers. But others soon followed Harvard's lead, or that of the AAUP, which in 1941 endorsed a 7-year probation for assistant professors. By the end of the 1930s, the structural features of the modern research university had begun to coalesce, largely in the institutions considered here, where, in the words of a government report, "the staffs of all departments are selected with a view to research ability, [and] facilities and time are specifically available for research."[42]

STUDENTS AND THE GREAT DEPRESSION

The stock market crash in the fall of 1929 initiated a downward spiral that culminated in economic paralysis by 1932. For higher education, relatively few baneful effects were felt until the 1931 academic year, and hardship then became nearly

---

42   Geiger, *To Advance Knowledge,* 214–64; Ruthven, *Naturalist,* 118–19; Van de Water, *Ruthven,* 206–31; National Resource Committee, *Research—A National Resource,* 175.

universal from 1932 to 1934. The New Deal brought a fitful recovery for the economy, but higher education was more fortunate. The last half of the 1930s registered sustained growth in enrollments, albeit amidst continued penury. Colleges and universities generally emerged from the decade financially weakened but academically more developed.

Colleges and universities weathered the Depression far better than most other institutions (save the federal government). Few faculty lost their jobs. Most had to absorb salary reductions, typically 10 to 15 percent; but the cost of living declined by as much as 20 percent. Adjusted for deflation, professors at the end of the decade had their highest real incomes of the interwar period. However, this fact alone is misleading: universities employed large numbers of assistants and instructors, who were no doubt thankful for these opportunities in spite of low pay. For the research universities discussed in the previous section, income was essentially flat from 1929 to 1939, but faculty ranks grew by 45 percent.[43]

Enrollments decreased from 1931 to 1934 but then increased rapidly for a combination of reasons: New Deal programs for student aid, slight improvement in the economy, and especially lack of alternatives. For want of jobs, more students finished high school, and many continued their education for the same reason. These effects extended to the graduate schools, which some students preferred to poor or no employment. When enrollments declined in 1932, institutions lowered standards in order to generate badly needed tuition revenues. Such practices were widespread at eastern private colleges.[44] The paucity of paying customers helps to explain the national recruitment strategies adopted by Harvard, Yale, and Princeton. Liberal arts colleges did much the same by enlarging recruitment geographically and, sometimes, religiously.

Financially, the impact of the Depression was initially most severe for public colleges and universities, which depended on appropriations from hard-pressed state legislatures. However, enrollment trends in the 1930s favored the public sector. The preponderance of students had limited means and, by necessity, attended schools that were inexpensive and local. These conditions favored public junior colleges, which rose from 45,000 students in 1931 to 140,000 in 1940—10 percent of enrollments. State universities offered students greater possibilities for supporting themselves, and nearly two-thirds on average worked while studying, compared with fewer than half before 1930. Branch campuses became a popular means for meeting local demand from homebound students. In Pennsylvania,

---

43   Geiger, *To Advance Knowledge*, appendices B and C.

44   Jerome Karabel, *The Chosen: The Hidden History of Admission and Exclusion at Harvard, Yale, and Princeton* (Boston: Houghton Mifflin, 2005), 200; David O. Levine, *The American College and the Culture of Aspiration, 1915–1940* (Ithaca: Cornell University Press, 1986), 192–93.

where the state government had an aversion to supporting public higher education, branch campuses were originally launched by private schools—Bucknell and Juniata colleges and the University of Pittsburgh—and later extended by Penn State. Branch campuses proved far more robust in cities, and urban universities exploited them to expand their services and enrollments in the 1930s. In fact, all forms of mass higher education described in chapter 10 expanded in the 1930s as hard-pressed students sought locally available and career-oriented courses.[45]

These students tended to live at home, work part-time if possible, and have little involvement with campus life. Student culture was still largely defined by full-time residential attendees, the predominant constituency of colleges and universities.[46] For 2 years after the stock market crash, the mostly upper-middle-class students who embodied the youth culture were relatively unaffected by the deteriorating economy. Campus activities, rituals, athletics, and Greek life dominated student culture from the eastern colleges to the more democratic western universities. By 1932, at the depth of the Depression, effects were everywhere evident, from the sufferings of the unemployed to attrition of hard-pressed fellow students. Professional families, while better off, experienced significant shrinkage of income. Even the citadels of privilege were affected: Yale canceled Derby Day celebrations, and Vassar engaged in a polarizing debate before proceeding with its extravagant junior prom. A perceptible change in campus atmosphere occurred. The frivolity and social snobbery of the peer culture was eclipsed by a more serious approach to academic study. Students who struggled financially to remain in college could not afford the collegiate life style that had been glorified in the 1920s and instead appreciated their precarious opportunity to learn. The prestige of Greek life correspondingly eroded throughout the decade, although remaining a fundamental component of campus life. Underlying these trends was an apparent loss of faith in the 1920s' dogma that becoming a Big Man on Campus (BMOC) produced later economic success. This shift was given some empirical backing when a Harvard graduate, John R. Tunis (1911), unsettled his classmates by analyzing subsequent patterns of success. Phi Beta Kappas and unaffiliated graduates had by 1936 handily outperformed the BMOCs of athletics,

45 Geiger, *To Advance Knowledge*, 246–50; Levine, *American College*, 185–93; Michael Bezilla, *Penn State: An Illustrated History* (University Park: Pennsylvania State University Press, 1985), 153–55, 175, 217–20; U.S. Office of Education, *Biennial Survey of Education, 1938–40, 1940–42*, 2 vol., chapter IV (Washington, D.C.: GPO, 1944), 10–13.

46 By one undocumented estimate from the midthirties: "it seems probable that about 30 percent of the youth of college age among the people in the upper three deciles of economic ability go to college, less than 1 percent of those in the lowest three deciles enter college": National Resource Committee, *Research—A National Resource*, 184.

clubs, and activities. Also fading in the 1930s was the apolitical nature of campus culture as students expressed growing concern for political and social issues.[47]

Radical politics were virtually absent from American campuses in the 1920s. The Bolshevik Revolution had divided international socialism, and the purges of the postwar Red Scare scattered American radicals. The Young Communist League, taking its marching orders from the Soviet Comintern, focused on the proletariat and disdained college students as hopelessly bourgeois. Anti-Soviet American socialists organized the League for Industrial Democracy (LID) in 1921, successor to the Intercollegiate Socialist Society organized by Upton Sinclair in 1905. LID's approach to students in the 1920s was essentially didactic, presenting lectures on economic and socialist principals and organizing interested students into study groups. More concerned with addressing adult voters, it never attempted to mobilize a student movement or address campus issues. At the end of the decade it counted barely 1,000 student members. As an organized movement, radicalism was virtually a New York City phenomenon.[48] Instead, the most active campus force for liberal politics in the 1920s was the YMCA.

In an effort to remain relevant to its membership after the upheavals of the war years, the Campus Y embraced the social gospel. As the leadership explained, "now religion has to be concerned with the wider social conditions on campus, in racial and industrial affairs, and in international relations." In the 1920s The Y had little company in pursuing programs in those three areas. Its internationalism stressed first Christian, then ecumenical, world solidarity. It also rallied support for the League of Nations but then drifted toward disarmament and pacifism. Where the prewar Y had sponsored charity for the poor, the postwar Y inquired into structural forces that generated poverty, corporate greed, and inequality. Here too, there was a leftward drift; by 1930 both YM and YWCA joined forces with the LID to advocate economic justice, urging students to recognize their privileged status and its dependence on the sacrifices of labor. A growing concern for racial justice was certainly consistent with Christian morality, especially compared to the mushy thinking on internationalism and economic justice. Still, the Y had difficulty negotiating with its own Colored Work Department, and it was only partially successful in integrating its meetings—although this took heroic efforts in the Jim Crow South. These social

47   Robert Cohen, *When the Old Left Was Young: Student Radicals and America's First Mass Student Movement, 1929–1941* (New York: Oxford University Press, 1993), 3–21; Helen Lefkowitz Horowitz, *Campus Life: Undergraduate Cultures from the End of the Eighteenth Century to the Present* (Chicago: University of Chicago Press, 1987), 114–17; Robert Nisbet, *Teachers and Scholars: A Memoir of Berkeley in Depression and War* (New Brunswick: Transaction, 1992), 17–97; John R. Tunis, *Was College Worth While?* (New York: Harcourt, Brace, 1936).

48   Cohen, *Old Left*, 22–34.

commitments cost the Y a good deal of its former constituency. The prewar Y had broad appeal to evangelicals as well as BMOCs who preferred a comfortable, nondenominational piety. The postwar social gospel was profoundly out of step with the predominant collegiate culture, and both these types abandoned the Y. Students enrolled in its Bible-study classes—a staple of the prewar Y—declined from 38,000 in 1915 to 4,000 in 1930.[49]

In 1931, controversy over the suppression of a radical journal at City College led first to the mobilization of mostly Marxist radicals across New York universities and then to the organization of the National Student League (NSL).[50] Its first convention the next year attracted representatives from twenty-five colleges. While each chapter differed, most were directed by communist leaders who loosely adhered to the party line. The existence of the NSL stimulated a militant faction of LID students to organize their own publication and in 1933 to start calling themselves the *Student* League for Industrial Democracy (SLID). Both organizations were Marxist and endorsed the gamut of other radical causes, but the issue that had greatest resonance with American students was the antiwar movement. Widespread disillusionment with American involvement in World War I was galvanized in 1933 by the Oxford Union Pledge, a resolution passed by Oxford debaters "in no circumstance [to] fight for King and country." The NSL and SLID incorporated the Oxford Pledge into a National Student Strike Against War—a 1-hour "strike" and demonstration held on April 13, 1934, the anniversary of United States entry into World War I. With 25,000 students participating, this was the largest coordinated student action in the history of American higher education, even if 60 percent were in New York City. However, the 1935 strike far surpassed this total. The Y and other groups now signed on as sponsors, and 175,000 students joined from colleges across the country, including nearly 10,000 in California. The antiwar movement carried a radical message well beyond pacifism. It critiqued American involvement in World War I—"the Great Betrayal of 1917"—for furthering economic imperialism, capitalist profiteering, and the suppression of civil liberties at home.

The participation in the 1935 strike of about 15 percent of American college students indicated a rising degree of leftist sympathy on campus. That a substantial student movement emerged in the 1930s was in itself remarkable. The dominant political orientation of campus administration and faculty was tacitly Republican conservative. Most administrators, from presidents to deans, were horrified

---

49   David P. Setran, *The College 'Y': Student Religion in the Era of Secularization* (New York: Palgrave, 2007), 221–44, quote p. 221.

50   The following account of the student movement draws from Cohen, *Old Left*, passim, quote p. 79.

in 1934–1935 by the NSL strikes and their radical leaders. Upholding the doctrine of in loco parentis, they felt obligated to protect students from the contagion of communist or socialist ideas. They readily shared information on radicals with the FBI, which was assembling dossiers on thousands of college students. More directly, they banned antiwar demonstrations on campus, suspended or expelled radicals, and censored student publications. On some campuses conservative fraternity members and football players were encouraged to disrupt rallies. Among these nonspontaneous reactions, at Michigan State rally leaders were dumped into the Red Cedar River, and in Madison speakers at NSL and SLID gatherings were thrown into Lake Mendota. City College surpassed all other campuses in expulsions—some forty-three in 1933–1934—to little effect. Ohio State expelled seventeen, Columbia, at least seven, and Michigan, four.

These actions, and the suppression of student speech on campus, had precisely the opposite of the intended effect. Student sympathy for those victimized and outrage at the denial of civil liberties motivated ever-larger attendance at student rallies. The provost of UCLA, who was exceptionally paranoid even for this era, expelled five students for merely planning an "open forum." Huge protests in Los Angeles and Berkeley forced the intervention of President Sproul, who was no less opposed to student radicals but equally chary of negative publicity for the university. After investigating, he reinstated all five students but also promulgated a general policy prohibiting political advocacy on UC campuses.[51] Expulsions and suppression of student speech proved so counterproductive that universities largely abandoned these policies after 1935. But the political landscape changed as well.

The success of the 1935 strike led to a merger of the NSL and SLID to form the American Student Union (ASU). They papered over (temporarily) a fundamental rift between communists, who approved of any war for revolution or defense of the Soviet Union, and pacifist socialists, who clung to the Oxford Pledge.[52] That year marked the start of the Popular Front, when Comintern instructed communists to join other liberal and leftist groups, chiefly to oppose fascism. The next three student strikes, in 1936–1938, were larger than ever, mobilizing about 500,000 students and uniting a phalanx of socialist and liberal groups. The ASU consisted of just 20,000 members, but they supplied the principal leaders of the student movement. These individuals also retained affiliations with the NSL and the Young Communist League. However, the ASU now embraced the

---

51   Overcoming this policy of prohibiting political speech or activity on UC campuses became the object of the celebrated "Free Speech Movement" in 1964.

52   Collaboration in the ASU did not affect the core commitment of communists to the Young Communists League or of socialists to the Young People's Socialist League.

New Deal, becoming increasingly supportive of the Roosevelt administration and befriended in turn by the First Lady.[53] Identifying itself as liberal, the ASU advocated the peace movement, greater federal benefits for students, civil rights, and solidarity with the labor movement. The group now cooperated with university officials in planning symbolic strikes. The substantial participation in the student movement thus represented left-liberal sympathies for the New Deal combined with residual allegiance to the peace movement—all the while under covert communist leadership. Events soon undermined this precarious coalition.

The Spanish Civil War raged from 1936 to 1939, pitting the Spanish Republic, deprived of foreign aid by the very neutrality laws endorsed by the peace movement, against General Francisco Franco's fascist Nationalists, receiving substantial aid from Nazi Germany and Fascist Italy. American communists, following the lead of the Soviet Union, sought aid for the Republic, while most American socialists clung to antiwar convictions, causing a serious rift in the antiwar student movement.[54] Discord also plagued the leftists who fought for the Republic, resulting in turmoil throughout the American Left. Franco crushed the disunited Republican forces and Spanish democracy. Then, in August 1939, Hitler and Stalin signed the Nazi-Soviet Nonaggression Pact and proceeded to dismember Poland, thereby launching World War II in Europe. American communists performed an astonishing about face, repudiating the Popular Front against fascism and now rationalizing Nazi and Soviet aggression. This stark reversal of their former positions destroyed a common student movement in the United States. If any doubters remained, the perfidy of American communists was confirmed in November by their support for the Soviet invasion of defenseless Finland. American communism shriveled to a disciplined sect, faithful to the directives of the Soviet Union. The American student movement became fragmented and largely leaderless. Students were more concerned than ever about the situation in Europe but were now divided, like the nation, between advocates for readiness and opponents of intervention.[55]

The student movement of the 1930s was a new element in American higher education, but it coexisted with other crosscurrents on Depression-era campuses.

---

53 Eleanor Roosevelt and the president directly supported the American Youth Congresses, which was organizationally parallel to the ASU but inclusive of all youth and, hence, more politically potent. The ASU worked with the administration for passage of the American Youth Act, which would have expanded programs benefiting students but was not enacted.

54 Eileen Eagan, *Class, Culture, and the Classroom: The Student Peace Movement of the 1930s* (Philadelphia: Temple University Press, 1981), 169–82. For controversy on one campus: Peckham, *University of Michigan*, 213–23.

55 Conservative isolationism on campus was epitomized by the America First Committee, largely organized at Yale: Geoffrey Kabaservice, *The Guardians: Kingman Brewster, His Circle, and the Rise of the Liberal Establishment* (New York: Henry Holt, 2004), 72–82.

The majority of students came from middle-class families that suffered lower incomes even when still employed. The collegiate culture that had dominated in the 1920s persisted throughout the Depression, despite growing challenges, and was fundamentally antithetical to the student movement. That culture was both apolitical, in ignoring national issues, and Republican by default. The presidential election of 1936 revealed a changing political landscape on campuses when the Republican candidate received a minority of student votes (44 percent). The plurality of votes won by Roosevelt (48.3 percent) may have included the solidly Democratic South, but it clearly indicated that New Deal sympathies now contested bedrock collegiate conservatism. This change was reflected in elections to student government and liberal and radical editors of student newspapers. The newfound political activism arose not from despair at the Depression's depths, but afterward from the relative success of the New Deal and the proselytizing of the student movement. It was evident on working-class campuses like City, Hunter, and Brooklyn Colleges; at elite schools like Harvard, Columbia, Vassar, and Bryn Mawr; and at middle-class state universities. Its popularity was inextricably linked with antiwar sentiment—a temporary strength but longer term, a fatal flaw. The peace, or antiwar, movement was built upon a backward-looking disillusionment with the conduct and consequences of World War I. In retrospect, the war had failed to justify its overblown propaganda—neither making the world safe for democracy nor managing to end all war. Squabbles over reparations and war debts seemed to justify critics who explained the conflict in terms of imperialism and economic determinism. From the 1920s to the 1930s the consequences appeared increasingly perverse. The best and the brightest of the 1930s student generation, on the Left and on the Right, were deeply cynical toward their elders' pieties. Students were scarcely alone in allowing these "lessons" to blind them to the global realities of the 1930s. Certainly by 1940 this conventional wisdom was dangerously irrelevant, but only the Japanese attack on Pearl Harbor would banish it.

AMERICAN HIGHER EDUCATION IN 1940

American higher education in 1940 pressed forward with quotidian tasks despite premonitions of the turmoil ahead. No one knew that higher education stood at the end of an era—that soon the campuses would be emptied of students and converted to war work; that peace would bring a flood of demobilized soldiers and a new partnership with the federal government—in short, that the postwar world would bring a new era for American colleges and universities. Remarkably, at the end of the difficult 1930s, higher education had largely fulfilled the agenda of an era that stretched back to the Civil War. The last decades of the nineteenth century experienced three revolutions, both aspirational and actual, that transformed all aspects of higher education. The land grant revolution sought to expand access to higher education to a larger portion of the population and introduce curricula relevant to the productive economy. The academic revolution altered the foundations of the college curriculum and joined American scholars with international communities of peers dedicated to the advancement of knowledge. The collegiate revolution transformed the experience of college for residential students and the image of college in American society. Adapting to changes of this magnitude was an ongoing process, materially affected by developments and actors outside of higher education proper. For the most part, the first four decades of the twentieth century, and especially the 1930s, saw the gradual consolidation of those three revolutions into what became the modern American system of higher education. To appreciate this prolonged and multifaceted evolution requires viewing separate components of this system as they appeared in the years before the deluge of the 1940s.

STUDENTS. The 1940 census was the first to obtain data on educational attainment. It reported that 4.6 percent of adults (older than 24 years) had graduated from college, and another 5.5 percent had attended between 1 and 3 years without graduating. Thus, 1 in 10 American adults had matriculated at an institution of higher education, by far the highest proportion in the world. The ratio was highest in California at 1 of 7 and lowest in the east-central South at half that level. Those figures were sure to grow: by 1940 higher education enrollments had regained the pre-Depression growth curve with more than 15 percent of the age cohort attending—1.5 million regular students.[56]

Where did they come from? Public high schools. The number of high school graduates roughly doubled in the 1920s and again in the 1930s, reaching the unprecedented level of 51 percent of 17-year-olds. First-time students in higher education in 1939 represented 36 percent of those graduates. Contemporaries were aware of pronounced social stratification. Estimates for college attendance among the top third of family income ranged from 20 to 30 percent of college-age youth. College-going among those at the bottom of the economic pyramid was close to nil, as it probably always had been.[57]

Where did they go? Enrollment growth in the 1930s was strongly influenced by the hardships of the Depression. With many students forced to live at home

---

56   U.S. Office of Education, *Biennial Survey of Education, 1938–40, 1940–42*, 2 vol. (Washington, D.C.: GPO, 1944), II, 4: 5–20.

57   Robert Lincoln Kelly, *The American Colleges and the Social Order* (New York: Macmillan, 1940), 205; National Resources Committee, *Research—A National Resource*, I, 184.

and able to afford only low tuition, the institutions of mass higher education absorbed much of the growth. Junior colleges added 100,000 students in the decade, one-fourth of the total growth. Teachers colleges and normal schools tended to be more rural and failed to grow. Junior colleges grew from 15 to 20 percent of public enrollments, while teachers schools fell from 18 to 14 percent. Urban universities are not recorded as a separate category. However, from the late twenties to 1939, the New York City colleges and New York and Wayne universities added nearly 50,000 students. Beyond these trends, institutions varied considerably in their growth, with older institutions less likely to expand than new campuses serving local clientele. Research universities showed little growth, except for the urban campuses of California (Los Angeles) and Minnesota.

Secular trends favored the public sector. When junior and teachers colleges are counted, the public and private sectors neared parity by 1940. However, for 4-year colleges, universities, and professional schools, public enrollments increased from 39 to 45 percent in the 1930s. More important, there were three times as many private institutions, and public universities were on average four times larger. Size was a crucial advantage for incorporating modern curricula. Moreover, when states are compared, a large public sector and low tuition correlated with higher rates of enrollment and larger percentages of women. Superficially, women appeared to lose ground in the 1930s as their share of total enrollments shrank from 44 to 40 percent. Hard-pressed families probably placed a higher priority on educating sons than daughters. But women who did attend college supplied a steady 40 percent of the growing number of graduates. Data on college graduation corroborate reports that students became more serious toward their studies in the 1930s: while enrollments rose by 27 percent, graduates increased by more than 50 percent. Finally, American higher education was heavily professional. Just 45 percent of first degrees were awarded in arts and sciences. Among professional degrees, 20 percent were in education, and engineering and business had 7 percent each.[58]

MEDICAL SCHOOLS. The changing relationship between collegiate and professional education was one of the starkest transformations of this era. In the 1890s more law and medical degrees were awarded than bachelor's; furthermore, most of those degrees were awarded by proprietary schools to students who had not attended college. By 1940, both medical and legal education were dominated by the leading universities, which required for admission 2 or 3 years of college, if not graduation. Higher standards and selective admissions raised the level of

58   *Biennial Survey*, author's calculations; Claudia Goldin and Lawrence F. Katz, *The Race between Education and Technology* (Cambridge: Harvard University Press, 2008), 194–285.

instruction, especially in medicine. For both professions, the decade of the 1930s solidified these advances.

Conditions for professional education were set by state licensing authorities, professional associations, and associations of professional schools. The latter tended to institute the practices of the leading universities and accept as members only those institutions honoring them. For medicine in the decades after the 1910 Flexner Report, all three made it a common cause to raise qualifications for students and standards for instruction. By the early 1920s, the number of medical schools was halved, and medical student numbers dropped by 40 percent. Most schools now required 2 years of college science for admission. This was just the foundation for a modern system of medical education. Its subsequent evolution was largely propelled by internal factors.[59]

The Roaring Twenties were a golden age for medical schools, with unprecedented voluntary support and ample appropriations at state schools as well. Faculty numbers multiplied, and enrollments grew as almost all qualified applicants were admitted. Among the seventy-seven schools still remaining, Harvard displaced Johns Hopkins as the nation's largest and most fully developed. Another fifteen emulated those two leaders in conducting some research and keeping abreast with the frontiers of medical science. Perhaps forty more schools performed little research but offered sound, up-to-date medical education. In fact, the MD course had become sufficiently standardized that students received similar training at any of these schools. Only at the bottom, largely impecunious schools faced a constant struggle to meet rising standards, but even there, accreditors now worked to improve these schools, not shut them down.

The Depression forced some retrenchment at medical schools and ended expansion, but overall the 1930s brought consolidation and improvements in quality. Research intensified, in part stimulated by rapid progress in treating acute disease and the prestige this brought to medical science. The emphasis on clinical sciences in the 1920s, though perhaps overdone by Flexner, encouraged close attention to patient observation and care. American medical schools also dominated preclinical sciences, especially biology and biochemistry, so that basic science developed in close proximity with medical science. Finally, philanthropy sustained the expansion of research: in the first third of the twentieth century; nearly one-half of foundation-giving to higher education went to medical schools ($154 of $339 million), and Abraham Flexner claimed that the $50 million of Rockefeller money he disbursed from 1919 to 1927 was leveraged by a factor of ten. In 1928, the foundation switched its grants from medical education

---

59 The following draws on Kenneth M. Ludmerer, *Time to Heal: American Medical Education from the Turn of the Century to the Era of Managed Care* (New York: Oxford University Press, 1999), 26–101.

to medical research, contributing to the concentration of research funding in medicine. These exertions made American medical science the best in the world and enhanced education as well.[60]

By the late 1920s medical schools limited enrollments in response to a rising tide of applicants. With less than half of applicants being admitted, the abilities of medical students rose significantly. By the late 1930s, one-half of medical students were college graduates, and attrition was only 15 percent. Medical students were likely the most adept group of American students, and their course may have been the most demanding—20 hours of class per week, supplemented by dissections, laboratories, and ward visits. In the 1920s internships became standard following the MD, and in the 1930s residencies for medical specialties became the rule for top students. The culture of medical schools supported close contact between students and professors, so that training kept pace with the latest findings of medical research. By 1940, medical schools had largely achieved the integration of research, education, and service that would characterize postwar universities, but they also epitomized the social prejudices of the era. Medical schools were the most blatantly anti-Semitic precincts of the higher-education establishment; African Americans knew not to bother applying; women were admitted by quota, if at all (6 percent in 1939). In all things except medical science, the medical professoriate, mirroring the profession, would long be the most conservative element in a generally conservative academy.

LEGAL EDUCATION. University legal educators aspired to follow the professionalizing path of medicine but faced conditions much like pre-Flexner medical schools: burgeoning enrollments in low-quality commercial schools for mostly part-time students. After 1920, the American Bar Association (ABA) and the Association of American Law Schools (AALS), which consisted mostly of members recognized by the ABA, were the foremost exponents of reform. Their menu for the upgrading of legal education included: a 3-year course of full-time study (or 4 years part-time); adoption of the case method; 2 years of prelegal college study for admission; a minimum library of 7,500 volumes; at least 3 full-time instructors; and the requirement of legal education to take the state bar exam. But reformers had little leverage as long as states failed to raise requirements for taking the bar examination and practicing law. Unaccredited schools, moreover, resisted or evaded any tightening of standards. When some states required high school graduation, for example, proprietary schools established their own 1-year high school course for their students.

60   Geiger, *To Advance Knowledge*, 252–53.

At the end of the 1920s, as total enrollments peaked above 46,000, the 67 law schools with ABA accreditation enrolled only one-third of law students. At this point the tide began to turn. One state after another mandated 2 years of prelegal college education. The Depression seemed to accelerate this process, as rather self-serving complaints were widely voiced of overcrowding in the legal profession. In 1940 one reformer could declare a victory of sorts: "the most significant trend in the legal education field today is toward elimination of unapproved law schools and adoption by the states of a requirement prescribing law study in a recognized law school." Now, 102 of the 180 law schools were approved by the ABA, and they enrolled two-thirds of law students. Legal education was dominated by the university party in the ABA and AALS, which sought to impose a high bar academically and socially. However, law remained less socially exclusive than medicine, since non-ABA schools still provided a social safety valve. If not yet a postgraduate course, the study of law had definitely become a postcollege subject.[61]

BUSINESS EDUCATION. For 17 years after its 1881 founding, Penn's Wharton School was the only collegiate school devoted to the study of commercial subjects. Across the country, however, a rising tide of instruction in high schools and private schools taught business skills from typewriting to bookkeeping. In 1898, the universities of California and Chicago established colleges of commerce, and business took off as a university subject. By 1913, 25 university business schools were operating, including graduate programs at Dartmouth (1901) and Harvard (1908). A decade later, 132 colleges and universities offered business majors. In the mid-1920s, perhaps 60,000 students were studying commerce or business administration, and 5,500 annually earned bachelor's degrees. Business studies originated with the academic leaders of American higher education but quickly became a growing component of mass higher education. As with other professions, the academic leaders soon sought some measure of control. In 1916, 16 business school deans met at the University of Chicago and laid the basis for the American Association of Collegiate Schools of Business (AACSB). Their ambition from the outset was to transform their colleges into professional schools and obtain recognition for business graduates as professionals. As a profession similar to medicine and the law, they envisioned businesspeople having stature in the community, assuming social responsibilities, and playing a role in public affairs. This was largely an academic vision, nurtured by deans who

---

61 Robert Stevens, *Law School: Legal Education in America from the 1850s to the 1980s* (Chapel Hill: University of North Carolina Press, 1983), 155–204; American Council on Education, *American Universities and Colleges*, 4th ed. (Washington, D.C.: ACE, 1940), quote pp. 122–23.

directed AACSB schools. The same vision had motivated a few business leaders, notably Joseph Wharton and Edward Tuck, who endowed Dartmouth's Tuck School of Administration and Finance. It was regarded with some skepticism by most academics, who doubted that business had sufficient theoretical knowledge to justify a place in the academy, and by a good many corporate leaders, only half of whom were college graduates. Nor was it clear how professional status might be achieved. Make business a *wissenschaftlich* academic field, as first attempted by Edmund James at Wharton and later by the University of Chicago's PhD program (1920)? Aim for the formation of a managerial elite, with suitable cultural and intellectual grounding to lead American corporations? Or, develop the technical specialties that are the lifeblood of the business economy?[62]

The AACSB promulgated fairly lenient standards for membership: a separate school or college in a reputable university, degree requirements including both liberal and business subjects, and qualified faculty. However, in 1930 just forty-two schools were members (fifty-two in 1940)—prominent public and private universities and a few private urban universities. Even this select group harbored great variety. Collegiate business education assumed four basic patterns. A bare majority of AACSB members offered a 4-year undergraduate course in the business school: most others, especially in the Midwest, began business studies with the junior year after 2 years of liberal arts; Dartmouth and Michigan offered a master's degree in 5 years—3 undergraduate and 2 in business, and Harvard, later joined by Stanford, offered business only as a graduate, master's course. Harvard's graduate business school was most adamantly fixated on elevating management to professional status. It borrowed the case method from the law school and used it to good advantage. Debating cases in class allowed the school to instill a management perspective toward firms and industries, but this approach was too demanding to be adopted in undergraduate programs. With a liberal arts education, a Harvard MBA, and school or family connections, Harvard graduates could aspire to be gentleman stewards of business enterprises. Lacking such inherent advantages, Dartmouth sought to advance the careers of its graduates by cultivating social networks and esprit de corps and additionally established the first placement office. The Wharton School, in contrast, was recognized for teaching the technical specialties of business practice, and its experience was probably closer to the mainstream for business schools.[63]

---

62   Rakesh Khurana, *From Higher Aims to Hired Hands: The Social Transformation of Business Schools and the Unfulfilled Promise of Management as a Profession* (Princeton: Princeton University Press, 2007).

63   James H. S. Bossard and J. Frederic Dewhurst, *University Education for Business: A Study of Existing Needs and Practices* (Philadelphia: University of Pennsylvania Press, 1931); Khurana, *From Higher Aims*, 100–136.

Enrollments at Wharton mushroomed after the war until they were capped in the midtwenties at around 2,200, with hundreds more in extension and evening classes. With the second-largest business faculty (after NYU), Wharton offered more than 100 individual courses covering numerous special topics. The main subjects taught everywhere were (under various titles) marketing, management, accounting, and finance, but Wharton also taught insurance, transportation, real estate, advertising, and more. Only the certified public accountant course had state licensing, like medicine and law. This represented one model of professionalization—monopolization of a critical technical skill. Wharton hoped (in vain) to duplicate this pattern with a certificate in insurance, where it had the premier program, but this credential reflected only the department's reputation. Wharton's older alumni were dismayed by the influx of middle-class, careerist students, criticizing it as "mass education"—exactly what it was. The market forces driving enrollments in business education and the revenues of business schools were those described in chapter 10 as mass higher education; but such conditions were a far cry from elevating management to a genuine profession.[64]

The discontent at Wharton generated a reform movement in the 1920s that sought to deemphasize specializations in favor of more generic business principles. The movement was led by Joseph Willits, a Wharton PhD with industry experience, who was named head of the "Department of Geography and Industry" in 1919. Under Willits this department became the home of management studies, particularly his own specialty of personnel management. As head of the curriculum committee, Willits advocated a greater emphasis on science and fundamental business courses and specifically sought to have specialization delayed from the second to the third year. Behind these issues lay the domination of the school by the powerful heads of the specialized departments.

To strengthen his case, Willits commissioned an exhaustive study, *University Education for Business*, by two Wharton faculty. Based on a survey of Wharton alumni and data from AACSB schools, the authors found that only one-third of the alumni were employed in the specialized fields they had studied and that alumni rated general business and liberal arts courses more highly than specialty courses, which most considered excessive. Perhaps more discouraging for Wharton, graduates from the lower third of the classes seemed to have more successful careers (i.e., higher earnings) than classmates in the top third. The data on faculty were also dismaying. Just over one-quarter of business school faculty held a PhD, but about the same number had only a bachelor's degree or less (the rest had mostly master's degrees). Patterns at other business schools varied

64 Steven A. Sass, *The Pragmatic Imagination: A History of the Wharton School, 1881–1981* (Philadelphia: University of Pennsylvania Press, 1982), 163–200.

widely, but the largest programs seemed to depend most heavily on what today are called adjunct faculty. At Wharton 32 of 138 faculty were full or associate professors and at Illinois, the third-largest school, 19 of 80. Without naming names, the study observed that some business faculties "show a preponderance of time servers and mediocre neophytes who have just drifted or been shifted together." After prolonged debate, in 1932 the Wharton faculty voted for a new curriculum that aimed to teach business fundamentals in the first 2 years and reserve specialization for upper-division studies. Actual change was incremental but indicative of the school's direction. The next year Willits was named dean and soon addressed the faculty issue.[65]

Willits' signal objective was to raise the academic stature of the Wharton School. Perhaps one in six faculty engaged in original investigation, which was at least as good as any other business school. Some schools had research bureaus that conducted descriptive studies of or for industries, but they employed full-time research staff, who had little connection with faculty. Willits directed a more ambitious Industrial Research Department that tapped foundation support for academic studies, but it too was unconnected with instruction. The Wharton faculty was heavily inbred, and its powerful department chairmen placed little value on scholarship or research. Willits quickly altered this regime by requiring a PhD degree and intellectual accomplishment for hiring and promotion to regular faculty positions. He also leavened the faculty with external scholars, most notably future Nobel laureate Simon Kuznets. Willits and Kuznets, soon joined by others, formed an ongoing research relationship with the National Bureau of Economic Research in New York, and applied economics emerged as Wharton's outstanding research thrust.

With this newly concentrated expertise, Wharton faculty addressed issues arising from the national economic crisis. Rather than clinging to laissez faire doctrines, Willits led the Wharton faculty in studying topics vital to the New Deal, such as labor economics and national accounts. Elsewhere among AACSB schools, the Depression brought considerable soul searching and a revival of the quest to establish business as a profession, especially one that would mobilize the social responsibility of businessmen to ameliorate the crisis. According to business school historian Rakesh Khurana, these efforts were the last gasp of the professionalizing project, which would fade away with the war. The Wharton School under Willits, on the other hand, achieved a more durable form of professionalism by joining business studies to the rigor of academic disciplines. Although still providing "mass education" to undergraduate

---

65   Bossard and Dewhurst, *University Education*, passim, quote p. 531; Sass, *Pragmatic Imagination*, 178–97.

and part-time students, Wharton exemplified a movement toward academic consolidation.[66]

LIBERAL ARTS COLLEGES. The Bureau of Education listed 734 colleges and universities in the United States in 1940. Although colleges and universities might be distinguishable as ideal types, the bureau included both types in this category, as well as some in between. Still, despite a few professional or graduate programs, three-quarters of those institutions operated and identified as private colleges, and together they enrolled perhaps one-third of undergraduate students in this category. America was still a "Land of Colleges," as David Potts had described it in 1828. As then, colleges varied enormously in terms of resources and academic development, but before 1860 they were the foremost institutions of higher education. By 1940 they were underdogs, defending their model within an increasingly crowded higher-education system.[67]

In 1939 the Association of American Colleges (AAC) celebrated its twenty-fifth anniversary. Evolving from the Council of Church Boards of Education, its core was and remained private liberal arts colleges, most of which were still controlled by or related to a denomination. However, the difficulty of representing the interests of so heterogeneous a collection of schools was an ongoing challenge. The result was a rather diffuse organization, lacking leadership from among its natural constituency. It made, and then withdrew, overtures to junior colleges and, then welcomed the liberal arts units of universities; soon some public universities joined as well. Representatives of private universities were the chief spokespersons to and for the AAC on national issues and the principal interpreters of liberal education. On issues directly affecting the colleges, the AAC membership was decidedly defensive. Most AAC colleges faced the challenge of catching up with the academic revolution. Members were united in opposing the creation of additional, competing colleges, and the prevailing trend toward standardization threatened to impose requirements they could scarcely meet.[68] Each of these colleges served a more-or-less defined constituency, and the greatest concern was sustaining or augmenting the flow of students, revenues, and gifts from those sources. Adaptations to national trends in admissions, curriculum, or

66   Sass, *Pragmatic Imagination*, 201–32; Khurana, *From Higher Aims*, 176–92. In 1939 the talented Willits was appointed Director of the Social Science Division of the Rockefeller Foundation, the most influential position in American social science.

67   Institutional data are derived from the *Biennial Survey, 1939–1940*; and the American Council on Education, *American Universities and Colleges* (1940).

68   Hugh Hawkins, *Banding Together: The Rise of National Associations in American Higher Education, 1887–1950* (Baltimore: Johns Hopkins University Press, 1992), 16–19, 41–44, 88–90, 97–103; "The Efficient College," *AAC Bulletin*, 2, 1 (Feb. 1916): 13–14.

student activities had to be filtered through those imperatives. Few of the experiments in undergraduate education of the previous decades affected rank-and-file AAC colleges.

Private colleges benefited from the prosperity of the Roaring Twenties by expanding enrollments, adding faculty, and increasing tuition. By the end of the 1930s, AAC colleges focused on a new set of issues. The 311 members of the National Conference of Church-Related Colleges were apprehensive about the waning ties with their sponsoring churches. Financial contributions from the faithful were falling, and support from the churches was disappearing. Children of church members attending colleges of their faith also registered notable declines for all but Catholics and Southern Baptists. These trends seemed to be undermining the finances, mission, and constituencies of church-related colleges.[69]

The decline of liberal arts majors, blamed on the Depression, was a national concern. Although often publicized by university presidents, it was a survival issue for the colleges. Nationally, freshman enrollment in liberal arts colleges declined from 75 to 60 percent in the 1930s. Although the AAC spoke principally for liberal arts colleges and the members embraced that identity, they were, in fact, part of the problem. Like the multipurpose colleges of the nineteenth century, they offered practical courses, often of dubious quality, to please their constituencies and buoy enrollments. The head of the AAC exclaimed, "Colleges of liberal arts in too many cases are adding as many courses as they can from the curricula of universities." In 1939, for example, 8.5 percent of bachelor's degrees in liberal arts were awarded to students majoring in commerce.[70] In another sense, the AAC defense of liberal education rang increasingly hollow. Meiklejohn's notion of the "Liberal College" was routinely invoked, but seemingly without his insistence on the "life intellectual." Robert Kelly, longtime head of the AAC, would have the American liberal college embrace just about everything—"science and philosophy and religion . . . things domestic, ethical, civic, social . . . things [that] are beautiful in God's creation and in human character . . . [and] things [that] have been made beautiful by the rare gift of man's artistic touch." A definition of the liberal college encompassing all of these subjects was no definition at all.[71]

Some dismay was expressed at the AAC about the vast increase in college going. Allusions were made to Minnesota's General College, where "almost any

69　Kelly, *American Colleges*, 266–84. Kelly was executive director of the AAC from 1917 to 1937 and received a grant from the Carnegie Foundation to write this overview.

70　James L. McConaughy, "Report of the President," *Bulletin of the AAC*, 24, 1 (Mar. 1938): 90–97; John L. Seaton, "Report of the President of the Association of American Colleges," *Bulletin of the AAC*, 25, 1 (Mar. 1939): 88–98, quote p. 87.

71　Kelly, *American College*, 216, 205.

one who manages to get through a high school may be admitted." The AAC also expressed concern for the opposite situation—talented students who were unable to attend higher education. Of the top 2 percent in terms of IQ, by one estimate, only one-half were able to attend college. The Association recommended that existing scholarship aid be redirected to increase the numbers of superior students.[72]

Finally, the federal government under the New Deal emerged as a phenomenon the colleges could not ignore. In 1938 Congress contemplated providing financial aid to public institutions and changing student aid under the National Youth Administration in ways that favored public institutions (neither enacted). At the same time, several state governments floated measures to tax private colleges. The AAC had from the first opposed government intrusions into higher education and often expressed the threat posed by the steady expansion of tax-supported institutions. Now they found their financial health directly imperiled. In response, the president resolved to move AAC headquarters from New York to Washington, D.C.[73]

Although each private college was unique, some sense of the sector can be had by examining it in the populous, industrial state of Pennsylvania. For the 1939 academic year, the Bureau of Education identified 45 private colleges of all types.[74] They can be divided between the 18 colleges on the "approved list" of the Association of American Universities (AAU) and the other 27 colleges. Since 1913 the AAU had certified a list of institutions whose graduates were assumed to be prepared for graduate study. At first, the qualifications were largely based on college resources, but in 1924 inspection visits were added. Precise standards are murky, but institutions on the approved list clearly aspired to be recognized as having academically credible programs. The majority of American colleges not included on the list, by implication, did not choose to compete at that level, that is, preparing students for graduate study. Hence, a meaningful difference in academic standards distinguished the 161 colleges (of 250 institutions on the approved list) from the rest.

Among Pennsylvania's approved colleges, 3 belonged to the highest echelon in terms of endowments (> $11,000/student) and students per faculty member (< 8). Bryn Mawr was a women's college, Haverford, a men's, and Swarthmore, coeducational—and all were outside Philadelphia with Quaker roots. The remaining 15 Pennsylvania colleges were remarkably similar and broadly representative. Three women's colleges had 300 to 400 students, $1,000 to 2,000

72   Seaton, "Report," 97; McConaughy, "Report," 94–95: This talent loss would only be recognized as a national problem in the 1950s.

73   McConaughy, "Report," 91–93; Kelly, *American College*, 285–99.

74   The following institutional data are derived from the *Biennial Survey, 1939–1940*; and the American Council on Education, *American Universities and Colleges* (1940).

endowment per student, low student/faculty ratios, but relatively few faculty PhDs. The 4 men's colleges were strongest on average, with 500 to 900 students, endowed at $1,300 to $4,000, and near 50 percent faculty PhDs. The 8 coeducation colleges had 500 to 900 students (except for outlier Bucknell with 1,300), 12 to 18 students per faculty, and endowments of $1,000 to $2,000 per student. All these institutions were substantially dependent on student tuition for their operating income, in part because tuition had been raised considerably since 1920.[75]

By the late thirties, these colleges tended to be dominated by one or more powerful alumni trustees, who wished to discard outmoded practices, strengthen the colleges academically, and bolster their reputations.[76] Businessmen trustees generally sought to displace lingering clerical influence, overcome logrolling by a complacent faculty, and improve the academic performance and college experience of students. Franklin & Marshall was particularly effective in these areas after its wealthy trustees appointed an alumnus from industry as president. Known for a premier premedical program, the college had sought to maintain tuition revenues with virtually open enrollments, even failing to drop students for academic reasons. In order to attract better students, President John Schaeffer (1935–1941) copied the Harvard and Swarthmore practice of offering merit scholarships—with similar positive results. He went further in mobilizing faculty and alumni to actively recruit for the college. By 1940, the college had boosted its enrollment by more than a third from the depression low, upgraded the quality of students and faculty, and substantially enlarged the physical facilities.[77]

Modernization at Bucknell University occurred in two stages. Homer Rainey was a rising star in college administration when he was recruited to the presidency (1931–1935). One of the few college leaders to articulate a coherent vision of liberal education, he pledged to transform Bucknell to "keep pace with changing social demands." He launched a thorough survey by the faculty of all its activities. The resulting recommendations, accepted in 1932, centralized the administration and reorganized the university into lower and upper divisions with comprehensive examinations required for advancement. Rainey aspired to

75 Tuition ranged from $300 to $400, and $1,000 of endowment in 1939 would produce at most $40 of annual income. Tuition growth at Gettysburg College was typical: $100 in 1915, $200 in 1924, $300 in 1929, and $350 in 1939: Charles H. Glatfelter, *A Salutary Influence: Gettysburg College: 1832–1985*, 2 vol. (Gettysburg, PA: Gettysburg College, 1987), II, 428. Having 50 percent of faculty with PhDs was quite good, but this figure often reflected the subjects being taught, since PhDs were scarce in fields outside the arts and sciences.

76 These developments continued the changes described by W. Bruce Leslie: *Gentlemen and Scholars: Colleges and Community in the Age of the University* (New Brunswick: Transaction Publishers, 2005 [1986]).

77 Sally F. Griffith, *Liberalizing the Mind: Two Centuries of Liberal Education at Franklin & Marshall College* (University Park: Pennsylvania State University Press, 2010), 181–203.

do much more, especially to raise the conditions and accomplishments of the faculty, However, the depths of the Depression prompted retrenchment instead. When Rainey moved on in 1935, the trustees appointed one of their own, Arnaud Marts (1935–1945), first as acting and then as full president. Marts proved successful at fund-raising and expanding the campus, but he was also committed to enhancing the school's prestige for teaching and learning. He placated faculty members unsettled by Rainey's reforms, and he made developing the library a high priority as an indispensable component of academic respectability. He bolstered the engineering programs so that they qualified for national accreditation. In 1940 Bucknell received a chapter of Phi Beta Kappa—a symbolic marker of quality and commitment to the liberal arts.[78]

Similar accounts could be given of other Pennsylvania colleges. At Methodist Dickinson, the president of the Board of Trustees dominated the college after 1934 through his activism and philanthropy. Neither a Methodist nor a teetotaler, he relentlessly pursued modernization and secularization in emulation of leading eastern private colleges. The Lutherans of Gettysburg College were more insular, but they steadily displaced Lutheran minister trustees with successful alumni from business.[79] In general, the experiences of these Pennsylvania colleges were representative of national trends. Many colleges adopted a divisional structure, which was a convenient way to unseat superannuated heads of tiny departments. Programs in music and fine arts were often established. Departments were invigorated through the hiring of newly minted PhDs, and greater academic respectability brought increasing support from alumni and the local business community. This trend no doubt reflected the academic consolidation taking place in universities and among the top echelon of colleges.

Private colleges nonetheless remained intensely focused on their students. Efforts to improve performance with comprehensive examinations were common. Colleges took a critical stance against intercollegiate athletics, especially football, prompted in part by a 1929 exposé published by the Carnegie Foundation.[80] They also took measures to mitigate the excesses of freshman hazing and barbarous fraternity rituals. But fraternities were an integral part of college life and, often, the principal provider of student residences. The prominence of collegiate activities and athletics appeared to be rebounding by the end of the 1930s, epitomized by the fad of goldfish swallowing sparked by Harvard in 1939. Despite the trials

78   J. Orin Oliphant, *The Rise of Bucknell University* (New York: Appleton-Century-Crofts, 1965), 269–303. Marts was head of a fund-raising firm.

79   Charles Coleman Sellers, *Dickinson College: A History* (Middletown, CT: Wesleyan University Press, 1973), 341–60; Glatfelter, *Gettysburg College*.

80   Howard J. Savage, *American College Athletics* (New York: Carnegie Foundation for the Advancement of Teaching, 1929).

of the Depression, private colleges, or at least those on the AAU approved list, ended the decade with more and better faculty and, often, sounder finances.

UNIVERSITIES AND AMERICAN SCIENCE. The most fateful achievement of higher education in the interwar years was the ascent of American science to preeminence in the world. In the mobilization of science during World War II, both the depth of expertise and the sheer number of experts provided a marked superiority over the Axis powers. By 1940, the best of those scientists were associated with universities and, if anything, more concentrated in the research universities than ever before. Thus, as the locus of scientific and academic expertise, universities were indispensable in developing this capacity. Here, only a sample of fields can be highlighted.

The rise of American physics was the most dramatic exemplar. Americans already were accomplished experimentalists, but significant theoretical advances all took place in Europe. The last half of the 1920s witnessed a revolution in the understanding of atomic theory, and in this case Americans participated as eager students and postdocs. As Americans returned and assumed university posts, the United States became the locus for extending and exploiting these breakthroughs. By 1930–1933, the American *Physical Review* was the most cited journal in the field. In 1932, three discoveries by American physicists would subsequently win Nobel prizes. Institutional factors lay behind these achievements. The postdoctoral fellowships funded by the Rockefeller Foundation allowed Americans to attend European centers of theoretical physics and join the revolution. Other foundation support brought young European physicists to American universities. This international community of physicists found a congenial and supportive home in American universities. Leading universities eagerly hired atomic physicists and provided them with support unequaled elsewhere. The careers of Oppenheimer and Lawrence at Berkeley, described earlier, exemplify this process. The twenty leading departments in the 1920s employed 40 percent of physics teachers, produced 75 percent of articles in *Physical Review*, and trained 90 percent of physics PhDs. Physics PhDs nearly doubled in the 1930s—the largest relative increase of any major discipline. This thriving field was further enriched by the immigration of displaced or discouraged European physicists, who readily found refuge at these same universities.[81]

American medical science distinguished itself earlier than physics. By the 1920s the United States surpassed all other nations in medical discoveries. The

81 Spencer B. Weart, "The Physics Business in America, 1919–1940: A Statistical Reconnaissance," in Nathan Reingold, ed., *The Sciences in the American Context: New Perspectives* (Washington, D.C.: Smithsonian Institution Press, 1979), 295–358; Kevles, *Physicists*, 267–86; Geiger, *To Advance Knowledge*, 233–45.

causes were similar: the institutionalization of research and a research ethos at the principal medical schools and ample funding from both foundations and internally generated funds. At Harvard, the nation's wealthiest medical school, expenditures rose from $300,000 in 1912 to $1,200,000 in 1935 while class size remained stationary at 125. Harvard also set a pattern for the increasing autonomy of medical schools, largely based on their capacity to raise external funds through research grants and philanthropy. These two revenue streams were complementary and not just at Harvard—philanthropy built the faculty and facilities that earned research awards, which in turn enhanced prestige and further giving. Medical science also forged into new areas of inquiry. Lawrence garnered additional funding for his ever-larger cyclotrons by employing them for radiation therapy, in itself an important advance. Biochemistry, largely developed in medical schools, oriented toward medical applications. When it was recognized as a separate discipline, it awarded the third-largest number of science PhDs (122 in 1939). Genetics and molecular biology were American-dominated fields closely related to medicine and also receiving significant foundation sponsorship. The preeminence of American medical science was recognized by twelve Nobel Prizes from 1925 to 1950.[82]

American achievements in the human sciences were evident in the two most organized fields, psychology and economics. In both cases, developments during the interwar years were largely achieved by university-based scholars, but developments in both disciplines were accelerated by wartime applications. Experimental psychology in the United States had been inspired by Wilhelm Wundt, whose student, Edward Titchener, became its foremost exponent and teacher at Cornell. A self-consciously pure *wissenschaftlich* science, psychology was mobilized during the war for mental testing. Afterward, experimental psychology would thrive in university departments, complemented by psychological laboratories, but further interest arose from demand for applications to mental testing and education. Psychology doctorates quadrupled from 1915 to 1929, with Columbia in the forefront. In 1929, when the Ninth International Congress of Psychology was hosted by Yale, the United States contained more professional psychologists than the rest of the world combined, and they produced one-third of published papers in the field. Membership in the American Psychological Association would continue to grow in the 1930s (150 percent). American psychology encompassed a host of different theories and approaches, but it clearly was ascendant in both the number of researchers, quantity of empirical findings, and established applications.[83]

82   Ludmerer. *Time to Heal*, 30–39.

83   James H. Capshew, *Psychologists on the March: Science, Practice, and Professional Identity in America, 1929–1969* (New York: Cambridge University Press, 1999), 15–38: two-thirds of psychology

For economics, the wartime need for accurate data for the mobilization of the American economy prompted empirical research for the War Industries Board. The desire to extend and complete this work was seized upon by economists who wished to transform their field through rigorous quantitative investigations. They chartered the National Bureau of Economic Research (NBER) in 1920 under Columbia economist Wesley Mitchell (1920–1945), the foremost American economist of the era. During the 1920s NBER studies sought to probe the workings of the economy through detailed quantitative studies of national income and business cycles, among other topics. With the onset of the Depression, the need for such data became all the more urgent. The NBER was committed to deriving economic facts without suggesting policies, which suited its foundation supporters, principally the Rockefeller group. The research was accomplished chiefly by university professors, who were paid for part of their time. NBER studies produced authoritative knowledge of previously uncharted aspects of the American economy and solidified a tradition of rigorous quantitative economic research. However, this institutionalist approach was superseded in the next decade by new economic theories.[84]

The most renowned economist of the 1930s was John Maynard Keynes, but the academic work that most advanced the discipline largely occurred in the United States, chiefly at Harvard. According to Paul Samuelson, the Harvard department contained the best and the worst of the discipline. However, it was "in the forefront of the three great waves of modern economics": the Keynesian Revolution, in which Harvard clearly led; "the monopolistic or imperfect competition revolution"; and the mathematical and econometric analysis of economic phenomena. The economists who led these revolutions—the best of the department—were all recruited to Harvard in the 1930s. In other words, Harvard's leadership was scarcely accidental. This work, and soon Samuelson's own work, established the foundation of American predominance in economics, which became glaringly obvious after World War II.[85]

The rise of American science occurred without an appreciable contribution from the federal government. Although this suited the scientific leadership of

---

PhDs in the 1920s were awarded by Columbia, Chicago, Iowa, Johns Hopkins, Cornell, Stanford, Harvard, and Pennsylvania (p. 21).

84   Solomon Fabricant, "Toward a Firmer Basis of Economic Policy: The Founding of the National Bureau of Economic Research" (NBER, 1984); Mark C. Smith, *Social Science in the Crucible: The American Debate Over Objectivity and Purpose, 1918–1941* (Durham, NC: Duke University Press, 1994), 49–83; Yuval P. Yonay, *The Struggle over the Soul of Economics: Institutionalist and Neoclassical Economists in America between the Wars* (Princeton: Princeton University Press, 1998).

85   Paul A. Samuelson, "Economics in a Golden Age: A Personal Memoir," in *The Making of Modern Science: Biographical Studies* (New York: Norton, 1972), 155–70, quote p. 164. After the war, Harvard forfeited that leadership through timid appointments: Keller and Keller, *Making Harvard Modern*, 80–85.

the 1920s, the situation changed as private monies dried up in the Depression. MIT President Karl Compton used his position as chairman of the Science Advisory Board (1933–1935) to advocate federal support for nongovernmental science. President Roosevelt appeared to be persuaded, requesting a proposal and a budget. Compton overcame opposition from conservative scientists on the board and submitted a plan for annual federal expenditures of $5 million for scientific research. This plan was then torpedoed by social scientists on the National Research Board, who objected to a policy that funded only the natural sciences. Instead, they proposed to develop a more comprehensive plan that would aid all academic fields and government science bureaus too. However, no general support for science would emerge from the New Deal. Proposals foundered on how research funds would be allocated: by peer-reviewed, best-science awards vetted by the national academies, the approach favored by the scientific community, or distributed to states, like land grant funds, the formula favored by most state universities and their legislators. Instead, the National Resources unit produced a comprehensive description of research in the United States, intended as both a factual depiction and an implicit case for new federal policies.[86]

Research—A National Resource, adopting a fairly loose definition, estimated that 50,000 research workers were employed in the country in 1938, 15,000 in universities. Although universities were awarding 2,700 PhDs annually, only one-fourth to one-third of them persisted in research positions. Consequently, it argued, universities were training roughly half the number needed simply to replenish the ranks of research workers. Total research expenditures at universities were generously estimated to be $50 million: $16 million from government sources for agriculture and another $3 million from states for other purposes.[87] Of the rest, $17 million was estimated to come from endowments and another $12 million from foundation grants and private gifts. Thus, outside of agriculture, university research was overwhelmingly dependent on past and present private philanthropy. The report included a lengthy list of measures to strengthen university research. It particularly emphasized attracting and supporting more and better graduate students through fellowships, selective admissions, and postdoctoral awards. However, the growing needs of university research required more money. For this the report looked chiefly to the federal government, without offering any specifics. In Washington fashion,

---

86   Geiger, *To Advance Knowledge,* 255–62.

87   The $50 million figure for 1938 is a generous figure that includes estimates for faculty time, etc. The NSF figure for *separately budgeted university research* for 1953, the first year such calculations were made, was $37 million, or $20 million in 1938 dollars.

Research—A National Resource merely presented carefully selected facts and invited legislators to act.[88]

THE AMERICAN SYSTEM OF HIGHER EDUCATION

The Roaring Twenties was a decade of explosive growth in students, innovations, financial resources, and popular notoriety and admiration of higher education. The depression decade of the 1930s was a time of consolidation and standardization in which the multiple components of the American system of higher education crystalized. Together, these entities constituted what sociologists have termed an *organizational field*—"organizations that, in the aggregate, constitute a recognized area of institutional life." Organizational fields, once established, strongly support tendencies for institutions to become more alike: emulation of more prestigious or successful institutions; the coordinating influence of associations of like institutions; pressure from organizations representing essential activities; strengthening professional networks and norms; and the influence of vital constituencies.[89] All these processes were evident in the interwar consolidation of American higher education. In fact, they were present in the three major revolutions that shaped twentieth-century higher education.

The land grant movement affected American higher education directly through the institutions it spawned and indirectly through the values it inculcated of broad access and advanced instruction in practical fields. By the 1930s agriculture, originally the most problematic field, had evolved into the most organized system, uniting autonomous university colleges of agriculture with the federal Department of Agriculture and corresponding state units. The 1887 Hatch Act, funding agricultural experiment stations, inaugurated the building of this multilayered system. The 1914 Smith-Lever Act provided the keystone of this structure by creating the Agriculture Extension System. County extension agents, supported by federal and state funds, linked the expertise of the agricultural colleges with the knowledge needs of practicing farmers. The 1917 Smith-Hughes Act added funds for education in agriculture and home economics, and subsequent legislation embellished these benefits. Colleges of agriculture became more closely tied to state and federal governments than to their own universities.[90] Interestingly, the universities that adhered most

---

88   National Resources Committee, *Research*, I, 167–91.

89   Paul J. DiMaggio and Walter W. Powell, "The Iron Cage Revisited: Institutional Isomorphism and Collective Rationality," in Walter W. Powell and Paul J. DiMaggio, eds., *The New Institutionalism in Organizational Analysis* (Chicago: University of Chicago Press, 1991), 63–82, quote p. 64.

90   Nathan M. Sorber and Roger L. Geiger, "The Welding of Opposite Views: Land-Grant Historiography at 150 Years," *Higher Education Handbook of Theory and Research,* forthcoming.

narrowly to this system seemed to have difficulty adapting to other aspects of the American system. The Ag and A&M colleges of the nineteenth century were anachronisms after 1900, their deficiency becoming most glaring in doctoral education.[91]

The system of engineering education and research, which evolved partly under private auspices, encompassed more than land grant institutions, although they harbored most large departments. The associations of the different branches of engineering date from the 1880s, and the joint Society for the Promotion of Engineering Education dates from 1893. Best practices and mutual concerns were addressed periodically through surveys sponsored by the engineering societies, the Carnegie Foundation, and the U.S. Office of Education. In 1932 seven engineering associations jointly formed the Engineers' Council for Professional Development, which undertook responsibility for accrediting engineering programs. Accreditation by the 1930s had become the chief means for voluntary quality control. By 1940, the Engineer's Council had approved some 500 programs in 118 of the 150 institutions offering engineering degrees. By that date, 38 states had established engineering research stations. All attempts to garner federal support for them failed, and they were poorly supported by their respective states. However, their chief purpose was to provide a venue for contract research for industry. Such activities were widespread in the major engineering schools as well as their respective stations and formed another means of coordination. Engineering was, consequently, heavily oriented toward the practical needs of industry both in education and research.[92]

In the twentieth century, leadership in new practical arts passed from the land grants, except for subjects linked with agriculture (home economics, veterinary medicine). The largest addition was business, and here flagship and urban universities dominated the AACSB-approved list, not A&Ms. Much the same could be said for thirty-two programs in journalism and thirty in library science approved by their respective professional associations. Perhaps the largest addition of applied studies after 1900 was the elevation of teacher education, where accreditation in 1940 was controlled by the American Association of Teachers Colleges. In the most notable change, three-quarters of students at teachers colleges now took a 4-year degree course. More vocational still was the advocacy for

91   Roger L. Geiger, "Land Grant Colleges and the Pre-modern Era of American Higher Education," Morrill Act Land Grant Conference, Mississippi State University (October 3–6, 2012). Iowa State University was a partial exception, being the first to grant PhDs: in 1928 it conferred 26 of 36 PhDs awarded by A&M schools. Doctoral production at A&M's improved by 1935–1937: National Resources Committee, *Research*, I, 172: Penn State ranked twenty-ninth with 69 doctorates; Purdue was thirty-third with 58.

92   Institutional information from ACE, *American Universities and Colleges* (1940); Seely, "Research, Engineering, and Science," 344–86.

terminal education within the junior college movement. The practical arts and expanded access went hand in hand. For the first generation of land grants, the access frontier was the island communities of rural America, but in the twentieth century that frontier was in the cities. Land grant universities—and non–land grant public universities—had provided most of the places for burgeoning cohorts of high school graduates. However, by the interwar years, urban universities and junior colleges accommodated a new constituency of location-bound students. By 1940 the land grant movement was probably more influential in promoting the ideal of expanding higher education to all classes; certainly it had no special claim to enrolling such students.

The collegiate revolution might appear to be quintessentially a local phenomenon, since its principal agents were fixated on their own campuses. However, systemic elements were long present and became more pronounced in the 1930s. The fraternity movement, dating from the 1820s, was the first effort by students at coordination across campuses and became a salient feature of college life. Extensive coordination of student life and activities was accomplished by the Campus Y, whose huge membership was overseen by a central administration. An additional dimension of coordination evolved out of necessity in athletics. Originally organized solely by students, an enormous amount of planning and management was required to arrange matches, rules, travel, logistics, and leagues. The ephemeral American Student Union may have been a new departure, but students had long forged links across campuses to promote their interests.

After 1900, as universities gradually displaced student control in assuming responsibilities for these activities, new forms of coordination were called for. The National Collegiate Athletic Association (1905) initiated more extensive and orderly coordination of athletics—a never-ending task. For other aspects of collegiate life, the process was more protracted. Well into the twentieth century, many of the tasks of orienting students, finding lodgings, and organizing activities were handled by the Campus Y. Universities appointed deans of women in the 1890s to deal with the special needs of coeds; deans of men were appointed after 1900 largely to handle—or prevent—disciplinary problems as well as to oversee student organizations, especially fraternities. Deans of women began to confer informally in 1903 and formed an association in 1916; deans of men did the same in 1919. Regular communications among deans thus tended to standardize the handling of student issues. By the late 1930s, both men's and women's deans were challenged by the rise of student personnel services. Focused on guidance and counseling, proponents of student personnel took a more professional approach to these tasks and fit more readily into the bureaucratization of all student services, a trend that triumphed after 1945. With bureaucratization, the deans' original role as advocates for students was eclipsed by efforts to promote efficiency and order.[93]

The academic revolution ushered in a thoroughgoing system of intellectual authority. Disciplinary associations and publications created an organizational superstructure for academic subjects in which the scientists and scholars who made the greatest contributions were accorded the greatest authority and resources. The reward system of science thus served as a kind of gyroscope guiding the advancement of knowledge and the development of the research universities. The contributions of foundations proved strategic because they tapped into this system—relying on individuals whose knowledge and integrity had been certified in their respective disciplines. This ideal largely informed the scientific-academic system, but its assimilation into universities was a prolonged and incremental process. From the academic revolution of the 1890s, universities—in fact, just a small set of universities—gradually conformed their practices in hiring, promotion, graduate education, and encouragement of research to the norms of this system. Already in 1906 this value system allowed Cattell to identify the "leading American men of science," and the 1920s saw explicit rankings of departments and universities. Foundations accelerated academic advancement in the 1920s and 1930s by providing the resources and incentives to motivate universities in these directions. They also sustained intermediate organizations, such as the National Research Council and the Social Science Research Council, that furthered these ends.

The formation of the Association of American Universities (AAU) in 1900 appeared to provide an elite coordinating body for the system of research universities, and, indeed, university presidents debated fundamental questions during its first decade. After World War I, however, it devolved into a meeting of graduate deans, preoccupied with the "minutia of graduate education." Nor was the AAU particularly effective in this domain, since progress on rationalizing doctoral education occurred only in the 1930s and still left much room for improvement. Similarly, standards for promotion and tenure were clarified only at the end of the 1930s, despite consistent prodding by another coordinating body, the American Association of University Professors. In fact, despite the achievements of American science already noted, the number of institutions identifying with the practices of research universities remained limited. The fourteen institutions identified by Edwin Slosson in 1909 as the "Great American Universities" employed the largest numbers of starred (distinguished) scientists 30 years later

93 Robert Schwartz, *Deans of Men and the Shaping of Modern College Culture* (New York: Palgrave, 2010); Jana Nidiffer, *More Than Wise and Pious Matrons: Pioneering Deans of Women* (New York: Teachers College Press, 2000).

(from 33 to 113). Universities invited to join the AAU after World War I had from 4 to 21 starred scientists. A similar pattern existed for the number of PhDs awarded, particularly in the arts and sciences. These very large discrepancies are a telling indicator of stasis among the academic leaders of the university system. They suggest, first, that for all the benefits of foundation patronage, it provided incentives only for a limited number of institutions to commit resources to academic advancement. Even these universities advanced to varying degrees, but elsewhere universities were likely to impose heavy teaching loads and make few provisions for research. Second, as a system, universities were relatively inefficient in terms of research. These deficiencies were listed in *Research—A National Resource*, but in essence, too many American PhDs, the stock of potential researchers, were either not motivated to engage in research or held positions that made it difficult.[94] American science in 1940 rested on a solid, but narrow, academic base.

Indeed, the American system of higher education in 1940 was highly segmented. The numerous supporting organizations served to make that segmentation—and hierarchy—more explicit. At the top of the hierarchy, the most prestigious institutions rested on their individual reputations but still were choosy about the company they kept. The AAU was formed as an elite organization but gradually admitted additional institutions. Although membership henceforth still carried some distinction, the diminished cachet may have been a factor in the desertion of the presidents. The elite women's colleges began informal discussions in 1915 and in the 1920s organized the Seven College Conference, better known as the Seven Sisters. Harvard, Yale, and Princeton concluded a Three Presidents Agreement over athletics after World War I, and in the 1930s, sportswriters referred to a larger group of "ivy colleges." But an athletic agreement between the Big Three and "a few of our other natural rivals and friends" waited until 1945.[95] The rank and file of colleges and universities could be sorted into tiers. Having a chapter of Phi Beta Kappa marked a commitment to liberal arts and a respectable curriculum. In the 1930s it had 125 chapters and twice as many inquiries to form new chapters. The AAU Approved List continually expanded in the interwar years, reaching 250 institutions in 1940. Less demanding still, approximately 700 colleges and universities were accredited by the five regional associations. And below them were unaccredited institutions.

---

94 Audrey N. Slate, *AGS: A History* (Washington, D.C.: Association of Graduate Schools, 1994), quote p. 41; National Research Committee, *Research*, 171–89.

95 Hawkins, *Banding Together*, 37–41; Mark K. Bernstein, *Football: The Ivy League Origins of an American Obsession* (Philadelphia: University of Pennsylvania Press, 2001), 177–80: other members of the Ivy League were Brown, Columbia, Cornell, Dartmouth, and Penn. The Seven Sisters were: Barnard, Bryn Mawr, Mount Holyoke, Radcliffe, Smith, Vassar, and Wellesley.

An institution's position in the vast American system was thus pegged by these many independent organizations.[96]

In most countries, the role and status of institutions of higher education would be determined largely by governments. This was the case for only minor parts of the American system. Teachers colleges, for example, remained largely under the thumbs of state departments of education; state universities operated under constraints, mostly fiscal, imposed by legislatures. In the main, however, the American system of higher education was a fluid free market with multiple actors. To participants it may have appeared less as a system than a number of subsystems—one for student issues, another for faculty, and others for athletics, research, revenues, and each of the professions. Presidents might ignore any of these subsystems at their peril. From this perspective, one can explain the short-comings of the wunderkind presidents of the interwar years—Hutchins, Frank, and Meiklejohn at Amherst—who had much less freedom than they imagined. They overemphasized pet projects and slighted other basic functions, but per-haps their chief failing was to disregard the feedback from offended or neglected constituencies. Conversely, radical departures from systemic norms seemed viable only in small, insular settings—generally with extraordinary support—as at Reed or Swarthmore.

This organizational field promoted both stability and change. The voluntary associations were effective conduits of best practices and timely innovations. An-nual meetings and publications communicated new ideas to members, which might or might not be adopted. How this worked reveals the dynamics of Amer-ican higher education. In some cases the direction of progress was evident, at least to some strategic actors. The associations governing medicine and law all endeavored to narrow the gateways to their professions and raise the qualifi-cations of practitioners, and by 1940 they had largely succeeded. The scientific method underlying the advancement of knowledge made progress axiomatic in the sciences, so that foundations understood the end purposes, if not always the means. In less obvious cases the direction of change advocated by external or-ganizations could be misguided. The ACE under George Zook, for example, promoted causes like terminal courses in junior colleges and the aggrandizement of the personnel movement, which were little supported in affected institutions. Teachers colleges, being under closer government control, were bureaucratically held to a vocational role despite higher aspirations among students and institu-tions. Even normally acute leaders sometimes confronted intractable realities: Abraham Flexner's vision of full-time clinical professors was neither feasible nor

---

96 Richard Nelson Current, *Phi Beta Kappa in American Life: The First Two-Hundred Years* (New York: Oxford University Press, 1990), 140–51; ACE, *Universities*.

desirable, and Beardsley Ruml's quest to transcend disciplinary hegemony in the social sciences was quixotic. What seemed to be good ideas sometimes failed to persuade the individuals or institutions they were meant to affect. Such situations are characteristic of systems, where each component affects and is constrained by other components. In this sense, the matrix of subsystems promoted stability by giving voice to multiple interests and tempering change through multiple feedbacks.

The systemic features of American higher education help to explain how significant progress occurred in the 1930s despite the dire hardships of the Depression. The multiple crises confronting institutions opened paths for meaningful reform. But reform first required recognition of problems, and second awareness of feasible means for addressing them. Being embedded in a system facilitated both these processes. Accreditation established minimum standards that became all but mandatory; eligibility for the AAU approved list raised that bar; criteria for a Phi Beta Kappa chapter were more stringent yet; and relatively strong colleges looked to imitate leaders like Swarthmore. Standards of quality in collegiate education became recognized systemwide, measured by admission requirements, comprehensive examinations, and faculty PhDs. Academic standards in the disciplines became more generalized and more imperative. The expansion of faculty authority previously noted was one significant consequence. Academic leaders recognized that the academic barons who had built departments and schools could become obstacles to further academic advancement. The professional associations, by accrediting individual programs, became advocates for their subjects in the polities of universities. For universities undertaking doctoral education, the AAU provided approved procedures; those addressing the logjam of junior faculty could find guidelines from the AAUP. Colleges and universities thus existed in a highly normative universe, where failure to measure up to expectations resulted in negative feedback and improvement within those norms brought tangible rewards. Systemic norms, at the same time, coexisted with an extraordinary diversity of institutions and institutional types, each adjusting in its own ways to both academic norms and the specific requirements of the unique students, faculty, and supporters on which it depended. The unplanned and undirected American system of higher education thus achieved order, unity, and growth amidst a profusion of distinctive institutions.

★ 12 ★

CULTURE, CAREERS,
AND KNOWLEDGE

THIS HISTORY OF AMERICAN HIGHER EDUCATION
has focused on institutions—colleges and universities legally empowered to award the degrees that certify advanced education.
These institutions by 1940 constituted a system whose structure,
formal rules, and powerful traditions had evolved over three centuries. This evolution was affected by features of American society
outside of higher education, most importantly *culture, careers, and knowledge*.
These phenomena are multifaceted, change over time, and defy precise definition. Their influence is occasionally obvious but is more often subtly manifested
in beliefs, expectations, and behavior. Their effects have influenced American
higher education in an evolving manner from the founding of Harvard College
to World War II.

Culture and careers are basic components of social class, a much broader
phenomenon. Sociologists have addressed class and education in terms of origins and destinations—where students come from socially and where graduates end up. Higher education is inherently connected with expectations about
such destinations; it is the means to achieve a desired end. So, who attended
American colleges, and why, become fundamental questions. The first answer
is: mostly sons (and later daughters) from the upper range of middle-class
families—specifically, families owning property, having some discretionary
wealth, and having respected standing in their communities. Few students came
from the propertyless lower class, chiefly because such children lacked access to
the necessary preparatory instruction. As for the wealthiest, they had little need
for college education and indulged only sporadically, at least before the late
nineteenth century. Colleges were always open to capable middle-class youth
who worked to attend or received some aid, and this social stratum for most
of these years encompassed relatively prosperous farmers. But the dominance
of the upper-middle class is confirmed by complaints of exclusiveness from the
Early Republic to 1940. On the other hand, low participation rates—less than
3 percent before 1900—suggest that aptitude and interest played a large role
in determining the small minority who went to college, regardless of social

background. Despite a persistent social bias, American college students were a fairly mixed bunch.

Upper-middle-class families looked to colleges chiefly to accomplish what today is called social reproduction. This required the acquisition of a cultural foundation, based ostensibly on academic knowledge, but also other aspects of the college experience. Such a foundation supported numerous possible careers—in family business, the professions, civic affairs, managing family properties, or some combination of these. Of course, for many students, such activities and lifestyles represented social advancement. Rural students in particular used college as a path from the agrarian to the town or urban world. Their college education did not prepare them for any particular occupation, outside of the humble post of schoolteacher, but rather taught them how to conduct themselves among what were called the upper ranks of society, genteel society, or the bourgeoisie.

The liberal education that colleges offered was always a cultural artifact, from the seventeenth to the twentieth century. This had important implications for the colleges. Knowledge was only loosely connected with the cultural value of college. Advanced learning has commanded enormous respect within higher education throughout its history. But such knowledge did not become integral to the curriculum until the academic revolution and was resisted by some even then. Earlier, the subject knowledge incorporated into a college course was almost arbitrary compared with knowledge recognized as having cultural value. Instrumental knowledge relevant to employment also remained largely separate from college education before the Civil War. Although reformers periodically sought to connect curricula with careers, their efforts almost always anticipated a demand for such instruction rather than responding to one.

Culture has thus played a critical role. In ways less tangible than the advancement of knowledge or education for careers, culture affected curricula, institutional mission, and student life. The interplay of these factors presents a kaleidoscope of changing patterns over the history of American higher education.

★　★　★

The founding of Harvard and Yale during the Puritan century embodied a consensus among those communities over culture, careers, and knowledge. Cultural objectives were clearly uppermost—to inculcate the intensely religious worldview of Calvinist Puritanism, but also to educate gentlemen who would become the leaders in church and state. The only "career" existing in this society was that of minister, and most students at some time considered the ministry as a potential calling. But the colleges did not train ministers, at least not as undergraduates. Ministers were expected to be educated men who could explain and interpret worldly events as well as theology to their congregations. This was accomplished with the traditional "arts" course, a legacy of medieval universities imported from contemporary Oxford and Cambridge. However, worldly knowledge was a small component of the course. Besides infusing all activities with Puritan religiosity and perfecting competence in Latin and (some) Greek, the arts course chiefly emphasized speaking skills—disputations to hone logic for argumentation and declamations to practice rhetoric. Secular knowledge was largely derived from the philosophies of Aristotle and was inherently limited. This education prepared graduates for the status of gentlemen, chiefly by the combination of these elements. Graduates acquired knowledge of the world, such as it was, literacy in the language of learning, capability for public speaking, and social skills imbued by collegiate living. This was a valuable skill set, whether or not one chose to join the ministry, since it prepared men for a variety of life tasks among the upper ranks of colonial social hierarchy. Hence it needed little adjustment, even as fewer graduates entered the ministry.

The Enlightenment undermined the knowledge base of the old arts course. The curriculum was altered to encompass the Newtonian cosmos, but the implications drawn from this worldview—natural religion and philosophical Anglicanism—had a greater impact. Calvinists struggled to retain control of the colleges in order to enforce their theological views, but religious beliefs inexorably changed. As the secular Enlightenment's influence deepened, the lure of a gentleman's life style strengthened as well. In New York and Philadelphia, in particular, colleges consciously mimicked the mores and fashions of the English upper class. Even the evangelical colleges were not immune. John Witherspoon brought enlightenment toleration, intellectual advance, and social ambitions to pious Princeton.

After 1760 the leading colleges taught an extensively updated curriculum, including Newtonian science, Scottish moral philosophy, and English belles lettres. The growing conflict with England made older material, such as natural law doctrines and Greek and Roman histories, highly relevant. Students focused on preparing to be gentlemen, and colleges openly identified with what Witherspoon called "persons in the higher ranks of life." Students further developed these traits in literary societies, which cultivated belles lettres, public speaking, and debate. College study now became more closely linked to careers in the law, although apprenticeship in a law office was still required. In medicine, however, the College of Philadelphia and King's College established medical courses to train gentleman physicians. Higher education reflected the relatively open, but inherently hierarchical, character of colonial America. Ambitious middle-class boys found ways to attend, and older students from humble backgrounds, aspiring to be ministers, worked their way to and through college. The colleges were well adapted to late colonial society, on the cusp of revolutionary change.

The American Revolution inspired the idea of republican universities, intended to propound new subjects befitting the new republic. Emphasis was variously placed on science, modern languages, government, and especially "useful knowledge," valued so highly by Enlightenment writers. The role of ancient languages was questioned, and religion largely honored outside the curriculum. Useful knowledge included the professions and at least implied a greater orientation toward careers. In terms of culture, the desirability of fostering a republican consciousness was frequently expressed, but it was still assumed that a republican citizen would be a gentleman of superior social rank. In fairly short order, republican universities failed on all these counts. With respect to knowledge, the Enlightenment promised far more than it could deliver. There was little useful knowledge to teach, scarcely anyone to teach it, and no apparent way to incorporate such subjects into the arts course. Rather than republicanizing the arts course, federalist educators soon found their institutions being attacked by more democratically inclined citizens as "aristocratic." By 1800 the arts course was a shambles, and the culture it embodied was on the defensive.

The first decades of the nineteenth century marked a low point in all the vital signs of American higher education. It had become ineffective in promoting culture, careers, or knowledge. The assumption of social superiority associated with collegiate education was resented and contested by democratic elements, especially in the expanding western settlements, but even in Federalist New England. Professional careers became increasingly dissociated from collegiate preparation. And what remained of the arts course proffered little general knowledge and nothing useful for careers. In newly established institutions, the skill set that colleges offered was greatly diluted; in established ones, its relevance seemed greatly diminished. After 1800, as the Second Great Awakening of evangelical piety swept the nation, emotional and anti-intellectual religious faiths specifically rejected college educated ministers. The path to rehabilitate the colleges seemed to lie with resuscitating the classical course—subjects the colleges were able to teach—and reasserting the role of religion.

The 1820s witnessed fruitless attempts to introduce useful knowledge. Perhaps the only success was the teaching of civil engineering at the United States Military Academy. Thomas Jefferson realized his vision of a republican university in Virginia, but in practice it served largely to provide acculturation to planters' sons, largely through student socialization. Instead, the chief contribution to rehabilitating the colleges was a reformulation of their cultural role. The Yale *Reports* of 1828 convincingly argued that a 4-year course of classical studies would, by instilling mental discipline, impart a superior culture beneficial for any calling. This assertion made explicit the eighteenth-century assumption that connected classical education with superior status in society. By 1828, this was a definition of means and ends that the higher-education community was ready to embrace. The message of the Yale *Reports* was buttressed by the American Education Society, which held that the thorough education of ministers required a 4-year classical course followed by 3 years of study in a theological seminary. It would be a century before this sequence of undergraduate-professional education was adopted in law and medicine. But in 1828 it underlined the foundational nature of a liberal education. Furthermore, it absolved the college course from teaching vocationally useful knowledge, as specifically rejected in the *Reports*.

The evangelical denominations of the Second Awakening soon recognized a need for colleges of their own. They had little interest in advanced knowledge but found ignorance a handicap. Developing communities needed educated people, and persons who valued them became dissatisfied with churches that did not. Education still conferred social status. In order to preserve their social base, evangelical churches after 1820 began establishing their own colleges, by no means confined to coreligionists. They all included preparatory departments, which often taught the majority of students, many of whom never attended the college. These multilevel institutions were an important community educational resource. But at the collegiate level they perpetuated the classical course, no matter how poorly taught. The denominational colleges thus conveyed little advanced knowledge, provided a rather superficial form of culture by the criteria of the Yale *Reports*, and awarded bachelor's degrees that had no value in the labor market. They nevertheless offered the promise of entrée into the developing bourgeoisie.

In the mid-nineteenth century, rapid growth and tentative innovation were premonitions of four major challenges that after 1870 would transform American higher education: (1) Higher education for women raised questions of how male patterns of culture, careers, and knowledge related to a woman's place in society. (2) The growth of scientific knowledge forced consideration of how it could be incorporated into the colleges. (3) The issue of teaching useful knowledge presented itself in ever-more pressing terms. And (4), collegiate culture transcended alleged effects of the ossified classical course and passed into the hands of students themselves. Each of these developments was strongly affected by the regionalization of higher education—the emergence of distinctive patterns in the Northeast, the South, and the West.

The traditional forms and customs of American colleges scarcely suited the condition of nineteenth-century women. The culture of mental discipline was hardly needed for students who had no access to the professions and whose social status would be determined by marriage, not career. A different approach to these issues was taken in each region. Southern female seminaries served women who would marry but not work. They conveyed a suitable culture of ornamental subjects and a light touch of general knowledge to rather young students. In Massachusetts at Mount Holyoke, Mary Lyon addressed somewhat older women who expected to have careers as teachers or minister's wives, and she aimed to provide subject knowledge comparable to that taught in men's colleges, sans classical languages. In the "West," evangelical Oberlin provided an experiment in equal coeducation, although most women took the nonclassical lady's course. But Oberlin feminists resisted social conventions by aspiring to enter the professions. The gap between male and female cultures and careers was too large to bridge at this juncture and would be a formidable obstacle long afterward. However, the better female colleges distinguished themselves by thorough teaching of English and science. Access to academic knowledge had to await endowed women's colleges and coeducational universities after the Civil War.

The classical AB degree possessed an implicit cultural significance, but the degree alone had limited value, and this fact was reflected in student attitudes toward their studies. Young men aspiring to the status of gentlemen instead sought recognition from their peers. This phenomenon was most exaggerated in Southern state universities, where planters' sons above all sought to establish their character and honor through exploits far from the classroom. Some of these students may have sought careers as professionals, but campus life largely reflected the culture of the plantations. In the North, rapidly spreading fraternities allowed midcentury students to cultivate the affects of gentlemanly status. Increasingly, this ideal mirrored the culture of the urban haut-bourgeoisie. Fraternities soon played a huge role in campus activities, but their tacit agenda for members was to learn and practice the manners and mores of the class they aspired to join. Culture, far more than curriculum was the most critical attribute for future careers.

By the 1850s some colleges felt the need to enlarge their teaching in response to the expansion of knowledge. Civil engineering was now taught beyond West Point, and Francis Wayland created a sensation by introducing practical subjects at Brown. Wayland's flawed reforms did not last long, and only piecemeal efforts to teach practical knowledge were made in the East. The exceptions were the new scientific schools at Harvard and Yale. There the desire to advance scientific knowledge was linked with practical applications. Freedom from a fixed curriculum allowed these schools to pursue both objectives, more pure science at Harvard and more applied at Yale. Such studies were off limits to students in the classical course and thus free from its limitations. In the West, the multiplying colleges represented community assets. They assumed additional roles to accommodate multiple educational needs, becoming multipurpose colleges. Typically, besides the classical AB course, they offered scientific, English, and teachers' courses, but all these provided different versions of general education, not preparation for careers. Only Michigan under Henry Tappan consciously aspired to become a true university in the breadth and depth of its offerings.

By the Civil War, American higher education was on the cusp of separate revolutions in each of its fundamental functions: the land grant revolution in introducing practical subjects; the academic revolution in committing to the advancement of knowledge; and the collegiate revolution in defining the experience and meaning of college for undergraduate students.

The 1862 Morrill Act implanted the practical arts as a permanent presence among other liberal subjects. Agriculture was the most radical addition, despite a few precursors, since it presupposed a body of relevant knowledge and a population of educable practitioners. In fact, it took 50 years: additional federal legislation and subsidies created experiment stations to develop agricultural science and cooperative extension to bring the results to farmers. Engineering required less assistance. Civil engineering was well established by the Civil War, and although Justin Morrill's conception of mechanic arts proved a blind alley, the major fields of engineering emerged in the 1880s and were readily incorporated into land grant and non–land grant universities alike. The Morrill Act hastened the incorporation of truly useful knowledge by establishing a network of what became relatively strong institutions dedicated, at least in part, to this mission.

American universities developed as compartmentalized institutions, capable of adding additional units for business, education, music, fine arts, and others, without disturbing core commitments to the liberal arts and sciences. Higher education now offered subjects directly relevant to careers. Meanwhile, cultural subjects were transformed by the academic revolution.

The academic revolution posited the systematic pursuit of new knowledge, embodied in research and graduate education, as a central mission of universities. The organization of academic disciplines provided a new knowledge base throughout higher education, rendering the fixed classical course obsolete. Traditionalists lamented this presumed loss of culture. However, Harvard President Eliot maintained that a liberal education was best achieved by allowing undergraduate students to choose their own courses in the arts and sciences. Practical and professional subjects, he felt, should be taught in separate institutions or as graduate subjects. Johns Hopkins promoted a different ideal—the relentless advance of knowledge through empirical investigation. Although originally focused on the arts and sciences, the spirit of research—and its benefits—were appropriated by the practical arts as well. American universities ignored Eliot's distinction and pursued the advancement of knowledge in all its domains. Knowledge was no longer an external influence affecting universities but rather an internal agent for continual change. However, generating new knowledge through research and graduate education required a scale of operation and expenditure that only a handful of universities could achieve. The rest of American higher education became largely consumers and disseminators of the new academic knowledge.

The majority of college students in the late nineteenth century were more concerned with culture, even if subconsciously, than with practical arts or academic knowledge. Increasingly, the culture they valued came from interactions with peers, not faculty. The rapid growth of student-run activities and organizations was the third revolution in higher education. First developed most vigorously in eastern private colleges, it spread rapidly across the country. Students judged their classmates and themselves on achievements outside the classroom and dismissed achievements within it. The rise of intercollegiate athletics epitomized these developments, but it was only one manifestation of the culture dominating campus life. After 1900, an idealized depiction of this culture was projected in popular media and uncritically digested by middle-class Americans. The collegiate culture was presumed to produce character, "manliness," and subsequent success in the business world. This image popularized colleges and, ironically, associated mere attendance with successful careers. A pronounced social bias in campus cultures, dominated by men's and women's fraternities and costly social activities, increased markedly after 1900. But even the socially homogeneous eastern colleges believed that this culture recognized character and merit.

These three revolutions pulled American higher education in different directions, at least in theory. In practice, these tendencies more often coexisted with little apparent tension. For example, the majority of Cornell students at the turn of the nineteenth century majored in some of the country's leading engineering departments and belonged to fraternities. However, the underlying logics of these revolutions shaped divergent developments in the twentieth century.

The collegiate culture gained momentum and reached a kind of apotheosis during the Roaring Twenties. But much earlier, university leaders had become disturbed by student aversion to serious study. Critics were most concerned with rehabilitating the cultural value of a liberal education, which they saw as having two components: they wished to preserve the spirit and social solidarity of campus culture, but they also felt that students should learn something. Negatively, they specifically attacked the other two revolutions: they denounced "vocational" courses as superficial and culturally barren, and they criticized "excessive specialization" by the professoriate as inappropriate for undergraduate learning. Woodrow Wilson at Princeton and Abbott Lawrence Lowell at Harvard were most prominent in imposing greater structure and rigor on the undergraduate curriculum, but this was a project of decades rather than a single reform. The

1920s witnessed numerous attempts to improve or reinvent the college course. Initiatives compatible with the curricular hegemony of the academic disciplines generally had the intended effect, like Harvard's and Swarthmore's honors programs, but attempts to reject specialization largely failed. Liberal culture could eschew applied subjects but not the academic revolution.

The second development linked with liberal culture focused on the social environment of colleges. If student socialization formed the peer culture, then it mattered who the peers were. As applicant numbers mushroomed, the eastern private colleges, led by Columbia, Harvard, Princeton and Yale, all resorted to discriminatory selective admissions, generally to preserve their social base but specifically to screen out Jewish applicants. High social status was more valuable for the culture they wished to instill than high IQs. This conscious effort to groom a social elite in democratic America might be compared with earlier preoccupations with culture—the gentleman ideal of mid-nineteenth century or the preoccupation with social rank in colonial and Federalist society. However, charters from colonial times forward stipulated that a college would not exclude any student on the basis of religion. Now they did.

The provision of practical courses of study accelerated after 1900 with the advent of mass higher education. Land grant institutions continued to provide instruction in the practical arts, but they were now complemented by the explosive growth of urban universities. These institutions also had significant enrollments in the liberal arts. Older urban universities, especially Catholic ones, had a base of traditional students, and many new students sought some combination of cultural and intellectual learning. Urban universities often separated their liberal and professional campuses, with mixed success. Nonetheless, they responded to the preferences of their clienteles, which were heavily weighted toward professional and career education. Accounting may be the best example of a demand-driven subject. The popularity of accounting courses allowed universities to develop larger offerings in business and commerce, thus expanding service to this clientele. Older students or working students were particularly drawn to career education, constituting the huge part-time and evening enrollments at New York City colleges. The latent prestige of the arts and sciences, among students and education policy makers, produced some tension with instrumental courses. The campaign for terminal junior college courses, or the efforts to restrict the offerings of teachers colleges, implicitly intended to distance the liberal arts from both. Similarly, the elevation of law and medicine to postgraduate courses testified to the cultural significance of an arts and sciences degree.

Once the advancement of knowledge was embraced as a university mission, the progress of the academic revolution became inexorable but not its velocity or its impact on higher education as a whole. Three factors determined the incidence of the academic revolution in the first four decades of the twentieth century. First was the narrow base of universities significantly engaged in research and doctoral education. Fifteen institutions could be called research universities after 1900, and only Caltech joined that select circle before 1940. This base may have been constrained by the limitation of inputs—a limited number of active scholars and scientists and the inefficiency of doctoral education. Inputs from universities were also crucial. Even research universities could divert few internal resources to research per se, and their leaders varied widely in the priorities accorded to academic development. Thus, second, the pace of advancement was powerfully shaped by the foundations. They made concentrated investments in a small number of institutions and on the whole appear to have invested effectively. They also mitigated the shortfall of academic researchers through extensive fellowship programs. Foundations invested heavily in academic science in the 1920s, contributing significantly to the achievements of American science that became evident by the 1930s. A third factor was the general acceptance of academic expertise as crucial for faculty and teaching among the better colleges and universities. Even research universities were slow to rationalize graduate education on a meritocratic basis and, more egregiously, to regularize academic criteria for hiring and promotion. By the end of the 1930s, these practices were spreading among the more ambitious universities. And liberal arts colleges perceived that academic respectability brought greater prestige and financial rewards. Viewed from the top, American science and American universities had attained world-leading positions; but viewed from below, the advancement of knowledge and expertise was only *becoming* generalized throughout a good portion of American higher education.

★　★　★

American higher education in 1940 reflected American society, for good and for ill, as it always had. The new palatial residential colleges at Yale and Harvard intentionally aimed to reproduce an exclusive, elite culture, although always reserving some space for the merely talented. The elevation and professionalization of medical education allowed gatekeepers to exercise social as well as intellectual selection. Ethnically and religiously insular communities preferred to educate their children in colleges under their own control, with little regard for accreditation or conventional notions of quality. A huge gulf separated African Americans from mainstream institutions in higher education and all other aspects of their lives. Leaders of the higher education community shared the inclination of traditionalists to divert the educational ambitions of many aspirants to terminal 2-year institutions. The low status of teachers, mostly female, was reflected in the restricted resources and curricula of teachers' colleges. And women, generally, had relatively broad access to higher education but faced employment opportunities that failed to match their educational attainments.

However, American society was still more open and democratic than any other developed country. That openness was reflected in a system of secondary education that graduated 50 percent of 18-year-olds and a diverse array of colleges and universities that offered places to nearly a third of those graduates. Individual colleges and universities, not government ministries, found ways to bring instruction to those who sought it in accordance with their own institutional incentives. Nuances of prestige still existed among different curricula and different institutions, and they continued to shape student choice. However, graduation from college was recognized as signifying acquisition of some combination of useful and liberal knowledge, a foundation for successful careers. American youth enrolling in 1940 acted on just such a belief. More socially diverse than ever before, they found opportunities for better futures across a panoply of institutions that offered culture and knowledge for future careers.

Less evident but more portentous for the future, American higher education exerted a reciprocal influence on American society. Such influence had no doubt been growing slowly since at least the Civil War. However, in 1940, the higher-education system was poised to assume a strategic role in shaping national developments that would emerge only after World War II.

First, the notion of liberal education, now sometimes called general education, which had been a signature feature since the founding of Harvard, survived as a bedrock foundation defining colleges and universities. The intense interwar scrutiny of this idea and the many proposed reformulations changed little but, rather, cemented its centrality. The concern to privilege instruction in the arts and sciences explains the huge postwar interest in the Harvard Redbook, *General Education in a Free Society*, which affirmed that central role. Vocational instruction might be offered in short courses or through extension, but graduation from a chartered college signified the attainment of some degree of disinterested, noninstrumental knowledge. A&M colleges and teachers colleges eventually rose to that standard, obviating the invidious distinction that existed in other countries between university degrees and nondegree courses for teachers and technicians. In the United States, college graduate was a universally recognized level of cultural attainment, which was consciously replicated in the great postwar expansion.

Second, Justin Morrill's instinctive belief that practical forms of advanced education should be elevated to the same plane as liberal education was fully realized in the United States by 1940. This feature of American higher education, again in stark contrast with coeval developed nations, provided an untold supply of practitioners and "know-how" to the economy. Every country trained engineers, but the University of Illinois, for example, prepared engineering specialists in twelve fields; MIT, in fourteen. Curricula in business administration was less developed, but fifty-two accredited schools or colleges in universities were dedicated to imparting the managerial skills utilized by growing corporations. Colleges of agriculture, through their federal partnership, not only drove technological progress but also conveyed the results to family farms. More generally, American colleges and universities had no compunction against establishing professional schools wherever demanded, which by 1940 included journalism, library science, forestry, social work, and home economics—and in the future would include still more fields. Besides training practitioners, such schools fostered expertise from dedicated faculty who hastened the pace of technological change. Science-based fields like engineering and agriculture, moreover, advanced further and faster given proximity with basic university research. The existence of such assets in 1940 meant that know-how and expertise would be multiplied after World War II by the massive influx of veterans under the GI Bill, supplying an extra impetus to the world's leading economy. As a bonus, the rapid escalation of college graduates did not produce a queue of unemployed university degree holders expecting civil service positions; American graduates with their useful skills were absorbed into the productive economy.

Third, the ascendancy of American science to world leadership, described above, brought incomparable advantages, not just in waging war but for technological and industrial development after 1945. Of course, both wartime and postwar federal science policies amounted to a gigantic mobilization of scientific expertise, but it was mobilization of a base that had been formed in universities during the interwar years. In 1940, just sixteen institutions merited the title research university, but their academic culture and practices would be progressively adopted across the university sector after 1945, creating an incomparable array of what are now called world-class universities.

Fourth, the postwar embrace of limitless expansion of higher education was premised on the historical dynamics of American colleges and universities. During the interwar years, pundits in foundations and government expressed concerns that too many students were going to college. They would have preferred higher standards for fewer students and possibly diverting the less fit into terminal programs. Such wisdom had no effect (Minnesota's General College notwithstanding) on the ballooning of enrollments to 15 percent of age cohorts. Colleges and universities, acting independently, sought students in order to serve their constituencies and balance their budgets. After the war, these institutional imperatives, heightened by the deluge of GI Bill students, evolved into a national consensus. The liberal President's Commission argued in 1947 that one-half of all students were capable of benefiting from higher education and should, by 1960, have such opportunities. The conservative rejoinder, while emphasizing academic standards, still recommended that higher education should serve 25 percent of American youth—two-thirds more than in 1940. The new national consensus in favor of expansion would soon be endorsed by state legislatures with appropriations to build flagship, regional, and community college campuses, altering the structure of American higher education but not the dynamics of independent colleges and universities serving the public good while pursuing their own institutional incentives.

For three centuries in preindustrial and industrializing America, higher education had largely responded to the demand for genteel culture, opportunities for careers, and the inexorable growth of knowledge. While those influences would remain, by 1940 an extensive and highly organized system of higher education was on the cusp of assuming a larger role, contributing to the shaping of American society. Unforeseen in 1940, American universities would soon be recognized as central institutions of postindustrial society.

INDEX